THE
unofficial GUIDE®
ᵀᴼUniversal
Orlando®

2019

COME CHECK US OUT!

Supplement your valuable guidebook with tips, news, and deals by visiting our websites:

theunofficialguides.com
touringplans.com

Also, while there, sign up for The Unofficial Guide newsletter for even more travel tips and special offers.

Join the conversation on social media:

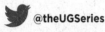 @theUGSeries   theUnofficialGuides

 theUGSeries   theUGSeries

#theUGseries

Other Unofficial Guides

The Disneyland Story: The Unofficial Guide to the Evolution of Walt Disney's Dream

Universal vs. Disney: The Unofficial Guide to American Theme Parks' Greatest Rivalry

The Unofficial Guide Color Companion to Walt Disney World

The Unofficial Guide to Disney Cruise Line

The Unofficial Guide to Disneyland

The Unofficial Guide to Las Vegas

The Unofficial Guide to Mall of America

The Unofficial Guide to Walt Disney World

The Unofficial Guide to Walt Disney World with Kids

The Unofficial Guide to Washington, D.C.

THE *unofficial* GUIDE®

TO Universal Orlando®

2019

SETH KUBERSKY *with*
BOB SEHLINGER & LEN TESTA

Published by:
AdventureKEEN
2204 First Avenue South, Suite 102
Birmingham. AL 35233

Cover design by Scott McGrew

Text design by Vertigo Design with modifications by Annie Long

For information on our other products and services or to obtain technical support, please contact us from within the United States at 888-604-4537 or by fax at 205-326-1012.

AdventureKEEN also publishes its books in a variety of electronic formats. Some content that appears in print may not be available in electronic formats.

ISBN 978-1-62809-089-5; eISBN: 978-1-62809-090-1

Distributed by Publishers Group West

Manufactured in the United States of America

5 4 3 2

CONTENTS

LIST *of* MAPS

ABOUT *the* AUTHORS

Seth Kubersky is the coauthor of *The Unofficial Guide to Disneyland* and a contributor to *The Unofficial Guide to Walt Disney World* and *The Unofficial Guide to Las Vegas*. A resident of Orlando since 1996, Seth is a former employee of Universal Orlando's entertainment department. He covers arts and attractions for the *Orlando Weekly* newspaper, *Attractions Magazine*, AAA's *Via Magazine*, and other publications. You can find Seth online at sethkubersky.com or on Twitter @skubersky.

Bob Sehlinger is the author of *The Unofficial Guide to Walt Disney World* and *The Unofficial Guide to Las Vegas* and is also the publisher of The Unofficial Guide series.

Len Testa is the coauthor of *The Unofficial Guide to Walt Disney World* and has contributed to *The Unofficial Guide to Disneyland* and *The Unofficial Guide to Las Vegas*. He is also the webmaster of touringplans.com, the sister website of The Unofficial Guides.

INTRODUCTION

WHY "UNOFFICIAL"?

DECLARATION OF INDEPENDENCE

THE AUTHORS AND RESEARCHERS of this guide specifically and categorically declare that they are and always have been totally independent. The material in this guide originated with the authors and has not been reviewed, edited, or in any way approved by Universal Orlando or any other companies whose travel products are discussed.

The purpose of this guide is to provide you with the information necessary to tour with the greatest efficiency and economy and with the least hassle and stress. In this guide we represent and serve you, the consumer. If a restaurant serves bad food, a gift item is overpriced, or a certain ride isn't worth the wait, we can say so, and in the process we hope to make your visit more fun, efficient, and economical.

DANCE TO THE MUSIC

A DANCE HAS A BEGINNING and an end. But when you're dancing, you're not concerned about getting to the end or where on the dance floor you might wind up. In other words, you're totally in the moment. That's the way you should be on your Universal Orlando vacation.

You may feel a bit of pressure concerning your vacation. Vacations, after all, are very special events—and expensive ones to boot. So you work hard to make your vacation the best that it can be. Planning and organizing are essential to a successful Universal Orlando vacation, but if they become your focus, you won't be able to hear the music and enjoy the dance.

So think of us as your dancing coaches. We'll teach you the steps to the dance in advance, so that when you're on vacation and the music plays, you'll dance with effortless grace and ease.

A BETTER MOUSETRAP?

DIE-HARD DISNEY DEVOTEES may want to cover their mouse ears because we are about to utter the ultimate blasphemy: it is possible to enjoy an awesome Orlando vacation without spending a single minute in Mickey's world. For much of the past four decades, the notion of spending a holiday in Central Florida without seeing Walt Disney's sprawling wonderland seemed silly. While visitors might take a day or two out of their trip to explore independent attractions such as Sea-World, Busch Gardens, or Kennedy Space Center, the Magic Kingdom and its sister parks were seen by most as the area's main draw.

Much to the Mouse House's dismay, that situation is swiftly shift-ing. While Walt Disney World is in no danger of closing for lack of interest, its share of Orlando's lucrative tourism market has been steadily and significantly swinging in favor of an energetic upstart located a few miles up I-4: the Universal Orlando Resort.

Originally opened in 1990 as a single theme park packed with advanced but unreliable attractions, Universal Orlando has matured into a full-service, fully immersive vacation destination with enough world-class activities to keep a family occupied for four days or more. Universal Studios Florida, a longtime rival of Disney's Hollywood Stu-dios that draws its inspiration from movies and television, has been almost entirely overhauled since its debut, and it now houses one of the world's top collections of cutting-edge attractions. Universal's Islands of Adventure debuted in 1999 as the most modern, high-tech theme park in the United States, featuring an all-star lineup of thrill rides that makes it the best park in town for older kids and young-at-heart adults.

Together, the two parks are home to the game-changing Wizarding World of Harry Potter, a meticulously imagined multilayered experi-ence that's drawing millions of Muggle fans from around the world to the hallowed halls of Hogwarts Castle and Gringotts Bank. Surround-ing the two parks are six immaculately appointed on-site resort hotels, the elaborately themed Volcano Bay water park, and the CityWalk nightlife complex full of restaurants, nightclubs, and entertainment options appealing to families and adults. And Universal Orlando has already begun developing land it owns outside of the resort's current boundaries, both on the former home of Wet 'n Wild—which will soon hold a pair of value-priced resort hotels—and on about 1,000 acres that Universal purchased near the Orange County Convention Center. Over the coming decades, those parcels will be populated with new hotels, entertainment complexes, and next-generation themed attractions, probably featuring characters from Nintendo video games and DreamWorks animated films.

Universal Orlando's ascendancy is not about to bankrupt Walt Disney World, and likely never will—Disney's nearly unlimited dominion over its vast 43-square-mile kingdom practically ensures its dominance. But those who approach Universal with open eyes will find that the resort can provide just as much magic and fantasy in its own fashion. Universal Orlando has an energy, pace, and attitude all its own that might appeal to the most adamant anti–amusement park person, and could even convert confirmed Disney customers. Instead of opting for the same old rat race, consider spending your next vacation playing Quidditch with Harry, saving New York with Spidey, and drinking a Duff with the Simpsons. You may just find yourself asking, "Mickey who?"

IT TAKES MORE THAN ONE BOOK TO DO THE JOB RIGHT

WE'VE BEEN COVERING CENTRAL FLORIDA tourism for almost 40 years. We began by lumping everything into one guidebook, but that was when the Magic Kingdom and Epcot were the only theme parks at Walt Disney World, at the very beginning of the boom that has made Central Florida one of the most visited tourist destinations on Earth. As the area grew, so did our guide, until eventually we needed to split the tome into smaller, more in-depth (and more portable) volumes. These titles are designed to work both individually and together. All provide specialized information tailored to specific Central Florida visitors. Though some tips (such as arriving at the parks early) are echoed in all the guides, most of the information in each book is unique.

The Unofficial Guide to Walt Disney World is the centerpiece of our Central Florida coverage because, well, Walt Disney World is the centerpiece of most Central Florida vacations. *The Unofficial Guide to Walt Disney World* is evaluative, comprehensive, and instructive—the ultimate planning tool for a successful Disney World vacation, including a condensed version of this book's Universal Orlando information.

The Unofficial Guide to Walt Disney World is supplemented by these additional titles:

- *The Unofficial Guide Color Companion to Walt Disney World,* by Bob Sehlinger and Len Testa
- *The Unofficial Guide to Walt Disney World with Kids,* by Bob Sehlinger and Liliane J. Opsomer with Len Testa

The Unofficial Guide Color Companion to Walt Disney World is a visual feast that proves a picture is worth 1,000 words.

The Unofficial Guide to Walt Disney World with Kids offers a wealth of planning and touring tips for a successful Disney family vacation.

Finally, you hold our in-depth guide dedicated to the attractions and amenities of the Universal Orlando Resort. All of the guides are available at most bookstores and in digital ebook editions.

THE DEATH OF SPONTANEITY

ONE OF OUR ALL-TIME favorite letters came from a man in Chapel Hill, North Carolina:

Your book reads like the operations plan for an amphibious landing: Go here, do this, proceed to Step 15. You must think that everyone is a hyperactive, type-A theme park commando. What happened to the satisfaction of self-discovery or the joy of spontaneity? Next you'll be telling us when to empty our bladders.

As it happens, Unofficial Guide researchers are a pretty existential crew who are big on self-discovery. But Universal Orlando—especially for first-time travelers—probably isn't the place you want to "discover" the spontaneity of needless waits in line or mediocre meals when you could be doing better.

In many ways, Central Florida's theme parks are the quintessential system, the ultimate in mass-produced entertainment and the most planned and programmed environment anywhere. Lines for rides form in predictable ways at predictable times, for example, and you can either learn here how to avoid them or "discover" them on your own.

We aren't saying that you can't have a great time at Universal Orlando, and enjoying the resort requires much less advance planning

than the equivalent vacation at Walt Disney World. What we *are* saying is that you should think about what you want to do before you go. The time and money you save by planning will help your family have more fun.

THE SUM OF ALL FEARS

EVERY WRITER WHO EXPRESSES an opinion is accustomed to readers who strongly agree or disagree: it comes with the territory. Extremely troubling, however, is the possibility that our efforts to be objective have frightened some readers away from Universal Orlando or made others apprehensive.

For the record, if you love theme parks, Universal Orlando is as good as it gets—absolute nirvana. If you arrive without knowing a thing about the place and make every possible mistake, chances are about 90% that you'll have a wonderful vacation anyway. The job of

a guidebook is to give you a heads-up regarding opportunities and potential problems. We're certain that we can help you turn a great vacation into an absolutely *superb* one.

THE UNOFFICIAL TEAM

THIS BOOK WAS AUTHORED by Seth Kubersky, building on decades of research from The Unofficial Guides by Bob Sehlinger, Len Testa, and the rest of the Unofficial team. Derek Burgan is our Universal food consigliere and contributed vital research to this guide's dining chapter. Our prologue is excerpted from Sam Gennawey's *Universal vs. Disney: An Unofficial Guide to American Theme Parks' Greatest Rivalry.* Special thanks to Genevieve Bernard for research assistance, proofreading, and patience. Amber Kaye Henderson edited the book, Chris Eliopoulos and Tami Knight drew the cartoons, Steve Jones and Cassandra Poertner created the maps, and Meghan Brawley indexed the book; thanks go to each of them.

UPDATES AND BREAKING NEWS

LOOK FOR THESE at the Unofficial Guide website, theunofficial guides.com, and at our sister website, touringplans.com. See page 24 for a complete description of the sites.

LETTERS AND COMMENTS FROM READERS

MANY OF THOSE WHO USE The Unofficial Guides write us to make comments or share their own strategies for visiting Central Florida. We appreciate all such input, both positive and critical, and encourage our readers to continue writing. Readers' comments and observations are frequently incorporated into revised editions of The Unofficial Guides and have contributed immeasurably to their improvement. If you write us, you can rest assured that we won't release your name and address to any mailing lists, direct-mail advertisers, or other third party.

Reader Survey

After your vacation, please fill out our reader survey by visiting touring plans.com/universal-orlando/survey. Unless you instruct us otherwise, we will assume that you do not object to being quoted in a future edition.

How to Write the Authors

Seth Kubersky and Bob Sehlinger c/o The Unofficial Guides
2204 First Ave. S, Ste. 102
Birmingham, AL 35233
unofficialguides@menasharidge.com

When you write by mail, put your address on both your letter and envelope, as sometimes the two get separated. It is also a good idea to include your phone number. If you email us, let us know where you're from. And remember, as travel writers, we're often out of the office for long periods of time, so forgive us if our response is slow.

UNIVERSAL ORLANDO:
An Overview

PROLOGUE: AMERICAN THEME PARKS' GREATEST RIVALRY

UNIVERSAL STUDIOS DID NOT SET OUT to challenge The Walt Disney Company in the theme park business. The men who ran the Music Corporation of America (MCA) were quite happy with the industrial tour they created in 1964 at Universal City. The Universal Studio Tour took visitors behind the scenes of the largest and busiest back lot in Hollywood to show how motion pictures and television programs were manufactured. People came from around the world with the hope of catching a glimpse of their favorite star. Unlike Disneyland, Walt Disney's fantasy theme park in nearby Anaheim, the Universal Studio Tour provided an authentic experience not found anywhere else. It was something entirely new, entertaining, and very profitable.

In 1979 MCA bought land in Orlando 10 miles north of Walt Disney World and later announced that it was going to build a motion picture and television production studio. The new studio would have also featured a tour just like the one in California. Lew Wasserman, MCA's legendary chief executive, knew better than to compete with Disney and its dominance with fantasy landscapes. He enjoyed the fact that the two Southern California tourist attractions complemented each other, and he was making money with minimal investment.

Everything changed just a few years later. In 1984 Disney hired Michael Eisner as the new chief executive officer and Frank Wells as president. Before Disney, Eisner had been president of Paramount Pictures Corp., and Wells had been a well-respected executive at Warner Bros. Within two weeks of the Disney leadership change, MCA president and Wasserman's protégé, Sidney Sheinberg, sent a letter to his old friends proposing a meeting to discuss ideas that would be in the mutual interest of both companies.

It made sense to turn to Michael Eisner. While he was at Paramount, Sheinberg had shown him MCA's Florida plans with the hopes of forming a partnership. Eisner liked what he saw. When nothing came of the talks, Eisner blamed the impasse on powers higher up the corporate food chain at Paramount's parent company, Gulf and Western. Now that Eisner was in charge of Disney, Sheinberg thought Eisner would be excited to become MCA's partner in Florida.

During the call, a confident Sheinberg suggested to Eisner, "Let's get together on a studio tour in Orlando. We tried with your predecessors, but they were unresponsive. We think we can help you."[1] Much to the surprise of the MCA executives, Eisner told his old friend, "We're already working on something of our own."[2]

---

1 Ellen Farly, "Behind the MCA-Disney War in Fla.," *The Los Angeles Times,* 23 April 1989.

2 Michael D. Eisner with Tony Schwartz, *Work in Progress: Risking Failure, Surviving Success* (New York: Hyperion, 1998).

That was not the reaction Wasserman and Sheinberg was expecting. "Ultimately, we were informed that they might want to do one of these tours themselves and they did not want to be accused of somehow, whatever the word was, stealing or acting improperly, if we had a meeting and they later decided to go on their own," Sheinberg later explained. "That signal really surprised us, to put it mildly. It was our first indication that they were off on a plan to do this."[3]

Then, on February 7, 1985, Michael Eisner made headlines at his first meeting with Walt Disney Productions shareholders. Before a packed house at the Anaheim Convention Center, he announced that Disney would soon start construction of a third theme park at Walt Disney World. The heart of Disney's park would be a real working production studio with two sound stages and a working animation studio. Eisner said this "was a way to make the experience more authentic, but these decisions would also serve our production needs as they grew." Regarding the plans, Eisner said they were "the most exciting to come out of Walt Disney Imagineering (WDI) in a long time." He also told the gathering, "We're definitely doing it within a year."[4]

The men at MCA were livid. After reviewing Disney's plans, Sidney Sheinberg claimed that Michael Eisner stole the idea he heard at the 1981 pitch at Paramount. For his part, Eisner claimed the presentation occurred "many, many years" ago and added "when I arrived at [Disney], the studio tour was already on the drawing boards and had been for many years."[5] Eisner ordered his team to work fast. For him, beating Sidney Sheinberg and MCA was critical. "They invaded our home turf," he told *Business Week*. "We will not be intimidated."[6]

A bitter Sheinberg replied, "You're going to have to work awfully hard to convince me that [Eisner] didn't know about [MCA's plans]. That's ridiculous. He was a member of the inner circle at Paramount." He added, "Disney obviously felt they were in trouble and felt they had to do something about it. Disney announced it would do the theme park and would have you believe it's been in the works since 1926—if you believe in mice, you probably believe in the Easter Bunny also."[7] At MCA, you do not get mad. You get even. This is how the greatest rivalry in the theme park industry began.

A UNIVERSAL PRIMER

THE UNIVERSAL ORLANDO RESORT is located on 840 acres inside the city of Orlando, about 8 miles northeast of Walt Disney World (which is actually in Lake Buena Vista). The resort consists of two theme parks—**Universal Studios Florida** and **Universal's Islands of Adventure**—along with the **Volcano Bay** water park, six (soon to be

---

3   Farly, "Behind the MCA-Disney War in Fla."

4   Walt Disney Productions (minutes of annual meeting, Anaheim, CA, 6 Feb. 1985), Anaheim History Room, Anaheim Public Library, Anaheim, CA.

5   Kathryn Harris, "Florida Fund may Invest in MCA Park," *The Los Angeles Times*, 20 May 1985.

6   Ron Grover, *The Disney Touch: How a Daring Management Team Revived an Entertainment Empire* (Homewood, IL: Business One Irwin, 1991).

7   Farly, "Behind the MCA-Disney War in Fla."

eight) Loews-operated Universal hotels, and the **CityWalk** dining, nightlife, and shopping complex.

Universal Studios Florida (USF) opened in June 1990. It debuted a year after the similarly themed Disney–MGM Studios (now known as Disney's Hollywood Studios) but made almost four times the area of its facility accessible to visitors. USF's original attractions focused on characters and situations from familiar Universal films, from *Jaws* and *King Kong* to *Earthquake* and *E.T.* Unfortunately, while the opening-day rides incorporated state-of-the-art technology and lived up to their billing in terms of creativity and uniqueness, several lacked the capacity or reliability to handle the number of guests who frequent major Florida tourist destinations.

With only one theme park, Universal played second fiddle to Disney's juggernaut for almost a decade. Things began to change when Universal opened Islands of Adventure (IOA) in 1999. Adding a second park, along with the CityWalk nightlife complex and three on-site resort hotels, made Universal a legitimate two-day destination and provided Universal with enough critical mass to begin serious competition with Disney for tourists' time and money.

IOA opened to good reviews and sizable crowds, and it did steady business for the first few years. Ongoing competition with Disney, however, and a lack of money to invest in new rides eventually caught up with IOA. Attendance dropped from a high of 6.3 million visitors in 2004 to a low of 4.6 million in 2009, less than half of Animal Kingdom, Disney's least-visited park in Orlando that year.

In the middle of this slide, Universal's management made one bold bet: securing the rights in 2007 to build a Harry Potter–themed area within IOA. Harry, it was thought, was possibly the only fictional character extant capable of trumping Mickey Mouse, and Universal went all out, under author J. K. Rowling's watchful and exacting eye, to create a setting and attractions designed to be the envy of the industry.

The first phase of **The Wizarding World of Harry Potter,** as the new land was called, opened at IOA in 2010 and was an immediate hit. Its headliner attraction, **Harry Potter and the Forbidden Journey,** broke new ground in its ride system and immersive storytelling. Families raced to ride the attraction, and IOA's attendance grew 28% in 2010 and another 28% in 2011.

Harry Potter single-handedly upended the power structure in Florida's theme parks. Emboldened by its success, Universal's new owner, Comcast—which acquired a majority stake in the NBCUniversal conglomerate in 2011 and purchased full ownership from General Electric in 2013—embarked on an unprecedented wave of expansions, rapidly adding new attractions and extensions, including **The Wizarding World of Harry Potter–Diagon Alley** at Universal Studios Florida and additional on-site hotels.

continued on page 12

Universal Orlando

Universal's Islands of Adventure

To Tampa &
Walt Disney
← World

Turkey Lake Road

Universal's Cabana Bay Beach Resort

The Wizarding World
of Harry Potter–
Hogsmeade

Hollywood Way

Universal's Volcano Bay

Universal's
Aventura Hotel

Loews Sapphire
Falls Resort

Loews Royal Pacific Resort

Main
Entrance

Universal's
Endless Summer
Resort
(opens 2019)

Universal CityWalk

Universal Blvd.

American Way

Hollywood Way

400

4

400

4

435   Parking Garages

435

Grand National Dr.

4

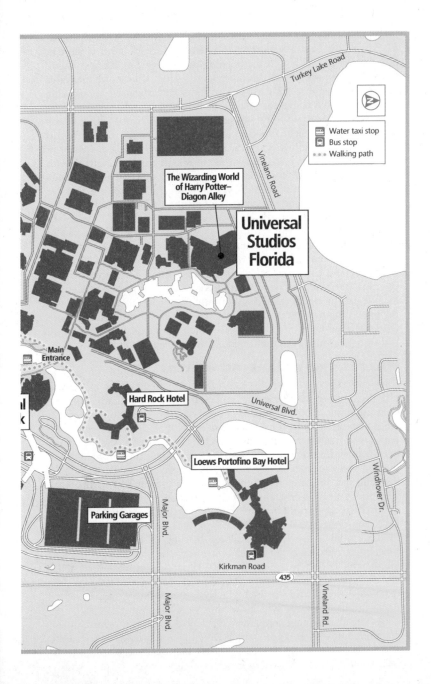

continued from page 9

While Disney responded to the Potter phenomenon by slowly building Avatar and Star Wars attractions, Universal struck another blow in the summer of 2017 with the opening of Volcano Bay, its first highly themed on-site water park. Volcano Bay aims to revolutionize the water park experience through cutting-edge slides and advanced Virtual Line technology. Like Universal Studios Florida and Islands of Adventure, Volcano Bay is a state-of-the-art park vying with Disney parks, whose attractions are decades older on average. Despite Walt Disney World deploying a wave of upgrades ahead of the resort's 50th anniversary in 2021, Universal's ever-accelerating expansion appears undaunted, with a pair of value-priced hotels set to open in 2019 and 2020 just outside the main resort on the former Wet 'n Wild property, and a massive second campus currently under development a few miles to the south.

The gamble appears to be paying off for Universal. Comcast's theme parks reported an 8.6% increase in revenue for the first half of 2018, and the Themed Entertainment Association estimated a 94.4% increase in attendance at USF and IOA between 2009 and 2017.

Disney and Universal officially downplay their fierce competition, pointing out that any new theme park or attraction makes Central Florida a more marketable destination. Behind closed doors, however, the two companies share a Pepsi-versus-Coke rivalry that keeps both working hard to gain a competitive edge. The good news is that all this translates into better and better attractions for you to enjoy.

WHAT IS THE WIZARDING WORLD?

UNIVERSAL HAS BEEN OPERATING ATTRACTIONS in Central Florida for more than a quarter century, but if it only recently attracted your attention, a certain superstar boy wizard is likely responsible. In what may prove to be the competitive coup of all time between theme park archrivals Disney and Universal, the latter inked a deal with Warner Brothers Entertainment to create "fully immersive" Harry Potter–themed environments based on the best-selling children's books by J. K. Rowling and the companion blockbuster movies from Warner Brothers. The books have been translated into 80 languages, with more than 500 million copies sold in more than 200 territories around the world. Factoring in the Fantastic Beasts prequels, the movies have grossed more than $8.5 billion worldwide, making Rowling's Wizarding World the third highest-grossing film franchise in history (behind Marvel and Star Wars). The project was blessed by Rowling, who is known for tenaciously protecting the integrity of her work. In the case of the films, she demanded that Warner Brothers be true, to an almost unprecedented degree, to the books on which the films were based.

As the Potter juggernaut took the world by storm, entertainment conglomerates began approaching Rowling about theme park rights. When she spurned a Universal Studios Florida concept for a show based on the Potter characters, industry observers were certain that she had struck a deal with Disney. In fact, Disney was in talks with Rowling about a stand-alone Harry Potter theme park. For her part, Rowling had no problem visualizing what she wanted in a theme park, but from Disney's point of view, what Rowling wanted was operationally problematic, if not altogether impossible. Never an entity to concede control, Disney walked.

Universal caught Rowling on the rebound and brought her to Orlando to tour Islands of Adventure. Among other things, they squired her around the Lost Continent section of the park, impressing her with its detailed theme execution and showing her how, with a little imagination, it could be rethemed. Rowling saw the potential but wasn't much more flexible with Universal than she was with Disney. From her perspective, getting a themed area right couldn't be any harder than getting a movie right, so she insisted that Stuart Craig, her trusted production designer for the films, be responsible for faithfully re-creating sets from the movies. Universal, on fire to land Harry Potter, became convinced that the collaboration could work.

But theme parks and movies are two very different things. With a film, a set has to look good only for a few moments and then it's on to something else. With a theme park, a set has to look good 12–16 hours a day, in all manner of weather, and with tens of thousands of tourists rambling through it in need of food, drink, restrooms, protection from rain, and places to rest. With The Wizarding World–Hogsmeade, Rowling's insistence on authenticity occasioned conundrums not anticipated by the theme park designers, who, for example, logically assumed that guests would like to see the interior of Hagrid's Hut. No problem—a walk-through attraction will serve nicely. Of course, there's the Americans with Disabilities Act, so we'll need ramps both in and out of the hut. No way, say the movie people: Hagrid's Hut in the films had steps, so the theme park version must have them too.

Similarly, you can't snag a photo op with Harry and his crew at Universal because Rowling decreed that no Daniel Radcliffe look-alike will ever be hired to stand in for him at the theme parks. The same rule applies to all the other important personas portrayed in the Potter movies, which is why Hogsmeade and Diagon Alley are populated by characters of whom you've never heard before.

To be frank, Universal shot itself in the foot by initially promoting the original Wizarding World as a "theme park within a theme park." While arguable from the aspect of immersive theming, the phrase implied a lot more content than what guests got back in 2010: a single land with only three rides, two of which were repurposed roller coasters. It also created a false impression that admission to the Harry Potter area was separate from the existing parks, or involved an additional charge. Now that Diagon Alley has been added, along with a train attraction connecting the two areas, the "theme park within a theme park" moniker is perhaps more apropos. But though The Wizarding Worlds will be the resort's top draw for years to come, they still represent just a sliver of what Universal Orlando's theme parks have to offer.

Bone Up

We don't have room to explain all the Potter allusions and icons incorporated into The Wizarding Worlds. Because they so accurately replicate scenes from the books and films, it helps immeasurably to be well versed in all things Harry. If it's been a while since you've seen one of the movies or read one of the novels, you can brush up by watching the first four flicks in the series, in particular *Harry Potter and the Prisoner of Azkaban* and *Harry Potter and the Sorcerer's Stone* (*Harry Potter and the Philosopher's Stone* outside of India and the United States). Escape from Gringotts is drawn directly from the first half of the final film, so you'll want to rewatch *Harry Potter and the Deathly Hallows: Part 2* before heading to the bank vaults. For an easy memory jog, check out the films' trailers on YouTube. If you know nothing at all about Harry Potter, you'll still have fun, but to truly appreciate the nuance and detail, we suggest you hit the books.

THE UNIVERSAL DIFFERENCE

IN MANY WAYS, UNIVERSAL ORLANDO will never achieve parity with Walt Disney World. It's minuscule compared to the 27,000-odd acres of Walt Disney World and will still be significantly smaller even after Universal's 1,000-acre expansion property is fully developed. And while guest service at Universal is generally exceptional by industry standards, there's something special about the "Disney Way" that some visitors will inevitably prefer. But in the areas where it *can* compete with Disney—namely, in theme park design and attraction quality—Universal has pulled even, if not ahead.

Even hard-core Disney fans, such as this Moncton, Nebraska, reader, are beginning to pay attention:

> I'm a huge fan of all things Disney, so it pains me a little to say that the highlight of our most recent trip was actually Universal Orlando. Not because Disney World isn't spectacular—it always is— but because Universal's themed Harry Potter experience is by far the most immersive I've ever had. Disney has to be a little nervous.

A dad from Montclair, New Jersey, compares Disney and Universal when it comes to value:

> After many Disney trips, we finally went to Universal last year. We'll never switch our allegiance, but Universal taught me some lessons about how to blow minds using new technology—and Disney needs to pay a little attention. Time at Disney isn't cheap, but I always tell people that it isn't a bad value; still, that high cost puts Disney in a position where if it doesn't deliver 100%, it looks awfully greedy, whether it's a tasteless muffin or a lame new attraction.

Or consider this, from a family of four from Kansas City:

> Our family loved our Universal experience more than Disney. The parks are close together, so park-hopping doesn't require a shuttle ride.

Mouse Jabs

THERE'S NOTHING WRONG with a little friendly competition, and outside the theme park world, we've seen plenty of examples of the No. 2 brand poking a little fun at the No. 1 brand. Pepsi and Coke, Marvel and DC, Burger King and McDonald's, and . . . Universal and Disney? That's right; while you won't find any references to Universal at Walt Disney World, Derek Burgan—author of the weekly "Saturday Six" column on touringplans.com—has cataloged a whole bunch of funny jabs at the Mouse House down the street.

6. Men in Black Alien Attack's Preshow The entire facade and framing story for Men in Black Alien Attack is a spoof on Disney's iconic attractions from the 1964–1965 New York World's Fair, as recreated in the 2015 film *Tomorrowland*. Before being ushered into the "elevator," and again as they exit, guests hear a scrap of narration that pays tribute to Walt's groundbreaking educational rides like *Carousel of Progress* and Ford's Magic Skyway.

5. The Simpsons Ride's Queue The Simpsons Ride is a hilarious send-up of all theme parks (including Universal). You'll see giant posters referencing several Disney rides, including The Jungle Cruise and Pirates of the Caribbean. Once you get inside the building, the first preshow is filled with hilarious nods to Disney attractions, including The Haunted Mansion, *The Hall of Presidents,* and even *Kitchen Kabaret.*

4. Dudley Do-Right's Ripsaw Falls One of the most underrated attractions in all of Universal, Dudley Do-Right's queue and ride are filled with clever gags that fit right in with the spirit of the old Jay Ward cartoons. Keep an eye open for the movie posters making fun of such films as Star Wars and *Three Men and a Baby*. While most people don't think of *Three Men and a Baby* as a Disney film, it was actually the first hit of CEO Michael Eisner's reign.

3. Duff Brewery Standing in front of Duff Brewery in Springfield are the Seven Duffs topiaries. A takeoff on Disney's Seven Dwarfs, the Seven Duffs are pretty much the exact opposites of Disney's lovable dwarfs. While the dwarfs are short, the Duffs are tall. All of Disney's dwarfs talk except one (Dopey), but only one of the Seven Duffs talks (Surly). The names of the Seven Duffs are Dizzy, Tipsy, Sleazy, Queasy, Surly, Edgy, and Remorseful, and together they are one of the best photo ops in the park.

2. *Shrek 4-D*'s Queue The *Shrek 4-D* queue is filled with fake attraction posters that reference Disneyland rides: *Great Moments with Mr. Farquaad* (*Great Moments with Mr. Lincoln*), *Enchanted Tick Room* (*Enchanted Tiki Room*), and Donkbo (Dumbo) are just some of the great posters you'll see while in line.

1. Jurassic Park River Adventure's Queue Without a doubt, the most famous Walter Elias Disney quote of all is: "I only hope that we don't lose sight of one thing— that it all started by a mouse." Guests in the Jurassic Park River Adventure queue have an opportunity to see Universal have a little fun with this quote during the cheesy video loop playing. The narrator says, "But in the words of our founder, John Hammond, 'I hope we never lose sight of one thing—that it all started with a mosquito.'"

Bonus Lost Disney Reference In the preshow of the now-extinct *Twister: Ride It Out* attraction, a wrecked automobile hung suspended from the ceiling. Squashed to the car's spinning tire: a classic Mickey Mouse ear hat!

From a Scarborough, Maine, reader:

Going to Universal is much less stressful than going to Disney. Even though we could go to the parks early, at Universal we slept in and still walked on most rides.

A woman from Noblesville, Indiana, says:

This was the first non-Disney theme park that I felt could have been a Disney-owned theme park. It was clean and well themed, with fun rides and wonderful team members. I truly enjoyed Universal as much (and in some ways more) than my trips to Disney World.

A Lake Frederick, Virginia, family agrees:

After being loyal to Disney for years, my family wanted to visit The Wizarding World. I was really impressed with Universal! Everyone we talked to was very nice. It was even more pleasant than dealing with Disney people—pretty surprising. I kept thinking of the old Avis slogan: "We try harder" [which was based on it being the second-largest car rental agency]. We thoroughly enjoyed our time at Universal and can't wait to go back!

Finally, this father from Rigby, Idaho, cuts to the chase:

Universal was less crowded and less expensive, and frankly, the rides were more fun and appropriate for all but the youngest of kids. EVERYONE, all ages, far preferred Universal over Disney World. That wasn't true 25 years ago, when our then-younger and smaller family first visited these places—but it is certainly true now.

To be fair, we also get occasional missives that dissent from our praise for Universal's product, such as this one from a multigenerational matriarch in New York City:

Universal's attractions were indeed state of the art, and the Harry Potter areas were amazing, but I didn't feel that magic that I did when we visited Disney three years ago. I don't know if my expectations were too high, or if it was because we were with a more diverse group age-wise, or what. Overall, I have no burning desire to return anytime soon, unlike with Disney, when I couldn't wait to go back.

Or this, from the parent of a pair of teens in Verona, New Jersey:

I like Universal fine, and The Wizarding World stuff is pretty neat, but two days is more than enough at these parks. We started at Disney and then moved to Universal for the end of our trip and were happy to be leaving. We are always much sadder leaving Disney. For a place that is making a mint of money off a magic franchise, it's not a very magical place.

Or this, from a mother of two in Arlington, Virginia:

Some of the rides were super impressive and fun, but too much of it was screen based, and there was very little that all four of us could handle (and therefore do together). I'm sure my teens would like to return, but I'll let them save that for their school band trips; as a family it's WDW all the way.

A handful of readers have criticized this book for mentioning Disney at all, including this online reviewer:

If I wanted a book about Disney, I would have purchased a book about Disney. I'm going to Universal; I don't care about what Disney does or offers.

In our defense, the majority of first-time Universal visitors (and hence, our readers) have previously been to Walt Disney World or another Disney attraction. Disney's product practically defines *theme park* in the public imagination, even among people who have never visited a Disney park, and its Florida resort sets the standard against which the entire industry is judged, not only in Orlando but around the world. So we point out parallels between Disney and Universal where appropriate only to give you a clearer picture of what to expect from your visit and how to spend your time.

We see the three Universal parks and the six Disney World parks (including water parks) as rough equals, and every one is world-class. Both Universal and Disney have splendid on-site hotels, with Universal offering more perks to its guests. There will always be those who miss the indescribable "magic" for which Disney World is famous. But here are five important arenas in which we think Universal currently has an advantage in the Orlando theme park wars:

MORE ADULT   If there's one distinguishing element that most separates Universal from Disney, it's the distinctly adult attitude that informs the resort's attractions and ambience. While Walt wanted to build a park that appealed equally to parents and their children, the majority of entertainment in today's Walt Disney World focuses on themes and characters catering to little kids. (That's not to say that there aren't plenty of adults who enjoy singing "Let It Go" at the top of their lungs, but the less said about that the better.) The same goes for most Disney rides, which emphasize visual charm over physical intensity; aside from the half dozen "mountains," you could probably take a nap on any given WDW attraction.

Universal, on the other hand, sets its sights slightly higher demographically, with a much higher proportion of attractions aimed at tweens, teens, and young (or young-at-heart) adults. Many of Universal's properties are based on PG-13 or R-rated movies; even their animated ambassadors, such as Shrek and Despicable Me's Minions, are a bit edgier than Mickey and friends. Don't try to fall asleep on Universal's simulators and scream machines, which range in intensity from pleasantly discombobulating to, "Dear Lord, what have I done?"

This parent from the Dallas area agrees:

Universal is PG-13 regarding its rides, while Disney is PG. Universal's rides are amazing, while Disney's seem dated. We might not have noticed if we had visited Disney first. The thrill rides were the most important experience for my teens, who tremendously enjoyed their time on their own at Universal.

Universal offers the CityWalk nightclub venue, just outside the park gates, for those with the energy to make a night of it; WDW's closest equivalent, the sprawling Disney Springs complex, is far more sedate. And observant audience members will also notice that the scripts at Universal have a subversively snarky, postmodern spin that flies over youngsters' heads but serves as a welcome antidote to pixie-dusted perfection. After all, as the host in *Universal Orlando's Horror Make-Up Show* jokes, "This isn't Disney. We don't have to be nice to you!"

All this isn't to imply that there's nothing for wee tykes to enjoy at Universal; on the contrary, the playgrounds in IOA's Seuss Landing and Jurassic Park are as good as any at WDW, and Universal's child-swap policy is arguably more user-friendly than Disney's. But rather than spending the day focused on fulfilling their offspring's fantasies, parents at Universal get to realize some of their own along the way.

MORE ADVANCED Universal has been technologically ascendant for several years, introducing revolutionary motion systems and special effects in both rides and theater performances. As a dad from Mount Desert Island, Maine, wrote us:

> *Our family toured both Disney and Universal for the first time this trip, beginning our stay at Disney. The difference in ride quality and technology was striking. It would've been difficult to go the other way (Universal to Disney), as the rides at Disney seemed dated and carnival-like by comparison.*

A father from Conway, Arkansas, agrees, adding:

> *Magic Kingdom and Epcot are full of old technology and uninteresting rides. New attractions are badly needed, especially to keep up with Universal.*

While Disney relies conservatively on a combination of highly detailed themed areas, beloved characters, and inspiration from classic animated features (that many young people under age 16 have never seen), Universal takes more technological swings for the fences.

Granted, Disney parks do have their share of high-tech attractions—particularly Pandora's Flight of Passage, which outdoes Universal simulators in sheer gee-whiz factor—and not all Universal attractions approach the creative genius of Harry Potter and the Forbidden Journey or Escape from Gringotts. But while guests at both Disney and Universal report high levels of satisfaction, it's the next-gen technology manifested in Universal's headliners that delivers true "Wow!" moments. Plus, **Port of Entry** and **Jurassic Park** at Islands of Adventure—along with **The Wizarding World of Harry Potter,** encompassing both **Hogsmeade** at IOA and **Diagon Alley** at USF—clearly demonstrate that Universal can create exquisitely detailed and totally immersive themed areas.

MORE CURRENT Doc Brown's time-traveling DeLorean from *Back to the Future* may be parked at USF, but Orlando's real time machine is found at Walt Disney World's theme parks. WDW's recent top attractions are all inspired by intellectual properties that date from the 1930s (Seven Dwarfs Mine Train) through the 1990s (Toy Story Land)—with the exception of *Frozen* and *Avatar,* both of which have cooled in the pop-culture consciousness—and much of its older inventory is even more old-fashioned. Epcot is finally sweeping away its detritus of dated celebrities for a future of Pixar and Marvel intellectual properties, and Disney's Hollywood Studios is inching toward completion of a sure-to-be-popular Star Wars expansion, but both parks are still works in progress at press time.

Universal, on the other hand, has been relentlessly aggressive about constantly updating its lineup with currently relevant characters. The best example of this is its Wizarding World of Harry Potter, the first phase of which debuted while the record-breaking film franchise was still in theaters. Potter mania has seen a revival thanks to the Fantastic Beasts film series and *Harry Potter and the Cursed Child* play, while Marvel's superheroes, Despicable Me's Minions, and Jurassic Park's dinosaurs remain hot box office commodities. King Kong's 2016 resurrection at the resort presaged his 2017 big-screen comeback, and the recent Fast & Furious ride opened only about a year after the franchise's eighth cinematic installment.

The downside to Universal's obsession with staying on the cultural cutting edge is a sense of impermanence that prevents the resort from retaining its rich history. Disney's blessing of size allows it to preserve the type of long-in-the-tooth attractions that space-squeezed Universal often sacrifices for the next generation. As a result, repeat visitors to WDW develop a sense of nostalgia over a lifetime of revisiting beloved rides, whereas those returning to Universal after a long absence are more likely to be befuddled; for a fun (and dangerous) drinking game, stand outside Diagon Alley and take a sip every time someone asks, "Where's Jaws?"

But Universal's weaker sense of tradition is offset by the thrill of the new; while the Magic Kingdom has now gone more than a quarter century without a brand-new E-ticket, you can count on a major attraction opening at Universal Orlando nearly every year, and even bigger things—such as a significant expansion of the resort's borders and yet another theme park—are on the horizon.

MORE COMPACT While the lack of available elbowroom hurts Universal in some ways, it's a huge advantage in others. Anyone who has stayed on-site at WDW (especially in a hotel not serviced by the monorail) can testify how arduous navigating Mickey's vast transportation system can be. Taking the Disney bus to Animal Kingdom sometimes seems to take longer than an actual African safari, and if you want to transfer from Disney Springs to a theme park, you'd better pack a lunch.

At Universal, on the other hand, you can go your whole vacation without ever taking a ride (other than the amusement kind) because everything is within easy walking distance. Even the most remote hotel room is only a 15- or 20-minute walk from the park gates, which are themselves separated by only a few hundred yards, making park-hopping at Universal a no-brainer. If your feet do get tired, a fleet of water taxis, pedicabs, and colorful buses are available to transport you, usually with much less waiting than their WDW equivalents. As one reader put it:

What we appreciated about USF and IOA more than Disney is how compact the entire area is. We thought it was incredibly easy to park in one of the large garages and walk to the theme parks. And they are so close together that you can easily walk from one park to another.

In fact, if Universal Orlando closely compares to any Disney resort, it is not Walt Disney World but Disneyland in California. Both properties boast two first-rate theme parks in close proximity to each other, with an adjoining entertainment complex and nearby hotels for easy pedestrian access. If you've ever enjoyed the Disneyland Resort's intimacy, in contrast to Disney World's overwhelming scale, you'll feel right at home at Universal Orlando.

MORE MANAGEABLE   Universal's smaller scale also has both logistical and psychological benefits. Walt Disney World is so vast that there is no way to do it all, even if you were to stay for weeks. For some travelers, that overabundance of options creates anxiety and a fear of missing out or not getting your money's worth. Universal has plenty to occupy your attention—you could stay for a week without getting bored—but the list of choices is much more manageable.

More important, once you choose what you want to do at Universal, you can usually just go ahead and do it without jumping through the hoops now found at Disney World. Despite Disney's investment of well over a billion dollars, many guests find WDW's MyMagic+ vacation-planning service—and the ability (read: necessity) to book FastPass+ attraction reservations weeks in advance—to be a royal hassle. Universal's Express line-cutting service, which is included free with every room at the top three on-site hotels, can be used at any time without prior arrangement, so you don't have to decide what time you want to ride Dudley Do-Right's Ripsaw Falls two months from now.

Universal Express was a big hit with this Texas family:

Universal resorts' inclusion of the Express Pass [is] genius. My girls couldn't stop raving about the pass. They had gotten spoiled going to any ride and using the Express Pass with less than 10 minutes of wait time. Disney's FastPass had mixed results with us.

Likewise, WDW may have many more table-service restaurants inside and outside its parks, but good luck getting a seat in a popular eatery without booking your table six months in advance; at Universal, walk-ups are often accommodated, or you can simply make a reservation with your smartphone a few days (or even hours) before you want to eat.

SHOULD I GO TO UNIVERSAL ORLANDO IF I'VE SEEN UNIVERSAL HOLLYWOOD?

UNIVERSAL STUDIOS HOLLYWOOD (USH) in California shares much in common with its younger sibling in Orlando, including several headliner attractions. So is it worth visiting UOR if you've already done USH? In a word, "Absolutely!"

The Hollywood park is primarily a working movie studio with a park bolted on, making it less than cohesive as a themed attraction. There's nothing in Orlando that can compare to USH's justly famous Studio Tour, though some of its sights (the 3-D King Kong encounter and the Fast & Furious segment) have stand-alone analogues on the East Coast. But aside from the tram tour and the *WaterWorld* stunt show, the bulk of USH's limited lineup consists of virtual clones of attractions found in Orlando, only in less immersive environments. And though USH's CityWalk complex is larger than Orlando's, its offerings are less unique, featuring a number of familiar chains.

USH is looking better than ever, thanks to an ambitious multiyear expansion plan, which has renovated three-quarters of the park over the past decade and will bring new attractions, amenities, and production facilities to the California complex during the next few years. The initial phases of this makeover resulted in a colorfully rethemed area around the new Despicable Me attraction, an expansive Springfield district adjacent to The Simpsons Ride, and the 2016 debut of Harry Potter's West Coast digs. But even with USH's Wizarding World open, it only reproduces the Hogsmeade area from IOA; for the full Diagon Alley and Hogwarts Express experience, Orlando continues to be your only option.

The bottom line is that Universal Studios Hollywood makes a fine daylong diversion from a Disneyland vacation, but it is not yet big enough by itself to build a trip around. Universal Orlando, on the other hand, has nearly everything USH has, plus a whole lot more.

Critical Comparison of Attractions Found at Both UNIVERSAL STUDIOS HOLLYWOOD and UNIVERSAL ORLANDO
Animal Actors on Location About the same at both parks.
Despicable Me Minion Mayhem USH has an elaborate interactive exterior and much higher capacity; the ride itself is the same at both parks.
Flight of the Hippogriff Track layout and queue look about the same, but USH's ride feels much smoother.
Harry Potter and the Forbidden Journey The USH version boasts scarier animatronics and enhanced lighting and scenery, but it is essentially the same ride.
Jurassic Park River Adventure USH's version is being rethemed in 2019 to the Jurassic World franchise, with new dinosaurs and special effects. IOA's drop is slightly taller, but USH's is much wetter in warm weather. Otherwise, the rides are similar.
Revenge of the Mummy—The Ride Much longer with better effects at USF.
The Simpsons Ride Ride is about the same at both parks, but USH has a less claustrophobic queue and an on-ride photo op.
Transformers: The Ride 3-D About the same at both parks.

UNIVERSAL-SPEAK POCKET TRANSLATOR AND GUIDE TO COMMON ABBREVIATIONS

IT MAY COME AS A SURPRISE TO MANY, but Universal Orlando (like Walt Disney World) has its own somewhat peculiar language. The following table lists some terms and abbreviations that you're likely to bump into, both in this guide and in the larger Universal (and Disney) community.

UNIVERSAL LEXICON IN A NUTSHELL
ATTRACTION Ride or show
AUDIENCE Crowd
BACKSTAGE Behind the scenes, out of view of customers
CHARACTER Cartoon or movie character impersonated by an employee • **Animated Character** A character who wears a head-covering costume (Scooby-Doo, the Minions, the Simpsons) • **Face Character** A "celebrity" character who doesn't wear a head-covering costume (Doc Brown, Marilyn Monroe, and the like)
COSTUME Work attire or uniform
DARK RIDE Indoor ride
DAY GUEST Any customer not staying at a Universal resort
EARLY PARK ADMISSION (EPA) Morning hour at Universal's theme parks for eligible guests (*Early Entry, Magic Morning,* or *Extra Magic Hour* in Disney-speak)
GENERAL PUBLIC Same as day guest
GREETER Employee positioned at an attraction entrance
GUEST Customer
ON-SITE One of the Loews-operated resort hotels located on Universal Orlando property
ONSTAGE In full view of customers
PRESHOW Entertainment at an attraction before the feature presentation
QUICK-SERVICE RESTAURANT Counter-service or fast food–style restaurant
RESORT GUEST A customer staying at a Universal resort hotel
ROLE A team member's job
TEAM MEMBER Employee (*cast member* in Disney-speak)
TECHNICAL REHEARSAL Opening a park or attraction before its stated opening date (*soft opening* in Disney-speak)

COMMON ABBREVIATIONS AND WHAT THEY STAND FOR
AP Annual pass
EPA Early Park Admission
I-DRIVE International Drive (major Orlando thoroughfare)
IOA Universal's Islands of Adventure theme park
TM Team member
USF Universal Studios Florida theme park
UOR Universal Orlando Resort
UX or UEx Universal Express
VB Volcano Bay
WWoHP Wizarding World of Harry Potter

UPCOMING AT UNIVERSAL ORLANDO RESORT

AT ISLANDS OF ADVENTURE, The Wizarding World will welcome an innovative new family-friendly roller coaster inspired by Hagrid's magical creatures in 2019. Jurassic Park is also ripe for a major renovation; its Hollywood cousin is already being converted into Jurassic World, and updated animatronic dinos and another new roller coaster are rumored to be in development for Orlando. The Lost Continent lost its *Eighth Voyage of Sindbad Stunt Show* in 2018, and Hyrule from Nintendo's Zelda games has been hinted at as a possible future replacement for the entire island.

At Universal Studios Florida, a new spy-themed stunt show will debut in 2019, replacing the former *Terminator 2: 3-D* attraction. The next attractions rumored to be on the chopping block are *Fear Factor Live* (for a Harry Potter Ministry of Magic attraction) and *Shrek 4-D* (for a *Secret Life of Pets* dark ride). Most important, long-rumored plans to replace Woody Woodpecker's KidZone (including Curious George Goes to Town, *A Day in the Park with Barney,* and Woody Woodpecker's Nuthouse Coaster) have been repeatedly postponed, but a new all-ages attraction—perhaps featuring Nintendo's Pokémon games or DreamWorks' popular Trolls characters—could be in the works for the area. And an expansion of Volcano Bay should add additional sliding capacity to the water park in the next year.

Outside of the theme parks, Universal debuted the Aventura Hotel, a 600-room ultramodern tower with rooftop views of the Volcano Bay water park, in 2018. It will follow up in 2019 by opening the first phase of Endless Summer Resort, comprised of a pair of hotels with 2,800 value-priced rooms and suites, on the former Wet 'n Wild land along International Drive. Farther off, roads and other infrastructure are already being constructed on the 1,000 acres Universal acquired near the convention center. Trademarks have been filed for the names Universal's Fantastic Worlds and Epic Universe, and Comcast CEO Steve Burke confirmed to investors that development of an entire new theme park—expected to include Super Nintendo World, starring video game icons Mario and Donkey Kong—is now under way.

PART ONE

PLANNING *Before* YOU LEAVE HOME

GATHERING INFORMATION

IN ADDITION TO READING THIS GUIDE, we recommend that you visit our website, theunofficialguides.com, which is dedicated to news about our guidebooks, as well as a blog with posts from Unofficial Guide authors. You can also sign up for the "Unofficial Guide Newsletter," containing even more travel tips and special offers.

Our sister website, touringplans.com, offers essential tools for planning your trip and saving you time and money. At blog.touringplans .com you will find breaking news for the Universal Orlando Resort (UOR) and Universal theme parks worldwide. The site also offers computer-optimized touring plans for Universal Studios Florida (USF) and Islands of Adventure (IOA), as well as complete dining menus, including wine lists, for every food cart, stand, kiosk, counter-service restaurant, and sit-down restaurant in the resort.

IMPORTANT UNIVERSAL ADDRESSES

- **THEME PARKS & CITYWALK PARKING GARAGE ADDRESS**
  6000 Universal Boulevard, Orlando, FL 32819
- **GPS COORDINATES FOR UNIVERSAL ORLANDO PARKING GARAGE**
  Latitude: N28° 28.439'   Longitude: W81° 27.737'
- **GUEST SERVICES & CORPORATE OFFICES**
  Universal Orlando Resort, 1000 Universal Studios Place, Orlando, FL 32819
- **HARD ROCK HOTEL**   5800 Universal Boulevard, Orlando, FL 32819
- **LOEWS PORTOFINO BAY HOTEL**   5601 Universal Boulevard, Orlando, FL 32819
- **LOEWS ROYAL PACIFIC RESORT**   6300 Hollywood Way, Orlando, FL 32819
- **LOEWS SAPPHIRE FALLS RESORT**   6601 Adventure Way, Orlando, FL 32819
- **UNIVERSAL'S AVENTURA HOTEL**   6725 Adventure Way, Orlando, FL 32819
- **UNIVERSAL'S CABANA BAY BEACH RESORT**
  6550 Adventure Way, Orlando, FL 32819
- **UNIVERSAL'S ENDLESS SUMMER RESORT**
  7000 Universal Boulevard, Orlando, FL 32819

UNIVERSAL ORLANDO PHONE NUMBERS	
Universal Orlando Main Information	☎ 407-363-8000
Guest Relations	☎ 407-224-4233 (press 2 for Lost and Found)
Tickets by Mail	☎ 407-224-7840
Merchandise	☎ 888-762-0820
Vacation Packages	☎ 877-801-9720
Vacation Packages Deaf or Hard of Hearing TDD	☎ 800-447-0672
On-Site Hotel Reservations	☎ 888-273-1311
Meeting Attendees/Individual Call-In for Group Blocks	☎ 866-360-7395
Universal In-Park Dining and Character Meals	☎ 407-224-3663
Universal Resort Dining and Character Meals	☎ 407-503-3463
Mandara Spa at Portofino Bay	☎ 407-503-1244
Hard Rock Hotel	☎ 407-503-ROCK (2000)
Loews Portofino Bay Hotel	☎ 407-503-1000
Loews Royal Pacific Resort	☎ 407-503-3000
Loews Sapphire Falls Resort	☎ 407-503-5000
Universal's Aventura Hotel	☎ 407-503-6000
Universal's Cabana Bay Beach Resort	☎ 407-503-4000
Universal's Endless Summer Resort	☎ 407-503-7000

Another really popular part of touringplans.com is the Crowd Calendar, which shows crowd projections for USF and IOA for every day of the year. Look up the dates of your visit, and the calendar will not only show the projected wait times for each day but will also indicate for each day which theme park will be the least crowded. Historical wait times are also available, so you can see how crowded the parks were last year for your upcoming trip dates.

Much of the content on touringplans.com—including the menus and resort photos and videos—is completely free for anyone to use. Access to part of the site, most notably the Crowd Calendar, additional touring plans, and in-park wait times, requires a small subscription fee (current-book owners get a substantial discount). This nominal charge helps keep the site online and costs less than lunch at the Leaky Cauldron restaurant in Diagon Alley. Plus touringplans.com offers a 45-day money-back guarantee.

UNIVERSAL ON THE WEB

THOUGH SOME DISNEY-CENTRIC SITES cover Universal in some (usually minimal) way, independent sites dedicated to Universal Orlando are much rarer. Of the independent Disney sites that deal with Universal, we recommend mousesavers.com for hotel and admission bargains.

For the latest Universal updates and rumors, try orlandoinformer.com, orlandoparkstop.com, parkscope.net, and the discussion boards at insideuniversal.net. For crowd projections and touring tips, check touringplans.com. Attractionsmagazine.com, themeparkinsider.com, screamscape.com, and behindthethrills.com are all reliable sites covering Central Florida attractions, including Universal. Local news and theme park developments are available at orlandosentinel.com, orlando.bizjournals.com, and orlandoweekly.com. Jimhillmedia.com offers insider information on attractions, new technologies, and changes in the parks. Finally, there's the official Universal Orlando website, universalorlando.com. Annual pass holders may want to visit uoapfb.com to join the official UOAP Facebook group, which is a rich source of both breaking news and petty griping.

BEST UNIVERSAL MOBILE APPS Universal offers a free smartphone app for Apple and Android devices that displays wait times and interactive maps while you're inside the parks, using the resort's free Wi-Fi (connect to "xfinitywifi" and accept the legal terms to access). Park admission can also be purchased through the app and stored in a digital wallet. You'll need the app to secure Virtual Line ride reservations inside USF without visiting a kiosk, or to set up your TapuTapu account before visiting Volcano Bay, so be sure to install it before your arrival.

We also recommend **Lines,** the mobile app of touringplans.com, available for the Apple iPhone and iPad at the iTunes Store (search for "TouringPlans") and for Android devices at the Google Play Store. Owners of other phones can use the web-based version at m.touringplans .com. The app is free to download, but you'll need to log in with a paid TouringPlans subscription to access most of its features.

The touringplans.com website's touring plans, menus, Crowd Calendar, and more are available in Lines, which provides continuous real-time updates on wait times at Universal Orlando. Using in-park staff and updates sent in by readers, Lines shows you the current wait times at every attraction in every park, as well as estimated actual waits for these attractions for the rest of today. For example, Lines will tell you that the posted wait time for Harry Potter and the Escape from Gringotts is 60 minutes, and that based on what they know about how Universal manages Gringotts' queue, the actual time you'll probably wait in line is 48 minutes. Lines is the only Universal app that shows you both posted and actual wait times.

You can update the touring plans when you're in the parks too. The ability to redo your plan allows you to recover from any situation while still minimizing your waits for the rest of the day. Lines also has an online chat feature, where folks can ask questions and give travel tips. Hundreds of "Liners" interact every day in discussions that stay remarkably on-topic for an internet forum.

As long as you have that smartphone handy while visiting the parks, we and your fellow Unofficial Guide readers would love it if you could report on the actual wait times you get while you're there. Run Lines, log in to your user account, and click "+time" in the upper right corner to help everyone out. We'll use that information to update the wait times for everyone in the park and make everyone's lives just a little bit better.

BEST UNIVERSAL PODCASTS   The best podcast devoted to Universal is **"UUOP: The Unofficial Universal Orlando Podcast"** (uuopodcast.com), which features regular reports from this book's author on "all the little things" that are new around the resort; ironically, the podcast is based not in Orlando but in the United Kingdom. **Parkscope** and **Inside Universal** also produce irreverent podcasts focusing on UOR. The **"E-Ticket Report,"** cohosted by irrepressible Touring Plans contributor Derek Burgan, frequently features Universal content. **"Orlando Tourism Report"** (orlandotourismreport.com) often breaks local attraction news. **Season passpodcast.com** and **coasterradio.com** have breaking news and in-depth interviews with theme park designers and executives from parks around the world.

BEST UNIVERSAL TWITTER FEEDS   If you want your Universal news and rumors in 280 character bites, follow these prolific park Tweeters: @universalorl, @parkscope, @insideuniversal, @themepark, @theme parks, @attractions, @horrornightsorl, @behindthrills, @aliciastella, @orlandoinformer, @thrillgeek, @richobj, @hatetofly, @thenjbrandon, @bioreconstruct, @derekburgan, @touringplans, and @skubersky.

TIMING YOUR VISIT

TRYING TO REASON WITH THE TOURIST SEASON

CENTRAL FLORIDA THEME PARKS and attractions are busiest the last week or so of December and the first few days of January. Next busiest is the spring break period from mid-March through the week of Easter, then Thanksgiving week. Following those are June–mid-July, when summer vacation is at its peak, and the week of Presidents' Day.

The least busy time is from the middle of August through the beginning of October. Next slowest are the weeks in mid-January after the Martin Luther King Jr. holiday weekend up to Presidents' Day in February. The weeks after Thanksgiving and before Christmas are less crowded than average, as is mid-April–mid-May, after spring break, and before Memorial Day.

Late February, March, and early April are dicey. Crowds ebb and flow according to spring break schedules and the timing of Presidents' Day weekend. Besides being asphalt-melting hot, July brings throngs of South American tourists on their winter holiday.

unofficial **TIP**
Though crowds have grown in September and October as a result of promotions aimed at the international market and families without school-age children, these months continue to be good for touring.

THE DOWNSIDE OF OFF-SEASON TOURING

THOUGH WE STRONGLY RECOMMEND going to Universal Orlando in the fall, winter, or spring, there are a few trade-offs. The parks often close early during the off-season, either because of low crowds or special events such as the Halloween and Rock the Universe events at Universal

Studios Florida. This drastically reduces touring hours. Even when crowds are small, it's difficult to see everything at Universal Studios Florida (USF) or Islands of Adventure (IOA) between 9 a.m. and 6 p.m. Early closing also usually means no evening lagoon show. And because these are slow times, some rides and attractions may be closed. Finally, Central Florida temperatures fluctuate wildly during late fall, winter, and early spring; daytime highs in the 40s and 50s aren't uncommon.

Given the choice, however, smaller crowds, bargain prices, and stress-free touring are worth risking cold weather or closed attractions. Touring in fall and other off periods is so much easier that our research team, at the risk of being blasphemous, would advise taking children out of school for an Orlando visit.

Most readers who have tried Central Florida's attractions at various times agree. A New Hampshire parent writes:

> I took my grade-school children out of school for a few days to go during a slow time and would highly recommend it. We communicated with the teachers about a month before traveling to seek their preference for whether classwork and homework should be completed before, during, or after our trip. It's so much more enjoyable to be [in Orlando] when your children can experience rides and attractions . . . rather than standing in line. And traveling at a time of year when it's not unbearably hot makes such a difference as well. I would be hard-pressed to go during a hot or busy time ever again.

There's another side to this story, and we've received some well-considered letters from parents and teachers who don't think taking kids out of school is such a hot idea. From a father in Fairfax, Virginia:

> My wife and I are disappointed that you seem to be encouraging families to take their children out of school to avoid the crowds [in Orlando] during the summer months. My wife is an eighth-grade teacher of chemistry and physics. She has parents pull their children, some honor roll students, out of school for vacations, only to discover when they return that the students are unable to comprehend the material. Parents' suspicions about the quality of their children's education should be raised when children go to school for 6 hours a day yet supposedly can complete this same instruction with less than an hour of homework each night.

A Martinez, California, teacher offers this compelling analogy:

> There are a precious 180 days for us as teachers to instruct our students, and there are 185 days during the year for [vacation]. I have seen countless students during my 14 years of teaching struggle to catch up the rest of the year due to a week of vacation during critical instructional periods. It's like walking out of a movie after watching the first 5 minutes, and then returning for the last 5 minutes and trying to figure out what happened.

But a teacher from Penn Yan, New York, sees things differently:

> I've read the comments by teachers saying that they all think it's horrible for a parent to take a child out for a vacation. As a teacher and

a parent, I disagree. If a parent takes the time to let us know that a child is going to be out, we help them get ready for upcoming homework the best we can. If the child is a good student, why shouldn't they go have a wonderful experience with their family? I also don't understand when teachers say they can't get something together for the time the student will be out. We all have to plan ahead, and we know what we are teaching days, if not weeks, in advance. Take 20 minutes out of your day and set something up. Learn to be flexible!

BE UNCONVENTIONAL Orlando's Orange County Convention Center (OCCC) hosts some of the largest conventions and trade shows in the world. Universal is far enough from the OCCC that it isn't usually affected by events, but hotel rooms anywhere around International Drive can be hard to find (and expensive) when there's a big convention. You can check the convention schedule at the OCCC for the next six months at calendar.occc.net/calendar.

DON'T FORGET AUGUST Kids go back to school pretty early in Florida (and in a lot of other places too). This makes mid- to late August a good time to visit Universal Orlando for families who can't vacation during the fall. A New Jersey mother of two school-age children spells it out:

The end of August is the PERFECT time to go (just watch out for hurricanes; it's the season). There were virtually no wait times, 20 minutes at the most.

A mom from Rapid City, South Dakota, agrees:

School starts very early in Florida, so our mid-August visit was great for crowds but not for heat.

And from a family from Roxbury, New Jersey:

I recommend the last two weeks of August for anyone traveling there during the summer. We have visited twice during this time of year and have had great success touring the parks.

Though we recommend off-season touring, we realize that it's not possible for many families. We want to make it clear, therefore, that you can have a wonderful experience regardless of when you go. Our advice, irrespective of season, is to arrive early at the parks and avoid the crowds by using one of our touring plans. If attendance is light, kick back and forget the touring plans.

WE'VE GOT WEATHER! Long before theme parks, tourists visited Florida year-round to enjoy the temperate tropical and subtropical climates. The best weather months generally are October, November, March, and April. Fall is usually dry, whereas spring is wetter. December, January, and February vary, with average highs of 72°–73°F intermixed with highs in the 50°–65°F range. May is hot but tolerable. June, July, August, and September are the warmest months. Rain is possible anytime, usually in the form of scattered thunderstorms. An entire day of rain is unusual, but midafternoon downfalls occur so regularly during the summer that you can practically set your watch by them. These squalls, with lightning and gale-force winds, can temporarily shutter attractions but typically disperse in under an hour. Immediately after a storm is an ideal time to experience rides with little wait, especially at Volcano Bay.

UNIVERSAL ORLANDO CLIMATE											
JAN	FEB	MAR	APR	MAY	JUN	JUL	AUG	SEP	OCT	NOV	DEC
AVERAGE DAILY HEAT INDEX (TEMPERATURE + HUMIDITY)											
76°F	75°F	80°F	88°F	104°F	109°F	116°F	117°F	110°F	92°F	80°F	74°F
AVERAGE DAILY LOW											
50°F	53°F	57°F	62°F	68°F	73°F	76°F	76°F	74°F	68°F	60°F	54°F
AVERAGE RAINFALL PER MONTH											
2.9"	2.7"	4.0"	2.3"	3.1"	8.3"	7.0"	7.7"	5.1"	2.5"	2.1"	2.9"
NUMBER OF DAYS OF RAIN PER MONTH											
6	6	7	5	8	14	16	16	13	8	5	6

Source: U.S. Climate Data

HOW MUCH TIME TO ALLOCATE

PRIOR TO THE DEBUT of The Wizarding Worlds, some visitors found that they could see everything of note at both Universal parks within a single day. Not anymore: Touring Universal Studios Florida, including one meal and a visit to Diagon Alley, takes about 10–12 hours, while a comprehensive tour of Islands of Adventure will take a couple hours less.

For that reason, we recommend devoting a minimum of a full day to each Universal Orlando theme park, especially if this is your first visit. Three days is ideal, particularly with a park-to-park pass, as it will allow you to fully explore each park and revisit your favorite attractions. Add an extra day to your trip if you plan on going to Volcano Bay, which you'll want to visit both during early morning and after sunset. An on-site stay of four or more days will allow you to sample the parks in smaller bites while taking full advantage of the resort's other amenities.

unofficial **TIP**
Get to the park with your admission already purchased about 30–45 minutes before official opening time. Arrive 45–60 minutes before official opening time if you need to buy admission. Be aware that you can't do a comprehensive tour of both Universal theme parks in a single day.

Some Universal Orlando attractions don't open until 10 a.m. or later. Most theater attractions don't schedule performances until 11 a.m. or after. This means that early in the day, all park guests are concentrated among the limited number of attractions in operation.

As a postscript, you won't have to worry about any of this if you use our Universal Orlando touring plans. We'll keep you one jump ahead of the crowd and make sure that any given attraction is running by the time you get there.

SELECTING THE DAY OF THE WEEK FOR YOUR VISIT

WHEN READERS ASKED, "What is the best day to visit Universal Orlando?," we used to reply that Sunday was the least crowded day at the resort (presumably because people are starting their vacations at Walt Disney World [WDW]), followed by Monday and Saturday, and that Thursday was the most crowded. While that still generally holds true, there are too many other variables—including weather and special events—to make this a reliable rule of thumb.

The best way to know which day to visit Universal Orlando is with the Crowd Calendar at touringplans.com/universal-orlando/crowd-calendar. No matter which day you visit, arriving early and following a touring plan makes a much bigger difference than what day of the week it is.

INTEGRATING A UNIVERSAL ORLANDO VISIT WITH A WDW VACATION

WHILE UNIVERSAL ORLANDO has recently made strides in convincing visitors to make UOR their primary destination, for many travelers a stop at Universal is a side trip in their Walt Disney World–centric vacation. If you are devoting the bulk of your Orlando holiday to Disney but still want to make a detour to Universal, you have three primary options:

THE DAY TRIP   Most Disney guests who want to sample Universal take a single day out of their vacation to visit USF and/or IOA. This solution is simplest for guests with their own cars, or shuttle transportation between the resorts can be arranged (see page 139). The day trip has a couple of drawbacks: the per-day cost can be high, especially if you want to visit both UOR theme parks, and (depending on transportation arrangements) you may be unable to arrive before rope drop (essential for optimal touring) or have to depart before closing time.

THE WDW/UOR/WDW SANDWICH   An increasing number of guests take a night or two out of the middle of their WDW trip and stay on property at Universal. Again, transportation can be handled through a private car or shuttle bus. This method allows you to explore Universal over the course of two or three days and enjoy the perks of staying on-site, such as Early Park Admission to The Wizarding World. You can also use Disney's Magical Express for free transfers from and to the airport at the beginning and end of your trip. The main drawback is that you must check in and out (and back in again) at your Disney hotel, or pay for nights in a WDW bed you won't be using.

THE SPLIT TRIP   The best option if you want to divide your vacation roughly equally between Disney and Universal is a split trip, where you stay at one resort for the first half of your visit, and then transfer to the other for the remainder. You'll only be able to use Disney's Magical Express on one end of your vacation (arriving or departing), so look into the three-way transportation offered by outfits such as Quicksilver (see page 137). To decide which resort to visit first, check Touring Plans' Crowd Calendars for both properties, and visit Disney on the days it will be less busy, because crowds can make a bigger difference there than at Universal. If possible, this reader from upstate New York suggests saving your Universal visit for last to diminish disappointment:

> We visited Universal Orlando first and were blown away by the technology of the rides and the quality of the attractions, especially in the newer Harry Potter sections. When we got to Disney, we had fun, but we weren't nearly as impressed. We enjoyed the attractions, but some of them seemed dated and a little less than spectacular.

A mom from Missouri City, Texas, reported a similar experience:

> For families planning a combined UOR/Disney trip, especially for those who like thrill rides but whose kids are older and the Disney magic may not be as exciting as it used to be, I recommend going to WDW parks before UOR. For my 13-year-old, who was at WDW in 2013 (at 8 years) and Disneyland/Universal Hollywood in 2016 (at 11 years), it seemed like the Disney rides were too tame after having done two days first at UOR. He specifically called out Space Mountain for not being as thrilling as he remembered.

WHICH PARK TO VISIT?

UNIVERSAL ORLANDO'S TWO THEME PARKS are both spectacular, so if you can only visit one, you can't really go wrong. If you've visited Universal since 2010, when the first Wizarding World opened, but have not yet seen Diagon Alley, you'll want to go to Universal Studios Florida. If you've never been to Universal Orlando, or at least not in this decade, the decision is down to what type of attractions you prefer. If you are a fan of simulators, screen-based experiences, and live shows, then USF is right for you. If you prefer big outdoor roller coasters and wild water rides, IOA is your destination. Of course, if you are a Harry Potter devotee, you're going to have to visit both parks to get the full Wizarding World experience. Incidentally, USF is a much better park to visit during inclement weather, due to its larger percentage of indoor attractions. Finally, waterslide enthusiasts will want to spend at least one full day of their vacation at Volcano Bay.

ARRIVAL AND DEPARTURE DAY ACTIVITIES

GUESTS STAYING AT UNIVERSAL'S ON-SITE RESORTS can take advantage of all provided theme park perks—including early admission and Express Passes—from dawn on their arrival day until midnight on their day of departure. However, that requires using a full day's park admission for what may be only a few hours of entertainment, depending on your travel plans. Here are some suggestions on how to spend that spare half day at the start or end of your vacation:

- Explore Universal's resort hotels using the garden walking paths and free water taxis.
- Relax at your hotel pool if the weather is clear, or spend some quarters inside the game room if it's inclement.

- Play a round at the Hollywood Drive-In Mini-Golf, or catch a first-run flick at the Universal Cinemark at CityWalk (see pages 365 and 362).

- Take the free Vibe tour of musical memorabilia at the Hard Rock Cafe (see page 237).

- Drive to the nearby Fun Spot America amusement park (fun-spot.com) for a few laps around the multilevel go-cart tracks, then ride the White Lightning and Freedom Flyer roller coasters.

- Indulge in some retail therapy at the Orlando Premium Outlets shopping mall on International Drive (see page 257).

- Visit the Icon Orlando 360 complex (iconorlando.com) on International Drive, home to the world's tallest StarFlyer swing ride and an enormous observation wheel, as well as a wax museum and an aquarium.

OPERATING HOURS

THE UNIVERSAL ORLANDO WEBSITE publishes preliminary park hours up to six months in advance, but schedule adjustments can happen at any time, including the day of your visit. Check tinyurl.com /unihrs or call ☎ 407-363-8000 for the exact hours before you arrive. Off-season, parks may be open as few as 9 hours (9 a.m.–6 p.m.). At busy times (particularly holidays), they may operate 8 a.m.–10 p.m., while 9 a.m.–9 p.m. is the standard summer schedule.

Volcano Bay opens to the public at 9 a.m. (10 a.m. in the fall and winter) and stays open as late as 9 p.m. during the summer. While closing time can be as early as 5 p.m. during the off-season, Volcano Bay was designed for nighttime operation, with the majestic waterfalls cascading down the park's centerpiece transforming into blazing lava after sunset. If the park is open late during your visit, even if you exit during the afternoon, try to return during the closing hours to experience Volcano Bay's beauty after dark.

Universal's website publishes the official operating hours, but on most days, the parks open earlier. If the official hours for both theme parks are 9 a.m.–9 p.m., for instance, turnstiles for the park (or parks) participating in Early Park Admission will open between 7:30 a.m. and 8 a.m., and the one not offering early entry may still open its gates as early as 8:45 a.m.

Queues to attractions usually close to new guests at exactly the park's official closing time; if you are already in line at closing, you will be permitted to stay as long as it takes for you to ride, barring technical malfunctions. (Exceptions are popular rides such as Skull Island and Harry Potter and the Escape from Gringotts, which may close their queues before the rest of the park if the estimated wait significantly exceeds the time remaining in the operating day.) The main gift shops near the front of each park remain open 30 minutes to an hour after the rest of the park has closed. Universal's closing times are often earlier than its competition's, as an Auburn, Alabama, father of three pointed out:

I wish the parks would have stayed open later than 9 p.m. Everyone is not a morning person. Why can't Universal stay open at least until 10 p.m., 11 p.m., or midnight like Disney?

ALLOCATING MONEY

UNIVERSAL ORLANDO TICKETS

UNIVERSAL OFFERS TICKETS good for one to five days of admission to its theme parks. The **1-Day Base Ticket** includes entry to one theme park per day. If you buy a 2-Day Base Ticket, you can visit Islands of Adventure on one day and Universal Studios Florida on the next. You may not use a 2-Day Base Ticket to visit both parks in one day, but you can exit and return to the same park on the same day, in case you want to head back to your hotel for a nap.

If you want to visit both Universal Studios Florida (USF) and Islands of Adventure (IOA) on the same day, purchase the **Park-to-Park admission** option, which allows you to move freely between both parks on the same day. It takes about 12–15 minutes to walk from the entrance of one park to the next, or you can take the 4-minute Hogwarts Express trip between The Wizarding Worlds. Be aware that you *must* have park-to-park admission to ride the Hogwarts Express train between IOA and USF; you can upgrade single-park tickets at Guest Services or at the King's Cross (USF) or Hogsmeade (IOA) train stations.

All single-day theme park tickets are priced according to seasonal demand. Universal charges $9 less for one-day Value tickets that are valid only on select days, as indicated on the calendar at universal ticketcalendar.com. Anytime one-day tickets and all multiday tickets may be used on any day of the year.

Admission to the Volcano Bay water park costs $80 per day for adults ($75 for kids); Florida residents can save up to $10 on select days during the off-season. Volcano Bay access can be added to multiday 1-Park and Park-to-Park tickets for $55–$75, depending on ticket length.

A 1-Park, 1-Day Base Ticket is on par with those at the Disney parks, and a 2-Park, 1-Day Ticket is slightly more expensive than a one-day pass to all four Disney World gates. Multiday tickets can be much more expensive at Disney, where, for example, a 4-Day Park Hopper ticket costs about 50% more than what you'd pay at Universal; Disney's 4-Day Park Hopper Plus with water park admission is about 30% more than Universal's equivalent 3-Park pass.

All multiday tickets expire six days after the first use. Kids under age 3 are free, but tickets for ages 3–9 are discounted only a few dollars from the adult prices, despite the large number of rides with height requirements at Universal. Prices listed in the table on the facing page are for online sales before tax; gate prices for multiday tickets are $20 higher.

UNIVERSAL ORLANDO ANNUAL PASSES

UNIVERSAL ORLANDO offers some of the best deals on annual passes in town, not only for locals but also for anyone visiting the resort more than four days out of the year. The entry-level 2-Park Seasonal Pass costs about the same as a 4-Day Park-to-Park ticket, and Universal's most expensive 3-Park Premier Annual Pass is about the price of two 3-Park, 4-Day Park-to-Park tickets. The 3-Park Premier Pass is also about 20% cheaper than Walt Disney World's Platinum Plus Annual Pass, and while Disney has several more parks included in its annual passes, Universal throws in some great perks (depending on pass level) to compensate.

Universal annual passes include park-to-park admission to USF and IOA, including special events that don't require a separate ticket, such as Mardi Gras (except Seasonal Pass holders on concert nights), Grinchmas, and Universal's Holiday Parade, as well as discounts on those that cost extra, such as Halloween Horror Nights and Rock the Universe.

UNIVERSAL ORLANDO ADMISSIONS		
	ADULTS	CHILDREN (ages 3–9)
1-Day Single-Park (USF/IOA)	$115–$124	$110–$119
1-Day Volcano Bay	$80	$75
1-Day Park-to-Park (USF/IOA)	$170–$179	$165–$174
2-Day Single-Park (USF/IOA)	$204.99	$194.99
2-Day Park-to-Park (USF/IOA)	$264.99	$254.99
2-Day Park-to-Park (USF/IOA/VB)	$319.99	$309.99
3-Day Single-Park (USF/IOA)	$224.99	$214.99
3-Day Single-Park (USF/IOA/VB)	$279.99	$269.99
3-Day Park-to-Park (USF/IOA)	$284.99	$274.99
3-Day Park-to-Park (USF/IOA/VB)	$339.99	$329.99
4-Day Single-Park (USF/IOA)	$234.99	$224.99
4-Day Single-Park (USF/IOA/VB)	$299.99	$289.99
4-Day Park-to-Park (USF/IOA)	$299.99	$289.99
4-Day Park-to-Park (USF/IOA/VB)	$364.99	$354.99
5-Day Single-Park (USF/IOA)	$244.99	$234.99
5-Day Single-Park (USF/IOA/VB)	$319.99	$309.99
5-Day Park-to-Park (USF/IOA)	$314.99	$304.99
5-Day Park-to-Park (USF/IOA/VB)	$389.99	$379.99
2-Park Seasonal Annual Pass	$304.99	$304.99
2-Park Power Annual Pass	$354.99	$354.99
2-Park Preferred Annual Pass	$394.99	$394.99
2-Park Premier Annual Pass	$559.99	$559.99
3-Park Seasonal Annual Pass	$403.99	$403.99
3-Park Power Annual Pass	$463.99	$463.99
3-Park Preferred Annual Pass	$503.99	$503.99
3-Park Premier Annual Pass	$733.99	$733.99

Any annual pass can be purchased with access to all three parks, which includes Volcano Bay water park. Three-Park Annual Passes cost $99 more than 2-Park passes at the Seasonal level, an additional $109 for Power and Preferred Passes, and $174 more for Premier. Current 2-Park pass holders can upgrade to 3-Park access for the same prices, but no prorated discounts are given. All annual passes except 3-Park Premier are blocked from entry into the water park before 4 p.m. mid-July–mid-August; Seasonal passes are also blocked during spring break.

All annual pass holders receive up to 30% off room rates at on-site hotels, 20% off up to six select Blue Man Group Orlando adult tickets, 25% off Budget rental car base rates and free upgrades, $8 admission all day at Universal Cinemark, and other discounts as detailed below. Here are the four types of annual passes offered by Universal:

Seasonal Pass
- Valid for one year, but with about eight weeks of blockout dates, including spring break, all of July, and Christmas week at USF and IOA, and all concert nights at USF only; Volcano Bay blockouts in April and July–August
- No free parking
- No food or merchandise discounts at parks or CityWalk; 10%–15% off at select resort hotel locations
- 10% off gate prices for additional multiday park tickets

Power Pass
- Valid for one year, but with about four weeks of blockout dates at USF and IOA, including spring break and Christmas week; Volcano Bay blockouts in July–August
- 50% discount on self-parking (after the first visit)
- No food or merchandise discounts at parks or CityWalk; 10%–15% off at select resort hotel locations
- 15% off gate prices for additional multiday park tickets

Preferred Annual Pass
- Valid 365 days at USF and IOA; Volcano Bay blockouts in July-August
- Early Park Admission 1 hour before official opening to USF and/or IOA; not valid on about 72 mornings per year, including spring break, Thanksgiving, Christmas week, and select Saturdays
- Free standard self-parking and discounted prime self-parking and valet (after the first visit)
- 10% off most in-park restaurants and merchandise (outdoor carts and alcohol excluded)
- 10%–15% off food and merchandise at select CityWalk and resort hotel locations
- 15% off gate prices for additional multiday park tickets
- 10% off My Universal Photos
- Additional discounts at CityWalk and the resort hotels

Premier Annual Pass
- Valid 365 days at all parks
- Early Park Admission 1 hour before official opening to USF and/or IOA; valid 365 mornings per year

- Free prime self-parking and valet and discounted Red Carpet Valet (after the first visit)
- 15% off most in-park restaurants and merchandise (outdoor carts and alcohol excluded)
- Free Universal Express at USF and IOA after 4 p.m. every day (one time per participating attraction)
- One free Halloween Horror Nights ticket (valid select off-peak nights only)
- 10%–20% off food and merchandise at select CityWalk and resort hotel locations
- 15% off gate prices for additional multiday park tickets
- 15% off My Universal Photos
- Free admission to CityWalk clubs, and free admission for one guest (excludes concerts and special events)
- Additional discounts at CityWalk and the resort hotels

In addition, all annual pass holders get a quarterly newsletter with announcements of special limited-time perks, such as exclusive merchandise or pass holder–only events during Passholder Appreciation Days, held in the off-season; see tinyurl.com/uniappdays for details. And if you can't handle the cost of a pass in one big bite, Universal's FlexPay service will (after a substantial down payment) split the remaining bill into interest-free payments as low as $17 a month. Be aware that you'll have to pay off your balance in full before upgrading your pass tier. After the initial yearlong payment contract is complete, FlexPay will automatically renew on a month-to-month basis with a significantly higher monthly payment. FlexPay customers do not get the renewal discount offered to paid-in-full pass holders, but they may be eligible for bonus months during seasonal sales promotions. Annual pass pricing and benefits change regularly, so visit tinyurl.com/UORAnnualPass for the latest offers.

So, should you buy a Universal Orlando annual pass, and if so, which one? If you are making only one trip to Universal within the year, are staying off-site, and plan to spend four days or fewer in the parks, then you should stick with standard tickets. If, however, you plan to spend five or more days at Universal's parks, anticipate returning to Universal within the year, or want to stay at an on-site hotel for even one night, it is well worth your while to run the numbers on an annual pass.

As for which one to buy, first double-check the current Seasonal and Power Pass blockout dates on Universal's website to ensure they don't conflict with your trip. Even if you're in the clear, at least one member of your party will want to pick up at least a Preferred Pass for its discounts, especially if you are driving to the resort; four days of self-parking at $25 per day adds up to $100, which is more than the difference in price between the Seasonal and Preferred Passes. The Power Pass is currently only $40 cheaper than the Preferred Pass ($30 for

unofficial **TIP**
If you're trying to book a room on the Universal Orlando or Loews websites with an annual pass discount, enter promo code "APH" on the search screen to see pass holder rates.

Florida residents), less than the cost of four visits with discounted self-parking; after factoring in the blockout dates and lack of discounts, the Power Pass is a poor value for most guests. (Note that free or discounted parking only applies after your first visit; you must first activate your annual pass at a park gate before receiving free parking.)

If—and only if—you take advantage of all its amenities, the Premier Annual Pass is an amazing value. At a $13.75-per-month upcharge from the 2-Park Preferred Pass, you can easily get your money's worth in free valet parking alone, and the free Universal Express after 4 p.m. is especially useful when the parks are open late. (See the Universal Express section on page 57 for more details.) The free Halloween Horror Nights pass isn't valid on most nights in October and can't be upgraded or transferred to another person, which limits its value if you are also planning to buy a Frequent Fear Pass.

BUYING ADMISSION TO UNIVERSAL ORLANDO

ONE OF OUR BIG GRIPES ABOUT UNIVERSAL is that there are never enough ticket windows open in the morning to accommodate the crowds. That means that guests wait in long ticket lines during the peak holiday and summer seasons just to reach a sales window before they can enjoy more waits at the turnstiles and attractions. You can purchase Volcano Bay tickets at the Volcano Bay bus stop inside the parking structure or at the park entrance. However, we strongly recommend that you buy your admission in advance. Passes are available directly from Universal at universalorlando.com or by phone at ☎ 800-711-0080; at the concierge desks or attraction box offices of many Orlando-area hotels; and through Guest Services at the DoubleTree at Universal hotel (☎ 407-351-1000), at the intersection of Major Boulevard and Kirkman Road.

Many hotels and some ticket brokers that sell Universal Orlando admissions don't issue actual passes. Instead, the purchaser gets a voucher that can be redeemed for a pass at the theme park. Fortunately, the voucher-redemption window is separate from the park's ticket-sales operation, but it's still quicker to get a ticket that you can take straight to the gate. If you downloaded the official Universal Orlando app on your smartphone, you can purchase single or multi-day admission directly on your mobile device, which will display a bar code that serves as your ticket, avoiding the need for paper altogether. Prices for passes purchased through the app are the same as on Universal's website.

SAVING MONEY ON ADMISSION TO UNIVERSAL ORLANDO

UNIVERSAL'S ADMISSION DISCOUNTS change too rapidly to comprehensively cover in this guide. The best online clearinghouse for keeping up with the latest available offers is mousesavers.com/universal -orlando-discounts-and-deals.

Ticket Savings Direct from Universal Orlando

Universal offers discounts when you purchase passes online at universal orlando.com, including $20-per-ticket discounts on multiday tickets plus other time-limited specials. Tickets purchased online can be printed at home and used at the turnstiles without the need to exchange them at a box office, or they can be retrieved using the credit card they were purchased with from automated will call kiosks outside each park; look for the ATM-like terminals to the right of the Guest Services window at USF, or to the left of Toothsome Chocolate Emporium outside IOA. Tickets purchased online (including annual passes) do not begin expiring until first activated at a park entrance.

Multiday tickets purchased online directly from Universal include a coupon booklet with "up to $150 in savings" on food, merchandise, and hotel services. Universal also offers a best-price guarantee: if you buy park tickets through Universal's website and then find them cheaper online within seven days, Universal Orlando will give you a gift card (good at restaurants and shops around the resort) refunding the price difference. The price guarantee is only on regular admission tickets (not Express or special-event tickets) available to the general public from US-based websites, and it excludes time-share promotions, group rates, or other special discounts. To claim your refund, call ☎ 877-589-4783 or send an email via visitorsatisfaction.com/contactus.

Florida (and sometimes Georgia) residents can take advantage of an ever-changing array of price breaks, often tied to a fast-food chain or soft drink promotion. Local resident tickets expire 59 days after first use for two-day tickets and 179 days after for three- to five-day tickets, unlike regular multiday tickets, which expire after a week. These specials require valid photo ID proving residency to redeem, so don't try using one if you aren't eligible. Current annual pass holders get a modest 10%–15% price break when buying additional multiday tickets at the gate but may do better with the standard online discount. Visit tinyurl.com/UniversalLocal to see the locals' latest discounts.

Universal Orlando frequently offers online-only specials that are usually superior to any other available discount. For example, in late 2018 Universal sold two-day 2-Park and 3-Park tickets with an extra two days free. These tickets have to be used before a certain expiration date, and blockout days may apply, but the savings can be substantial.

Ticket Savings from Third-Party Vendors

The lowest possible prices on electronically delivered Universal tickets that we're aware of are through **Orlando Ticket Connection** (orlando ticketconnection.com), which undercuts Universal's online prices on park-to-park tickets by $5–$10. We asked readers who had used Orlando Ticket Connection to write in and received this reply:

> *I ordered tickets for SeaWorld and Universal from Orlando Ticket Connection late on Thursday night (around midnight), and at 9:08 on Friday morning I received my tickets by email. It was quick, and*

they were actual tickets that you take directly to the turnstile. I used them both at the parks today and had no problems whatsoever. I would order tickets from them again without a second thought.

Best of Orlando (bestoforlando.com) and **Official Ticket Center** (officialticketcenter.com) are also reliable vendors that sell print-at-home tickets for a few dollars (or sometimes cents) more or less than Orlando Ticket Connection.

Dreams Unlimited Travel (dreamsunlimitedtravel.com) charges the same or more for Universal tickets as the official website, but it does offer exclusive one- and two-day park-to-park tickets bundled with discounted round-trip transportation from Disney-area hotels via Quick Transportation (quicktransportation.com). Its tickets are processed through Universal's secure website and can be printed at home or retrieved from will call kiosks.

Universal charges $14 for domestic FedEx shipping of tickets ($19 for international delivery). If you want physical tickets mailed to you for the cheapest price and can order at least two weeks before your trip, consider using an online ticket wholesaler, such as **Official Ticket Center** (officialticketcenter.com) or **Undercover Tourist** (undercovertourist.com). Official Ticket Center advertises all its prices inclusive of tax and USPS Certified shipping, and it has the lowest bottom line cost on physical Universal Orlando tickets that we've found, usually within pennies of Orlando Ticket Connection's e-delivery price. Both OTCs often match or beat the short-term deals that Universal offers on its own website.

If you are visiting from the United Kingdom, check out **Attraction Tickets Direct** (attraction-tickets-direct.co.uk) for good deals on 14-day tickets.

DISCOUNTS AT UNIVERSAL ORLANDO

UNIVERSAL ORLANDO PROVIDES DISCOUNTS on tickets, dining, and lodging to members of many travel organizations, including automobile clubs such as AAA and CAA. Discounts are also available to Universal Orlando annual pass holders. This section is a guide to finding the best discounts for members of these groups and the general public.

Admission

In addition to the previously mentioned discounts, AAA members save $4–$5 on multiday tickets at the gate. Some regional AAA offices also sell discounted Universal Orlando passes to members in advance, but prices vary by area. The closest Auto Club South office to Universal Orlando is at 7339 W. Sand Lake Road, Ste. 424, in Bay Hill; call ☎ 407-351-5610 for hours and directions. AAA South members can buy discounted tickets, annual passes, and vacation packages online at aaa.com/universal. *Note:* You must purchase your park admission through AAA and show the Discounts and Rewards voucher included with your ticket to receive any AAA food or merchandise discounts inside Universal's parks.

Costco Wholesale clubs sometimes sell discounted Universal Orlando tickets to members.

Active duty and retired members of the United States armed forces should visit universalorlando.com/military for exclusive deals on tickets and hotel packages. A typical military discount package includes three nights of accommodations in an on-site or partner hotel and a 3-Park, 4-Day Park-to-Park Ticket. Universal Orlando tickets are available at most base Leisure Travel offices, as well as at Shades of Green at Disney World.

Resorts

All annual pass holders (including Seasonal and Power Pass holders) receive discounts of up to 30% on resort lodging, depending on availability. If you're staying at a Universal resort for two or more days, you may save enough on lodging to offset the cost of an annual pass for the adult booking the room. Similar (and sometimes superior) seasonal Florida resident discounts are detailed at tinyurl.com/uniflres.

AAA members can book on-site rooms and vacation packages at a modest discount, usually 5%–25%. You must call AAA or Loews directly to get the discount; it cannot be applied online.

Cheaptickets.com and orbitz.com often offer discount codes for up to 20% their already-discounted Universal Orlando room rates; Google "Orlando hotel promo codes" or use a site such as retailmenot.com to find the latest offers.

Check the mousesavers.com website, which lists seasonal and specialized discounts for Universal's resorts, such as discounts available to residents of certain states.

The Hard Rock Rewards frequent-stay program at Hard Rock Hotel offers free priority late checkout and points toward free stays; you can learn about the program and sign up in advance at members .hardrock.com. Note that the perks sometimes cannot be used in conjunction with discounted rates. (A similar Loews YouFirst loyalty program at the other on-site hotels has been discontinued.)

Dining

AAA members receive 10% off food and nonalcoholic beverages at most restaurants inside USF and IOA, as well as 10% off at the Hard Rock Hotel's Palm Restaurant for groups of up to seven. *Note:* You must purchase your park admission through AAA and show the Discounts and Rewards voucher included with your ticket to receive any AAA food discounts inside Universal's parks.

American Express members save 10% off the Quick-Service Universal Dining Plan with Coca-Cola Freestyle cup; you must buy the dining plan on an American Express card and use your smartphone to show the American Express offer in the Universal Orlando mobile app at the time of purchase to receive the discount.

If you are visiting during September, several Universal resort restaurants participate in Orlando's Magical Dining Month, when you can order three courses from special prix fixe menus for only $35; visit visitorlando.com/magicaldining for details.

See page 36 for discounts offered to annual pass holders.

Merchandise

AAA members receive 10% off with a minimum pretax purchase of $50, or 15% off with a minimum of $75, of most merchandise (excluding carts and kiosks) inside Universal's theme parks and at CityWalk's Universal Studios Store. *Note:* You must purchase your park admission through AAA and show the Discounts and Rewards voucher included with your ticket to receive any AAA merchandise discounts inside Universal's parks. See page 36 for discounts offered to annual pass holders.

American Express members save 10% off merchandise with a $75 minimum purchase when using their AmEx card at Universal-owned shops (excluding inside The Wizarding Worlds). You must use your smartphone to show the American Express offer in the Universal Orlando mobile app at the time of purchase to receive the discount.

Entertainment and Other Discounts

Preferred Annual Pass holders receive 10% off services at Portofino Bay's Mandara Spa, and Premier Pass holders save 20% (Monday–Thursday only; some services excluded). Discounted Mandara Spa packages are also regularly offered on Groupon.

AAA members receive 10% off Blue Man Group tickets in Tier 1 or Tier 2 seating, while all annual pass holders (including Seasonal and Power Pass) receive 20% off; limit six seats per transaction.

Preferred Pass holders save 20% on CityWalk Party Passes (up to four per day); Premier Pass holders get Party Passes free for themselves, and for one guest.

Preferred and Premier Pass holders receive discounts on an 18-hole round at Hollywood Drive-In Mini-Golf for up to five players; Preferred Pass holders save 10%, while Premier Pass holders save 15%.

All annual pass holders pay the senior/child discounted rate of only $8 for adult admission to any Universal Cinemark showing (3-D films cost $3.50 extra).

Preferred and Premier Pass holders get a $5 discount on Classic Albums Live concert tickets at the Hard Rock Live box office.

Preferred Pass holders get 10% off all in-park rock climbing walls; Premier Pass holders save 15% per climb.

All annual pass holders (including Seasonal Pass holders) get 10%–20% off inflatable pool tubes, cabana rentals, and souvenir cups at Cabana Bay Beach Resort, and 50% off virtual reality games at Aventura Hotel's arcade.

All annual pass holders can save up to 25% off base rates and get a free upgrade at Budget rental cars.

Finally, you *might* save money at Universal Orlando by booking a package with tickets and lodging through **Universal Orlando Vacations** (☎ 877-801-9720; universalorlandovacations.com), the official travel company of Universal Orlando. It advertises packages with attractive-sounding rates, like "only $149 per adult per night," but you must take full advantage of every package component (including food or photos you may not want) to realize a modest 5% discount over buying each component separately.

For a full breakdown of Universal Orlando Vacations bundles, see page 94.

MAKING *the* MOST *of* YOUR TIME *and* MONEY *at* UNIVERSAL ORLANDO

THE CARDINAL RULES FOR SUCCESSFUL TOURING

MANY VISITORS DON'T HAVE three or four days to devote to Universal Orlando. Some are en route to other destinations or are visiting Universal as a sideline to their Disney World vacation. For these visitors, efficient touring is a must.

Even the most time-effective touring plan won't allow you to comprehensively cover more than one Universal theme park in one day. Plan to allocate an entire day to each park. An exception to this is when the parks close at different times, allowing you to tour one park until closing and then proceed to another.

One-Day Touring

A comprehensive tour of *both* Universal Orlando theme parks in one day is virtually impossible. A comprehensive one-day tour of Universal Studios Florida (USF) *or* Islands of Adventure (IOA) is possible but requires knowledge of the park, good planning, good navigation, and plenty of energy and endurance. One-day touring leaves little time for sit-down meals, prolonged browsing in shops, or lengthy breaks. One-day touring can be fun and rewarding, but allocating at least three full days to enjoy the two theme parks is preferable.

We provide one-day plans for each Universal park, plus one-day and two-day plans for those with park-to-park access. We also provide touring advice for Volcano Bay, though due to the water park's use of Virtual Line technology, a step-by-step touring plan isn't possible. Guests with three days should use our comprehensive two-day/two-park plan, followed by one of our specialized one-day plans; guests with more than three days can try multiple specialized one-day plans, or spend their additional days at leisure exploring without an itinerary.

Even if you are on a relaxed schedule, following a touring plan can still enhance your trip, according to this reader from Rockford, Michigan:

> *While we had four days to explore Universal, we followed the two-day park-to-park plan the first day, and it worked amazingly! It allowed us to get so much in that we could relax the rest of the trip and see and do everything we wanted, plus repeat rides everyone liked.*

Successfully touring USF or IOA in one day hinges on three rules:

1. Determine in Advance What You Really Want to See

Which attractions appeal to you most? Which ones would you like to experience if you have time left? What are you willing to forgo?

To help you set your touring priorities, we describe the theme parks and their attractions in detail in Parts Seven and Eight. In each description, we include the author's evaluation of the attraction and the opinions of Universal Orlando guests expressed as star ratings. Five stars is the highest rating.

Finally, because attractions range from midway-type rides and walk-through exhibits to high-tech extravaganzas, we have developed a hierarchy of categories to pinpoint an attraction's magnitude:

SUPER-HEADLINERS   The best attractions the theme park has to offer. Mind-boggling in size, scope, and imagination. Represent the cutting edge of attraction technology and design.

HEADLINERS   Multimillion-dollar, full-scale, themed adventures and theater presentations. Modern in technology and design and employing a full range of special effects.

MAJOR ATTRACTIONS   More modestly themed adventures, but ones that incorporate state-of-the-art technologies, or larger-scale attractions of older design.

MINOR ATTRACTIONS   Midway-type rides, small theater presentations, and elaborate walk-through attractions.

DIVERSIONS   Exhibits, both passive and interactive. Includes playgrounds, video arcades, and street theater.

Though not every attraction fits neatly into these descriptions, the categories provide a comparison of size and scope. Remember: bigger and more elaborate doesn't always mean better or more popular. Flight of the Hippogriff, a kiddie coaster in The Wizarding World of Harry Potter–Hogsmeade, sometimes attracts a longer line than the larger Harry Potter and the Forbidden Journey. Likewise, for many young children, no attraction, regardless of size, surpasses One Fish, Two Fish, Red Fish, Blue Fish, a simple Seussian spinner.

2. Arrive Early! Arrive Early! Arrive Early!

This is the single most important key to efficient touring and avoiding long lines. First thing in the morning, there are no lines and fewer people.

The same four rides you experience in 1 hour in early morning can take as long as 3 hours after 10:30 a.m. Eat breakfast before you arrive; don't waste prime touring time sitting in a restaurant.

The earlier a park opens, the greater your advantage. This is because most vacationers won't rise early and get to a park before it opens.

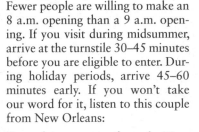

Fewer people are willing to make an 8 a.m. opening than a 9 a.m. opening. If you visit during midsummer, arrive at the turnstile 30–45 minutes before you are eligible to enter. During holiday periods, arrive 45–60 minutes early. If you won't take our word for it, listen to this couple from New Orleans:

Your advice to get to the parks 30 minutes before they open (we did not have early admission) was spot on. We could pretty much get on almost any ride with little to no wait until about 10:30–11 a.m. each day we were there.

3. Avoid Bottlenecks

Helping you avoid bottlenecks is what *The Unofficial Guide* is about. This involves being able to predict where, when, and why bottlenecks occur. Concentrations of hungry people create gridlocks at restaurants during lunch and dinner; concentrations of people moving toward the exit near closing time cause gift shops en route to clog; concentrations of visitors at new and popular rides, and at rides slow to load and unload, create logjams and long lines.

Our solution for avoiding bottlenecks: touring plans for USF and IOA. We also provide detailed information on rides and performances, enabling you to estimate how long you may have to wait in line and allowing you to compare rides for their crowd capacity. All touring plans are in the back of this book, following the index. Plans for Universal Studios Florida begin on page 387, and for Islands of Adventure, on page 390. One-day and two-day touring plans for both USF and IOA are provided for those with park-to-park admission.

WHAT'S A QUEUE?

THOUGH IT'S NOT COMMONLY USED in the United States, *queue* (pronounced "cue") is the universal English word for a line, such as one in which you wait to cash a check at the bank or to board a ride at a theme park. Queuing theory, a mathematical area of specialization within the field of operations research, studies and models how lines work. Because *The Unofficial Guide* draws heavily on this discipline, we use some of its terminology. In addition to the noun, the verb *to queue* means "to get in line," and a *queuing area* is "a waiting area that accommodates a line."

OF UTMOST IMPORTANCE: READ THIS!

IN ANALYZING READER SURVEYS, we were astonished by the percentage of readers who *don't* use our touring plans. Scientifically tested and proven, these plans can save you 4 entire hours or more of waiting in line in a single day—4 fewer hours of standing, 4 hours freed up to do something fun. Our groundbreaking research that created the touring plans has been the subject of front-page articles in *The Dallas Morning News* and *The New York Times* and has been cited in numerous scholarly journals. So why would you not use them?

We get a ton of reader mail—98% of it positive—commenting on our touring plans. From an Edmonds, Washington, family who used one of our touring plans for IOA:

> It worked like a charm! I've always wondered how it feels to follow your plans not ever having seen the park before, and now I know— it was easy!

Another reader reports:

> We didn't have early entry and got there 30 minutes before the official opening time of 9 a.m. and walked on the first three rides on the plan. We spent two days at both parks and got on everything twice. Never waited more than 45 minutes.

TOURING PLANS: WHAT THEY ARE AND HOW THEY WORK

FROM THE FIRST EDITION OF The Unofficial Guide, minimizing our readers' waits in line has been a top priority. We know from our research and that of others that theme park patrons measure overall satisfaction based on the number of attractions they're able to experience during a visit: the more attractions, the better. Thus, we developed and offered our readers field-tested touring plans that allow them to experience as many attractions as possible with the least amount of waiting in line.

Our touring plans have always been based on theme park traffic flow, attraction capacity, the maximum time a guest is willing to wait, walking distance between attractions, and waiting-time data collected at every attraction in every park, every day of the year.

The Unofficial Guide touring plan program contains two algorithms that allow it to quickly analyze tens of millions of possible plans in a very short time. The program can analyze standby wait times and estimate the time saved by using Universal Express Passes. The software can also schedule rest breaks throughout the day and estimate walking times to meals if you specify a preferred restaurant.

Numerous other features are available, many of which we'll discuss in the next section.

Over the years, this research has been recognized by the travel industry and academe, having been cited by such diverse sources as *The New York Times, USA Today, Travel Weekly, Bottom Line, Money, Operations Research Forum,* CBS News, Fox News, the BBC, the Travel Channel, *The Dallas Morning News,* and *The Atlanta Journal-Constitution.* The methodology behind our touring plans was also used as a case study in the 2010 book *Numbers Rule Your World* by Kaiser Fung.

Customize Your Touring Plans

The attractions included in our touring plans are the best and most popular as determined by our expert team and reader surveys. If you've never been to Universal Orlando, we suggest using the plans in this book. They'll ensure that you see the best Universal attractions with as little waiting in line as possible.

If you're a return visitor, your favorite attractions may be different. One way to customize the plans is to go to touringplans.com or use the Lines app to create personalized versions. Tell the software the date, time, and park you've chosen to visit, along with the attractions you want to see. The plan will tell you, for your specific travel date and time, the exact order in which to visit the attractions to minimize your waits in line. Lines also supports child swap (see page 188) on thrill rides. Besides rides, you can schedule shows, meals, breaks, character greetings, and more. You can even tell Lines how fast you plan to walk, and whether or not you'll be using Universal Express, and it will make the necessary adjustments.

Alternatively, some changes are simple enough to make on your own. If a plan calls for an attraction in which you're not interested, simply skip it and move on to the next one. You can also substitute similar attractions in the same area of the park. If a plan calls for, say, riding Cat in the Hat and you'd rather not, but you would enjoy the Caro-Seuss-el (which is not on the plan), then go ahead and substitute that for Cat. As long as the substitution is a similar attraction—substituting a show for a ride won't work—and is pretty close by the attraction called for in the touring plan, you won't compromise the plan's overall effectiveness. If all else fails and you need some extra hand-holding, the author of this book provides personalized tour-planning services for all Universal parks; visit sethkubersky.com for pricing and details.

OVERVIEW OF THE TOURING PLANS

OUR TOURING PLANS ARE STEP-BY-STEP GUIDES for seeing as much as possible with a minimum of standing in line, and without needing Universal Express Passes. They're designed to help you avoid crowds and bottlenecks on any day of the year. The plans will save time on days when attendance is lighter (see "Trying to Reason with the

Tourist Season," page 27), but on those days, they won't be as critical to successful touring.

What You Can Realistically Expect from the Touring Plans

Though we present one-day/two-park plans for Universal Orlando, Universal Studios Florida and Islands of Adventure together have more attractions than you can reasonably expect to see in one day. You can either see all of The Wizarding World in depth or highlights of the rest of the resort, but not both in a single visit. Because our two-day plans for Universal Orlando are the most comprehensive, efficient, and relaxing, we strongly recommend them over the one-day/two-park plans. However, if you must cram your visit to both parks into a single day, the one-day plans will allow you to see as much as is humanly possible.

Variables That Affect the Success of the Touring Plans

The plans' success will be affected by how quickly you move from ride to ride; when and how many refreshment and restroom breaks you take; when, where, and how you eat meals; and your ability (or lack thereof) to find your way around. Smaller groups almost always move faster than larger groups, and parties of adults generally cover more ground than families with young children. Child swap (see page 188), also known as rider swap, baby swap, or switching off, inhibits families with little ones from moving as expeditiously as possible among attractions.

Plus, some folks simply cannot conform to the plans' "early to rise" conditions, as this reader from Cleveland Heights, Ohio, recounts:

> Our touring plans were thrown totally off by one member who could not be on time for opening. Even in October, this made a huge difference in our ability to see attractions without waiting.

And a family from Centerville, Ohio, says:

> The toughest thing about your touring plans was getting the rest of the family to stay with them. Getting them to pass by attractions to hit something across the park was no easy task.

If you have young children, the appearance of a cartoon character (especially Dora the Explorer or the Minions) can stop a touring plan in its tracks, and even adults will detour to snap a selfie with Optimus Prime or the Hogwarts Express conductor. While some characters stroll the parks, it's equally common that they assemble in a specific venue where families queue up for photos and autographs. Meeting characters and getting autographs aren't as popular pastimes at Universal as at Disney but can still burn valuable touring time. If your kids collect character autographs, you need to anticipate these interruptions by including character greetings when creating your online touring plans, or else negotiate some understanding with your children about when you'll collect autographs.

Some things are beyond your control. Chief among these are the manner and timing of bringing a particular ride to capacity. For example, Harry Potter and the Escape from Gringotts, an indoor roller coaster in USF, has nine trains, one of which is kept as a spare. On any given morning, it may begin operation with four or five trains running, and then add two to four more as needed. If the waiting line builds rapidly before operators go to full capacity, you could have a long wait, even in early morning.

A variable that can give your touring plans a boost is the singles line (see page 64), as this English reader explains:

> We used the touring plans to the letter and found that not only did they work, but they also worked even better in conjunction with single-rider queues. The only rides that we queued up for normally were ones with a 20-minute-or-less queue time and wet rides.

Another variable is your arrival time for a theater show. You'll wait from the time you arrive until the end of the presentation in progress. Thus, if a show starts every 30 minutes and you arrive 1 minute after it has begun, your wait will be 29 minutes. Conversely, if you arrive just before the next show begins, your wait will be only a minute or two.

While we realize that following the plans isn't always easy, we nevertheless recommend continuous, expeditious touring until around noon. After that, breaks and diversions won't affect the plans significantly.

What to Do if You Lose the Thread

We suggest sticking to the plans religiously, especially in the mornings, if you're visiting during busy times. The consequence of touring spontaneity in peak season is hours of standing in line. When using the plans, however, relax and always be prepared for surprises and setbacks. If unforeseen events interrupt a plan:

1. If you're following a touring plan in the Lines app (touringplans.com/lines), just press OPTIMIZE when you're ready to start touring again. Lines will figure out the best possible plan for the remainder of your day.

2. If you're following a printed touring plan, skip a step on the plan for every 20 minutes' delay. For example, if you lose your wallet and spend an hour hunting for it, skip three steps and pick up from there.

3. Forget the plan and organize the remainder of the day using the standby wait times listed in the Lines app.

Even if you aren't strictly following a touring plan, remember to refresh the Lines app after a detour, as a father of three from Sydney, Australia, advises:

> When using Lines and seeing what the attraction wait times are, make sure to refresh it first so you can see the up-to-date wait times, not the wait times from 2 hours ago when you last refreshed it. I may have been guilty of not doing this, as I took the family from one side of the park to the other to go to Transformers, and then waited

40 minutes for the ride when I told everyone that it was a 15-minute line. Or it might have been the two restroom stops on the way?

Clip-Out Touring Plans

For your convenience, the touring plans combine itineraries with numbered maps. Select the plan appropriate for your party, and get familiar with it. Then clip the pocket version from the back of this guide and carry it with you as a quick reference at the theme park.

Will the Plans Continue to Work Once the Secret Is Out?

Yes! First, all the plans require that a patron be there when a park opens. Many Universal Orlando patrons simply won't get up early while on vacation. Second, less than 2% of any day's attendance has been exposed to the plans—too few to affect results. Last, most groups tailor the plans, skipping rides or shows according to taste.

How Frequently Are the Touring Plans Revised?

We revise them every year, and updates are always available at touring plans.com. Be prepared for surprises, though: opening procedures and showtimes may change, for example, and you can't predict when an attraction might break down.

Tour Groups on Steroids

We've discovered that tour groups of up to 200 people sometimes use our plans. Unless your party is as large as that tour group, this development shouldn't alarm you. Because tour groups are big, they move slowly and have to stop periodically to collect stragglers. The tour guide also has to accommodate the unpredictability of five dozen or so bladders. In short, you should have no problem passing a group after the initial encounter.

"Bouncing Around"

Some readers object to crisscrossing a theme park as our touring plans sometimes require. A woman from Decatur, Georgia, told us she "got dizzy from all the bouncing around." Believe us, we empathize.

We've worked hard over the years to eliminate the need to crisscross a theme park in our touring plans. (In fact, our customized software can minimize walking instead of waiting in line, if that's important to you.) Occasionally, however, it's possible to save a lot of time in line with a few extra minutes of walking.

The reasons for this are varied. Sometimes a park is designed intentionally to require walking. In USF, for example, the most popular attraction (Harry Potter and the Escape from Gringotts in Diagon Alley) is placed at the farthest corner from the front gate, so that guests are more evenly distributed throughout the day. Other times, you may be visiting just after a new attraction has opened that everyone wants to try. In that case, a special trip to visit the new attraction may be required earlier in the day than normal to avoid longer waits later. And live shows, especially at USF, sometimes have performance schedules so at odds with each other (and the rest of the park's schedule) that orderly touring is impossible.

If you want to experience headliner attractions in one day without long waits, you can see those first (which requires crisscrossing the park), use Universal Express and single-rider lines (if available), or hope to squeeze in visits during parades and the last hour the park is open (which may not work).

If you have two days to visit Universal Orlando, use the two-day touring plans (see pages 307–308). These spread the popular attractions over two mornings and work great even when the parks close early.

Touring Plan Rejection

Some folks don't respond well to the regimentation of a touring plan. If you encounter this problem with someone in your party, roll with the punches, as this Maryland couple did:

> The rest of the group was not receptive to the use of the touring plans. I think they all thought I was being a little too regimented about planning this vacation. Rather than argue, I left the touring plans behind as we ventured off to the parks. You can guess the outcome. We took videos and watched them when we returned home. About every 5 minutes or so, there's a shot of us all gathered around a park map trying to decide what to do next.

Finally, as a Connecticut woman alleges, the touring plans are incompatible with some readers' bladders, as well as their personalities:

> When you write those plans next year, can you schedule bathroom breaks in there too? You expect us to be at a certain ride at a certain time and with no stops in between. The schedules are a problem if you are a laid-back, slow-moving, careful detail noticer. What were you thinking when you made these schedules?

Before you injure your urinary tract, feel free to deviate from the touring plan as necessary to heed the call of nature. If you are using a customized plan in Lines, you can build in as many breaks (bathroom or otherwise) as you like, and the optimizer will plan around them.

WHAT TO EXPECT WHEN YOU ARRIVE AT THE PARKS (ROPE DROP)

BECAUSE MOST TOURING PLANS ARE BASED ON being present when the theme park opens, you need to know about opening procedures. Universal Orlando's on-site resort transportation to the parks via buses and water taxis begins 2 hours before official opening, or 1 hour before Early Park Admission (see page 54). Guests staying on-site during peak periods will want to catch the first ride of the morning (or start walking around the time it leaves) to be the first into The Wizarding World during the early-entry period. Off-season visitors should arrive at the gates 10–20 minutes before Early Park Admission (EPA) begins.

The parking garage also opens 2 hours before official opening, but on days of exceptional attendance (like the grand opening of a new attraction), the garage has opened as early as 3 a.m. If you are driving to the resort and are not eligible for EPA, plan to arrive at the Universal parking garage 45–60 minutes prior to official opening. If you need to purchase park admission, add another 15 minutes to that. It takes approximately 10–15 minutes to walk from the parking garage to the parks' entrance turnstiles, so you should arrive at the turnstiles 30–45 minutes before the park opens.

There are fewer turnstiles at USF and IOA than at Disney's Magic Kingdom or Epcot, and the turnstiles are not spread out over as much ground. Consequently, lines tend to be evenly distributed at each turnstile. If you see a shorter line, however, get in it, especially if portable ticket scanners (which are usually faster than the fixed turnstiles) have been set up in front of the center gate.

Universal's turnstiles use a biometric scanner that will record your fingerprint (for guests age 10 and older only) when using your ticket for the first time. Be sure to remember which finger you used to speed reentry. You'll also be asked to sign your pass, so that you don't mix it up with those of other family members. Universal's finger scanners don't seem nearly as efficient as the ones Disney uses, so be prepared for slowdowns at entry, as one Orchard Park, New York, family found:

> *The finger scanning going into the park and at Hogwarts Express did not work well. It randomly did not work for some in our party—very annoying and time-consuming.*

Rope Drop at Universal Studios Florida

USF team members select a "first family" from the early risers at the turnstiles each morning and usher them in a few minutes early to open the park with an old-fashioned movie clapboard. It's no Magic Kingdom character welcome, but it is a cute moment worth catching if you can.

Once the gates open, there is no mad dash for Diagon Alley, nor is a literal rope dropped. When USF's turnstiles open for EPA, resort guests walk straight toward Revenge of the Mummy and are escorted to The Wizarding World via San Francisco. Day guests are restricted to the front of the park, where Despicable Me Minion Mayhem opens to all guests 30–45 minutes before the official opening.

On days when USF does not officially offer EPA, the gates may still open 15 minutes (or more) before opening, with Despicable Me typically running for all early guests. Guests can enter the Harry Potter and the Escape from Gringotts queue before official opening, but the ride may not begin running until park opening (or a few minutes before) on non-EPA mornings.

Most of the crowd will head for The Wizarding World of Harry Potter's Gringotts ride, which usually sees its longest waits between opening and early afternoon. Despicable Me, located a short distance past the entrance, also attracts large crowds, as do Transformers: The Ride 3-D and Hollywood Rip Ride Rockit. A smaller number of visitors will head for The Simpsons Ride or Revenge of the Mummy, but these attractions usually don't get crowded until an hour or two after the park has opened.

unofficial **TIP**
Decorative planters inhibit lines from forming at the center turnstiles, making the outside lines longer. Squeeze through to the middle lanes for quicker entry.

Rope Drop at Islands of Adventure

At the end of Port of Entry, hotel guests are walked to the right through Seuss Landing to The Wizarding World of Harry Potter–Hogsmeade, while day guests are sent to Marvel Super Hero Island, where they will be held near Cafe 4 until opening time. Once released into the park, most guests turn counterclockwise through Seuss Landing and make a beeline for Hogsmeade as soon as the park is open. A smaller number of guests will head clockwise for The Incredible Hulk Coaster (which may allow guests to ride a few minutes before the official opening time) and then continue through Toon Lagoon to Skull Island.

Unless you have early entry, our advice is to see Hulk, The Amazing Adventures of Spider-Man, and Reign of Kong first and save The Wizarding World until late in the day. Note that when one park opens before the other, guests arriving on the first Hogwarts Express train from the early-entry park will reach the opposite Wizarding World at the same time or slightly after those entering from the front gates. And when EPA hour concludes, guests already inside Hogsmeade have the advantage in queuing for Reign of Kong, reaching Skull Island via Jurassic Park a few moments before the general public is released from the Marvel area.

Rope Drop at Volcano Bay

Arrival for Volcano Bay visitors is complicated by the fact that there is no parking at the water park itself, so all guests must be bused in from the main parking garage or resorts. Guests begin arriving at the turnstiles up to an hour before the park opens, but distribution of the mandatory TapuTapu wristbands doesn't begin until moments before early entry starts. Once it does, hotel guests and off-site visitors alike are allowed in, with those eligible for EPA funneled to the left for admittance to the attractions. Day guests are herded to the right, where they may rent lockers and purchase food while awaiting their release into the rest of the park, which may happen up to 30 minutes before official opening. Upon entering, most bolt for the lockers and beach chairs, with all the prime spots around the wave pool usually snapped up within an hour of opening. Long lines for guests trying to rent cabanas also immediately form at the concierge hut closest to the entrance. All slides start the day with "Ride Now" status, but queues build swiftly, and Virtual Line waits for popular slides may exceed an hour by 11 a.m.

EARLY PARK ADMISSION (EARLY ENTRY)

THE MOST VALUABLE PERK available for free to all Universal on-site resort hotel guests is Early Park Admission (EPA, also sometimes referred to as Early Entry), which grants entry to The Wizarding World of Harry Potter 1 hour before the general public. An hour or more of early entry is also offered every morning at the Volcano Bay water park. In addition to guests staying at on-site hotels, guests holding certain designated vacation packages—purchased through Universal Orlando Vacations (☎ 877-801-9720; universalorlandovacations.com) and including both accommodations at an off-site Universal partner hotel *and* theme park admission—are allowed in early. Premier Pass holders can take advantage of EPA at USF or IOA on any morning, as can Preferred Pass holders on select days (blockouts apply).

Which park you may enter on any particular day, and which attractions will be operating, are at Universal's discretion and will vary with the attendance seasons. The turnstiles to the park(s) participating in early entry will open 60–90 minutes before the official opening time. Both hotel and day guests will be admitted to the park, and each EPA-eligible guest (including children) will need to show his or her own room key or annual pass to pass beyond the park's entry plaza during the early admission hour. Guests not eligible for EPA will be held in an alternate area to await the official opening time.

During EPA, all of the attractions, shops, and restaurants in the participating Wizarding World area should be open, along with select attractions outside the Harry Potter area. Attractions offer standby queues during EPA (along with single-rider lines and child swap, where available), but Express Passes are valid only during regular operating hours. EPA, when available at USF, allows early birds to ride Escape from Gringotts with a minimal wait, as this father from New York City experienced:

> We got to the Universal Studios turnstiles at 10 minutes before 6 [for 7 a.m. Early Park Admission] and had only five people in front of us. Soon there were plenty behind us, however! They let us in at about 6:20, and we were among the first 100–150 people to enter Diagon Alley and subsequently Gringotts. We essentially walked onto the ride, slowed only by our amazed awe at walking through the Gringotts lobby and seeing all the astonishing attractions in the line. We were through so quickly that we immediately got in the singles line and literally walked on the ride a second time, and then a third time with the singles line, which by this time was backed up a bit toward the steps leading to the loading platform, resulting in about a 20-minute wait. It was now 8 a.m. and we had been on the ride three times. The non-resort guests were now streaming into Diagon Alley to be welcomed by a standby entrance to Gringotts, which was marked 180 minutes.

However, because EPA crowds are concentrated in The Wizarding World, it can quickly become overcrowded, particularly on days when only one park participates. If you aren't at the front of the pack when the turnstiles open, but you are eligible for Express access, you may be better off riding Gringotts just as EPA ends, according to this reader from Natick, Massachusetts:

> *The early-entry hour was a bit disappointing because it was soooo crowded in Diagon Alley. It was absolute gridlock in the wand shop from the moment the park opened. We waited about half an hour for Gringotts during that first hour. Then immediately afterward, at 9 a.m., when we could use Express, we walked right onto Gringotts.*

Similarly, when IOA opens early, the Forbidden Journey ride typically operates only about 20% of its ride vehicles during EPA, which makes the queue move maddeningly slow. If you aren't among the first few dozen at the gates, you may want to enjoy the other Hogsmeade attractions and save Forbidden Journey until afternoon, lest you spend most of the hour inching through Hogwarts's boarding area. Also, if the Gringotts or Forbidden Journey attractions are not operational when early entry begins, skip them and try again late in the day; by the time they begin running in the morning, there will be a huge backlog of riders.

Universal publishes its EPA calendar several months in advance at tinyurl.com/UniEPA, but procedures seem to change often and arbitrarily with no warning. Ask at your hotel's front desk to find out what opening procedures are in effect during your visit.

IOA-Only Early Park Admission

At certain off-peak times, only Islands of Adventure (and not Universal Studios Florida) may admit eligible guests for Early Park Admission. IOA-only EPA was suspended for most of 2018 but returned late in the year.

The following attractions should be available during IOA-only Early Park Admission:

• Caro-Seuss-el *(seasonally)*	• Harry Potter and the Forbidden Journey
• Flight of the Hippogriff	• Ollivanders Wand Shop

On days that only IOA offers Early Park Admission, USF may still unofficially open 15 minutes early, with Despicable Me Minion Mayhem open for all guests (hotel and off-site alike).

Guests entering USF early may also enter the queue for Escape from Gringotts, though the ride itself usually won't begin running until just before the park officially opens.

The first Hogwarts Express train from Hogsmeade Station should depart shortly after USF opens its gates for the day. The first trainload of guests riding from IOA will enter Diagon Alley around the same time or shortly after the first guests entering through USF's front gates. Early-entry guests at IOA are held at the bridge between Hogsmeade and Jurassic Park until the park's official opening time, at which point they may proceed to Skull Island: Reign of Kong or any other attraction.

USF-Only Early Park Admission

For much of 2018, Early Park Admission was confined to Universal Studios Florida. The following attractions should be available during USF-only EPA:

• Harry Potter and the Escape from Gringotts	• Fast & Furious: Supercharged
• Ollivanders Wand Shop	

In addition, Despicable Me Minion Mayhem usually opens to all park guests 15–30 minutes after EPA begins. Day guests are also allowed to queue for Transformers: The Ride 3-D and Hollywood Rip Ride Rockit prior to the official park opening time.

The Hogwarts Express train from King's Cross Station will not begin running to The Wizarding World of Harry Potter–Hogsmeade in IOA until both parks have opened their gates to guests. The first trainload of guests riding from USF will enter Hogsmeade around the same time or shortly after the first guests entering through IOA's front gates.

Two-Park Early Park Admission (Peak Season)

Universal Orlando only guarantees early admission to one park per day, but during the busiest times of the year—primarily the weeks around Easter and Christmas—Universal offers EPA to The Wizarding World of Harry Potter areas at both USF (Diagon Alley) and IOA (Hogsmeade).

When both parks are scheduled to open at the same time, Hogwarts Express will begin running when EPA starts.

The following attractions should be available during peak season early entry:

UNIVERSAL STUDIOS FLORIDA

• Despicable Me Minion Mayhem	• Ollivanders Wand Shop
• Harry Potter and the Escape from Gringotts	• Fast & Furious: Supercharged
• Hogwarts Express *(only if IOA is open)*	

ISLANDS OF ADVENTURE

• Caro-Seuss-el *(seasonally)*	• Hogwarts Express *(only if USF is open)*
• Flight of the Hippogriff	• Ollivanders Wand Shop
• Harry Potter and the Forbidden Journey	

Volcano Bay Early Park Admission

In addition to the early entry offered at USF and IOA, Volcano Bay also opens 60–90 minutes early every morning for all on-site resort hotel guests, with all or most of its attractions operating. (In the winter months, only select slides may operate during EPA.) While EPA is a wonderful luxury in The Wizarding World, at the water park it is an absolute necessity. Because the entire park often closes for capacity on busy days within minutes of the official opening time, early admission is the only way to be guaranteed admittance to Volcano Bay, much less have a chance to enjoy most of the slides.

During the early-entry hour, most, if not all, of the slides are kept at "Ride Now" status, allowing guests to take advantage of the relatively short lines. During peak season, using EPA is just about the only way to experience all the slides in one day without purchasing an Express Pass, as one woman from Stamford, Connecticut, found:

> You are only able to get the "Ride Now" signs if you come for early admission. The moment the park opens to the public, the waiting times for the attractions increase fast. If you do not have early admission privileges, you may be able to do three or four rides during the day, as waiting times longer then 100 minutes are typical. We came at 7:30 and did the rides we wanted, then left in the afternoon.

Off-site guests who aren't eligible for early entry should still try to get to the gates an hour before official opening, potentially getting up to a 30-minute head start on the slides. If you aren't able to arrive that early, save yourself a lot of frustration and skip Volcano Bay until you can. Alternatively, use a multiday park-to-park pass to sample some slides in the late afternoon (preferably post-rainstorm) after spending the morning in USF or IOA.

To prevent overcrowding, Universal caps attendance inside Volcano Bay at 8,000–10,000 guests, a limit that can be reached within minutes after opening during the peak summer period. When the park approaches maximum capacity, Universal first restricts day visitors, then on-site guests. The park usually reopens its gates as guests depart in the afternoon, but tickets are not date-specific, so no refunds or rain checks are issued if you are refused entry after capacity is reached.

Annual Pass Holder Early Park Admission

Premier Pass holders may use EPA at USF or IOA on any day of the year, while Preferred Pass holders can enter USF or IOA early on most days (see tinyurl.com/APearly for details). During Annual Passholder Appreciation Days, held in the off-season, Power and Seasonal Pass holders can use EPA at IOA or USF on select dates, and all 3-Park pass holders can take advantage of EPA at Volcano Bay without having to stay on-site.

UNIVERSAL EXPRESS

THIS SYSTEM ALLOWS GUESTS to "skip the line" and experience an attraction via a special queue with little or no waiting. Guests approach the marked Universal Express entrance at participating attractions, present their Universal Express Pass to the greeter for scanning, and proceed to

unofficial **TIP**
Universal Express is now valid at all Harry Potter attractions, including Forbidden Journey, Escape from Gringotts, and Hogwarts Express.

a significantly reduced wait—usually 20% or less of the posted time, or no more than a 15- to 20-minute wait. For rides that use Virtual Line like Race Through New York Starring Jimmy Fallon, you'll be able to enter the attraction lobby whenever you like without a prearranged return time.

Though both let guests bypass the typical wait, there are three major differences between Disney's FastPass+ and Universal Express. While Disney's system requires scheduling your ride reservation hours or days ahead of time, Universal Express involves no advance planning; simply visit any eligible operating attraction whenever you choose, no return time windows required. Also, FastPass+ is only offered at a select list of designated attractions, while nearly all the attractions at Universal (with a couple exceptions, noted later) accept Express. Finally, unlike FastPass+, Universal Express is not free.

Three versions of Universal Express are available, all of which require you to cough up more money beyond your park admission:

UNIVERSAL EXPRESS PASS Available for purchase online or in the parks, allowing one person one ride on each attraction that participates in Universal Express. (Note that for single-use Express, each Hogwarts Express station counts as a separate attraction, so you can ride the train once in each direction.)

UNIVERSAL EXPRESS UNLIMITED PASS Available for purchase online or in the parks (either bundled with admission or separately), allowing one person an unlimited number of rides on any attraction that participates in Universal Express.

ON-SITE HOTEL UNIVERSAL EXPRESS UNLIMITED PASS Included for all guests at the top three Universal Resort hotels (Hard Rock, Portofino Bay, and Royal Pacific) at no extra cost, allowing each person staying on-site an unlimited number of rides on any attraction that participates in Universal Express. Note that the free Express Passes are not valid at Volcano Bay.

No matter which version of Universal Express you use, it works the same: present your pass to a greeter at each attraction entrance, get it scanned for verification, and enjoy your expedited entertainment. (Universal has been experimenting with a facial-recognition system for identifying Express Pass holders, but it has not been fully rolled out yet.) At shows, you can produce your pass for priority seating 15 minutes before showtime, but that's less of a perk because Universal's large theaters rarely fill up.

It's worth noting that, while almost all the Express queues are themed, in a few cases (Revenge of the Mummy and Men in Black Alien Attack at USF; Doctor Doom's Fearfall and Skull Island: Reign of Kong at IOA), they sacrifice significant scenic elements and story setup that the standby line sees.

Finally, be aware that Pteranodon Flyers at IOA, a slow-loading children's ride with limited capacity, does not accept Universal Express.

Neither do the Ollivanders wandkeeper presentations. Further, all of the Express types (including the free passes for resort guests) are valid only during regular operating hours and not during separately ticketed events. Separate Express Passes are available at an additional cost for special events such as Rock the Universe and Halloween Horror Nights.

PREMIER PASS UNIVERSAL EXPRESS AFTER 4 P.M.   Holders of the top-of-the-line Premier Pass get free Universal Express access every day from 4 p.m. until park closing (excluding special events like Halloween). Even though it's officially valid only once per attraction per day, we've rarely been denied a re-ride and can sometimes bring a companion along.

Universal Express and Express Unlimited for Purchase

Anyone can purchase Universal Express for one or both theme parks and for either single (one ride only on each participating attraction) or unlimited use, and from one to four days. The number of Express Passes is limited each day, and they can sell out. Increase your chances of securing passes by buying and printing them at home from Universal's website. They are available up to eight months in advance at tinyurl.com /UORExpress. You'll need to know when you plan on using it, though, because prices vary depending on the date.

Universal Express Pass prices range from $79.99 for a one-park single-use pass in slow season to $159.99 for a two-park unlimited pass on a holiday; the top-tier passes are significantly cheaper when bundled with a park-to-park multiday pass. Incidentally, the online calendar of Express Pass prices is a great indicator of how crowded Universal will be on any given day; the more expensive the passes, the more packed the park will be.

You can also buy Universal Express at the theme parks' ticket windows, just outside the front gates, but it's faster to do so inside the parks. Express Passes are sold at the large stores near the front of each park and in most major gift shops. Universal also sells Express from freestanding kiosks that seem to proliferate around the parks like mushrooms during peak seasons. When the park is open late, Universal sometimes sells an unadvertised Express Pass valid after 4 p.m. only for about $35; ask at any Express sales location for details.

Universal Express for Resort Guests

This program allows guests at Universal's three original luxury resorts (Hard Rock, Portofino Bay, and Royal Pacific) to bypass the regular lines at USF and IOA and use the Express entrance any time and as often as desired. Guests of one of the above-mentioned hotels may simply present their room key card for admission through any Universal Express attraction entrance inside USF or IOA.

Universal Express for resort guests is available from the moment of check-in until closing time on the day of checkout. And even though check-in time at Universal's on-site hotels isn't until 4 p.m., guests can retrieve room keys and Express Passes as early in the morning as they are able to arrive, and guests may drop their luggage in the lobby and head to the parks until their room is ready. Therefore, a single night's stay on-site yields two full days of Universal Express access. This perk far surpasses any benefit accorded to guests of Disney resorts; combined with the hour of Early Park Admission to The Wizarding World, it helps make touring Universal Orlando a remarkably low-stress experience for on-site guests, even during peak attendance periods.

A father from Snellville, Georgia, did the math and discovered that it was cheaper for his family to stay at a Universal resort than buy Universal Express:

> *The benefits of staying on-property are worth it, with early entry to The Wizarding World and Express Unlimited privileges at both parks. We got a room at the Royal Pacific Resort for $349 on a Saturday night, which allowed us to use Universal Express Saturday and Sunday. The room cost $43.63 per person per day, while an [à la carte] Express Pass this same weekend would have cost $56 per person per day, and we still would have had to pay for a hotel.*

Universal Express at Volcano Bay

Universal Express Passes valid at Volcano Bay are sold on select days inside the park at the concierge stands or in advance online. Volcano Bay's basic Universal Express Passes cost $19.99–$69.99 (depending on the season). Express Passes are valid for one ride each on select slides, which include the Krakatau Aqua Coaster and Honu ika Moana but exclude the Kala & Tai Nui body slides, Ohyah & Ohno drop slides, and Ko'okiri Body Plunge. A 1-Day Universal Express Plus Pass costs $39.99–$99.99 for a single trip down every slide in the park; at press time, no unlimited usage Express option was available. Express allows you to act as if participating attractions say "Ride Now," but even though you won't need a TapuTapu return time, you'll still experience some waiting before your slide.

Is Universal Express Worth It?

No matter when you use it, Universal Express will significantly reduce the amount of time you spend waiting in queues at Universal Orlando. But whether or not that time saving is worth it depends on the season you visit, hours of park operation, and crowd levels.

During busy periods, Universal Express users should wait no more than 15–20 minutes for a ride, even when the standby wait is well over an hour; the one exception is Despicable Me Minion Mayhem, whose Express queue can approach an hour at peak times due to its limited guest capacity. That's a significant time savings and may make the difference between seeing all your favorite headliners in a single day or going home disappointed.

During slow periods, Express users should experience little to no wait at most attractions and can practically walk on to most rides.

However, the standby waits will typically top out between 15 and 30 minutes at these times, making the total minutes saved with Express much less impressive.

Attendance has jumped at both parks since the opening of each Harry Potter land, especially at USF since Diagon Alley debuted. And now that the big-ticket Harry Potter rides in Hogsmeade and Diagon Alley participate in Universal Express, the passes are even more valuable.

However, Universal Express is *not* mandatory for enjoying the parks (as we've heard some claim), just so long as you show up bright and early with a well-organized agenda. If you want to sleep in and arrive at a park after opening, Express is an effective, albeit expensive, way to avoid long lines at the headliner attractions, especially during holidays and busy times. If, however, you arrive at least 30 minutes before park opening and you use our touring plans (see pages 387–400), you should experience the lowest possible waits.

If you are not eligible for free Express Passes, we encourage you to try the touring plans first, but if waits for rides become intolerable, you can always buy Express in the parks (provided they haven't sold out, an infrequent occurrence).

A New York mom had a trouble-free experience, but she questions the value of the investment:

> Universal Express was neither necessary nor consistently effective. By arriving at park opening, we were able to see many attractions right away without needing the passes at all. The passes helped on about three attractions between the two parks—a poor return for an investment of $156, but it was like life insurance: good to have just in case. On Dudley Do-Right's Ripsaw Falls, we still had to wait 30 minutes even with Express, whereas with Disney's free FastPass+ we never waited more than 5 minutes for an attraction. The only aspect of UE that was better than FP+ is that touring order was unaffected: UE could be used whenever you first approached an attraction instead of your having to come back later.

On the other hand, this Kansas City family thought very highly of the Express Unlimited Passes included in their Royal Pacific Resort stay:

> The free Express Pass you get by staying at one of the top three resorts is a lifesaver. We never waited in line more than 15 minutes, and it was usually closer to 5. For my roller coaster–loving family, this was great. We didn't have a scheduled time to ride anything like at Disney, so we could stray from our plan and re-ride The Incredible Hulk Coaster or Hollywood Rip Ride Rockit over and over again.

Another reader from San Jose, California, concurred:

> In 90°F heat and 80% humidity, having an Express Pass by staying at the Royal Pacific made all the difference. The ability to get through the ride queues quickly easily made up for the higher cost of the room.

A dad from Conway, Arkansas, chimed in:

Universal Express Pass is totally worth it. We applied for the American Express card at the entrance to the park and got the passes for free. After having used them, we would pay for them next time.

And this mom from Massachusetts agreed:

Universal Express did not disappoint. We walked on to every ride we wanted to, and we could easily and immediately re-ride our favs with no wait. I would definitely either stay at Royal Pacific or spring for Universal Express on my next trip. It was wonderful to have that flexibility with our kids. We could wait to ride Gringotts the first day, until our 8-year-old had worked up the nerve. Then we could spontaneously ride again—right away with no wait!

Finally, you'll want to devise a convenient way to keep track of your pass, as this Endicott, New York, reader suggests:

The paper Express Passes were not nearly as user friendly as Disney's MagicBands. The lanyard was a lifesaver, or we surely would have lost something.

Universal will happily sell you a souvenir lanyard with a plastic pouch, so you can proudly wear your admission around your neck for all to see. Universal's lanyards start at around $10 and come in a variety of themes, including the colors of each Hogwarts house. You can also pick up equally usable and far cheaper (though less magical) versions at your local office supply store.

How Universal Express Affects Crowd Conditions at Attractions

Guests using Universal Express don't have to modify their touring behavior in any way; simply visit any attraction at will and enjoy the shorter waits. However, the Express effect can be somewhat less salutary for guests without Express. The standby and Express queues at each attraction meet up shortly before the boarding area, and attendants are supposed to merge them so that Express guests wait 15 minutes or less, without the standby guests' wait being inflated beyond the estimate posted outside.

Typically, this means about half of each ride's capacity is dedicated to Express guests, which ordinarily keeps both queues flowing smoothly. The catch is that, because Universal Express guests (unlike Disney FastPass+ users) don't schedule ride times in advance, the number of them waiting in a queue at any given time is highly variable and unpredictable, as one Highlands Ranch, Colorado, reader pointed out:

The Universal Express Pass is not the same as Disney's FastPass. If everyone holding an Express Pass decides to use it at the same time on the same ride, wait times can get very long, making the pass seem less of a bargain. That being said, an Express Pass almost seemed a necessity on the day we were there because it was a short day due to Halloween Horror Nights and we weren't able to make it there for park opening.

As a result, an unexpected backlog of Express guests—either because of a sudden influx of pass users or a temporary technical breakdown that pauses the line—can force Universal to increase the ratio of Express to standby, slowing non-Express guests' progress to a crawl.

While that's great news for Universal Express users, this can dramatically affect crowd movement (and touring-plan usage) for those without it, as a woman from Yorktown, Virginia, writes:

People in the Express line were let in at a rate of about 10 to 1 over the regular-line folks. This created bottlenecks and long waits for people who didn't have the Express privilege at the very times when it's supposed to be easier to get around!

A Potter fan from Brevard, North Carolina, didn't appreciate the advantage afforded Express guests:

It was obvious that anyone who paid for an Express Pass had preferential treatment—they let in eight Express guests to one standby guest at the Gringotts ride after I had stood in line for almost 2½ hours. I feel like people who buy "normal" tickets are second-class citizens.

If you encounter this situation while waiting standby, simply grit your teeth and take some deep yoga breaths; the situation normally clears up quickly, and your total wait should still be approximately as originally advertised. In case of a major traffic jam where the standby line stops moving altogether, calculate how much time you've invested already, and consider hopping out of line and returning later when things are running more smoothly. And for those who really can't stand watching Express guests pass them by: If you can't beat 'em, join 'em.

U-BOT

THIS RIDE-RESERVATION SYSTEM incorporates the small U-Bot device. These water-resistant egg-shaped gadgets (provided by Accesso, the same company behind the FlashPass and U-Bot services at Six Flags and other regional parks) closely resemble the Tamagotchi virtual pet toys that were briefly popular in the 1990s.

U-Bot is only available seasonally and is not advertised or offered online, and some Express vendors don't even know it exists. Guests can only purchase access to the device at the Rental Services window inside each park. Once you have your U-Bot, you can use the small built-in screen to reserve ride times for any Universal Express attraction. Note that you can make only one reservation at a time; you must use or cancel your first reservation before making another.

Your minimum wait time before you can experience an attraction with U-Bot will be the same as the ride's current standby wait; that is, if a ride's posted wait time is 1 hour, you can enter the attraction any time 1 hour or more after making your reservation. The U-Bot will vibrate and display a message telling you when it's time to ride. Next, you take your U-Bot to the ride's Express entrance, where the attraction greeter will scan your device and admit you to the Express queue.

U-Bot costs $29.99–$39.99 for one use per ride, and an additional $10 for unlimited use. A single U-Bot can be used by up to six guests, though the full per-person price still applies. U-Bot can be rented for either park. When renting a U-Bot, you'll be asked to provide a credit card, which will be charged $50 if you fail to return your device to a designated location near the park exit at the end of the day.

Despite the lower price and geeky tech appeal of the U-Bots, they aren't nearly as popular as Universal Express Passes, largely because they lack the latter's "use anytime" ease. If managed efficiently, U-Bot can help cut time spent standing in queues, but only if you can slip into another attraction while waiting for your next reservation time to come around. Otherwise, most visitors are better off saving their money or investing in Express.

VIRTUAL LINES

UNIVERSAL HAS INTRODUCED another line-skipping service to its theme parks, but unlike the aforementioned Express options, Virtual Line is completely free for all park guests, regardless of hotel or ticket type. Virtual Line works much like the same-day FastPass service still found at Disneyland: guests may claim time slots for certain rides on a first-come, first-served basis and can experience the attraction with a minimal wait after returning during their assigned hour-long window. The service is mandatory for most slides at Volcano Bay, where it is tied to the TapuTapu wristbands; see page 345 for a detailed explanation. The method and usefulness of Virtual Line varies depending on the attraction. In USF, Virtual Line is mandatory at Race Through New York Starring Jimmy Fallon during select times of day and is offered as an option at Fast & Furious: Supercharged; return times are available at kiosks outside each attraction or through the official Universal Orlando mobile app. In IOA, Virtual Line is sometimes available for Pteranodon Flyers at a kiosk outside Camp Jurassic; all riders must be present to make a reservation.

SINGLE-RIDER LINES

ONE OTHER TIME-SAVING OPTION available to all Universal Orlando guests without extra charge is the single-rider (or singles) line. Several attractions at USF and IOA have this special line for guests traveling alone, or at least willing to be temporarily separated from their companions. Single riders wait in a separate queue and are slipped into vacant seats left by large groups without (theoretically) impacting the other lines. Disney also offers single-rider queues, but at fewer attractions across all four Disney World parks than Universal has in its two, making it a great alternative for those unable or unwilling to cough up the dough for Universal Express Passes.

The singles line is often just as fast as the Express line. However, because the speed of the singles line is highly dependent on the flow of odd-numbered parties through the other queues, the wait time can be extremely unpredictable. At some times we've walked onto Forbidden

Journey via the singles line when the standby wait time was more than an hour; at others we've stood longer in Hollywood Rip Ride Rockit's singles line than the posted standby wait.

Single-rider lines open at the discretion of the ride attendants and may temporarily close if crowds are very light (because they aren't needed) or very heavy (when the singles queue becomes filled to capacity, which happens frequently at Gringotts). In the latter case, try hanging around the entrance for 15 or 20 minutes, which is usually how long it takes for the singles line to shrink enough to be reopened.

Also note that some queues (particularly those of Forbidden Journey and Escape from Gringotts) are attractions in themselves and deserve to be experienced during your first ride. Even so, we strongly recommend using the singles line whenever possible—it will decrease your overall wait and leave more time for repeat rides or just bumming around the parks.

Singles lines are almost always available at the following attractions:

SINGLE-RIDER LINES AT UNIVERSAL STUDIOS FLORIDA	SINGLE-RIDER LINES AT ISLANDS OF ADVENTURE
Fast & Furious: Supercharged	The Amazing Adventures of Spider-Man
Harry Potter and the Escape from Gringotts	Doctor Doom's Fearfall
Hollywood Rip Ride Rockit	Harry Potter and the Forbidden Journey
Men in Black Alien Attack	The Incredible Hulk Coaster
Revenge of the Mummy	Jurassic Park River Adventure
Transformers: The Ride 3-D	Skull Island: Reign of Kong

In addition, Universal intermittently offers single-rider access at Dudley Do-Right's Ripsaw Falls in IOA and E.T. Adventure in USF.

VIP TOURS

FOR THE ULTIMATE no-expenses-spared Universal Orlando experience, book a VIP tour of one or both parks. VIP guests are given the red-carpet treatment at both parks and never have to worry about waiting in line. And don't worry if you aren't a genuine VIP—or even a social media pseudo-celebrity—because at Universal, anyone can be treated like the rich and famous . . . for a price.

Universal offers two types of VIP tours: nonexclusive and private. On nonexclusive tours, your party of up to 6 guests will be paired with other guests to form a group of up to 12. Nonexclusive tours begin at 11 a.m. and last 5–7 hours. Your guide will expedite you onto a minimum of 8 attractions (10 if you take the two-park option) based on group consensus.

Private tours give you free reign to set your start time and make your own itinerary because the guide is dedicated to only your party for a full 8 hours. Private tours are mandatory if your party has seven or more members. You can even ride your favorite ride over and over all day, if you like.

Either way, your VIP experience begins with free valet parking and a complimentary Continental breakfast in the private guest services lounge. In addition to backdooring you into rides—bypassing even the Universal Express queues—and getting you reserved seating at shows, VIP tour guides are a font of trivia about the history and operations of the parks and can even grant backstage access to see how some of the magic is done, like a glimpse underneath Revenge of the Mummy's ride track or inside Transformer's high-tech control booth. VIP tours also include access to the American Express lounge in USF and a complimentary midday meal. Nonexclusive tour guests each get a one-day Quick-Service Universal Dining Plan to use where they wish on an entrée and snacks, while exclusive VIP tour guests get to pick from an array of full-service options, including an exclusive lunch inside USF's Cafe La Bamba, where chefs will prepare a sampling of signature dishes from restaurants around the resort. At the end of the tour, your souvenir VIP lanyard serves as an Express Unlimited Pass for the rest of the day and offers discounts on food and merchandise.

Perhaps most important, VIP tours are the quickest way to skip the queues at the headlining Harry Potter attractions during peak times, when even the Express entrances can be overwhelmed; during the height of Diagon Alley's opening summer, when guests were waiting more than 4 hours just for Gringotts, Bob and Len were able to experience everything in both Wizarding Worlds (including lunch and ice cream) plus other park highlights in a little more than 5 hours.

Of course, this kind of star treatment doesn't come cheap. While VIP tours start at $189 on select dates during the slowest seasons, at most times, a one-day, one-park nonexclusive VIP tour of USF or IOA will run you $209 per person. A one-day tour of both parks starts at $199 and is typically $219. However, during peak pricing times (the weeks around Christmas and Easter), those rates jump as high as $429 for one park, and $449 for both.

Private-tour pricing approaches "if you have to ask, you can't afford it" territory, starting at $3,099 for a day in both parks; one-park exclusive tours are available during off-peak periods on special request, but you will only save a couple hundred dollars off the two-park price. That flat rate is good for one to five guests; additional guests (up to a total of 10) cost another $375 each for a two-park tour. During peak times (Christmas and spring break), those base prices increase to $3,999, plus $450 for each additional guest. Finally, if you splurge on the ultimate two-day, two-park private tour, you'll be poorer by $4,899 ($6,699 during peak periods).

Before you break out your credit card, there's one final catch: in addition to not including tax, the aforementioned prices are on top of admission, which is required and not included with any VIP tour.

Whether the VIP tours are worth it depends largely on your net worth and your tolerance for any type of wait. Having taken them many times over the years, we can say that the experience is a dream come true for theme park junkies, who will get their money's worth in insider info alone, as well as anyone allergic to rubbing elbows with unwashed hordes. If you were already planning to pony up for Express Unlimited Passes, the extra couple hundred per person (depending on the season) could seem a bargain in the heat of summer. For most visitors, a stay at a luxury on-site hotel (with free Express Unlimited included) is probably a more economical investment, but no one we know who has taken a VIP tour has regretted it.

Nonexclusive tours can be booked online through an interactive calendar with availability and pricing at tinyurl.com/univip, but private tours must be booked by phone at ☎ 866-346-9350. If you want to take a VIP tour, order early because they can fill up quickly at busier times.

Note that all of the previously mentioned tours are offered only during regular daytime operating hours. Different VIP tours with their own pricing may be available during separately ticketed special events such as Halloween Horror Nights (see page 298).

FREE BEHIND-THE-SCENES TOURS

IF YOU WANT TO FEEL LIKE A VIP but can't afford the fare, Universal generously offers unpublicized free backstage tours at several attractions to any guest who inquires (subject to staff availability). For details on these "secret" behind-the-scenes experiences, read the attraction descriptions for Men in Black Alien Attack, Race Through New York Starring Jimmy Fallon, and Revenge of the Mummy at USF in Part Seven; and The Incredible Hulk Coaster, Jurassic Park Discovery Center, and Skull Island: Reign of Kong at IOA in Part Eight.

TECHNICAL REHEARSALS

TECHNICAL REHEARSALS, OR SOFT OPENINGS as they are commonly called, are when Universal uses its paying guests as guinea pigs and allows them to preview an attraction that isn't yet ready for prime time. Technical rehearsals may be held anywhere from a few weeks to a few days before a new ride officially opens, but they are never preannounced or guaranteed; frontline employees may be instructed to deny that any opening is possible until the moment they open the queue. In exchange for bragging rights that they were the first inside a hot new attraction, technical rehearsal participants must accept the possibility of waiting a long time without ever getting to ride, as the soft opening may end at any moment.

For theme park junkies who live in the area, technical rehearsals can be both a blessing and a curse; some folks stood in front of Diagon Alley for more than 30 consecutive days waiting for a soft opening, and even then the Gringotts ride never had a public preview before grand opening. Similar scenes occurred at USF in the spring of 2018 prior to Fast & Furious: Supercharged's opening, as fans waited fruitlessly for weeks, fueled by rumors on social media. You can expect the technical rehearsal groupies to regroup ahead of the new Harry Potter coaster's debut in 2019. Unless you are a local with lots of time on your hands, or on an extended vacation and obsessed with the about-to-open attraction, avoid spending any of your valuable time waiting for a ride that may or may not open. Instead, enjoy everything else the parks have to offer, and keep your ears open (and an eye on the @touringplans Twitter feed) just in case.

QUITTING TIME

BECAUSE THE DAY PARKING for the Universal theme parks and the CityWalk shopping, dining, and entertainment complex is consolidated in the same parking structures, chaos can ensue on days when both parks close at the same time, resulting in an epic flood of humanity heading to the parking garages.

An Orlando woman, obviously very perturbed, comments:

Both Universal Studios and Islands of Adventure share the same parking lot. IT MAKES NO SENSE for the two theme parks to close at the same time. I cannot even explain the amount of people. It was insane at closing (and other people were coming IN to go to City-Walk, so it was SUCH a big mess)!

If you are unlucky enough to find yourself in such a situation, we suggest taking a side trip to CityWalk and sitting out the stampede with a snack or drink. If you haven't yet exited the park, you can try lingering inside the gates as long as possible, browsing the shops that remain open past closing time. Security guards will eventually gently shoo you out, but not until most of the parking mess has cleared.

PART TWO

ACCOMMODATIONS

The BASIC CONSIDERATIONS

WHILE YOU'LL SURELY HAVE FUN inside Universal's parks wherever you spend the night, your choice of hotel is critical to the overall success of your vacation. Visitors to Universal face the basic question of whether to stay inside the resort—where room rates range from less than $100 on an off-season weeknight at a Value resort to more than $560 per night for a peak-season luxury property—or outside Universal, where rooms are as low as $50 a night. Affordability and easier access to non-Universal attractions must be weighed against the convenience and comfort of staying on property.

Universal Orlando currently operates six on-site resorts, with a total of 6,200 rooms. An additional 2,800 rooms and suites will open during 2019 and 2020 on the former Wet 'n Wild property, bringing the count up to 9,000 rooms. NBCUniversal CEO Stephen Burke has said that the resort could someday support up to 20,000 rooms.

Compared to the more than 30,000 rooms Walt Disney World has spread across nearly 30 hotels, your choice of an on-site hotel at Universal is a lot simpler, but you may find limited room availability during busy times. On the other hand, Universal's hotels (all operated by the highly regarded Loews chain) boast service and amenities equal to or better than the competition, and usually at a lower cost; Universal's Preferred property is often priced like Disney's Moderates, and its Prime Value–priced resorts outshine Disney's All-Star and Pop Century hotels. You should also consider the superior benefits granted to Universal's on-site guests, a couple of which can make the difference between a marvelous vacation and a miserable one.

Whether you decide to stay on-site or off, this chapter will help you get a grip on the multitude of lodging options in the Universal Orlando area and find the property that fits your family's needs.

THE TAX MAN COMETH

SALES AND LODGING TAXES can add a chunk of change to the cost of your hotel room. Cumulative tax in Orange County, which includes the Universal Orlando area and International Drive, is 12.5%.

ABOUT HOTEL RENOVATIONS

WE INSPECT SEVERAL HUNDRED HOTELS in the Orlando area to compile *The Unofficial Guide*'s list of lodging choices. Each year we call each hotel to verify contact information and inquire about renovations or refurbishments. If a hotel has been renovated or has refurbished its guest rooms, we reinspect it, along with any new hotels, for the next edition of the guide. Hotels reporting no improvements are rechecked every two years. We inspect most Universal-owned hotels every 6–12 months and no less than once every two years.

Many hotels more than five years old refurbish 10%–20% of their guest rooms each year. This incremental approach minimizes disruption, but it makes your room assignment a crapshoot—you might luck into a newly renovated room, or you might be assigned a threadbare one.

Universal reservationists won't guarantee you a recently refurbished room but will note your request and try to accommodate you. On the other hand, off-site hotels will often guarantee you an updated room when you book.

BENEFITS OF STAYING ON-SITE AT UNIVERSAL ORLANDO

UNIVERSAL OFFERS PERKS to get park visitors into its hotels. All guests at any Universal Orlando Resort on-site hotel can take advantage of the following:

- Early Park Admission to The Wizarding World and Volcano Bay 1 hour before the public (see page 54)
- The ability to charge in-park purchases to the hotel-room key
- Free package delivery to the hotel room for items purchased in the parks
- Free parking at the main CityWalk parking garage
- Free transportation to the parks and CityWalk
- Pool-hopping privileges to use any hotel's recreational facilities
- Free Wi-Fi in all hotel rooms and public areas (faster speeds available for a fee)
- Free scheduled transportation to SeaWorld and Aquatica (see page 139)
- Preferred tee times and complimentary transportation (for foursomes) to participating golf courses
- Free admission to CityWalk clubs (excludes concerts and special events).

In addition, every guest staying at Portofino Bay, Hard Rock, or Royal Pacific receives the following benefits:

- Free Universal Express Unlimited Passes for both theme parks (see page 57)
- Priority seating at select restaurants in the parks and CityWalk

All these benefits are available from the moment you arrive until midnight on the day you check out. Even if your room won't be ready until the afternoon, you can register at your hotel as early in the morning as you like, leaving your bags and retrieving your Express Passes (if eligible) in time for the Early Park Admission hour. Then linger at the resort after your checkout time, taking advantage of your pool privileges until late in the evening.

The most valuable of these perks is admission to The Wizarding World of Harry Potter and Volcano Bay 1 hour before the general public each morning, along with the Universal Express Unlimited Passes for guests of the top three hotels. It's hard to put a dollar value on the Early Park Admission, but two-park Universal Express Unlimited Passes are sold to the general public for $99.99–$159.99 per day, per person, plus tax, depending on the time of year you visit. Universal says the pass is "a value of $129.99 per person, per day," which works out to $520 per day for a family of four. One night at Universal's Royal Pacific hotel costs anywhere from $284 to $494, plus tax, depending on the season. If you were planning on staying at a comparable off-site deluxe hotel anyway, staying at the Royal Pacific gets your family two days of Universal Express Unlimited at no additional cost. During busy season, this can be a huge boon for parties of four or five, though be aware that an additional $35-per-night fee applies to each adult beyond the first two staying in the room. If you are traveling solo or as a couple, or are visiting at a slow time of year, calculate the cost of staying at Sapphire Falls or one of the Prime Value hotels and buying Express Passes on arrival if they turn out to be necessary.

Some of the benefits are of questionable value. Free parking at the parks, for example, is of little use to anyone staying at the resort because it's probably just as much walking from the resort as it is from the garages.

Having stayed at each of Universal's hotels, we think a sometimes-overlooked benefit is the ability to walk to the parks from your hotel. And it's not just the convenience—the walkways are pretty and almost serene at night, if you can ignore the roars from The Incredible Hulk Coaster.

This Dallas-area family found foot accessibility to the parks to be Universal's biggest advantage over Walt Disney World's on-site hotels:

> The simple convenience of being able to walk everywhere whenever you wanted was definitely worth the expense. Disney's shuttle and parking systems are extensive. We tried the bus, but it gets bogged down by the stops. Parking your own vehicle meant parking and then using a tram to get to the gate. Magic Kingdom was the worst with its off-site parking. You can't hop from park to park quickly. At Universal, with one parking area, everything was easily and quickly reachable. The girls could enjoy the park early (with little wait time), walk back to the hotel to nap, and then go back to the park or CityWalk. They felt very grown up being on their own without us adults to slow them down. This was inconvenient at Disney due to the transport time.

UNIVERSAL ORLANDO RESORT HOTELS 101

UNIVERSAL HAS SIX RESORT HOTELS. The 750-room **Portofino Bay Hotel** is a gorgeous property set on an artificial bay and themed like an Italian coastal town. The 650-room **Hard Rock Hotel** is an ultracool "Hotel California" replica, and the 1,000-room, Polynesian-themed **Royal Pacific Resort** is sumptuously decorated and richly appointed. All three are on the pricey side. The retro-style **Cabana Bay Beach Resort,** Universal's largest hotel, has 2,200 moderate-priced rooms, plus amenities (a bowling alley and lazy river) not seen at comparable Disney resorts. The Caribbean-styled **Sapphire Falls Resort** offers 1,000 rooms priced between Royal Pacific and Cabana Bay. **Aventura Hotel,** Universal's 600-room sixth property, opened in 2018 next to Sapphire Falls and across from the similarly priced Cabana Bay; it's a Miami-style modern high-rise with a Y-shaped glass tower and rooftop lounge. **Endless Summer Resort,** Universal's new value-priced option, consists of the 750-room Surfside Inn and Suites and the 2,050-room Dockside Inn and Suites, which will open in phases in 2019 and 2020.

Before you make any decisions, understand these basics regarding Universal Orlando Resort hotels.

UNIVERSAL ORLANDO RESORT HOTEL POLICIES

Resort Classifications

Universal's hotels fall into four categories. The three most expensive on-site hotels—**Portofino Bay Resort, Hard Rock Hotel,** and **Royal Pacific Resort**—are called Premier resorts, and their perks include Universal Express Unlimited, priority restaurant seating, and water taxi transportation to CityWalk. **Sapphire Falls Resort** is labeled a Preferred resort; it's a AAA Four Diamond–awarded hotel, just like the Premier properties, and offers water taxi service but lacks free Universal Express or priority restaurant seating.

Cabana Bay Beach Resort and the **Aventura Hotel** represent the Prime Value resorts. Both have bus and pedestrian access to the attractions (including Volcano Bay), but neither is connected to the water taxi system. The **Endless Summer Resort** hotels will be the first designated as Value hotels, as well as the first located a brief bus ride across I-4 from Universal proper. Regardless of classification, all on-site Universal guests enjoy amenities that surpass any other value-priced hotels in the area.

Seasonal Rates

Universal uses so many adjectives—*Value, Regular, Summer, Holiday,* and *Peak*—to describe its seasonal calendar that it's hard to keep up. Plus, Universal also changes the price of its hotel rooms with the day of the week, charging more for the same room on Friday and Saturday nights. Universal no longer makes a breakdown of its hotel seasons and corresponding rack (or nondiscounted) rates accessible online, but each Universal hotel profile (see pages 81–94) includes the lowest rack rate (Value season) and the highest rack rate (Holiday season). These prices are for a weeknight stay in a basic room with a standard view, usually of a "garden" or parking lot; upgrades to pool or bay views start at $25–$50. Rates include a maximum of two adults per room, plus any children up to the room's capacity; additional adults each incur a $35-per-night surcharge. Rack rates do not include taxes or parking, but no hidden resort fees are tacked on at Universal's hotels.

Discounts

Universal hotel rack rates are just the starting point, and most clever visitors can save substantially on their stay with a little legwork because Universal frequently offers sizable percentage-off deals to fill its rooms.

Start by reviewing the resort discount information in Part One (see page 41), and then visit universalorlando.com and click on "Places to Stay" then "Special Offers" to view the latest deals. Next, visit loews hotels.com to pick your hotel and dates; then select "Promotion" and enter "APH" (for annual pass holders) in the code box, or "FLO")for Florida residents). You don't have to prove eligibility to book with these codes, but you will need to show appropriate ID upon check-in.

If you are staying multiple nights, Universal's "Stay More, Save More" pricing structure kicks in. Stays in any on-site hotel standard room (or family suite at Cabana Bay) of four to seven nights save 10%–25% during holiday, peak, and summer seasons, and stays of three to seven nights save 10%–35% during regular and value seasons.

Making Reservations

The easiest way to book a room at Universal Orlando is online through universalorlando.com, or by phone at ☎ 888-273-1311. If you are attending a meeting or event, call ☎ 866-360-7395 for your group block room.

Cancellations

A credit card deposit equal to one night's room rate (plus tax) is required when booking. Cancellations made six or more days prior to check-in receive a full refund. Cancellations five or fewer days before check-in forfeit the deposit. However, Universal's "No Questions Asked" severe-weather policy says that if you are not able to travel to Orlando due to an "active named storm impacting your travel," you can reschedule your vacation or receive a full refund. This applies only for rooms or vacation packages booked directly with Loews and Universal; if you use a third-party reseller, you'll need to consult its cancellation policy.

Check-In and Checkout

Check-in time at all Universal hotels is 4 p.m., and checkout is 11 a.m.; if you ask nicely, you can usually get a noon checkout for free. Remember that all on-site hotel benefits—including Express Unlimited Passes for guests of the top three hotels and Early Park Admission—begin the first morning of your stay and last until midnight after you check out. So even if you can't get into your room, you can preregister as early as you like, leave your luggage, grab your Express Passes (at the top three hotels), and hit the parks at rope drop. Checkout can be done at the front desk, through the interactive TV system, or via Express with your bill emailed to you.

Age Requirements

The minimum age to book a hotel room at Universal Orlando is 21, and valid ID is required at check-in. At least one guest staying in the room must be age 21 or older.

Accessibility

All Universal Orlando hotels have wheelchair-accessible public areas and offer designated accessible rooms for mobility-, sight-, and/or hearing-impaired guests. Accessibility features include 36-inch-wide entry doors, peepholes at 3½ feet from the floor, closets with rods at 48 inches high, toilets with hand bar, and roll-in shower stalls or combination shower/tubs with adjustable showerheads. Sight- and hearing-impaired features include Braille room numbers, closed-caption televisions, smoke detectors with lights, and Hearing-Impaired Kits, including a TDD-relay service that may be used in any guest room.

Pets

Loews "loves pets" and is one of the few luxury chains to allow cats and dogs in its rooms. It even has a special (and expensive) room service menu for four-legged guests. There are some restrictions, starting with a $100 flat fee per stay for a maximum of two pets per guest room. Guests will be assigned a pet-friendly room category on arrival, which includes garden- and bay-view rooms at the Portofino Bay, garden-view rooms at the Hard Rock, and standard rooms at the Royal Pacific and Sapphire Falls. Club rooms don't participate in the pet program, nor do any of the Prime Value properties, such as Cabana Bay Beach Resort and Aventura Hotel.

Dogs may be walked only in designated areas and are not allowed in the pool/lounge or restaurant areas. Arrangements must be made with housekeeping for daily room cleaning, and there is a $10-per-hour "time-out" fee if they find your pet left unattended. If other guests complain about your pet's behavior, you may be asked to board it off-site. You must provide current vaccination records from a licensed veterinarian on request. Read the full Loews Loves Pets policy at tinyurl.com/LoewsPets.

Smoking

All Universal Orlando Resort hotels are smoke-free. Smoking is only permitted outdoors in designated locations. If you light up in your room, you'll be burned with a $250 cleaning fee.

Hard Rock Rewards

Hard Rock Hotel accepts the Hard Rock Rewards loyalty card, which offers free priority late checkout and other perks; visit hardrock.com /rewards to join. Be warned that discounted room bookings may not qualify for reward program benefits. The similar Loews YouFirst program previously offered at the other on-site hotels has been discontinued.

UNIVERSAL ORLANDO RESORT HOTEL SERVICES *and* AMENITIES

DINING

TO KEEP YOU FED, every Universal on-site hotel has multiple restaurants, a spot for coffee and grab-and-go snacks, and at least two bars. The Premier and Preferred properties each have sit-down restaurants, including one family-friendly eatery, while Cabana Bay has a counter-service food court, as well as table-service munchies in the bowling alley. Aventura Hotel has an upscale food court with international dishes and a rooftop bar that serves small plates. The Premier and Preferred hotels also have 24-hour room service menus, while Cabana Bay and Aventura offer pizza delivery to the rooms until midnight (1 a.m. on Friday and Saturday).

The primary downside to staying on-site at Universal is the cost of food at the Premier hotels' restaurants, which seem to be priced as if everyone staying at the hotels is on a corporate expense account. Fortunately, many good, cheaper restaurant choices are within a few minutes' drive of the hotels on Major Boulevard, International Drive, and Sand Lake Road. Hotel guests also have easy access to CityWalk, which has some cheaper choices for dining.

POOLS AND RECREATION

SWIMMING IS MANY GUESTS' NO. 1 priority (after the parks, of course), so you'll find some of Orlando's best pools at Universal's hotels. Each resort has at least one themed swimming facility for guests. The main pool is the more active, family-centric one, where you'll find playground equipment and organized activities, both for kids (water-based games and contests) and adults (free smoothies and cool towels). Most resorts (except Royal Pacific and Aventura) have a waterslide, and Cabana Bay has a lazy river. On most nights (weather permitting) a PG or PG-13 "dive-in" movie is projected on an outdoor screen, with the Harry Potter, Marvel, and Transformers flicks in heavy rotation.

The secondary pools at Portofino Bay are usually slightly more sedate and attract a more adult clientele. All pools are staffed with trained lifeguards during operating hours (which vary seasonally, typically 8 a.m.–10 p.m.) and have adjacent whirlpool tubs, changing facilities, and drink services. Towels are free with resort ID, and hotel guests are free to pool-hop from one resort to another; ask an attendant for access if your room key won't open another hotel's security gate.

Each hotel's main pool (except Aventura's) has private cabanas for rent, which start around $100 per day. Aside from providing shade and cushioned lounge chairs, cabanas come with ceiling fans, TVs, a refrigerator, free soft drinks, food and drink delivery, and a personal safe. Reserve a cabana by calling ☎ 407-503-4175 at Cabana Bay, ☎ 407-503-5200 ext. 35235 at Sapphire Falls, ☎ 407-503-3235 at Royal Pacific, ☎ 407-503-2236 at Hard Rock, or ☎ 407-503-1200 at Portofino Bay. Same-day cancellations incur a 50% penalty fee. You'll also find a variety of recreational activities around the pools, from a bocce court at Portofino Bay to a croquet lawn at the Royal Pacific; free equipment can be checked out to play.

KIDS' ACTIVITIES AND KIDS' SUITES

THE LOEWS LOVES KIDS PROGRAM means that there's always something at the hotel to keep the rug rats occupied when your family isn't in the parks. Free lending libraries of games and sports equipment are available at every hotel, and a schedule of supervised activities is offered at each main pool (or indoors on rainy days). The Minions (or other Universal characters) make regular meet and greet appearances at Cabana Bay Beach Resort on Friday evenings. In addition, the kids' clubs at the top three hotels offer evening childcare for a fee (see page 194), and every hotel has an arcade with video games; Cabana Bay's Game-O-Rama is the biggest, and Aventura Hotel's arcade includes virtual reality headsets.

If you want to go all out and amaze the kids (at the expense of your bank account), reserve one of the elaborately decorated **Kids' Suites.** Portofino Bay's Despicable Me suites look like Gru's laboratory, with missile-shaped beds and vaultlike doors. Royal Pacific's Jurassic World suites have appropriately dinosaurish decor, with high-tech headboards and jungle graphics. The Hard Rock's Future Rock Star suites give kids a pint-size stage to shred on. Aventura's and Sapphire Falls's Kids' Suites have a separate kids' room with TV and child-size furniture but no whimsical theming. All the Kids' Suites have separate bedrooms for the kids that only open on the parents' room (not the hallway). You'll get some extra privacy but pay a hefty price with the resort's highest room rates (outside the outrageous presidential suites). Still, these rooms are almost always booked up, so someone is willing to pay for them. Cabana Bay and Endless Summer don't offer Kids' Suites, but they do have Family Suites, without the private kids' quarters, for a much lower cost.

PARKING

UNIVERSAL'S THREE PREMIER HOTELS all charge a $24-per-night self-parking fee ($33 for valet) for registered guests; day guests pay $26 for self-parking and $38 for valet at Portofino Bay and Hard Rock, while

Royal Pacific charges day guests $45 for self-parking longer than 30 minutes and $34 for valet. Sapphire Falls overnight guests pay $22 for self-parking and $29 for valet; day guests pay $45 for self-parking longer than 30 minutes and $34 for valet. Cabana Bay and Aventura charge $14 for overnight guests (self-parking only) and Endless Summer charges $12; all three bill $45 per day for day visitors.

Most of the hotel restaurants (including Bice and Mama Della's at Portofino, Jake's and Islands Dining Room at Royal Pacific, Strong Water Tavern and Amatista Cookhouse at Sapphire Falls, and Bar 17 Bistro at Aventura) will validate diners for free self-parking or a discounted rate of $5 valet parking; The Palm at Hard Rock Hotel offers complimentary valet. You must spend at least $25 on food or beverages to receive parking validation. There are no annual pass discounts on parking at the hotels. The hotels don't charge for another night until midnight, so you can leave your car in the lot long past your checkout time without paying extra.

ATTRACTION TICKET CENTER

THOUGH THE PARTNERSHIP between Universal and Loews is largely harmonious, it does have one quirk: Loews staff have no authority over park tickets or anything else involving the attractions, so if you ask the front desk or concierge about park admission and the like, you'll be directed to the Universal Orlando Attraction Ticket Center. Typically located in the main hotel lobby (though the one at Portofino Bay is tucked around a secluded corner), the Ticket Center can help you purchase park tickets (or pick up ones you preordered), as well as arrange for Universal Express Passes, dining reservations, off-site transportation, and other amenities. The Ticket Center in each hotel is usually open daily, 7 a.m.–9 p.m.

INTERNET

ALL UNIVERSAL ORLANDO HOTELS offer free Wi-Fi in their public areas and guest rooms for up to four devices. The service is somewhat spotty but good enough for email and social media. If you plan to stream videos or upload large photos, you may want to pay $15 per 24 hours for Premium Plus Internet, which affords higher bandwidth (we've achieved more than 30 megabits-per-second downloads) on up to eight devices.

BUSINESS CENTERS

EACH OF THE PREMIER AND PREFERRED HOTELS has a fully equipped business center offering internet-connected computers with printers, copy and fax services, and mail facilities through FedEx and UPS. Portofino Bay's and Royal Pacific's business centers are open Monday–Friday, 7 a.m.–5:30 p.m., and Saturday, 7 a.m.–noon (closed Sunday). Hard Rock Hotel's and Sapphire Falls's business centers are open 24-7, and the others may be accessed during off-hours by contacting the front desk. Fees apply for certain services such as copying and faxing. Aventura Hotel has no business center, but the lobby has a couple of touch screens for printing airline boarding passes. Cabana Bay's diner has a quiet corner with phone booths but no printers.

CRIBS AND ROLLAWAY BEDS

COMPLIMENTARY CRIBS ARE AVAILABLE in all rooms. Rollaway beds can be requested at Premier and Preferred hotels on a first-come, first-serve basis for $25 per day, plus 12.5% sales tax. Only one rollaway per room is allowed, and they are not available at Cabana Bay Beach Resort or Aventura Hotel.

LAUNDRY

ALL THE HOTELS EXCEPT PORTOFINO BAY offer self-service Laundromats. Machines take quarters or credit cards and cost $3 per load to wash, and the same to dry. At all the Preferred and Premier hotels, you can also avail yourself of valet laundry, dry cleaning, quick pressing, and shoeshines, with express same-day service available daily, 9 a.m.–7 p.m.; pricing and instructions can be found inside your closet.

MICROWAVES AND REFRIGERATORS

ALL HOTEL ROOMS include small refrigerators, and the family suites at Cabana Bay and Endless Summer have kitchenettes with a microwave and sink. Microwaves are available on a first-come, first-serve basis for $15 each per day, plus 12.5% sales tax.

TRANSPORTATION AND CAR RENTAL

ALL OF UNIVERSAL'S HOTELS OFFER free transportation via bus and/or water taxi to CityWalk and the parks, as well as well-lit landscaped walking paths connecting the resort. Water taxis depart from each of the Premier and Preferred hotels every 15–20 minutes, while the buses from Cabana Bay and Aventura run almost continuously. Either transportation method takes about 15 minutes to reach the park entrances, while walking takes between less than 5 minutes from the Hard Rock Hotel to 15 or 20 minutes from Cabana Bay and Portofino Bay.

If you are staying at one resort but wish to dine at another, ask the concierge where to catch the free hotel dining shuttle, which circulates among the Loews properties every 30 minutes 6 p.m.–10 p.m. A final alternative to walking are the pedicabs operated by Orient Express Rickshaw. Drivers ply the pathways between the resorts and CityWalk, working for tips ($5 per passenger is typical). You can flag down an empty rickshaw, or call OER at ☎ 407-385-0471 to reserve one. Rickshaws run Monday–Friday, 7 a.m.–midnight, and until 2 a.m. Saturday–Sunday.

Free daily transportation for hotel guests to SeaWorld and Aquatica is available (see page 139). This service is poorly advertised, but a limited number of seats are available on a first-come, first-serve basis, so check with your hotel's Ticket Center a day in advance for the schedule and boarding passes.

Another free bus from Universal's parking hub to Busch Gardens Tampa is available to anyone holding a paid park ticket; visit secure .mearstransportation.com/MearsExpress/BuschGardens.asp or call ☎ 800-221-1339 for details. For a fee, the concierge desk will arrange for Mears Transportation to take you to Walt Disney World or the airport. If you want to rent a car, Avis rental-car service desks operate inside each hotel daily, 8 a.m.–6 p.m.

FITNESS CENTERS AND MANDARA SPA

IF YOU WANT TO STAY IN SHAPE while vacationing, every Universal hotel has a well-appointed fitness center filled with the latest in exercise equipment. The expansive Jack LaLanne–themed workout room at Cabana Bay Beach Resort, as well as the somewhat smaller workout rooms in the other hotels, are free for all hotel guests to use.

Whether you are staying at a Universal hotel or not, you may book services at Portofino Bay's Mandara Spa, which is attached to the hotel's fitness center. Access to the spa's shower and sauna facilities costs $10 per day for guests of any on-site resort and is free for club-level guests or anyone purchasing spa services. If you aren't staying on-site, you can get access to the spa (though not the nearby Beach Pool) with a $25 day pass, which also includes free self-parking or $5 valet parking at the hotel entrance.

Universal Orlando's Mandara Spa was renovated in 2017, enhancing its changing and sauna facilities while retaining its Asian ambience despite its location in an Italy-themed resort. We like the contrast, though, and find it slightly exotic. Waiting areas are decorated in comforting earth tones; treatment rooms feature silk-draped ceilings. Changing and bathroom areas are spacious and clean, but they also include less-than-subtle advertisements for products sold on premises. The treatment rooms feature additional decorative lighting and accessories.

The emphasis on tranquility extends to the stellar spa services, which include free self-heating oil for massages. Men and women enjoy separate steam and sauna facilities; the whirlpool tub is unisex. The Portofino's sand-bottom pool is conveniently located near the entrance to the spa, as are nail services. The fitness center is still on the other side of the glass wall, however, so you may feel a bit like that doggy in the window.

We rate the Mandara Spa at Portofino Bay as 4 stars, just behind the spas at Disney's Grand Floridian, the Waldorf Astoria, and the Four Seasons and equivalent to the spas at the Ritz-Carlton, Saratoga Springs, and Gaylord Palms. Prices range from $75 for a 25-minute myofascial release to $390 for an 80-minute couple's massage package. Hair salon and makeup services are also on the menu. A 20% automatic gratuity applies to all services, and Preferred and Premier Annual Pass holders can save 10%–20% on services (Monday–Thursday only). Groupon frequently offers discounted Mandara Spa packages, but you'll be charged gratuity based on the full value.

Purchase of most massages and treatments also includes access to the fitness center for the day. Call ☎ 407-503-1244 for reservations, or visit tinyurl.com/PBHMandaraSpa to preview the price list.

CLUB LEVEL

THE THREE TOP HOTELS each offer club-level rooms or suites that allow access to an exclusive lounge, where you'll find a complimentary Continental breakfast, afternoon snacks, hot and cold evening hors d'oeuvres with free beer and wine, and after-dinner desserts. Club-level guests also get free fitness center access, discounted poolside cabana rentals, personal concierge service, evening turndown service, and other luxurious touches. Hard Rock Hotel's Rock Royalty and Royal Pacific's Royal Club Lounges are on the seventh floor, while Portofino Bay's Portofino Club Lounge is in the lobby; all are open daily, 7 a.m.–10 p.m. Most of our readers who stay in a club-level room seem happy with their choice, like this family from Kansas City:

> We stayed on the club level of the Royal Pacific. Absolutely worth the money. It not only includes breakfast every morning but also includes sodas all day and cocktails in the evening with heavy appetizers, which we usually made a meal out of. There was always a salad and then something hot. One night it was beef stew, then fried rice, and then chicken potpie. And if you weren't full, they put out dessert 8–9 p.m. This ended up saving us money, and we were usually tired from the day, so just walking down the hall was fabulous.

This family from St. Louis also felt that the club level's cost was money well spent:

> Club level was only $40 more, and we easily had this covered with breakfast and dinner that we didn't eat out, along with soda and water taken into the park. For a family of four, it was well worth it. When my son became ill, the concierge service connected us with an urgent care that stayed open late. Amazing service.

WEDDINGS

SEEING HOW SUCCESSFUL THE NUPTIAL BUSINESS has been for Disney, it was only a matter of time before Universal got into the matrimony game. There is no dedicated wedding pavilion at Universal (yet), but each hotel has facilities for staging fairy-tale ceremonies, large or small. Intimate weddings with 50 or fewer guests start at $1,500 for a simple ceremony, plus $300 for a cake or $99 per guest for a 1-hour cocktail reception. A Signature wedding for more than 50 guests starts at $2,500–$4,500 for the ceremony and $160-plus per plate for a dinner reception. To Universal's credit, it doesn't quote an hourly rate for having Minions attend your bachelorette party, but this is Orlando: money talks. Visit tinyurl.com/uniweddings to download brochures with pricing and menus, and start planning your Universal union today.

UNIVERSAL ORLANDO RESORT HOTEL PROFILES

Hard Rock Hotel Orlando ★★★★½

Rate per night $324–$569. **Pool** ★★★★. **Fridge in room** Yes.
Shuttle to parks Yes (Universal, SeaWorld, Aquatica). **Maximum
number of occupants per room** 5 (two queens) or 3 (king). **Comments** Pets welcome (2/room; $100/stay).

5800 Universal Blvd.
Orlando
☎ 407-503-2000 or
888-273-1311
hardrockhotelorlando.com

FOR YOUNGER ADULTS AND FAMILIES with older kids, the Hard Rock
Hotel is the hippest place to lay your head. Opened in 2001, the Hard
Rock Hotel is the closest resort to Universal's theme parks. The exterior
has a California Mission theme, with white stucco walls, arched entry-
ways, and rust-colored roof tiles. Inside, the lobby is a tribute to rock-
and-roll style, all marble, chrome, and stage lighting. The lobby's walls are
decorated with enough concert posters, costumes, and musical instruments to start another wing of Cleveland's Rock and Roll Hall of Fame.
Exhibits include Lady Gaga and Rihanna, and QR codes near each artifact
let you take a self-guided memorabilia tour via your smartphone.

The eight floors hold 650 rooms, including 29 suites, with the rooms
categorized into standard, deluxe, and Rock Royalty club-level tiers. Standard rooms are 375 square feet, slightly larger than rooms at Disney's
Moderate resorts and a bit smaller than most Disney Deluxe rooms. The
rooms feature light-gray walls and linens, pastel furniture, and colorful
retro-inspired accents, such as throw pillows crocheted with phrases such
as "Quiet Please" and "Be Nice." To be frank, the style looks more bubble-
gum pop than hard rock, but the brighter look is a bit more soothing after
you stumble back from a fatiguing day in the parks.

Standard rooms are furnished with two queen beds, with plush, comfortable linens and more pillows than you'll know what to do with. Rooms
also include a flat-panel HDTV, refrigerator, coffee maker, and an alarm
clock with an iPhone docking port.

A six-drawer dresser and separate closet with sliding doors ensure
plenty of storage space. In addition, most rooms have a reading chair and
a small desk with two chairs. An optional rollaway bed, available at an
extra charge, allows standard rooms to sleep up to five people.

Each room's dressing area features a sink and hair dryer. The bathroom
is probably large enough for most adults to get ready in the morning
while another person gets ready in the dressing area.

Guests staying in standard rooms can choose from one of three views:
standard, which can include anything from walkways and parking lots to
lawns and trees; garden view, which includes the lawn, trees, and (in
some rooms) the waterway around the resort; and pool view, which
includes the Hard Rock's expansive pool.

A step up from standard rooms are deluxe rooms. Deluxe rooms with
king beds are around 500 square feet and can accommodate up to
three people with an optional rollaway bed rental. These rooms feature

a U-shaped sitting area in place of the second bed, and the rest of the amenities are the same as in standard rooms. Deluxe queen rooms are also 500 square feet and can hold up to five people using a pullout sofa, located in a small cubby just off the room's entrance.

For families, each 800-square-foot Future Rock Star suite features an authentic piece of music memorabilia, along with a simulated stage inside the separate kids' bedroom. Or you can really live like The King in the 2,000-square-foot Graceland Suite, which comes complete with a baby grand piano and fireplace.

The zero-entry pool is an attraction unto itself; it is the place to see and be seen. Situated in the middle of the resort's C-shaped main building, the 12,000-square-foot pool includes a 250-foot waterslide (the longest at any Universal hotel), a sand beach, and underwater speakers so you can hear the music while you swim. Adjacent to the pool are a fountain play area for small children, a sand volleyball court, hot tubs, and a poolside bar. The entire pool area is lined with tall palm trees, but if they don't provide enough shade (or you just want to make an impression), private cabanas are available for rent. The Hard Rock also has a small, functional fitness center, but for spa services you'll have to go to the Mandara at Universal's nearby Portofino Bay. Like all Universal Orlando Resort hotels, the Hard Rock has a business center and video arcade.

On-site dining includes The Kitchen, a casual full-service restaurant open for breakfast, lunch, and dinner that features American food such as burgers, steaks, and salads. The Kitchen hosts strolling magicians on Wednesday and Friday, Kids Can Cook activities on Tuesday and Thursday, and random celebrity-chef sightings. The Palm Restaurant is an upscale steak house available for dinner only. There is also an Emack & Bolio's ice cream shop and grab-and-go marketplace on the lower level; the stylish Velvet Bar in the lobby for drinks after dark and monthly Velvet Sessions rock-and-roll cocktail parties (visit velvetsessions.com for the schedule and to purchase tickets); and the BeachClub bar and grill by the pool. And, of course, the Hard Rock Cafe is just a short distance away at Universal CityWalk. Oenophiles will want to keep an eye on tinyurl.com/HRHWineRiffs for announcements about periodic Wine Riffs events ($125 plus tax and gratuity), which pair five courses of vino and victuals with a carefully curated soundtrack.

If all that musical immersion puts you in the mood to jam, you can borrow a Crosley turntable with a stack of vinyl records or 1 of 20 Fender guitars—including Stratocasters, Telecasters, and even bass guitars—with amp and headphones for free (after a $1,000 credit card deposit) through the hotel's The Sound of Your Stay program; ask the front desk for details. Alternatively, investigate the Rock Om in-room yoga program (hardrock hotelorlando.com/rock-om.htm) if you yearn to achieve a state of Zen.

We rate the rooms at Hard Rock slightly ahead of the more-expensive Portofino Bay. In fact, Hard Rock Hotel is so popular with families that, during certain seasons when school is out of session, it can command a higher nightly rate than Portofino Bay. While not exactly cheap, Hard Rock is a good value compared to, say, Disney's Yacht & Beach Clubs.

What you're paying for at the Hard Rock is a short walk to the theme parks and Universal Express Unlimited first, and the room second.

While the hotel can get a bit loud, especially in areas facing the pool, it gets high marks from families with teenagers, like this Texas parent with two daughters ages 15 and 17:

> *One word: "WOW!" My group loved it! We splurged for a club room. My teenagers liked the club lounge . . . allowing them to pop in for food whenever they wanted. The beds were super comfortable, soft instead of firm mattresses. The pool was a big hit with the girls. We all liked the convenience of being so close to walk to the parks.*

Loews Portofino Bay Hotel ★★★★½

Rate per night $339–$564. **Pools** ★★★★. **Fridge in room** Yes. **Shuttle to parks** Yes (Universal, SeaWorld, Aquatica). **Maximum number of occupants per room** 5 (two queens) or 3 (king). **Comments** Pets welcome (2/room; $100/stay).

5601 Universal Blvd. Orlando
☎ 407-503-1000 or 888-273-1311
loewshotels.com /portofino-bay-hotel

IF YOU WANT THE ULTIMATE European-style, spare-no-expense on-site experience, look no further than the Portofino Bay Hotel. Universal's top-of-the-line hotel evokes the Italian seaside city of Portofino, complete with a man-made Portofino Bay past the lobby. To Universal's credit, the layout, color, and theming of the guest room buildings are a good approximation of the architecture around the harbor in the real Portofino (Universal's version has fewer yachts, though).

The front of the Portofino continues the theme, with a trio of Vespa-like scooters parked around a burbling fountain. Deep-green tapestries hang from the sand-colored porte cochere, which is flanked by narrower recessed arches. It's a convincing transition from the nearby parking deck.

Inside, the lobby is decorated with pink marble floors, white wood columns, and arches. The space is both airy and comfortable, with side rooms featuring seats and couches done in bold reds and deep blues.

Most guest rooms are 450 square feet and have either one king bed or two queen beds. King rooms sleep up to three people with an optional rollaway bed; the same option allows queen rooms to sleep up to five. Two room-view types are available: garden rooms look out over the landscaping and trees (many of these are the east-facing rooms in the resort's east wing; others face one of the three pools); bay-view rooms face either west or south and overlook Portofino Bay, with a view of the piazza behind the lobby too. A very small number of rooms have working balconies; you can't reserve one in advance but may upgrade at check-in if one is available for $15–$30 extra.

Rooms come furnished with a 42-inch flat-panel HDTV, a small refrigerator, a coffee maker, and an alarm clock with an iPhone docking port. Other amenities include a small desk with two chairs, a comfortable reading chair with lamp, a chest of drawers, and a standing closet. Beds are large and comfortable. You'll have a hard time in the morning convincing yourself that getting out of them and going to a theme park is the best option you have.

Guest bathrooms at Portofino Bay are the best on Universal property. We've seen smaller New York apartments! Speakers inside the bathroom transmit the audio from whatever is playing on the room's television. The best thing is the shower, which has enough water pressure to strip paint from old furniture, not to mention an adjustable spray nozzle that varies the water pulses to simulate everything from monsoon season in the tropics to the rhythmic thumps of wildebeest hooves during migrating season. We love it.

Portofino Bay has three pools, the largest of which is the Beach Pool, on the west side of the resort. Two smaller quiet pools sit at the far end of the east wing and to the west of the main lobby. The Beach Pool has a zero-entry design and a waterslide themed after a Roman aqueduct, plus a children's play area, hot tubs, and a poolside bar and grill. The Villa Pool has private cabana rentals for that Italian Riviera feeling and a bocce ball court with free equipment for that Jersey shore feeling. Rounding out the luxuries are the full-service Mandara Spa; a complete fitness center with weight machines, treadmills, and more; a business center; and a video arcade.

On-site dining includes three sit-down restaurants serving Italian cuisine, a deli, a pizzeria, and a café serving coffee and gelato. Two bars round out the food offerings at Portofino. The Portofino has 10 separate convention meeting rooms and is a popular destination for small to mid-size groups. Perhaps because Universal figures that most guests have an expense account, some of the food prices go well beyond what we'd consider reasonable, even for a theme park hotel.

While we think Portofino Bay has some of Universal's best rooms, certain areas are starting to show their age, and the prices put it on par with the Ritz-Carlton, something its good points can't quite justify. On the other hand, the Ritz isn't a short walk from Harry Potter, and the Portofino is significantly cheaper than the hotels along Disney's monorail, as this Shelby, North Carolina, reader remarked:

> We stayed at Portofino Bay for three nights before transferring to Disney's Contemporary Resort, and we liked the Portofino much better for half the price!

If you can't swing a stay here, at least take a complimentary sunset water taxi ride to the harbor for Musica della Notte, the free mini-concert of romantic operatic pop tunes belted from Portofino's bayside balconies daily at sunset (weather permitting). Four times each year, Harbor Nights are held on the plaza, with free-flowing wine, heavy hors d'oeuvres, and live music. Tickets are $55 (plus tax) for general admission and $90 for VIP admission with reserved seating and private food stations. The experience is like attending an upscale wedding without having to bring a gift, and it makes for a wonderfully romantic date night. See tinyurl.com/PBH HarborNights for details on the next date.

Loews Royal Pacific Resort   ★★★★½

Rate per night $284–$494. **Pool** ★★★★. **Fridge in room** Yes. **Shuttle to parks** Yes (Universal, SeaWorld, Aquatica). **Maximum number of occupants per room** 5 (two queens) or 3 (king). **Comments** Character breakfast on Saturday. Pets welcome (2/room, $100/stay).

A FAVORITE OF YOUNG FAMILIES and solo travelers alike, the Royal Pacific is the least expensive and most relaxing of Universal's top hotels. You may be tempted, as we were initially, to write off the Royal Pacific, which opened in 2002, as a knockoff of Disney's Polynesian Village Resort. There are indeed similarities, but the Royal Pacific is attractive enough, and has enough strengths of its own, for us to recommend that you try a stay there to compare for yourself.

6300 Hollywood Way Orlando
☎ 407-503-1000 or 888-273-1311
loewshotels.com /royal-pacific-resort

The South Seas–inspired theming is both relaxing and structured. Guests enter the lobby from a walkway two stories above an artificial stream that surrounds the resort. Once you're inside, the lobby's dark teakwood accents contrast nicely with the enormous amount of light coming in from the windows and three-story A-frame roof. Palms line the walkway through the lobby, which surrounds an enormous outdoor fountain.

The Royal Pacific's 1,000 guest rooms are spread among three Y-shaped wings attached to the resort's main building. Standard rooms are 335 square feet and feature one king or two queen beds. The beds, fitted with 300-thread-count sheets, are very comfortable.

The rooms feature modern monochrome wall treatments and carpets, accented with boldly colored floral graphics. Rooms include a flat-panel LCD HDTV, a refrigerator, a coffee maker, and an alarm clock with an iPhone docking port. Other amenities include a small desk with two chairs, a comfortable reading chair, a chest of drawers, and a large closet.

As at the Hard Rock, rooms at the Royal Pacific have a dressing area with sink, separated from the rest of the room by a wall. Adjacent to the dressing area is the bathroom, with a tub, shower, and toilet. While they're acceptable, the bathroom and dressing areas at the Royal Pacific are our least favorite in the upscale Universal resorts.

The Royal Pacific was one of the first Orlando hotels to offer themed rooms for kids with its Jurassic Park Kids' Suites, which were refurbished in 2018 to fit the Jurassic World franchise. These two-room suites have a door connecting the kids' room to the main hotel room, but only the main room has a door out to the hallway. The kids' room has two twin beds with headboards that look like Gyrospheres, as well as a wall-size mural of dinosaurs.

Some standard-view rooms look out over the Royal Pacific's green landscape, while others see the parking lot or nearby roads. Water-view rooms facing the pool or lagoon are also available, many of which have a great look at Hogwarts Castle. Guests in north- and west-facing rooms in Tower 1 are closest to the attractions at Islands of Adventure (IOA) and can hear the roar from IOA's Incredible Hulk Coaster throughout the day and night. East-facing rooms in Towers 1 and 2 are exposed to traffic noise from Universal Boulevard and, more distantly, I-4. Quietest are south-facing pool-view rooms in Tower 1 and south-facing rooms in Tower 3.

Like the Hard Rock, the Royal Pacific's zero-entry pool includes a sand beach, volleyball court, play area for kids, hot tub, and cabanas for rent, plus a poolside bar and grill. Designed to look like a cross between a tropical island and cruise ship pool (complete with faux exhaust tower and observation deck), the swimming complex pool is huge; it does not, however, have a waterslide. Lounge chairs line most of the walkway around the pool, and portable folding umbrellas provide shade where the palm trees and lush green plants can't. A free torch-lighting ceremony with Polynesian dances, music, and fire juggling is held by the pool around sunset on select nights (usually Tuesday, Friday, and Saturday during the summer). For the full island experience, the *Wantilan Luau* is held every Saturday night year-round; see the review on page 248.

The Royal Pacific includes a 5,000-square-foot fitness facility, with free weights and machines, treadmills, stair-climbers, elliptical machines, and exercise bikes, plus separate lockers, dressing areas, and sauna rooms for men and women. The Royal Pacific's expansive convention facilities cover more than 132,000 square feet and connect to the Sapphire Falls Resort via an air-conditioned bridge. A business center and video arcade round out the on-site amenities.

On-site dining includes a full-service restaurant, three bars, and a luau. Islands Dining Room is open daily for breakfast; its buffet is stocked with the usual eggs, bacon, pancakes, and French toast, or you can order more exotic eye-openers à la carte. At dinner, Islands has better-than-average international cuisine. Another breakfast option is the grab-and-go Continental-style breakfast in the lobby's marketplace kiosk. Jake's American Bar serves a casual sit-down menu for lunch and dinner, along with late-night bar snacks. On Saturday mornings, the Tahitian Room (formerly Emeril's Tchoup Chop restaurant) opens for a character breakfast with the Minions and their Despicable Me pals; see page 198 for details. Several casual bar areas—including Jake's American Bar, the Orchid Court Lounge & Sushi Bar, and the poolside Bula Bar & Grille with neighboring ice cream stand—are located in the resort.

Though nice, the rooms alone aren't worth the rates, but adding in Universal Express Unlimited and a short walk to the parks makes it the best deal among Universal's top hotels.

Loews Sapphire Falls Resort ★★★★

6601 Adventure Way
Orlando
☎ 407-503-5000 or
888-273-1311
loewshotels.com
/sapphire-falls-hotel

Rate per night $209–$324. **Pool** ★★★★. **Fridge in room** Yes. **Shuttle to parks** Yes (Universal, SeaWorld, Aquatica). **Maximum number of occupants per room** 5 (two queens) or 3 (king). **Comment** Pets welcome (2/room, $100/stay).

SAPPHIRE FALLS RESORT brings a sunny Caribbean island vibe to the moderate market with its 1,000 rooms (including 77 suites), which opened in summer 2016. Sandwiched between Royal Pacific and Cabana Bay—both physically and price-wise—Sapphire Falls sports most of the amenities of Universal's three fanciest hotels, including water taxi transportation to the parks, with the crucial exception of complimentary Express Passes.

Rather than replicating the stereotypical pastel palette seen at Disney's Caribbean-themed hotel, Sapphire Falls's designers went with a cooler blue-and-white color scheme for the exterior. The lobby continues the modern reinterpretation of island aesthetics with a playful hanging sculpture of wicker beach balls and a massive floor-to-ceiling window providing a postcard-perfect view of the rear lagoon, with the towers of Doctor Doom's Fearfall posing in the background. Public spaces fuse seemingly ancient structures—such as a stunning stone silo, complete with authentic-looking mill equipment—with starkly minimalist architecture and contemporary artwork. The mix can prove somewhat jarring; we sometimes emerged from a richly detailed space into a barren white hallway and wondered if we'd taken a wrong turn into an employee-only area. But we've come to appreciate the Sapphire Falls Resort's casually sophisticated vibe, which hits a sweet spot between the family-friendly freneticism of Cabana Bay and the elegance of Universal's more upscale hotels.

Water figures heavily at Sapphire Falls, whose namesake waterfalls form the scenic centerpiece of the resort. The 16,000-square-foot main pool boasts 3,500 square feet of white sand on which to set your lounger, a 100-foot waterslide, children's play areas, fire pits, a hot tub, and cabanas for rent. There are two zero-entry points near the middle of the pool on opposite sides, which allow you to pretend to walk across the water. A fitness room holds a sauna; table tennis (free to use) and a pool table (nominal fee per game) are available outside near the small arcade.

On the lower level, Amatista Cookhouse offers à la carte or buffet American breakfast, followed by table-service Caribbean food for lunch and dinner. Drhum Club Kantine serves tapas-style small plates, sandwiches, and massive bowls of alcohol near the pool bar's fire pit. New Dutch Trading Co., an island-inspired grab-and-go marketplace, has ice cream, coffee, hot entrées and sandwiches, refillable Coke Freestyle cups, and packaged snacks. Strong Water Tavern in the lobby offers rum tastings and freshly made ceviche, and a Universal Studios Store in the lobby sells sundries and resort souvenirs. The *Caribbean Carnaval,* held every Friday, is an interactive dinner show combining an island-inspired buffet with live music and dancing; see the review on page 233.

The rooms range from 322 square feet in a standard queen or king to 529 square feet in the 36 Kids' Suites, up to 1,353 square feet in the 15 Hospitality Suites, which are appointed with charming rustic light fixtures and are sizable enough to live in long-term. All rooms include a 49-inch flat-panel HDTV, an alarm clock with iPhone dock, in-wall USB charging ports, minifridge, and coffee maker. The rooms are aesthetically acceptable but a bit antiseptic, aside from a garishly colored mirror frame and metallized photos above the beds, and they are barely bigger than the standard Cabana Bay rooms. The layout is perfectly functional, but there are some odd design quirks, such as a sliding door to the toilet that doesn't latch; don't plan on doing your business in private if you have inquisitive kids.

Sapphire Falls also contains nearly 115,000 square feet of meeting space and a business center. Covered walkways connect to a parking structure, which in turn connects to the meeting facilities at Royal Pacific, making the sister properties ideal for conventions.

Water taxi transportation to Sapphire Falls takes only a few minutes longer than sailing to Royal Pacific, though boats may be delayed by traffic congestion under the bridge between the hotels and CityWalk. A pedestrian pathway to the parks starts near the boat dock, joining up with the Royal Pacific garden path near that hotel's convention center entrance. If you want to walk from Sapphire Falls to Cabana Bay, note that there's no pedestrian crosswalk at the heavily trafficked intersection that separates the two hotels; instead, walk to the corner of Hollywood Way and use the garden bridge to cross over Adventure Way, or use the path between Aventura and Volcano Bay to walk beneath the busy road.

Sapphire Falls occupies an interesting spot in Universal's hotel spectrum, appealing to people turned off both by the mid-century aesthetics of Cabana Bay (or Aventura's ultramodernism) and the higher price tags of the resort's other properties. If water taxi transportation is important to you, but Express Unlimited access is not, Sapphire Falls is your spot. Otherwise, search for photos online to see if you like the resort's look, and carefully compare the rates to both Cabana Bay and Aventura Hotel for the time of your planned visit.

Universal's Aventura Hotel ★★★★

6725 Adventure Way
Orlando
☎ 407-503-6000
or 888-273-1311
loewshotels.com
/universals-aventura-hotel

Rate per night $149–$254. **Pools** ★★★½. **Fridge in room** Yes. **Shuttle to parks** Yes (Universal, SeaWorld, Aquatica). **Maximum number of occupants per room** 4 (two queens or king with pull-out) or 6 (Kids' Suites). **Comment** Pets not permitted.

IN THE SUMMER OF 2018, Universal's Aventura Hotel opened as the resort's sixth property and second Prime Value option. Squeezed next to the lushly tropical Sapphire Falls and across the street from the colorfully retro Cabana Bay, Universal's Aventura Hotel may seem a bit under-themed in comparison to its neighbors. But if you've ever seen the luxury skyscrapers lining Miami's waterfronts, this 16-story Y-shaped tower will make you feel right at home with its ultramodern curvilinear glass-covered design (which looks suspiciously similar to a giant fidget spinner).

From the sleek, spacious lobby to the streamlined guest rooms, Aventura embodies that trendy aesthetic that Universal describes as simplified style, and which cynics might describe as IKEA stark; if you've stayed in a European micro-hotel, Aventura's rooms will feel familiar. Standard rooms start at a miniscule 238 square feet for a king room with a pullout couch, while the standard room (with two queen beds), at 314 square feet, is a smidgen smaller than those at Sapphire Falls next door. Deluxe rooms, available with two queen beds or a single king, have a little more elbowroom at 395 square feet but still sleep a maximum of four. Because the deluxe rooms are located at the ends of the hotel's wings, you'll wake up to a dramatic 180-degree view. If you need more room, 16 Kids' Suites are available; at 575 square feet, they have space for six, including a separate interior room with two twin beds and a play area with a pullout couch.

Unusually, room upgrades are priced not based on direction of view but altitude: "skyline" rooms on the topmost floors charge an extra $25 per night for panoramic views of the City Beautiful from one side of the tower or of Universal Orlando from the others. Odd-numbered rooms XX01–XX15 and even-numbered rooms XX30–XX44 face I-4 and International Drive; odd-numbered rooms XX31–XX45 and even-numbered rooms XX50–XX64 face Cabana Bay and Volcano Bay; and even-numbered rooms XX00–XX14 and odd-numbered rooms XX51–XX65 face toward Sapphire Falls and Islands of Adventure.

All of the hotel's rooms share the same minimalist design scheme, featuring faux-wood tile floors and a monochromatic palette with a noticeable absence of color or artwork. Floor plans are oddly shaped, owing to the hotel's curved footprint, but floor-to-ceiling windows and translucent dividers between the bed and bath help the rooms feel more spacious. In addition to the standard amenities, such as separate vanity and toilet areas, minifridge, coffee maker, and 43-inch flat-panel TV, Aventura's rooms integrate advanced smart home technology that will make gadget geeks drool. Not only are USB plugs preinstalled in the power outlets for recharging your digital devices, but every room also includes a tablet that you can use to adjust the air-conditioning, tune the TV, or even order a pizza and clean towels. If you have a Chromecast-compatible device or subscribe to Netflix or Amazon Prime, you can stream your own videos on the TV set. The iPad integration is innovative but also annoying if you need to use the sink in the middle of the night; thankfully, there are still physical switches for illuminating the toilet.

The pool at Aventura Hotel is also in the chic South Floridian style, with a compact crescent-shaped main pool surrounded by white decks and strategically placed palm trees. There's a splash pad and underwater speakers (all the better to hear the dive-in movies) for the kids, and a fire pit and hot tub for the grown-ups; anyone with a couple of bucks can enjoy the Foosball and pool tables. Rainy day recreation includes a free fitness room, a Universal Studios Store, and an arcade with HTC Vive virtual reality headsets ($10 for 5 minutes of game play; 50% discount for annual pass holders). Aventura is also home to Universal Orlando's first V-Hub lounge, where Virgin Holidays travelers staying at any on-site hotel can stash their luggage, grab some snacks, and relax on their departure day.

Aventura Hotel is the first Universal on-site resort without a full-service restaurant, but that doesn't mean you'll starve. Along with the de rigueur Starbucks in the lobby, you'll also find Urban Pantry, a fast-casual food hall serving international entrées like ramen, artisanal pizza, and rotisserie chicken, plus a rooftop bar that serves craft cocktails and small plates. There are two additional bars, in the lobby and at the pool, but you'll want to take the dedicated elevator up to Bar 17 Bistro on the rooftop for its million-dollar views of Volcano Bay's namesake peak and the surrounding city.

Like Cabana Bay, Aventura lacks direct water taxi service to CityWalk, though you can easily walk over to Sapphire Falls and use its boats. Bus service delivers guests to the parking hub, and there is direct pedestrian access to all three parks, including a dedicated sidewalk past the pool to Volcano Bay.

Valet parking is not offered, and self-parking is $14 per night for hotel guests. Visitors are charged a hefty $45 for parking to discourage them from using Aventura to access Volcano Bay.

Rack rates for Aventura are essentially identical to Cabana Bay, and both Prime Value properties include Early Park Admission but not Universal Express. So the choice between them might come down to whether your preferred style is cutting-edge cool or vibrant vintage.

Universal's Cabana Bay Beach Resort ★★★★

6550 Adventure Way
Orlando
☎ 407-503-4000 or
888-273-1311
loewshotels.com
/cabana-bay-hotel

Rate per night $149-$254. **Pools** ★★★★½. **Fridge in room** Yes. **Shuttle to parks** Yes (Universal, SeaWorld, Aquatica). **Maximum number of occupants per room** 4 (two queens) or 6 (family suites). **Comments** Character greeting in lobby on Friday. Pets not permitted.

IF YOU'RE OBSESSED WITH VINTAGE 1950s and 1960s designs, and with finding a good value (we're guilty on both accounts), you may just fall in love with Cabana Bay Beach Resort, Universal's first Prime Value hotel. The mid-century modern aesthetic starts with the neon signage that welcomes you outside and continues inside with lots of windows, bright colors, and period-appropriate lighting and furniture. The designers were inspired by classic seaside hotels such as the doo-wop Caribbean Motel in Wildwood Crest, New Jersey, and the original Americana Hotel in Bal Harbour, Florida. We think that the resort would be right at home in the deserts of Palm Springs or Las Vegas, while our British friends say the decor reminds them of Butlin's Bognor Regis resort circa 1985.

Whatever Cabana Bay reminds you of, we think you'll like it. Kids will love the two large and well-themed pools (one with a lazy river), the amount of space they have to run around in, the vintage cars parked outside the hotel lobby, and the video arcade. Adults will appreciate the sophisticated kitsch of the decor, the multiple lounges, and the on-site Starbucks. We think Cabana Bay is an excellent choice for price- and/or space-conscious families visiting Universal.

The hotel's closest competitor in the Orlando area is Disney's Art of Animation Resort, and the two share many similarities. Both have standard rooms and family suites. At 430 square feet per suite, Cabana Bay suites are about 135 square feet smaller than comparable suites at Art of Animation and have only one bathroom. We found them well appointed for two to four people per room (though not for the six Loews claims as its capacity). Rates for the suites are about $140–$300 per night less than Art of Animation's. Standard rooms are only 300 square feet but can frequently be had for around $115 a night after discounts, undercutting Disney's cheapest rooms.

Each family suite has a small bedroom with two queen beds and a 40-inch flat-panel HDTV, divided from the living area and kitchenette by a sliding screen; a pullout sofa in the living area offers additional sleeping space and a second 40-inch TV. The bath is divided into three sections: toilet, sink area, and shower room with additional sink; all are separated by doors, so three people can theoretically get ready at once. Retro theming even extends to the toiletries, which include the fondly remembered Zest and VO5 brands. The kitchenette has a microwave, coffee maker, and minifridge. A bar area allows extra seating for quick meals, and a large closet has enough space to store everyone's luggage. Built-in USB charging outlets for your devices are a thoughtful touch. Standard rooms have the same two queen beds but without the living area, kitchenette, or three-way bathroom. Instead, they get a minifridge with coffee maker and an average-size single bathroom.

Cabana Bay's rooms are divided among five long structures and two towers, arranged around two pool courtyards and connected in the center by the lobby facilities. The Castaway, Thunderbird, and Starlight (designated buildings 1, 2, and 3, respectively, each proudly identified in glowing neon script) are motel-style structures with exterior entrances surrounding the Cabana Courtyard. The Continental (building 4) and Americana (buildings 5 and 6) frame the Lazy River Courtyard and have hotel-style interior hallways. At the far end of the Continental and Americana buildings, Universal built the Bayside (building 7) and Beachside (building 8) expansion towers with 400 additional guest rooms, 20 of which are expansive 772-square-foot two-bedroom suites with stunning views of the Volcano Bay water park. Buildings 4 (rooms XX00–XX21) and 5 (rooms XX00–XX24) are closest to the bus loop and cafeteria, while some north-facing rooms in building 2 have a view of Hogwarts Castle.

Cabana Bay's two large pools both have artificial beaches and zero-entry sloping bottoms. The Cabana Courtyard Pool is more active, with a splash-pad playground and 100-foot waterslide wrapped around a central diving tower (which you can't actually dive off of, for safety reasons). The Lazy River Courtyard is a little more laid-back, with classic rock music (as opposed to the top 40 usually played around the Cabana Courtyard) and a lushly landscaped circular stream in which to relax; flotation toys are sold for $4–$15 plus tax, inflation and deflation included. Cabana Bay even sells watertight cups at the pool bar, so you can sip your cocktail while circulating in the lazy river.

Indoor recreational options include the Game-O-Rama arcade (well stocked with late-model machines and classic carnival-style redemption games) and the 10-lane Galaxy Bowl, modeled after the Hollywood Star Lanes featured in *The Big Lebowski*. Bowling costs $16.99 per adult, $10.99 per kid age 12 and under, for 45–75 minutes of play with shoe rental. Everyone bowls for $9 with the 20-minute Speed Bowling special. Waits for a lane can get long, especially on rainy days. Other diversions include poolside table tennis and billiards, as well as a large Jack LaLanne fitness center for free. An activity room with board games and beanbag chairs opens on rainy days. Finally, outdoor movies are shown nightly near both pools, and the food court sells $8 s'mores kits to roast over the gas-fueled fire pits.

In addition to the lobby's full-service Starbucks, the cavernous cafeteria-style Bayliner Diner food court serves breakfast, lunch, and dinner, with Coke Freestyle dispensers and giant screens in the seating area showing 1960s TV clips. Swizzle Lounge in the lobby, two pool bars (both with attached counter-service grills), in-room pizza delivery, and table-service snacks and sandwiches at the Galaxy Bowl round out the on-site dining options. The Universal Gift Shop is the largest hotel store in the resort and stocks candy and clothes exclusive to Cabana Bay.

Colorful buses head to the parks' main parking hub from outside Cabana Bay's food court. The bus service is amazingly efficient; we've never waited more than 5 minutes for one to arrive, and the total transit time to the attractions is usually less than 15 minutes. It takes about the same amount of time to walk to CityWalk along the landscaped garden walkway, which passes the Sapphire Falls Resort before joining up with the walking path to Royal Pacific. And with an exclusive on-site entrance into Volcano Bay just for Cabana Bay guests, rolling out of bed just in time for early admission at the water park is a breeze; request the Bayside tower or Americana building 6 for the shortest walk.

Self-parking is $14 for overnight guests, which is significantly less than parking at Universal's Premier hotels, but there is no valet, and daily parking is a steep $45 for visitors. Day guests who want to check out Cabana Bay should take the bus there from the parking hub because the garden walk's gate requires a key card for hotel access. Take care when driving into and out of the hotel's driveway on Adventure Way. If you miss the entrance, or make a right when exiting, you'll find yourself on a one-way road to I-4 West toward Disney, and you won't be able to correct your course until the FL 528 expressway.

We've received rave reviews of Cabana Bay from our readers, like this mom from Putney, Vermont:

> *I LOVED the hotel. I usually share a standard room with my two children, but after trying the (very reasonably priced) family suites, I don't think I can go back! We each had our own bed, and it was wonderful. The pullout bed was hard but perfect for my back. The theming of the hotel is so fun. The kids loved the lazy river. The food court is fun too. There's an Icee station and a frozen yogurt station.*

Remember, Cabana Bay guests are eligible for Early Park Admission at Universal but do not receive complimentary Express Passes.

Universal's Endless Summer Resort *(opens 2019–2020)*

7000 Universal Blvd.
Orlando
☎ 407-503-7000 or
888-430-4999
loewshotels.com
/surfside-inn-and-suites

Rate per night $99–$204. **Pools** ★★★½. **Fridge in room** Yes. **Shuttle to parks** Yes (Universal, SeaWorld, Aquatica). **Maximum number of occupants per room** 4 (two queens) or 6 (suites). **Comments** Pets not permitted.

FOR ANYONE WHO FONDLY REMEMBERS the eponymous seminal 1966 surfing documentary, the phrase *Endless Summer* conjures images of pristine oceans, epic waves, and limitless freedom. Universal's Endless Summer Resort, a 2,800-room complex of value-priced rooms that will open in phases during 2019 and 2020, is built along an inland lake that was previously home to the Wet 'n Wild water park, so the only waves it has ever known were man-made. But the resort does offer liberation of a sort, both from the traditional boundaries of Universal's property and from the limitation that park-owned hotels must always cost more than their off-site competition.

Endless Summer Resort is actually comprised of two sibling hotels, which sit across from each other on Universal Boulevard. Surfside Inn and Suites, located to the south on the land originally occupied by Wet 'n Wild's attractions, will open in summer 2019 with 750 rooms along the shoreline surrounding a surfboard-shaped pool. Dockside Inn and Suites, situated on the north side of the street in the water park's former parking lot, will boast a substantial 2,050 rooms, supported by a separate lobby and two organically shaped pools. Both properties share a similar sunny aesthetic, with abstract images of seaside fun etched into the hotels' multistory cement towers.

Despite being the first to sport Universal's Value label, the 313-square-foot standard room with two queen beds is nearly identical in size to those at the Prime Value locations. And they aren't cheap from an aesthetic perspective either, as long as you appreciate the shabby chic look popular at vintage beachside hotels. In this modernized reinterpretation of a hippie hangout, the floors and furniture resemble reclaimed driftwood, and the tie-dyed curtains and vibrant wall art recall the summer of love. Thankfully, unlike the bohemian beach shacks of yore, at Endless Summer all the modern amenities are included: separate vanity and toilet areas, minifridge, 43-inch flat-panel TV, smart home controls for the temperature, and built-in USB charging outlets.

A little more than half the rooms at each Endless Summer complex are 440-square-foot suites with two bedrooms (three queen beds) and a kitchenette complete with sink, microwave, and a kitschy picnic table for dining alfresco indoors.

The pool at Surfside Inn will feature a splash pad for the kids and hold organized family activities like bingo and hoop contests. Each hotel also includes a free fitness room, a Universal Studios Store, and a video arcade. Full-service dining isn't offered, but food courts, lobby and pool bars, and pizza delivery are all available.

Because it's located on the opposite side of International Drive and I-4 from the rest of Universal Orlando, walking to the parks from Endless Summer isn't practical with preschoolers in tow, so a fleet of free buses is provided. The ride to the parking hub from here is actually slightly shorter than the one from Cabana Bay. Self-parking in one of several giant garages costs $12 per night for hotel guests and $45 for day guests; valet parking isn't available.

Universal advertises Endless Summer's rates as "starting from $73 per night," which is based on a 7-night stay during the value season. Even at full rack rate, the hotel's competitive pricing undercuts many of its independent I-Drive neighbors, whose aging amenities will struggle to compete with Universal's 800-pound gorilla.

UNIVERSAL ORLANDO VACATION PACKAGES

UNIVERSAL FREQUENTLY OFFERS VACATION packages including hotel accommodations and park tickets via its in-house travel company, Universal Orlando Vacations. You can book a package yourself by calling ☎ 877-801-9720 or by visiting universalorlandovacations .com, or you can contact your preferred travel agent. Universal Orlando Vacations booked more than 45 days in advance require only a $50-per-person deposit (airfare fully due at time of booking) that is fully refundable until 45 days out; after that, the penalty is $200 per package, though some event tickets may be nonrefundable.

Universal Orlando Vacations also handles group sales; if you want to organize a family reunion at Cabana Bay, call ☎ 800-224-4489 and choose option 3, or visit res.universalorlandovacations .com/Group/Groups.aspx.

Universal advertises its packages with enticing taglines like, "The Wizarding World from only $169 a night!" You have to do the math, though, because it's difficult for package purchasers to save money over buying à la carte unless they fully exploit every included component.

Here's an example. A Wizarding World of Harry Potter Vacation Package in late 2018 offered a family of four (two adults and two kids under age 10) these components:

1. Four nights at a Universal on-site hotel (or off-site partner hotel)
2. Four days of park-to-park admission to all three parks, including Volcano Bay
3. Breakfast at The Three Broomsticks (one per person)
4. Breakfast at Leaky Cauldron (one per person)
5. Photography session at Shutterbutton's in Diagon Alley, including souvenir DVD in a collectible tin
6. Early Park Admission to The Wizarding World of Harry Potter and Volcano Bay 1 hour before the general public
7. CityWalk Party Pass

At Royal Pacific Resort, the package started at $2,773, including tax, during the value season (January–February), and cost $2,899 during regular season (October–November). There were significant restrictions, including blackout dates around spring break, Easter, and Memorial Day, and the stay had to occur on a Sunday–Thursday to qualify for that low rate; weekend nights were more expensive.

Here's the first thing to recognize: the last two items—early admission to The Wizarding World and a CityWalk Party Pass—are automatically given to everyone who stays at a Universal resort and purchases a multiday ticket, so they don't have any value by themselves.

There are only four components to price: the hotel, tickets, the Shutterbutton's session, and the breakfasts at The Three Broomsticks and Leaky Cauldron. We checked Universal's website for the cost of the other components using various dates in late 2018 and ensured those dates would also qualify for the aforementioned package. Here's a typical cost per component:

- $1,022.40 for four nights (using "Stay More, Save More" discount) at Royal Pacific Resort during value season, including tax (regular seasonal rate $1,148.40, including tax)
- $1,447.16 for two-day park-to-park tickets with the third and fourth day free from orlandoticketconnection.com
- $125.16 for breakfast for four at The Three Broomsticks and Leaky Cauldron, including tax
- $74.55 for the Shutterbutton's DVD, or $53.25 if you purchase a photo package, including tax

The total cost if you bought each component separately is $2,669.27 during value season, or $2,795.27 during regular season, which means that shopping à la carte saves you $104. However, if you were to forgo the breakfasts and Shutterbutton's video, you'd save $303.71 by buying separately. You can still reserve breakfast in The Wizarding World through your hotel's Ticket Center without a package, or even just walk up to the restaurants on many mornings. Universal's price for the breakfast is $18.09 per adult and $13.20 per child, including tax, so it's easy enough to figure out what it costs. Unless you're certain that you want the breakfasts and DVD, you're better off having lunch at the Leaky Cauldron with the money you'll save by buying each item of the package separately.

Even if it won't save you money, there are a few reasons why you might still want to book a Universal Orlando Vacations package. The first is if you can't afford to stay on-site but still want Early Park Admission to The Wizarding World and Volcano Bay. Booking a room at a Universal-area partner hotel as part of a package through Universal Orlando Vacations is the *only* way to get guaranteed early entry to the Harry Potter attractions and the water park, other than staying in an on-site hotel.

Another reason is if you are attending a special event at Universal Orlando that offers exclusive experiences for package buyers. For example, the now-discontinued Celebration of Harry Potter fan convention held an after-hours party in The Wizarding World just for vacation-package purchasers. Occasionally, packages are offered with truly unique perks: before the openings of Hogsmeade and Diagon Alley, a limited number of package holders were allowed into the new Wizarding Worlds weeks before the general public. These rare opportunities are only for the diehards because uncontrollable technical delays can always preempt previews without refunds.

One worthwhile package to consider is the Volunteer Vacation, which combines three nights of accommodations with two-day park-to-park tickets and a 4-hour volunteer opportunity at Give Kids the World Village, a nonprofit resort for kids with serious illnesses and their families. Universal will provide round-trip transportation to your volunteer shift and donate $100 to the organization per package purchased. Visit universalorlandovacations.com/vacation-deals /volunteer-vacation-packages for details.

If you opt to book through Universal Orlando Vacations, be sure to pay very close attention during the confirmation process, as a mom of three from Arlington, Virginia, explains:

> We did not get the package we thought we were getting because we didn't catch the omission when the phone attendant confirmed our travel plans. When we called back about it, they went back to the recording transcripts and said that because we had not caught the omission then, it was our fault, and they didn't have to reinstate that portion of the package. I was miffed.

Finally, if you insist on prepaying for your table-service meals, the Table-Service Universal Dining Plan is available exclusively as an add-on to any Universal Orlando Vacations package. The adult plan costs $59.99 plus tax per person, per day, and includes one table-service meal (entrée, nonalcoholic beverage, and select dessert), one quick-service meal (entrée and nonalcoholic beverage), one snack, and a third nonalcoholic beverage. The child plan costs $22.99 plus tax and includes one table-service meal and one quick-service meal from the kids' menu, plus a regular snack and soft drink. Neither plan's price includes gratuities, which are expected at table-service restaurants based on the value of your meal. Eligible table-service restaurants are restricted to the two sit-down restaurants at each theme park, plus a handful of CityWalk locations, the best of which are The Cowfish, Vivo Italian Kitchen, and Antojitos Authentic Mexican Food. Bafflingly, none of the restaurants inside the resort's hotels accept the dining plan, making it even more pointless for on-site guests. Occasionally, Universal will run booking specials offering free dining credit at your resort hotel's restaurants, a much better bargain.

Suffice it to say that there are much better ways to spend $60-plus a day on dining at Universal, and you'll have to order very carefully to get your money's worth from every table-service meal. A quick service–only dining plan ($23.99 for adults, $15.99 for kids, plus tax) is also sold to the general public; there's no real benefit to buying it in advance in a package. For more information on Universal's dining plans, see page 199, and visit universalorlando.com/web /en/us/tickets-packages/universal-orlando-dining-plan/index.html.

OFF-SITE LODGING OPTIONS

SELECTING AND BOOKING A HOTEL

LODGING COSTS IN ORLANDO vary incredibly. If you shop around, you can find a clean motel with a pool for as low as $50 a night. Because of hot competition, discounts abound, particularly for AAA and AARP members. There are four primary areas to consider:

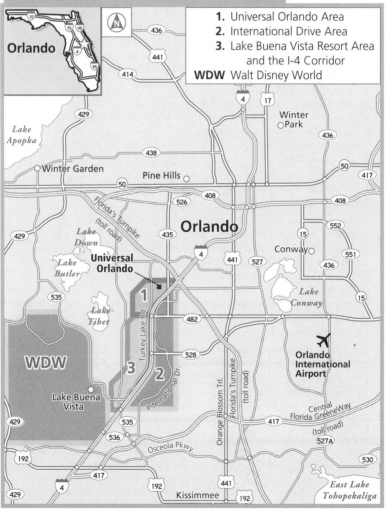

Hotel Concentrations Around Universal Orlando

Orlando

1. Universal Orlando Area
2. International Drive Area
3. Lake Buena Vista Resort Area and the I-4 Corridor
WDW Walt Disney World

1. UNIVERSAL ORLANDO AREA In the triangular area bordered by I-4 on the southeast, Vineland Road on the north, and Turkey Lake Road on the west are Universal Orlando and the hotels most convenient to it. Running north–south through the middle of the triangle is Kirkman Road, which connects to I-4. On the east side of Kirkman are a number of independent hotels and restaurants. Universal hotels, parks, and CityWalk are west of Kirkman. Traffic in this area is not nearly as congested as on nearby International Drive, and there are good interstate connections in both directions.

2. INTERNATIONAL DRIVE AREA This area, about 5 minutes from Universal, parallels I-4 on its eastern side and offers a wide selection of hotels and restaurants. Prices range from $56 to $400 per night. The chief drawbacks of this area are its terribly congested roads, countless traffic signals, and inadequate access to I-4 West. While International's biggest bottleneck is its intersection with Sand Lake Road, the mile between Kirkman and Sand Lake Roads is almost always gridlocked.

Regarding traffic on International Drive (known locally as I-Drive), a conventioneer from Islip, New York, weighed in with this:

> We wasted huge chunks of time in traffic on International Drive. Our hotel was in the section between the big McDonald's [at Sand Lake Road] and Universal Boulevard. There are practically no left-turn lanes in this section, so anyone turning left can hold up traffic for a long time.

Traffic aside, a man from Ottawa, Ontario, sings the praises of his I-Drive experience:

> International Drive is the place to stay in Orlando. Your description of this location failed to point out that there are several discount stores, boutiques, restaurants, mini-putts, and other entertainment facilities all within walking distance of remarkably inexpensive accommodations and a short drive away from the attractions.

International Drive hotels are listed in the *Official Visitors Guide.* To obtain a copy, call ☎ 800-972-3304 or 407-363-5872, or go to visitorlando.com.

3. LAKE BUENA VISTA AND THE I-4 CORRIDOR A number of hotels are along FL 535 and west of I-4 between Disney World and I-4's intersection with Florida's Turnpike. They're easily reached from the interstate and are near many restaurants, including those on International Drive. Traffic on I-4 can be a real slog, so avoid it during rush hours. (See the map on page 134.)

WDW We've also included a few hotels on the northeast side of Walt Disney World property, due to their proximity to Universal Orlando. We have not included other hotels on Disney property, nor have we included hotels along US 192 or those in Kissimmee.

International Drive & Universal Areas

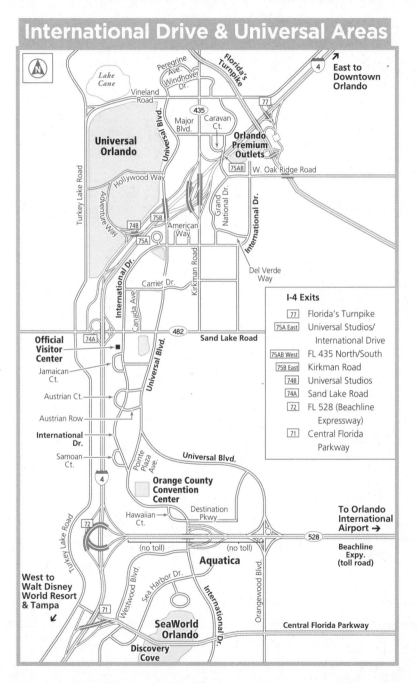

I-4 Exits

77	Florida's Turnpike
75A East	Universal Studios/ International Drive
75AB West	FL 435 North/South
75B East	Kirkman Road
74B	Universal Studios
74A	Sand Lake Road
72	FL 528 (Beachline Expressway)
71	Central Florida Parkway

Lake Buena Vista Resort Area & the I-4 Corridor

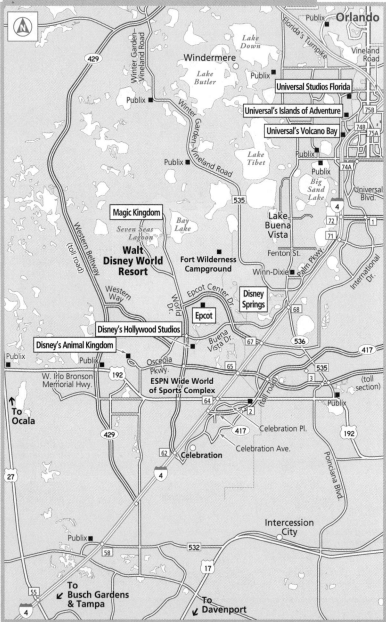

HOTEL SHOPPING

OTAS AND THE MERCHANT MODEL   Online travel agencies (OTAs) sell travel products from a wide assortment of suppliers, often at deep discounts. These sites include such familiar names as **Travelocity, Orbitz, Priceline, Expedia, Hotels.com,** and **Hotwire.** Under a merchant model, hotels provide an OTA with a deeply discounted room rate that the OTA then marks up and sells. The difference between the marked-up price and the discounted rate paid to the hotel is the OTA's gross profit. If, for example, a hotel makes $120 rooms available to an OTA at a 33% discount, or $80, and the OTA sells the room at $110, the OTA's gross profit is $30 ($110-$80=$30).

OTAs don't have to commit to a specified volume of sales or keep discounted room rates hidden within a bundled price. What's more, doing business with OTAs is very expensive for hotels. Let's say a hotel sells a $100 room for six nights on its own website. The booking would cost the hotel around $12, or $2 per night, including site hosting and analytics, marketing costs, and management fees. If an OTA books the same room, having secured it from the hotel at a 30% discount, the hotel receives $70 per night from the OTA. Thus the hotel's cost for the OTA booking is $30 per night, or $180 for six nights—15 times as costly as selling the room online with no middleman.

In the hotel industry, occupancy rates are important, but simply getting bodies into beds doesn't guarantee a profit. A more critical metric is revenue per available room (RevPAR). For a hotel full of guests booked through an OTA, RevPAR will be 20%–50% lower than for the same number of guests who booked the hotel directly, either through the hotel's website or by phone.

The better-known OTAs draw a lot more web traffic than a given hotel's (or even hotel chain's) website. So the challenge for the hotel becomes how to shift room-shoppers away from the OTAs and channel them to its website. A number of hotel corporations, including Choice, The Hotel Group (Hilton, DoubleTree, Marriott, and Comfort Inn), Hyatt, InterContinental, and Wyndham, have risen to that challenge by forming their own OTA called **Room Key** (roomkey.com). The participating chains hope that working together will generate enough visitor traffic to make Room Key competitive with the Expedias and Travelocities of the world.

MORE POWER TO THE SHOPPER   Understanding the market dynamics we've described gives you a powerful tool for obtaining the best rates for the hotel of your choice. It's why we tell you to shop the web for the lowest price available and then call your travel agent or the hotel itself to ask if they can beat it. Any savvy reservationist knows that selling you the room directly will both cut the hotel's cost and improve gross margin. If the reservationist can't help you, ask to speak to his or her supervisor. (We've actually had to explain hotel economics to more than a few clueless reservation agents.)

As for travel agents, they have clout based on the volume of business they send to a particular hotel or chain and can usually negotiate a rate even lower than what you've found online. Even if the agent can't beat the price, he or she can often obtain upgrades, preferred views, free breakfasts, and other deal sweeteners. When we bump into a great deal on the web, we call our agent. Often she can beat the deal or improve on it, perhaps with an upgrade. *Reminder:* Except for special arrangements agreed to by you, the fee or commission due to your travel agent will be paid by the hotel.

THE SECRET When we're really hungry for a deal, there are a number of sites that we always check out:

OUR FAVORITE ONLINE HOTEL RESOURCES	
HOTELCOUPONS.COM	Self-explanatory
ORLANDOVACATION.COM	Great rates for condos and home rentals
VISITORLANDO.COM	Good info; not user-friendly for booking

We scour these sites for unusually juicy hotel deals that meet our criteria (location, quality, price, and amenities). If we find a hotel that fills the bill, we check it out at other websites and comparative travel search engines such as **Kayak** (kayak.com), **Hotels.com,** and **Mobissimo** (mobissimo.com) to see who has the best rate. (As an aside, Kayak used to be purely a search engine but now sells travel products, raising the issue of whether products not sold by Kayak are equally likely to come up in a search. Mobissimo, on the other hand, only links potential buyers to provider websites.) Another site is **Trivago** (trivago.com). Your initial shopping effort should take about 15–20 minutes, faster if you can zero in quickly on a particular hotel.

Next, armed with your insider knowledge of hotel economics, call the hotel or have your travel agent call. Start by asking about specials. If there are none, or if the hotel can't beat the best price you've found on the internet, share your findings and ask if the hotel can do better. Sometimes you'll be asked for proof of the rate you've discovered online—to be prepared for this, go to the site and enter the dates of your stay, plus the rate you've found to make sure it's available. If it is, print the page or take a screenshot of this information and have it handy for your travel agent or for when you call the hotel. (*Note:* Always call the hotel's local number, not its national reservations number.)

INDEPENDENT AND BOUTIQUE HOTEL DEALS While chain hotels worry about sales costs and profit margins, independent and so-called boutique hotels are concerned about discoverability—making themselves known to the traveling public. The market is huge, and it's increasingly hard for these hotels to get noticed, especially when they're competing with major chains. For these hotels, substantially discounting rates is part of their marketing plan to build a client base. Because such hotels get lost on the big OTA sites and on search engines such as Kayak and Google, they offer almost irresistible rates on daily-coupon sites such as **Groupon** and **LivingSocial,** allowing them to get their product in front of thousands of potential guests.

These offers are very generous but also time-limited. If you're in the market, though, you'll be hard-pressed to find better deals. While an OTA such as Expedia generally obtains rooms at a 20%–35% discount off the hotel's published rate, flash sites cut deals at an extra-deep discount. This allows their subscribers to bid on or secure coupons for rooms that are often as much as 50% lower than the hotel's standard rate, and the coupons frequently include perks such as meals, free parking, waived resort fees, shopping vouchers, spa services, and entertainment. On Groupon's home page, click "Getaways" or just wait for Getaway coupons by email as part of your free subscription. On LivingSocial you have to specifically subscribe to "Travel"; otherwise, you'll receive only non-travel-related offers. We've also had great results using **HotelTonight.com**'s free smartphone app around the country and in Europe. If you don't mind not knowing where you'll rest your head until a few days (or even hours) in advance, you can score tremendous savings on properties near Universal, though not on-site.

ANOTHER WRINKLE Finally, a quick word about a recent trend: bidding sites. On these sites you enter the type of accommodation you desire and your travel dates, and hotels bid for your reservation. Some sites require that you already have a confirmed booking from a hotel before you can bid. A variation is that you reserve a room at a particular hotel for a set rate. If the rate drops subsequently, you get money back; if the rate goes up, your original rate is locked in. TripAdvisor's **Tingo** (tingo.com) and Montreal-based **BackBid** (backbid.com) both claim to be able to beat rates offered by hotel websites and OTAs.

AIRBNB Airbnb (airbnb.com) hooks up travelers with owner-hosted alternative lodging all over the world, from spare bedrooms in people's homes to private apartments, vacation homes, and even live-in boats. It's also rattled the hotel industry because it's not subject to most of the regulations and taxes that dedicated hotels must observe.

We use Airbnb extensively in our personal and professional travel, including for most of our work in New York City and Washington, D.C. But we find that Airbnb is not as useful in Orlando for a couple of reasons. One is the enormous supply of vacation home rentals and hotel rooms, which keeps prices down for lodging around Universal. Second are Universal's incentives for staying on property, including extra time in the parks and Universal Express Unlimited. Airbnb users seem to agree: while Orlando is one of the country's biggest travel destinations, it's not one of Airbnb's top 10 markets.

IS IT WORTH IT? You might be asking yourself if it's worth all this effort to save a few bucks. Saving $10 on a room doesn't sound like a big deal, but if you're staying six nights, that adds up to $60. Earlier we referred to unusually juicy deals, deep discounts predicated by who-knows-what circumstances that add up to big money. They're available every day, and with a little perseverance, you'll find them. Happy hunting!

TWO OTHER DISCOUNT SOURCES WORTH MENTIONING

VISIT ORLANDO DEALS   Obtain a Vacation Planner and the *Visit Orlando Official Visitors Guide* (both free) from the Visit Orlando Official Visitor Center. The discounts cover hotels, restaurants, ground transportation, shopping malls, dinner theaters, and non-Disney theme parks and attractions. View the deals at visitorlando.com and click on "Discounts." To order the accommodations guide, call ☎ 800-643-9492. For more information and materials, call ☎ 407-363-5872 Monday–Friday, 8:30 a.m.–6:30 p.m. Eastern time, or go to visitorlando.com.

HOTELCOUPONS.COM FLORIDA GUIDE   This book of coupons for lodging statewide is free in many restaurants and motels on main highways leading to Florida. Because most travelers make reservations before leaving home, picking up the book en route doesn't help much. To view it online or to sign up for a free monthly guide sent by email, visit hotel coupons.com. For a hard copy ($4 for handling, $6 if shipped to Canada), call ☎ 800-222-3948 Monday–Friday, 8 a.m.–5 p.m. Eastern time.

New Is Better—and Sometimes Cheaper

New hotels rarely burst on the scene at 100% occupancy. During a hotel's first year, when it strives to generate buzz and attract clientele, it often offers deeply discounted rooms. This is true even of prestigious brands. One thing's for sure: a new hotel will charge less the first few months it's open than subsequently, and a hotel that opens during low season will discount more than hotels that come on line during high season.

SCRATCH THAT ITCH . . . FOR INFORMATION

GRANTED, IT WON'T HELP YOU FIND good deals on hotels, but **The Bedbug Registry** (bedbugregistry.com) is nonetheless a useful resource, allowing you to peruse reports of bedbug and other insect infestations at any hotel in the United States. Simply enter the name, city, and state of the property in question; you can also submit a report of your own. Understand that bedbug outbreaks are usually confined to particular rooms and that the creepy-crawlies were probably brought in by previous guests. If you suspect an infestation, report it to management immediately.

CONDOMINIUMS AND VACATION HOMES

BECAUSE CONDOS TEND TO BE part of large developments (frequently time-shares), amenities such as swimming pools, playgrounds, game arcades, and fitness centers often rival those found in the best hotels. Generally speaking, condo developments don't have restaurants, lounges, or spas. In a condo, if something goes wrong, there will be someone on hand to fix the problem. Vacation homes rented from a property-management company likewise will have someone to come to the rescue, though responsiveness tends to vary vastly from company to company. If you rent directly from an owner, correcting problems is often more difficult, particularly when the owner doesn't live in the same area as the rental home.

In a vacation home, all the amenities are contained in the home (though in planned developments, there may be community amenities available as well). Depending on the specific home, you might find a small swimming pool, hot tub, two-car garage, family room, game room, and even a home theater. Features found in both condos and vacation homes include full kitchens, laundry rooms, TVs, DVD players, and frequently stereos. Interestingly, though almost all freestanding vacation homes have private pools, very few have backyards. This means that, except for swimming, the kids are pretty much relegated to playing in the house.

Time-share condos are clones when it comes to furniture and decor, but single-owner condos and vacation homes are furnished and decorated in a style that reflects the taste of the owner. Vacation homes, usually one- to two-story houses in a subdivision, very rarely afford interesting views (though some overlook lakes or natural areas), while condos, especially the high-rise variety, sometimes offer exceptional ones.

How the Vacation Home Market Works

In the Orlando area, there are more than 26,000 rental homes, including stand-alone homes, single-owner condos (that is, not time-shares), and townhomes. The same area has about 129,000 hotel rooms. Some owners deal directly with renters, while others enlist the assistance of a property-management company.

Incredibly, about 700 property-management companies operate in the Orlando market. Most of these are mom-and-pop outfits that manage an inventory of 10 homes or fewer (probably fewer than 70 companies oversee more than 100 rental homes).

Homeowners pay these companies to maintain and promote their properties and handle all rental transactions. Some homes are made available to wholesalers, vacation packagers, and travel agents. A wholesaler or vacation packager will occasionally drop its rates to sell slow-moving inventory, but more commonly the cost to renters is higher than when dealing directly with owners or management companies: because most wholesalers and packagers sell their inventory through travel agents, both the wholesaler/packager's markup and the travel agent's commission are passed along to the renter. These costs are in addition to the owner's cut and/or the fee for the property manager.

Along similar lines, logic may suggest that the lowest rate of all can be obtained by dealing directly with owners, thus eliminating middlemen. Though this is sometimes true, it's more often the case that property-management companies offer the best rates. With their marketing expertise and larger customer base, these companies can produce a higher occupancy rate than the owners themselves can. What's more, management companies, or at least the larger ones, can achieve economies of scale not available to owners regarding maintenance, cleaning, linens, and even acquiring furniture and appliances (if a house is not already furnished). The combination of higher occupancy rates and economies of scale adds up to a win-win situation for owners, management companies, and renters alike.

Location, Location, Location

The best vacation home is one that is within easy commuting distance of the parks. If you plan to spend some time at Walt Disney World and SeaWorld in addition to the Universal parks, you'll want something just to the southwest of Universal Orlando (between Walt Disney World and Orlando).

Zoning laws in Orange County (which also includes most of Orlando, Universal Studios, SeaWorld, Lake Buena Vista, and the International Drive area) used to prohibit short-term rentals of homes and single-owner condos, but in recent years the county has loosened its zoning restrictions in a few predominantly tourist-oriented areas. So far, practically all of the vacation-rental homes in Orange County are in the Floridays and Vista Cay developments.

By our reckoning, about half the rental homes in Osceola County and all the rental homes in Polk County are too far away for commuting to be practical. You might be able to save a few bucks by staying farther out, but the most desirable homes to be found are in Vista Cay and in developments no more than 10 miles south of Universal's main entrance, from west of John Young Parkway to east of the FL 429 Western Beltway.

To get the most from a vacation home, you need to be close enough to commute in 20 minutes or less to your Orlando destination. This will allow for naps, quiet time, swimming, and dollar-saving meals you prepare yourself.

Shopping for a Vacation Home

There are three main types of websites in the home-rental game: those for property-management companies, which showcase a given company's homes and are set up for direct bookings; individual owner sites; and third-party listings sites, which advertise properties available through different owners and sometimes management companies as well. Sites in the last category will usually refer prospective renters to an owner's or management company's site for reservations.

We've found that most property-management sites are not very well designed and will test your patience to the max. You can practically click yourself into old age trying to see all the homes available or figure out where on earth they are. Nearly all claim to be "just minutes from Universal [or Disney]." (By that reasoning, we should list Bob's home; it's also just minutes from Universal . . . 570 minutes, to be exact!)

Many websites list homes according to towns (such as Clermont, Lake Buena Vista, Windermere, and Winter Garden) or real estate developments (including Eagle Pointe, Floridays, Golden Oaks, and Vista Cay) in the general Universal area, none of which you're likely to be familiar with. The information that counts is the distance of a vacation home or condo from Universal; for that, you often must look for something like "4 miles from Universal" embedded in the home's description.

The best websites provide the following:

- Numerous photos and in-depth descriptions of individual homes to make comparisons quick and easy
- Overview maps or text descriptions that reflect how far specific homes or developments are from your Orlando destination
- The ability to book the specific rental home of your choice on the site
- An easy-to-find phone number for bookings and questions

The best sites are also easy to navigate, let you see what you're interested in without your having to log in or divulge any personal information, and list memberships in such organizations as the Better Business Bureau and the Florida Vacation Rental Managers Association (visit fvrma.com for the association's code of ethics).

Recommended Websites

After checking out dozens upon dozens of sites, here are the ones we recommend. All of them meet the criteria listed on the following pages. If you're stunned that there are so few of them, well, so were we. (For the record, we elected not to list some sites that met our criteria but whose homes are too far away from the Orlando-area attractions.)

#1 Dream Homes (floridadreamhomes.com) has a good reputation for customer service and has photos of and information about the homes in its online inventory.

Vacation Rentals by Owner (vrbo.com) is a nationwide vacation-homes listings service that puts prospective renters in direct contact with owners. The site is straightforward and always lists a large number of rental properties in Celebration, Disney's planned community situated about 15–20 minutes from the Universal theme parks. Two similar listings services with good websites are **Vacation Rentals 411** (vacationrentals411.com) and **Last Minute Villas** (lastminutevillas.net).

Think Vacation Homes (thinkvacationhomes.com) took over All Star Vacation Homes, our previous pick for best management company; we're eager for feedback from readers who have experience with the new operators.

The website for **Visit Orlando** (visitorlando.com) is the place to go if you're interested in renting a condominium at one of the many time-share developments (click on "Places to Stay" at the site's home page). You can call the developments directly, but going through this website allows you to bypass sales departments and escape their high-pressure invitations to sit through sales presentations. The site also lists hotels and vacation homes. For all types of accommodations, you can sort by distance from where you'll spend your touring time. Distance-sorting categories include Universal, Walt Disney World, the Orange County Convention Center, and downtown Orlando, among others.

Making Contact

Once you've found a vacation home you like, check around the website for a Frequently Asked Questions (FAQ) page. If there's not an FAQ page, here are some of the things you'll want to check out on the phone with the owner or rental company.

1. How close is the property to my vacation destination?
2. Is the home or condominium that I see on the internet the one I'll get?
3. Is the property part of a time-share development?
4. Are there any specials or discounts available?
5. Is everything included in the rental price, or are there additional charges? What about taxes?
6. How old is the home or condo in which I'm interested? Has it been refurbished recently?
7. What is the view from the property?
8. Is the property near any noisy roads?
9. What is your smoking policy?
10. Are pets allowed? This consideration is as important to those who want to avoid pets as to those who want to bring them.
11. Is the pool heated?
12. Is there a fenced backyard where children can play?
13. How many people can be seated at the main dining table?
14. Is high-speed internet access available?
15. Are linens and towels provided?
16. How far are the nearest supermarket and drugstore?
17. Are childcare services available?
18. Are restaurants nearby?
19. Is transportation to the parks provided?
20. Will we need a car?
21. What is required to make a reservation?
22. What is your change/cancellation policy?
23. When is checkout time?
24. What will we be responsible for when we check out?
25. How will we receive our confirmation and arrival instructions?
26. What are your office hours?
27. What are the directions to your office?
28. What if we arrive after your office has closed?
29. Whom do we contact if something goes wrong during our stay?
30. How long have you been in business?
31. Are you licensed by the state of Florida?
32. Do you belong to the Better Business Bureau and/or the Florida Vacation Rental Managers Association?

We frequently receive letters from readers extolling the virtues of renting a condo or vacation home. This endorsement by a family from Ellington, Connecticut, is typical:

> *Our choice to stay in a vacation home was based on cost and sanity. We've found over the last couple of years that our children can't share the same bed. We have also gotten tired of having to turn off the lights at 8 p.m. and lie quietly in the dark waiting for our children to fall asleep. With this in mind, we needed a condo/suite layout. We decided on the Sheraton Vistana Resort. We had a two-bedroom villa with full kitchen, living room, three TVs, and washer/dryer. I packed for half the trip and did laundry almost every night. The facilities offered a daily children's program and several pools, kiddie pools, and playscapes. Located on FL 535, we had a 5- to 10-minute drive to most attractions, including SeaWorld, Disney, and Universal.*

THE BEST HOTELS FOR FAMILIES NEAR UNIVERSAL ORLANDO

WHAT MAKES A SUPER FAMILY HOTEL? Roomy accommodations, in-room fridge, great pool, complimentary breakfast, childcare options, and programs for kids are a few of the things *The Unofficial Guide* hotel team researched in selecting the top hotels for families from among hundreds of properties in the Universal Orlando area. Some of our picks are expensive, others are more reasonable, and some are a bargain. Regardless of price, be assured that these hotels understand a family's needs.

Though all of the following hotels offer some type of shuttle to the parks, some offer very limited service. Call the hotel before you book and ask what the shuttle schedule will be when you visit. Because families, like individuals, have different wants and needs, we haven't ranked the following properties here; they're listed alphabetically. All of the properties profiled below are along International Drive, with the exception of Rosen Shingle Creek, which is located on Universal Boulevard.

Castle Hotel ★★★½

Rate per night $110–$332. **Pool** ★★★. **Fridge in room** Yes ($15/day). **Shuttle to parks** Yes (Universal, SeaWorld). **Maximum number of occupants per room** 4. **Comment** Pets up to 40 pounds welcome ($150 nonrefundable fee). $15 daily parking fee.

8629 International Dr. Orlando
☎ 407-345-1511 or 877-317-5753
castlehotelorlando.com

YOU CAN'T MISS THIS ONE: it's the only castle on I-Drive and is part of Marriott's Autograph Collection. Inside you'll find royal colors (purple predominates), opulent fixtures (antlers are a recurring motif), European art, and Renaissance music.

The 214 rooms and suites also retain the royal treatment, but the decor is a bit more tasteful and streamlined. All rooms are fairly large and well equipped with a 37-inch flat-panel HDTV, free Wi-Fi, coffee maker, iron and board, hair dryer, and safe. The Garden Bistro & Bar off the lobby serves full or Continental breakfast. For lunch or dinner, you might walk next door to Vito's Chop House (dinner only) or Café Tu Tu Tango (an Unofficial favorite). The heated circular pool is 5 feet deep and features a fountain in the center, a poolside bar, and a hot tub. There's no separate kiddie pool. Other amenities include the Poseidon Spa, a fitness center, gift shop, lounge, valet laundry service and facilities, and guest services desk with park passes for sale and babysitting recommendations. Security feature: Elevators require an electronic key card.

CoCo Key Hotel & Water Resort–Orlando ★★★½

7400 International Dr.
Orlando
☎ 407-351-2626 or
877-875-4681
cocokeyorlando.com

Rate per night $110–$179. **Pools** ★★★★½. **Fridge in room** Yes. **Shuttle to parks** Yes (Universal, Aquatica, SeaWorld: free; Disney: $18/person round-trip). **Maximum number of occupants per room** 4. **Comments** $32/night resort fee for use of the water park; day guests may use the water park for $29.95/person.

NOT FAR FROM THE UNIVERSAL ORLANDO parks, CoCo Key combines a tropical-themed hotel with a canopied water park featuring three pools and 14 waterslides, as well as poolside food and arcade entertainment. A full-service restaurant serves breakfast and dinner; a food court offers family favorites such as burgers, chicken fingers, and pizza.

A unique feature of the resort is its cashless payment system, much like that on a cruise ship. At check-in, families receive bar-coded wristbands that allow purchased items to be easily charged to their room.

The spacious guest rooms include 37-inch flat-panel TVs, free Wi-Fi, granite showers and countertops, and plentiful outlets for electronics.

DoubleTree by Hilton Orlando at SeaWorld ★★★★½

10100 International Dr.
Orlando
☎ 407-352-1100 or
800-327-0363
doubletreeorlando
idrive.com

Rate per night $89–$249. **Pools** ★★★½. **Fridge in room** Standard in some rooms; available in others for a fee. **Shuttle to parks** Yes (Universal, Aquatica, SeaWorld: free; Disney: $8/person). **Maximum number of occupants per room** 4. **Comments** $19.95/night resort fee. Good option if you're visiting SeaWorld or Aquatica. Pets welcome (1/room, 25-pound limit, $75).

ON 28 LUSH, TROPICAL ACRES with a Balinese feel, the DoubleTree is adjacent to SeaWorld and Aquatica water park. The 1,094 rooms and suites—classified as resort or tower—are suitable for business travelers or families. We recommend the tower rooms for good views and the resort rooms for maximum convenience. Laguna serves steak and seafood, along with breakfast; you can also get a quick bite at The Market or the pool bar. Relax and cool off at one of the three pools (there are two more just for kids), or indulge in a spa treatment. A fitness center, minigolf course, children's day camp, and game area afford even more diversions. The resort is about a 12-minute drive to Universal, a 15-minute drive to Walt Disney World, or a short walk to SeaWorld.

Holiday Inn Resort Orlando Suites–Waterpark ★★★½

14500 Continental
Gateway, Orlando
☎ 407-387-5437
hisuitesorlando.com

Rate per night $129–$500. **Pools** ★★★★½. **Fridge in room** Yes. **Shuttle to parks** Yes (Universal, SeaWorld, Disney). **Maximum number of**

occupants per room 8. **Comment** $33.75/night resort fee. $12/day self-parking ($17/day for additional vehicle).

FOLLOWING A $30 MILLION RENOVATION IN 2016, the hotel formerly known as the Nickelodeon Suites Resort is now the Holiday Inn Resort Orlando Suites–Waterpark. Sadly, all of the Nickelodeon experiences are gone: no Double Dare, no getting slimed, no characters. However, the resort is still impressive—and newly renovated.

The 777 suites come in one-, two-, and three-bedroom varieties and each suite contains a minifridge, microwave, flat-panel TV, and high-speed internet. The resort also boasts two water parks with 13 slides, a 4-D Experience, Laser Challenge, and a 3,000-square-foot arcade, along with cabanas, a poolside bar, and casual dining.

Rosen Shingle Creek ★★★★

Rate per night $165–$253. **Pools ★★★★**. **Fridge in room** Yes. **Shuttle to parks** Yes (Universal, SeaWorld, Discovery Cove, Aquatica). **Maximum number of occupants per room** 4. **Comment** Pets welcome ($150 nonrefundable fee). $18/day self-parking; $26/day valet.

9939 Universal Blvd.
Orlando
☎ 407-996-9939 or
866-996-6338
rosenshinglecreek.com

BEAUTIFUL ROOMS (EAST-FACING ONES HAVE GREAT VIEWS) and excellent restaurants distinguish this mostly meeting- and convention-oriented resort. The pools are large and lovely and include a lap pool, a family pool, and a kiddie wading pool. There's an 18-hole golf course on-site, as well as a superior spa and an adequate fitness center. Childcare is provided as well.

Though a state-of-the-art video arcade will gobble up your kids' pocket change, the real kicker, especially for the 8-years-and-up crowd, is a natural area encompassing lily ponds, grassy wetlands, Shingle Creek, and an adjacent cypress swamp. Running through the area is a nature trail complete with signs to help you identify wildlife. Great blue herons, wood storks, coots, egrets, mallard ducks, anhingas, and ospreys are common, as are sliders (turtles), chameleons, and skinks (lizards).

If you stay at Shingle Creek and plan to visit the theme parks, you'll want a car. Shuttle service is limited, departing and picking up at rather inconvenient times and stopping at three other hotels before delivering you to your destination.

HOTELS AND MOTELS:
Rated and Ranked

IN THIS SECTION, WE COMPARE HOTELS in four main areas outside Universal Orlando (see page 113) with those inside the resort. Additional hotels can be found at the intersection of US 27 and I-4, on US 441 (Orange Blossom Trail), and in downtown Orlando. Most of these require more than 30 minutes of commuting to the Orlando-area attractions and thus are not rated. We also haven't rated lodging along US 192.

WHAT'S IN A ROOM?

EXCEPT FOR CLEANLINESS, STATE OF REPAIR, and decor, travelers pay little attention to hotel rooms. There is, of course, a clear standard of quality and luxury that differentiates Motel 6 from Holiday Inn, Holiday Inn from Marriott, and so on. Many guests, however, fail to appreciate that some rooms are better engineered than others. Making the room usable to its occupants is an art that combines both form and function.

Decor and taste are important. No one wants to stay in a room that's dated, garish, or ugly. But beyond decor, how "livable" is the room? In Orlando, for example, we've seen some beautifully appointed rooms that aren't well designed for human habitation. Even more than decor, your room's details and design elements are the things that will make you feel comfortable and at home.

ROOM RATINGS

TO EVALUATE PROPERTIES FOR THEIR QUALITY, tastefulness, state of repair, cleanliness, and size of their standard rooms, we have grouped the hotels and motels into classifications denoted by stars—the overall star rating. Star ratings in this guide apply only to Orlando-area properties and don't necessarily correspond to ratings awarded by Frommer's, Forbes, AAA, or other travel critics. Because stars have little relevance when awarded in the absence of recognized standards of comparison, we have tied our ratings to expected levels of quality established by specific American hotel corporations.

Overall star ratings apply only to room quality and describe the property's standard accommodations. For most hotels, a standard accommodation is a room with one king bed or two queen beds. In an all-suite property, the standard accommodation is either a studio or a one-bedroom suite. In addition to standard accommodations, many hotels offer luxury rooms and special suites, which aren't rated in this guide. Star ratings for rooms are assigned without regard to whether a property has restaurant(s), recreational facilities, entertainment, or other extras.

OVERALL STAR RATINGS		
★★★★★	Superior rooms	Tasteful and luxurious by any standard
★★★★	Extremely nice rooms	What you'd expect at a Hyatt Regency or Marriott
★★★	Nice rooms	Holiday Inn or comparable quality
★★	Adequate rooms	Clean, comfortable, and functional without frills —like a Motel 6
★	Super-budget	These exist but are not included in our coverage

In addition to stars (which delineate broad categories), we use a numerical rating system—the room quality rating. Our scale is 0–100, with 100 being the best possible rating and zero (0) the worst. Numerical ratings show the difference we perceive between one property and another. For instance, rooms at both the Best Western Plus Universal Inn and the Fairfield Inn & Suites Near Universal Orlando Resort are rated

3.5 stars (★★★½). In the supplemental numerical ratings, the former is a 75 and the latter an 80. This means that within the 3.5-star category, Fairfield Inn & Suites has slightly nicer rooms than Best Western Plus.

The location column identifies the area where you'll find a particular property. A 1 means it's in the Universal Orlando area. A 2 means it's on or near International Drive. All others are marked with 3 and for the most part are along FL 535 and the I-4 corridor, though some are in nearby locations that don't meet any other criteria. WDW, of course, indicates hotels located near Walt Disney World property.

LODGING AREAS *(see map on page 97)*	
1 Universal Orlando Area	**2** International Drive
3 Lake Buena Vista and I-4 Corridor	**WDW** Walt Disney World Resort

Cost estimates are based on the hotel's published rack rates for standard rooms. Each $ represents $50. Thus a cost symbol of $$$ means that a room (or suite) at that hotel will be about $150 a night; amounts more than $200 are indicated by $ x 5 and so on.

We've focused on room quality and excluded consideration of location, services, recreation, or amenities. In some instances, a one- or two-room suite is available for the same price or less than that of a single standard hotel room.

unofficial **TIP**
The key to avoiding disappointment is to snoop in advance. Ask how old the hotel is and when its guest rooms were last renovated.

If you've used a previous edition of this guide, you'll notice that new properties have been added and many ratings and rankings have changed, some because of room renovation or improved maintenance or housekeeping. Lax housekeeping or failure to maintain rooms can bring down ratings.

Before you shop for a hotel, consider this letter from a man in Hot Springs, Arkansas:

> *We canceled our room reservations to follow the advice in your book and reserved a hotel highly ranked by* The Unofficial Guide. *We wanted inexpensive but clean and cheerful. We got inexpensive but also dirty, grim, and depressing. The room spoiled the holiday for me aside from our touring.*

This letter was as unsettling to us as the bad room was to the reader—our integrity as travel journalists is based on the quality of the information we provide. When rechecking the hotel, we found our rating was representative, but the reader had been assigned one of a small number of threadbare rooms scheduled for renovation.

Be aware that some chains use the same guest room photo in promotional literature for all their hotels and that the rooms at a specific property may bear no resemblance to the photo in question. When you or your travel agent calls, ask how old the property is and when the guest room you're being assigned was last renovated. If you're assigned a room that is inferior to your expectations, demand to be moved.

A WORD ABOUT TOLL-FREE TELEPHONE NUMBERS

AS WE'VE REPEATED several times in this chapter, it's essential to communicate with the hotel directly when shopping for deals and stating your room preferences. Most toll-free numbers are routed directly to a hotel chain's central reservations office, and the customer service agents there typically have little or no knowledge of the individual hotels in the chain or of any specials those hotels may be offering. In our Hotel Information Chart (pages 120–127), therefore, we list the toll-free number only if it connects directly to the hotel in question; otherwise, we provide the hotel's local phone number.

The 30 BEST HOTEL VALUES

IN THE CHART ON THE FACING PAGE, we look at the best combinations of quality and value in a room. Rankings are made without consideration for location or the availability of restaurant(s), recreational facilities, entertainment, and/or amenities.

A reader wrote to complain that he had booked one of our top-ranked rooms in terms of value and had been very disappointed in the room. We noticed that the room the reader occupied had a quality rating of ★★½. Remember that the list of top deals is intended to give you some sense of value received for dollars spent. A ★★½ room at $40 may have the same value as a ★★★★ room at $115, but that doesn't mean the rooms will be of comparable quality. Regardless of whether it's a good deal, a ★★½ room is still a ★★½ room.

THE 30 BEST HOTEL VALUES

	HOTEL	LODGING AREA	OVERALL QUALITY RATING	ROOM QUALITY RATING	COST ($ = $50)
1.	Allure Resort	2	★★★	68	$
2.	Motel 6 Orlando–I-Drive	2	★★★	66	$+
3.	Hyatt House Across from Universal Orlando	1	★★★★½	91	$$+
4.	InTown Suites Orlando Universal	2	★★½	63	$
5.	Caribe Royale All-Suite Hotel & Convention Center	2	★★★★½	90	$$$–
6.	Avanti Palms Resort and Conference Center	2	★★★½	77	$$–
7.	Clarion Inn & Suites Universal	1	★★★½	82	$$
8.	Legacy Vacation Club Lake Buena Vista	3	★★★★	85	$$+
9.	Hawthorn Suites Lake Buena Vista	3	★★★★	85	$$+
10.	Extended Stay America Orlando Lake Buena Vista	3	★★★★	83	$$+
11.	Parc Corniche Resort	2	★★★½	82	$$
12.	Marriott's Grande Vista	2	★★★★½	93	$$$+
13.	Westgate Lakes Resort & Spa	3	★★★★½	92	$$$+
14.	Hilton Orlando	2	★★★★½	92	$$$+
15.	Best Western Plus Universal Inn	1	★★★½	75	$$+
16.	DoubleTree Universal	1	★★★★	89	$$$–
17.	DoubleTree by Hilton Orlando at SeaWorld	2	★★★★½	92	$$$+
18.	Sheraton Lake Buena Vista Resort	3	★★★★	88	$$$–
19.	Sunsol International Drive	2	★★★	72	$$–
20.	Rosen Inn International Hotel	2	★★★	70	$$–
21.	Staybridge Suites Lake Buena Vista	3	★★★★½	90	$$$+
22.	Quality Suites Turkey Lake	3	★★★	74	$$
23.	Hilton Grand Vacations Club at Tuscany Village	2	★★★★	88	$$$
24.	Hyatt Regency Orlando	2	★★★★½	90	$$$$–
25.	Hilton Orlando Lake Buena Vista	WDW	★★★★	87	$$$
26.	Sheraton Vistana Resort Villas	3	★★★★	89	$$$+
27.	Four Points by Sheraton Orlando Studio City	2	★★★★½	90	$$$$–
28.	Las Palmeras by Hilton Grand Vacations	2	★★★★	87	$$$+
29.	Cypress Pointe Resort	3	★★★★½	90	$$$$–
30.	Hilton Grand Vacations Club at SeaWorld	2	★★★★½	95	$$$$–

How the Hotels Compare

HOTEL	LOCATION	OVERALL QUALITY	ROOM QUALITY	COST ($ = $50)
Four Seasons Resort Orlando at Walt Disney World Resort	WDW	★★★★★	98	$ x 15
Hilton Grand Vacations Club at SeaWorld	2	★★★★½	95	$$$$-
Rosen Centre Hotel	2	★★★★½	95	$$$$+
The Ritz-Carlton Orlando, Grande Lakes	2	★★★★½	94	$- x 8
Hard Rock Hotel Orlando	1	★★★★½	93	$+ x 8
Marriott's Grande Vista	2	★★★★½	93	$$$+
Waldorf Astoria Orlando	WDW	★★★★½	93	$+ x 7
DoubleTree by Hilton Orlando at SeaWorld	2	★★★★½	92	$$$+
Hilton Orlando	2	★★★★½	92	$$$+
Hyatt Regency Grand Cypress	3	★★★★½	92	$$$$$-
Loews Portofino Bay Hotel	1	★★★★½	92	$$+ x 9
Westgate Lakes Resort & Spa	3	★★★★½	92	$$$+
Hyatt House Across from Universal Orlando	1	★★★★½	91	$$+
Rosen Plaza Hotel	2	★★★★½	91	$$$$$-
Caribe Royale All-Suite Hotel & Convention Center	2	★★★★½	90	$$$-
Cypress Pointe Resort	3	★★★★½	90	$$$$-
Four Points by Sheraton Orlando Studio City	2	★★★★½	90	$$$$-
Hyatt Regency Orlando	2	★★★★½	90	$$$$-
Loews Royal Pacific Resort	1	★★★★½	90	$+ x 7
Marriott's Harbour Lake	3	★★★★½	90	$$$$-
Orlando World Center Marriott Resort	3	★★★★½	90	$$$$-
Renaissance Orlando at SeaWorld	2	★★★★½	90	$$$$$
Staybridge Suites Lake Buena Vista	3	★★★★½	90	$$$+
Staybridge Suites Orlando at SeaWorld	2	★★★★½	90	$$$$+
Courtyard Orlando Lake Buena Vista at Vista Centre	3	★★★★	89	$$$$-
DoubleTree Universal	1	★★★★	89	$$$-
Sheraton Vistana Resort Villas	3	★★★★	89	$$$+
Floridays Resort Orlando	2	★★★★	88	$$$+
Hilton Grand Vacations Club at Tuscany Village	2	★★★★	88	$$$
Hilton Orlando Bonnet Creek	WDW	★★★★	88	$$$$$
Rosen Shingle Creek	2	★★★★	88	$$$$$+
Sheraton Lake Buena Vista Resort	3	★★★★	88	$$$-
Sheraton Vistana Villages Resort	2	★★★★	88	$$$$+
WorldQuest Orlando Resort	2	★★★★	88	$$$+
Hilton Orlando Lake Buena Vista	WDW	★★★★	87	$$$
Las Palmeras by Hilton Grand Vacations	2	★★★★	87	$$$+
Residence Inn Orlando at SeaWorld	3	★★★★	87	$- x 6

How the Hotels Compare (continued)

HOTEL	LOCATION	OVERALL QUALITY	ROOM QUALITY	COST ($ = $50)
Residence Inn Universal Studios	2	★★★★	87	$$$$+
Embassy Suites Orlando-Lake Buena Vista Resort	3	★★★★	86	$$$$+
Hilton Orlando Buena Vista Palace Resort	WDW	★★★★	86	$$$+
Marriott's Cypress Harbour	2	★★★★	86	$$$$$
Marriott's Imperial Palms	2	★★★★	86	$$- x 6
Marriott's Royal Palms	2	★★★★	86	$$$$$+
Hawthorn Suites Lake Buena Vista	3	★★★★	85	$$+
Homewood Suites by Hilton LBV-Orlando	3	★★★★	85	$$$$+
Homewood Suites by Hilton Orlando Theme Parks	2	★★★★	85	$$$$-
Legacy Vacation Club Lake Buena Vista	3	★★★★	85	$$+
Sonesta ES Suites	2	★★★★	85	$$$$$-
SpringHill Suites Orlando at SeaWorld	2	★★★★	85	$$$$+
Wyndham Orlando Resort I-Drive	2	★★★★	85	$$$$
Extended Stay America Convention Center/Westwood	2	★★★★	84	$$$+
Homewood Suites by Hilton near Universal	2	★★★★	84	$$$$$+
Hyatt Place Orlando Lake Buena Vista	3	★★★★	84	$$$$
Hyatt Place Orlando/Universal	1	★★★★	84	$$$$+
Loews Sapphire Falls Resort	1	★★★★	84	$$$$$
The Point Hotel & Suites Orlando Resort	2	★★★★	84	$$$+
TownePlace Suites Orlando at SeaWorld	2	★★★★	84	$$$$-
Buena Vista Suites	2	★★★★	83	$$$+
Embassy Suites Orlando I-Drive/Jamaican Court	2	★★★★	83	$$$$+
Extended Stay America Orlando Lake Buena Vista	3	★★★★	83	$$+
Residence Inn Orlando Lake Buena Vista	3	★★★★	83	$$$$-
Universal's Aventura Hotel	1	★★★★	83	$$$
Universal's Cabana Bay Beach Resort	1	★★★★	83	$$$
B Resort	WDW	★★★½	82	$$$$-
Castle Hotel	2	★★★½	82	$ x 6
Clarion Inn & Suites Universal	1	★★★½	82	$$
CoCo Key Water Resort-Orlando	2	★★★½	82	$$$-
Four Points By Sheraton Orlando Convention Center	2	★★★½	82	$$$+
Hilton Garden Inn Orlando I-Drive North	2	★★★½	82	$$$$$-
Holiday Inn Resort Lake Buena Vista	3	★★★½	82	$$$
Holiday Inn Resort Orlando Suites-Waterpark	2	★★★½	82	$$$+
Parc Corniche Resort	2	★★★½	82	$$
Radisson Hotel Orlando Lake Buena Vista	3	★★★½	82	$$$$-

How the Hotels Compare (continued)

HOTEL	LOCATION	OVERALL QUALITY	ROOM QUALITY	COST ($ = $50)
Stay Sky Suites I-Drive Orlando	2	★★★½	82	$$$
Hawthorn Suites Orlando I-Drive	2	★★★½	81	$$$$−
Homewood Suites by Hilton I-Drive	2	★★★½	81	$$$$$−
Quality Suites Lake Buena Vista	3	★★★½	81	$$$+
Courtyard Orlando I-Drive	2	★★★½	80	$$$+
Courtyard Orlando Lake Buena Vista in Marriott Village	3	★★★½	80	$$$+
Fairfield Inn & Suites near Universal Orlando Resort	1	★★★½	80	$$$$
Fairfield Inn & Suites Orlando at SeaWorld	2	★★★½	80	$$$$+
Hilton Garden Inn Orlando at SeaWorld	2	★★★½	80	$$$$+
Residence Inn Orlando Convention Center	2	★★★½	80	$ x 6
SpringHill Suites Orlando Convention Center	2	★★★½	80	$− x 6
Holiday Inn in the Walt Disney World Resort	WDW	★★★½	79	$$$+
Hampton Inn & Suites Sea World	2	★★★½	78	$$$$−
Holiday Inn Express & Suites Orlando at SeaWorld	2	★★★½	78	$$$$
Avanti Palms Resort and Conference Center	2	★★★½	77	$$−
Best Western Orlando Gateway Hotel	2	★★★½	77	$$$−
Crowne Plaza Universal Orlando	2	★★★½	77	$$$
Delta Hotels by Marriott Lake Buena Vista	3	★★★½	76	$$$+
Wingate by Wyndham Universal Studios	1	★★★½	76	$$$−
Best Western Plus Universal Inn	1	★★★½	75	$$+
Embassy Suites Orlando I-Drive	2	★★★½	75	$$$$$−
Extended Stay America Deluxe Orlando Theme Parks	1	★★★½	75	$$$−
Extended Stay America Orlando Theme Parks	1	★★★½	75	$$$−
Holiday Inn & Suites Orlando Universal	1	★★★½	75	$$$−
Rosen Inn at Pointe Orlando	2	★★★½	75	$$$−
Wyndham Lake Buena Vista Resort	WDW	★★★½	75	$$$$−
Avanti Resort Orlando	2	★★★	74	$$$+
Best Western Lake Buena Vista Resort Hotel	WDW	★★★	74	$$$$−
Fairfield Inn & Suites Orlando International Drive	2	★★★	74	$$$$$+
Hampton Inn South of Universal	2	★★★	74	$$$$−
Holiday Inn Express & Suites International Drive	2	★★★	74	$$$+
Quality Inn at International Drive	2	★★★	74	$$$+
Quality Suites Turkey Lake	3	★★★	74	$$

How the Hotels Compare (continued)

HOTEL	LOCATION	OVERALL QUALITY	ROOM QUALITY	COST ($ = $50)
Ramada Plaza Resort and Suites Orlando I-Drive	2	★★★	74	$$$$$–
Extended Stay America Orlando Convention Center	2	★★★	72	$$$–
La Quinta Inn Orlando Universal Studios	1	★★★	72	$$+
Sunsol International Drive	2	★★★	72	$$–
Rosen Inn near Universal	2	★★★	71	$$+
Comfort Suites Universal	1	★★★	70	$$$+
Hampton Inn I-Drive/Convention Center	2	★★★	70	$$$$–
Monumental Hotel	2	★★★	70	$$
Rosen Inn International Hotel	2	★★★	70	$$–
Allure Resort	2	★★★	68	$
Westgate Palace	2	★★★	68	$$$$$–
The Enclave Hotel & Suites	2	★★★	67	$$+
Hampton Inn Universal	1	★★★	67	$$$
Comfort Inn I-Drive	2	★★★	66	$$$+
Motel 6 Orlando-I-Drive	2	★★★	66	$+
Best Western I-Drive	2	★★★	65	$$$$–
Ramada Convention Center I-Drive	2	★★★	65	$$
Clarion Inn & Suites at I-Drive	2	★★½	64	$$+
Clarion Inn Lake Buena Vista	3	★★½	64	$$–
Country Inn & Suites Orlando Universal	2	★★½	63	$$$+
The Floridian Hotel & Suites	2	★★½	63	$$$–
InTown Suites Orlando Universal	2	★★½	63	$
Monumental Movieland Hotel	2	★★½	63	$$–
Extended Stay Orlando Convention Center	2	★★½	58	$$$–

Hotel Information Chart

Allure Resort ★★★
8444 International Dr.
Orlando, FL 32819
☎ 407-345-0505
allureresortidriveorlando.com

LOCATION 2
ROOM RATING 68
COST ($=$50) $
RESORT FEE $15

Avanti Palms Resort and Conference Center ★★★½
6515 International Dr.
Orlando, FL 32819
☎ 407-996-0900
avantipalmsresort.com

LOCATION 2
ROOM RATING 77
COST ($=$50) $$-
RESORT FEE $12

Avanti Resort Orlando ★★★
8738 International Dr.
Orlando, FL 32819
☎ 407-313-0100
avantiresort.com

LOCATION 2
ROOM RATING 74
COST ($=$50) $$$+
RESORT FEE $12

Best Western Orlando Gateway Hotel ★★★½
7299 Universal Blvd.
Orlando, FL 32819
☎ 407-351-5009
bworlando.com

LOCATION 2
ROOM RATING 77
COST ($=$50) $$$-
RESORT FEE $5.50

Best Western Plus Universal Inn ★★★½
5618 Vineland Road
Orlando, FL 32819
☎ 407-226-9119
tinyurl.com/bwuniversal

LOCATION 1
ROOM RATING 75
COST ($=$50) $$+
RESORT FEE $2.99

Buena Vista Suites ★★★★
8203 World Center Dr.
Orlando, FL 32821
☎ 407-239-8588
bvsuites.com

LOCATION 2
ROOM RATING 83
COST ($=$50) $$$+
RESORT FEE $12.32

Clarion Inn & Suites Universal ★★★½
5829 Grand National Dr.
Orlando, FL 32819
☎ 407-351-3800
tinyurl.com/clarionuniversal

LOCATION 1
ROOM RATING 82
COST ($=$50) $$
RESORT FEE No

Clarion Inn Lake Buena Vista ★★½
8442 Palm Pkwy.
Lake Buena Vista, FL 32836
☎ 407-996-7300
clarionlbv.com

LOCATION 3
ROOM RATING 64
COST ($=$50) $$-
RESORT FEE No

CoCo Key Water Resort–Orlando ★★★½
7400 International Dr.
Orlando, FL 32819
☎ 407-351-2626
cocokeyorlando.com

LOCATION 2
ROOM RATING 82
COST ($=$50) $$$-
RESORT FEE $32

Courtyard Orlando I-Drive ★★★½
8600 Austrian Ct.
Orlando, FL 32819
☎ 407-351-2244
tinyurl.com/courtyardidrive

LOCATION 2
ROOM RATING 80
COST ($=$50) $$$+
RESORT FEE No

Courtyard Orlando Lake Buena Vista at Vista Centre ★★★★
8501 Palm Pkwy.
Lake Buena Vista, FL 32836
☎ 407-239-6900
tinyurl.com/courtyardlbv

LOCATION 3
ROOM RATING 89
COST ($=$50) $$$$-
RESORT FEE No

Courtyard Orlando Lake Buena Vista in Marriott Village ★★★½
8623 Vineland Ave.
Orlando, FL 32821
☎ 407-938-9001
tinyurl.com/courtyardlbvmarriott village

LOCATION 3
ROOM RATING 80
COST ($=$50) $$$+
RESORT FEE No

DoubleTree by Hilton Orlando at SeaWorld ★★★★½
10100 International Dr.
Orlando, FL 32821
☎ 407-352-1100
dtresortorlando.com

LOCATION 2
ROOM RATING 92
COST ($=$50) $$$+
RESORT FEE $20

DoubleTree Universal ★★★★
5780 Major Blvd.
Orlando, FL 32819
☎ 407-351-1000
doubletreeorlando.com

LOCATION 1
ROOM RATING 89
COST ($=$50) $$$-
RESORT FEE No

Embassy Suites Orlando I-Drive ★★★½
8978 International Dr.
Orlando, FL 32819
☎ 407-352-1400
embassysuitesorlando.com

LOCATION 2
ROOM RATING 75
COST ($=$50) $$$$$-
RESORT FEE No

Extended Stay America Convention Center/Westwood ★★★★
6443 Westwood Blvd.
Orlando, FL 32821
☎ 407-351-1982
tinyurl.com/extendedstaywestwood

LOCATION 2
ROOM RATING 84
COST ($=$50) $$$+
RESORT FEE No

Extended Stay America Deluxe Orlando Theme Parks ★★★½
5610 Vineland Road
Orlando, FL 32819
☎ 407-370-4428
tinyurl.com/esvineland

LOCATION 1
ROOM RATING 75
COST ($=$50) $$$-
RESORT FEE No

Extended Stay America Orlando Convention Center ★★★
6451 Westwood Blvd.
Orlando, FL 32821
☎ 407-352-3454
tinyurl.com/extendedstayocc

LOCATION 2
ROOM RATING 72
COST ($=$50) $$$-
RESORT FEE No

B Resort ★★★½
1905 Hotel Plaza Blvd.
Lake Buena Vista, FL 32830
☎ 407-828-2828
bresortlbv.com

LOCATION WDW
ROOM RATING 82
COST ($=$50) $$$$–
RESORT FEE $30.38

Best Western I-Drive ★★★
8222 Jamaican Ct.
Orlando, FL 32819
☎ 407-345-1172
tinyurl.com/bwidrive

LOCATION 2
ROOM RATING 65
COST ($=$50) $$$$–
RESORT FEE $17.90

**Best Western Lake Buena Vista
Resort Hotel** ★★★
2000 Hotel Plaza Blvd.
Lake Buena Vista, FL 32830
☎ 407-828-2424
lakebuenavistaresorthotel.com

LOCATION WDW
ROOM RATING 74
COST ($=$50) $$$$–
RESORT FEE $27.98

**Caribe Royale All-Suite Hotel &
Convention Center** ★★★★½
8101 World Center Dr.
Orlando, FL 32821
☎ 407-238-8000
cariberoyale.com

LOCATION 2
ROOM RATING 90
COST ($=$50) $$$–
RESORT FEE $25

Castle Hotel ★★★½
8629 International Dr.
Orlando, FL 32819
☎ 407-345-1511
castlehotelorlando.com

LOCATION 2
ROOM RATING 82
COST ($=$50) $$$$$$
RESORT FEE No

**Clarion Inn & Suites at
I-Drive** ★★½
9956 Hawaiian Ct.
Orlando, FL 32819
☎ 407-351-5100
tinyurl.com/clarionidrive

LOCATION 2
ROOM RATING 64
COST ($=$50) $$+
RESORT FEE $4

Comfort Inn I-Drive ★★★
8134 International Dr.
Orlando, FL 32819
☎ 407-313-4000
tinyurl.com/comfortidrive

LOCATION 2
ROOM RATING 66
COST ($=$50) $$$+
RESORT FEE $9

Comfort Suites Universal ★★★
5617 Major Blvd.
Orlando, FL 32819
☎ 407-363-1967
tinyurl.com/csuniversal

LOCATION 1
ROOM RATING 70
COST ($=$50) $$$+
RESORT FEE No

**Country Inn & Suites Orlando
Universal** ★★½
7701 Universal Blvd.
Orlando, FL 32819
☎ 407-313-4200
countryinns.com/orlandofl
_universal

LOCATION 2
ROOM RATING 63
COST ($=$50) $$$+
RESORT FEE No

Crowne Plaza Universal Orlando
★★★½
7800 Universal Blvd.
Orlando, FL 32819
☎ 407-355-0550
cporlando.com

LOCATION 2
ROOM RATING 77
COST ($=$50) $$$
RESORT FEE No

Cypress Pointe Resort ★★★★½
8651 Treasure Cay Ln.
Orlando, FL 32836
☎ 800-438-2929
cypresspointe.net

LOCATION 3
ROOM RATING 90
COST ($=$50) $$$$–
RESORT FEE $7

**Delta Hotels by Marriott Lake
Buena Vista** ★★★½
12490 Apopka-Vineland Road
Lake Buena Vista, FL 32836
☎ 407-387-9999
tinyurl.com/deltaorlando

LOCATION 3
ROOM RATING 76
COST ($=$50) $$$+
RESORT FEE No

**Embassy Suites Orlando I-Drive/
Jamaican Court** ★★★★
8250 Jamaican Ct.
Orlando, FL 32819
☎ 407-345-8250
tinyurl.com/jamaicancourt

LOCATION 2
ROOM RATING 83
COST ($=$50) $$$$+
RESORT FEE No

**Embassy Suites Orlando–Lake
Buena Vista Resort** ★★★★
8100 Lake St.
Orlando, FL 32836
☎ 407-239-1144
embassysuiteslbv.com

LOCATION 3
ROOM RATING 86
COST ($=$50) $$$$+
RESORT FEE $20

The Enclave Hotel & Suites ★★★
6165 Carrier Dr.
Orlando, FL 32819
☎ 407-351-1155
enclavesuites.com

LOCATION 2
ROOM RATING 67
COST ($=$50) $$+
RESORT FEE No

**Extended Stay America Orlando
Lake Buena Vista** ★★★★
8100 Palm Pkwy.
Orlando 32836
☎ 407-239-4300
tinyurl.com/extendedlbv

LOCATION 3
ROOM RATING 83
COST ($=$50) $$+
RESORT FEE No

**Extended Stay America Orlando
Theme Parks** ★★★½
5620 Major Blvd.
Orlando, FL 32819
☎ 407-351-1788
tinyurl.com/extendeduniversal

LOCATION 1
ROOM RATING 75
COST ($=$50) $$$–
RESORT FEE No

**Extended Stay Orlando Convention
Center** ★★½
8750 Universal Blvd.
Orlando, FL 32819
☎ 407-903-1500
tinyurl.com/esccuniversal

LOCATION 2
ROOM RATING 58
COST ($=$50) $$$–
RESORT FEE No

Hotel Information Chart *(continued)*

Fairfield Inn & Suites near Universal Orlando Resort ★★★½ 5614 Vineland Road Orlando, FL 32819 ☎ 407-581-5600 tinyurl.com/fairfielduniversal	**Fairfield Inn & Suites Orlando at SeaWorld** ★★★½ 10815 International Dr. Orlando, FL 32821 ☎ 407-354-1139 tinyurl.com/fairfieldsw	**Fairfield Inn & Suites Orlando International Drive** ★★★ 8214 Universal Blvd. Orlando, FL 32819 ☎ 407-581-9001 tinyurl.com/fairfieldidrive
LOCATION 1 ROOM RATING 80 COST ($=$50) $$$$ RESORT FEE No	LOCATION 2 ROOM RATING 80 COST ($=$50) $$$$+ RESORT FEE No	LOCATION 2 ROOM RATING 74 COST ($=$50) $$$$$+ RESORT FEE $20
Four Points by Sheraton Orlando Studio City ★★★★½ 5905 International Dr. Orlando, FL 32819 ☎ 407-351-2100 fourpointsorlandostudiocity.com	**Four Seasons Resort Orlando at Walt Disney World Resort** ★★★★★ 10100 Dream Tree Blvd. Lake Buena Vista, FL 32836 ☎ 407-313-7777 fourseasons.com/orlando	**Hampton Inn & Suites Sea World** ★★★½ 7003 Sea Harbor Dr. Orlando, FL 32821 ☎ 407-778-5900 tinyurl.com/hamptoninnseaworld
LOCATION 2 ROOM RATING 90 COST ($=$50) $$$$- RESORT FEE No	LOCATION WDW ROOM RATING 98 COST ($=$50) $ x 15 RESORT FEE No	LOCATION 2 ROOM RATING 78 COST ($=$50) $$$$- RESORT FEE No
Hard Rock Hotel Orlando ★★★★½ 5800 Universal Blvd. Orlando, FL 32819 ☎ 407-503-2000 hardrockhotels.com/orlando	**Hawthorn Suites Lake Buena Vista** ★★★★ 8303 Palm Pkwy. Orlando, FL 32836 ☎ 407-597-5000 hawthornlakebuenavista.com	**Hawthorn Suites Orlando I-Drive** ★★★½ 7975 Canada Ave. Orlando, FL 32819 ☎ 407-345-0117 tinyurl.com/hawthornidrive
LOCATION 1 ROOM RATING 93 COST ($=$50) $$$$$$$$+ RESORT FEE No	LOCATION 3 ROOM RATING 85 COST ($=$50) $$+ RESORT FEE $12.95	LOCATION 2 ROOM RATING 81 COST ($=$50) $$$$- RESORT FEE No
Hilton Grand Vacations Club at Tuscany Village ★★★★ 8122 Arrezzo Way Orlando, FL 32821 ☎ 407-465-2600 tinyurl.com/hgvtuscany	**Hilton Orlando** ★★★★½ 6001 Destination Pkwy. Orlando, FL 32819 ☎ 407-313-4300 thehiltonorlando.com	**Hilton Orlando Bonnet Creek** ★★★★ 14100 Bonnet Creek Resort Ln. Orlando, FL 32821 ☎ 407-597-3600 hiltonbonnetcreek.com
LOCATION 2 ROOM RATING 88 COST ($=$50) $$$ RESORT FEE $15	LOCATION 2 ROOM RATING 92 COST ($=$50) $$$+ RESORT FEE $27	LOCATION WDW ROOM RATING 88 COST ($=$50) $$$$$ RESORT FEE $35
Holiday Inn Express & Suites International Drive ★★★ 7276 International Dr. Orlando, FL 32819 ☎ 407-535-4100 tinyurl.com/hiexpressidrive	**Holiday Inn Express & Suites Orlando at SeaWorld** ★★★½ 10771 International Dr. Orlando, FL 32821 ☎ 407-996-4100 tinyurl.com/holidaysw	**Holiday Inn in the Walt Disney World Resort** ★★★½ 1805 Hotel Plaza Blvd. Lake Buena Vista, FL 32830 ☎ 407-828-8888 hiorlando.com
LOCATION 2 ROOM RATING 74 COST ($=$50) $$$+ RESORT FEE No	LOCATION 2 ROOM RATING 78 COST ($=$50) $$$$ RESORT FEE No	LOCATION WDW ROOM RATING 79 COST ($=$50) $$$+ RESORT FEE $17
Homewood Suites by Hilton LBV-Orlando ★★★★ 11428 Marbella Palm Ct. Orlando, FL 32836 ☎ 407-239-4540 tinyurl.com/homewoodsuiteslbv	**Homewood Suites by Hilton near Universal** ★★★★ 5893 American Way Orlando, FL 32819 ☎ 407-226-0669 tinyurl.com/homewoodnearuni	**Homewood Suites by Hilton Orlando Theme Parks** ★★★★ 6940 Westwood Blvd. Orlando, FL 32821 ☎ 407-778-5888 tinyurl.com/homewoodorl
LOCATION 3 ROOM RATING 85 COST ($=$50) $$$$+ RESORT FEE No	LOCATION 2 ROOM RATING 84 COST ($=$50) $$$$$+ RESORT FEE No	LOCATION 2 ROOM RATING 85 COST ($=$50) $$$$- RESORT FEE No

Floridays Resort Orlando ★★★★
12562 International Dr.
Orlando, FL 32821
☎ 407-238-7700
floridaysresortorlando.com

LOCATION 2
ROOM RATING 88
COST ($=$50) $$$+
RESORT FEE $15

The Floridian Hotel & Suites
★★½
7531 Canada Ave.
Orlando, FL 32819
☎ 407-212-3021
floridianhotelorlando.com

LOCATION 2
ROOM RATING 63
COST ($=$50) $$$-
RESORT FEE $5

**Four Points By Sheraton Orlando
Convention Center** ★★★½
6435 Westwood Blvd.
Orlando, FL 32821
☎ 407-351-6600
fourpointsorlandocc.com

LOCATION 2
ROOM RATING 82
COST ($=$50) $$$+
RESORT FEE No

**Hampton Inn I-Drive/Convention
Center** ★★★
8900 Universal Blvd.
Orlando, FL 32819
☎ 407-354-4447
tinyurl.com/hamptonocc

LOCATION 2
ROOM RATING 70
COST ($=$50) $$$$-
RESORT FEE No

Hampton Inn South of Universal
★★★
7110 S. Kirkman Road
Orlando, FL 32819
☎ 407-345-1112
tinyurl.com/hamptonkirkman

LOCATION 2
ROOM RATING 74
COST ($=$50) $$$$-
RESORT FEE No

Hampton Inn Universal ★★★
5621 Windhover Dr.
Orlando, FL 32819
☎ 407-351-6716
tinyurl.com/hamptonuniversal

LOCATION 1
ROOM RATING 67
COST ($=$50) $$$
RESORT FEE No

**Hilton Garden Inn Orlando at
SeaWorld** ★★★½
6850 Westwood Blvd.
Orlando, FL 32821
☎ 407-354-1500
tinyurl.com/hgiseaworld

LOCATION 2
ROOM RATING 80
COST ($=$50) $$$$+
RESORT FEE No

**Hilton Garden Inn Orlando I-Drive
North** ★★★½
5877 American Way
Orlando, FL 32819
☎ 407-363-9332
tinyurl.com/hiltonidrive

LOCATION 2
ROOM RATING 82
COST ($=$50) $$$$$-
RESORT FEE No

**Hilton Grand Vacations Club at
SeaWorld** ★★★★½
6924 Grand Vacations Way
Orlando, FL 32821
☎ 407-239-0100
tinyurl.com/seaworldhgv

LOCATION 2
ROOM RATING 95
COST ($=$50) $$$$-
RESORT FEE $25

**Hilton Orlando Buena Vista Palace
Resort** ★★★★
1900 E. Buena Vista Dr.
Lake Buena Vista, FL 32830
☎ 407-827-2727
buenavistapalace.com

LOCATION WDW
ROOM RATING 86
COST ($=$50) $$$+
RESORT FEE $30

**Hilton Orlando Lake Buena
Vista** ★★★★
1751 Hotel Plaza Blvd.
Lake Buena Vista, FL 32830
☎ 407-827-4000
hilton-wdwv.com

LOCATION WDW
ROOM RATING 87
COST ($=$50) $$$
RESORT FEE $30

**Holiday Inn & Suites Orlando
Universal** ★★★½
5905 Kirkman Road
Orlando, FL 32819
☎ 407-351-3333
hiuniversal.com

LOCATION 1
ROOM RATING 75
COST ($=$50) $$$-
RESORT FEE No

**Holiday Inn Resort
Lake Buena Vista** ★★★½
13351 FL 535
Orlando, FL 32821
☎ 407-239-4500
hiresortlbv.com

LOCATION 3
ROOM RATING 82
COST ($=$50) $$$
RESORT FEE $19.95

**Holiday Inn Resort Orlando
Suites-Waterpark** ★★★½
14500 Continental Gateway
Orlando, FL 32821
☎ 407-387-5437
hisuitesorlando.com

LOCATION 2
ROOM RATING 82
COST ($=$50) $$$+
RESORT FEE $33.75

Homewood Suites by Hilton I-Drive
★★★½
8745 International Dr.
Orlando, FL 32819
☎ 407-248-2232
tinyurl.com/homewoodidrive

LOCATION 2
ROOM RATING 81
COST ($=$50) $$$$$-
RESORT FEE No

**Hyatt House Across from
Universal Orlando** ★★★★½
5915 Caravan Ct.
Orlando, FL 32819
☎ 407-352-5660
acrossfromuniversalorlando.house
.hyatt.com

LOCATION 1
ROOM RATING 91
COST ($=$50) $$+
RESORT FEE No

**Hyatt Place Orlando
Lake Buena Vista** ★★★★
8688 Palm Parkway
Orlando, FL 32836
☎ 407-778-5500
orlandolakebuenavista.place.hyatt
.com

LOCATION 3
ROOM RATING 84
COST ($=$50) $$$$
RESORT FEE No

Hyatt Place Orlando/Universal
★★★★
5895 Caravan Ct.
Orlando, FL 32819
☎ 407-351-0627
orlandouniversal.place.hyatt.com

LOCATION 1
ROOM RATING 84
COST ($=$50) $$$$+
RESORT FEE No

Hotel Information Chart *(continued)*

Hyatt Regency Grand Cypress
★★★★½
1 Grand Cypress Blvd.
Orlando, FL 32836
☎ 407-239-1234
grandcypress.hyatt.com
LOCATION 3
ROOM RATING 92
COST ($=$50) $$$$$–
RESORT FEE $30

Hyatt Regency Orlando ★★★★½
9801 International Dr.
Orlando, FL 32819
☎ 407-284-1234
orlando.regency.hyatt.com
LOCATION 2
ROOM RATING 90
COST ($=$50) $$$$–
RESORT FEE $25

InTown Suites Orlando Universal
★★½
5615 Major Blvd.
Orlando, FL 32819
☎ 407-370-3734
tinyurl.com/intownsuitesorlando
LOCATION 2
ROOM RATING 63
COST ($=$50) $
RESORT FEE No

Loews Portofino Bay Hotel
★★★★½
5601 Universal Blvd.
Orlando, FL 32819
☎ 407-503-1000
loewshotels.com/portofino-bay
-hotel
LOCATION 1
ROOM RATING 92
COST ($=$50) $$$$$$$$$+
RESORT FEE No

Loews Royal Pacific Resort
★★★★½
6300 Hollywood Way
Orlando, FL 32819
☎ 407-503-3000
loewshotels.com/royal-pacific
-resort
LOCATION 1
ROOM RATING 90
COST ($=$50) $$$$$$$+
RESORT FEE No

Loews Sapphire Falls Resort
★★★★
6601 Adventure Way
Orlando, FL 32819
☎ 407-503-5000
loewshotels.com/sapphire-falls
-resort
LOCATION 1
ROOM RATING 84
COST ($=$50) $$$$$
RESORT FEE No

Marriott's Imperial Palms ★★★★
8404 Vacation Way
Orlando, FL 32821
☎ 407-238-6200
tinyurl.com/imperialpalmvillas
LOCATION 2
ROOM RATING 86
COST ($=$50) $$$$$$$–
RESORT FEE No

Marriott's Royal Palms ★★★★
8404 Vacation Way
Orlando, FL 32821
☎ 407-238-6200
tinyurl.com/marriottsroyalpalms
LOCATION 2
ROOM RATING 86
COST ($=$50) $$$$$+
RESORT FEE No

Monumental Hotel ★★★
12120 International Dr.
Orlando, FL 32821
☎ 407-239-1222
monumentalhotelorlandofl.com
LOCATION 2
ROOM RATING 70
COST ($=$50) $$
RESORT FEE $6.75

Parc Corniche Resort ★★★½
6300 Parc Corniche Dr.
Orlando, FL 32821
☎ 407-239-7100
parccorniche.com
LOCATION 2
ROOM RATING 82
COST ($=$50) $$
RESORT FEE $7.95

Quality Inn at International Drive
★★★
8300 Jamaican Ct.
Orlando, FL 32819
☎ 407-351-1660
tinyurl.com/qualityinnidrive
LOCATION 2
ROOM RATING 74
COST ($=$50) $$$+
RESORT FEE $5.95

Quality Suites Lake Buena Vista
★★★½
8200 Palm Pkwy.
Orlando, FL 32836
☎ 407-465-8200
qualitysuiteslbv.com
LOCATION 3
ROOM RATING 81
COST ($=$50) $$$+
RESORT FEE $4.95

Ramada Convention Center I-Drive
★★★
8342 Jamaican Ct.
Orlando, FL 32819
☎ 407-363-1944
tinyurl.com/ramadaidrive
LOCATION 2
ROOM RATING 65
COST ($=$50) $$
RESORT FEE $4.99

**Ramada Plaza Resort and Suites
Orlando I-Drive** ★★★
6500 International Dr.
Orlando, FL 32819
☎ 407-345-5340
tinyurl.com/ramadaplazaidrive
LOCATION 2
ROOM RATING 74
COST ($=$50) $$$$$–
RESORT FEE No

**Renaissance Orlando at
SeaWorld** ★★★★½
6677 Sea Harbor Dr.
Orlando, FL 32821
☎ 407-351-5555
tinyurl.com/renorlandoseaworld
LOCATION 2
ROOM RATING 90
COST ($=$50) $$$$$
RESORT FEE $25

Residence Inn Universal Studios
★★★★
5616 Major Blvd.
Orlando, FL 32819; ☎ 407-313-1234
marriott.com/hotels/travel/mcotw
-residence-inn-near-universal
-orlando
LOCATION 2
ROOM RATING 87
COST ($=$50) $$$$+
RESORT FEE No

**The Ritz-Carlton Orlando,
Grande Lakes** ★★★★½
4012 Central Florida Pkwy.
Orlando, FL 32837
☎ 407-206-2400
grandelakes.com
LOCATION 2
ROOM RATING 94
COST ($=$50) $$$$$$$$–
RESORT FEE $35

Rosen Centre Hotel ★★★★½
9840 International Dr.
Orlando, FL 32819
☎ 407-996-9840
rosencentre.com
LOCATION 2
ROOM RATING 95
COST ($=$50) $$$$+
RESORT FEE No

La Quinta Inn Orlando Universal Studios ★★★
5621 Major Blvd.
Orlando, FL 32819
☎ 407-313-3100
tinyurl.com/lquniversal

LOCATION 1
ROOM RATING 72
COST ($=$50) $$+
RESORT FEE No

Las Palmeras by Hilton Grand Vacations ★★★★
9501 Universal Blvd.
Orlando, FL 32819
☎ 407-233-2200
tinyurl.com/laspalmerashilton

LOCATION 2
ROOM RATING 87
COST ($=$50) $$$+
RESORT FEE $25

Legacy Vacation Club Lake Buena Vista ★★★★
8451 Palm Pkwy.
Lake Buena Vista, FL 32836
☎ 407-238-1700
legacyvacationresorts.com

LOCATION 3
ROOM RATING 85
COST ($=$50) $$+
RESORT FEE $4

Marriott's Cypress Harbour ★★★★
11251 Harbour Villa Road
Orlando, FL 32821
☎ 407-238-1300
tinyurl.com/cypressharbourvillas

LOCATION 2
ROOM RATING 86
COST ($=$50) $$$$$
RESORT FEE No

Marriott's Grande Vista ★★★★½
5925 Avenida Vista
Orlando, FL 32821
☎ 407-238-7676
tinyurl.com/marriottsgrandevista

LOCATION 2
ROOM RATING 93
COST ($=$50) $$$+
RESORT FEE No

Marriott's Harbour Lake ★★★★½
7102 Grand Horizons Blvd.
Orlando, FL 32821
☎ 407-465-6100
tinyurl.com/harbourlake

LOCATION 3
ROOM RATING 90
COST ($=$50) $$$$-
RESORT FEE No

Monumental Movieland Hotel ★★½
6233 International Dr.
Orlando, FL 32819
☎ 407-351-3900
monumentalmovielandhotel.com

LOCATION 2
ROOM RATING 63
COST ($=$50) $$-
RESORT FEE $2.50

Motel 6 Orlando-I-Drive ★★★
5909 American Way
Orlando, FL 32819
☎ 407-351-6500
tinyurl.com/motel6idrive

LOCATION 2
ROOM RATING 66
COST ($=$50) $+
RESORT FEE No

Orlando World Center Marriott Resort ★★★★½
8701 World Center Dr.
Orlando, FL 32821
☎ 407-239-4200
marriottworldcenter.com

LOCATION 3
ROOM RATING 90
COST ($=$50) $$$$-
RESORT FEE $28.13

Quality Suites Turkey Lake ★★★
9350 Turkey Lake Road
Orlando, FL 32819
☎ 407-351-5050
qualitysuitesorlandofl.com

LOCATION 3
ROOM RATING 74
COST ($=$50) $$
RESORT FEE $4.50

The Point Hotel & Suites Orlando Resort ★★★★
7389 Universal Blvd.
Orlando, FL 32819
☎ 407-956-2000
thepointorlando.com

LOCATION 2
ROOM RATING 84
COST ($=$50) $$$+
RESORT FEE $13

Radisson Hotel Orlando Lake Buena Vista ★★★½
12799 Apopka-Vineland Road
Orlando, FL 32836
☎ 407-597-3400
tinyurl.com/radissonlbv

LOCATION 3
ROOM RATING 82
COST ($=$50) $$$$-
RESORT FEE No

Residence Inn Orlando at SeaWorld ★★★★
11000 Westwood Blvd.
Orlando, FL 32821
☎ 407-313-3600
tinyurl.com/residenceinnseaworld

LOCATION 3
ROOM RATING 87
COST ($=$50) $$$$$$-
RESORT FEE No

Residence Inn Orlando Convention Center ★★★½
8800 Universal Blvd.
Orlando, FL 32819
☎ 407-226-0288
tinyurl.com/resinnconventioncenter

LOCATION 2
ROOM RATING 80
COST ($=$50) $$$$$$
RESORT FEE No

Residence Inn Orlando Lake Buena Vista ★★★★
11450 Marbella Palm Ct.
Orlando, FL 32836
☎ 407-465-0075
tinyurl.com/residenceinnlbv

LOCATION 3
ROOM RATING 83
COST ($=$50) $$$$-
RESORT FEE No

Rosen Inn at Pointe Orlando ★★★½
9000 International Dr.
Orlando, FL 32819
☎ 407-996-8585
roseninn9000.com

LOCATION 2
ROOM RATING 75
COST ($=$50) $$$-
RESORT FEE No

Rosen Inn International Hotel ★★★
7600 International Dr.
Orlando, FL 32819
☎ 407-996-1600
roseninn7600.com

LOCATION 2
ROOM RATING 70
COST ($=$50) $$-
RESORT FEE No

Rosen Inn near Universal ★★★
6327 International Dr.
Orlando, FL 32819
☎ 407-996-4444
roseninn6327.com

LOCATION 2
ROOM RATING 71
COST ($=$50) $$+
RESORT FEE No

Hotel Information Chart *(continued)*

Rosen Plaza Hotel ★★★★½ 9700 International Dr. Orlando, FL 32819 ☎ 407-996-9700 rosenplaza.com **LOCATION** 2 **ROOM RATING** 91 **COST ($=$50)** $$$$$– **RESORT FEE** No	**Rosen Shingle Creek** ★★★★ 9939 Universal Blvd. Orlando, FL 32819 ☎ 866-996-9939 rosenshinglecreek.com **LOCATION** 2 **ROOM RATING** 88 **COST ($=$50)** $$$$$+ **RESORT FEE** No	**Sheraton Lake Buena Vista Resort** ★★★★ 12205 S. Apopka-Vineland Road Orlando, FL 32836 ☎ 407-239-0444 sheratonlakebuenavistaresort.com **LOCATION** 3 **ROOM RATING** 88 **COST ($=$50)** $$$– **RESORT FEE** $24
SpringHill Suites Orlando at SeaWorld ★★★★ 10801 International Dr. Orlando, FL 32821 ☎ 407-354-1176 tinyurl.com/springhillsw **LOCATION** 2 **ROOM RATING** 85 **COST ($=$50)** $$$$+ **RESORT FEE** No	**SpringHill Suites Orlando Convention Center** ★★★½ 8840 Universal Blvd. Orlando, FL 32819 ☎ 407-345-9073 tinyurl.com/shsconventioncenter **LOCATION** 2 **ROOM RATING** 80 **COST ($=$50)** $$$$$$– **RESORT FEE** No	**Stay Sky Suites I-Drive Orlando** ★★★½ 7601 Canada Ave. Orlando, FL 32819 ☎ 407-581-2151 stayskysuitesidriveorlando.com **LOCATION** 2 **ROOM RATING** 82 **COST ($=$50)** $$$ **RESORT FEE** $4.95
TownePlace Suites Orlando at SeaWorld ★★★★ 10731 International Dr. Orlando, FL 32821 ☎ 407-996-3400 tinyurl.com/towneplacesw **LOCATION** 2 **ROOM RATING** 84 **COST ($=$50)** $$$$– **RESORT FEE** No	**Universal's Aventura Hotel** ★★★★ 6725 Adventure Way Orlando, FL 32819 ☎ 407-503-6000 loewshotels.com/universals -aventura-hotel **LOCATION** 1 **ROOM RATING** 83 **COST ($=$50)** $$$ **RESORT FEE** No	**Universal's Cabana Bay Beach Resort** ★★★★ 6550 Adventure Way Orlando, FL 32819 ☎ 407-503-4000 loewshotels.com/cabana-bay-hotel **LOCATION** 1 **ROOM RATING** 83 **COST ($=$50)** $$$ **RESORT FEE** No
Wingate by Wyndham Universal Studios ★★★½ 5661 Windhover Dr. Orlando, FL 32819 ☎ 407-226-0900 wingateorlando.com **LOCATION** 1 **ROOM RATING** 76 **COST ($=$50)** $$$– **RESORT FEE** No	**WorldQuest Orlando Resort** ★★★★ 8849 WorldQuest Blvd. Orlando, FL 32821 ☎ 407-387-3800 worldquestorlando.com **LOCATION** 2 **ROOM RATING** 88 **COST ($=$50)** $$$+ **RESORT FEE** $19.95	**Wyndham Lake Buena Vista Resort** ★★★½ 1850 Hotel Plaza Blvd. Lake Buena Vista, FL 32830 ☎ 407-828-4444 wyndhamlakebuenavista.com **LOCATION** WDW **ROOM RATING** 75 **COST ($=$50)** $$$$– **RESORT FEE** $25

Sheraton Vistana Resort Villas
★★★★
8800 Vistana Centre Dr.
Orlando, FL 32821
☎ 407-239-3100
tinyurl.com/vistanavillas

LOCATION 3
ROOM RATING 89
COST ($=$50) $$$+
RESORT FEE No

Sheraton Vistana Villages Resort
★★★★
12401 International Dr.
Orlando, FL 32821
☎ 407-238-5000
tinyurl.com/sheratonvillages

LOCATION 2
ROOM RATING 88
COST ($=$50) $$$$+
RESORT FEE No

Sonesta ES Suites ★★★★
8480 International Dr.
Orlando, FL 32819
☎ 407-352-2400
tinyurl.com/sonestaorlando

LOCATION 2
ROOM RATING 85
COST ($=$50) $$$$$-
RESORT FEE $8

**Staybridge Suites
Lake Buena Vista** ★★★★½
8751 Suiteside Dr.
Orlando, FL 32836
☎ 407-238-0777
tinyurl.com/staybridgelbv

LOCATION 3
ROOM RATING 90
COST ($=$50) $$$+
RESORT FEE No

**Staybridge Suites Orlando at
SeaWorld** ★★★★½
6985 Sea Harbor Dr.
Orlando, FL 32821
☎ 407-917-9200
tinyurl.com/staybridgesw

LOCATION 2
ROOM RATING 90
COST ($=$50) $$$$+
RESORT FEE No

Sunsol International Drive ★★★
5859 American Way
Orlando, FL 32819
☎ 407-203-2664
sunsolhotels.net/internationaldrive

LOCATION 2
ROOM RATING 72
COST ($=$50) $$-
RESORT FEE $9

Waldorf Astoria Orlando
★★★★½
14200 Bonnet Creek Resort Ln.
Orlando, FL 32821
☎ 407-597-5500
waldorfastoriaorlando.com

LOCATION WDW
ROOM RATING 93
COST ($=$50) $$$$$$$+
RESORT FEE $35

Westgate Lakes Resort & Spa
★★★★½
10000 Turkey Lake Road
Orlando, FL 32819
☎ 407-345-0000
westgateresorts.com/lakes

LOCATION 3
ROOM RATING 92
COST ($=$50) $$$+
RESORT FEE $14.50

Westgate Palace ★★★
6145 Carrier Dr.
Orlando, FL 32819
☎ 407-996-6000
westgateresorts.com/palace

LOCATION 2
ROOM RATING 68
COST ($=$50) $$$$$-
RESORT FEE $10

Wyndham Orlando Resort I-Drive
★★★★
8001 International Dr.
Orlando, FL 32819
☎ 407-351-2420
wyndham.com/hotels/MCOWD

LOCATION 2
ROOM RATING 85
COST ($=$50) $$$$
RESORT FEE $24.70

PART THREE

ARRIVING *and* GETTING AROUND

GETTING THERE

DIRECTIONS TO UNIVERSAL ORLANDO

UNIVERSAL ORLANDO IS LOCATED within the Orlando city limits, a short distance from I-4 and Florida's Turnpike. You can access the resort from I-4 East by taking Exit 75A and turning left at the top of the ramp onto Universal Boulevard. If you're traveling on I-4 West, use Exit 74B and then turn right onto Hollywood Way. Entrances are also located off Kirkman Road to the east, Turkey Lake Road to the west, and Vineland Road to the north. Universal Boulevard connects the International Drive area to Universal via an overpass bridging I-4. Grand National Drive has been extended with another I-4 overpass that connects Major Boulevard on the east side of Universal with International Drive's northernmost end. Turkey Lake and Vineland Roads are particularly good alternatives when I-4 is gridlocked. See pages 130–131 and page 134 for maps of the area.

Signs for Universal's hotels and theme parks are easy to find and read as soon as you've left the interstate. Once on Universal property, follow the signs to the parking garage or your hotel.

FROM THE ORLANDO INTERNATIONAL AIRPORT (MCO) Take FL 528/Beachline Expressway, a toll road, west for about 12 miles to the intersection with I-4. Bear right and go east 2 miles on I-4 to Exit 75A, marked UNIVERSAL/INTERNATIONAL DRIVE, and make a left at the end of the exit ramp. Tolls cost $2.25 each way, and we advise bringing quarters if your car doesn't have a SunPass or E-Pass transponder for the automated toll lanes.

FROM WALT DISNEY WORLD Go east on I-4, take Exit 75A (marked UNIVERSAL/INTERNATIONAL DRIVE), and make a left at the end of the exit ramp.

FROM DAYTONA, SANFORD INTERNATIONAL AIRPORT (SFB), OR ORLANDO Head west on I-4 through Orlando. Take Exit 74B toward Universal Orlando.

FROM MIAMI, FORT LAUDERDALE, OR SOUTHEASTERN FLORIDA Head north on Florida's Turnpike to Exit 259, and merge onto I-4 West toward Tampa. Take Exit 74B toward Universal Orlando.

FROM TAMPA AND SOUTHWESTERN FLORIDA Take I-75 North to I-4. Go east on I-4, take Exit 75A (marked UNIVERSAL/INTERNATIONAL DRIVE), and make a left at the end of the exit ramp.

FROM FLORIDA'S TURNPIKE SOUTH Take Exit 259 to merge onto I-4 West toward Tampa, and then take Exit 74B toward Universal Orlando.

FROM I-10 Take I-10 East across Florida to I-75 South at Exit 296A/Tampa; then take Florida's Turnpike (toll road) southbound at Exit 328 (on the left) toward Orlando. Take Exit 259 to merge onto I-4 West toward Tampa; then take Exit 74B toward Universal Orlando.

FROM I-75 SOUTH Take I-75 South onto Florida's Turnpike via Exit 328 (on the left) toward Orlando. Take Exit 259 to merge onto I-4 West toward Tampa, and then take Exit 74B toward Universal Orlando.

FROM I-95 SOUTH Take Exit 260B to merge onto I-4 West, and then take Exit 74B toward Universal Orlando.

Universal Orlando Exits off I-4

West to east (in the direction of Tampa to Orlando), six I-4 exits serve Universal Orlando.

Exit 74A (Sand Lake Road) serves the southern edge of Universal's property, with access to the resort from Turkey Lake Road, which lies just west of the exit. This exit also provides access to the attractions on the southern end of International Drive, heading toward the Orange County Convention Center, as well as the Restaurant Row dining options on West Sand Lake Road. Be warned that this exit can get quite congested with I-Drive traffic.

Exit 74B (Adventure Way) is only accessible from I-4 West and serves as the primary entrance to Universal Orlando Resort from that direction. The exit ramp leads directly to the Cabana Bay Beach and Sapphire Falls Resorts. Make a right at the light past the hotels to reach the Universal Orlando parking garage. Note that you can't return to I-4 East via this exit.

Exit 75A (Universal Boulevard/International Drive) serves as the primary entrance to Universal Orlando Resort for visitors coming from Walt Disney World on I-4 East. Make a left at the end of the ramp into Universal property, and the parking garage will be ahead on your right. Make a right off this exit to take Universal Boulevard south across International Drive to the Endless Summer Resort hotels; it then parallels that busy road, making it a perfect bypass to south International Drive and the convention center.

continued on page 132

South Orlando

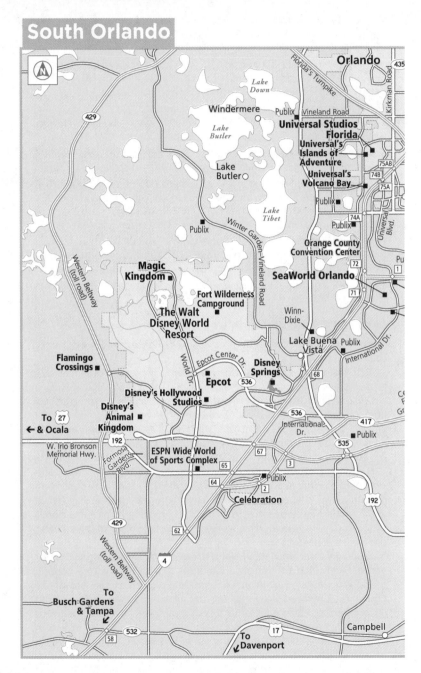

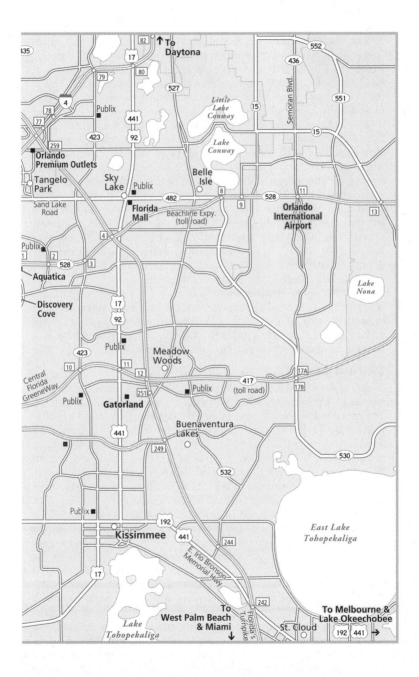

continued from page 129

Exit 75B (Kirkman Road North) leads drivers from I-4 East north to the Kirkman Road entrance on the east side of Universal Orlando Resort. Stay in the left lane after exiting, then turn left at the first traffic signal onto Major Boulevard to enter Universal property. This is the closest exit to the Portofino Bay and Hard Rock Hotels, as well as most off-site hotels within walking distance.

Exit 75AB (Kirkman Road/International Drive) is the recently redesigned exit from I-4 West to Kirkman Road just south of Universal. Stay to the right after Florida's Turnpike to take Exit 75. Bear left when the exit ramp splits for 75B to Kirkman Road southbound, toward the shopping and attractions on north International Drive, or stay right on Exit 75A to Kirkman Road northbound and Universal Orlando. A barrier prevents drivers exiting I-4 West from making a left turn directly into the resort, but you can make a right at the first intersection onto Major Boulevard, followed by a U-turn at Grand National Drive back toward Universal. Alternatively, make the next left off Kirkman onto Vineland Road, and then turn left onto Universal Boulevard to enter the resort from the north.

Exit 78 (Conroy Road/Millenia) is an option for westbound drivers when traffic is backed up approaching Florida's Turnpike. Make a right off the exit (at The Holy Land Experience theme park), and then make an immediate left onto Vineland Road. Universal Boulevard will be your second left after crossing Kirkman Road.

THE I-4 BLUES

OVER MANY YEARS OF COVERING Orlando's attractions, we've watched I-4 turn from a modern interstate highway into a parking lot. The greatest congestion used to be between the Universal Orlando–International Drive area and downtown Orlando, but the section to the southwest serving the Disney World exits has become the new choke point, seemingly irrespective of the time of day. If you're going from Walt Disney World toward Universal Orlando (east), the jam usually breaks up after you've passed the FL 535 exit. As you head west toward Tampa, traffic calms down after the US 192 interchange.

Ameliorating (or complicating) the situation, the state of Florida is renovating a 21-mile stretch of I-4, from FL 434 in the northeast to Kirkman Road in the southwest, to improve traffic flow and capacity in these areas. The construction project will renovate 15 of the busiest interchanges, build 56 new bridges, and replace more than 70 overpasses, plus add four variable-charge toll lanes to help pay for the $2 billion estimated cost. The bad news is that construction, which was supposed to wrap up by 2021, is significantly behind schedule. Lane and exit ramp closures frequently occur between 10 p.m. and 6 a.m., which can snarl night owls exiting from CityWalk or early birds arriving before Early Park Admission. Real-time road conditions are available at i4exitguide.com/i-4-traffic, and an interactive map showing all active construction projects in Florida can be found at fdot.gov/agencyresources/maps/projects. Info about construction in Orlando and the tourist areas is available at Central Florida Roads (cflroads.com), an FDOT website. For information and current conditions on area toll roads, see cfxway.com.

On long road trips, we always use a GPS device that's smart enough to accept traffic updates and route us around delays. TomTom GPS units, for example, have an accessory cable that picks up traffic signals from HD radio broadcasts. If you have a smartphone, the free mobile app Waze (waze.com; iOS and Android) also does this trick.

If the I-4 traffic becomes intolerable, it's pretty easy to commute from the Universal Orlando–International Drive area to Walt Disney World via Turkey Lake Road, connecting to Palm Parkway and FL 535 on the northwest side of I-4, or on the southernmost section of I-Drive, connecting to FL 536 on the southeast side of the interstate.

SNEAK ROUTES

WE'RE CONSTANTLY LOOKING for ways to avoid traffic snarls. For some roads and areas, there are no alternative routes. For others, we've discovered sneak routes. These suggestions will not only help you avoid congestion, but they're also great ways to discover local restaurants outside the theme park orbit.

International Drive (I-Drive) is by far the most difficult area to navigate without long traffic delays. Most hotels on I-Drive are between Kirkman Road to the north and FL 417 (Central Florida GreeneWay) to the south. Between Kirkman Road and FL 417, three major roads cross I-Drive: From north to south on I-Drive, the first is Universal Boulevard. Next is Sand Lake Road (FL 482), pretty squarely in the middle of the hotel district. Finally, the Beachline Expressway (FL 528) connects I-4 and the airport. The southern third of I-Drive can be accessed via Central Florida Parkway, connecting I-4 and Palm Parkway with the SeaWorld area of I-Drive, and by Daryl Carter Parkway, connecting Palm Parkway with the Orlando Vineland Premium Outlets.

I-Drive is a mess for a number of reasons: scarcity of left-turn lanes, long multidirectional traffic signals, and, most critically, limited access to westbound I-4. From the Orange County Convention Center south to the Beachline Expressway and FL 417/Central Florida GreeneWay, getting on westbound I-4 is easy, but in the stretch where the hotels are concentrated (from Kirkman to about a mile south of Sand Lake), the only way most visitors know to access I-4 westbound is to slog through the gridlock of the I-Drive–Sand Lake Road intersection en route to the I-4–Sand Lake Road interchange. A combination of a long, long traffic signal; a sea of motorists; and insufficient turn lanes makes this about as much fun as a root canal.

To travel between Universal and the northernmost end of International Drive (near the outlet mall), use the Grand National Drive overpass between Oak Ridge Road and Major Boulevard. If your hotel is north of Sand Lake, access Kirkman Road by going north on I-Drive

I-Drive Area Sneak Routes

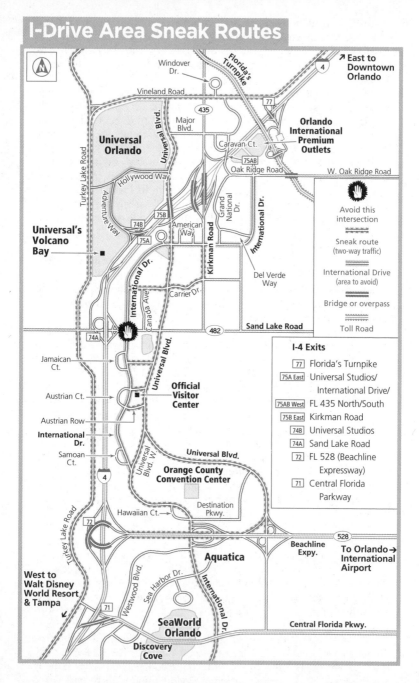

East to Downtown Orlando

Windover Dr.

Florida's Turnpike

Vineland Road

77

Orlando International Premium Outlets

Major Blvd.

435

Caravan Ct.

75AB

Oak Ridge Road

W. Oak Ridge Road

Universal Orlando

Hollywood Way

Adventure Way

75B

74B

American Way

75A

Grand National Dr.

Kirkman Road

International Dr.

Universal's Volcano Bay

Turkey Lake Road

International Dr.

Canada Ave.

Carrier Dr.

Del Verde Way

74A

482

Sand Lake Road

Jamaican Ct.

Universal Blvd.

Austrian Ct.

Official Visitor Center

Austrian Row

International Dr.

Samoan Ct.

4

Universal Blvd. W.

Universal Blvd.

Orange County Convention Center

Destination Pkwy.

Hawaiian Ct.

72

Turkey Lake Road

528

Beachline Expy.

To Orlando → International Airport

Aquatica

Westwood Blvd.

Sea Harbor Dr.

International Dr.

West to Walt Disney World Resort & Tampa

71

SeaWorld Orlando

Central Florida Pkwy.

Discovery Cove

Avoid this intersection

Sneak route (two-way traffic)

International Drive (area to avoid)

Bridge or overpass

Toll Road

I-4 Exits

77	Florida's Turnpike
75A East	Universal Studios/ International Drive/
75AB West	FL 435 North/South
75B East	Kirkman Road
74B	Universal Studios
74A	Sand Lake Road
72	FL 528 (Beachline Expressway)
71	Central Florida Parkway

(in the opposite direction of the heaviest traffic) to the Kirkman Road intersection and turning left, or by cutting over to Kirkman via eastbound Carrier Drive. You can also go north on Universal Boulevard, which parallels I-Drive to the east; after you cross I-4 onto Universal property, stay right and follow the signs for the parking garage, or take two left turns to reach I-4 westbound.

If your hotel is south of Sand Lake Road but north of Austrian Court, use Austrian Row or Jamaican Court to cut over to Universal Boulevard. If south of Austrian Court, continue south until you intersect the Beachline Expressway (FL 528); then take the Beachline west to I-4 (no toll).

SECURITY AT ORLANDO INTERNATIONAL AIRPORT

THIS AIRPORT HANDLES about 45 million passengers a year. It's not unusual to see lines from the checkpoints snaking out of the terminal and into the main shopping corridor and food court. Airport officials sometimes actually shut down moving sidewalks to use them for more queuing space. A number of passengers have reported missing their flights even when they arrived at the airport 90 minutes before departure. System improvements have alleviated some, but by no means all, of the congestion. Most waits to clear security are less than 30 minutes on average, compared with as many as 55 minutes before the improvements. Even so, there are substantial fluctuations, with peak waits nearing an hour. Check orlandoairports.net or download the free MCO mobile app for current security wait times.

unofficial **TIP**
We recommend arriving at MCO 90 minutes–2 hours before your scheduled departure.

ALTERNATIVE AIRPORTS

A SHORT DISTANCE NORTHEAST of Orlando is **Sanford International Airport** (SFB; orlandosanfordairport.com). Small, convenient, and easily accessible, it's low hassle compared with the huge Orlando International Airport (MCO) and its block-long security-checkpoint lines.

The primary domestic carrier serving Sanford International is **Allegiant Air** (☎ 702-505-8888; allegiantair.com), with service from large and small airports throughout the Eastern and Midwestern United States. International carriers include **Surinam Airways** (South America: flyslm.com) and **TUIFly** (Netherlands, Belgium, UK: ☎ 855-808-4015; tui.nl).

A reader from Roanoke, Virginia, uses Sanford frequently, writing:

> The 45-minute drive to [Orlando] is more than made up for by avoiding the chaos at Orlando International, and it's stress free.

The downside is that Sanford is 35 miles from Universal Orlando. A one-way taxi ride will cost over $100 with tip, and a ride-share service will charge about $40 or more. One reader recommends **Better Deal Transport** (☎ 407-470-4121; betterdealtransport.com), which advertises $140 round-trip transportation for up to five guests:

I couldn't be happier with our car service out of Sanford. Our driver was great—flexible, patient, and in touch through the day as we dealt with delays. [It] couldn't have been better.

Other readers, like this couple from White Township, New Jersey, prefer flying into Tampa instead:

We've found that flying from Newark to Tampa instead of Orlando saves us money and our sanity. It means significantly lower fares, fewer children on the plane, and shorter security lines.

(Note that it's an 84-mile drive from Tampa International Airport to Universal Orlando—about an hour and 20 minutes.)

GETTING TO UNIVERSAL ORLANDO FROM THE AIRPORT

YOU HAVE FIVE OPTIONS FOR GETTING from Orlando International to Universal Orlando:

1. TAXI **Mears Transportation Group** (☎ 888-983-3346; mearstransportation.com) has a near monopoly on taxi service in Central Florida and operates multiple brands (Yellow Cab Company, Checker Cab Company, and City Cab Company) with identical rates. Taxis carry four to eight passengers (depending on vehicle type). Rates vary according to distance. If your hotel is on Universal property, or nearby on International Drive or Major Boulevard, your fare will be about $45–$50, plus tip. Download the Mears Taxi app for Apple or Android to estimate the cost of your trip, but it's buggy, so don't rely on it to hail your ride; report to the dispatch stand on level two outside baggage claim.

2. SHUTTLE SERVICE **Mears Transportation Group** (☎ 888-983-3346; mearstransportation.com) also dominates shared shuttle service and provides the transportation for many third-party vacation packages that include airport transfers. Non-package travelers can also use the service. The shuttles collect passengers until a van (or bus) is filled. The vehicles are then dispatched. Mears charges *per-person* rates (children under age 3 ride free). A one-way adult fare is $21 ($16 for children ages 4–11); round-trip is $33 for adults ($25 for children). Reserve online using discount code WEB10 to save 10%. Mears's competitor **Super-Shuttle** (☎ 800-258-3826; supershuttle.com) also offers shared vans to Universal for $21 per person one way, or $40 round-trip.

Universal offers **SuperStar Shuttle** airport transfers only to on-site guests who book their stay through a Universal Vacations package. The shuttle costs $39 per adult, $29 per child ages 3–9 round-trip (kids under age 3 ride free). Guests arriving between 7:30 a.m. and 8:30 p.m. are welcomed at the Hotel Transportation Desk on the first floor of the airport terminal, where they receive a preprinted packet containing any tickets purchased with their vacation package; those with earlier or later flights will need to call ☎ 407-888-9795 for pickup. SuperStar service will not deliver luggage to your room like Disney's Magical Express, so you'll need to retrieve it from baggage claim yourself before checking in, and you'll have to provide your own child car seats. As a bonus, SuperStar service includes a complimentary three-month family membership in CLEAR (clearme.com), a prescreening service that can speed your way through security at Orlando International and a dozen other airports; you'll have to activate your membership at the Enrollment Center (located inside the airport) before your departure to take advantage of the offer. SuperStar airport transfers can be added to an existing Universal Vacations reservation by calling ☎ 800-407-4275. For more information, visit tinyurl.com/unishuttle or call ☎ 866-604-7557 (daily, 8 a.m.–5:30 p.m.). A reader from Exton, Pennsylvania, warns against taking Universal's shuttle service:

> The SuperStar Shuttle (which cost extra, even though we were staying at an on-site property) was a dark spot on an otherwise great trip. After our arrival in Orlando, we ended up waiting over an hour to get picked up. The first shuttle that came was too small to fit all of the people waiting for it. Why does Universal require advance reservations with flight arrival times if it won't be prepared for the amount of people it needs to transport?

When using any shared transportation service, you might have to wait at the airport until a vehicle fills. Once under way, the shuttle will probably stop several times to discharge passengers before reaching your hotel. Obviously, it takes less time to fill a van than a bus, and less time to deliver and unload those passengers.

From your hotel to the airport, you will likely ride in a van (unless you're part of a tour group, for which the company might send a bus). Because shuttles make several pickups, they ask you to leave much earlier than you'd depart if you were taking a cab or returning a rental car.

3. TOWN CAR SERVICE Like a taxi, a town car service will transport you directly from the airport to your hotel. The driver will usually be waiting for you in your airline's baggage-claim area. If saving time and hassle is worth the money, book a town car.

Each town car service we surveyed offers large, well-appointed late-model sedans, such as the Lincoln Town Car series, or limousines. These hold four persons; trunks easily hold golf bags. Some services also offer roomier luxury SUVs and vans for an extra fee. To reserve a child's car seat, call ahead.

Tiffany Towncar Service (☎ 888-838-2161 or 407-370-2196; tiffanytowncars.com) provides a prompt, clean ride. The round-trip fee to the Universal area in a town car is $135 plus tip; one-way is $75. Tiffany charges an extra $10 for pickups before 6 a.m. but offers a free 30-minute stop at a supermarket en route to your hotel with a round-trip booking.

Quicksilver Tours & Transportation (☎ 888-GO-TO-WDW [468-6939] or 407-299-1434; quicksilver-tours.com) offers 8-person limos and 10-person vans in addition to 4-person town cars. Round-trip in a town car from MCO to the Universal area and back (with a free 30-minute grocery stop on the way) is $125; round-trip in a van costs $140; the round-trip limo rate is $240. Quicksilver also offers a three-way trip from the airport to Walt Disney World, then to Universal Orlando, and finally back to the airport, starting at $170—perfect for those splitting their vacation between the two resorts.

Mears Transportation Group (☎ 407-423-5566; mearstransportation .com) also offers a town car service for a flat $79 each way, as does **SuperShuttle** (☎ 800-258-3826; supershuttle.com) for $77 each way.

4. RENTAL CARS   Short- and long-term rentals are available. Most companies allow drop-off at certain hotels or subsidiary locations in the Universal area if you don't want the vehicle for your entire stay. Likewise, any time during your stay, you can pick up a car at those hotels and locations. Check mousesavers.com for rental-car discount codes.

The preferred routes to Universal Orlando (as well as Walt Disney World, International Drive, and US 192) all involve toll roads. Some roads require exact change to enter or exit via automated gates, and manned tollbooths will not accept any denomination bill higher than $20. So before you leave the airport, make sure you're armed with at least $3 in quarters and some lower-denomination currency.

5. RIDE-SHARE SERVICES   This somewhat controversial option is represented in Orlando by the companies **Uber** and **Lyft.** You start by downloading a service's app to your smartphone (Apple or Android) and registering an account with a form of payment. When you want to hail a ride, the app shows you what available drivers are nearby and estimates the time and cost to your destination. You can follow your car's progress via GPS, and you can add an optional gratuity through the app.

Uber and Lyft can pick you up and drop you off at the Orlando airport, as well as transport you around and between the theme park resorts. A four-passenger UberX or Lyft from the airport to Universal will cost about $30 (versus more than $45 for a traditional taxi), and UberX will provide a car seat for a few dollars more; a six-passenger UberXL or LyftPlus is around $40. Pickups for most ride-shares are on the airport's second level, the same as where passengers are picked up by family and friends; luxury ride-shares like UberSelect use the Express Pickup Tunnel near the rental car desks on level one.

If you've used Uber or Lyft elsewhere and are comfortable with them, consider using them for transportation around Orlando or back to the airport. We recommend Lyft over Uber. While both companies offer about the same service at about the same cost, Uber's surge pricing policy makes its fare estimates unreliable.

Dollars and Sense

Which option is the best deal depends on how many people are in your party and how much you value your time. If you're traveling solo or have only two in your party and you're pretty sure that you won't need a rental car, the shuttle is your least-expensive bet.

A cab for two makes sense if you want to get to your hotel faster than the shuttle can arrange. The cab will cost about $50–$55, including tip. That's $25–$28 per person. The shuttle will cost about $16 each one-way if you buy round-trip transfers, saving $9–$12. You must decide whether the cab's timeliness and convenience are worth the extra bucks.

A one-day car rental costs $40–$70, plus you have to take time to complete the paperwork, get the vehicle, and fill the tank before you return it. The more people you have in your group, the more economical the cab becomes over the shuttle. Likewise with the rental car, though the cab or ride share will get you there faster.

GETTING TO UNIVERSAL ORLANDO FROM WALT DISNEY WORLD

DRIVING FROM WALT DISNEY WORLD to Universal Orlando along I-4 takes about 15 minutes with light traffic, or as much as 40 minutes during rush hour. If you're staying at Walt Disney World and you don't have a car, **Mears Transportation** will shuttle you from your hotel to Universal and back for $21 ($16 for children ages 4–11). To schedule a shuttle, call ☎ 855-463-2776.

From three Denver college-aged women who tried Mears:

We took a Mears shuttle from Disney to Universal, and we don't recommend it. It takes a very long time to get you there—it stops at Sea-World and a couple of other places before Universal—plus we waited 45 minutes for the shuttle back to the hotel.

Taxis and ride-share services (**Uber** and **Lyft**) are also readily available to and from the resorts. A one-way taxi ride is $35–$45 (plus tip), depending on which Disney hotel you are leaving from, and may be cheaper than a shuttle if you have three to five people. A ride-share will cost about half that, and you can usually get picked up from any WDW hotel in less than 15 minutes. All transportation services drop off at and pick up from the lower level of Universal's main parking hub, from which you can walk to CityWalk and the parks. This family of five from Texas shares its positive experience getting to Universal from WDW via taxi:

It worked out cheaper for us to get a cab for five people than to hire a service like Mears or to rent a car for two days and pay for parking. We just walked to the front of our resort (Port Orleans River-side), they hailed a waiting cab/van, and off we went. At the end of the day at Universal, we walked to the cab drop-off and pickup, got right into a cab, and headed back to our resort.

UNIVERSAL PARTNER HOTEL CONNECTOR SHUTTLE

UNIVERSAL OFFERS FREE scheduled transportation to SeaWorld and Aquatica for its on-site hotel guests via the Universal Partner Hotel Connector Shuttle (sometimes referred to as the Super Star Shuttle, not to be confused with the paid SuperStar airport shuttle service previously discussed). Departure and return times are limited and are based on regular park operating hours; typically there are three outbound trips to SeaWorld and Aquatica in the morning and three returning runs in the evening. Boarding passes are required and available at the Ticket Center in each hotel lobby up to one day in advance and until 30 minutes prior to departure; guests with accessibility needs (including wheelchairs and service animals) must make a reservation 24 hours in advance. The shuttle picks up guests directly at Universal's Premier and Preferred hotels; guests at Cabana Bay and Aventura must transfer to the parking hub and catch the shuttle there. As with other free shuttles that service multiple hotels, your free ride may cost you valuable park time with its roundabout route; rope drop enthusiasts may want to rely on ride share or rental cars instead.

OFF-SITE HOTEL SHUTTLES

MANY INDEPENDENT HOTELS AND MOTELS near Universal Orlando provide free shuttle buses to the resort. Some properties participate in the same Universal Partner Hotel Connector Shuttle program that services SeaWorld and Aquatica for Universal's on-site hotel guests, while others operate their own transportation. The shuttles are fairly carefree, depositing you at the parking garages' central hub and saving you parking fees. The rub is that they might not get you there as early as you desire (a critical point if you take our touring advice) or be available when you wish to return to your lodging. Each service is different; check details before you make reservations.

Some shuttles go directly to Universal, while others stop at other hotels en route. This can be a problem if your hotel is the second or third stop on the route. During periods of high demand, buses frequently fill up at the first stop, leaving little or no room for passengers at subsequent stops. Before booking, inquire how many hotels are on the route and the sequence of the stops. The hotels are often so close together that you can easily walk to the first hotel on the route and board there. Similarly, if there's a large hotel nearby, it might have its own dedicated bus service that is more efficient. Use it instead of the service provided by your hotel. The majority of Universal-area shuttles work on a fixed schedule, typically with three or four departures in the morning and a similar or smaller number of returns around closing. Knowing exactly when a bus will depart makes it easier to plan your day.

At closing or during a hard rain, more people will be waiting for the shuttle than it can hold, and some will be left behind. Most shuttles return for stranded guests, but guests may wait 20 minutes to more than an hour.

If you're depending on shuttles, leave the park at least 45 minutes before closing. If you stay until closing and don't want the hassle of the shuttle, take a cab or request a ride share. Cab stands and guest pickup/drop-off are located on the lower level of the main parking hub, near the bus stops, and at each on-site hotel.

I-RIDE TROLLEY

THE **I-Ride Trolley** (☎ 407-248-9590; iridetrolley.com) is cheap, convenient transportation servicing the International Drive area. Trolley-shaped buses circulate from the Orlando Vineland Premium Outlets on the south side of town to the hotels near Universal on Major Boulevard, with stops at SeaWorld and the Orange County Convention Center along the way.

A single one-way fare costs $2 for adults ($1 for kids ages 3–9; $0.25 for seniors age 65 and older) and must be paid in cash using exact change. You can prepurchase unlimited ride passes for 1 day ($5) to 14 days ($18) via the website or at participating hotels and attractions listed at iridetrolley.com/passes.asp.

The only problem with the I-Ride Trolley is that it doesn't stop at Universal Orlando. The closest stop is at the DoubleTree hotel on the corner of Kirkman Road and Major Boulevard (marked G4 on the trolley route map). From there you can walk to the Universal parks (see below).

WALKING TO UNIVERSAL ORLANDO FROM YOUR HOTEL

UNIVERSAL ORLANDO has a number of nearby off-site hotels that are within walking distance of the resort's attractions. The closest off-site hotels to Universal are along Major Boulevard near the intersection with Kirkman Road, at the eastern entrance to Universal property. The DoubleTree hotel on this corner isn't much farther from Universal's parks than the on-site Portofino Bay. To reach the parks from this area, cross Kirkman at Major from the northeast corner (where a new pedestrian bridge is currently under construction), and follow the sidewalks to Universal Boulevard. Cross Universal Boulevard and turn left, and then walk to the escalators leading up to CityWalk from the valet parking circle. You should be able to walk the 0.5 mile from the DoubleTree to CityWalk in about 15 minutes.

Farther away, but still within walking distance, are the hotels and motels on International Drive near Universal Boulevard, neighboring Universal's Endless Summer Resort. This route requires walking north along Universal Boulevard, over the I-4 overpass, and into the bus and taxi parking loop on the lower level of the parking hub. While there are sidewalks and pedestrian traffic signals the entire way, this is at least a 0.75-mile walk alongside busy traffic and isn't recommended for families with young children.

THE PUBLIC TRANSPORTATION ALTERNATIVE

SOME OFF-SITE HOTEL SHUTTLES don't operate early enough to get you to the parks before opening. An alternative is the **LYNX** public bus system, which costs $2 (exact change required) for a single one-way fare, with discounted all-day, weekly, and monthly passes available for advance purchase online.

If you're staying in downtown Orlando, you can take the LYNX #21 or #40 bus from the central bus station to Universal's parking garage.

To reach Walt Disney World, take LYNX #40 from Universal and transfer at Grand National Drive onto #8 (or the I-Ride Trolley from Kirkman and Major) to SeaWorld, and then transfer to LYNX #50 to the Magic Kingdom's Transportation and Ticket Center. The buses begin running daily hours before the parks open to accommodate commuting employees, but service to Universal is limited after 8 p.m. on Fridays, weekends, and holidays. Precise hours of service vary depending on where along the route you are. Use the online trip planner at golynx .com or call ☎ 407-841-LYNX (5969) for travel information.

GETTING ORIENTED

PARKING AT UNIVERSAL ORLANDO

UNIVERSAL IS HOME to two massive multistory parking garages, holding a combined total of 20,000 cars. According to Forbes, they form the world's largest parking complex, dwarfing Disney Springs's 6,000-space garages. Signs route you from each of the five resort entrances to the parking structures.

The two rectangular garages lie along a north-south axis, with the pedestrian walkways leading to the theme parks running along the west, or long, side of each building. Sections are named for classic Universal movies and characters found in the parks: Jurassic Park, King Kong, and Jaws in the north garage, and E.T., Spider-Man, and Cat in the Hat in the south structure. The first numeral following the section name tells you on which deck level you are located, and the remaining numbers specify the row. So if a sign tells you that you're on King Kong 409, you're in the King Kong section on the fourth floor in row nine. We strongly recommend that you take a photo of the name and number of your section, level, and row.

unofficial **TIP**
When the tollbooths before the garages are backed up, the farthest left one is often the swiftest.

Guests driving to Universal Orlando's attractions have three parking options:

SELF PARKING   Parking in the main garage costs $25 for cars and $30 for RVs, trailers, and other large rigs. Regular parking is free for everyone after 6 p.m., except on Halloween Horror Nights when a fee is charged until 10 p.m. Parking is free for Preferred and Premier Annual Pass holders, and half price for Power Pass holders. Self parking is valid all day long, so if you want to leave the resort and return in the evening, just show your paid receipt at the parking booths for free reentry.

PRIME SELF PARKING   For $40, you will be parked on the garages' central level in the closest available section to the central hub. These spots are supposed to be the second closest to the parks, after the handicapped parking section. However, we've scored spaces just as good or better using the regular parking, especially when we've arrived before 10:30 a.m. Because the garages are two-thirds as wide as they are long, the farther your parking place is from the west side, the worse it will be. This is why prime parking is often not as close as regular parking—with the former, you'll be closer to the covered walkways to the parks, but if your particular space is toward the east side of the garage, you'll end up farther away than a guest who chose regular parking and was assigned a space closer to the west side of the structure.

An advantage of prime parking, however, is that you'll park faster because the ratio of cars choosing prime to regular is about 1 to 13. If you are picking prime, a piece of paper will be tucked under your windshield wiper at the tollbooth, and you'll be asked to turn your hazard blinkers on before following signs to the prime parking section. Prime parking is free for Premier Annual Pass holders and costs $10 for Preferred Pass holders. Cars rented from Avis and Budget at Orlando International Airport include vouchers for a free upgrade to prime with paid standard parking.

VOLCANO BAY PARKING   There is no dedicated guest parking at Volcano Bay itself. Instead, visitors pay the usual rates to park on the first level of the southern parking structure used by other Universal theme park guests. Stay in the marked lanes when approaching the parking garage tollbooths and follow the signs for Volcano Bay parking.

VALET PARKING   In addition to the self-parking garages, valet parking is available at CityWalk for $25 for a visit of up to 2 hours, or $50 for longer than that ($45 if arriving after 6 p.m.). Red Carpet Valet costs $60 ($55 if arriving after 6 p.m.) and guarantees that your car will be kept close for a quick exit at the end of your evening. The entrance to the valet parking circle is on Universal Boulevard, across the street from the parking garages' taxi and bus loop. After dropping off your car, ascend the escalator adjacent to the miniature golf course and turn right to enter the CityWalk complex. Forgo valet parking if you're headed to Volcano Bay because you'll have to backtrack through the parking hub to reach the buses.

Premier Pass holders valet park for free (tip not included) or can upgrade to Red Carpet for $20; Preferred Pass holders can valet for $20, or use Red Carpet for $35. Pass holder valet discounts aren't valid on July 4, December 31, or Mardi Gras and Halloween event nights after 7 p.m., but Premier Pass holders can valet on event nights for just $20 if they prepay when dropping off. Select CityWalk restaurants will validate for up to 2 hours of valet if you eat lunch Monday–Friday, 11 a.m.–2 p.m. Stay past 2 hours and you'll be charged full freight. And be warned that if you imbibe too much and have to leave your car at valet overnight, you'll have to pay a $60 fine in the morning.

Dropping off your car is usually quick, and our favorite unadvertised feature of the valet circle is its private security checkpoint, which usually has little wait. But beware that retrieving your car at the end of the evening can sometimes take up to half an hour, especially after a concert or special event in CityWalk or the parks. Premier Pass holders, Red Carpet guests, and anyone else who prepays can cut the line by using the automated kiosks to the right of the valet windows; just scan your parking ticket and pass or receipt for priority vehicle retrieval.

Guest Drop-Off

If you aren't parking at the resort but only dropping off passengers, find the Universal Boulevard entrance to the taxi and bus loop beneath the central parking hub, across the street from valet parking. This is also the best spot to pick up departing guests at the end of the day. Some guests try to use the valet parking circle for this purpose, but it is officially not permitted.

Another option is to drop off at the lobby of the Hard Rock Hotel, which is a short walk from Universal Studios Florida's front gates if you cut through the pool. However, you can't backtrack through the pool at the end of the day without a resort key card.

Speaking of the hotels, don't attempt to save money by parking at one of the resorts. Unless you are eating at a hotel restaurant that validates, off-site guests are charged a hefty fee for parking at the hotels.

SECURITY SCREENINGS AT UNIVERSAL ORLANDO

CENTRAL FLORIDA'S THEME PARKS use uniformed and undercover security to screen and monitor guests entering their parks. Every single guest arriving at Universal Orlando must either pass through a full-body scanner or be screened with a hand-held detection wand, and also submit any bags for inspection, before continuing on to CityWalk and the parks.

On a busy day, the crowd queuing for inspection in the parking garage rotunda may appear mind-boggling at first glance, but fortunately there is a phalanx of scanning machines, and Universal's security team could teach the TSA a thing or two about courtesy and efficiency. If you really hate to start your day with waiting, arrive extra early, or opt for valet parking, which has its own dedicated screening checkpoint. Guests staying at the resort hotels will be inspected before boarding the water taxis, and additional security screens pedestrians on the pathways near Margaritaville and Hard Rock Hotel.

Volcano Bay guests get screened at a dedicated security checkpoint on the garage's bottom floor before boarding special shuttle buses that transport them along dedicated lanes to Volcano Bay's entrance. Hotel guests (and day guests on slower days) are screened by security upon arriving at the water park's bus stop. The entire process is not particularly pleasant and can be time-consuming, so arrive on Universal property 45–60 minutes before you want to actually get to Volcano Bay.

We've rarely experienced a serious issue with Universal's security procedures, but some guests (like this reader from Waipahu, Hawaii) found their efforts intrusive:

> *Security checks at the hotel prior to getting on the boat shuttle are the most thorough I've been through (more than TSA). On my last day I encountered an employee who was overzealous in her checks and left me feeling very uncomfortable, and I heard others comment the same.*

FINDING YOUR WAY AROUND

THERE ARE NO PARKING TRAMS, so depending on where in the garage your car is parked, you'll have an 8- to 20-minute hike to the theme park entrances. From the garages, (sometimes) moving sidewalks deliver you first to the central hub between the two garages. In this area, you'll find wheelchair rentals, a snack and souvenir stand, and escalators leading down to bus and taxi parking. To proceed to CityWalk and the parks, you'll need to pass through the aforementioned security screening checkpoint. To reach Volcano Bay, follow signs to park on the lowest level of the south garage, where you'll find ticket booths, security screenings, and dedicated shuttle buses that will transport you to and from the water park.

unofficial **TIP**
You can cut through the Quiet Flight Surf Shop (which exits into The Island Clothing Co.) as a shortcut to Universal Studios Florida.

Upon exiting the parking structure, you'll pass the Universal Cinemark on your right and Starbucks (always open early for that essential morning caffeine jolt) on your left before reaching CityWalk's central plaza. From here, you walk straight toward the lighthouse to reach the main entrance of Islands of Adventure, or bear right at the Fossil store toward the big globe for Universal Studios Florida's front gate.

TRANSPORTATION BETWEEN UNIVERSAL RESORTS AND PARKS

UNIVERSAL OFFERS WATER TAXI SERVICE between each of its Preferred and Premier hotels and the two theme parks. The boat service uses a dock in CityWalk near the bridge to Universal Studios Florida as a hub, which is great if you're going from one of the hotels to a theme park. If you're traveling between hotels for a meal, however, you'll need to switch boats. Boats depart about every 15 minutes, from 1 hour before Early Park Admission begins until after CityWalk shuts down at 2 a.m.; allow 20–25 minutes for each leg of your journey by boat.

Universal also offers an evening shuttle bus service that circulates every 30 minutes between its on-site hotels during dinnertime (6–10 p.m.), which is often faster than its boats for getting from one resort to another; tell the driver your destination when boarding. In addition, Minion-themed buses frequently run between Cabana Bay Beach Resort and Aventura Hotel and the parking hub, from which you must walk to CityWalk or the theme parks. All of the hotels also offer free shuttle buses to Volcano Bay, except Cabana Bay and Aventura, which provide pedestrian access to the water park. Don't attempt to park at Cabana Bay or Aventura and walk to Volcano Bay if you aren't a registered guest; day visitors are charged $45 for self-parking, and key cards are inspected at the exclusive hotel entrance.

Finally, walking from any resort hotel to either theme park takes a maximum of about 15 minutes using the resort's beautifully landscaped (though frustratingly winding) garden pathways. Hard Rock Hotel is the closest to the parks, being only steps away from

Universal Studios Florida's front gates, while Portofino and Cabana Bay are the farthest. To walk between Portofino and Cabana Bay takes 30–40 minutes.

You'll find more about Universal Orlando resort transportation in Part Two (see page 78).

LEAVING UNIVERSAL ORLANDO

AT THE END OF YOUR VISIT, retrace your steps to your vehicle and follow directional signage to depart the resort. From the south garage, you have little option but to follow the arrows to I-4 or International Drive. If you exit the north garage onto Universal Boulevard, you can reach I-4 West by turning right onto Major Boulevard and then right onto Kirkman Road; reach I-4 East by making a U-turn onto Universal Boulevard southbound at Major Boulevard, and then turn left onto the interstate after passing the garage. Practice deep breathing if you're departing with the masses at park closing on a crowded day because the backups on the parking garages' exit ramps may induce road rage.

PART FOUR

BARE NECESSITIES

▌▌ MONEY, ETC.

ATMS AND BANKING SERVICES

BANKING AT UNIVERSAL ORLANDO is limited to ATMs, which are marked on the park maps. There are a half dozen ATMs in each theme park, plus three in CityWalk, one in each hotel, and one at Volcano Bay. Most major banking networks are accepted.

The closest full-service bank to Universal Orlando is the Regions Bank at the corner of Kirkman and Vineland Roads (5401 S. Kirkman Road).

USF ATM LOCATIONS	IOA ATM LOCATIONS	CITYWALK ATM LOCATIONS	VOLCANO BAY ATM LOCATIONS
Outside the park entrance to the right of the Guest Services window	Outside the park entrance to the right of the Guest Services window	Downstairs to the left of the Guest Services window	Outside Volcano Bay to the right of the main entrance
Front Lot near First Aid and Lost and Found	Marvel Super Hero Island near The Amazing Adventures of Spider-Man	Upstairs by the second-level exit of the movie theater	
New York near Revenge of the Mummy	Jurassic Park by the exit of Jurassic Park River Adventure	To the left of The Groove	
Outside Diagon Alley to the right of King's Cross Station	Hogsmeade outside of the Three Broomsticks		
World Expo at the *Fear Factor Live* restrooms	Lost Continent outside Mythos Restaurant		
Springfield: Home of the Simpsons along Fast Food Boulevard			

CHECKS

UNIVERSAL ORLANDO ONLY ACCEPTS personal checks that are preprinted, are drawn on US banks, and are made out for the exact amount of the purchase, and they are only accepted at the front gate. A valid photo ID is required, and your check will be submitted to an online verification system.

Traveler's checks in US currency are accepted throughout the resort but must be signed by the bearer in front of the cashier and be presented with photo ID.

Business checks, cashier's checks, and school checks are only accepted if they are drawn on US banks, are preprinted, are made out for the exact amount of purchase, and are presented with photo ID.

CREDIT CARDS

AMERICAN EXPRESS, DINERS CLUB, DISCOVER CARD, Master-Card, and Visa are accepted throughout the Universal Orlando Resort. The hotels also accept Japanese Credit Bureau and Carte Blanche. Most point-of-sale registers at Universal now feature the more-secure chip scanners and offer tap-to-pay transactions for mobile devices, such as ApplePay.

American Express is the official card of Universal Orlando, and members get several discounts and perks, including access to a private **American Express VIP Lounge** hidden behind the Classic Monsters Cafe near the front of Universal Studios Florida (USF); look for the door to the left of the Shrek meet and greet. Inside you'll find free bottled water, potato chips, granola bars, and smartphone charging stations, as well as air-conditioning and a respite from the crowds. In addition, a full-time concierge inside can assist you with information or reservations. The lounge is open daily, noon–5 p.m., and up to six people can enter per American Express card. Technically, you must have purchased your Universal admission (park-to-park tickets or annual pass) with your American Express, and your purchase history may be inspected for verification. If you don't yet have an AmEx card, you can stop by its membership center next to security in the parking hub and receive free Universal Express Passes or Quick-Service Dining Plans in exchange for filling out an application. For additional details and current discounts, visit tinyurl.com /UniAmEx or download the "Amex Special Offers" tab inside Universal's smartphone app.

CURRENCY EXCHANGE

EXCHANGE YOUR EUROS, KRONER, OR ZLOTYS for good ol' American greenbacks (the only form of cash accepted at Universal Orlando) at either theme park's Guest Services window, or at any hotel front desk. There may be a daily limit on how much you can exchange (around $500), and a nominal transaction surcharge applies.

A LICENSE TO PRINT MONEY

AFTER DECADES OF WATCHING DISNEY literally mint money with its **Disney Dollars** (which were discontinued in 2016), Universal got into the currency game with **Gringotts Wizarding Bank Notes.** Available exclusively at the Gringotts Money Exchange shop in USF's Diagon Alley, these handsome bills are available in $10 or $20 denominations, and there is no extra fee to exchange your Muggle money for some.

The bank notes can be redeemed virtually anywhere on Universal Orlando property (even for valet parking) at a one-for-one exchange rate. While you won't lose any money on Wizarding currency as long as you spend it before leaving the resort, most guests (intentionally or unintentionally) take them home as souvenirs, making a healthy profit for Universal's goblin accountants. Less magical credit card–style Universal Orlando gift cards with various designs are also sold (in $5 increments up to $500) and accepted all around the resort; you can buy them online at universalorlando.com/web/en/us/gift-cards/index.html.

SALES TAX

A COMBINED STATE AND LOCAL SALES TAX of 6.5% applies to all purchases made at Universal Orlando. Hotels also charge a 6% Orange County occupancy tax, for a total of 12.5%. All prices listed in this book are before tax, unless otherwise noted.

PROBLEMS *and* UNUSUAL SITUATIONS

ATTRACTION CLOSURES

FIND OUT IN ADVANCE what rides and attractions are scheduled to be closed for repair during your visit. For complete refurbishment schedules, check online at Universal's official operating calendar (tinyurl.com/unihrs) and TouringPlans' Universal Orlando closures page (touringplans.com/universal-orlando/closures), or use the mobile app Lines.

Universal's attractions are technically complex, so it's almost inevitable that you will experience some unscheduled downtime during your visit. If a ride is temporarily closed, ask the attendants outside if there is an estimated reopening time (usually they can't tell you) and continue with your touring, returning later if possible. If a ride stops running while you are already in the queue, decide whether to stay based on how long the posted wait was when you entered and how much time you've already invested. Most "brief operational delays" are resolved in about 15 minutes, but there are no guarantees.

If a ride halts unexpectedly while you are on it, remain calm and rest assured that Universal has extremely safe evacuation procedures for every contingency. Stay seated and listen for announcements, and be patient because employees may need to evacuate ride vehicles one at a time in a specific order. On the plus side, you may get an exclusive backstage view of how the ride operates, and you should be offered either an immediate re-ride (if the attraction resumes operating) or a return ticket to let you skip the standby line later on.

CAR TROUBLE

UNIVERSAL ORLANDO OFFERS complimentary vehicle assistance—including battery jumps—to guests parked in its garage. Raise your car's hood (if possible) and flag down a parking attendant, or use one of the security call boxes located in each parking section.

If you have more serious car trouble, the nearest repair facility is the **Universal Service Center** in the Speedway gas station located on the west side of Universal property at 5989 Turkey Lake Road (☎ 407-345-4860; universalservicecenter.net).

GASOLINE

THERE IS ONE SPEEDWAY GAS STATION on Universal property. It is on the west side of the resort, adjacent to the corporate offices and employee parking lot. The address is 5981 Turkey Lake Road. From the guest parking garages, take Hollywood Way west to Turkey Lake Road; turn right, and the station will be ahead on your right.

CELL PHONE SNAFUS

CELL PHONE SERVICE CAN BE SPOTTY at Universal Orlando, especially on days of high attendance. Cell and Wi-Fi coverage is especially poor inside Volcano Bay, so lock the phone away and bring a book for the beach. A woman from Leawood, Kansas, tells it like it is:

In our group, we were using three different carriers, and we all had problems sending and receiving texts and calls.

The problem of signal strength is compounded by crowd noise and the ambient music played throughout the parks. Even if you have a decent signal, it's an exasperating challenge to find some place quiet enough to have a conversation. When possible, opt for texting.

Smartphone data speeds can be especially sluggish when the park is packed with guests trying to Facebook over LTE. Luckily, Universal's Wi-Fi service is free and fairly stable throughout the theme parks and CityWalk; you can even get decent reception inside Gringotts' vaults. Log into "xfinitywifi" and accept the nonsubscriber agreement before opening your browser or social media apps. You may have to log in again every day or so.

LOST AND FOUND

IF YOU LOSE (OR FIND) SOMETHING in USF, go to the Lost and Found counter to the right of the main gate as you enter. At Islands of Adventure (IOA), Lost and Found is located near stroller rental to the left of the park's entrance. At Volcano Bay visit Guest Services at the front of the park. If you discover your loss after you've left the park(s), call ☎ 407-224-4233 and choose option 2.

It's better not to lose anything in the first place, but if you do, there is hope: we've had an excellent track record with Universal's Lost and Found, which has recovered errant hats and keys for us over the years.

MEDICAL MATTERS

HEADACHE RELIEF Sample sizes of some over-the-counter medications are available for free from the First Aid Stations. For the locations of the

First Aid Stations in the parks and CityWalk, see page 154. Aspirin and other sundries are sold at the Universal Studios Store in USF, at Islands of Adventure Trading Co. in IOA, and at Krakatoa Katy's in Volcano Bay; they are held behind the counter, so you must ask an employee for them.

ILLNESSES REQUIRING MEDICAL ATTENTION   Off property, the closest walk-in clinic is **Centra Care** (8014 Conroy Windermere Road; ☎ 407-291-8975; centracare.org). The clinic is open Monday–Friday, 8 a.m.–8 p.m., and Saturday–Sunday, 8 a.m.–5 p.m.; Centra Care also operates a 24-hour physician house call service and runs a free shuttle (call ☎ 407-938-0650 to arrange pickup).

The Medical Concierge (☎ 855-932-5252; themedicalconcierge .com) has board-certified physicians available 24-7 for house calls to your hotel room. It offers in-room X-rays and IV therapy service, as well as same-day dental and specialist appointments. It also rents medical equipment. Insurance receipts, insurance billing, and foreign-language interpretation are provided. Walk-in clinics are also available. You can also inquire about transportation arrangements.

DOCS (Doctors on Call Service; ☎ 407-399-3627; doctorson callservice.com) offers 24-hour house call service. All physicians are certified by the American Board of Medical Specialties. A father of two from O'Fallon, Illinois, gives them a thumbs-up:

My wife's cold developed into an ear infection that required medical attention, and DOCS was able to respond in 40 minutes. The doctor had medicine with him and was very professional and friendly.

Physician Room Service (☎ 407-238-2000; physicianroomservice .com) provides board-certified doctor house calls to Universal Orlando–area guest rooms for adults and children. In case of a life-and-death emergency, the nearest fully equipped emergency room is at **Dr. Phillips Hospital** (9400 Turkey Lake Road; ☎ 407-351-8500).

DENTAL NEEDS   Call **Celebration Dental Group** (☎ 407-351-9704; celebrationdentalgroup.com), located at 6001 Vineland Road, Ste. 106.

PRESCRIPTION MEDICINE   The nearest pharmacy to Universal Orlando is **Walgreens** (☎ 407-248-0315) at 5501 Kirkman Road, in the shopping plaza across from the resort. Google will tell you that there is a Walgreens at 1000 Universal Studios Plaza, but that is a backstage clinic for employees only. **Turner Drugs** (☎ 407-828-8125; turnerdrug .com) charges $15 to deliver a filled prescription to your hotel's front desk ($7.50 for Disney hotels).

Sergeant Blisterblaster's Guide To Happy Feet

1. ON YOUR FEET!   You can easily log 5–10 miles a day at the Universal Orlando parks, and a reader told us she clocked 13.5 (more than a half-marathon!), so now is the time to shape up. Start with short walks around the neighborhood. Increase your distance gradually until you can do 6 miles without CPR.

2. A-TEN-SHUN!   During your training program, pay attention when those puppies growl. They'll give you a lot of information about your feet and the appropriateness of your shoes. Listen up! No walking in flip-flops, loafers, or sandals. Wear well-constructed, broken-in running or hiking shoes. If you feel a hot spot, that means a blister is developing. The most common sites for blisters are heels, toes, and balls of the feet. If you develop a hot spot in the same place every time you walk (a clue!), cover it with a blister bandage before you set out.

3. SOCK IT UP, TRAINEE!   Good socks are as important as good shoes. When you walk, your feet sweat like a mule in a peat bog, and the moisture only increases friction. To minimize friction, wear a pair of socks, such as Smartwool or Coolmax, that wicks perspiration away from your feet (Smartwool makes socks of varying thicknesses). To further combat moisture, dust your dogs with antifungal talcum powder.

4. WHO DO YOU THINK YOU ARE? JOHN WAYNE?   Don't be a hero. Take care of a foot problem the minute you notice it. Carry a small foot-emergency kit for your platoon. Include gauze, antibiotic ointment, moleskin, and blister bandages. Extra socks and talcum powder are optional.

5. BITE THE BULLET!   If you develop a hot spot, cover it ASAP with a blister bandage. If you develop a blister, air out and dry your foot. Clean the area with antibiotic ointment and place a blister bandage over the blister. The bandages come in several sizes, including specially shaped ones for fingers and toes; they're also good for covering hot spots. If you don't have blister bandages, don't cover the hot spot or blister with adhesive bandages; they'll slip and wad up. Moleskin, the old-fashioned hiker's standby for covering blisters, can still be useful for lining the roughened inner surface of shoe heels and toes to prevent further foot damage.

6. TAKE CARE OF YOUR PLATOON.   If you have young, green troops in your outfit, they might not sound off when a hot spot develops. Stop several times a day and check their feet. If you forgot your emergency kit and a problem arises, visit the park's First Aid. It will have all the stuff you need to keep your command in action.

RAIN

WEATHER BAD? GO TO THE PARKS anyway. The crowds are lighter, and most attractions and waiting areas are under cover. Showers, especially during warmer months, are short and frequently occur in the late afternoon around 4 p.m.

If picking among the parks, know that USF is a much better park to tour in the rain, as almost all of its headliner attractions (except Hollywood Rip Ride Rockit) are indoors. While the many outdoor attractions at IOA can operate in a moderate downpour, they must all shut down when lightning is in the vicinity. That leaves Harry Potter and the Forbidden Journey, The Amazing Adventures of Spider-Man, Reign of Kong, and Cat in the Hat as virtually the only rides at IOA that

unofficial **TIP**
Raingear isn't always displayed in shops, so you may have to ask for it.

can operate during severe weather. Volcano Bay will let you keep swimming in a moderate rain, but as soon as lightning is detected in the vicinity, everyone must get out of the water. Many guests will flee when a downpour starts, but you should find some shelter and stay put (hey, you came here to get wet, right?). Once the weather clears, you'll have all the slides to yourself, making poststorm summer afternoons the best time to enjoy the water park without crowds.

Ponchos are $10 for adults and $9 for children; umbrellas cost $12–$20. All ponchos sold at Universal Orlando are made of clear plastic (though ones sold within The Wizarding World have a special insignia), so picking out somebody in your party on a rainy day can be tricky. Stores such as Target sell inexpensive solid-color ponchos that will make your family bright beacons in a plastic-covered sea of humanity.

A Wilmington, North Carolina, mom thinks high-quality raingear is worth the investment:

> *It rained every day on our trip, driving many people out of the parks and leaving others looking miserable in their ponchos. Meanwhile, we hardly noticed the rain from inside our high-end rain jackets as we walked right on to many of the attractions.*

Some unusually heavy rain precipitated (no pun intended) dozens of reader suggestions for dealing with soggy days. The best came from this Memphis, Tennessee, mom:

1. *Raingear should include ponchos and umbrellas. When rain isn't beating down on your ponchoed head, it's easier to ignore.*

2. *Buy blue ponchos at Walgreens. We could keep track of each other more easily because we had blue ponchos instead of clear ones.*

3. *If you're using a stroller, bring a plastic sheet or extra poncho to protect it from rain. (Ponchos cover only single strollers.) Carry a towel in a plastic bag to wipe off your stroller after experiencing an attraction during a rainfall.*

Unofficial Guide researcher Connie Wolosyk adds, "It helps to wear a baseball cap under the poncho hood—without it, the hood never covers your head properly, and your face always gets wet."

HOW TO LODGE A COMPLAINT WITH UNIVERSAL

GUEST SERVICES at the front of each Universal park will be happy to listen to any complaints and will be even happier to pass along praise for any exceptional employees you encounter. Minor problems are often addressed with a sincere apology and a pass to skip an attraction queue. You usually will find Universal folks highly responsive to guests' issues. However, a more global gripe, or one beyond an on-site manager's ability to resolve, is likely to founder in the labyrinth of Universal bureaucracy. To contact Guest Services after your trip, use the email contact form at visitorsatisfaction.com/contactus.

SERVICES

CELEBRATION BUTTONS

CELEBRATING A BIRTHDAY, ANNIVERSARY, honeymoon, engagement, or Bat Mitzvah at Universal? Or just celebrating the fact that its your first visit to the parks? Stop by Guest Services for a free celebration button to wear during your special day. Buttons come in "It's My Birthday!" and more generic "I'm Celebrating!" varieties. At a minimum, you'll have employees (and fellow guests) shouting you warm wishes all day long. And if you're lucky, you might find yourself treated to preferred seating, a special meet and greet, or other unexpected perks, as this Endicott, New York, reader happily discovered:

> *A birthday button earned many greetings, two free deserts, and a free drink.*

CELL PHONE CHARGING

UNIVERSAL ORLANDO HAS NOT permanently installed any dedicated cell phone charging stations in the parks, so pack a power cable and wall plug if you want to steal juice from accessible outlets you find along the way. The exception is the American Express VIP Lounge discussed previously, which stocks charging adapters for most Apple and Android devices (including micro-USB and Lightning). If you prefer to charge on the go, we use Jackery external batteries for our devices, available on amazon.com.

Universal has experimented with renting precharged Go Puck 5x battery packs from MIB Gear in USF and Island Market & Export in IOA. They rent for $20 per day (with an $80 credit card hold for deposit), but you can buy one online for under $60, so we don't recommend it unless you are desperate to replenish.

FIRST AID

EACH PARK HAS A Walgreens-sponsored first aid center. In USF, it's located on Canal Street behind Louie's Italian Restaurant, on the border between New York and San Francisco. In IOA, it is in the Lost Continent near The Mystic Fountain; look for the red cross behind the coin vendor. In both parks, the Family Services nursing facilities and companion restroom are right next to First Aid. Volcano Bay's First Aid is just inside the park entrance. CityWalk's first aid facility is located near Guest Services, at the end of the hallway behind Cold Stone Creamery. Guests who use the service are generally very positive about it; Seth once sought treatment for a minor flesh wound and was patched up and riding rides again in a matter of minutes.

GROCERIES

EACH UNIVERSAL RESORT HOTEL has a shop or food court selling sundries, snacks, and grab-and-go breakfast foods. While their locations make them undeniably convenient, the selection is poor, and you'll find the prices higher and more frightening than Doctor Doom's Fearfall. For down-to-earth prices, try **Publix,** located north of Universal at the intersection of Kirkman and Conroy Roads (4606 S. Kirkman Road; ☎ 407-293-7673), or for fancier fare visit **Whole Foods,** located southwest of Universal on Sand Lake Road near I-4 (8003 Turkey Lake Road; ☎ 407-355-7100).

If you don't have a car or you don't want to take the time to go to the supermarket, **Orlando Grocery Express** (orlandogroceryexpress .com) and **WeGoShop.com** will both shop for you and deliver your groceries. The best way to compile your order for either is online before you leave home. Orlando Grocery Express's website lets you select from a wide selection of items (listed with photos and prices), while WeGoShop simply takes your typed shopping list to the grocery store you request and buys at market rates. Both deliver to all on-site Universal resorts, but Orlando Grocery Express requires Hard Rock Hotel, Sapphire Falls, and Cabana Bay guests to be present 9–11 a.m. to accept delivery in person; Portofino Bay and Royal Pacific will hold deliveries at bell service. Orlando Grocery Express charges a flat $14 delivery with a $40 minimum order; orders over $200 are delivered free. WeGoShop charges on a sliding scale, from $21 for up to a $50 grocery bill, to 15% of the total for bills over $300; a $3 fuel surcharge is levied on all orders, and a 15% mandatory gratuity is added for deliveries left at bell services. Finally, Amazon Prime subscribers can try ordering groceries through **Prime Now Pantry** (primenow.amazon.com). The selection is limited and there's a $20 minimum per order, but delivery is free within a 2-hour window, and 1-hour delivery is available. You must be present for delivery of perishables, alcohol, or orders over $500.

LOCKERS

WHEN VISITING UNIVERSAL'S PARKS, we try to pare down our gear to a bare minimum and only bring those necessities that fit comfortably in our pockets: admission, ID, a credit card or cash, and a cell phone. Many guests keep their tickets handy in a plastic lanyard (readily available around the resort for around $9 and up), and Seth swears by cargo shorts with zippered pockets, for function if not fashion. However, many guests (especially those accompanying young children or those with special needs) find that they simply can't travel that light. When your burden becomes too much to bear, make a beeline for a bank of lockers and lighten your load.

Incidentally, Universal strictly enforces its restrictions on what items guests are allowed to bring into its parks. Obviously, any form of weapon or illegal substance is prohibited, as is clothing with "offensive language or content" or that "represents someone as emergency personnel." You are also disallowed from entering with large duffel bags, folding chairs, beach umbrellas, or hard-sided coolers. Packing picnics is officially prohibited; however, you may bring bottled water and small snacks, along with any medically necessary nutritional items and baby food, as long as it is nonalcoholic, is not in glass containers, and is carried in a soft-sided cooler or bag no bigger than 8½ inches by 6 inches by 6 inches. There are also no facilities for refrigerating or reheating outside food in the park. Keep in mind that all items are subject to inspection before entering CityWalk, so be prepared to open your bags at the security checkpoint.

All of Universal Orlando's lockers are automated and use a computerized locking system. The locker banks are easy to find, and each bank has a small touch screen computer in the center. Begin by approaching a locker computer, selecting your language, and touching RENT A LOCKER. (When the sun is bright, the screen is almost impossible to read, so have someone block the sun or use a different computer.) After selecting your language and locker type or location (if applicable), most lockers ask you to press your thumb onto the keypad and have your fingerprint scanned. We've seen people walk away cursing at this step, having repeated it over and over with no success. Don't press down too hard—the computer can't read your thumbprint that way. Instead, take a deep breath and lightly place your thumb on the scanner. The newest lockers (currently located at The Incredible Hulk Coaster and Revenge of the Mummy) scan your admission ticket instead of your thumb. This method is far faster and more reliable, so we're happy to see that the finger scanners are being phased out as more lockers are converted to this system.

After you scan your thumb or ticket, you'll receive a locker number. Commit it to memory, or write it down! Place your property in the indicated locker, which should have a flashing green light, and press the illuminated button after you have closed the door to lock it.

When you are ready to retrieve your belongings, go to the same kiosk machine, select REOPEN YOUR LOCKER, enter your locker number, and scan your thumb or ticket again. Remember that only the person who used his or her thumb to get the locker can retrieve anything from it. The locker should relinquish its contents; if you have any trouble, find a nearby employee to assist.

Universal Orlando offers three types of lockers, described on the following pages.

Paid All-Day Lockers

These lockers charge one flat rate for a full day and can be opened and relocked as many times as you like during your visit using a six-digit code that you select. All-day lockers in the theme parks come in two categories: regular (approximately 9½ inches wide by 16 inches high by 15½ inches deep) for $10 per day, or roomier family size (approximately 12½ inches wide by 16 inches high by 23½ inches deep) for $12 per day. Lockers inside Volcano Bay cost $8–$15 per day, depending on size, and are controlled with the TapuTapu wristbands. Volcano Bay has four locker facilities arrayed around the park's perimeter, plus one outside the entrance; see page 348 for details.

All-day lockers can be found in the following locations:

UNIVERSAL STUDIOS FLORIDA ALL-DAY LOCKERS
• Next to the Studio Audience Center inside the front gate (regular size)
• Behind the restrooms near the Studio Audience Center (family size)
• Near the exit turnstiles, next to wheelchair and stroller rental (regular size)
ISLANDS OF ADVENTURE ALL-DAY LOCKERS
• Inside the front gate near wheelchair and stroller rental (regular and family size)

Free Short-Term Lockers

Universal enforces a mandatory locker system at its big thrill rides. Lockers outside these attractions are free for an amount of time that varies with the length of the standby line. So if the line is 30 minutes, for example, and the ride itself is 10 minutes, you get 40 minutes plus a small cushion of about 15 minutes. The lockers then cost $3 for each 30 minutes after that, with a $20 daily maximum.

The free lockers at most attractions are slightly smaller than the standard paid all-day lockers (approximately 9½ inches wide by 11½ inches high by 15½ inches deep). The newer ticket-scanning lockers at The Incredible Hulk Coaster and Revenge of the Mummy come in two varieties. A limited number are the same size as the older biometric ones, but most are half-size (approximately 12 inches wide by 5 inches high by 15½ inches deep) and barely large enough for a few cell phones and wallets, as this reader from Brooklyn, New York, was frustrated to find:

> I wish I had known how SMALL the mandatory lockers at Universal are. I was very frustrated trying to fit my bag into the lockers, which are seemingly designed to fit only a small backpack or purse.

Free short-term lockers are located at the following attractions:

UNIVERSAL STUDIOS FLORIDA FREE SHORT-TERM LOCKERS	
• Harry Potter and the Escape from Gringotts	• Hollywood Rip Ride Rockit
• Men in Black Alien Attack • Revenge of the Mummy	
ISLANDS OF ADVENTURE FREE SHORT-TERM LOCKERS	
• Harry Potter and the Forbidden Journey • The Incredible Hulk Coaster	

On most of the aforementioned rides, all bags, purses, and other objects too large to be secured in a pocket must be placed in a free locker during your ride; wallets, phones, and compact cameras are generally permitted, as are small hip belts or fanny packs that can be securely fastened and tucked beneath a shirt.

Universal strictly enforces a "no loose items" policy at The Incredible Hulk Coaster and Hollywood Rip Ride Rockit. At these rides, guests are required to pass through an airport-style security screening (complete with walk-through metal detectors and electronic scanning wands) to ensure no phones, keys, or even spare change enter the queue. You should be permitted to keep your prescription eyeglasses and ticket lanyard.

If the ride breaks down while you are in line and you exceed your free usage period through no fault of your own, a locker attendant can override the charge on request. You may need to be firm to avoid paying an overage fee, as this reader found:

> Watch out for the MIB lockers. We went over our allotted time because of ride issues, but the [attendant] kept insisting that we had to pay. Only after standing our ground did the [attendant] finally check with others and confirm that there were ride issues.

When you want to ride a thrill ride but don't want to bother with a locker, you can use each attraction's child-swap area (see page 188) as a bag swap, and leave a nonrider with your belongings. This is an especially useful technique for the Harry Potter rides because the free lockers are too small to hold some wand boxes from Ollivanders (at 19 inches, the Rowan, Oak, and Alder boxes are all too long), and the locker banks for Forbidden Journey and Gringotts are frequently overcrowded.

Paid Short-Term Lockers

Universal does not enforce mandatory locker usage on its water rides, but it does conveniently (or capitalistically) provide paid short-term lockers outside each attraction that is likely to soak you and your belongings. The lockers are the same size as the free ones (approximately 9½ inches wide by 11½ inches high by 15½ inches deep) and operate identically. The difference is that they cost $4 for the first 90 minutes, and $3 for each additional hour after that, with a $20 daily maximum.

Paid short-term lockers are located only at IOA at the following attractions:

ISLANDS OF ADVENTURE PAID SHORT-TERM LOCKERS
• Dudley Do-Right's Ripsaw Falls   • Jurassic Park River Adventure
• Popeye & Bluto's Bilge-Rat Barges

PACKAGE PICKUP AND DELIVERY

COMPLIMENTARY PACKAGE PICKUP is available at USF and IOA. Ask the salesperson to send your purchases to Package Pickup. When you leave the park, they'll be waiting for you. At USF, Package Pickup is at the It's a Wrap gift shop immediately adjacent to the exit turnstiles. At IOA, it is at Port Provisions at the park exit. Volcano Bay does not hold packages until the end of the day but will deliver merchandise to on-site hotel rooms.

If you're staying at a Universal Orlando resort, you can also have the packages delivered directly to your hotel room by the following day for free. If you're leaving within 24 hours, however, take them with you or use the in-park pickup location.

If you get home and realize you missed an essential souvenir, shop for Universal Orlando tchotchkes online at shop.universalorlando.com.

PET CARE

UNIVERSAL ORLANDO'S KENNEL FACILITY boards dogs and cats (no exotic or native species allowed) on a first-come, first-serve basis. You can find the facility by following the signs to RV and camper parking after passing through the tollbooths; the kennel is located on the corner of the oversize parking lot. The kennel opens at 8 a.m. and does not take reservations. The cost is $15 per pet, per day. All cats and dogs under 39 pounds are kept indoors in air-conditioning. Dogs weighing 39 pounds and up are kept outdoors with shade and fans.

An attendant remains on duty at the kennel until 2 hours after the last park closes, but you can retrieve your pet until 3 a.m. by using the phone outside the kennel to call for assistance. The kennel provides water, but you need to bring your own food and toys and return to walk your dog at least once during the day.

Note: You must provide written proof from a veterinarian of current vaccination (rabies, Bordetella, and DHPP for dogs; rabies, calicivirus, panleukopenia, and rhinotracheitis for cats) either at check-in or by fax at ☎ 407-224-9516. Call ☎ 407-224-9509 or visit tinyurl.com /uniservices for more information.

MY UNIVERSAL PHOTOS

WHILE SOME GUESTS STILL FIND their point-and-shoot or camera phone sufficient for documenting their vacation, Universal (in partnership with Colorvision's Amazing Pictures) has capitalized on advancing digital photo and social media technology with its My Universal Photos program (formerly known as Photo Connect). All the images captured during your day by Universal—either by roving paparazzi near the park entrances, at organized character meet and greets, or inside attractions— can be collected on plastic cards (distributed free from every photo location) and retrieved at the end of the day at the photography shops at the front of the parks: On Location at USF, DeFotos Expedition Photography at IOA, or Krakatau Katy's and Waturi Marketplace at Volcano Bay.

Photos can be purchased à la carte, which quickly gets expensive at $19.95 for a single 5-by-7-inch print or digital download ($21.95 gets you both). You can also print your prom picture with Optimus Prime on a poster ($24.95), mug ($9.95), or mouse pad. A better value are the My Universal Photos daily packages, which offer 1, 3, or 14 days of unlimited digital photos and a souvenir lanyard to hold your My Universal Photos card. With a My Universal Photos package, you receive two free printed photos (one 4-by-6-inch and one 5-by-7-inch) as well as deep discounts on videos ($20 for Hollywood Rip Ride Rockit) and additional prints ($2 for 4-by-6-inch; $5 for 5-by-7-inch; $10 for 8-by-10-inch), along with 20% off Amazing Pictures green screen photo ops. The package includes all street photographers, on-ride still images, and even unique photo ops such as E.T.'s flying bicycle.

The digital images can be downloaded at myuniversalphotos.com or through the free Apple or Android app (search for "Amazing Pictures Mobile" in your app store or visit amazingpictures.com/app), from where they can be emailed, shared on Facebook and Twitter, or saved at a resolution good enough for printing (though not for poster-size enlargements).

To use the My Universal Photos package, simply present your card to every Universal photographer you approach, or at the photo counters at the exits of rides. Ride photos can be edited to zoom in on your party, and some photographers can set up special effects shots. Universal also has automated My Universal Photos kiosks at the exits of select attractions, including Men in Black Alien Attack, Revenge of the Mummy, and The Incredible Hulk Coaster, so you can register your photos without waiting in line, though My Universal Photos team members are still available to help find and edit your photos if you don't want to use the self-service stations. You get two cards per My Universal Photos package, in case your party splits up, and any additional images you get on other photo cards can be added to your My Universal Photos account at any photo service center.

In addition to on-ride pictures and wandering photogs, you'll find a few automated photo ops scattered around the parks, including the Back to the Future car in USF, the Jurassic Park spinosaurus in IOA, and several selfie stations at Volcano Bay. Scan your My Universal Photos card (or TapuTapu wristband) at the kiosk, then pose at the designated spot while the camera counts down to the flash.

If you prepurchase your My Universal Photos package online at pre sale.amazingpictures.com/universalflorida.aspx or universalorlando .com/web/en/us/my-universal-photo/index.html, it won't begin expiring until you activate it upon visiting the parks. Once activated at the photography shop near the front of each park, My Universal Photos packages are valid for the purchased number of consecutive days. Online prices (plus tax) are $69.99 for a single day, $89.99 for 3 days, and $139.99 for a 14-day package. Annual pass holders can get a full year of My Universal Photos service for $139.99 and renew for $99. You can extend a package for $49.99 per day. A one-day photo pass valid only at Volcano Bay is $39.99, and a package combining a three-day My Universal Photos package with a video session at Shutterbutton's in Diagon Alley (see page 281) costs $139.99 online. My Universal Photos packages cost $10 more if purchased inside the park.

We used to be big fans of My Universal Photos, especially the yearlong package for annual pass holders, before the last few rounds of steep price hikes. If you are the type of person who buys ride and character photos, you'll still save money over buying à la carte, and if not, the freedom of unlimited snapshots may seduce you. But Universal's offer is no longer a superior value to Walt Disney World's similar Memory Maker package, which costs $199 for 30 days ($169 if ordered online at least three days in advance) and is included with Gold level or better annual passes.

There are some deficits and gotchas to My Universal Photos that you should be aware of before buying. For starters, My Universal Photos photographers can be found at each park's entrance, and occasionally at an impromptu character greeting, but they aren't on every corner. You can sometimes find an exceptional Universal photographer who will spend time posing with your family in various locations, but you're equally likely to encounter a meet and greet where the photog has gone mysteriously MIA. You certainly should not leave your camera at home with the expectation that My Universal Photos will be able to capture all your vacation memories.

Second, if you want to purchase any photos, you must do so (or buy and activate a My Universal Photos package) before you leave the park; once you exit at the end of the day, photos not paid for or not connected to an active My Universal Photos account will be erased. Likewise, if any photographers asked you to pose pointing or with your empty palm, you should stop by the photo store before leaving to have special effects characters layered into the image; otherwise you'll look pretty silly in the shots. Even if you didn't take any "magic" photos, you should still review your pictures from the day on your phone or at a photo center before exiting because images sometimes get mysteriously lost on the way to your account.

Finally, a few specific attractions have their own quirks. All digital photos in The Wizarding Worlds are included with My Universal Photos, but if you want to use your included free prints for the Forbidden Journey or Gringotts ride, you must get your photo printed at those attractions. All other attraction pictures may be printed at any photo-service location. For the record, here is where you can always find My Universal Photos locations throughout Universal's parks:

MY UNIVERSAL PHOTOS LOCATIONS

UNIVERSAL STUDIOS FLORIDA

- Park entrance
- Meet and greet near *Shrek 4-D* exit
- SpongeBob StorePants in Woody Woodpecker's KidZone
- Transformers meet and greet
- E.T. Toy Closet
- Men in Black Alien Attack on-ride photo
- Revenge of the Mummy on-ride photo
- Hollywood Rip Ride Rockit on-ride photo
- Minions meet and greet at the Despicable Me Minion Mayhem ride exit
- Harry Potter and the Escape from Gringotts queue photo
- Back to the Future car automated photo op
- Roaming photographers during Halloween Horror Nights and other events (seasonal)

ISLANDS OF ADVENTURE

- Park entrance
- The Incredible Hulk Coaster on-ride photo
- The Amazing Adventures of Spider-Man on-ride photo
- Spider-Man meet and greet
- Dudley Do-Right's Ripsaw Falls on-ride photo
- Jurassic Park spinosaurus automated photo op
- Jurassic Park River Adventure on-ride photo
- Harry Potter and the Forbidden Journey on-ride photo
- The High in the Sky Seuss Trolley Train Ride! queue photo (standby only)
- Raptor Encounter
- Grinch meet and greet during Grinchmas (seasonal)

VOLCANO BAY

- Park entrance
- Krakatau Aqua Coaster on-ride photo
- Ohyah & Ohno Drop Slides on-ride photo
- Tonga and Raki of Taniwha Tubes on-ride photo
- Honu and ika Moana on-ride photo
- Punga Racers on-ride photo
- Volcano, Family, and Hug a Mo Selfie Station automated photo ops

RELIGIOUS SERVICES

THE CLOSEST CHURCHES TO UNIVERSAL ORLANDO are the nondenominational **I Drive Church** (7440 Universal Blvd.; ☎ 407-573-8743; idrivechurch.org) and the enormous **First Baptist Orlando** (3000 John Young Pkwy.; ☎ 407-425-2555; firstorlando.com). The nearest Catholic Mass is held at **Holy Family** at 5125 S. Apopka-Vineland Road (☎ 407-876-2211; holyfamilyorlando.org), and the nearest synagogue is **Southwest Orlando Jewish Congregation** at 11200 S. Apopka-Vineland Road (☎ 407-239-5444; sojc.org). For a complete list of religious services in the Orlando tourist area, see allears.net/btp/church .htm and wdwinfo.com/tips_for_touring/churchservices.htm. Christian visitors may also be interested in the **Rock the Universe** religious music weekend held in early February (see page 295).

VACATION SERVICES

THROUGHOUT THE PARKS, you'll spot stands marked VACATION SERVICES, staffed by chatty team members who will ask you where you're from as you pass. Most guests hurry by, assuming—correctly—that these outposts serve as sales pitches for time-shares. But Universal's Vacation Services actually serves a number of other useful functions. In addition to selling Universal Orlando gift cards, meal plans, Express Passes, and Blue Man Group tickets, it can help book dining reservations and answer many Guest Services questions. If you have an issue, stop by one of these locations before walking back to the front of the park.

WINE, BEER, AND LIQUOR

ALCOHOL IS WIDELY AVAILABLE by the pint, glass, or shot throughout Universal's parks, hotels, and CityWalk. You can also buy wine by the bottle in the resort's table-service restaurants and some hotel shops. Note that while you can walk freely with a drink within the parks or CityWalk, due to liquor-license laws, you may not pass from CityWalk into a park or hotel (or vice versa) with an open container in hand.

Wine and beer are also sold off property in grocery stores, convenience stores, and liquor stores. The best range of adult beverages is sold by **Grand Liquors** at 5601 International Dr. (☎ 407-751-4517). The **Walgreens** across Kirkman Road from Universal also has a decent, if slightly expensive, liquor selection.

Remember that the minimum age to buy or consume alcohol in Florida is 21, and anyone who looks 30 or younger should plan to present government-issued photo ID (valid driver's license or passport) when purchasing. At CityWalk you'll be tagged with a paper bracelet while drinking, to take home as a hair-snagging reminder of your debauched revels.

UNIVERSAL ORLANDO *for* GUESTS *with* SPECIAL NEEDS

UNIVERSAL ORLANDO MAKES EFFORTS to accommodate every visitor, in accordance with the Americans with Disabilities Act (ADA). The resort offers a free **"Rider's Guide for Rider Safety & Guests with Disabilities"** describing each attraction's restrictions and requirements in detail at tinyurl.com/UniADA. You can download the booklet for each of the three parks in PDF format before your visit (which we highly recommend) or get printed copies at Guest Services, at resort front desks, or at wheelchair-rental locations inside the parks. The limitations you will face at Universal Orlando, and the accommodations you can take advantage of, will vary according to the nature of your special needs.

MOBILITY RESTRICTIONS

UNIVERSAL ORLANDO IS FAIRLY FRIENDLY for nonambulatory guests to navigate, and the resort has repaved some bumpy streets (such as the uneven paving stones in USF's San Francisco district) to be more comfortable for wheelchair users.

Universal provides close(r)-in parking for disabled visitors; ask for directions when you pay your parking fee. These spots are located on the main level of each parking garage, nearest to the central hub. You'll still have a substantial trip to CityWalk and the parks from even the best handicapped parking spot.

The entire Universal Orlando Resort transportation system is also disabled-accessible. Water taxis have roll-on ramps for easy boarding, and bus routes are served by vehicles with wheelchair lifts that can accommodate all but the largest motorized scooters.

All shopping, dining, and restroom facilities at the parks, City-Walk, and hotels are generally ADA compliant for wheelchair access. Some fast-food queues and shop aisles (especially in The Wizarding World of Harry Potter) are too narrow for wheelchairs. At these locations, ask a team member for assistance. All shows and performances (including parades) also have designated disability sections for guests in wheelchairs and their parties.

In addition, all attraction queues in USF and IOA (with the exception of Pteranodon Flyers in IOA) are fully wheelchair accessible, so you can enjoy the full preshow experience. Alternative routes (such as elevators to bypass stairs at Harry Potter and the Escape from Gringotts, Revenge of the Mummy, and Men in Black Alien Attack) and accessible boarding procedures (such as the stationary loading station at Harry Potter and the Forbidden Journey) are provided wherever necessary; be sure to read the specific instructions posted outside each attraction, and bring your needs to the attention of the first attendant to greet you for further instructions. At Volcano Bay, only the Krakatau

Aqua Coaster and Maku Puihi Round Raft Rides have elevators; for all other slides, you must be able to climb stairs to the top.

Strollers are not normally permitted inside most attractions, so if your child's stroller doubles as his or her wheelchair, swing by Guest Services for a special pass that will allow you to roll it through queues.

None of Universal's ride vehicles (except the Hogwarts Express trains) are able to accommodate electric convenience vehicles (ECVs) or motorized wheelchairs, though a handful have special cars that can carry a manual wheelchair. At those rides, guests can transfer from their powered chair to a standard one that will be provided at each applicable attraction. Even if an attraction doesn't accommodate wheelchairs of any kind, nonambulatory guests may ride if they can transfer from their wheelchair to the ride's vehicle. Universal's staff, however, aren't trained or permitted to assist with transfers—guests must be able to board the ride unassisted or have a member of their party assist them. Either way, members of the nonambulatory guest's party will be permitted to ride with him or her.

Regarding Universal's accessibility for the mobility impaired, a reader from upstate New York wrote:

My husband used a scooter throughout our trip because, though he can walk short distances, he has leg weakness and balance problems from an incomplete spinal cord injury. Whenever we approached a ride or attraction at Universal, the employees were always very attentive and willing to help. When he was using the scooter, they guided him to accessible areas, and when he chose to walk into attractions (with an obvious gait issue), they always very politely showed him the easiest route (avoiding stairs or steep ramps, opening the unused roped-off queuing areas to avoid having to walk around them) or offered wheelchair transport.

Wheelchair Rentals

Any guest may rent a wheelchair, with no proof of medical need required. Most rides, shows, attractions, restrooms, and restaurants accommodate the nonambulatory disabled. If you're in a park and need assistance, go to Guest Services. Be aware that, as almost all attraction queues are wheelchair accessible, using one does not automatically allow you to skip the standby line or shorten your wait.

Wheelchairs rent for $12 per day (tax included) with a fully refundable $50 deposit (cash or credit card) required. Standard wheelchairs are available at the central parking hub before you reach CityWalk and inside each park near the front gates.

A limited number of ECVs are available for rent at USF and IOA (not Volcano Bay). Easy to drive, they give nonambulatory guests tremendous freedom and mobility. ECVs are $50 per day (tax inclusive) with no deposit required. An upgraded model with a canopy is an extra $70. ECVs are popular and tend to sell out by midmorning on peak days, so call Guest Services (☎ 407-224-4233, option 3) at least a week in advance to reserve one. ECVs are only available inside the parks; you can rent a standard wheelchair at the parking hub and upgrade to an ECV once you reach the park. A reader from Newbury, Ohio, found the entire ECV rental process to be user-*un*friendly:

> *You have to fill out paperwork to rent a wheelchair to get to the ECV rental area, where you have to fill out more paperwork to get the ECV, after traversing a long distance through the entrance terminal, over a long bridge, and through CityWalk. You can't use the ECVs in lines for the attractions, which doesn't matter, I guess, because most attractions are too turbulent for handicapped, older, or larger guests!*

If you need an ECV to travel around the resort hotels or City-Walk, consider renting one from a third-party company such as **Walker Mobility** (☎ 407-518-6000; walkermobility.com) or **Scooter Vacations** (☎ 855-939-7266; scootorlando.com). Both will deliver a scooter and all necessary accessories to your hotel (including Universal Orlando on-site resorts) for about $25–$40 per day, a worthwhile investment per this reader from Middletown, Delaware:

> *We rented an ECV for my mother-in-law. We doubled our time in the parks, and she enjoyed the day with dignity. The rental is worth it for the long haul from the parking lot to Diagon Alley alone. The staff on Hogwarts Express are phenomenal with getting the ECV to the queue and embarking and disembarking the train.*

Finally, those who normally rent ECVs may want to forgo them in favor of manual wheelchairs during evening special events when the streets are especially dark and densely crowded, according to this Illinois reader:

> *Taking an ECV during Halloween Horror Nights is not practical. It became more of a hassle than it helped. You cannot take the ECV inside the haunted houses. You have to park it at the entrance, sometimes far away from the entrance of the house you just came out of, and then you have to backtrack to get your ECV and then back to where you exited. It was a pain in the posterior.*

FAMILY RESTROOMS

IF A MEMBER OF YOUR PARTY needs assistance using the restroom, check the park map for designated family or companion restrooms, which are large enough for two adults to access. Family restrooms are located in USF near the front of the park near the Studio Audience Center, in Springfield outside Fast Food Boulevard, in San Francisco across from Richter's Burger Co., at First Aid behind Louie's Italian Restaurant in New York, and outside Mel's Drive-In across from the Transformers gift shop. In IOA, the family restrooms are found at Guest Services near the entrance and at First Aid in Lost Continent. In Volcano Bay, family restrooms are located at the First Aid Station, under the Ohyah and Ohno slides, and near the entrance to Honu ika Moana.

SERVICE ANIMALS

SERVICE ANIMALS ARE WELCOME at the Universal Orlando Resort, and all the Premier and Preferred Loews hotels accommodate even nonservice pets. Working companion animals are allowed inside all Universal restaurant and merchandise locations, attraction queues, and most other locations throughout the resort. Specific guidelines for each attraction are posted at the queue entrance and listed in the "Rider's Guide." For attractions where the service animal cannot safely enter, portable kennels are provided.

When nature calls, service-animal relief areas are marked on the park map. There are two designated walking areas in USF (Woody Woodpecker's KidZone behind the NBC Media Center and World Expo between Men in Black Alien Attack and *Fear Factor Live*) and three in IOA (Marvel Super Hero Island between The Amazing Adventures of Spider-Man and Doctor Doom's Fearfall, Jurassic Park behind Pizza Predattoria, and Seuss Landing behind One Fish, Two Fish, Red Fish, Blue Fish). Volcano Bay's service-animal relief areas are near Honu ika Moana and next to Maku Puihi.

DIETARY RESTRICTIONS

UNIVERSAL ORLANDO RESTAURANTS WORK very hard to accommodate guests' special dietary needs. If properly informed, Universal's chefs can prepare food that is vegetarian or vegan; kosher or halal; or dairy-free, gluten-free, or nut-free. When you make a dining reservation, either online at tinyurl.com/unidinres or by phone (☎ 407-224-FOOD [3663] for restaurants in the parks and CityWalk, or ☎ 407-503-DINE [3463] for hotel dining), you'll be asked about food allergies and the like. The host or hostess and your server will also ask about this and send the chef out to discuss the menu; if you're not asked, just talk to your server when you're seated.

Kosher meals ($29.95 plus tax and gratuity) must be ordered through Guest Services (☎ 407-224-4233) at least 72 hours in advance and can be delivered to Lombard's or Finnegan's in USF, Confisco or Mythos in IOA, or Kohola Reef or Bambu in Volcano Bay.

At counter-service restaurants, ask to see the menu book with ingredient and allergen info. Unfortunately, one place that does not get high marks for dietary accommodation is the Leaky Cauldron in Diagon Alley. There is virtually nothing on the menu that's vegan, and not much more for the gluten-free or lactose intolerant. In general, those on restricted diets will find many more options at Universal's table-service eateries.

Be aware also that Universal Orlando does not have separate kitchen facilities in which to prepare allergen-free foods, so there is always a slight possibility of inadvertent allergen contamination before or during preparation. You are welcome to bring your own food into the resort, as long as you let security know that you have a dietary issue and follow the restrictions on items permitted inside the parks (no glass containers nor large or hard coolers).

For more information, email your specific dietary requests to food servicecuf@universalorlando.com and visit universalorlando.com/web /en/us/things-to-do/dining/food-allergies/index.html.

HEARING IMPAIRMENT

GUEST SERVICES AT THE PARKS PROVIDES free assistive-technology devices to hearing-impaired guests with a refundable deposit (depending on the device). Hearing-impaired guests can benefit from amplified audio on many attractions, and closed-captioning is available on request for queue video monitors. Select shows offer reflective captioning as well. Guest Services can also provide a printed script to many of the attractions for you to peruse.

In addition, Universal provides complimentary sign language interpretations of live shows at the theme parks daily. There is typically only one interpreted performance of each show per day, so check the show schedule in the park map as soon as you arrive and plan your visit accordingly. Even if you don't understand sign language, it's well worth seeing for how animated and expressive the interpreters are—they truly steal the show.

While we're on the subject of sound, Universal loves to assail its guests with multiple overlapping background tracks, all cranked up to 11 for maximum impact. Even if you didn't have a hearing problem before arriving at Universal Orlando, the overwhelming amplification employed by many of the resort's attractions may leave your eardrums ringing. Anyone with a touch of tinnitus, or who is simply sensitive to loud noise, should heed this advice from a New Orleans parent and pack some hearing protection:

> I would recommend earplugs for almost every dark ride, especially for kids, to protect the ears. Most of those rides were so loud that earplugs or special [noise-canceling] headphones would not lessen the enjoyment at all.

VISION IMPAIRMENT

PARK INFORMATION GUIDES, restaurant menus, and attraction scripts are available at Guest Services in large print and embossed Braille. Some rides can accommodate guests with white canes (a collapsible cane is recommended), while at others an attendant will hold the cane and return it to the guest immediately at the unload area.

MISSING AND PROSTHETIC LIMBS

ALL GUESTS MUST BE ABLE to hold themselves upright and continuously grasp a safety restraint with at least one extremity to experience most rides. Guests with prosthetic limbs may ride with them securely attached on most rides. Those with prosthetic arms or hands may need to demonstrate that they can grip the safety restraints. All prosthetic limbs need to removed before riding Pteranodon Flyers (both natural legs must extend to the edge of your seat or terminate below the knee) or Hollywood Rip Ride Rockit (must have one full natural leg and one natural leg that extends to the edge of the seat or terminates below the knee). Consult the "Rider's Guide" for details.

LARGER GUESTS

THRILL-SEEKING GUESTS OF SIZE will discover that several of Universal's rides are unfriendly toward those of generous girth. The Harry Potter headliners are the most notorious for excluding plus-size riders, though both have certain seats—the outside seats on Harry Potter and the Forbidden Journey, and rows three and six on Harry Potter and the Escape from Gringotts—that are more accommodating to most body shapes. Likewise, the big roller coasters at IOA have designated seats with double seat belts designed for bigger guests, and row three at Revenge of the Mummy offers extra legroom.

In all cases, these safety restrictions are based less on weight than torso circumference; some guests with large chests (40" or greater) who would not otherwise be considered overweight may find the restraint harnesses challenging to lock properly. Before getting into line for any attraction, check out the sample ride vehicle at the entrance, and discuss your concerns with the attraction's greeter.

At Volcano Bay, most body slides and raft rides have weight limits, which are posted on each attraction's information sign. Every queue has a scale built into the ground (either at the base of the steps for body slides or at the top for raft slides), which is discreetly checked by an attendant to ensure compliance. Guests weighing more than 300 pounds will find themselves excluded from several slides. Some rafts have an overall weight limit, so even parties of four or more average-size adults may struggle to squeeze everyone into some multirider rafts.

OXYGEN TANKS AND CONCENTRATORS

FOR SAFETY REASONS, OXYGEN TANKS are not allowed on most moving attractions at Universal Orlando. The only rides that permit oxygen tanks are Hogwarts Express and Despicable Me Minion Mayhem (stationary seating only). Oxygen tanks are permitted inside all shows and playgrounds, and portable oxygen concentrators are allowed on most rides, as long as they don't interfere with the safety restraints.

NONAPPARENT DISABILITIES

WE RECEIVE MANY LETTERS from readers whose traveling companion or child requires special assistance but who, unlike a person in a wheelchair, is not visibly disabled. Autism, for example, makes it very difficult or impossible for someone with the disorder to wait in line for more than a few minutes or in queues surrounded by a crowd.

A trip to Universal Orlando can be nonetheless positive and rewarding for guests with autism and similar conditions. And while any theme park vacation requires planning, a little extra effort to accommodate the affected person will pay large dividends.

Our first suggestion is to visit the website autismattheparks.com and study its extensive information on visiting Universal Orlando. It's the best independent source we know for dealing with neurological or sensory issues at the attractions, and it is filled with practical first-hand advice.

Next, you'll want to familiarize yourself with two programs Universal offers to make your visit a little smoother, discussed below.

Universal's Attractions Assistance Pass (AAP)

For years, Universal has been offering assistance to impaired guests through its **Attractions Assistance Pass** (**AAP**). AAP is designed to accommodate guests who can't wait in regular standby lines. You must first obtain an AAP card at Guest Services of the first park you visit. AAP cards are good for parties of up to six people, but all members of your party who will use the service must have their admission tickets scanned at Guest Services. The same card is valid in the theme parks for the length of your vacation, or up to 14 days for annual pass holders.

When you get to Guest Services, you'll need to present identification and describe your or your family member's limitations. You don't need to disclose a disease or medical condition—by federal privacy law, they are forbidden to ask. Rather than an attempt to have you prove your condition, the goal here is to get you the right level of assistance.

Be as detailed as possible in describing limitations. For instance, if your child is on the autism spectrum, has trouble waiting in long lines, and has sensory issues that make it difficult for him or her to stand or be subjected to loud noises, you need to let the team member know each of these things. "He doesn't wait in lines" isn't enough to go on. A doctor's note explaining the necessary accommodations can be very helpful.

AAP cards can be used at any ride or attraction, even if it doesn't have a Universal Express entrance. Present the card to a team member at the attraction you want to ride. If the ride's standby wait time is less than 30 minutes, you'll usually be escorted through the Universal Express entrance. If the standby time is higher than 30 minutes, the team member will enter on the AAP card the attraction name, time of day, wait time, and a return time for you to come back to ride. The return time will be based on the current wait time, so if you get to The Amazing Adventures of Spider-Man at 12:20 p.m. and the standby time is 40 minutes, your return time will be 40 minutes later, at 1 p.m.

You may return at the specified time or at any time thereafter, but you can't get another AAP return time until you have used or forfeited the first. When you return, you'll be given access to the Universal Express line, where you should face a wait of 15 minutes or less. The card holder need not be present to obtain a return time but must be present with his or her party for anyone to gain admission. Because all Volcano Bay guests are eligible to use the Virtual Line system, no AAP cards are available at the water park.

Universal's Guest Assistance Pass (GAP) Entry Cards

If the AAP doesn't meet your family's needs, Universal makes a small number of **Guest Assistance Pass** (**GAP**) Entry cards available on a strictly limited basis. Basically, a GAP Entry card is identical to a one-day/two-park Universal Express Unlimited Pass and provides immediate entry to any attraction's Universal Express queue, regardless of the standby wait. Like the Universal Express Pass, GAP Entry is only valid at attractions that offer Universal Express, which excludes Pteranodon Flyers, so you'll still want an AAP card or Virtual Line reservation for that attraction.

If you want a GAP because long standby lines are rendering the AAP unworkable for your party, be prepared to plead your case to a Guest Services supervisor and endure some time-consuming scrutiny. If you're turned down, or prefer not to deal with the hassle, you can always purchase Express Passes (subject to availability).

FRIENDS OF BILL W.

FOR INFORMATION ON THE NEAREST **Alcoholics Anonymous** meetings to Universal Orlando (held daily, except Wednesday), visit cflintergroup.org or call ☎ 407-260-5408 for additional information. For information on **Al-Anon/Alateen** meetings in the area, visit al-anon orlando.org or call ☎ 407-253-9848.

INTERNATIONAL VISITORS

UNIVERSAL ORLANDO PROVIDES PARK MAPS in a number of different languages and maintains special websites designed for visitors from Brazil, Latin America, and the United Kingdom. Click the language box at the top-center of the universalorlando.com home page to see the international options.

PART FIVE

UNIVERSAL ORLANDO *with* KIDS

IT'S *a* SMALL UNIVERSE, AFTER ALL

SINCE THE OPENING OF ISLANDS OF ADVENTURE'S (IOA's) coasters and CityWalk's nightclubs, Universal Orlando (UOR) has positioned itself as an edgier, more adult alternative to the Mouse. Even Disney diehards will admit that Universal Orlando sports more attractions aimed at older teens and young adults than Walt Disney World (WDW) currently does. But the commonly heard rejoinder is that there's "nothing" for little kids to do at Universal's parks.

That stereotype has seeds of truth. While the Magic Kingdom can claim more than a dozen rides with no height restrictions, Universal Studios Florida (USF) and IOA combined have only seven rides that accommodate kids less than 34 inches tall. And as popular as Universal characters like the Minions and SpongeBob are with the single-digit set, it's tough to compete with the multibillion-dollar marketing machine behind Mickey's menagerie. But numbers alone don't tell the tale because a vacation at UOR can actually be a better experience for the youngest visitors (and therefore the family members around them) than the equivalent WDW escape.

For starters, while Universal lacks many moving attractions for tots, it makes up for it with the best themed playgrounds in town, as this family from Lancaster, Pennsylvania, learned:

> We were concerned about the big rides at Universal leaving our youngest child (age 5) bored. In actuality, she had a blast at Fievel's Playland, Seuss Landing, and Camp Jurassic. Even the older kids joined her to play at these areas whenever we got back together.

Second, without FastPass+ reservations and 180-day Advanced Dining Reservations to worry about, a stay at Universal Orlando requires much less preplanning, which means less damage to your day when the inevitable toddler tantrum derails your carefully laid touring plans. Universal's parks are more compact than Magic Kingdom and Epcot, which means that little legs won't tire as quickly. Also, on any given day, the crowds are likely to be lighter at UOR, welcome news for anyone shoving a stroller through the streets. Finally, it's far easier to travel from Universal's on-site hotels to its parks and back, a key benefit when heading back to your room for that essential midday nap.

Ideally, your kids should be at least 42 inches tall to experience the bulk of the parks' dark rides and simulators, or 54 inches tall to brave the biggest roller coasters. But traveling to Universal Orlando with a toddler, or even infant, can be equally rewarding, as long as you know what you're getting into and prepare thoroughly. The biggest danger is in dealing with a child who's barely under the minimum for something they'll "just die" without riding, so read up on height requirements (see page 188) in advance to avoid disappointment on the day.

When you're planning a Universal Orlando vacation with young children, consider the following:

AGE   Though Universal Orlando's color and festivity excite all children (with specific attractions that delight toddlers and preschoolers), and there's no admission fee for those under 3 years old, Universal's entertainment is generally oriented to older children and adults. Children should be a fairly mature 8 years old to appreciate USF, and a bit older to tackle the thrill rides in IOA, as this reader recommended:

> *Wait to visit until your children are tall enough, brave enough, and/or interested enough to ride at least most of the rides. USF and IOA have a much different vibe from the Disney theme parks. If your children can't or won't ride most of the rides, it will just be a waste of money.*

Note that Universal considers all kids ages 3–9 as children for pricing purposes, regardless of height or ability to experience rides.

WHEN TO VISIT   Avoid the hot, crowded summer months, especially if you have preschoolers. Go in October, November (except Thanksgiving), early December, January, February, or May. If you have children of varied ages and they're good students, take the older ones out of school and visit during the cooler and less congested off-season. Arrange special assignments relating to the educational aspects of Universal Orlando. If your children can't afford to miss school, take your vacation as soon as the school year ends. Alternatively, try late August before school starts. Please understand that you don't have to visit during one of the more ideal times of year to have a great vacation.

unofficial **TIP**
Coupled with a sense of humor and a little preparedness on your part, our touring plans and tips for families ensure a super experience at any time of year.

A Peterborough, England, woman agrees:

> *We visited at the end of August, and we expected that the crowds would be almost unbearable. However, we were surprised to find that because most local schools were back in session, we could walk on*

most headliner rides up until late afternoon, and even then there was only a short wait—some rides at Universal Studios didn't even open until 11 a.m. because we were visiting on a low-attendance day! We'd recommend that more people go this time of year, especially those people whose children don't return to school until later.

BUILD NAPS AND REST INTO YOUR ITINERARY The parks are huge: don't try to see everything in one day. Tour in the early morning and return to your hotel around 11:30 a.m. for lunch, a swim, and a nap. Even during off-season, when crowds are smaller and the temperature is more pleasant, the size of the parks will exhaust most children younger than age 8 by lunchtime. Return to the park in the late afternoon or early evening and continue touring. A family from Texas underlines the importance of naps and rest:

Probably the most important tip your guide gave us was going to the hotel to swim and regroup during the day. The parks became unbearable by noon—and so did my husband and boys. The hotel was an oasis that calmed our nerves! After about 3 hours of playtime, we headed out to [the other park] for dinner and a cool evening of fun.

Regarding naps, this mom doesn't mince words:

For parents of small kids: Take the book's advice, get out of the park, and take the nap, take the nap, TAKE THE NAP! Never in my life have I seen so many parents screaming at, ridiculing, or slapping their kids. (What a vacation!) [The parks can be] overwhelming for kids and adults.

If you plan to return to your hotel at midday and want your room made up, let housekeeping know.

WHERE TO STAY The time and hassle involved in commuting to and from the theme parks will be less if your hotel is on Universal property. It's hard to overemphasize how convenient it is to commute between your room and the parks when staying at the top Loews resorts, and even the value-priced Cabana Bay is only a 15-minute stroller push away from IOA's front gates. A number of off-site hotels along Major Boulevard and International Drive (see page 109) are also within walking distance, but you may not feel comfortable crossing busy roads with small kids in tow.

BE IN TOUCH WITH YOUR FEELINGS When you or your kids get tired and irritable, call a time-out. Trust your instincts. What would feel best? Another ride, an ice cream break, or going back to the room for a nap?

LEAST COMMON DENOMINATORS Somebody is going to run out of steam first, and when he or she does, the whole family will be affected. Sometimes a snack break will revive the flagging member. Sometimes, however, it's better to return to your hotel. Pushing the tired or discontented beyond their capacity will spoil the day for them—and you. Energy levels vary. Be prepared to respond to members of your group who poop out. *Hint:* "We've driven a thousand miles to take you to Harry Potter and now you're ruining everything!" is not an appropriate response.

BUILDING ENDURANCE   Though most children are active, their normal play usually doesn't condition them for the exertion required to tour an Orlando park. Start family walks four to six weeks before your trip to get in shape. A mother from Wescosville, Pennsylvania, reports:

> We had our 6-year-old begin walking with us a bit every day one month before leaving—when we arrived [in Orlando], her little legs could carry her, and she had a lot of stamina.

From a Middletown, Delaware, mom:

> You recommended walking for six weeks prior to the trip, but we began months in advance. My husband lost 10 pounds, and we met a lot of neighbors! We wouldn't have made it without you—thanks!

SETTING LIMITS AND MAKING PLANS   To avoid arguments and disappointment, establish guidelines for each day and get everybody committed. Include the following:

1. Wake-up time and breakfast plans
2. When to depart for the park
3. What to take with you
4. A policy for splitting the group or for staying together
5. What to do if the group gets separated or someone is lost
6. What you want to see, including plans in the event an attraction is closed or too crowded
7. A policy on what you can afford for snacks
8. How long you plan to tour in the morning and what time you'll return to your hotel to rest
9. When you'll return to the park and how late you'll stay
10. Dinner plans
11. A policy for buying souvenirs, including who pays: Mom and Dad or the kids
12. Bedtimes

BE FLEXIBLE   Any day at Universal Orlando includes surprises; be prepared to adjust your plan. Listen to your intuition, and take advantage of the Lines app's optimization tool to update your itinerary after any unexpected detours.

ABOUT *the* UNOFFICIAL GUIDE TOURING PLANS

PARENTS WHO USE OUR TOURING PLANS are often frustrated by interruptions and delays caused by their young children. Here's what to expect:

1. CHARACTER ENCOUNTERS CAN WREAK HAVOC WITH THE TOURING PLANS.   Many children will stop in their tracks whenever they see a cartoon character like Shrek or Scooby-Doo. Attempting to haul your child away before he has satisfied his curiosity is likely to cause anything from whining to full-scale revolt. Either go with the flow or specify a morning or afternoon for photos and autographs. Luckily, queues for autographs at Universal aren't nearly as long as at Disney World.

2. OUR TOURING PLANS CALL FOR VISITING ATTRACTIONS IN A SEQUENCE, OFTEN SKIPPING ATTRACTIONS ALONG THE WAY. Children don't like to skip anything! If something catches their eye, they want to see it that moment. Some kids can be persuaded to skip attractions if parents explain their plans in advance. Other kids flip out at skipping something, particularly in Seuss Landing and The Wizarding Worlds.

3. IF YOU'RE USING A STROLLER, YOU WON'T BE ABLE TO TAKE IT INTO ATTRACTIONS OR ONTO RIDES. You'll need to leave your stroller (personal or rented) outside each attraction, unless you have a special pass indicating a medical need (see page 169). An exception is the Hogwarts Express train, which provides transportation between the parks and accommodates personal strollers; rentals will be swapped for free at the stations. Well-marked stroller parking is available throughout the parks.

unofficial **TIP**
Keep little ones well covered in sunscreen and hydrated with fluids. Don't count on hydrating young children with soft drinks and stops at water fountains. Carry refillable bottles of water. Bottles with screw caps are sold across the resort for about $3. *Remember:* Excited kids may not tell you when they're thirsty or hot.

4. YOU PROBABLY WON'T FINISH THE TOURING PLAN. Varying hours of operation, crowds, your group's size, your children's ages, and your stamina will all affect how much of the plan you'll complete. Tailor your expectations to this reality, or you'll be frustrated.

While our touring plans allow you to make the most of your time at the parks, it's impossible to define what *most* will be. It differs from family to family. If you have two young children, you probably won't see as much as two adults will. If you have four children, you probably won't see as much as a couple with only two children.

STUFF *to* THINK ABOUT

BLISTERS AND SORE FEET   In addition to wearing comfortable shoes, bring along some blister bandages if you or your children are susceptible to blisters. These bandages (which are also available at First Aid, if you didn't heed our warnings) offer excellent protection, stick well, and won't sweat off. Remember, a preschooler may not say anything about a blister until it's already formed, so keep an eye on things during the day. For an expanded discussion, see page 151.

OVERHEATING, SUNBURN, AND DEHYDRATION   These are the most common problems of younger children at Universal Orlando. Use sunscreen. Apply it on children in strollers, even if the stroller has a canopy.

To avoid overheating, stop for rest regularly in the shade, in a restaurant, or at a show with air-conditioning.

FIRST AID   If you or your children have a medical problem, go to a First Aid Station (see page 154). They're friendlier than most doctor's offices and are accustomed to treating everything from paper cuts to allergic reactions. And if your kid just needs some rehydration and a short nap, they can provide a quiet cot.

CHILDREN ON MEDICATION   Some parents of hyperactive children on medication discontinue or decrease the child's dosage at the end of the school year. If you have such a child, be aware that Universal Orlando might overstimulate him or her. Consult your physician before altering your child's medication regimen.

GLASSES AND SUNGLASSES   If your kids (or you) wear them, attach a strap to the frames so the glasses will stay on during rides and can hang from the child's neck while indoors.

THINGS YOU FORGOT OR RAN OUT OF   Raingear, diapers, baby formula, sunburn treatments, memory cards, and other sundries are sold at the parks and at CityWalk. If you don't see something you need, ask if it's in stock. Basic over-the-counter meds are often available free in small quantities at the First Aid Stations in the parks.

INFANTS AND TODDLERS AT THE THEME PARKS   All Universal parks have centralized Family Services facilities for infant and toddler care adjacent to the First Aid Stations. Everything necessary for changing diapers, preparing formulas, and warming bottles and food is available. Supplies are for sale, and rockers and special chairs for nursing mothers are provided. In Universal Studios Florida, Family Services is located in the Front Lot near Lost and Found, and on Canal Street behind Louie's Italian Restaurant, on the border between New York and San Francisco. In Islands of Adventure, Family Services is in Port of Entry near Guest Services, and in The Lost Continent near the Mystic Fountain; look for the red cross behind the coin vendor. In Volcano Bay, Family Services is immediately on your left as you enter the park. Dads are welcome at the centers and can use most services. In addition, most men's restrooms in the resort have changing tables.

RUNNING OUT OF GAS   When Bob was preparing to hike from the Colorado River to the rim of the Grand Canyon—a 5,000-foot ascent—a park ranger told him to mix an electrolyte-replacement powder in his water and eat an energy-boosting snack at least twice every hour. While there's not much ascending to do at Universal, battling the heat, humidity, and crowds contributes to pooping out, especially where kids are concerned. Limiting calorie consumption to mealtimes just won't get it, as an experienced and wise grandma points out:

> *Children who get cranky during a visit often do so from all that time and energy expended without food. Feed them! A snack at any price goes a long way to keeping the little ones happy and parents sane. Oh, and the security people are very nice about you taking snacks or drinks in, but DO NOT bring glass containers!*

STROLLERS

STROLLERS ARE AVAILABLE for rent inside Universal Studios and Islands of Adventure (but not Volcano Bay) to the left of the front gates as you enter. A single stroller is $14.99 (tax included) per day, and a double stroller is $24.99. Kiddie cars have plastic steering wheels attached, so your child can pretend he or she is driving; they come in single and double sizes and cost $3 more than the price of a standard stroller. A $50 deposit (cash or credit card) is required, which will be fully refunded when you return your stroller. If you leave the park and return, or switch parks during the day, you can get a fresh stroller for free by showing your receipt.

Strollers are a must for infants and toddlers, but we've seen many sharp parents rent strollers for somewhat older children—the stroller spares parents from having to carry kids when they sag, and it provides a convenient place to tote water and snacks.

A family from Tulsa, Oklahoma, recommends a double stroller:

We rented a double for baggage room or in case the older child gets tired of walking.

But a New Lenox, Illinois, family advocates not leaving anyone out:

If your kids are 8 or under, rent strollers for all of them! An 8-year-old will fit in a stroller, and you can fit up to four kids in two doubles. My husband suggested getting a stroller for our 6-year-old and the two "babies" (ages 4 and 3). We plowed through crowds, and the kids didn't get nearly as tired because they could be seated whenever they wanted.

However, a McKean, Pennsylvania, reader thinks the situation has gotten out of hand:

Please tell parents their children don't have to be in strollers if (a) they're old enough to vote, (b) they've served in the armed services, (c) they smoke, and/or (d) they have kids of their own. It's gotten really ridiculous—this last visit we saw more 10-plus-year-olds in strollers than sub-10-year-olds. Strollers add congestion, especially with dingbat parents using them to blast through crowds like child-first battering rams. I never knew walking was bad for you.

A Charleston, West Virginia, mom recommends a backup plan:

Strollers are not allowed in lines for rides, so if you have a small child (ours was 4) who needs to be held, you might end up holding him a long time. If I had it to do over, I'd bring along some kind of child carrier for when he was out of the stroller.

Rental strollers are too large for all infants and many toddlers. If you plan to rent a stroller for your infant or toddler, bring pillows, cushions, or rolled towels to buttress him or her in. Bringing your own stroller is permitted. Your stroller is unlikely to be stolen, but mark it with your name.

STROLLER-RENTAL OPTIONS   Several Orlando companies are able to undercut the parks' prices, provide more comfortable strollers, and deliver them to your hotel. Most of the larger companies offer the same stroller models (the Baby Jogger City Mini Single, for example), so the primary differences between the companies are price and service.

To rate stroller companies, we had Unofficial Guide researchers rent the same strollers from each company, use the strollers in the parks, and return them. Our evaluation covers the overall experience, from the ease with which the stroller was rented to the delivery of the stroller, its condition upon arrival, and the return process.

Kingdom Strollers (☎ 407-271-5301; kingdomstrollers.com) topped our list, getting top marks for website ease of use, stroller selection, condition, and overall service. The stroller was also much easier to use than Universal's standard model, had more storage, and had an easier-to-use braking system. A rental of one to three nights costs $45; four to seven nights is $65. That makes the break-even point for choosing Kingdom Strollers over Universal at three days. At Universal's on-site resorts, you may have to manually enter your hotel name when booking online, and confirm your stroller delivery with the bell services manager on arrival.

We also recommend **Orlando Stroller Rentals, LLC** (☎ 800-281-0884; orlandostrollerrentals.com), which has similar prices plus an excellent website that allows you to easily compare the features of different strollers. It also requires you to be present to drop off and pick up your stroller (unless you can cajole the bell captain into arranging otherwise) but is more flexible about arranging a meeting time.

STROLLER WARS   Sometimes strollers disappear while you're enjoying a ride or show. Universal staff will often rearrange strollers parked outside an attraction. This may be done to tidy up or to clear a walkway. Don't assume that your stroller is stolen because it isn't where you left it. It may be neatly arranged a few feet away—or perhaps more than a few feet away, as this Skokie, Illinois, dad reports:

The stroller reorganizations while you're on rides are a bit unnerving. More than once, our stroller was moved out of visible distance from the original spot. On one occasion, it was moved to a completely different stroller-parking area near another ride, and no sign or team member was around to advise where. We had to track down a team member, and she had to call in to find out where it had been moved. Be prepared for this.

Sometimes, however, strollers are taken by mistake or ripped off by people not wanting to spend time replacing one that's missing. Don't be alarmed if yours disappears. You won't have to buy it, and you'll be issued a new one.

*un*official **TIP**
Don't try to lock your stroller to a fence, post, or anything else at Universal. You'll get in big trouble.

While replacing a stroller is no big deal, it's inconvenient. Through our own experiments and readers' suggestions, we've developed a technique for hanging on to a rented stroller: affix something personal (but expendable) to the handle. Evidently, most strollers are pirated by mistake (they all look alike) or because it's easier to swipe someone else's than to replace one that has disappeared. Because most stroller "theft" results from confusion or laziness, the average pram-pincher will hesitate to haul off a stroller containing another person's property. We tried several items and concluded that a bright, inexpensive scarf or bandanna tied to the handle works well as identification. A sock partially stuffed with rags or paper works even better (the weirder and more personal the object, the greater the deterrent). A multigenerational family from Utah went a step further:

> We decorated our stroller with electrical tape to make it stand out, and my son added a small cowbell to make it clang if moved.

STROLLERS AS LETHAL WEAPONS   A middle-aged couple from Brunswick, Maine, lobbies for a temporary stroller ban:

> As an over-45 couple, we couldn't believe the number and sizes of strollers and those ubiquitous scooters. You had to be constantly vigilant or you would have your foot run over or path slowed down by them. We've decided that one day a week, in one theme park, there should be a "no wheels" day.

You'd be surprised at how many people are injured by strollers pushed by parents who are driving aggressively or in a hurry. Given the number of strollers, pedestrians, and tight spaces, mishaps are inevitable on both sides. A simple apology and a smile are usually the best remediation.

LOST CHILDREN

THOUGH IT'S AMAZINGLY EASY TO LOSE a child (or two) in the parks, it usually isn't a serious problem: Universal employees are schooled in handling the situation. If you lose a child in the resort, report it to the nearest Universal employee, and then check at Guest Services. Paging isn't used, but in an emergency, an all-points bulletin can be issued throughout the park(s) via internal communications.

Sew a label into each child's shirt that states his or her name, your name, the name of your hotel, and your cell phone number. Accomplish the same thing by writing the information on a strip of masking tape.

An easier and trendier option is a temporary tattoo with your child's name and your phone number. Unlike labels, ID bracelets, or wristbands, the tattoos cannot fall off or be lost. Temporary tattoos last about two weeks, won't wash or sweat off, and are not irritating to the skin. They can be purchased online from SafetyTat at safetytat .com, or from Tattoos with a Purpose at tattooswithapurpose.com. Special tattoos are available for children with food allergies or cognitive impairment such as autism.

A Kingston, Washington, reader recommends recording vital info for each child on a plastic key tag or luggage tag and affixing it to the child's shoe. This reader also snaps a photo of the kids each morning to document what they're wearing. A mother from Rockville, Maryland, reported a strategy one step short of a cattle brand:

> *Traveling with a 3-year-old, I was very anxious about losing him. I wrote my cell phone number on his leg with a permanent marker and felt much more confident that he'd get back to me quickly if he became lost.*

One way to better keep track of your family is to buy each person a Universal uniform—in this case, the same brightly and distinctively colored T-shirt. A Yuma, Arizona, family tried this with great success:

> *We all got the same shirts (bright red) so that we could easily spot each other in case of separation (VERY easy to do). It was a lifesaver when our 18-month-old decided to get out of the stroller and wander off. No matter what precautions you may try, it seems that there are always those opportunities to lose a child, but the recognizable shirts helped tremendously.*

HOW KIDS GET LOST

CHILDREN GET SEPARATED from their parents every day at Universal parks under remarkably similar (and predictable) circumstances:

1. PREOCCUPIED SOLO PARENT   The party's only adult is preoccupied with something like buying refreshments, reading a map, or using the restroom. Junior is there one second and gone the next.

2. THE HIDDEN EXIT   Sometimes parents wait on the sidelines while two or more young children experience a ride together. Parents expect the kids to exit in one place and the youngsters pop out elsewhere. Exits from some attractions are distant from entrances. Know exactly where your children will emerge before letting them ride by themselves.

3. AFTER THE SHOW   At the end of many shows and rides, a Universal staffer announces, "Check for personal belongings and take small children by the hand." When dozens, if not hundreds, of people leave an attraction simultaneously, it's easy for parents to lose their children unless they have direct contact.

4. RESTROOM PROBLEMS   Mom tells 6-year-old Tommy, "I'll be sitting on this bench when you come out of the restroom." Three possibilities: One, Tommy exits through a different door and becomes disoriented (Mom may not know there's another door). Two, Mom decides she also will use the restroom, and Tommy emerges to find her gone. Three, Mom pokes around in a shop while keeping an eye on the bench but misses Tommy when he comes out.

If you can't find a companion- or family-accessible restroom, make sure there's only one exit. Designate a distinctive meeting spot and give clear instructions: "I'll meet you by this flagpole. If you get out first, stay right here." Have your child repeat the directions back to you.

5. PARADES   There are many parades and shows at which the audience stands. Children tend to jockey for a better view. By moving a little this way and that, the child quickly puts distance between you and him before either of you notices.

6. MASS MOVEMENTS   Be on guard when huge crowds disperse after fireworks or a parade, or at park closing. With 20,000–40,000 people at once in an area, it's very easy to get separated from a child or others in your party. Use extra caution after the afternoon Superstar Parade and evening lagoon show in Universal Studios Florida. Plan where to meet in the event you get separated.

7. CHARACTER GREETINGS   When the Universal characters appear, children can slip out of sight.

UNIVERSAL, KIDS, *and* SCARY STUFF

THOUGH THERE'S PLENTY FOR YOUNGER children to enjoy at the Universal parks, most major attractions can potentially make kids under age 8 wig out. To be frank, they freak out a fairly large percentage of adults as well. On average, Universal's rides move more aggressively and feature more intense (some would say assaultive) audiovisual effects than their Disney counterparts. There are attractions with menacing mummies, exploding insects, and man-eating dinosaurs—not to mention demonic soul-sucking Dementors and fire-breathing dragons. And while Walt Disney World rides always end on a happy note, Universal is equally as apt to send you out with a final scare or snarky parting shot, which is less likely to soothe shaken nerves. Universal also sets surprisingly strict minimum height requirements for some kid-centric rides, ruling out attractions such as Cat in the Hat and The High in the Sky Seuss Trolley Train Ride! for the infants who might enjoy them most.

You can reliably predict that a visit to Universal Orlando will, at one time or another, send a young child into system overload. Be sensitive, alert, and prepared for almost anything, even behavior that is out of character for your child. Most children take Universal's macabre trappings in stride, and others are easily comforted by an arm around the shoulder or a squeeze of the hand. Parents who know that their children tend to become upset should take it slow and easy, sampling milder adventures like the E.T. Adventure, gauging reactions, and discussing with the children how they felt about what they saw. If your child has difficulty coping with the cartoon creatures in Despicable Me Minion Mayhem and Men in Black Alien Attack, you should think twice before exposing him or her to the photo-realistic Lord Voldemort in Harry Potter and the Escape from Gringotts, as this reader from Finstadjordet, Norway, wrote us to emphasize:

Please remember: children are different. My 8-year-old boy found Revenge of the Mummy a bit scary and a bit fun, but he was super-scared on both Harry Potter rides because they seemed "too real" compared to the other rides. It can be difficult to tell in advance what will scare your child, but try to read your child while waiting in line. Universal has excellent child-swap systems, and if in doubt, use them.

Sometimes young children will rise above their anxiety in an effort to please their parents or siblings. This doesn't necessarily indicate a mastery of fear, much less enjoyment. If children leave a ride in apparently good shape, ask if they would like to go on it again (not necessarily now but sometime). The response usually will indicate how much they actually enjoyed the experience.

Evaluating a child's capacity to handle the visual and tactile effects of Universal Orlando requires patience, understanding, and experimentation. Each of us has our own demons. If a child balks at or is frightened by a ride, respond constructively. Let your children know that lots of people, adults and children, are scared by what they see and feel. Help them understand that it's OK if they get frightened and that their fear doesn't lessen your love or respect. Take pains not to compound the discomfort by making a child feel inadequate; try not to undermine self-esteem, impugn courage, or ridicule. Most of all, don't induce guilt by suggesting the child's trepidation might be ruining the family's fun. It's also sometimes necessary to restrain older siblings' taunting.

A visit to Universal Orlando is more than an outing or an adventure for a young child. It's a testing experience, a sort of controlled rite of passage. If you help your little one work through the challenges, the time can be immeasurably rewarding and a bonding experience for you both.

THE FRIGHT FACTOR

WHILE EACH YOUNGSTER IS DIFFERENT, following are seven attraction elements that alone or combined could push a child's buttons and indicate that a certain attraction isn't age appropriate for that child:

1. NAME OF THE ATTRACTION Young children will naturally be apprehensive about something called, say, Skull Island or *Horror Make-Up Show.*

2. VISUAL IMPACT OF THE ATTRACTION FROM OUTSIDE Doctor Doom's Fearfall, Dudley Do-Right's Ripsaw Falls, The Incredible Hulk Coaster, Jurassic Park River Adventure, Reign of Kong, and Hollywood Rip Ride Rockit look scary enough to give adults second thoughts, and they terrify many young children.

3. VISUAL IMPACT OF THE INDOOR-QUEUING AREA The dark forest inside E.T. Adventure and the castle dungeon of Harry Potter and the Forbidden Journey can frighten children, and the creepy creatures

continued on page 186

SMALL-CHILD FRIGHT-POTENTIAL TABLE

This is a quick reference to identify attractions to be wary of, and why. The table represents a generalization, and all kids are different. It relates specifically to kids ages 3–7. On average, children at the younger end of the range are more likely to be frightened than children in their sixth or seventh year.

Universal Studios Florida

PRODUCTION CENTRAL

DESPICABLE ME MINION MAYHEM   Universal's mildest simulator motion-wise, but the huge 3-D images and loud soundtrack may startle preschoolers. Stationary benches are available in the front row to avoid the moving seats. Child swap available (see page 188).

HOLLYWOOD RIP RIDE ROCKIT   The tallest roller coaster at Universal Orlando, with loud music to cover your screams. May terrify guests of any age. Child swap available (see page 188).

SHREK 4-D   Intense, loud, and disrespectful toward beloved fairy-tale icons. Stationary seating is available to avoid the jerky moving chairs. Child swap available (see page 188).

TRANSFORMERS: THE RIDE 3-D   Intense, bloodlessly violent virtual reality simulator may frighten younger children and deafen guests of any age. Child swap available (see page 188).

NEW YORK

RACE THROUGH NEW YORK STARRING JIMMY FALLON   Moderate simulator motion, intense 3-D imagery, loud sounds, and the comedy stylings of Jimmy Fallon may disturb younger kids (and adults who remember Johnny Carson).

REVENGE OF THE MUMMY   Very intense roller coaster in the dark with angry mummies, bugs, and fireballs. May frighten guests of any age. Child swap available (see page 188).

SAN FRANCISCO

FAST & FURIOUS: SUPERCHARGED   Parental guidance suggested for intense simulated street-racing action with blasts of fog, loud noises, and improper use of turn signals. The actual motion of the vehicle is very mild. Child swap available (see page 188).

THE WIZARDING WORLD OF HARRY POTTER–DIAGON ALLEY

HARRY POTTER AND THE ESCAPE FROM GRINGOTTS   Visually intimidating with intense 3-D effects and brief moments of moderately fast roller coaster motion. Less frightening than Harry Potter and the Forbidden Journey but may still rattle some riders. Child swap available (see page 188).

HOGWARTS EXPRESS: KING'S CROSS STATION   Brief encounter with Dementors may scare some preschoolers; otherwise, not frightening.

OLLIVANDERS   Not frightening in any respect.

WORLD EXPO

FEAR FACTOR LIVE   An intense stunt show featuring people wearing and/or eating live insects. Explosive ending may startle preschoolers; may nauseate guests of any age.

MEN IN BLACK ALIEN ATTACK   Dark ride with spinning cars and comical aliens may frighten some preschoolers. Child swap available (see page 188).

SPRINGFIELD: HOME OF THE SIMPSONS

KANG & KODOS' TWIRL 'N' HURL   Dumbo-style midway ride. A favorite of many young children. Child swap available (see page 188).

THE SIMPSONS RIDE   Extremely intense visually, with USF's strongest simulated motion. May frighten many adults as well as kids. Child swap available (see page 188).

WOODY WOODPECKER'S KIDZONE

ANIMAL ACTORS ON LOCATION!   Not frightening in any respect, unless you have an animal phobia.

CURIOUS GEORGE GOES TO TOWN   Not frightening in any respect, but your kid may get soaked.

A DAY IN THE PARK WITH BARNEY   Not frightening in any respect, unless you have a purple-dinosaur phobia. Kids typically handle a brief period of darkness, as well as a few seconds of thunder and lightning, well.

E.T. ADVENTURE   Dark ride with simulated flight and psychedelic creatures. A little intense for a few preschoolers, but the end is all happiness and harmony. Child swap available (see page 188).

SMALL-CHILD FRIGHT-POTENTIAL TABLE *(continued)*

Universal Studios Florida *(continued)*

WOODY WOODPECKER'S KIDZONE *(continued)*

FIEVEL'S PLAYLAND Not frightening in any respect, except for the big slide that may scare some preschoolers.

WOODY WOODPECKER'S NUTHOUSE COASTER A beginner's roller coaster; safe for all but the most timid tykes. Child swap available (see page 188).

HOLLYWOOD

SPY STUNT SHOW (OPENS 2019) Intense action-movie fight choreography, including live gunfire, may startle viewers of all ages.

UNIVERSAL ORLANDO'S HORROR MAKE-UP SHOW Gory props and film clips, presented educationally and humorously, may wig out wee ones, but most children seem to handle it disturbingly well. Interestingly, very few families report problems with this show.

UNIVERSAL ORLANDO'S CINEMATIC CELEBRATION Oversize images of dinosaurs and Dementors, accompanied by loud fireworks, may startle small children.

Islands of Adventure

MARVEL SUPER HERO ISLAND

THE AMAZING ADVENTURES OF SPIDER-MAN Immersive 3-D effects and spinning simulator movement may frighten younger kids, but most take the comic book mayhem in stride. Technically similar to Transformers at USF but significantly less intense. Child swap available (see page 188).

DOCTOR DOOM'S FEARFALL Visually intimidating to all guests, with an intense launch and brief weightlessness. The actual plummeting is less protracted than on WDW's Tower of Terror. Child swap available (see page 188).

THE INCREDIBLE HULK COASTER Very intense looping roller coaster with a high-speed launch. This is a scary roller coaster by any standard. Child swap available (see page 188).

STORM FORCE ACCELATRON Teacups-type midway ride can induce motion sickness in all ages, though most kids seem to love it. Child swap available (see page 188).

TOON LAGOON

DUDLEY DO-RIGHT'S RIPSAW FALLS Visually intimidating from outside, with several intense, potentially drenching plunges. A toss-up, to be considered only if your kids like water-flume rides. Child swap available (see page 188).

ME SHIP, *THE OLIVE* Not frightening in any respect.

POPEYE & BLUTO'S BILGE-RAT BARGES Potentially frightening and certainly soaking for guests of all ages, but most younger children handle it well. Child swap available (see page 188).

SKULL ISLAND

SKULL ISLAND: REIGN OF KONG The ride vehicle's motion is fairly mild, but don't let the low minimum height fool you: the 3-D visuals of mutant bugs are grosser than anything outside *Fear Factor Live,* and the queue is even more frightening, with sections that resemble a haunted house. Child swap available (see page 188).

JURASSIC PARK

CAMP JURASSIC Some preschoolers may be spooked by the dark caves and dinosaur sounds; guests who are afraid of heights should avoid the net climb.

JURASSIC PARK DISCOVERY CENTER Not frightening in any respect.

JURASSIC PARK RIVER ADVENTURE Visually intimidating boat ride with life-size dinosaurs and an intense flume finale. May frighten and dampen guests of any age. Child swap available (see page 188).

PTERANODON FLYERS A short, slow suspended roller coaster. Frightens some children who are scared of heights and bores most adults who ride with them. Child swap available (see page 188).

RAPTOR ENCOUNTER The velociraptor makes loud, growling noises and sudden, snapping movements that startle even some adults.

THE WIZARDING WORLD OF HARRY POTTER–HOGSMEADE

FLIGHT OF THE HIPPOGRIFF Another beginner coaster, comparable to The Barnstormer at the Magic Kingdom. May frighten some preschoolers. Child swap available (see page 188).

HAGRID'S MAGICAL CREATURES COASTER *(OPENS 2019)* A moderately intense outdoor coaster with no loops, but forward and backward launches, dramatic drops, and close encounters with magical creatures may intimidate younger Muggles. Child swap available (see page 188).

HARRY POTTER AND THE FORBIDDEN JOURNEY Extremely intense special effects and macabre visuals with wild simulated movement that may frighten and discombobulate guests of any age. Child swap available (see page 188).

HOGWARTS EXPRESS: HOGSMEADE STATION Not frightening in any respect.

THE LOST CONTINENT

POSEIDON'S FURY Loud explosions, water effects, and brief periods of pitch darkness may scare younger children. You must remain standing through the entire attraction.

SEUSS LANDING

CARO-SEUSS-EL Not frightening in any respect. Child swap available (see page 188).

THE CAT IN THE HAT Mild spinning motion and modest visual effects may frighten a small percentage of preschoolers. Child swap available (see page 188).

THE HIGH IN THE SKY SEUSS TROLLEY TRAIN RIDE! May scare children who are afraid of heights; otherwise, not frightening in any respect. Child swap available (see page 188).

IF I RAN THE ZOO Not frightening in any respect.

ONE FISH, TWO FISH, RED FISH, BLUE FISH A tame midway ride that is a great favorite of most young children, though they will likely get wet. Child swap available (see page 188).

Volcano Bay

THE VOLCANO

VOL'S CAVERNS Dark pathways may spook sensitive toddlers; otherwise, not frightening.

RAINFOREST VILLAGE

KALA & TAI NUI SERPENTINE BODY SLIDES Even more terrifying than Ko'okiri, with twisting enclosed tubes and extreme g-forces.

MAKU ROUND RAFT RIDE Maku is one of the milder family raft rides in the park, with mostly open troughs and gentle curves. Don't mix it up with Puihi!

OHYAH AND OHNO DROP SLIDES The shortest twisting tube slides in the park, but the final drop of 4–6 feet can knock the wind out of weak swimmers.

PUIHI ROUND RAFT RIDE Puihi is among the scariest family raft rides in the park, with sharp turns that seem to nearly toss you onto the interstate.

PUKA ULI LAGOON Not frightening in any respect.

PUNGA RACERS Enclosed tubes may upset claustrophobes; otherwise, not frightening.

TANIWHA TUBES A moderately fast-moving raft slide with some surprising twists and drops. Each of the four tubes has a different configuration; accompany smaller kids on a two-seater raft, and ask for a green Tonga slide with more open-air sections if you get claustrophobic.

TEAWA THE FEARLESS RIVER Swift current can swamp smaller swimmers; life jackets are available in all sizes.

RIVER VILLAGE

HONU SLIDE Honu's hair-raising highly banked walls will wig out almost anyone. Don't confuse it with its sibling, ika Moana.

IKA MOANA SLIDE Ika Moana is a mild raft ride that most kids can handle.

KOPIKO WAI WINDING RIVER A brief segment floats through a dark, foggy cave; otherwise, not frightening in any respect.

KRAKATAU AQUA COASTER Roller coaster-style dips and brief enclosed tunnels may scare younger kids, but most find it thrilling.

RUNAMUKKA REEF Not frightening in any respect.

TOT TIKI REEF Not frightening in any respect.

WAVE VILLAGE

KO'OKIRI BODY PLUNGE High-speed vertical drop slide that will scare anyone silly.

THE REEF Not frightening in any respect.

WATURI BEACH Larger waves may overwhelm little ones; otherwise, not frightening in any respect.

continued from page 182

lurking inside Skull Island: Reign of Kong's temple ruins may induce an emergency undergarment change.

4. INTENSITY OF THE ATTRACTION   Some attractions inundate the senses with sights, sounds, movement, and even smell. USF's *Shrek 4-D,* for example, combines loud sounds, lights, water spray, and moving seats with 3-D cinematography to create a total sensory experience.

A Johnston, Iowa, mom describes the situation well:

> *The 3-D and 4-D experiences are way too scary for even a very brave 5-year-old girl. The shows that blew things on her, shot smells in the air, had bugs flying, etc. scared the bejabbers out of her.*

5. VISUAL IMPACT OF THE ATTRACTION   Sights in various attractions range from falling fish to flying bats, from grazing dinosaurs to gory body parts. What one child calmly absorbs may scare the bejabbers out of another the same age.

6. DARK   Many Universal attractions operate indoors in the dark. For some kids, this triggers fear. A child who gets frightened on one dark ride (E.T. Adventure, for example) may be unwilling to try other indoor rides.

7. THE TACTILE EXPERIENCE   Some rides are wild enough to cause motion sickness, wrench backs, and discombobulate guests of any age.

As a footnote, be aware that a kid's courage and confidence in regard to riding attractions doesn't necessarily increase as he or she gets older. A ride that delights a child at age 4 may scare them to death at 5; by 6 years old they may be fine again. As a dad from Maryland explains:

> *Just because a child loves a ride at one age doesn't mean that he or she will love it on the next trip.*

A BIT OF PREPARATION

WE RECEIVE MANY TIPS from parents about how they prepared their young children for their theme park experience. A common strategy is to acquaint children with the characters and stories behind the park attractions by reading Universal-related books and watching movies at home.

Universal Studios Florida's attractions prominently feature the family-friendly film series Despicable Me and Shrek (*E.T.* should already be on your kids' required viewing list), as well as Men in Black, Transformers, Fast & Furious, and The Mummy (only bother with the Boris Karloff and Brendan Fraser versions) if they are old enough for PG-13 entertainment. *The Simpsons* are in perpetual reruns, so refreshing your memory of Homer and family shouldn't be hard. For extra credit, screen Jaws and Back to the Future movies, and then hunt for hidden tributes to their extinct attractions.

Islands of Adventure was inspired by literature, so start by reading the classics before bedtime—Dr. Seuss, Stan Lee's superheroes, ancient mythology, and the Sunday funnies. For Jurassic Park, you can cheat and watch the original Spielberg film; for King Kong (the exception to the literary rule), watch the 2005 Peter Jackson remake, even though the 1933 original is still superior. Of course, you'll want to be well versed in all seven volumes of Harry Potter's academic career (along with the associated films, short stories, and spin-offs) to fully appreciate both Wizarding Worlds; if that's too much work, at a minimum you must watch the first movie before visiting Hogsmeade, and the last one before delving into Diagon Alley.

A more direct approach is to watch videos that show the attractions. Online, you'll find good point of view videos of most Universal attractions from TouringPlans, *Attractions Magazine,* Inside the Magic, and other bloggers. Videos of dark indoor rides—especially those that use 3-D glasses—never do the attractions justice, but they usually show enough for you to judge whether your child can comfortably handle the real thing. A Lexington, Kentucky, mom reports:

My timid 7-year-old daughter and I watched rides and shows on You-Tube, and we cut out all the ones that looked too scary.

ATTRACTIONS THAT EAT ADULTS

YOU MAY SPEND SO MUCH ENERGY worrying about Junior that you forget to take care of yourself. The following attractions can cause motion sickness or other problems for older kids and adults:

Potentially Problematic Attractions for Grown-Ups
UNIVERSAL STUDIOS FLORIDA
PRODUCTION CENTRAL Despicable Me Minion Mayhem | Hollywood Rip Ride Rockit | Transformers: The Ride 3-D
NEW YORK Revenge of the Mummy
THE WIZARDING WORLD OF HARRY POTTER–DIAGON ALLEY Harry Potter and the Escape from Gringotts
WORLD EXPO Men in Black Alien Attack
SPRINGFIELD: HOME OF THE SIMPSONS The Simpsons Ride
ISLANDS OF ADVENTURE
MARVEL SUPER HERO ISLAND The Amazing Adventures of Spider-Man | Doctor Doom's Fearfall | The Incredible Hulk Coaster | Storm Force Accelatron
TOON LAGOON Dudley Do-Right's Ripsaw Falls
THE WIZARDING WORLD OF HARRY POTTER–HOGSMEADE Harry Potter and the Forbidden Journey | Hagrid's Magical Creatures Coaster (opens 2019)
VOLCANO BAY
KRAKATAU Kala & Tai Nui Serpentine Body Slides | Ko'okiri Body Plunge
RAINFOREST VILLAGE Ohyah and Ohno Drop Slides | Puihi Round Raft Ride
RIVER VILLAGE Honu Raft Slide

A WORD ABOUT HEIGHT REQUIREMENTS

ALL ATTRACTIONS AT UNIVERSAL ORLANDO require that children be at least 48 inches tall to ride without a supervising companion, also known as an older family member or guardian. Most moving attractions at Universal Orlando require children to meet additional minimum height requirements. If you have children too short to ride, instead of skipping the ride or splitting up your group, consider using child swap (see below). For more information, see the table on the facing page. Regardless of height requirements, all guests must be able to sit up unassisted on all rides. Handheld infants are welcome in all shows, playgrounds, and walk-through attractions, but the only rides that accommodate handheld infants are Caro-Seuss-el and One Fish, Two Fish, Red Fish, Blue Fish in IOA; Kang & Kodos' Twirl 'n' Hurl and Despicable Me Minion Mayhem (ask for stationary seating) in USF; and Hogwarts Express.

Please note that height requirements only relate to the physical needs of a ride's safety restraints and are not a measure of whether an attraction is intellectually or psychologically appropriate for a given child, as this Illinois parent discovered too late:

> It is very important to stress that height requirements are NOT a good indicator for whether a child is ready for a ride. My almost 4-year-old is a big Harry Potter and Transformers fan and met the height requirements for Transformers and Escape from Gringotts, so we let him go on. He went through the entire ride without crying or screaming, but immediately upon the ride stopping in the bay, he turned to me and said, "I am NOT going on that ride again!" In retrospect, it was waaay too intense for a child of that age, whether he met the height requirement or not.

Child Swap (also known as Rider Swap, Baby Swap, or Switching Off)

Most Universal Orlando attractions have minimum height requirements. Some couples with children too small or too young forgo these attractions, while others take turns riding. Missing some of Universal's best rides is an unnecessary sacrifice, and waiting in line twice for the same ride is a tremendous waste of time.

Instead, take advantage of child swap, also known as baby swap, rider swap, or switching off. To child swap, there must be at least two adults. Adults and children wait in line together. When you reach a team member at the entrance of an attraction, say you want to child swap. The employee will allow everyone, including young children, to enter the attraction. When you reach the loading area, one adult rides while the other waits in a special child-swap holding area with the kids. Then the riding adult disembarks and takes charge of the children while the other adult rides. A third member of the party, either an adult or an older child, can ride twice, once with each switching-off adult, so that the switching-off adults don't have to ride alone.

Attraction Height Requirements

UNIVERSAL STUDIOS FLORIDA

Despicable Me Minion Mayhem	40" minimum height
E.T. Adventure	34" minimum height
Fast & Furious: Supercharged	40" minimum height
Harry Potter and the Escape from Gringotts	42" minimum height
Hollywood Rip Ride Rockit	51" minimum height; 79" maximum height
Men in Black Alien Attack	42" minimum height
Revenge of the Mummy	48" minimum height
The Simpsons Ride	40" minimum height
Transformers: The Ride 3-D	40" minimum height
Woody Woodpecker's Nuthouse Coaster	36" minimum height

ISLANDS OF ADVENTURE

The Amazing Adventures of Spider-Man	40" minimum height
The Cat in the Hat	36" minimum height
Doctor Doom's Fearfall	52" minimum height
Dudley Do-Right's Ripsaw Falls	44" minimum height
Flight of the Hippogriff	36" minimum height
Harry Potter and the Forbidden Journey	48" minimum height
The High in the Sky Seuss Trolley Train Ride!	36" minimum height
The Incredible Hulk Coaster	54" minimum height
Jurassic Park River Adventure	42" minimum height
Popeye & Bluto's Bilge-Rat Barges	42" minimum height
Pteranodon Flyers (Guests taller than 56" must be accompanied by a guest 36"–56".)	36" minimum height; 56" maximum height
Skull Island: Reign of Kong	36" minimum height

VOLCANO BAY

Honu Raft Slide	48" minimum height
ika Moana Raft Slide	42" minimum height
Kala & Tai Nui Serpentine Body Slides	48" minimum height
Ko'okiri Body Plunge	48" minimum height
Krakatau Aqua Coaster	42" minimum height
Maku Round Raft Ride	42" minimum height
Ohyah and Ohno Drop Slides	48" minimum height
Puihi Round Raft Ride	42" minimum height
Puka Uli Lagoon	under 48" must wear life vest
Punga Racers	42" minimum height
The Reef	under 48" must wear life vest
Taniwha Tubes: Tonga and Raki	42" minimum height
TeAwa the Fearless River	42" minimum height
Waturi Beach	under 48" must wear life vest

Child swap at Universal is similar to Disney's version but superior in several respects. Instead of one adult waiting at the exit with the children

and returning after through the FastPass+ queue, at Universal the entire family goes through the whole line together before being split into riding and nonriding groups near the loading platform. The nonriding parent and child(ren) wait in a designated room, usually with some sort of entertainment (for example, Harry Potter and the Forbidden Journey at IOA shows the first 20 minutes of *Harry Potter and the Sorcerer's Stone* on a loop), a place to sit down, and sometimes restrooms with changing tables. And nearly every attraction at Universal offers child swap, which can even be used if you don't have children; it works equally well for skittish or infirm adults who don't like thrill rides, or for designated baggage handlers in families who hate to use lockers.

Attractions where switching off is practiced are oriented to more mature guests. Sometimes it takes a lot of courage for a child just to move through the queue holding Dad's hand. In the boarding area, many children suddenly fear abandonment when one parent leaves to ride. Prepare your children for switching off, or you might have an emotional crisis on your hands. A mom from Edison, New Jersey, writes:

Once my son came to understand that the switch off would not leave him abandoned, he did not seem to mind. Practice the switch off on some dry runs at home, so your child is not concerned that he will be left behind. At the very least, the procedure should be explained in advance so that the little ones know what to expect.

An Ada, Michigan, mother discovered that the child-swap procedure varies among attractions. She says:

Parents need to tell the very first attendant they come to that they would like to switch off. Each attraction has a different procedure for this. Tell every other attendant too because they forget quickly.

As at any theme park, the best tip we can give is to ask the greeter in front of the attraction what you're supposed to do.

UNIVERSAL CHARACTERS

THOUGH OFTEN OVERSHADOWED by the fur-clad cartoon celebrities down the street, Universal Orlando also has a stable of characters to call its own and will sell you a notebook to store your signatures, but the interest in oversize cartoon vermin isn't anywhere near as intense as at Disney World; you'll occasionally see a Minion getting mobbed or a couple dozen families queued to meet SpongeBob, but never anything like the hour-plus waits that Disney's princesses can draw at the Magic Kingdom.

PREPARING YOUR CHILDREN TO MEET THE CHARACTERS

ALMOST ALL CHARACTERS ARE quite large, and several, like Sideshow Bob, are huge! Small children don't expect this, and preschoolers especially can be intimidated.

Discuss the characters with your children before you go. On first encounter, don't thrust your child at the character. Allow the little one to deal with this big thing from whatever distance feels safe. If two adults are present, one should stay near the youngster while the other approaches the character and demonstrates that it's safe and friendly. Some kids warm to the characters immediately; some never do. Most take a little time and several encounters.

unofficial TIP
Don't underestimate your child's excitement at meeting the Universal characters—but also be aware that very small children may find the large costumed characters a little frightening.

There are two kinds of characters: animated, or those whose costumes include face-covering headpieces (including animal characters and humanlike cartoon characters such as the Simpsons), and celebrities or face characters, those for whom no mask or headpiece is necessary. The latter includes Marilyn Monroe, Doc Brown, and the Knight Bus and Hogwarts Express conductors, among others.

Only face characters speak. Because team members couldn't possibly imitate the animated characters' distinctive cinema voices, Universal has determined that it's more effective to keep such characters silent. Lack of speech notwithstanding, headpiece characters are

warm and responsive, and they communicate effectively with gestures. Tell children in advance that these characters don't talk. Exciting exceptions are character encounters such as the Shrek meet and greet with Donkey and the Transformers photo op, where hidden actors or prerecorded audio clips are employed to allow interaction between costumed characters and guests.

Some character costumes are cumbersome and give performers very poor visibility. (Eyeholes frequently are in the mouth of the costume or even on the neck or chest.) Children who approach the character from the back or side may not be noticed, even if the child touches the character. It's possible in this situation for the character to accidentally step on the child or knock him down. A child should approach a character from the front, but occasionally not even this works. If a character appears to be ignoring your child, the character's handler will get its attention. Finally, some characters can't sign autographs because of their costumes.

It's OK for your child to touch, pat, or hug the character. Understanding the unpredictability of children, the character will keep his feet still, particularly refraining from moving backward or sideways. Most characters will pose for pictures or sign autographs. Costumes make it difficult for characters to wield a normal pen. If your child collects autographs, carry a pen the width of a Magic Marker.

UNIVERSAL CHARACTER-GREETING LOCATIONS

SOME UNIVERSAL ORLANDO CHARACTERS are confined to a specific location and visit with guests on a schedule that is printed on the park map. Characters who appear in the Superstar Parade also make daily Character Party Zone appearances in Hollywood, which include a mini-show and meet and greet. Other characters appear at random times in a few regular areas. Most mornings you'll find a rotating collection of characters near the entrance of the park. Not every character will appear every day; the busier the season, the more likely lesser-known characters will come out.

See the facing page for a guide to the places you're likely to find famous friends in Universal's parks.

CHARACTER DINING

UNIVERSAL ORLANDO OFFERS character meals at both its theme parks and hotels, but unlike Walt Disney World's Cinderella's Royal Table, you have a reasonable shot of supping with Spider-Man or Gru on short notice.

CHARACTER-GREETING LOCATIONS

UNIVERSAL STUDIOS FLORIDA

CELEBRITIES *(Face Characters)*

Beetlejuice Hollywood; Classic Monsters Café

Doc Brown from Back to the Future Hollywood; at the DeLorean outside Fast Food Boulevard

Knight Bus Conductor and Talking Head London Waterfront outside Diagon Alley

Lucille Ball Hollywood

Marilyn Monroe Hollywood; New York near Macy's

The Men in Black Hollywood; World Expo outside Men in Black Alien Attack

ANIMATED *(Costumed Characters)*

Barney the Dinosaur, BJ, & Baby Bop Woody Woodpecker's KidZone at *A Day in the Park with Barney*

Despicable Me Minions Hollywood; exit of Despicable Me Minion Mayhem ride

Dora the Explorer and Diego Hollywood

Gru, Agnes, Edith, Margo, and Vector from Despicable Me Hollywood

Hello Kitty Hollywood outside her store

Homer, Marge, Bart, and Lisa Simpson Hollywood; Springfield outside Kwik-E-Mart

Madagascar Penguins Hollywood behind Cafe La Bamba

Optimus Prime, Bumblebee, and Megatron from Transformers Eighth Avenue between the *Shrek 4-D* exit and Mel's Drive-In

Poppy and Branch from DreamWorks' *Trolls* Woody Woodpecker's KidZone

Scooby-Doo, Shaggy, and the Mystery Van Hollywood; Woody Woodpecker's KidZone

Shrek, Donkey, and Princess Fiona Eighth Avenue across from the *Shrek 4-D* exit

Sideshow Bob and Krusty the Clown Springfield outside Kwik-E-Mart

SpongeBob SquarePants, Squidward, and Patrick Hollywood; Woody Woodpecker's KidZone inside SpongeBob StorePants

ISLANDS OF ADVENTURE

CELEBRITIES *(Face Characters)*

Betty Boop Toon Lagoon outside The Betty Boop Store

Captain America Marvel Super Hero Island outside Captain America Diner

Dinosaur Keeper Jurassic Park

The Grinch (live-action version) Seuss Landing inside All The Books You Can Read store (seasonally)

Hogwarts Express Conductor Hogsmeade across from Honeydukes

Popeye and Olive Oyl Toon Lagoon outside Comic Strip Cafe

Rogue, Storm, Wolverine, and Cyclops Marvel Super Hero Island outside Marvel Alterniverse Store

Spider-Man Marvel Super Hero Island inside Marvel Alterniverse Store

ANIMATED *(Costumed Characters)*

Beetle Bailey Toon Lagoon outside Comic Strip Cafe

Blue the velociraptor Jurassic Park outside the Discovery Center

Cat in the Hat, Thing 1, and Thing 2 Seuss Landing at *Oh! The Stories You'll Hear!*

Green Goblin and Doctor Doom Marvel Super Hero Island outside Doctor Doom's Fearfall

The Grinch (cartoon version) Seuss Landing at *Oh! The Stories You'll Hear!*

The Lorax and Sam-I-Am Seuss Landing at *Oh! The Stories You'll Hear!*

A Marvel character dinner, featuring favorites from the Avengers and X-Men, is held in Islands of Adventure every Thursday–Sunday. The Royal Pacific Resort hosts a Despicable Me character breakfast with the Minions every Saturday. During the holiday season, the Grinch hosts a breakfast at Islands of Adventure. For further details, see page 198.

▐ BABYSITTING

CHILDCARE CENTERS

CHILDCARE ISN'T AVAILABLE INSIDE THE PARKS, but the top three Loews hotels each offer on-site kids' clubs that operate in the evenings to allow Mom and Dad a night out alone at CityWalk. Only on-site hotel guests may use the clubs, which rotate their days of operation seasonally; guests of any on-site hotel can register their kids at another hotel's club if the club at their hotel is closed. **Camp Portofino** at Portofino Bay, **Camp Lil' Rock** at Hard Rock Hotel, and **The Mariner's Club** at Royal Pacific all feature story time, arts and crafts, computer games, and a movie room. There is one counselor for every 8–10 children; participants must be toilet-trained and between ages 4 and 14. Childcare costs $15 per hour, per child, and an additional $15 per meal if they stay through dinnertime. The clubs operate Sunday–Thursday, 5–11:30 p.m., and Friday–Saturday, 5 p.m.–midnight; hours vary seasonally and are subject to change. Call ☎ 407-503-1200 for information and reservations.

IN-ROOM BABYSITTING

A COUPLE OF COMPANIES PROVIDE in-room sitting in Universal Orlando and surrounding areas, but **Kid's Nite Out** (☎ 800-696-8105; kidsniteout.com) is the resort's preferred provider, and who the concierge will call if you ask for a babysitter; the company also staffs the hotels' childcare centers. Kid's Nite Out also serves hotels in the greater Orlando area, including downtown. It provides sitters older than age 18 who are insured, bonded, screened, reference-checked, police-checked, and trained in CPR; bilingual sitters are also available. In addition to caring for your kids in your room, the sitters will, if you direct (and pay), take your children to the theme parks or other venues. Kid's Nite Out cares for children as young as six weeks old and can care for kids with special needs as well; rates start at $18 per hour for one child, up to $26 per hour for four children.

PART SIX

DINING *and* SHOPPING *at* UNIVERSAL ORLANDO

WHEN FOODIES ARE ASKED TO NAME great gourmet vacation spots around the world—New York, Paris, Singapore—Orlando probably doesn't immediately pop to the top of their wish lists. But believe it or not, Central Florida has developed a substantial culinary culture, from the prototype concepts tested by Darden and other major chains along Sand Lake Road's Restaurant Row and lauded gastropubs that have sprouted around downtown, to the thriving local community of upscale food trucks.

Even so, while adventurous eaters have always known there's plenty to explore in the greater Orlando area, and even tourist-phobic locals have long been lured to Walt Disney World (WDW) property by its lengthy list of restaurants, Universal has often been left out of the conversation. Thanks to the uniform mediocrity of Universal Studios Florida's (USF's) counter-service food during the resort's formative years, the conventional wisdom was that Universal Orlando's food options simply weren't as delicious or as diverse as those at Disney.

The good news is that, today, food in Universal is almost always on par with, or a step ahead of, what you can find at WDW and other parks. Thanks largely to the efforts of the resort's award-winning executive chef Steven Jayson, more variety, better preparations, and more current trends are generally the rule at Universal. And best of all, a first-class meal at Universal will almost always leave less of a dent in your credit card than the equivalent repast would at Mickey's table.

Quick-service (or counter-service, as it is sometimes called) offerings inside USF and Islands of Adventure (IOA) are largely lackluster, but Harry Potter's **Leaky Cauldron** and **Three Broomsticks,** and The Simpsons' **Fast Food Boulevard,** set a new bar for theme park fast food, and the fare at Volcano Bay is far fresher and more diverse than you'd expect from a water park.

USF's two full-service restaurants are **Finnegan's Bar and Grill** in New York and **Lombard's Seafood Grille** in San Francisco. Finnegan's serves typical bar food—burgers and wings—as well as fresh fish-and-chips and other takes on Irish cuisine. Lombard's is the better restaurant, but it's not in the same stratosphere as Disney's Hollywood Brown Derby (in quality or price).

IOA has two sit-down restaurants: **Confisco Grille** in Port of Entry and **Mythos Restaurant** in The Lost Continent. Confisco is fine for pizza and drinks. Despite its Hellenic-sounding name, Mythos isn't a Greek restaurant; rather it serves something-for-everyone fusion fare, including Italian risotto, Asian noodles, and Mexican fish tacos, plus steaks and burgers. Diners with dietary restrictions will be happy to see that Mythos has more options for vegetarian, vegan, and gluten-free diners than almost any other in-park Universal restaurant.

For even better eating options, exit the parks into **CityWalk**, Universal's dining, shopping, and entertainment district. CityWalk has seen welcome upgrades to its restaurant lineup in recent years with the addition of **Vivo Italian Kitchen, Toothsome Chocolate Emporium,** and **Antojitos Authentic Mexican Food,** along with **NBC Sports Grill & Brew** and **The Cowfish**'s much-better-than-it-sounds burger/sushi bar. We also like **Bob Marley** and **Pat O'Brien's** for drinks and music.

Many of the older CityWalk restaurants' menus are similar to Applebee's or Chili's. Given the average entrée from **Hard Rock Cafe** or **Jimmy Buffett's Margaritaville,** it would be difficult for a blindfolded diner to be certain from which restaurant it came. That blindfolded diner would probably guess that any plate with shrimp on it had a decent chance of coming from the **Bubba Gump Shrimp Co.,** but there's little else of note on its menu.

Some of Universal's best sit-down restaurants are found at the resort hotels, where the Flavor by Loews program features locally produced ingredients such as bread, honey, and beer. **The Palm Restaurant,** an upscale steakhouse in the Hard Rock Hotel, serves grade A meat at prices to match. If you're in the mood for Italian, try **Bice** (expensive) or **Mama Della's Ristorante** (moderate), both at the Portofino Bay Hotel. Asian food is the specialty at Universal's Royal Pacific, where **Islands Dining Room** is the primary sit-down destination. **Amatista Cookhouse,** the table-service restaurant at Sapphire Falls Resort, tends toward Caribbean comfort food, but the tapas and rum at **Strong Water Tavern** upstairs are top-shelf, as are the small plates and craft cocktails at **Bar 17 Bistro,** on the roof of the neighboring Aventura Hotel. Probably because they handle a lot of convention traffic, menu prices at Universal's Premier and Preferred resorts tend to be higher than you might expect, though they are still easier to swallow than the bill at Disney's top tables.

RESERVATIONS

ONE OF THE BIGGEST DIFFERENCES BETWEEN Walt Disney World and Universal Orlando is the ease with which you can secure dining reservations at the latter resort. If you're used to frantically booking your Disney Advance Dining Reservations 180 days before your vacation, you can relax. During much of the year, you can walk up and get a table at most Universal Orlando eateries with only a modest wait; guests staying at an on-site Premier or Preferred hotel can flash their key card to get seated even sooner.

While reservations are often not needed at Universal, you can use opentable.com or the OpenTable smartphone app to search for a seating at most of the sit-down hotel restaurants. CityWalk locations and in-park table-service restaurants use zomato.com, which also offers an app. If you're not sure which reservation system to use, visit tinyurl.com/unidinres, and click the RESERVE NOW button next to the restaurant where you wish to dine to see availability and make special requests. Alternatively, you can call ☎ 407-224-FOOD (3663) for in-park and CityWalk dining reservations, and ☎ 407-503-DINE (3463) for hotel restaurants. No deposit is necessary to book a Universal restaurant reservation, so there's no penalty when your dinner plans inevitably change. Most of the CityWalk and in-park restaurants only take reservations 30 days in advance, but the hotel restaurants accept bookings 90 days out, and The Palm will let you reserve for next year. If you are visiting at a peak time of the year (such as Thanksgiving or late December) or during a major convention, we suggest making table-service reservations a couple of weeks to a month in advance.

DRESS

DRESS IS INFORMAL AT ALL park restaurants and in CityWalk's restaurants. At upscale resort restaurants such as Hard Rock's Palm Restaurant or Bice, men are not permitted to wear sleeveless shirts, and resort casual wear is appropriate (but not required) for dinner: khakis, dress slacks, jeans, or dress shorts with a collared shirt for men and Capris, skirts, dresses, jeans, or dress shorts for women.

FOOD ALLERGIES AND SPECIAL REQUESTS

FOR SIT-DOWN MEALS, if you have food allergies or observe a specific diet such as eating kosher or gluten-free, make your needs known when you make your dining reservation and again when your waiter introduces himself at your table. The waitstaff or chef will be able to tell you the kinds of accommodations the kitchen is prepared to make for your meal.

Accommodating dietary needs is more difficult at fast-food places because staff may not be as familiar with the menu's ingredients or preparation. Ask to see the allergen information book, which should be behind the counter at every quick-service location; it lists the menu items that can be made or modified for various diets. When our vegans and vegetarians have doubts about menu descriptions, their strategy is usually to default to the simplest, most-likely-to-be-acceptable item.

See page 166 for additional dietary details.

CHARACTER MEALS

UNIVERSAL OFFERS ONE YEAR-ROUND in-park character dinner, held every Thursday–Sunday starting at 5 p.m. at **Cafe 4** inside Islands of Adventure. During the **Marvel Character Dinner,** guests dine with characters from the X-Men like Wolverine and Storm, plus Spider-Man and Captain America from the Avengers. The cost is $49.99 for adults and $24.99 for kids; park admission is required and not included, nor is gratuity. A buffet meal with your choice of salads, pastas, pizzas, and Italian entrées is served, along with soft drinks and dessert. The food is a notch above Cafe 4's standard fare, with shrimp scampi, stuffed pasta shells, and chicken scaloppine on the menu. Attendees also get a digital photo card documenting their Marvel-ous meal. The half dozen assembled heroes circulate among the tables separately, and all excel at interacting with fans of every age. Days and times are subject to change; you can book online at tinyurl.com/marveldinner, but you must call ☎ 407-224-3663 at least 24 hours before your meal to reserve your table.

There's also a weekly character breakfast every Saturday morning at the **Tahitian Room** (formerly Emeril's Tchoup Chop) in the Royal Pacific Resort. Gru and his Minions from Despicable Me, along with sisters Margo, Edith, and Agnes, are the guests of honor. The cost is $34.99 for adults, $20.99 for kids ages 3–9. The meal includes a full breakfast buffet featuring an omelet station and a digital photo of your character encounter. Seatings are at 8, 9:30, and 11 a.m. You

Casting? There's been a mistake. We were supposed to get the Assorted Character Package with one SpongeBob, one Dora, one Gru . . .

must reserve at least 24 hours in advance by visiting loewscharacter breakfast.tix.com or by calling ☎ 407-503-DINE (3463).

During the holiday season, Universal offers a breakfast in Islands of Adventure's **Seuss Landing** with the Grinch, played by an extremely interactive actor in film-quality prosthetic makeup. This meal (which may include green eggs and ham, if you wish) is held only on select mornings in November and December, 8–10 a.m., and pricing and reservations info are the same as the Despicable Me breakfast.

UNIVERSAL ORLANDO DINING PLANS

UNIVERSAL OFFERS TWO FLAVORS of dining plans that allow guests to prepay for their food, and potentially save some money in the process. The **Quick Service Universal Dining Plan** provides one quick-service meal (including an entrée platter and soft drink), another soft drink, and one snack. The cost is $23.99 for adults and $15.99 for kids age 9 and younger. It's valid at most quick-service eateries in all three parks (including Three Broomsticks at The Wizarding World of Harry Potter–Hogsmeade, the Leaky Cauldron in Diagon Alley, and Fast Food Boulevard in Springfield), plus a smattering at Universal CityWalk, but not at any hotel eateries. You can view a complete list of participating restaurants at tinyurl.com/unidineplan.

Virtually every entrée at participating venues can be purchased with a quick-service meal credit, even combo platters that include a side salad or milkshake. A few of the most expensive items, such as whole pizzas, aren't covered. For your nonalcoholic beverages, you can choose from a regular-size fountain beverage; bottled water, juice, or sports drink; or coffee, cocoa, or tea (including tall Starbucks brews). Eligible snacks include churros, pretzels, popcorn, ice cream (regular-size cup or cone, or novelty bar), fruit, cookies, and pastries. Some larger items from snack vendors, such as turkey legs and hot dogs, count as a quick-service meal. Credits can even be used inside The Wizarding Worlds, though the Universal Dining eligibility logo doesn't appear on Potter menus for thematic reasons. However, signature beverages such as Butterbeer will count as a snack, not a drink.

If two sodas a day isn't enough for you, a souvenir Coca-Cola Freestyle cup can be added to any quick-service dining plan for an additional $6, which includes unlimited refills from the Freestyle machines found around the parks (see page 207).

Universal claims that the plan can save you up to 25%, but unless you use all your credits and order carefully, adults will probably do as well or better buying à la carte with an annual pass or AAA discount (which cannot be applied to purchasing the plan). We're also not big fans in principal of prepaying for meals, but thankfully Universal doesn't force you to book it for every day of your vacation or for every member of your party. It is possible to purchase the quick-service dining plan in advance when reserving your vacation, but there's really no need to.

Instead, take advantage of your ability to buy into the plan on a day-by-day basis at any participating restaurant *after* you've already made your menu selection. If your entrée and drink add up to at least $18 before tax, and you aren't eligible for any discounts, it's probably in your best interest to ask the cashier to sell you a quick-service plan. The extra few dollars will net another beverage (worth about $3–$4.50) and snack (worth $2.50–$7) for the afternoon, saving you up to $4–$5 on average. Order a ribs platter and pumpkin fizz from Three Broomsticks with a dining plan, and your second drink and snack are essentially free. On the other hand, if you order a vegan burger, two bottles of juice, and a giant cookie, you'll lose about $6 on the deal. As for the kids, the children's plan is almost universally a good deal. Because kids' meals all cost $6.99 without a beverage, even buying bottles of water and a banana puts you in the black. (And there's no law saying that adults with smaller appetites can't order from the children's menu.) Finally, the key to maximizing the value of your dining plan is using the snack credit on a Butterbeer. At $6.99, it's the most expensive eligible snack item in the parks, and arguably the tastiest; order one with the aforementioned ribs and you can save up to $10. The dining-plan cards aren't tied to a particular person, so they can be traded among family members, and they don't expire at the end of the day—unused credits hold their value as long as you hold onto the card. Just be aware that if you have a large group, juggling the plan's plastic can become a pain, because each person receives a separate card for every day.

A **Table Service Universal Dining Plan** is also offered to on-site hotel guests buying vacation packages, but it's a much worse bargain. The full-service plan costs $59.99 per adult per day ($22.99 for kids) and includes everything the quick-service plan does, plus one table-service meal (entrée, soft drink, and select dessert; gratuity not included) per day. Unfortunately, there are only a dozen participating restaurants on property, none of which are in the resort hotels—which is strange because the only way to buy the table-service plan is as part of a Universal Orlando Vacations hotel package. The table-service plan probably wouldn't be a great deal even if Universal gave it away "free"; at full price, you're basically throwing money away.

FAST FOOD *in* UNIVERSAL ORLANDO'S PARKS

FAST FOOD IS AVAILABLE THROUGHOUT Universal Studios Florida (USF), Islands of Adventure (IOA), Volcano Bay, and CityWalk. The food compares in quality to McDonald's, Arby's, or Taco Bell but is more expensive, though often served in larger portions. Quick-service prices are fairly consistent from park to park. Expect to pay about the same for your coffee or hot dog at USF or IOA as at WDW. Please note that the following menu prices do not include sales tax, unless otherwise noted.

QUICK-SERVICE RECOMMENDATIONS AT UNIVERSAL STUDIOS FLORIDA

MUCH OF THE QUICK SERVICE at USF is utterly unremarkable: burgers, pizza, pasta, chicken fingers, sandwiches, and salads. The mediocre food is matched by the predictable theming in the park's original fast-food joints: American diner? Check. New York Italian? Got it. We're a little surprised that there's not a Chinese-takeout place next to a laundry in the San Francisco section.

The Springfield: Home of the Simpsons themed area brings a number of wacky *Simpsons*-inspired eateries to life along **Fast Food Boulevard,** including **Krusty Burger, The Frying Dutchman** for seafood, **Cletus' Chicken Shack, Luigi's Pizza, Lard Lad Donuts, Lisa's Teahouse of Horror, Bumblebee Man's Taco Truck, Duff Brewery,** and **Moe's Tavern.** Serving sizes are large, and the food quality is an improvement over your run-of-the-mill theme park fare, with dozens of menu items (including tater tots and curly fries) that aren't available in any other quick-service location.

The best quick-service food in USF can currently be found at the **Leaky Cauldron.** Diagon Alley's flagship restaurant serves authentically hearty British pub fare such as bangers and mash, cottage pie, toad-in-the-hole, Guinness stew, and a ploughman's platter for two of Scotch eggs and imported cheeses. When you're done, head over to **Florean Fortescue's Ice-Cream Parlour** for some delicious Butterbeer ice cream.

QUICK-SERVICE RECOMMENDATIONS AT ISLANDS OF ADVENTURE

OF ISLANDS OF ADVENTURE'S quick-service offerings, we like **Three Broomsticks,** the counter-service restaurant in The Wizarding World of Harry Potter–Hogsmeade, which serves Boston Market–style rotisserie chicken, plus fish-and-chips, shepherd's pie, and barbecue ribs. The **Hog's Head** pub, attached to Three Broomsticks, serves beer, wine, mixed drinks, and the obligatory Butterbeer (see page 203).

We're also fond of the gyros at **Fire-Eater's Grill,** the kebabs at **Doc Sugrue's Kebab House,** and especially the ribs and roasted corn at **Thunder Falls Terrace.** Almost all of the other IOA counter-service places serve some variation of burgers, chicken, pizza, or pasta, and while your superhero-loving kids are going to be drawn toward Marvel Island's **Cafe 4** and **Captain America Diner** as if the Pied Piper himself was leading them there, avoid both, as there are much better places to eat.

QUICK-SERVICE RECOMMENDATIONS AT VOLCANO BAY

WHEN VOLCANO BAY FIRST OPENED, it made a big splash by offering exotic, island-inspired fare that far exceeded standard water park counter-service snacks. Early guests balked at both the unfamiliar ingredients and the long waits required to assemble them. As a result, some of the more upscale items, such as shrimp tacos, were swiftly swapped for old standbys like nachos. Happily, most of our favorite 86'd dishes—including the ahi tuna poké—have since been restored, so you can still eat exceptionally well at Volcano Bay.

At **Bambu** in Rainforest Village, we enjoy the grilled mahi-mahi sandwich with pineapple salsa, and the creamy coconut chicken salad. Also at Rainforest Village is **The Feasting Frog;** try the poké with plantain chips or carne asada tacos. At River Village, **Whakawaiwai Eats** is home to Hawaiian pizza (with caramelized pineapple, diced ham, and jalapeños) and mac and cheese with jerk shrimp. At **Kohola Reef Restaurant & Social Club** in Wave Village, we love slow-smoked ribs, the quinoa-edamame burger (topped with roasted shiitake mushrooms and sriracha mayo), and the coconut curry chicken with sweet plantains. For dessert, it's impossible to choose between chocolate lava cake and the pineapple upside-down cake—so order both! **Dancing Dragons Boat Bar** (Rainforest Village) and **Kunuku Boat Bar** (Wave Village) serve exotic drinks, but the signature cocktails are far too sugary for our taste. Stick with the locally brewed Volcano Blossom beer instead.

QUICK-SERVICE RECOMMENDATIONS AT CITYWALK AND RESORT HOTELS

DINING OPTIONS AT CITYWALK and the resort hotels are oriented toward sit-down restaurants, but there are some counter-service choices worth considering. The chain franchises on CityWalk's upper floor have a following for their familiarity, but **Hot Dog Hall of Fame, Fusion Bistro Sushi,** and **Bread Box** serve food that's a step above the drive-through. **Red Oven Pizza** is a fast-casual cross between quick-service and sit-down, and it's delicious no matter how you slice it. For a snack, **Menchie's Frozen Yogurt** and **Voodoo Doughnut** don't disappoint. The best quick-service hotel food is found at **Sal's Market Deli,** whose pies and salads are second only to Red Oven, and at Aventura's **Urban Pantry** food hall; Cabana Bay's **Bayliner Diner** food court has the widest range of selections.

QUICK-SERVICE COURTESY

GETTING YOUR ACT TOGETHER REGARDING quick-service restaurants in the parks is more a matter of courtesy than necessity. Rude guests rank fifth among reader complaints. A mother from Fort Wayne, Indiana, points out that indecision can be as maddening as outright discourtesy, especially when you're hungry:

Every fast-food restaurant has menu signs the size of billboards, but do you think anybody reads them? People waiting in line spend enough time in front of these signs to memorize them and still don't have a clue what they want when they finally get to the counter. If, by some miracle, they've managed to choose between the hot dog and the hamburger, they then fiddle around another 10 minutes deciding what size Coke to order. Folks, PULEEEZ get your orders together ahead of time!

On that note, it's also courteous to have your form of payment (cash, credit, hotel key, or dining-plan card) in hand by the time you approach the cashier.

A close second on the frustrating scale are folks without food who monopolize restaurant tables while others balance trays, searching for a place to sit and eat. It's polite to wait until you've received your food before claiming a seat, and employees may enforce this policy on busy days, as one family discovered:

> Many of the indoor counter-service restaurants require you to purchase your meal before they seat you. We were looking for a break from the sun with our turkey leg and other things bought from a cart. If we had known, we would have bought food from the specific counter-service place with indoor seating. We found that Circus McGurkus was the one place where we could bring in other food.

THE WIZARDING WORLD OF BEVERAGES: BUTTERBEER AND BEYOND

The Butterbeer Craze

In the fictional Wizarding World, **Butterbeer** is a mildly intoxicating treat favored by Harry Potter and other Hogwarts students. It made its first appearance in the book *Harry Potter and the Prisoner of Azkaban,* and ever since it has made fans' mouths water with dreams of the taste, enticingly described as "a little bit like less-sickly butterscotch."

In the real world, the Butterbeer served at Universal Orlando is a non-alcoholic beverage served from a tap, with a butterscotch-y marshmallow foam head that's added after the drink is poured; it's guaranteed to leave you with a selfie-worthy mustache. Whereas in the books Butterbeer can be bought cold in bottles or hot in "foaming tankards," at Universal there are three liquid varieties, none of which are packaged for taking home, plus three Butterbeer-flavored solid snacks. All were invented by chef Steven Jayson for The Wizarding World and had to meet J. K. Rowling's stringent specifications, which, among other things, required natural sugar (don't ask for Butterbeer Lite). We didn't expect to like it but were pleasantly surprised: it's tasty and refreshing, albeit really sweet.

First, there is the basic **cold Butterbeer,** which is a vanilla cream soda–style liquid with the foam topping. There's also a **frozen Butterbeer** that's sort of like a slush made from the same cream soda base, again topped with foam. Frozen is the only variety that comes with a straw; beware of putting a straw in the cold kind because stirring the liquid can cause an embarrassing eruption.

After the success of the first two temperatures, Universal introduced **hot Butterbeer,** which it brings back seasonally each year during the colder months of November–March (like Starbucks's pumpkin spice but more magical). The hot variety eschews the soda base for a rich, creamy beverage that resembles a vanilla chai latte, light on the chai. The signature foam stays on top, natch.

The cold and frozen versions go for $6.99 in a 16-ounce plastic cup. The same drink in a Harry Potter souvenir cup sells for an additional $6, but there is no discount on Butterbeer refills (you do get $1.49 refills on non-Freestyle soda outside The Wizarding World). The hot version is sold in a 12-ounce paper cup for $6.99.

Note that while Butterbeer is gluten-free, and the base of cold and frozen Butterbeer has no dairy products, the "nondairy" foam topping contains whey, a protein derived from milk. For licensing reasons, they refuse to serve the drinks without the topping, even if you are vegan or lactose intolerant.

Finally, Diagon Alley introduced the world to soft-serve **Butterbeer ice cream,** which tastes almost exactly like the drinks. You can get it at Florean Fortescue's in a cup ($5.49), waffle cone ($7.49), or plastic souvenir sundae glass ($10.99). If you want only a cup of Butterbeer ice cream without toppings, the soft-serve is also available off menu at The Hopping Pot and Fountain of Fair Fortune, where you'll find a shorter wait. A cart in Hogsmeade serves hard-packed Butterbeer ice cream in prepackaged cups ($5.49), but it isn't as good as the soft serve. In Diagon Alley you'll find **Butterbeer potted cream** in the Leaky Cauldron (a deliciously light butterscotch mousse) and **Butterbeer fudge** at Sugarplum's (inedibly saccharine with a candy corn–like crust).

If forced to choose among the different types of Butterbeer, Seth's hands-down favorite is the frozen version; the ice crystals seem to dull the overpowering sweetness. That is, unless it's cold out or early in the morning, in which case hot Butterbeer is the clear winner. Lastly, while it's officially forbidden to adulterate your Butterbeer, if you want to order a cup of the frozen stuff at the Hog's Head alongside a shot of, say, Irish cream . . . we won't tell if you pour it in while the barkeep's back is turned.

It seems that everyone in the parks is dead set on trying Butterbeer, as confirmed by Universal's 1 million sales of it within just the first seven months of offering the beverage. Unfortunately, in IOA's Hogsmeade, the ambrosial liquid is sold only at **Three Broomsticks,** at the **Hog's Head** pub, and by two street vendors. That can mean long waits, as many guests buy from the outside carts, waiting 30 minutes or more in line to be served. The outdoor vendors also charge a few pennies more and don't honor annual pass discounts. We recommend that you try your luck at the Hog's Head; the wait here is generally 10 minutes or less, and often there's nobody in line, even when the outdoor carts have lines 30 people deep only 20 feet away. Once served, you can relax with your drink at a table in the pub or out on the rear patio.

Universal learned its lesson and installed more Butterbeer taps around USF's Diagon Alley, where it flows freely in the **Leaky Cauldron, The Hopping Pot,** and **Fountain of Fair Fortune.** Unfortunately, it forgot to install enough seating to enjoy your drink. Once the picnic tables in Carkitt Market are full, your best bet is to squat on the "stairs to nowhere" next to Harry Potter and the Escape from Gringotts.

Beyond Butterbeer

Though Butterbeer gets most of the press, Hogsmeade has had a handful of other signature Harry Potter drinks since its inception, and Diagon Alley debuted many more. You might as well try one because you won't find any Coca-Cola products whatsoever inside The Wizarding World.

Foremost at both parks is **Pumpkin Juice,** which has a slightly pulpy texture and tastes like Thanksgiving dessert. It is available in a cup ($4.99) or a souvenir plastic bottle ($7.50); a sparkling **Pumpkin Fizz** version ($4.99) is served only in Hogsmeade. Refreshing nonalcoholic **Cider** ($3.69) is also on draft in apple or pear flavors. Other exclusive drinks in Diagon Alley include:

TONGUE TYING LEMON SQUASH ($5.49) A tart squeezed-to-order lemonade.

OTTER'S FIZZY ORANGE JUICE ($5.49) Lightly carbonated orange drink with a lip-smacking crust of cinnamon-sugar on the cup's rim; one of our favorites.

FISHY GREEN ALE ($5.49) Green cinnamon-mint boba tea with blueberry "fish eggs" that burst blueberry in your mouth when sucked through a straw. A must-try for the novelty factor but not necessarily a must-finish; many find it downright nasty.

PEACHTREE FIZZING TEA ($5.49) Lightly carbonated sweetened iced tea with peach and ginger flavors.

GILLYWATER ($4.50) A small plastic bottle of filtered water with a Harry Potter label. Seriously! For an extra $4.25 you can get it paired with a vial of flavored "magical elixir" available in four varieties—

Top Six Snacks Outside The Wizarding Worlds

FINE DINING IS ALL WELL AND GOOD, but many park visitors consume the majority of their calories enjoying the kind of pushcart sweets and midway treats that make it possible to walk 10 miles a day during your Orlando vacation and still gain weight. With that in mind, we turned to Universal Orlando eating expert Derek Burgan—author of the popular "Saturday Six" series on touringplans.com—for the best snacks to be found at USF and IOA, beyond the aforementioned Wizarding World exclusives:

6. CHURRO (both parks) The omnipresent churro, a cinnamon-sugar stick of fried dough, remains one of the tastiest treats in the theme park world; it's also the easiest to traverse the parks with.

5. CHEESECAKE (USF) Not just any cheesecake, Beverly Hills Boulangerie cheesecake. These massive slices will set your heart aflutter (both literally and figuratively).

4. LARD LAD'S BIG PINK DONUT (USF) Big enough to share, this doughnut from Springfield: Home of the Simpsons is guaranteed to put a smile on your face (if not send you straight into a diabetic coma). If you want to start a little smaller, try a standard-size doughnut crusted with crushed chocolate sandwich cookies, fruit cereal, or even bacon.

3. GOURMET APPLE (both parks) Candy apples at Universal are becoming works of art. One worth going out of your way to try is the Rocky Road Gourmet Apple. Covered with caramel, chocolate, pecans, and marshmallows, this apple is almost the size of a human head but much more delicious (no offense to our cannibal readers).

2. BROOKIE (both parks) The best thing since chocolate met peanut butter, the brookie fuses a brownie with a chocolate chip cookie, and it tastes just as good as it sounds.

1. BRAIN FREEZIN D'OH-NUT SUNDAE (USF) The combination of soft-serve ice cream sandwiched between halves of a warm doughnut turns out to be one of mankind's greatest creations. A culinary delight.

Before we go, let's also mention the *worst* snack outside The Wizarding World: **candy filled with insects** (both theme parks). You will be shocked at how many stores on property carry lollipops or other pieces of candy with actual insects (such as ants and scorpions) encased inside them. It's the closest we here in America can come to re-creating the dinner scene from *Indiana Jones and the Temple of Doom.*

Fire Protection (watermelon, peach, and strawberry), **Babbling Beverage** (fruit punch), **Draught of Peace** (blueberry, blackberry, and cherry), and **Euphoria** (pineapple and mint)—to enhance your water. The most magical thing about the elixirs is how much money Universal has made disappear from Muggles' wallets with fancy punch.

Finally, adults who imbibe shouldn't feel left out of the fun; Universal contracted Florida Beer Company to come up with a trio of exclusive beers served only inside The Wizarding World. In Hogsmeade, Three Broomsticks and Hog's Head pub serve **Hog's Head Brew,** a hoppy Scottish ale. Diagon Alley's Leaky Cauldron, The Hopping Pot, and Fountain of Fair Fortune pour **Wizard's Brew,** a heavy dark porter with chocolate notes, and **Dragon Scale,** a Vienna-style amber lager. All are served in 20-ounce cups for $8.99 and are poured from creative custom-carved taps. Ask your bartender about secret off-menu concoctions, such as the Triple (unofficially known as a Deathly Hallows), made from layers of Strongbow, Hog's Head ale, and Guinness. Cart vendors in the streets and queues around Diagon Alley also sell cans of "domestic" brews such as Stella Artois and Strongbow.

For an added kick, try **Blishen's Fire Whisky,** a 70-proof cinnamon-flavored liquor distilled exclusively for the parks by TerrePURE Spirits of South Carolina. The flavor is warm but wonderfully smooth, and much more drinkable than the superficially similar Fireball whiskey that was briefly in vogue. Fire Whisky is available at the Leaky Cauldron and Hopping Pot in USF and at the Hog's Head in IOA. It is served neat or on the rocks as single ($8.99) or double ($15.75) shots, or can be mixed in nonalcoholic apple or pear cider for the same price. A pint of Strongbow with a Fire shot is $13 and tastes like apple pie. While Fire Whisky can't officially be served in Butterbeer, we can vouch for a shot snuck into a cup of hot Butterbeer as a breakfast eye-opener.

REFILLABLE DRINKS AND POPCORN

ONE SMART WAY TO CUT snacking costs—if not calories—around Universal Orlando is by investing in refillable souvenir containers. Souvenir cups never expire and can be brought back to the park months or years in the future.

Universal sells two different types of refillable soft drink cups. The standard **collectible souvenir cups** are found around the resort in various styles for $7–$16, including your first fill-up, and can be refilled at almost any soda fountain in the parks or CityWalk for $1.49 plus tax. They can only be refilled for that price with regular fountain flavors—Coke, Diet Coke, Sprite, root beer, or Hi-C—and not with any specialty drinks. However, you do get a modest discount when using a souvenir cup to purchase an Icee, lemon slush, and some other specialty drinks. Pricier character cups (shaped like Transformers or Minions) and specialty souvenir cups (like Butterbeer mugs) can also be refilled with sodas for the same price, but you only get as much as those sometimes skimpy cups can contain.

In addition to the standard souvenir soda cups, Universal also sells **Coca-Cola Freestyle souvenir cups** at dining locations with Freestyle soda machines. These massive red marvels can mix dozens of different drink brands and additional flavorings together to dispense more than 100 soft drink combinations, including exclusive flavors such as Gamma Green and Celebrity Fizz; you haven't lived until you've had an Orange Coke. The self-service Freestyle fountains can only be activated by the RFID computer chip on the base of the cup. You can purchase a single-use Freestyle cup from select quick-service restaurants for $3.49, or buy a reusable souvenir cup that is valid for unlimited refills (with a 10-minute pause in between pours) for the entire day. Freestyle cups cost $15.99 plus tax for one, $14.99 each for two, or $12.99 each for three or more ($6 if purchased with a quick-service dining plan at participating in-park locations) and can be reactivated for an additional $7.99 per day; rinse and repeat for as many days as you like. Freestyle cups can also be refilled for free with frozen slush drinks. (Moose Juice and Goose Juice at IOA's Seuss Landing are eligible, but Springfield Squishees, alas, are not.) Freestyle cups cannot be refilled at regular soda fountains, and Freestyle machines aren't yet ubiquitous, with about a dozen dispensers in each theme park and a handful at Volcano Bay. You cannot get filtered water from Freestyle machines without an activated cup, but any restaurant will give you a cup of free ice water on request, which tastes much better than the sulfurous, lukewarm liquid flowing from the parks' drinking fountains.

A related program is the **Souvenir Cup Drink Package** sold exclusively at Aventura Hotel, Cabana Bay Beach Resort (where it is known as **Sonic Fill**), and Sapphire Falls Resort. This cup costs $9.99 plus tax for one day of use, $15.99 for three days, or $17.99 for the entire length of your stay at the resort. A day is considered a calendar day and ends at midnight. Souvenir mugs can be refilled at the Coke Freestyle soda stations in the Bayliner Diner, Galaxy Bowl, and pool areas at Cabana Bay; at Aventura's Urban Pantry; and in New Dutch Trading Co. and the pool area at Sapphire Falls. The cups are only compatible with the Freestyle machines at the hotel they were purchased at and can't be used inside the parks, nor can the parks' Freestyle cups be used at the hotels.

If you're looking for something harder to whet your whistle, all of the hotels' pool bars sell cocktails in souvenir cups for about $15 that can be refilled for only $10 at any of the other hotels, except Cabana Bay, whose refillable cups are larger and cheaper than those at the pricier resorts. Cabana Bay Beach Resort even sells a special watertight "pool cup" that allows you to drink while drifting on the lazy river, which is normally a no-no. Souvenir cocktail glasses are also available in CityWalk at Fat Tuesday's but are not honored at the freestanding bars. Souvenir beer pilsners are sold inside the parks at select bars (including Moe's Tavern and Chez Alcatraz in USF) for about $13; refills cost the same as a regular drink, but you get a couple extra ounces for free. Refillable cocktail cups with blinking lights (in case you get blind drunk?) are sold at a similar price during events like Halloween and Mardi Gras.

Lastly, street-cart vendors in Universal's parks sell fresh popcorn in either $4.79 single servings or $6.99 **souvenir popcorn buckets** that can be refilled as often as your sodium level can stand for only $1.99. Flavored varieties such as caramel or cheese can be refilled for $3.69, and (like the soda cups) buckets can be brought back on future trips.

CUTTING YOUR DINING TIME AT THE THEME PARKS

EVEN IF YOU CONFINE YOUR MEALS to vendor and quick-service fast food, you lose a lot of time getting food in the theme parks. Here are some ways to minimize the time you spend hunting and gathering:

1. Eat breakfast before you arrive. Restaurants outside the parks offer some outstanding breakfast specials. Plus, some hotels furnish small refrigerators in their guest rooms, or you can rent a fridge or bring a cooler. If you can get by on cold cereal, rolls, fruit, and juice, this will save a ton of time.

2. After a good breakfast, buy snacks from vendors in the parks as you tour, or stuff some snacks in a fanny pack.

3. All theme park restaurants are busiest between 11:30 a.m. and 2:15 p.m. for lunch and 6 and 9 p.m. for dinner. For shorter lines and faster service, don't eat during these hours, especially 12:30–1:30 p.m.

4. Many quick-service restaurants sell cold sandwiches. Buy a cold lunch minus drinks before 11:30 a.m., and carry it in small plastic bags until you're ready to eat (within an hour or so of purchase). Ditto for dinner. Buy drinks at the appropriate time from any convenient vendor.

5. Most fast-food eateries have more than one service window. Regardless of the time of day, check the lines at all windows before queuing. Sometimes a window that's staffed but out of the way will have a much shorter line or none at all. Note, however, that some windows may offer only certain items.

6. At press time, Universal Orlando had just begun testing a Mobile Express option, which allows guests to select and purchase their meals through the smartphone app. Menu prices are the same as if ordering in person, and you can customize some entrées and side items. The service is currently available only at a few select quick-service locations, and payment must be made by credit card (no discounts or dining plans accepted), but users get to bypass the queue for a cashier and skip directly to a designated pickup window upon arriving at the restaurant. Click "Order Food and Drinks" in the app's main menu to see which dining venues are participating.

7. If you're short on time and the park closes early, stay until closing and eat dinner outside the park before returning to your hotel. If the park stays open late, eat dinner about 4 or 4:30 p.m. at the restaurant of your choice. You should sneak in just ahead of the dinner crowd.

8. Be warned that if you wait until after the dinner rush to eat, you'll discover that most restaurants outside The Wizarding World stop serving at least an hour before the parks close, leaving CityWalk's eateries as your best option for a late supper.

Beyond Quick-Service: Tips for Saving Money on Food

Though buying food from quick-service restaurants and vendors will save time and money (compared with full-service dining), additional strategies can bolster your budget and maintain your waistline.

Our readers offer the following suggestions for stretching food dollars. A Missouri mom writes:

> We stocked our steel cooler with milk and sandwich fixings. I froze a block of ice in a milk bottle, and we replenished it daily with ice from the resort ice machine. I also froze small packages of deli meats for later in the week. We ate cereal, milk, and fruit each morning, with boxed juices. I also had a hot pot to boil water for instant coffee, oatmeal, and soup. Each child had a belt bag of his own, which he filled from a special box of goodies each day. Some things were actual food, such as packages of crackers and cheese, peanuts, and raisins. Some were worthless junk, such as candy and gum. Each child also had a small, rectangular plastic water bottle that could hang on the belt. We filled these at water fountains before getting into lines. We left the park before noon; ate sandwiches, chips, and soda in the room; and napped. We purchased our evening meal in the park at a quick-service eatery. We budgeted for both morning and evening snacks from a vendor but often didn't need them.

A Whiteland, Indiana, mom suggests:

> One must-take item if you're traveling with younger kids is a supply of small paper or plastic cups to split drinks, which are both huge and expensive.

The top budget-trimming tip that we can offer is to skip the soft drinks and instead order free ice water with every meal. It's far healthier and more hydrating than soda (sugared or artificially sweetened), and at $3.49 per fountain drink, you'll be shocked at how swiftly the savings add up. The parks' drinking fountains are potable in a pinch, but the filtered water that all counter-service restaurants (excluding vending carts) give away tastes as good as the bottled water they sell, which goes for $2.99 from outdoor vending carts and $4.50 at indoor restaurants.

UNIVERSAL ORLANDO QUICK-SERVICE RESTAURANT MINI-PROFILES

TO HELP YOU FIND FLAVORFUL FAST FOOD while staying fleet of foot, we've developed mini-profiles of Universal Orlando's quick-service restaurants. The restaurants are listed alphabetically by location. Detailed profiles of all Universal Orlando full-service restaurants begin on page 227.

The restaurants profiled in the following pages are rated for quality and portion size as well as value. The value rating ranges from A to F as follows:

A Exceptional value; a real bargain	**D** Somewhat overpriced
B Good value	**F** Extremely overpriced
C Fair value; you get exactly what you pay for	

Note: Because of special or unusual offerings, the three following quick-service restaurants are listed with the full-service restaurants:

Leaky Cauldron *(Universal Studios Florida)*	**Red Oven Pizza Bakery** *(CityWalk)*
Three Broomsticks *(Islands of Adventure)*	

UNIVERSAL STUDIOS FLORIDA
Ben & Jerry's

LOCATION	New York	QUALITY	Good	VALUE	C+	PORTION	Medium
READER-SURVEY RESPONSES	94% 👍	6% 👎					

SELECTIONS A large selection of ice cream, frozen yogurt, milkshakes, and smoothies. Adventurous families can try the Mini Vermonster (four scoops of ice cream topped with a freshly baked brownie, chocolate chip cookie, banana, hot fudge or caramel, whipped cream, and two spoonfuls of your four favorite toppings).

COMMENTS Located in the New York section of the park, the facade for Ben & Jerry's is the famous Hudson Street Home for Girls, the very orphanage in which Little Orphan Annie lived. While several places serve Ben & Jerry's soft-serve, this is the only place in the parks with a wide selection of hard-packed flavors, including Cherry Garcia and Stephen Colbert's Americone Dream.

Beverly Hills Boulangerie

LOCATION Hollywood **QUALITY** Fair–Good **VALUE** B– **PORTION** Medium–Large
READER-SURVEY RESPONSES 89% 👍 11% 👎

SELECTIONS Hot breakfast sandwiches; fresh panini; veggie, turkey, roast beef, tuna, or ham-and-Swiss sandwiches; cookies, cakes, and pastries; espresso, cappuccino, and coffee.

COMMENTS The pastries and coffee make an acceptable breakfast. Because it's at the front of the park, it's usually not as crowded as other restaurants for lunch. Most of the sandwiches are premade and cold, but you can get a hot pressed Italian melt on ciabatta or rosemary bread. The boulangerie has the largest selection of muffins, cookies, and cheesecakes in the park.

Bumblebee Man's Taco Truck

LOCATION Springfield **QUALITY** Good **VALUE** B– **PORTION** Medium
READER-SURVEY RESPONSES 88% 👍 12% 👎

SELECTIONS Chicken and beef soft-shell tacos served with tortilla chips; loaded nachos. Coca-Cola fountain products; Buzz Cola; Duff, Duff Lite, and Duff Dry beers.

COMMENTS Capitalizing on the popular trend of food trucks, Bumblebee Man's Taco Truck is the first eatery guests encounter walking into Springfield: Home of the Simpsons from the main gates. The truck is adorned with a huge taco on the front bumper and an even bigger Bumblebee Man head coming out of the roof. The theming continues inside the truck as team members are dressed up in cute little bee costumes, complete with antennae on their hats. Each of the selections is well done. While the guacamole and salsa seem to be off-the-shelf varieties, every other element tastes great. The quality is very competitive with the food at Moe's Southwest Grill in CityWalk. Our favorite picks are the carne asada and the Korean beef.

Cafe La Bamba *(open seasonally)*

LOCATION Hollywood **QUALITY** Good **VALUE** B+ **PORTION** Medium–Large
READER-SURVEY RESPONSES 96% 👍 4% 👎

SELECTIONS VIP dining events.

COMMENTS Modeled after the legendary Hollywood Hotel, home to many silent movie stars and captains of the film industry in the early 20th century, this is a lovely place to dine—if you can get inside. In the afternoons, it hosts a private gourmet buffet, where guests taking high-dollar exclusive VIP tours sample signature dishes from the parks' best restaurants (see page 65). Once in a blue moon during holidays, it opens to the public with a Southwestern menu of barbecue and burritos.

Chez Alcatraz

LOCATION San Francisco **QUALITY** Good **VALUE** B **PORTION** Medium–Large
READER-SURVEY RESPONSES 89% 👍 11% 👎

SELECTIONS Mixed drinks, beer, soda, and appetizers.

COMMENTS With usually little to no wait, Chez Alcatraz can be a great place to relax and unwind with an adult beverage and a quick snack (we recommend the seasoned house-made chips with chipotle ketchup). With plenty of seating, it's a great place to take a break from touring the park, and you just happen to be next to one of the best photo ops in USF (Bruce the shark from *Jaws*).

Duff Brewery

LOCATION	Springfield	QUALITY	Fair–Good	VALUE	C	PORTION	Medium
READER-SURVEY RESPONSES	91% 👍	9% 👎					

SELECTIONS Corn dogs, pretzels, and assorted snacks. Beverages include Coca-Cola products, Buzz Cola, Duff beer, and other *Simpsons*-related drinks. In *The Simpsons* TV show, Duff, Duff Lite, and Duff Dry are all the exact same beer, but the Duff beers at Duff Brewery are completely different from each other. Duff beer is most equivalent to Yuengling, Duff Lite is closer to your standard light beer (like Miller Lite), and Duff Dry is a stout dark beer that can be compared to Guinness but has a strong coffee taste. Seasonal brews like Dufftoberfest are periodically poured.

COMMENTS Duff Brewery is an outdoor bar area with plenty of seating nearby to relax. It is part of the larger Duff Gardens, which, in *The Simpsons* TV show, is a theme park run by a beer-brewing company. The character of Duffman is available for photo ops, and there are hilarious topiaries of the Seven Duffs (Tipsy, Queasy, Surly, Sleazy, Edgy, Dizzy, and Remorseful), a parody of Disney's Seven Dwarfs and the mascots of Duff Gardens. Duff beers are brewed exclusively for Universal by the Florida Beer Company, which also brews beers for The Wizarding World of Harry Potter. Because Duff Brewery is out in the open and in view of every guest, it can often attract a big crowd, especially on a hot day. The waterfront-viewing terrace is a fine place to enjoy the evening lagoon show if the Central Park viewing area is overcrowded. Order a drink here (the banana Squishee is especially tasty) with one of the giant Bavarian pretzels.

Fast Food Boulevard

LOCATION	Springfield	QUALITY	Good–Excellent	VALUE	A-	PORTION	Large
READER-SURVEY RESPONSES	82% 👍	18% 👎					

SELECTIONS Burgers, chicken, pizza, seafood, sandwiches, and salads. With different eateries pulled straight from *The Simpsons* TV series, guests dine on cleverly named selections from Krusty Burger, The Frying Dutchman, Flaming Moe's, Cletus' Chicken Shack, Luigi's Pizza, Lard Lad Donuts, and Lisa's Teahouse of Horror.

COMMENTS Besides the hilarious menus themselves (taste-tested by writers of *The Simpsons* TV show), Fast Food Boulevard contains items you can't get anywhere else in the park, including a pulled-pork sandwich, tater tots, and seasoned curly fries instead of the normal fries served everywhere else. Our favorites are the gloriously messy Clogger Burger, the tender fried calamari, and the chicken-and-waffle sandwich (with extra maple mayo on the side). And thanks in large part to Lisa's Teahouse of Horror, Fast Food Boulevard also has several options, outside of the ever-present salad, for the vegetarians and vegans in your party. Note that this is a very popular spot for lunch, and a long line can develop. Guests queue inside and are released to the serving stations in small groups. Once you order and receive your food, pay at the cashier, and an employee will find an empty table for you. The process can take a while on busy days, and the televisions broadcast a loop of classic *Simpsons* clips that is maddeningly brief. An Ambler, Pennsylvania, couple sampled the offerings:

> *The doughnuts at Lard Lad were fresh, flavorful, and surprisingly delicious. (Mmm . . . doughnuts.) The Flaming Moe is an overpriced glass of orange soda with dry ice on the bottom—for $9, it should have some alcohol in it or be larger. The queuing for Krusty Burger was frustrating during the lunch rush—they let only a few guests up to the food court at a time—but once you go through the line and pay, an employee shows*

you to a table. Lunch for the four of us cost $88 with two beers and that one overpriced Flaming Moe. Duff beer was essentially a less-delicious Heineken. My husband's Krusty Burger was pretty good; my chicken-and-waffle sandwich was excellent but had too much sauce on it.

Florean Fortescue's Ice-Cream Parlour

LOCATION Diagon Alley **QUALITY** Excellent **VALUE** B **PORTION** Medium–Large
READER-SURVEY RESPONSES 97% 👍 3% 👎

SELECTIONS Ice cream is served in cups, waffle cones, and plastic souvenir sundae glasses. A single order can contain two different flavors, and you can add unusual toppings such as shortbread crumbles and meringue pieces for under a dollar.

COMMENTS Readers of the Harry Potter books will remember Florean Fortescue's Ice-Cream Parlour for its prominent appearance in *Harry Potter and the Prisoner of Azkaban.* When Harry spent several weeks staying in a room above the Leaky Cauldron, he would spend time at the ice cream parlor, and Florean Fortescue himself gave Harry free ice cream sundaes every half hour. Now Muggles can have their own sundaes in this very establishment, with some very "magical" flavors, including Butterbeer-flavored ice cream. Our favorites are the salted caramel blondie and chocolate chili—but be warned, it has a bite!

Fountain of Fair Fortune

LOCATION Diagon Alley **QUALITY** Good-Excellent **VALUE** B- **PORTION** Medium
READER-SURVEY RESPONSES 98% 👍 2% 👎

SELECTIONS Potter-themed drinks, both soft and hard.

COMMENTS Named after a short story in *Tales of Beedle the Bard,* this pub sells Fishy Green Ale, Gillywater, Wizard's Brew, and Dragon Scale (see page 205)—and features an exclusive Butterbeer souvenir mug not found in Hogsmeade. You can also get a cup of Butterbeer soft-serve here, usually with a much shorter wait than at the ice cream shop next door.

The Hopping Pot

LOCATION Diagon Alley **QUALITY** Good-Excellent **VALUE** B- **PORTION** Medium
READER-SURVEY RESPONSES 99% 👍 1% 👎

SELECTIONS Potter-themed drinks, including all four varieties of Butterbeer: cold, frozen, hot, or soft-serve. If you're peckish, snack portions of meat pasties and bags of British potato crisps are also available.

COMMENTS Outdoor bar with eight different brews—including Wizard's Brew (a heavy porter) and Dragon Scale (a hoppy amber)—on draft, each with its own customized tap handle, along with the area's most complete selection of signature nonalcoholic drinks. Much better food is available elsewhere in Diagon Alley. Seating is at a limited number of picnic tables, within sight of the Carkitt Market stage.

KidZone Pizza Company *(open seasonally)*

LOCATION Woody Woodpecker's KidZone **QUALITY** Fair **VALUE** C **PORTION** Medium
READER-SURVEY RESPONSES 67% 👍 33% 👎

SELECTIONS Pizzas, pretzels, corn dogs, and milkshakes.

COMMENTS Located at the front of Woody Woodpecker's KidZone and directly next to the impressive SpongeBob StorePants, KidZone Pizza is only open during select seasons. There's no indoor seating, and even the few seats outdoors can fill up quickly during the busier times. The limited menu is missing the wow factor, as you can get better pizza at several other locations in the park.

London Taxi Hut

LOCATION Outside Diagon Alley **QUALITY** Fair–Good **VALUE** C **PORTION** Medium
READER-SURVEY RESPONSES 80% 👍 20% 👎

SELECTIONS You can get a jacket potato (baked potato to Americans) smothered with baked beans and cheese, broccoli and cheese, or the salty stuffing from a shepherd's pie. Bags of crisps (British potato chips), hot dogs, and canned European beers fill out the brief menu.

COMMENTS Outside the gorgeous London Waterfront facade in front of Diagon Alley are two "cabman shelter" kiosks. One sells London-themed merchandise such as T-shirts, and this one sells quick-service food and drink items. The signature item is an extralong hot dog in an odd tubelike bun; shape aside, it tastes about the same.

Louie's Italian Restaurant

LOCATION New York **QUALITY** Fair–Good **VALUE** C **PORTION** Medium
READER-SURVEY RESPONSES 82% 👍 18% 👎

SELECTIONS Spaghetti with meatballs; fettuccine Alfredo; cheese, pepperoni, or veggie pizza; Caesar salad; soup; cookies; cake; fruit cups; gelato; Italian ices; turkey legs; beer.

COMMENTS One of the largest indoor restaurants in the Studios and a good choice to get out of the hot sun. The name of the restaurant is an homage to the movie *The Godfather,* which had a very famous scene set at Louie's Restaurant. The food is nothing special, and the whole pies are outrageously overpriced at more than $35 apiece, but it's hard to screw up pizza and pasta. Guido's, a small counter in the corner, offers a limited selection of frozen Italian desserts. Be warned: It can be very crowded throughout the afternoon.

Mel's Drive-In

LOCATION Hollywood **QUALITY** Fair **VALUE** C **PORTION** Medium–Large
READER-SURVEY RESPONSES 73% 👍 27% 👎

SELECTIONS Hamburgers, cheeseburgers, veggie burgers, chicken fingers, grilled chicken sandwich, grilled chicken salad, fries, onion rings, and ice cream floats.

COMMENTS Based on the diner from the George Lucas movie *American Graffiti,* Mel's has several vintage automobiles in the parking lot that are always available for photo ops. Check out the license plates for some fun references. During Halloween Horror Nights, the neon lights in the Mel's Drive-in sign are creatively changed to Mel's Die-in.

More than half the menu lists some combination of hamburger patty, cheese, and bacon, with fries. The food is as bland as the selection. Root beer floats are available, but we wouldn't make a special trip here for anything.

Moe's Tavern

LOCATION Springfield **QUALITY** Good **VALUE** C+ **PORTION** Medium
READER-SURVEY RESPONSES 88% 👍 12% 👎

SELECTIONS Duff beer and Flaming Moe.

COMMENTS Grab a Duff beer (regular or Duff Lite on draft or in a bottle; Duff Dry in a bottle only) or a Flaming Moe from this replica of Homer and Barney's haunt from *The Simpsons* TV series. Filled with nods to the TV show, the tavern has a large photo op with Barney, along with a working Love Tester. If you're lucky and sitting by the red phone on the bar top, you just may happen to take a prank phone call. The Flaming Moe is the first signature drink "experience" we have seen to date. Pricey at about $9 each, a Flaming Moe comes in a souvenir cup that does a good job of hiding dry ice via a separate compartment. The orange soda-tasting drink bubbles up with smoke billowing out, giving a really good representation of being on fire. The nonalcoholic Flaming Moe is sure to be a hit with the younger set when they see it for the first time.

New York Craft Beer Cart

LOCATION	New York	QUALITY	Good	VALUE	B-	PORTION	Medium
READER-SURVEY RESPONSES	92% 👍	8% 👎					

SELECTIONS Craft beers, corn dogs, nachos, and chips.

COMMENTS We don't typically review outdoor vendor pushcarts, but we're making an exception here because BEER! This old-fashioned stand outside Ben & Jerry's doesn't even have a real name (the sign just says SNACKS & DRINKS), but it does stock a selection of real suds, with fine Florida breweries from Miami to Tampa proudly representing. Alas, all are served in cans rather than draft, but you can pair your brew with a corn dog to help soak up the alcohol.

Richter's Burger Co.

LOCATION	San Francisco	QUALITY	Fair	VALUE	C	PORTION	Medium-Large
READER-SURVEY RESPONSES	72% 👍	28% 👎					

SELECTIONS Burgers, chicken sandwiches, garden burgers, chili-cheese fries, salads, and milkshakes.

COMMENTS Near the Fast & Furious attraction, Richter's Burger Co. has a theme tied to the 1906 San Francisco earthquake. All of the menu items have earthquake-related names, and the decor around the surprisingly large seating areas includes photos from that era (including some wonderful ads for products that are just hilarious to read with 20/20 hindsight), as well as seismologist props. One of the more impressive elements in the restaurant is the faithful re-creation of the Louis Agassiz statue that fell off a Stanford University building during the 1906 earthquake; the statue lodged itself firmly into the concrete, head first. The food here is nothing to start quaking over, but there is a toppings bar for customizing your burger, and you can upgrade your sandwich with guacamole or sautéed mushrooms for an additional fee.

San Francisco Pastry Company

LOCATION	San Francisco	QUALITY	Fair	VALUE	C	PORTION	Medium-Large
READER-SURVEY RESPONSES	91% 👍	9% 👎					

SELECTIONS Soups; chicken, turkey, or ham-and-Swiss sandwiches; fruit plates; salads; cookies, cakes, pies, and pastries; espresso, cappuccino, and coffee; beer.

COMMENTS The selection is similar to Beverly Hills Boulangerie at the front of the park. The pastries and coffee make a good pick-me-up if you're in the area during the afternoon, but the sandwiches are premade and cold.

Schwab's Pharmacy *(open seasonally)*

LOCATION	Hollywood	QUALITY	Good	VALUE	C+	PORTION	Medium
READER-SURVEY RESPONSES	75% 👍	25% 👎					

SELECTIONS Ice cream sundaes and milkshakes.

COMMENTS Schwab's Pharmacy, modeled after the legendary drugstore counter where Lana Turner was supposedly discovered, serves frozen treats made with Ben & Jerry's ice cream. The selection is more limited here than at the other Ben & Jerry's location in New York. The medicines here are for display only; if you need a nostrum, head to First Aid. Schwab's is open for only a few hours each afternoon, and sometimes it doesn't open at all in the off-season.

Universal Studios' Classic Monsters Cafe

LOCATION Production Central **QUALITY** Good **VALUE** B **PORTION** Medium
READER-SURVEY RESPONSES 59% 👍 41% 👎

SELECTIONS Rotisserie chicken with roasted potatoes; turkey legs; barbecue brisket sandwich; salads; ribs; cheese or pepperoni pizza; crinkle-cut fries; cheesecakes and cookies; beer.

COMMENTS With a lot of indoor seating, Universal Studios' Classic Monsters Cafe can be a good place for a meal and to get out of the hot sun. The restaurant is filled with movie props from various monster films, including *The Creature from the Black Lagoon* and *The Mummy,* but also has references from *The Munsters* TV show. Food quality has greatly improved here since the chili-cheese dogs and burgers were bumped off the menu. Chicken and ribs are comparable to those at Three Broomsticks, the brisket sandwich is a delicious finger-licking mess, and the pizza slices are huge (and they better be for the monstrous price) and are much better than your average theme park pizza.

ISLANDS OF ADVENTURE
Blondie's

LOCATION Toon Lagoon **QUALITY** Fair-Good **VALUE** C+ **PORTION** Large
READER-SURVEY RESPONSES 62% 👍 38% 👎

SELECTIONS Dagwood deli sandwiches; made-to-order roast beef, turkey, tuna, and ham sandwiches; Nathan's hot dogs; brookies.

COMMENTS Avoid the signature sandwich—the Dagwood—which is premade and refrigerated until needed. It also has more bread than necessary, making it dry. If you're really in the mood for a sandwich, try one of the made-to-order turkey or ham subs; the roast beef is invariably too dry. Blondie's serves subs on white or multigrain rolls, accompanied by a side of potato salad. If you like Nathan's hot dogs, Blondie's serves the most styles in the parks (chili, Chicago, Reuben, and slaw) and pairs them with crinkle-cut fries.

The Burger Digs

LOCATION Jurassic Park **QUALITY** Fair **VALUE** C **PORTION** Medium-Large
READER-SURVEY RESPONSES 75% 👍 25% 👎

SELECTIONS Double cheeseburger, chicken sandwich, vegan burger, chicken tenders, and milkshakes.

COMMENTS Burger Digs has indoor seating. The burgers and chicken sandwiches are nothing special, though they come on kaiser rolls, and a cold toppings bar allows for customization. The specialty burger is topped with mango barbecue sauce, smoked Gouda, and coleslaw, and it can be ordered with a vegan patty made from brown rice and mushrooms. For a lighter meal, try the chicken spring salad with corn, black beans, and pineapple vinaigrette. If you're looking for better food, try Thunder Falls Terrace a little farther along in Jurassic Park.

Cafe 4

LOCATION Marvel Super Hero Island **QUALITY** Fair-Good **VALUE** C **PORTION** Medium
READER-SURVEY RESPONSES 61% 👍 39% 👎

SELECTIONS Pizza, pasta, meatball or chicken Parmesan sub, Caesar salad, and breadsticks.

COMMENTS The food is generic and fairly flavorless, but it is served rather speedily. However, Doctor Doom seems to think that an average price of $15 for a single slice of pizza and side salad (or a jaw-dropping $38 for a whole pie) is reasonable in a theme park setting. This is not Via Napoli by any "stretch" of the imagination (that one is for the Mr. Fantastic fans), but the café does make specialties such as barbecue chicken pizza. The exact same salads, meatball subs, and basic pastas and sauces that are served at Louie's in USF round out the not-so-Fantastic menu. At 5 p.m. on select nights, this location turns into a Marvel character buffet (see page 198).

Captain America Diner

LOCATION Marvel Super Hero Island **QUALITY** Fair **VALUE** C **PORTION** Medium–Large
READER-SURVEY RESPONSES 56% 👍 44% 👎

SELECTIONS Cheeseburgers, chicken sandwiches, chicken fingers, chicken salad, milkshakes, and onion rings.

COMMENTS The meat is entirely average but comes served on a sesame-seed bun, and the specialty burger is topped with barbecue pulled pork. While the name of the restaurant is Captain America Diner, the air-conditioned inside is themed to the Marvel Comics version of *The Avengers*, including references to C-level characters in the group such as the Black Knight and Wonder Man—even the flooring is themed. Inside seating features a gorgeous look outside into the lagoon (with a great view of Mythos and Hogwarts Castle).

Circus McGurkus Cafe Stoo-pendous

LOCATION Seuss Landing **QUALITY** Fair-Good **VALUE** C+ **PORTION** Medium–Large
READER-SURVEY RESPONSES 68% 👍 32% 👎

SELECTIONS Fried chicken, pasta, pizza, cheeseburgers, and Caesar salad. Dippin' Dots sundaes and floats for dessert.

COMMENTS This is certainly one of the more interesting counter-service venues. The High in the Sky Seuss Trolley Train Ride! passes overhead, and during inclement weather the *Oh! The Stories You'll Hear!* show takes place within the restaurant. The fried chicken is actually pretty good; it comes in two- or three-piece combos with corn on the cob and mashed potatoes with home-style gravy. Everything else on the menu is just average.

Comic Strip Cafe

LOCATION Toon Lagoon **QUALITY** Poor-Fair **VALUE** C- **PORTION** Medium–Large
READER-SURVEY RESPONSES 71% 👍 29% 👎

SELECTIONS Asian barbecue chicken, stir-fry, chicken fingers, fish-and-chips, personal pizza, pasta, salads, cheeseburgers, and chili dogs.

COMMENTS Long notorious for serving the worst fast food in IOA, Comic Strip Cafe attempts to serve something for everyone and ends up satisfying no one. The "Chinese" dishes are pretty dire. Better fish-and-chips can be found at Three Broomsticks, and better pizza is at Cafe 4. If you're hungry for funnel cake, try the bite-size funnel puffs.

Croissant Moon Bakery

LOCATION Port of Entry **QUALITY** Fair-Good **VALUE** B- **PORTION** Large
READER-SURVEY RESPONSES 88% 👍 13% 👎

SELECTIONS Deli sandwiches, panini, freshly baked pastries, funnel cakes, and Lavazza coffee.

COMMENTS Tucked into the right side of Port of Entry's main walkway as you enter the park, Croissant Moon Bakery is a good place to get a quick breakfast (its "on the run" Continental combo is a great deal) or a pastry and coffee pick-me-up between meals. Prices for fancy flavored lattes are lower here than at the Starbucks across the street. The cold sandwiches tend to be premade and refrigerated, so this isn't the best choice for subs, but you can get a hot pressed panini. The service is fast and friendly, and there's plenty of shaded seating outdoors, where you can people-watch.

Doc Sugrue's Kebab House

LOCATION The Lost Continent	QUALITY Good	VALUE B	PORTION Medium
READER-SURVEY RESPONSES 81% 👍 19% 👎			

SELECTIONS Meat and vegetarian kebabs, hummus, Greek salad, yogurt, and beverages.

COMMENTS The stand offers nicely seasoned beef and chicken kebabs, and it's also very vegetarian and vegan friendly, with hummus, fruit cups, Greek yogurt, and pretzels on the menu. This location also has several Coke Freestyle machines. Doc Sugrue's is in the unfortunate position of being between the popular eatery Mythos and The Wizarding World of Harry Potter. With many hungry guests making a beeline toward the Potter-themed food in Hogsmeade or the award-winning Mythos, both Doc Sugrue's and Fire-Eater's Grill in Lost Continent see little to no waits on most days.

Fire-Eater's Grill

LOCATION The Lost Continent	QUALITY Good	VALUE B-	PORTION Medium
READER-SURVEY RESPONSES 97% 👍 3% 👎			

SELECTIONS Gyros, chicken tenders, hot dogs, chili-cheese fries, and salads.

COMMENTS The lamb gyro sandwich with salad is the best combination here, and also the most popular. Vegetarians can request falafel as a meat substitute. You have to admire Universal's ability to combine the various entrées to make more meal options. One is a plain chicken tenders platter. Add hot sauce, and it becomes the Chicken Stingers platter. Omit the sauce and add lettuce, and it's the Crispy Chicken Salad. We're hoping for an entrée named Lamb Dog with Cheesy Chicken Stingers.

Hog's Head

LOCATION Hogsmeade	QUALITY Good	VALUE B-	PORTION Medium
READER-SURVEY RESPONSES 97% 👍 3% 👎			

SELECTIONS Butterbeer, Pumpkin Juice, beer, wine, and mixed drinks.

COMMENTS Wonderfully themed pub attached to the Three Broomsticks restaurant that offers both alcoholic and alcohol-free drinks. If you want a Butterbeer, the line is often shorter here than at either of the outdoor carts. A full liquor selection is kept behind the bar, but there are no sodas to mix with (only juice), nor are the bartenders allowed to add alcohol to nonalcoholic Potter drinks (which is not to say that you can't mix them yourself). There are also some potent secret cocktails available off-menu, like Hog's Tea (a raspberry Long Island iced tea) and a triple-layered cider/ale/porter potion that (for trademark reasons) you should definitely *not* refer to as a Deathly Hallows. The animatronic hog hanging behind the bar is known to snort and snarl if you slide the barkeep a tip.

Hop on Pop Ice Cream Shop

LOCATION Seuss Landing	QUALITY Fair	VALUE C	PORTION Medium
READER-SURVEY RESPONSES 89% 👍 11% 👎			

SELECTIONS Ice cream, waffle cones, root beer floats, and Dippin' Dots.

COMMENTS A small ice cream stand in Seuss Landing with no indoor seating. The Sundae on a Stick, a vanilla ice cream bar dipped in chocolate and sprinkles, is exceptionally messy on warm summer days.

The Mess Tent

LOCATION Skull Island	QUALITY Fair–Good	VALUE C+	PORTION Medium–Large
READER-SURVEY RESPONSES 100% 👍 0% 👎			

SELECTIONS Hot dogs, pretzels, churros, frozen slush, and beer.

COMMENTS Apparently, all an attraction needs to qualify as an entire island on Universal's map is an adjoining souvenir kiosk and snack stand, which explains the presence of this modest mess tent outside Reign of Kong's entrance. The appropriately oversize ⅓-pound foot-long hot dog comes topped with cheese sauce and relish on a pretzel roll in a Kong Combo. The banana slush tastes suspiciously like the banana Squishee served at USF's Duff Brewery, but it's still darn tasty.

Moose Juice, Goose Juice

LOCATION Seuss Landing	QUALITY Good	VALUE C	PORTION Small–Medium
READER-SURVEY RESPONSES 100% 👍 0% 👎			

SELECTIONS Corn dogs, pretzels, cookies, and churros; frozen orange, apple, watermelon, or grape juice.

COMMENTS Cartoon animal rights activists rest easy: no geese nor meese were harmed in the making of these drinks. Moose Juice is actually an orange tangerine-flavored frozen slush, and Goose Juice is a green sour apple–flavored slush. Both can hit the spot on a hot Florida day.

Pizza Predattoria

LOCATION Jurassic Park	QUALITY Fair–Good	VALUE C+	PORTION Medium
READER-SURVEY RESPONSES 75% 👍 25% 👎			

SELECTIONS Personal pizzas, meatball sub, Caesar salad, and brookies.

COMMENTS The meat-lovers pizza is decent, as far as theme park pizza goes. Stick to that or the salads. The brookie—a cookie-brownie hybrid—is a brilliant development in the history of desserts.

Thunder Falls Terrace

LOCATION Jurassic Park	QUALITY Excellent	VALUE A-	PORTION Large
READER-SURVEY RESPONSES 87% 👍 13% 👎			

SELECTIONS Rotisserie chicken, ribs, smoked turkey legs, soups, and salads.

COMMENTS A nice change from the usual theme park hamburgers and pizza served all over Islands of Adventure. The roasted corn on the cob and seasoned rice with beans are excellent. Thunder Falls is quite possibly the best bet for a meal in the park. It's not as busy as Three Broomsticks and serves food almost as good, making this location a winner.

The Watering Hole

LOCATION Jurassic Park	QUALITY Fair–Good	VALUE C	PORTION Medium
READER-SURVEY RESPONSES 100% 👍 0% 👎			

SELECTIONS Nathan's hot dogs, nachos, soft pretzels, frozen beverages, beer, and liquor.

COMMENTS A small takeaway food and drink stand in Jurassic Park. A few tables, some with umbrellas for shade, are nearby. The food is just a fig leaf; you're here for the libations.

Wimpy's *(open seasonally)*

LOCATION Toon Lagoon **QUALITY** Fair **VALUE** C **PORTION** Medium–Large
READER-SURVEY RESPONSES 100% 👍 0% 👎

SELECTIONS Bacon cheeseburgers, fish sandwiches, hot dogs, fries, and whoopie pie.

COMMENTS This outdoor-only burger stand, themed to Popeye's perpetually indebted pal, serves entirely unremarkable American standards on the handful of days each year when it is open. Seriously, this "seasonal" restaurant is seen operating so infrequently that it's become the white whale of Universal dining. We were about to write it off entirely, but Wimpy's briefly reopened in 2018, offering a new signature burger topped with spinach and a sunny-side up egg. If you happen to spy it open during your visit, snap a photo and send it to our dining consigliere Derek Burgan (he'll burn with envy), and then continue on to a better eatery.

VOLCANO BAY

Bambu

LOCATION Rainforest Vlg. **QUALITY** Good–Excellent **VALUE** B+ **PORTION** Medium–Large
READER-SURVEY RESPONSES 91% 👍 9% 👎

SELECTIONS Cheeseburgers, chicken sandwiches, chicken tenders, fish sandwiches, pork belly sandwiches, and salads.

COMMENTS Bamboo-shaded patios provide plenty of sheltered seating near the Maku Puihi slides. The grilled mahi-mahi sandwich with rémoulade and pineapple salsa is excellent, as is the pineapple upside-down cake. Volcano Bay Freestyle machines dispense Kunuku Cooler, a refreshing mixed-berry soda exclusive to the park.

The Feasting Frog

LOCATION Rainforest Vlg. **QUALITY** Good **VALUE** B **PORTION** Medium
READER-SURVEY RESPONSES 85% 👍 15% 👎

SELECTIONS Tacos, nachos, and tuna poké.

COMMENTS This charming amphibian-shaped hut serves pretty good carne asada and chicken tacos, though the shells seem to go stale swiftly in the Orlando humidity. Our favorite is the poké bowl, with sashimi-quality ahi tuna and crispy plantain chips. You can grab food and sit at the neighboring Kunuku Boat Bar, which serves a refreshing locally brewed Volcano Blossom beer and an array of supersweet signature cocktails.

Kohola Reef Restaurant & Social Club

LOCATION Wave Vlg. **QUALITY** Good–Excellent **VALUE** B+ **PORTION** Medium–Large
READER-SURVEY RESPONSES 89% 👍 11% 👎

SELECTIONS Hawaiian ribs, burgers, veggie burgers, pulled-pork sandwiches, chicken, pizzas, salads, and sushi.

COMMENTS As Volcano Bay's largest eatery and the one closest to the park's entrance, this is usually the most crowded restaurant at mealtimes. The burgers are served on Hawaiian rolls, but you're better off skipping them and the "longboard" pizzas in favor of more exotic entrées, like the braised chicken in green coconut curry, quinoa-edamame burger, smoked ribs, or mango barbecue pulled pork. For lighter fare, we like the island chicken salad and California rolls. Chocolate lava cake is the can't-miss dessert. If you want an adult beverage with your meal, step across the pathway to the nearby Dancing Dragons Boat Bar. Breakfast items are served here until 10:30 a.m., and this is the park's only eatery that stays open until closing time.

Whakawaiwai Eats

LOCATION	River Vlg.	QUALITY	Good	VALUE	B	PORTION	Medium
READER-SURVEY RESPONSES	90% 👍	10% 👎					

SELECTIONS Pizza, hot dogs, mac and cheese, and salads.

COMMENTS Somewhat isolated in the rear of the park, this is probably your best bet for getting food without a long wait, though the menu isn't particularly innovative. The same "longboard" pizzas served at Kohola Reef are also found here, plus Hawaiian varieties (for those blasphemers who believe caramelized pineapple belongs on pizza) and an Island BBQ version (chicken, Gouda, and mango sauce). The hot dogs are served on pretzel buns and topped with bacon and pineapple, and the upscale mac and cheese is stuffed with jerk-seasoned shrimp.

CITYWALK
Auntie Anne's

LOCATION	Waterfront	QUALITY	Good	VALUE	C	PORTION	Medium
READER-SURVEY RESPONSES	90% 👍	10% 👎					

SELECTIONS Pretzels, pretzel nuggets, pretzel dogs, and soft drinks.

COMMENTS The familiar twisted-dough franchise, with prices only slightly more exorbitant than what you'll pay at the mall. Pretzels are made in original or cinnamon-and-sugar varieties, and dipping sauces (cheese, caramel, or sweet glaze) are extra. Additional Auntie Anne's windows are located in IOA's Marvel area adjacent to The Amazing Adventures of Spider-Man ride and in USF's New York neighborhood next to the *Blues Brothers* stage.

BK Whopper Bar

LOCATION	Upper Level	QUALITY	Fair	VALUE	C	PORTION	Large
READER-SURVEY RESPONSES	58% 👍	43% 👎					

SELECTIONS A Burger King location with Whoppers of all kinds; fried chicken sandwich or strips; salads; fries; onion rings; shakes; sundae pie.

COMMENTS Because the menu is so familiar, long lines can develop here during lunchtime. Prices are markedly higher than your local drive-thru, and there's no value menu, but you are getting a double Whopper with unique toppings (such as blue cheese or angry onions), and the "small" fries and drink are the size of a medium elsewhere.

Bread Box Handcrafted Sandwiches

LOCATION	Upper Level	QUALITY	Good	VALUE	C–	PORTION	Small-Medium
READER-SURVEY RESPONSES	94% 👍	6% 👎					

SELECTIONS Hot and cold deli sandwiches, grilled cheese, house-made potato chips, soups, salads, milkshakes, beer, and wine.

COMMENTS The Bread Box claims that guests will be "transported back to your childhood kitchen or your favorite street corner deli" through its use of high-quality meats, vegetables, fresh bread, and simple preparation. Sounds good, and the menu indeed has a wide selection of grilled cheeses (stuffed with everything from bacon to pastrami to smoked brisket), along with house-made soups and various sandwiches made fresh to order. And you can't complain about Nutella milkshakes for dessert. The problem is that, while everything we've tasted at Bread Box has been yummy, you can't ignore how outrageously overpriced it is, especially compared to its noble competition; $12 will buy you a sandwich, though at least the fries or tater tots are included. If you want a high-quality, creative snack and can stomach the price, give one of the grilled cheese creations a go, but save some money for another meal later.

Cinnabon

LOCATION	Lower Level	QUALITY	Good	VALUE	B–	PORTION	Large
READER-SURVEY RESPONSES	92% 👍	8% 👎					

SELECTIONS Original Cinnabon, plus Pecanbons, Minibons, Seattle's Best Coffee, and soft-serve ice cream.

COMMENTS The same cinnamon-sugar goodness sold inside IOA can also be found in CityWalk on the way to and from the parks. This location, along with the Starbucks across the street, is usually the first thing to open each morning for breakfasting early birds.

Cold Stone Creamery

LOCATION	Lower Level	QUALITY	Good	VALUE	B–	PORTION	Medium
READER-SURVEY RESPONSES	94% 👍	6% 👎					

SELECTIONS Hard-packed ice cream with mix-in toppings, waffle cones, and milkshakes.

COMMENTS Using only the highest-quality ingredients, Cold Stone Creamery has made its name by preparing your ice cream creation in front of your eyes on a frozen granite slab. With a large selection of ice creams—and even larger choices of mix-ins—the possibilities seem almost endless. Cold Stone has a unique way of describing sizes with *Mine* (16 ounces), *Ours* (32 ounces), and *Everybody's* (480 ounces). This location is very popular with exiting guests and often sees a long line when the parks close.

Dockside and Shoreline

LOCATION	Waterfront	QUALITY	Good	VALUE	C+	PORTION	Medium
READER-SURVEY RESPONSES	100% 👍	0% 👎					

SELECTIONS Craft beer, mixed drinks, snacks, and pizza delivery.

COMMENTS Dockside and Shoreline are sibling outdoor bar areas with alfresco seating, allowing guests to take a break and enjoy a cool drink while touring the CityWalk waterfront. Dockside has a great view of Hollywood Rip Ride Rockit, where you can sit back with a Rose Mule (vodka, strawberry purée, and ginger beer) and listen to the screaming of thrilled riders. With outdoor seating and a half dozen different local craft beers in the cooler, Shoreline is a great place to relax with a cold brew while overlooking the lagoon. Red Oven Pizza Bakery is available for delivery as well.

Fat Tuesday

LOCATION	Upper Level	QUALITY	Good	VALUE	C	PORTION	Medium-Large
READER-SURVEY RESPONSES	100% 👍	0% 👎					

SELECTIONS Premium frozen daiquiris.

COMMENTS Fat Tuesday began on Bourbon Street in New Orleans more than 35 years ago and brings the Mardi Gras party atmosphere—and its world-famous frozen drinks—to CityWalk. Located between Pat O'Brien's and The Groove, Fat Tuesday is a to-go window with decent-size drinks for a fair price. Be careful, because adding floaters to the daiquiris can catch up to you fast. Some of the more popular drink combinations include Peaches & Cream (Bellini and piña colada), Superman (Eye Candy and Cat 5 Hurricane), and Mochalada (mudslide and piña colada). Fat Tuesday is open daily, 3 p.m.-1:45 a.m.

Fusion Bistro Sushi & Sake Bar

LOCATION	Upper Level	QUALITY	Good	VALUE	C–	PORTION	Small–Medium
READER-SURVEY RESPONSES	57% 👍	43% 👎					

SELECTIONS Raw and cooked sushi *nigiri* and *maki,* sake and Japanese beer, miso soup, edamame, hot appetizers, salads, and bento boxes.

COMMENTS This restaurant is operated by Sushi House, with other locations in Atlanta and Orlando's Florida Mall. Fusion Bistro's unusual sushi preparations mix traditional Japanese with tastes and ingredients from throughout Eastern Asia and the Pacific Rim, all made in a glassed-in kitchen that you can observe from outside. The sushi here ain't cheap, but it's quicker and less expensive than The Cowfish. Because of extended hours, you can get your fix until the wee hours. Quality is a cut above your local supermarket, but because everything is made from fairly pedestrian fish—tuna, salmon, tilapia, escolar, shrimp, and eel—sushi snobs will want to eat elsewhere. The spicy tuna rolls are acceptable. Add $5 to any roll to create a bento box with miso soup, salad, seaweed, rice, and a small cake.

Hot Dog Hall of Fame

LOCATION	Lower Level	QUALITY	Good	VALUE	C+	PORTION	Medium
READER-SURVEY RESPONSES	90% 👍	10% 👎					

SELECTIONS Vienna, Nathan's, Kayem, Farmer John, Sabrett, Koegel, and bratwurst sausages with a variety of toppings; fries; beer and soda.

COMMENTS Developed by Steven Schussler, the creative force behind Rainforest Cafe and T-REX, Hot Dog Hall of Fame is a tribute to the iconic baseball-park food. From the mustard bar curated by the National Mustard Museum in Wisconsin, to famous dogs from ballparks across the nation (such as the Dixie Dog and the Dirty Water Dog), Hot Dog Hall of Fame resonates with baseball enthusiasts and foodies alike. The venue features large-screen TVs and bleacher-type seating (from actual Major League Baseball parks) for those interested in catching a game. It also sells fun extras, such as "paint your wiener" (a blank vinyl wiener dog that guests can put their own designs on) and an electronic yodeling pickle. The sausages, buns, and toppings are all authentic and perfectly prepared, but the value will vary with the variety; $8.99 for a New York Sabrett with kraut sounds pretty steep, but the $9.99 Kansas City (pulled pork and coleslaw) and $8.99 Milwaukee (bratwurst and grilled onions) dogs deliver a good bang for the buck. There's even a 2-foot dog for just under twice the price, if you want to share. The posted price includes the pup and shoestring fries (subtract $2 for à la carte); roasted peanuts and Cracker Jacks (natch) are extra.

Lone Palm Airport

LOCATION	Waterfront	QUALITY	Good	VALUE	B–	PORTION	Medium
READER-SURVEY RESPONSES	100% 👍	0% 👎					

SELECTIONS Breakfast selections in the morning. Wings, nachos, shrimp, conch fritters, pretzel sticks, beer, and specialty drinks for lunch and dinner.

COMMENTS Across from Margaritaville lies the Lone Palm Airport tiki bar. A great place to grab your food and snacks on the go, the Lone Palm Airport is also home to Jimmy Buffett's seaplane, the *Hemisphere Dancer.* Outdoor seating makes the Lone Palm a great place to sit back with a nice cool drink and enjoy the atmosphere of Parakeet Beach (not to mention people-watch on CityWalk).

Menchie's Frozen Yogurt

LOCATION	Upper	Level	QUALITY	Good	VALUE	B-	PORTION	Varies
READER-SURVEY RESPONSES	96% 👍	4% 👎						

SELECTIONS Self-service frozen yogurt with toppings and bottled soft drinks.

COMMENTS Menchie's is a build-your-own yogurt chain that offers guests the ability to put themselves into a diabetic coma with an overwhelming amount of available toppings. Yes, there is fresh fruit for those who want to stay healthy, but for the rest of us there are sprinkles, Cinnamon Toast Crunch, Kit Kats, gummy bears, Cap'n Crunch, Twix, chocolate rocks, and more (MUCH more) to load on top of your yogurt. Just as Via Napoli imports its water from Pennsylvania, Menchie's brings its milk in from California. Why? We're not exactly sure, but this cartoon says it is better for you. Science, schmience—you put enough Oreo cookies in the yogurt, and the milk might as well be from Mars. Perhaps most important, one of the flavors in Menchie's regular rotation is Dole pineapple, otherwise known to Disney fans as the Dole Whip; there's also an equally luscious lime variety in rotation. This is one of the few places where the cult favorite flavor can be found outside Adventureland, and the only one where it can be topped with pink-frosted animal crackers and marshmallow sauce. Menchie's is located between the first and second levels of CityWalk, next to Bread Box. The price? Grab a cup (or a waffle bowl), and everything is $0.63 an ounce, so you can pay as much—or as little—as you'd like.

Moe's Southwest Grill

LOCATION	Upper	Level	QUALITY	Good	VALUE	B+	PORTION	Large
READER-SURVEY RESPONSES	100% 👍	0% 👎						

SELECTIONS Tacos, burritos, quesadillas, nachos, fajitas, and taco salads made with steak, ground beef, chicken, tofu, or veggies; chips and salsa; cookies; beer.

COMMENTS The Mexican-food equivalent of a Subway sandwich shop. You place your order (for example, steak tacos) at the front of a long assembly line, and then follow your plate down the line as it's passed from worker to worker, each of whom adds whatever garnishes, sides, and sauces you want. We like Moe's quite a bit. The menu is filled with references to TV shows and movies, such as the John Coctostan (from *Fletch*).

Panda Express

LOCATION	Upper	Level	QUALITY	Fair	VALUE	C	PORTION	Medium-Large
READER-SURVEY RESPONSES	83% 👍	17% 👎						

SELECTIONS Chinese food, including entrées of sweet-and-sour chicken, orange chicken, kung pao chicken, beef and broccoli, beef with mushrooms and asparagus, honey walnut shrimp, and eggplant tofu, with sides of mixed veggies, chow mein, and white or fried rice.

COMMENTS The kung pao chicken has a darker, smoky flavor than most we've tried, and the sauces are heavier than our local Chinese takeouts. Still, Panda Express is a hit with the kids in our group, who want to eat here every time they see it. Panda Express usually has the longest line of the three fast-food joints on CityWalk's upper level.

Starbucks

LOCATION	Lower	Level	QUALITY	Good	VALUE	C	PORTION	Medium
READER-SURVEY RESPONSES	98% 👍	2% 👎						

SELECTIONS Coffees and teas in many blends and flavors; espresso, cappuccino, frozen coffees, and smoothies; pastries; cookies; and sodas.

COMMENTS While the Starbucks locations in Islands of Adventure, Universal Studios Florida, and Cabana Bay Beach Resort feature the chain's full sandwich menu, this particular Starbucks offers a more limited selection of pastries. However, it does provide a large amount of seating (with free Wi-Fi and accessible power ports) both inside and out. Though this handsomely designed coffee shop has much more barista capacity than the average franchise, its ground-central location leads to long lines around park opening. *Note:* Starbucks loyalty stars can be earned at Universal locations, but rewards may not be redeemed here. Starbucks gift cards and Universal annual pass discounts are both honored here.

Voodoo Doughnut

LOCATION	Lower Level	QUALITY	Good	VALUE	B-	PORTION	Medium
READER-SURVEY RESPONSES	82% 👍	18% 👎					

SELECTIONS Raised yeast, cake, or vegan doughnuts, topped with everything from fruit cereal or orange powdered-drink mix to bacon; plus coffee to wash them down.

COMMENTS This Portland-based bakery, which has built a cult following for its outrageously shaped confections, took over the former Element skate shop at Universal Orlando in 2018. The signature Voodoo Doll (with a pretzel stake through its heart) is Instagram-worthy, but the original anatomically explicit menu items aren't sold at a family-friendly theme park. Expect long lines outside the shop at breakfast and as the parks empty. Call ☎ 407-224-2691 to order ahead if buying a dozen ($16–$28). Even if you don't get anything to eat, pose for a photo on the doughnut throne outside.

RESORT HOTELS

Bayliner Diner

LOCATION	Cabana Bay Beach	QUALITY	Good	VALUE	B	PORTION	Medium–Large
READER-SURVEY RESPONSES	87% 👍	13% 👎					

SELECTIONS Cheeseburgers, chicken sandwiches, hot dogs, beef churrasco, Cajun shrimp, chicken potpie, seared salmon, pizza, pasta, flatbread, panini, wraps, salad bar, and frozen yogurt.

COMMENTS Cabana Bay's Bayliner Diner is a food court–style cafeteria with several different stations offering a wide range of food options. The preparations are a cut above the counter service found inside the parks. The churrasco-style flat iron with creamy chimichurri is surprisingly tender and tasty for counter-service steak. For breakfast, the diner serves up all the usual suspects. Get waffles or French toast, or wait for a made-to-order omelet, but avoid the precooked eggs on the combo platter and the croissant sandwich. The seating area, filled with booths and tables, is large. Large screens play retro commercials to evoke a feeling of nostalgia. One thing noticeable is the amount of usable outlets to charge your phones and tablets, including one outside every booth. If you prefer to dine poolside, the Hideaway Bar & Grill by the lazy river slings burgers, fish tacos, Honolulu-style hot dogs, and Cuban sandwiches, while Atomic Tonic near the waterslide serves *döner* kebabs and falafel wraps.

Emack & Bolio's Marketplace

LOCATION	Hard Rock Hotel	QUALITY	Good	VALUE	C	PORTION	Medium
READER-SURVEY RESPONSES	92% 👍	8% 👎					

SELECTIONS Ice cream, sorbet, frozen yogurt, sundaes, Starbucks coffee, sandwiches, candy, pizza, snacks, soft drinks, cereal, and pastries.

COMMENTS Boston-based Emack & Bolio's has a long history of associating with rock stars (check out the vintage van doors outside) and naming ice cream flavors after their songs. Here you can have a cone or sundae made from Space Cake, Trippin' on Espresso, or Deep Purple Cow. This location also has a grab-and-go selection of snacks, cold breakfast foods, and Starbucks drinks to speed you through your morning, plus a decent selection of hot and cold snacks, sandwiches, and takeout pizzas (in 10- or 16-inch pies) after noon.

New Dutch Trading Co.

LOCATION Sapphire Falls **QUALITY** Good **VALUE** C+ **PORTION** Medium
READER-SURVEY RESPONSES 85% 👍 15% 👎

SELECTIONS Hot and cold sandwiches, soup, salads, coffee, pastries, hand-scooped ice cream, and milkshakes.

COMMENTS This white-tiled quick-service marketplace in the Sapphire Falls Resort lobby is far smaller than the food hall at Aventura next door, but it manages to pack a lot of options—including Cuban and grilled veggie sandwiches, tropical salads, specialty smoothies, and lattes blended with the house brew—into a small space. The eatery also doubles as a grab-and-go market for snacks and sundries; secure s'mores kits for the pool's fire pit, or stock up on Tortuga rum cake here and skip your next Caribbean cruise. About the only thing there isn't space for is seating, with only a handful of stools along a bar, so plan on eating on the run or bringing food back to your room. New Dutch Trading Co. opens at 6 a.m. for breakfast and stays open until 11 p.m., so you can refill the Coke Freestyle mugs available here (see page 207).

Sal's Market Deli

LOCATION Portofino Bay **QUALITY** Good–Excellent **VALUE** B- **PORTION** Medium–Large
READER-SURVEY RESPONSES 97% 👍 3% 👎

SELECTIONS Pizza, calzones, deli sandwiches, salads, wine, and beer.

COMMENTS This casual counter-service deli and pizzeria is practically the only affordable option on Portofino Bay property. The pizza is the best in Universal outside of Red Oven and can be made with gluten-free dough. Around the corner, a full-service Starbucks with an attached *gelateria* and bakery serves breakfast and desserts. Food can be packaged and taken back to your room, undercutting the expensive room service.

Urban Pantry Food Hall

LOCATION Aventura **QUALITY** Good–Excellent **VALUE** B+ **PORTION** Medium–Large
READER-SURVEY RESPONSES Too new to rate

SELECTIONS Burgers, pizzas, chicken, Asian dishes, and roasted meats.

COMMENTS In lieu of a full-service restaurant, Aventura Hotel has a fast-casual food court off the main lobby. Inspired by big-city indoor markets, this next-generation food hall follows all the hip foodie trends: individual feeding stations, each with its own open kitchen and cash register, serving healthier and more diverse dining, in a minimalist industrial environment. In the morning, breakfast sandwiches, omelets, and American breakfast standards—along with flatbreads and calzones made with eggs, goat cheese, or avocado—are served. For lunch and dinner, start at the sushi bar—with a limited but creative collection of rolls—and wok station, where chefs turn your pick of veggies, noodles, and protein into stir-fry or soup. The burger station grills thick patties (either Black Angus beef or the vegan Impossible meat substitute) with high-end condiments like bacon-fig jam and Gruyère; the roast station carves half chickens, prime ribs, and cedar-planked salmon, paired with Brussels sprouts and colorful carrots; and pizzas can be topped with artichokes or prosciutto (as well as pepperoni). End your meal with a scoop of gelato or a shot glass–sized cake.

UNIVERSAL ORLANDO FULL-SERVICE RESTAURANT PROFILES

TO HELP YOU MAKE CHOICES FOR SIT-DOWN meals at breakfast, lunch, or dinner, we've provided full profiles of Universal's full-service restaurants, most of which are located in the CityWalk complex. Each profile lets you quickly check the restaurant's cuisine, location, star rating, cost range, quality rating, and value rating. Profiles are listed alphabetically by restaurant. In addition to all full-service restaurants, we also list and profile a few quick-service eateries around the resort that transcend basic burgers, hot dogs, and pizza.

STAR RATING

THE STAR RATING REPRESENTS THE ENTIRE dining experience: style, service, and ambience, in addition to taste, presentation, and food quality. Five stars, the highest rating, indicates that the restaurant offers the best of everything. Four-star restaurants are above average, and three-star restaurants offer good, though not necessarily memorable, meals. Two-star restaurants serve mediocre fare, and one-star restaurants are below par. Our star ratings don't correspond to ratings awarded by AAA, Forbes, Zagat, or other restaurant reviewers.

COST RANGE

THE NEXT RATING TELLS HOW MUCH an adult full-service entrée will cost. Appetizers, sides, desserts, drinks, taxes, and tips aren't included. We've rated the cost as inexpensive, moderate, or expensive.

Inexpensive	under $15/person
Moderate	$15–$35/person
Expensive	over $35/person

QUALITY RATING

THE FOOD QUALITY IS RATED on a scale of one to five stars, five being the best. The quality rating is based on the taste, freshness of ingredients, preparation, presentation, and creativity of food. There is no consideration of price. If you want the best food available and cost is no issue, look no further than the quality ratings.

VALUE RATING

IF, ON THE OTHER HAND, you are looking for both quality *and* value, check the value rating, also expressed as stars:

★★★★★	Exceptional value; a real bargain
★★★★	Good value
★★★	Fair value; you get exactly what you pay for
★★	Somewhat overpriced
★	Extremely overpriced

continued on page 229

Universal Orlando Restaurants by Cuisine

CUISINE	LOCATION	OVERALL RATING	COST	QUALITY RATING	VALUE RATING
AMERICAN					
THE COWFISH SUSHI BURGER BAR	CITYWALK	★★★★	MOD	★★★★	★★★½
BAR 17 BISTRO	AVENTURA HOTEL	★★★½	MOD	★★★★	★★★½
TOOTHSOME CHOCOLATE EMPORIUM & SAVORY FEAST KITCHEN	CITYWALK	★★★½	MOD	★★★★	★★★
THE KITCHEN	HARD ROCK HOTEL	★★★½	MOD	★★★½	★★★
CONFISCO GRILLE	ISLANDS OF ADVENTURE	★★★	MOD	★★★	★★★
HARD ROCK CAFE	CITYWALK	★★★	MOD	★★★	★★★
JIMMY BUFFETT'S MARGARITAVILLE	CITYWALK	★★★	MOD	★★★	★★★
NBC SPORTS GRILL & BREW	CITYWALK	★★★	MOD	★★★	★★★½
ORCHID COURT LOUNGE & SUSHI BAR	ROYAL PACIFIC RESORT	★★★	MOD-EXP	★★★	★★
JAKE'S AMERICAN BAR	ROYAL PACIFIC RESORT	★★★	MOD	★★★	★★½
GALAXY BOWL	CABANA BAY BEACH RESORT	★★	INEXP	★★½	★★½
ASIAN					
ISLANDS DINING ROOM	ROYAL PACIFIC RESORT	★★★½	MOD	★★★½	★★★
WANTILAN LUAU	ROYAL PACIFIC RESORT	★★★½	EXP	★★★½	★★★
ORCHID COURT LOUNGE & SUSHI BAR	ROYAL PACIFIC RESORT	★★★	MOD-EXP	★★★	★★
BRITISH AND IRISH					
LEAKY CAULDRON	UNIVERSAL STUDIOS FLORIDA	★★★½	INEXP	★★★½	★★★★
THREE BROOMSTICKS	ISLANDS OF ADVENTURE	★★★	INEXP	★★★½	★★★
FINNEGAN'S BAR & GRILL	UNIVERSAL STUDIOS FLORIDA	★★★	MOD	★★★	★★★
CAJUN					
PAT O'BRIEN'S ORLANDO	CITYWALK	★★★	INEXP	★★★½	★★★½
CARIBBEAN/JAMAICAN					
STRONG WATER TAVERN	SAPPHIRE FALLS RESORT	★★★½	MOD	★★★★	★★½
CARIBBEAN CARNAVAL	SAPPHIRE FALLS RESORT	★★★½	EXP	★★★½	★★★
AMATISTA COOKHOUSE	SAPPHIRE FALLS RESORT	★★★	MOD	★★★	★★★
JIMMY BUFFETT'S MARGARITAVILLE	CITYWALK	★★★	MOD	★★★	★★★
BOB MARLEY— A TRIBUTE TO FREEDOM	CITYWALK	★★½	INEXP	★★★	★★★

Universal Orlando Restaurants by Cuisine

CUISINE	LOCATION	OVERALL RATING	COST	QUALITY RATING	VALUE RATING
ITALIAN					
BICE	PORTOFINO BAY HOTEL	★★★★½	EXP	★★★★½	★★★★
VIVO ITALIAN KITCHEN	CITYWALK	★★★★	MOD	★★★★	★★★★½
MAMA DELLA'S RISTORANTE	PORTOFINO BAY HOTEL	★★★★	MOD–EXP	★★★★	★★★½
RED OVEN PIZZA BAKERY	CITYWALK	★★★½	INEXP	★★★½	★★★★½
TRATTORIA DEL PORTO	PORTOFINO BAY HOTEL	★★★	MOD	★★★	★★
MEXICAN					
ANTOJITOS AUTHENTIC MEXICAN FOOD	CITYWALK	★★★½	MOD	★★★½	★★★½
SEAFOOD					
THE COWFISH SUSHI BURGER BAR	CITYWALK	★★★★	MOD	★★★★	★★★½
MYTHOS RESTAURANT	ISLANDS OF ADVENTURE	★★★½	MOD	★★★½	★★★★
LOMBARD'S SEAFOOD GRILLE	UNIVERSAL STUDIOS FLORIDA	★★★	MOD	★★★½	★★★
ORCHID COURT LOUNGE & SUSHI BAR	ROYAL PACIFIC RESORT	★★★	MOD–EXP	★★★	★★
THE BUBBA GUMP SHRIMP CO. RESTAURANT & MARKET	CITYWALK	★★½	MOD	★★★	★★
SOUTHERN					
THE BUBBA GUMP SHRIMP CO. RESTAURANT & MARKET	CITYWALK	★★½	MOD	★★★	★★
STEAK					
THE PALM	HARD ROCK HOTEL	★★★★	V. EXP	★★★★	★★½
MYTHOS RESTAURANT	ISLANDS OF ADVENTURE	★★★½	MOD	★★★½	★★★★
NBC SPORTS GRILL & BREW	CITYWALK	★★★	MOD	★★★	★★★½

continued from page 227

PAYMENT

ALL UNIVERSAL ORLANDO RESTAURANTS accept American Express, MasterCard, Visa, Discover, Diners Club, and Universal Resort hotel-room charges.

Amatista Cookhouse ★★★

CARIBBEAN	MODERATE	QUALITY ★★★	VALUE ★★★
READER-SURVEY RESPONSES 91% 👍	9% 👎		

Sapphire Falls Resort; ☎ 407-503-DINE (3463)

Customers Hotel guests. **Reservations** Accepted via OpenTable. **When to go** Breakfast or dinner. **Entrée range** $13–$28. **Service rating** ★★½. **Friendliness rating** ★★★. **Parking** $5 valet or free self-parking at hotel with validation. **Bar** Full service. **Wine selection** Modest. **Dress** Resort casual. **Disabled access** Good. **Hours** Daily, 7–11 a.m., 11:30 a.m.–2:30 p.m., and 5–10 p.m.

SETTING AND ATMOSPHERE A large, sunny room on Sapphire Falls Resort's lower level features an exhibition kitchen and indoor–outdoor seating with a view of the hotel's lagoon. Seating is in the open main area or one of the private dining rooms.

HOUSE SPECIALTIES Buffet breakfast with waffles and smoked salmon; rotisserie chicken, flatbreads, and sandwiches for lunch; Caribbean snapper, chargrilled steak, and slow-cooked pork chop for dinner.

SUMMARY AND COMMENTS Bright and clean, though a bit too big to be cozy, Amatista is the main table-service restaurant at Sapphire Falls and caters to families and conventioneers by serving comfort food favorites with an abundance of Caribbean creativity. We love the jerk-seasoned chicken wings, flaky empanadas, and juicy Angus burger, but the flatbread topped with blue cheese was too pungent for us to finish. Ordering breakfast à la carte quickly adds up, so if you want more than a muffin, spring for the buffet. Service, like that on the actual islands, is friendly but inconsistent; at lunch you may have the place all to yourself, but don't count on a quick dinner here if you are on a tight schedule. Preferred Annual Pass holders get a free wine or beer and a free kids' meal with the purchase of an adult dinner entrée.

Antojitos Authentic Mexican Food ★★★½

MEXICAN	MODERATE	QUALITY ★★★½	VALUE ★★★½
READER-SURVEY RESPONSES	88% 👍 12% 👎		

CityWalk; ☎ 407-224-FOOD (3663)

Customers Locals and tourists. **Reservations** Accepted via Zomato. **When to go** Dinner. **Entrée range** $13–$28. **Service rating** ★★★. **Friendliness rating** ★★★★. **Parking** Universal Orlando garage. **Bar** Full service. **Wine selection** Good. **Dress** Casual; *luchador* masks and sombreros optional. **Disabled access** Good. **Hours** Sunday–Thursday, 3 p.m.–midnight; Friday–Saturday, 3 p.m.–1 a.m.

SETTING AND ATMOSPHERE This festive postmodern tribute to Mexican street culture features a large open kitchen framed by graffiti graphics and eye-catching neon, with the central bar and surrounding booths fashioned from reclaimed wood and metal. The downstairs can get very noisy, so if you want a quieter meal, ask for one of the private rooms upstairs. Or grab a seat on the patio or balcony to watch the CityWalk crowds go by.

HOUSE SPECIALTIES Roasted corn (*elotes*), quesadillas, enchiladas, tacos, fajitas, grilled salmon, carnitas, roast pork loin, churrasco steak, and cheesecake chimichangas with sour cream ice cream.

ENTERTAINMENT A modern mariachi ensemble plays outside and inside Antojitos.

SUMMARY AND COMMENTS The colorful Antojitos sits next to Jimmy Buffett's Margaritaville. A Universal Studios concept, Antojitos offers unique and craveable tapas-style Mexican food, featuring handcrafted tortillas, made-while-you-watch guacamole, and fresh sauces for a taste of Mexico City without the high crime rate.

For starters, you'll probably want a drink, and Antojitos has Orlando's best tequila selection this side of Epcot's La Cava. Order from the four-sided bar on the ground floor or from the converted Volkswagen bus outside the entrance. If you don't do straight shots, try a signature drink such as The Horse You Rode In On (garnished with an expensive Amarena black cherry).

When it comes to the food, while it's pricier than your local taco joint, Antojitos prepares familiar plates with exceptionally fresh ingredients. The table-side guacamole is a must-have that will convert the most hardened avocado-hater, and the *elotes* (roasted corn with cotija cheese and jalapeño mayo) is almost a meal in itself. The portion sizes of the enchiladas and tacos aren't enormous, but you'll probably be full after the free chips (served hot with house-made salsa) and the excellent rice and beans accompanying most entrées. The *comidas de la casa* include some holdovers from the short-lived upscale menu briefly served on the second floor; the churrasco steak and pork loin are wonderfully seasoned, though the pork can be a bit dry. Leave room for dessert because the sour cream ice cream served with the molten *cajeta de leche* cake will make you shout, "Ay, caramba!"

Bar 17 Bistro ★★★½

AMERICAN	MODERATE	QUALITY ★★★★	VALUE ★★★½
READER-SURVEY RESPONSES	Too new to rate		

Aventura Hotel; ☎ 407-503-6000

Customers Locals and hotel guests. **Reservations** Not accepted. **When to go** Dinner. **Entrée range** $10–$18. **Service rating** ★★★. **Friendliness rating** ★★★½. **Parking** Free self-parking at hotel with validation. **Bar** Full service. **Wine selection** Limited. **Dress** Casual. **Disabled access** Good. **Hours** Daily, 5–11 p.m.; bar open 4 p.m.–2 a.m.

SETTING AND ATMOSPHERE Located on the roof of the Aventura Hotel, Bar 17 Bistro boasts a better view than any watering hole at Walt Disney World, with 360-degree views of Universal Orlando—including Volcano Bay—and International Drive.

HOUSE SPECIALTIES Chinese *bao* steamed buns; fried rice or egg noodles; small plates and tapas-style appetizers.

ENTERTAINMENT DJ on weekend evenings.

SUMMARY AND COMMENTS Even if you aren't staying at Aventura, you'll want to visit the hotel just to ride the dedicated elevator to the 17th floor and take in the picture-postcard panorama from the roof. But the carefully balanced craft cocktails and savory small plates of exotic flavors are what will make you want to linger at Bar 17 Bistro long past sunset.

Begin by picking one of the signature cocktails (Seth recommends the frozen bourbon-based Barrel) or a draft craft beer. Next, choose a trio of *bao,* which are the Asian fusion answer to tacos; they're on the small side, but their fillings pack a ton of flavor. Pork belly, Mongolian beef, tempura vegetables, and spicy shrimp are all excellent. Finally, don't forget a few of the bistro plates; the charcuterie board holds enough meat and cheese to share, and the beet salad and grilled octopus are each the equal of any appetizer from Emeril's now-shuttered restaurants.

A word of warning: Bar 17 Bistro's glorious open-air atmosphere includes complimentary exposure to wind and rain. In case of a severe storm, the entire establishment may temporarily shut down.

Bice ★★★★½

ITALIAN	EXPENSIVE	QUALITY ★★★★½	VALUE ★★★★
READER-SURVEY RESPONSES	91% 👍 9% 👎		

Portofino Bay Hotel; ☎ 407-503-1415

Customers Locals and tourists. **Reservations** Recommended via OpenTable. **When to go** Dinner. **Entrée range** $23–$48. **Service rating** ★★★★★. **Friendliness rating** ★★★★. **Parking** $5 valet or free self-parking at hotel with validation. **Bar** Full service. **Wine selection** Very good. **Dress** Resort dressy. **Disabled access** Good. **Hours** Daily, 5:30–10 p.m.

SETTING AND ATMOSPHERE Cedarwood and marble floors, crisp white linens, opulent flower arrangements, and waiters in black suits give Bice ("beach-ay") the feeling of a formal restaurant, but there is nothing stiff or fussy about the space or the staff. It is immaculately clean, beautifully lit, and relatively quiet even when crowded. Outdoor seating overlooking the bay is lovely on spring and fall evenings.

HOUSE SPECIALTIES Menu changes seasonally; selections may include prosciutto with fresh melon and baby greens; homemade braised beef spareribs ravioli with spinach in mushroom-Marsala sauce; veal Milanese with an arugula and cherry tomato salad; or risotto of the day.

ENTERTAINMENT Piano in bar.

SUMMARY AND COMMENTS This is part of a chain of very upscale and quite impressive restaurants found in New York, Tokyo, Las Vegas, and other international locales. The food is incredibly fresh, well prepared, and elegant, and the service is top-notch. But be prepared: Even a modest meal will put a dent in your wallet, and even though the food and service are definitely worth it, it may be too expensive for many vacationers. If you want to try a variety of things on the menu, split a salad, appetizer, or pasta dish between two people for a starter; portions are large enough for sharing, and the staff is more than happy to accommodate.

Our favorite appetizer is the fresh *burrata* mozzarella caprese. The other appetizers, mostly salads and antipasti of meats and cheeses, aren't bad, but you've probably had something similar already.

Among the best entrées is the breaded veal, which is pounded so thin that it takes up almost the entire plate. It's served with a small salad on top, and the salad's dressing serves to keep the veal juicy. The penne *all'arrabbiata* is even spicier than advertised.

We rate Bice as one of the best restaurants in all of Universal Orlando Resort, and it compares favorably to any of the similar restaurants at Walt Disney World. Because the Portofino gets a lot of business-convention traffic, it's probably easier to get a reservation at 5:30 p.m. than 7:30 p.m. As for reservations, you can make them in person, over the phone, or online at opentable.com.

Bob Marley—A Tribute to Freedom ★★½

JAMAICAN/CARIBBEAN	INEXPENSIVE	QUALITY ★★★	VALUE ★★★
READER-SURVEY RESPONSES	77% 👍	23% 👎	

CityWalk; ☎ 407-224-FOOD (3663)

Customers Locals and tourists. **Reservations** Accepted via Zomato. **When to go** Early evening. **Entrée range** $10–$18. **Service rating** ★★. **Friendliness rating** ★★★. **Parking** Universal Orlando garage. **Bar** Full service. **Wine selection** Poor. **Dress** Casual; dreadlocks if you have them. **Disabled access** Good. **Hours** Sunday–Thursday, 4–10 p.m.; Friday–Saturday, 4–11 p.m.; bar open daily, 3 p.m.–2 a.m.

SETTING AND ATMOSPHERE Set in a replica of reggae singer Bob Marley's Jamaican home, the building is filled with memorabilia and photos showcasing his career and life. Lots of lions, the colors of the Jamaican flag, and other Rastafarian influences pay tribute to the musician's career. Most of the area is open to the elements, and there's no air-conditioning, though there are shelters from the occasional rainstorm.

HOUSE SPECIALTIES Jerk-marinated chicken breast; smoky white-Cheddar cheese fondue; Jamaican vegetable patties; beef patties; yucca fries; oxtail stew.

ENTERTAINMENT Live reggae band and DJ in courtyard nightly; cover charge after 9 p.m.

SUMMARY AND COMMENTS None of the food is spectacular or particularly adventurous, but it's worth a visit for the laid-back atmosphere. Feel free to get up and dance.

The Bubba Gump Shrimp Co. Restaurant & Market ★★½

SOUTHERN/SEAFOOD	MODERATE	QUALITY ★★★	VALUE ★★
READER-SURVEY RESPONSES	81% 👍	19% 👎	

CityWalk; ☎ 407-224-2690

Customers Tourists. **Reservations** Not accepted. **When to go** Anytime. **Entrée range** $13–$29. **Service rating** ★★★. **Friendliness rating** ★★★★. **Parking** Universal Orlando garage. **Bar** Full service. **Wine selection** Minimal. **Dress** Casual. **Disabled access** Good. **Hours** Daily, 11 a.m.–midnight.

SETTING AND ATMOSPHERE The movie that inspired the chain, *Forrest Gump,* plays on TVs throughout but without sound, just closed-captioning. Movie memorabilia decorates the wooden walls of this seafood shanty. License plates that say RUN FORREST RUN on one side and STOP FORREST STOP on another help signal a waiter when you need service, and waiters may ask you trivia questions from the movie.

HOUSE SPECIALTIES Fried, stuffed, or grilled shrimp (and shrimp cooked almost every other way); burgers; salads; grilled salmon; fried chicken; baby back ribs. A gluten-free menu is also offered.

SUMMARY AND COMMENTS The theme may seem a little cheesy, but this is a fun and festive atmosphere to bring the kids. The food is no worse than your average seafood chain (think Red Lobster without the cheese biscuits) and is not too spicy.

Caribbean Carnaval ★★★½

CARIBBEAN	EXPENSIVE	QUALITY ★★★½	VALUE ★★★
READER-SURVEY RESPONSES	100% 👍	0% 👎	

Sapphire Falls Resort; ☎ 407-503-DINE (3463)

Customers Tourists. **Reservations** Required via caribbeancarnaval.eventbrite.com. **When to go** Dinner only. **Entrée range** Buffet: $75.62 adults, $38.34 children ages 3–9. (Prices include tax and gratuity for everyone, and planter's punch, wine, and beer for guests age 21 and older.) **Service rating** ★★★. **Friendliness rating** ★★★★. **Parking** Free valet or free self-parking at hotel with validation. **Bar** Rum punch, wine, and beer available. **Wine selection** Limited. **Dress** Caribbean casual. **Disabled access** Average. **Hours** Friday; seating begins at 6 p.m., with registration starting 30 minutes before.

SETTING AND ATMOSPHERE Outdoor hotel event pavilion masquerading as a tropical paradise.

HOUSE SPECIALTIES Buffet includes *mojo*-roasted suckling pig with spiced rum-soaked pineapple purée, grilled snapper, jerk chicken, *ropa vieja,* sweet plantains, and johnnycakes. Dessert buffet has rum cake and guava flan.

ENTERTAINMENT Caribbean dancing and live music.

SUMMARY AND COMMENTS Mardi Gras may come to Universal's theme parks only once a year, but this lively dinner show bids farewell to the flesh with Caribbean flair every week. The buffet features some of the tastiest Latin American dishes from Sapphire Falls's restaurants, and the live show after you eat delivers all the audience participation limbo and conga lines your rum-addled head can handle. Priority Seating reserves you a table near the front for an extra $10.65 per adult ($5.33 per kid), but it isn't necessary to get an acceptable view.

Confisco Grille ★★★

AMERICAN	MODERATE	QUALITY ★★★	VALUE ★★★
READER-SURVEY RESPONSES	91% 👍	9% 👎	

Islands of Adventure, Port of Entry; ☎ 407-224-4406

Customers Park guests. **Reservations** Accepted via Zomato. **When to go** Anytime. **Entrée range** $10-$22. **Service rating** ★★★. **Friendliness rating** ★★★★. **Parking** Universal Orlando garage. **Bar** Full service. **Wine selection** Moderate. **Dress** Casual. **Disabled access** Good. **Hours** Daily, 11 a.m.-7 p.m. (varies with park closing).

SETTING AND ATMOSPHERE A way station on the road to Morocco, perhaps? Actually, it's meant to look like a customs house. Look for "smuggled goods," representing the park's various islands, decorating the lobby's upper level. You'll see giant dinosaur skeletons from Jurassic Park, golden urns from Lost Continent, and even a wand from The Wizarding World of Harry Potter if you look hard enough.

HOUSE SPECIALTIES Wood-grilled pizzas; hummus served with a puffy lavash bread larger than most human heads; selection of salads; beef and chicken fajitas; grilled sandwiches and burgers; pad Thai.

SUMMARY AND COMMENTS Confisco isn't fine dining, but it does fine when you just can't stand in another line. Because of its varied menu of Mediterranean, Italian, Mexican, and Asian dishes, most people should find something to please them at Confisco Grille. Wood-grilled pizzas have a pleasing crust—check with your server to find out the daily special pies. More adventurous options include slow-braised beef in Bordelaise cream, Moroccan-spiced calamari, and curry chicken. Several menu items can be made vegetarian and vegan friendly. For dessert, indulge in a Brookieberry Treasure, a chocolate chip cookie baked inside a brownie, covered with vanilla ice cream, and smothered in strawberry and chocolate sauces. The adjoining Backwater Bar is a good spot to grab a cool sangria on a hot day.

The Cowfish Sushi Burger Bar ★★★★

AMERICAN/SUSHI	MODERATE	QUALITY ★★★★	VALUE ★★★½
READER-SURVEY RESPONSES	93% 👍	7% 👎	

CityWalk; ☎ 407-224-2690

Customers Locals and park guests. **Reservations** Accepted via Zomato before 5 p.m. **When to go** Early afternoon or late evening. **Entrée range** $12-$28. **Service rating** ★★½. **Friendliness rating** ★★★★. **Parking** Universal Orlando garage. **Bar** Full service. **Wine selection** Good. **Dress** Resort casual. **Disabled access** Good. **Hours** Sunday-Thursday, 11 a.m.-11 p.m.; Friday-Saturday, 11 a.m.-midnight.

SETTING AND ATMOSPHERE A photo op of this restaurant's mascot—a giant bug-eyed fish with a saddle on its back—should clue you in that this isn't the spot for stuffy food snobs. The Cowfish features colorful Pop Art, larger-than-life displays (including King Kong and a noodle-filled fishbowl), and silly signage—be sure to check out the restrooms. Guests can enter though the small lobby on the ground floor or the patio bar on the upper level; all seating—both indoors and out—is on the second and third floor, offering spectacular views over CityWalk.

Aside from table seating, there are multiple bars at Cowfish. Young children will enjoy the touch screen games and a make-your-own-fish app, which you can then watch swim in a virtual aquarium.

HOUSE SPECIALTIES Crab Rangoon dip, blackened tuna nachos, half-pound burgers, sushi and sashimi combos, fusion and Burgushi rolls and bento boxes, hand-spun milkshakes, specialty cocktails, and spiked shakes.

SUMMARY AND COMMENTS A one-of-a-kind dining concept that melds pan-Asian cuisine with the good ol' American burger, Cowfish brings something completely unique to the table. Like peanut butter and chocolate, The Cowfish's burgers and sushi both taste great, and taste great together.

The voluminous menu starts with familiar-sounding appetizers, such as Parmesan bacon truffle fries and tuna nachos, expertly prepared and presented in generous portions (a recurring theme). Next comes an extensive list of half-pound hormone-free hamburgers, with names such as the Jalapeño Popper Show-Stopper, Big Squeal, and Rise & Swine. Veggie and turkey burgers are also available, and all are served with seasoned fries, which can be substituted with seaweed salad, bacon coleslaw, or edamame. The Boursin Bacon Burger, with garlic-herb cheese and sautéed mushrooms, is a standout. Traditional sushi selections range from chef combos of sashimi and *nigiri*, classic makimono rolls, and fusion specialties stuffed with tuna, coconut shrimp, shiitake mushrooms, or crabmeat; the premium tuna and salmon on Jen's Fresh Find roll is particularly flavorful.

Finally, we arrive at the creative center of Cowfish's menu: the Burgushi. You can try a sushi roll made with lobster and filet mignon (The Prime Time), Angus beef and applewood bacon (The Taste Explosion), or pulled pork and barbecue sauce (High Class Hillbilly). Despite the bizarro pairing, all the ones we've sampled (with the exception of the What's Shakin' Tuna Bacon Sandwich) have been as delicious as they are odd, which is saying something; Doug's Filet Roll (with ginger dipping sauce for the steak) is a safe bet. If you are still apprehensive, try a bento box, which brings a slider mini-burger, sushi roll, and several side dishes together on a Japanese TV dinner tray.

The extensive craft cocktail list includes a bourbon and candied bacon concoction and old-fashioned mules made with ginger beer. Hand-spun milkshakes (nonalcoholic or spiked) headline the dessert menu, which also features sushi-shaped pastries exclusive to the Orlando location.

We love the overall atmosphere, but the time that it takes for a meal to come out can be painfully slow because the kitchen is undersized for the multistory dining rooms. The restaurant doesn't take reservations after 5 p.m., and the wait can be long on a busy weekend, but the host will take your cell phone number when you check in, allowing them to text you when your table is ready. In addition, a free app for Apple and Android phones (search in your app store for "The Cowfish Orlando") will let you join the wait list from anywhere within 0.5 mile of the restaurant; use it to check in while exiting a ride, but be sure to see the host once you arrive because the app isn't prompt at letting you know your table is ready.

Finnegan's Bar & Grill ★★★

IRISH	MODERATE	QUALITY ★★★	VALUE ★★★
READER-SURVEY RESPONSES	84% 👍	16% 👎	

Universal Studios Florida, New York; ☎ 407-363-8757

Customers Park guests. **Reservations** Accepted via Zomato. **When to go** Anytime. **Entrée range** $11–$22. **Service rating** ★★★. **Friendliness rating** ★★★★. **Parking** Universal Orlando garage. **Bar** Full service. **Wine selection** Limited. Ireland is not really known for its wines; good beer selection, though. **Dress** Casual. **Disabled access** Good. **Hours** Daily, 11 a.m.–7 p.m. (varies with park closing).

SETTING AND ATMOSPHERE Fashioned after an Irish bar in New York City, albeit one built as a movie set. Along with the requisite publike accoutrements—such as the tin ceiling and belt-driven paddle fans—are movie lights and half walls that suggest the back of scenery flats. Obligatory references to Guinness beer and New York City abound. The bar area is a popular gathering spot for locals and gets insanely busy during special events like Halloween.

HOUSE SPECIALTIES Shepherd's pie; fish-and-chips; Guinness beef stew; bangers and mash; Dingle seafood pie; Irish coffee.

ENTERTAINMENT Singer/guitarist in the bar.

SUMMARY AND COMMENTS The food is modest, but the entertainment is fun and the beer is cold; brew fans can happily explore a five-sample flight of international ales as they rest from the park. Add to that the fact that this is one of only two full-service spots in Universal Studios Florida, and the average pub fare starts to look a bit more attractive.

The fish-and-chips, which come wrapped in "newspaper," are about the same as those served in The Wizarding World. The shepherd's pie is bland, but the potato-leek soup is good, and the fried potato-onion "web" is addictive. For entrées, burgers, sandwiches, salads, and Guinness stew are safe choices.

Galaxy Bowl ★★

AMERICAN	INEXPENSIVE	QUALITY ★★½	VALUE ★★½
READER-SURVEY RESPONSES	79% 👍	21% 👎	

Cabana Bay Beach Resort; ☎ 407-503-4230

Customers Hotel guests. **Reservations** Not available. **When to go** Early afternoon or late evening. **Entrée range** $9–$14. **Service rating** ★★. **Friendliness rating** ★★★. **Parking** Universal Orlando garage or $45 for self-parking at hotel. **Bar** Full service. **Wine selection** Limited. **Dress** Casual. **Disabled access** Good. **Hours** Daily, noon–midnight.

SETTING AND ATMOSPHERE Galaxy Bowl, located on the second floor of the main Cabana Bay building directly above Starbucks, is the only full-service dining option inside the hotel. The 10-lane bowling alley is inspired by Hollywood Star Lanes, made famous in the film *The Big Lebowski.* The lanes are illuminated in trippy colors at night, and large projection screens broadcast sporting events.

HOUSE SPECIALTIES Loaded cheese fries, chicken wings, salads, sandwiches, burgers, and fried shrimp.

ENTERTAINMENT Bowling costs $16.99 for adults, $10.99 for kids age 12 and under, including shoe rental; 20-minute speed bowling sessions cost $8.99 per person, shoes included. Parties of one to three people get 45 minutes of lane time; four to eight people get 75 minutes.

SUMMARY AND COMMENTS Some people enjoy the athleticism of basketball, while others admire the grace and skill of soccer, but we at the Unofficials favor bowling as our preferred sport, as it is the only one in which you can participate while eating chili-cheese fries. Galaxy Bowl has several tables where you can enjoy a meal, but you can also order snacks and drinks while taking in a game of bowling. When the wait for a lane grows long (as it often does on rainy days), ask for a table, and order drinks and appetizers until your turn arrives.

The limited menu offers fast-food selections similar to items served downstairs in the Bayliner Diner, and quality is about on par for greasy bowling alley grub. Draft beer is served in pitchers, and the list of specialty drinks is nearly as long as the food menu. There are two Coke Freestyle machines at Galaxy Bowl for your Sonic Fill mugs. If you want the alcohol and appetizers without the ambience of falling pins, the hotel lobby's Swizzle Lounge serves pizza and wings with craft beers and classic cocktails; happy hour is daily from opening until 7 p.m.

Hard Rock Cafe   ★★★

AMERICAN	MODERATE	QUALITY ★★★	VALUE ★★★
READER-SURVEY RESPONSES	80% 👍 20% 👎		

CityWalk; ☎ 407-351-7625

Customers Tourists. **Reservations** Accepted via hardrock.com/reservations. **When to go** Afternoon or evening. **Entrée range** $10–$35. **Service rating** ★★★. **Friendliness rating** ★★. **Parking** Universal Orlando garage. **Bar** Full service. **Wine selection** Moderate. **Dress** Casual. **Disabled access** Good. **Hours** Daily, 8:30 a.m.–midnight.

SETTING AND ATMOSPHERE This is the biggest Hard Rock Cafe in the world (or in the Universe, as they like to say in this part of town). Shaped like the Roman Coliseum, the two-story dining room is a massive museum of rock art memorabilia. The circular center bar features a full-size pink 1959 Cadillac spinning overhead. If you need to be told that this is a noisy restaurant, you've never been to a Hard Rock Cafe before. Everyone, however, should visit a Hard Rock at least once.

HOUSE SPECIALTIES Chicken and waffles and eggs Benedict at breakfast. Barbecue pork sandwich, charbroiled burgers, barbecued ribs, grilled fajitas, New York strip steak, hot fudge brownie, and milkshakes.

ENTERTAINMENT Rock-and-roll records and memorabilia, the biggest such collection on display anywhere in the Hard Rock chain. Ask at the check-in podium about free guided Vibe tours of the restaurant; if you're lucky, you may get a glimpse of the VIP-only John Lennon Room upstairs.

SUMMARY AND COMMENTS The best meals we've had here are when we order only appetizers or only desserts, and drinks. The entrées are average, and you'd be hard-pressed to differentiate them from anything you'd get at, say, Margaritaville.

Hard Rock Cafe offers a 15% discount on food for Preferred and Premier Annual Pass holders and military personnel with ID; 10% AAA discounts also apply. You can sign up for a Hard Rock Rewards membership to get additional offers and earn points on purchases (including alcohol). Be aware that admission to the adjoining Hard Rock Live concert hall is completely separate from the restaurant, though you can sometimes order food from the venue's bar.

Islands Dining Room   ★★★½

PAN-ASIAN	MODERATE	QUALITY ★★★½	VALUE ★★★
READER-SURVEY RESPONSES	93% 👍 7% 👎		

Royal Pacific Resort; ☎ 407-503-DINE (3463)

Customers Hotel guests. **Reservations** Accepted via OpenTable. **When to go** Breakfast or character dinners. **Entrée range** Breakfast, $12–$17; dinner, $18–$35. **Service rating** ★★★. **Friendliness rating** ★★★. **Parking** Free self-parking at hotel with validation. **Bar** Full service. **Wine selection** Average. **Dress** Casual. **Disabled access** Good. **Hours** Monday–Friday, 7–11 a.m. and 6–10 p.m.; Saturday–Sunday, 7 a.m.–noon and 6–10 p.m.

SETTING AND ATMOSPHERE Pretty standard hotel dining room; big and open, and always spotless.

HOUSE SPECIALTIES Breakfast features waffles with mixed berries, Tahitian French toast à l'orange, and Hawaiian pancakes. Dinner options include family-style stir-fry, Filipino-style shrimp fried rice, honey-glazed salmon, and Korean bulgogi-style rib eye.

SUMMARY AND COMMENTS Breakfast here is a treat—the specialties are all tasty and (surprisingly) moderately priced, or go whole *pua'a* and order the breakfast buffet ($24 plus tax for adults, $14 for kids). The all-you-can-eat Wok Experience, available 6–9 p.m. on most Fridays and select other nights for $24 per person ($14 for kids), comes highly recommended by our resident gourmand Derek Burgan. Dinner is good too, but with all the other restaurants around, especially if you're spending the day in the parks, we suggest having a hearty breakfast here and an evening meal elsewhere.

Jake's American Bar ★★★

AMERICAN	MODERATE	QUALITY ★★★	VALUE ★★½
READER-SURVEY RESPONSES	84% 👍	16% 👎	

Royal Pacific Resort; ☎ 407-503-DINE (3463)

Customers Hotel guests. **Reservations** Accepted via OpenTable. **When to go** Early or late evening. **Entrée range** $13–$35. **Service rating** ★★★. **Friendliness rating** ★★★. **Parking** Free self-parking at hotel with validation. **Bar** Full service. **Wine selection** Average. **Dress** Resort casual. **Disabled access** Good. **Hours** Daily, 11 a.m.–1:30 a.m.

SETTING AND ATMOSPHERE Run-of-the-mill hotel bar and restaurant with a vaguely 1930s "Rick's Cafe" feel. The menu explains the backstory of Captain Jake McNally and his association with Royal Pacific Airways, continuing the overall theme of the resort, which centers on the golden age of travel.

HOUSE SPECIALTIES Homemade pretzel rods, charcuterie, *burrata* salad, flatbreads, beer-braised short ribs, rib eye and *frites,* seared sea bass, and grilled tomato-and-mozzarella sandwich.

ENTERTAINMENT Live music Wednesday, Friday, and Saturday.

SUMMARY AND COMMENTS This is a viable option if you're staying in the hotel, but as far as special meals go, this place doesn't deliver—and really isn't meant to.

Beer lovers will want to check out the four-sample flights, as well as the four-course pairing parties held on select nights (visit tinyurl.com/jakesbeer for Jake's Beer Dinner schedule). Jake's serves a limited late-night menu 10 p.m.–1:30 a.m. and is usually the only restaurant at the resort serving hot food after midnight.

Jimmy Buffett's Margaritaville ★★★

CARIBBEAN/AMERICAN	MODERATE	QUALITY ★★★	VALUE ★★★
READER-SURVEY RESPONSES	88% 👍	12% 👎	

CityWalk; ☎ 407-224-2155

Customers Local and tourist Parrotheads. **Reservations** Accepted via Zomato. **When to go** Early evening. **Entrée range** $15–$30. **Service rating** ★★★. **Friendliness rating** ★★★★. **Parking** Universal Orlando garage. **Bar** Full service. **Wine selection** Minimal. **Dress** Floral shirts and flip-flops. **Disabled access** Good. **Hours** Sunday–Thursday, 10:30 a.m.–midnight; Friday–Saturday, 10:30 a.m.–2 a.m.

SETTING AND ATMOSPHERE A boisterous tribute to the chief Parrothead, this two-story dining space has many large-screen TVs playing Jimmy Buffett music videos and scenes from his live performances. The focal point is a volcano that erupts occasionally, spewing margarita mix instead of lava.

HOUSE SPECIALTIES Cheeseburgers and margaritas, of course; volcano nachos; fish tacos; jambalaya; coconut shrimp; Key lime pie.

ENTERTAINMENT Live music on the porch early; band on inside stage late evening.

SUMMARY AND COMMENTS This is a relaxing, festive place, but it's not always worth the wait (especially if it's 2 hours, which it has been known to be). This place is wildly popular with Jimmy Buffett fans, who stand in line just to get a beeper, so they can stand in line some more and wait for a table. The atmosphere, though, is like a taste of the beach without having to travel to the coast.

The food is a mix of Floridian and Caribbean, so expect lots of seafood and Jamaican seasoning. The food is good, but not good enough for non-Buffett fans to make a special trip. If the line for a table is outrageous, see if you can sidle up to the bar for a margarita and appetizers, which is just as much—if not more—fun than actually having a full meal. None of the entrées, including the cheeseburger, will make you think that you're in paradise, but fans don't seem to care.

The Kitchen ★★★½

AMERICAN	MODERATE	QUALITY ★★★½	VALUE ★★★
READER-SURVEY RESPONSES	83% 👍	17% 👎	

Hard Rock Hotel; ☎ 407-503-2430

Customers Tourists. **Reservations** Recommended via OpenTable. **When to go** Breakfast or dinner. **Entrée range** $15–$42. **Service rating** ★★★. **Friendliness rating** ★★★★. **Parking** $5 valet or free self-parking at hotel with validation. **Bar** Full service. **Wine selection** Good. **Dress** Casual. **Disabled access** Good. **Hours** Sunday–Thursday, 7 a.m.–10 p.m.; Friday–Saturday, 7 a.m.–11 p.m. (may vary seasonally).

SETTING AND ATMOSPHERE With the appearance of a spacious kitchen in a rock megastar's mansion, The Kitchen features walls adorned with culinary-themed memorabilia from the Hard Rock Hotel's many celebrity guests. A colorful "kids' crib" adorned with beanbag chairs and TVs allows the adults to eat in peace.

HOUSE SPECIALTIES Breakfast choices include eggs Benedict, spinach-and-sausage frittata, and custom omelets. The lunch menu has salads, burgers, flatbreads, three-cheese mac and cheese, and chicken potpie. At dinner, seared ahi tuna, filet mignon, shrimp tacos, and grilled pork chops are served. A gluten-free menu is available.

ENTERTAINMENT Rock stars occasionally visit to cook their specialties at the Chef's Table, so call ahead to see if any rock stars will be in the kitchen—you may find yourself having dinner with Joan Jett or Bob Seger. Signed aprons and rock memorabilia hang on the walls. A magician performs table-side on Wednesdays and Fridays, 6–9 p.m. On Tuesdays and Thursdays at Kids Can Cook, kids create their own pizzas or quesadillas 5–7 p.m. For adults, wine and martini specials Sunday–Thursday (5 p.m.–close) offer discounted flights and bottles.

SUMMARY AND COMMENTS Though we must admit that our expectations weren't too high for this Hard Rock venture, we were pleasantly surprised with the food and service here. Though expensive, the food is actually quite good, and the setting is pretty fun. The 10-ounce Angus beef Kitchen Burger will set you back about $18, but the regular version is just as tasty and less expensive. Brave and/or crazy souls can take part in the Kitchen Sink Challenge, which consists of eating The Kitchen burger, a pound of fries, a fried pickle, and the humongous Kitchen Sink Cake within a 30-minute time limit. If dinner is a little out of your price range but you still want the experience, visit at lunchtime or go for the $23 breakfast buffet ($17 for kids ages 10–14 and $13 for ages 3–9; $8 7–9 a.m.), which includes a host of fresh, yummy selections and an omelet station; for an additional $15 Friday–Sunday, adults can upgrade to unlimited Bloody Marys or mimosas, always a smart choice before walking around a hot theme park all day.

Leaky Cauldron ★★★½

BRITISH	INEXPENSIVE	QUALITY ★★★½	VALUE ★★★★
READER-SURVEY RESPONSES	89% 👍	11% 👎	

Universal Studios Florida, The Wizarding World of Harry Potter–Diagon Alley; ☎ 407-224-4012

Customers Park guests. **Reservations** Breakfast only. **When to go** Early or late. **Entrée range** $10–$22. **Service rating** ★★★. **Friendliness rating** ★★★★. **Parking** Universal Orlando garage. **Bar** Beer and wine only. **Wine selection** Limited. **Dress** Casual. **Disabled access** Good. **Hours** Daily, park opening–10:30 a.m. and 11 a.m.–park closing.

SETTING AND ATMOSPHERE Modeled after the Leaky Cauldron in the Harry Potter books and films, this table-service restaurant is the flagship diner of Diagon Alley. A haunt of wizards, Leaky Cauldron was located outside The Wizarding World on Charing Cross Road in the novels and movies but is located inside Diagon Alley in the Universal Studios version. (You can find a non-opening replica of the pub door from the original film just outside Diagon Alley, tucked between the bookstore and record shop.) To get a sense of what the restaurant looks like, check out "Prisoner of Azkaban—The Leaky Cauldron" on youtube.com.

Meals are ordered and drinks received at a counter; then you are seated with a candlestick, which helps servers deliver food directly to your table.

HOUSE SPECIALTIES For breakfast, English bacon, black pudding, baked beans, and grilled tomato; pancakes with bacon; and an egg, leek, and mushroom pasty with breakfast potatoes. Lunch and dinner selections feature bangers and mash, cottage pie, toad-in-the-hole, Guinness stew, fish-and-chips, shepherd's pie, and a ploughman's platter for two of Scotch eggs and imported cheeses.

SUMMARY AND COMMENTS Diagon Alley's flagship restaurant, the Leaky Cauldron serves hearty British pub fare similar to that of Three Broomsticks but with even more authentically Anglo favorites. You can reserve breakfast by booking through your travel agent or the Ticket Center at your Universal Resort hotel; walk-ins for day guests are also usually available. The morning menu costs $16.99 plus tax for adults ($12.39 for kids) with a small drink and has a similar mix of American and British breakfast foods to Three Broomsticks. The breakfast is fair at best; the blood sausage and beans aren't bad if you have a taste for them, but the scrambled eggs are awful, and the oatmeal is outrageously overpriced, making the quichelike mushroom pasty your best bet. And yes, you can have hot or cold Butterbeer for breakfast. If you want to eat breakfast here, buy it with the Quick-Service Dining Plan for maximum value, and do it as late in the morning as possible; your early-entry time is better spent riding Harry Potter and the Escape from Gringotts.

The star of the lunch and dinner menu is the ploughman's platter for two, with an array of gloriously stinky imported cheeses. The bangers are also bang on, whether ordered with mash, in a sandwich, or (best of all) baked into a toad-in-the-hole with Yorkshire pudding. The fish-and-chips are the same as those served in Hogsmeade, as is the soup and salad (which isn't vegan). The fisherman's pie is extremely salty, as is the Guinness stew, which comes served in a nearly inedible bread bowl. Top off your meal with chocolate or Butterbeer potted cream or sticky toffee pudding for dessert. Children's menu items include macaroni and cheese, fish-and-chips, and mini meat pies (for your budding *Sweeney Todd* enthusiast).

Leaky Cauldron can be overwhelmed by Diagon Alley crowds. To avoid long waits, eat early or late.

Lombard's Seafood Grille ★★★

SEAFOOD	MODERATE	QUALITY ★★★½	VALUE ★★★
READER-SURVEY RESPONSES	78% 👍	22% 👎	

Universal Studios Florida, San Francisco; ☎ 407-224-6401

Customers Park guests. **Reservations** Recommended via Zomato. **When to go** Anytime. **Entrée range** $14–$25. **Service rating** ★★★. **Friendliness rating** ★★★. **Parking** Universal Orlando garage. **Bar** Full service. **Wine selection** Good. **Dress** Casual. **Disabled**

access Good. **Hours** Daily, 11:30 a.m.-2 hours before park closing or at park closing, depending on park attendance. Call to verify hours, as there is no set schedule.

SETTING AND ATMOSPHERE Situated on the park's main lagoon, Lombard's looks like a converted wharf-side warehouse. The centerpiece of the brick-walled room is a huge aquarium with bubble glass windows, and a fish-sculpture fountain greets guests. Private dining rooms upstairs have balconies that overlook the park.

HOUSE SPECIALTIES Shrimp cocktail, mahi-mahi sandwich, fried fisherman's basket, lobster roll, seafood cioppino, surf and turf, and fresh fish selections.

SUMMARY AND COMMENTS Universal Studios Florida's San Francisco–inspired seafood restaurant, where the emphasis is on deep-fried favorites and daily fresh fish specials. Originally an attempt at in-park fine dining, with whole live lobsters formerly on the menu, Lombard's Seafood Grille now has a more casual focus. Unfortunately, so does the kitchen. The cioppino (a bowl of fusilli and fragrant broth loaded with calamari and clams) is a standout, but the tuna poké is oddly salsalike with its tomato-heavy garnish, and the lemon-garlic shrimp penne was disappointingly bland and chewy. Stick to the grilled or fried fish, and you should be safe. There are arguably better food options in the park, but as one of only two full-service restaurants inside USF, it's your best choice for a quiet meal off your feet.

With two floors of seating, it's generally easy to get a table, even during the busier times.

Mama Della's Ristorante ★★★★

ITALIAN	MODERATE-EXPENSIVE	QUALITY ★★★★	VALUE ★★★½
READER-SURVEY RESPONSES	95% 👍	5% 👎	

Portofino Bay Hotel; ☎ 407-503-1432

Customers Hotel guests. **Reservations** Recommended via OpenTable. **When to go** Dinner. **Entrée range** $21–$38. **Service rating** ★★★★. **Friendliness rating** ★★★★. **Parking** $5 valet or free self-parking at hotel with validation. **Bar** Full service. **Wine selection** Good. **Dress** Nice casual. **Disabled access** Good. **Hours** Daily, 5:30–10 p.m.

SETTING AND ATMOSPHERE Just like being in the dining room of a Tuscan home, with hardwood floors, Provincial printed wallpaper, and wooden furniture. Check out the collection of chicken-themed tchotchkes adorning the walls.

HOUSE SPECIALTIES Veal scaloppine, pan-seared branzino, filet mignon with truffled potatoes, and lasagna.

ENTERTAINMENT Strolling musicians perform Italian American standards on select evenings.

SUMMARY AND COMMENTS This restaurant falls on the fancy scale somewhere between Bice and Trattoria del Porto. Traditional Italian food is served in a comfortable atmosphere conducive to a special meal but not quite as extravagant as its lavish neighbor, Bice. If you want food (almost) as tasty but for (a bit) less dough, Mama Della's is a great choice.

Mythos Restaurant ★★★½

STEAK/SEAFOOD	MODERATE	QUALITY ★★★½	VALUE ★★★★
READER-SURVEY RESPONSES	93% 👍	7% 👎	

Islands of Adventure, The Lost Continent; ☎ 407-224-4012

Customers Park guests. **Reservations** Recommended via Zomato. **When to go** Early evening. **Entrée range** $14–$25. **Service rating** ★★★½. **Friendliness rating** ★★★. **Parking** Universal Orlando garage. **Bar** Full service. **Wine selection** Good. **Dress** Casual. **Disabled access** Good. **Hours** Daily, 11 a.m.–4 p.m. or later; call ahead for closing time.

SETTING AND ATMOSPHERE A grottolike atmosphere suggests that you're eating in a cave. Large picture windows, framed by water cascading down from waterfalls on top of the restaurant, look out over the central lagoon to The Incredible Hulk Coaster. You can time your meal by coaster launchings.

HOUSE SPECIALTIES Fried calamari, meze platter, Greek salad, pan-roasted salmon, blue cheese–crusted pork, beef medallions, crab cake sandwich, blackened fish tacos, and seasonal risotto.

SUMMARY AND COMMENTS Outside the restaurant is a sign proclaiming that Mythos was voted BEST THEME PARK RESTAURANT. Read the fine print and you'll notice that the voting happened a decade ago and was done by visitors to a theme park–centric website. This was originally the park's one stab at fine dining, but few guests seemed to be looking for that sort of dining experience, especially after getting soaked on one of the water-based rides. Things are now more casual, much to the chagrin of those who remember the whole roasted lobster and chicken Oscar.

The food is well above average for theme park eats, and the setting provides a pleasant retreat. The spanakopita dip isn't far off from T.G.I. Friday's spinach dip, but the meze platter and deep-fried shrimp sushi roll are satisfying. Your best bets among the entrées are the cranberry pork chop (one of Seth's favorite entrées on property); a bacon cheeseburger; the Fork, Knife and Spoon Grilled Cheese (Derek Burgan's recommendation); or the daily risotto. Make your reservation early if you want to dine here on a busy day.

During the off-season, Mythos may close before dinnertime, as this reader discovered:

We were disappointed to find out that Mythos closed at 5 when the park closed at 7 p.m. Due to its popularity, only the Harry Potter area remained completely open until 7 p.m.

NBC Sports Grill & Brew ★★★

AMERICAN/STEAK	MODERATE	QUALITY ★★★	VALUE ★★★½
READER-SURVEY RESPONSES	82% 👍	18% 👎	

CityWalk; ☎ 407-224-FOOD (3663)

Customers Sports fans. **Reservations** Accepted via Zomato. **When to go** When the game is on. **Entrée range** $13–$30. **Service rating** ★★★. **Friendliness rating** ★★★½. **Parking** Universal Orlando garage. **Bar** Full service; more than 100 beers. **Wine selection** Average. **Dress** Casual. **Disabled access** Good. **Hours** Daily, 11 a.m.–1:30 a.m.

SETTING AND ATMOSPHERE NBC Sports Grill & Brew features nearly 100 big-screen high-definition TVs, so guests will have no problem ignoring their tablemates to watch the latest game. The decor is intended to evoke a luxury skybox (though it's more like sports bar industrial with dark concrete floors and exposed ductwork ceilings painted black), and the central show kitchen sports a signature open-flame kettle grill. Sadly, the giant steel fermenting tanks are only for show, as no brewing takes place on the premises. Bonus: Some dining tables are playable games (such as Foosball) with glass tops for the food. The exterior is distinguished by a super-size video screen that broadcasts games to all of CityWalk; during major events (like the Olympics), bleachers may be erected outside for alfresco viewing.

HOUSE SPECIALTIES Sliders, wraps, grilled wings, flatbreads, salads, ribs, steaks, and burgers.

SUMMARY AND COMMENTS With a large selection of burgers and beers, NBC Sports Grill & Brew is the go-to place at Universal to catch the latest game. The menu is surprisingly deep, and the open kitchen concept allows you to see the chefs in action. Beer lovers will be drawn to the large variety of selections (more than 100), including two brewed exclusively for the restaurant by Florida Beer Company, and a fresh firkin-contained ale that's hand-pumped from the cask.

As for the food, it's decent but not especially memorable. The grilled chicken wings are underwhelming, but the steaks and fresh fish sandwich are unexpectedly excellent, and the monster soft pretzel (served on its own stand with mustard and queso) has a cult following. Otherwise, stick to burgers and beer.

Orchid Court Lounge & Sushi Bar ★★★

AMERICAN/ASIAN/SUSHI	MODERATE-EXPENSIVE	QUALITY ★★★	VALUE ★★
READER-SURVEY RESPONSES	81% 👍	19% 👎	

Royal Pacific Resort; ☎ 407-503-3200

Customers Hotel guests. **Reservations** Not accepted. **When to go** Early or late evening. **Entrée range** $13–$72. **Service rating** ★★★. **Friendliness rating** ★★★. **Parking** Free self-parking at hotel with validation. **Bar** Full service. **Wine selection** Average, but an excellent sake selection. **Dress** Resort casual. **Disabled access** Good. **Hours** Monday–Friday, 6–11 a.m.; Saturday–Sunday, 6 a.m.–noon. Sushi: 5–11 p.m. Lounge: Daily, 5 p.m.–midnight.

SETTING AND ATMOSPHERE Located on the lobby level of the Royal Pacific Resort with gorgeous views of the pool and central reflecting fountain, the Orchid Court Lounge is decorated with inviting hand-carved Balinese furniture and flowering orchids. At one end of the lounge, you'll find a bar with coffee and liquor; at the other end, a traditional sushi bar with see-through seafood cases. In between, clusters of couches and armchairs separated by wooden screens form intimate seating areas.

HOUSE SPECIALTIES For breakfast, Starbucks coffee, cinnamon buns, pastries, cereal, and yogurt. The lounge menu has burgers, Asian chicken salad, a tomato-mozzarella sandwich, spring rolls, General Tso's chicken, and tuna tartare. The sushi bar offers miso soup, seaweed salad, edamame, tuna *tataki, nigiri*, sashimi, *maki* rolls, and cold and warm sake.

ENTERTAINMENT Live music Thursday–Friday.

SUMMARY AND COMMENTS The Orchid Court Lounge, which almost exclusively caters to guests staying at the Royal Pacific Resort, has a tripolar personality. In the morning, it's a quick-service stop for Starbucks coffee and Continental breakfast pastries. From 5 p.m. to midnight, it's a bar and lounge with free Wi-Fi and a brief menu that incongruously features bacon cheeseburgers and grilled mozzarella sandwiches alongside krab Rangoon and rice paper rolls. Also in the evenings, sushi chefs prepare fishy fare that falls (in terms of quality and creativity) somewhere between The Cowfish and Fusion Bistro at CityWalk. Most of the rolls are adequate executions of Japanese American standards—California, spicy tuna, spider, and volcano—though a couple, such as the Tropical, use more unusual ingredients such as kiwi and mango. This is the only place on Universal property to order some expert items such as *uni* (sea urchin), but be warned: they are formerly frozen and outrageously expensive. Ordering à la carte can quickly add up, but the combinations aren't cheap either: a 25-piece sashimi combo will set you back more than $60, and a Tahitian longboat for four is $120.

The Palm ★★★★

STEAK	VERY EXPENSIVE	QUALITY ★★★★	VALUE ★★½
READER-SURVEY RESPONSES	100% 👍	0% 👎	

Hard Rock Hotel; ☎ 407-503-7256

Customers Tourists. **Reservations** Recommended via OpenTable. **When to go** Dinner. **Entrée range** $26–$99. **Service rating** ★★★. **Friendliness rating** ★★★. **Parking** Free valet at hotel with validation. **Bar** Full service. **Wine selection** Very good. **Dress** Resort, business casual, or smart casual; no sleeveless men's shirts. **Disabled access** Good. **Hours** Sunday–Monday, 5–9 p.m.; Tuesday–Saturday, 5–10 p.m.

SETTING AND ATMOSPHERE Despite the celebrity caricatures drawn on the wall, the restaurant exudes sophistication due to the dark woods and white tablecloths. The chain's flagship location is in New York, and the decor reflects this. Waiters wear long, white aprons.

HOUSE SPECIALTIES New York strip, bone-in rib eye, lamb chops, veal parmigiana, whole live lobster, Chilean sea bass with corn relish, Atlantic salmon, and iceberg lettuce wedge salad.

SUMMARY AND COMMENTS The crowd here can get noisy, so The Palm may not be the best place for a romantic night out. However, if you're looking to celebrate with friends or family, this is a good, if very expensive, choice. Stick with the signature dishes: the steaks are done well, and the ginormous lobsters are impeccably prepared, while some of the other dishes could be better. The side dishes are meant for sharing, and the creamed spinach and Brussels sprouts are justly famous. If you want a taste of The Palm on a hamburger budget, drop by the bar during PrimeTime (Sunday–Friday, 5–7 p.m.) for discounted appetizers, or take advantage of the annual $99 summer special on 4-pound lobsters for two. If you dine here more than once a year, look into joining the 837 Club (thepalm.com/837 -Club) for discounts and exclusive event invitations.

Pat O'Brien's Orlando   ★★★

CAJUN	INEXPENSIVE	QUALITY ★★★½	VALUE ★★★½
READER-SURVEY RESPONSES	86% 👍	14% 👎	

CityWalk; ☎ 407-224-2106

Customers Tourists. **Reservations** Accepted via Zomato. **When to go** Anytime. **Entrée range** $10–$18. **Service rating** ★★. **Friendliness rating** ★★★. **Parking** Universal Orlando garage. **Bar** Full service. **Wine selection** Modest. **Dress** Casual. **Disabled access** Good. **Hours** Sunday–Thursday, 4–10 p.m.; Friday–Saturday, 4–11 p.m.; bar open daily, 4 p.m.–2 a.m.

SETTING AND ATMOSPHERE A fairly faithful rendition of the original Pat O'Brien's in New Orleans, from the redbrick facade to the fire-and-water fountain in the courtyard. The outdoor dining area is the most pleasant place to eat. Inside areas include a noisy "locals" bar and a dueling piano bar, featuring some of Orlando's most talented musicians 5 p.m.–2 a.m. nightly. A cover charge is levied after 9 p.m. because it's mostly a music venue that also serves food.

HOUSE SPECIALTIES Shrimp gumbo, jambalaya, muffuletta, and red beans and rice.

SUMMARY AND COMMENTS The food is surprisingly good and surprisingly affordable. Be careful about ordering a Hurricane, the restaurant's signature drink. Not only is it deceptively potent, but you are also automatically charged for the souvenir glass, and if you don't want it, you must turn it in at the bar for a refund.

Red Oven Pizza Bakery   ★★★½

ITALIAN	INEXPENSIVE	QUALITY ★★★½	VALUE ★★★★½
READER-SURVEY RESPONSES	89% 👍	11% 👎	

CityWalk; ☎ 407-224-2690

Customers Tourists. **Reservations** Not accepted. **When to go** Anytime. **Entrée range** $9–$14. **Service rating** ★★. **Friendliness rating** ★★★. **Parking** Universal Orlando garage. **Bar** Wine and beer only. **Wine selection** Limited. **Dress** Casual. **Disabled access** Good. **Hours** Sunday–Thursday, 11 a.m.–midnight; Friday–Saturday, 11 a.m.–1:30 a.m.

SETTING AND ATMOSPHERE Hardwood beams, colorful tile, and gleaming countertops make Red Oven look unexpectedly upscale for an open-air pizza joint. You
can pose for photos on the red scooter parked out front.

HOUSE SPECIALTIES White and red pizza with gourmet toppings, salads, and
imported beer and wine.

SUMMARY AND COMMENTS Red Oven Pizza Bakery may be seen as Universal's
answer to Via Napoli in Epcot, which brought high-quality pizza to the theme park
world. Only whole pies, not slices, can be ordered at Red Oven. However, with a
reasonable price of only $13–$14 per pizza, two people can eat very cheaply. The
six white and five red Neapolitan-style artisan pies are made with San Marzano
tomatoes, organic extra-virgin olive oil, buffalo mozzarella, fine-ground "00" flour,
and filtered water, and then baked in a 900°F oven while you watch. Salads and a
limited selection of beer and wine are available, with free refills on soda.

   After ordering your food and receiving your drinks, a server will seat you and
bring your order once it's ready. Plenty of covered outdoor seating is available, a welcome relief from the Florida sun (and rain). Because of its location in the main hub
of CityWalk, Red Oven is a great place to get a bite to eat and people-watch. Red
Oven can also be delivered to the freestanding bars along the CityWalk waterfront.

Strong Water Tavern   ★★★½

CARIBBEAN	MODERATE	QUALITY ★★★★	VALUE ★★½
READER-SURVEY RESPONSES	94% 👍	6% 👎	

Sapphire Falls Resort; ☎ 407-503-5447

Customers Hotel guests. **Reservations** Not accepted. **When to go** Evenings. **Entrée range** $8–$16. **Service rating** ★★★. **Friendliness rating** ★★★. **Parking** $5 valet or free self-parking at hotel with validation. **Bar** Full service with extensive rum selection. **Wine selection** Average. **Dress** Casual. **Disabled access** Good. **Hours** Daily 4 p.m.–2 a.m..

SETTING AND ATMOSPHERE One of the largest lobby bars at any Universal Resort
hotel, Strong Water Tavern—like the rest of Sapphire Falls Resort—fuses organically
aged objects and sleek modern elements. This New World watering hole sports
oversize vintage couches on which to sprawl, faux reclaimed rum barrels forming
the ceiling on the inside, and a spectacular view over the hotel's signature waterfalls from the patio. A video display wall, which usually broadcasts sports or a loop
of Universal advertisements, dominates one end of the room. The centerpiece of
Strong Water Tavern is the massive marble bar, which features a designated seating area for rum-tasting experiences.

HOUSE SPECIALTIES Ceviche, arroz con pollo, *ropa vieja,* roasted pork, empanadas,
and rum cocktails.

SUMMARY AND COMMENTS We love almost everything about Strong Water Tavern—
the contemporary Caribbean atmosphere, the variety of fresh ceviches, the
potent cocktails—except for the prices. Drinks are a bit steep ($12–$15, $75–$85
for a punch bowl that serves four to six) but not unreasonable considering the
top-shelf ingredients. A couple mugs of the Tavern Grog will make you want to
join the merchant marines, and the $18 tasting flight lets you sample three rums
that normally retail at up to $35 per shot; don't order the Hamilton 151 if you plan
on driving home. On the other hand, while those who enjoy authentic West
Indian, Cuban, and Puerto Rican recipes will feel right at home, your *abuela* would
never dream of charging this much for such tiny tapas-style servings. Pretty much

all the savory plates are overpriced, but the beef empanadas are probably the best buy. Dessert is a different story; at $6, the coconut milk cake with *dulce de leche* and almonds is a bargain.

Three Broomsticks ★★★

BRITISH	INEXPENSIVE	QUALITY ★★★½	VALUE ★★★
READER-SURVEY RESPONSES	89% 👍	11% 👎	

Islands of Adventure, The Wizarding World of Harry Potter–Hogsmeade;
☎ 407-224-4012

Customers Park guests. **Reservations** Breakfast only. **When to go** Early or late. **Entrée range** $10–$17. **Service rating** ★★★. **Friendliness rating** ★★★. **Parking** Universal Orlando garage. **Bar** Beer and wine only. **Wine selection** Limited. **Dress** Casual. **Disabled access** Good. **Hours** Daily, park opening–10:30 a.m. and 11 a.m.–park closing.

SETTING AND ATMOSPHERE Modeled after the Three Broomsticks inn in the Harry Potter books and films, this buffeteria is the most visually interesting eatery at Islands of Adventure. Open beams, dark furniture, and the contiguous Hog's Head pub (see page 218) make Three Broomsticks a place to linger and savor. The detail is incredible, and it's one of the best-themed restaurants we've seen. The amazing thing about the decor, aside from the vaulted ceiling, is that Universal's architects managed to hide virtually every modern convenience, such as air-conditioning vents, behind 18th-century facades. Alfresco dining is behind the restaurant.

HOUSE SPECIALTIES Breakfast items include English bacon, black pudding, baked beans, and grilled tomato; pancakes with bacon; and porridge with fruit. Lunch and dinner offerings are fish-and-chips, rotisserie chicken, smoked spareribs, shepherd's pie, Cornish pasty, turkey legs, and nonalcoholic Butterbeer. Children's menu items include chicken, macaroni and cheese, fish-and-chips, and chicken fingers.

SUMMARY AND COMMENTS Because it was converted from a larger restaurant during The Wizarding World development, quite a number of seats were sacrificed to achieve the desired look. The menu is very similar to Thunder Falls Terrace in Jurassic Park, with which it shares the title of best counter-service restaurant in IOA. The ribs or chicken, or the combo plate, are your best bets, though the tartar sauce is a tasty side to the fish-and-chips (made from fresh cod). The Great Feast family platter includes ribs, chicken, corn, potatoes, and salad for four for $59.99 ($14.99 each additional portion), a good value. As the only dining option in Hogsmeade, Three Broomsticks stays busy all day. Like the Leaky Cauldron, you can reserve breakfast at Three Broomsticks by booking through your travel agent or the Ticket Center at your Universal Resort hotel, and walk-ins for day guests are also usually available, but there are probably better uses of your morning touring time.

Toothsome Chocolate Emporium & Savory Feast Kitchen ★★★½

CHOCOHOLIC-AMERICAN	MODERATE	QUALITY ★★★★	VALUE ★★★
READER-SURVEY RESPONSES	89% 👍	11% 👎	

CityWalk; ☎ 407-224-FOOD (3663)

Customers Tourists and locals. **Reservations** Not accepted. **When to go** Dinner or late evening dessert. **Entrée range** $12–$47. **Service rating** ★★½. **Friendliness rating** ★★★★. **Parking** Universal Orlando garage. **Bar** Full service with craft cocktails. **Wine selection** Modest. **Dress** Casual. **Disabled access** Good. **Hours** Daily, 11 a.m.–11 p.m.

SETTING AND ATMOSPHERE Looming across the CityWalk lagoon like Willy Wonka's summer home, Toothsome Chocolate Emporium & Savory Feast Kitchen is an original concept from Universal Creative that draws heavily on both Roald Dahl's crazed confectioner (closer to the Johnny Depp version than Gene Wilder) and steampunk, the Jules Vern–influenced sci-fi style that ditches futuristic chrome for Victorian-era copper. This multistory brick-faced venue seems to be a whimsical factory from the outside, complete with billowing smokestacks, while the inside is a wonderland of imaginative industrial contraptions (both physical and projected on large video screens) adorned with antique doodads. Much of the ground floor is devoted to a takeaway milkshake counter; a glassed-in kitchen where you can watch sweets being assembled; and a shop full of chocolates, candies, and steampunk souvenirs. Upstairs seating includes decadent semicircular booths and a private dining room; make sure to get a good look at the fiber-optic ceiling sculpture near the serpentine second-floor bar.

HOUSE SPECIALTIES Warm chocolate almond bread, baked Brie, pork belly sliders, salads, flatbreads, sandwiches, hamburgers, pasta, steaks, and all-day brunch with quiche and crêpes. And of course, drinks, desserts, and milkshakes with lots and lots of chocolate.

ENTERTAINMENT Actors portraying proprietress Penelope Toothsome and her animatronic assistant Jacques roam the restaurant interacting with guests. Brush up on their backstory (found on the first page of the menu) before they arrive at your table for a more in-depth conversation.

SUMMARY AND COMMENTS Rising from the ashes of the largely reviled NBA City, Toothsome takes a trendy aesthetic and potentially gut-busting gastronomic concept and combines them into an unexpectedly upscale eating experience. Many (though not all) of the offerings include some form of cocoa, from the old-fashioned cocktails with chocolate bitters to the chocolate mole sauce served on the pork chop (ask for it as an accompaniment with the brisket and mushroom meat loaf). Prices are moderate, aside from the wallet-busting steaks, and portions are big enough to share or take home leftovers. Be sure to save room for the dark chocolate mousse, which is richer than any we've tasted outside Paris.

Toothsome's signature milkshakes have proved so popular that at peak times they may be unavailable for table service and are only served at the downstairs to-go counter. The $12–$13 price tag may have you quoting John Travolta in *Pulp Fiction,* particularly since the shakes themselves are achingly sweet and not especially thick or large. But they are served in a souvenir Mason jar and crowned with an absurd mountain of toppings, such as an entire cupcake, brownie, or slice of Key lime pie. Be warned that the sour ice cream used in some varieties lives up to its name. Our biggest problem with Toothsome is that it's extremely popular and doesn't accept reservations, leading to hour-plus waits at mealtimes; try to slip in around 4 p.m., or ask if you can sit at the second-floor bar. Once seated, the restaurant often seems understaffed for its size, so come expecting leisurely service.

Trattoria del Porto ★★★

ITALIAN	MODERATE		QUALITY ★★★	VALUE ★★
READER-SURVEY RESPONSES	93% 👍	7% 👎		

Portofino Bay Hotel; ☎ 407-503-1430

Customers Hotel guests. **Reservations** Suggested for dinner via OpenTable. **When to go** Breakfast or dinner. **Entrée range** Breakfast, $12–$17; lunch, $15–$25; dinner, $16–$34. **Service rating** ★★★. **Friendliness rating** ★★★. **Parking** $5 valet or free self-parking at hotel with validation. **Bar** Full service. **Wine selection** Average. **Dress** Resort casual. **Disabled access** Good. **Hours** Daily, 7–11 a.m. and 5:30–10:30 p.m. Select days, 11 a.m.–2 p.m.

SETTING AND ATMOSPHERE Like a boisterous down-home Italian kitchen. A play area lets kids watch cartoons while the grown-ups eat.

HOUSE SPECIALTIES　At breakfast, Belgian waffles, steak and eggs, and eggs Benedetto with prosciutto and arugula. At dinner, chicken pesto flatbread, salads, burgers, steaks, shrimp and grits, and make-your-own pasta combinations.

SUMMARY AND COMMENTS　Where Mama Della's succeeds in not feeling like a hotel restaurant, Trattoria del Porto does not. The food is perfectly fine and moderately priced (relatively speaking). The interactive Pasta Cucina is available every night until 10 p.m., allowing you to create your own entrée from a variety of noodles and sauces ($26.99 adults, $12 kids). Omelets at breakfast can set you back more than $14, so opt instead for the buffet offered in the mornings.

Vivo Italian Kitchen　★★★★

ITALIAN	MODERATE	QUALITY ★★★★	VALUE ★★★★½
READER-SURVEY RESPONSES　87% 👍　13% 👎			

CityWalk; ☎ 407-224-2318

Customers Locals and tourists. Reservations Accepted via Zomato. When to go Dinner. Entrée range $13–$27. Service rating ★★★. Friendliness rating ★★★. Parking Universal Orlando garage. Bar Full service. Wine selection Good. Dress Casual. Disabled access Good. Hours Daily, 4–11 p.m.

SETTING AND ATMOSPHERE　Sleek and contemporary without being stuffy, Vivo brings a touch of casual class to CityWalk's central crossroads. There are outdoor tables (with embedded chessboards) and a well-lit bar, along with plush semicircular booths surrounded by sinuous steel cages. But the real action is around the open kitchen; see if you can snag a seat at the food bar in front of the "tree" where fresh pasta is hung.

HOUSE SPECIALTIES　Freshly made pasta, homemade mozzarella, pizza, salads, lasagna, chicken Marsala, and risotto.

SUMMARY AND COMMENTS　Vivo is Universal's best Italian food outside Portofino Bay. The menu is filled with comfortingly familiar dishes—such as chicken piccata, veal parmigiana, spinach cannelloni, and spaghetti Bolognese—presented without unnecessary postmodern flourishes, just classic recipes prepared à la minute with the freshest ingredients. Best of all, you can dine here for half the price of Bice, Mama Della's, or one of Disney's Signature restaurants.

Start by ordering an enormous house-made meatball, hand-pulled mozzarella, or beet-and-Gorgonzola salad. Standout entrées include linguine with seasonal clams, black squid ink pasta with seafood, and risotto with short ribs. Save room for warm orange-walnut cake; the recipe came directly from chef Steven Jayson's grandmother. On a cost–quality basis, this may be the best table-service meal you'll have on Universal property.

Wantilan Luau　★★★½

HAWAIIAN	EXPENSIVE	QUALITY ★★★½	VALUE ★★★
READER-SURVEY RESPONSES　100% 👍　0% 👎			

Royal Pacific Resort; ☎ 407-503-DINE (3463)

Customers Tourists. Reservations Required via wantilanluau.eventbrite.com. When to go Dinner only. Entrée range Buffet: $75.62 adults, $38.34 children ages 3–9. (Prices include tax and gratuity for everyone, and mai tais, wine, and beer for guests age 21 and older.) Service rating ★★★. Friendliness rating ★★★★. Parking Free valet or free self-parking at hotel with validation. Bar Mai tais, wine, and beer available. Wine selection Limited. Dress Floral shirts, beachy casual. Disabled access Average. Hours Saturday; seating begins at 6 p.m., with registration starting 30 minutes before.

SETTING AND ATMOSPHERE Typical luau setting with tiki torches and wooden tables.

HOUSE SPECIALTIES Buffet includes pit-roasted suckling pig with spiced rum–soaked pineapple purée; Pacific catch of the day; Hawaiian chicken teriyaki; fire-grilled beef with mushrooms; and chicken fingers, mac and cheese, PB&J, and pizza for kids. Dessert buffet has white chocolate mousse shots and pineapple macadamia tarts.

ENTERTAINMENT Polynesian dancing, storytelling, hula dancers, and live music.

SUMMARY AND COMMENTS This is a fun diversion and a change of scenery from the other restaurants on Universal property. Though dinner is a bit expensive, it's the best food of any luau show in the area, and the entertainment is more energetic than *Disney's Spirit of Aloha Dinner Show*. Priority Seating reserves you a table near the front for an extra $10.65 per adult ($5.33 per kid), but either way the check-in process can take a while.

DINING *near*
UNIVERSAL ORLANDO

AS WE'VE MENTIONED PREVIOUSLY, guests staying at Universal Orlando's on-site resorts may find their dining options a bit limited and expensive compared to the restaurants found at some Walt Disney World hotels. The flip side is that, while Disney's resorts are largely isolated from the outside world, Universal hotel guests have an array of off-property eateries only a few minutes' drive—or even walk—away.

The closest off-site restaurants to Universal Orlando are found between the hotels along Major Boulevard, just east of the resort entrance on Kirkman Road. **Miller's Ale House** (5573 S. Kirkman Road; ☎ 407-248-0000; millersalehouse.com) is a popular after-hours hangout for Universal employees and serves the largest chicken nachos you'll ever see. Chefs at **Kobe Japanese Steakhouse & Sushi Bar** (5605 S. Kirkman Road; ☎ 407-248-1978; kobesteakhouse .com) perform at teppanyaki tables; ask about early bird and late-night specials. On the opposite side of Major Boulevard, you'll find a run-of-the-mill **T.G.I. Friday's** and **Tabla Restaurant** (5847 Grand National Dr.; ☎ 407-248-9400; tablacuisine.com), an upscale Indian/Thai/Chinese restaurant tucked into the back of a Clarion Inn. A **Wendy's** and **Burger King** round out the block; more fast-food franchises, **Soupa Saiyan** ramen bar (5689 Vineland Road; ☎ 407-930-3396; soupasaiyan.com), and a **Carrabba's Italian** are located across the street on the north side of Vineland Road. Continue a few lights farther north, and you'll find a strip mall at the corner of Kirkman and Conroy Roads, housing **Kim Wu Chinese Restaurant** (4904 S. Kirkman Road; ☎ 407-293-0752; kimwuorlando.com), with a popular lunch-only buffet; **Karen's Tasty Crabs** (4898 S. Kirkman Road; ☎ 407-293-3036; addicted2karens.com); a **Bubbalou's Bodacious Bar-B-Que** (5818 Conroy Road; ☎ 407-295-1212; kirkman.bubbalous.com); **Smashburger** (5812 Conroy Road; ☎ 407-440-3595; smashburger .com); and **Sloppy Taco Palace** (4892 S. Kirkman Road; ☎ 407-574-6474; sloppytacopalace.com), which lives up to its name.

Slightly farther afield, international treasures near Universal property along International Drive include **Aashirwad Indian Cuisine** (7000 S. Kirkman Road; ☎ 407-370-9830; aashirwadrestaurant .com), **Ichiban** sushi buffet (5529 International Dr.; ☎ 407-930-8889; ichibanbuffet.com), **Boi Brazil Churrascaria** (5668 International Dr.; ☎ 407-354-0260; boibrazil.com), **Sweet Tomatoes** salad buffet (6877 S. Kirkman Road; ☎ 407-363-1616; souplantation.com), **Thai Silk** (6803 S. Kirkman Road; ☎ 407-226-8997; thaisilkorlando.com), **Nile Ethiopian Restaurant** (7040 International Dr.; ☎ 407-354-0026; nile07.com), **World's Magic Indonesian Restaurant** (7044 International Dr.; ☎ 407-929-6194; worldsmagicrestaurant.com), and a 24-hour **Del Taco** (6855 Grand National Dr.; ☎ 407-363-0738; deltaco.com) for those late-night munchies. If you take Universal Boulevard south past I-Drive and Sand Lake Road, you can access rear entrances for I-Drive restaurants without the traffic, ending up at the **Pointe Orlando** shopping and dining complex. Finally, take Turkey Lake Road south from Universal to Sand Lake Road, and turn right toward Restaurant Row for a plethora of upscale chain restaurants, including **Seasons 52, Roy's, Bonefish Grill, Ocean Prime,** and many more.

If you want to take a drive to downtown Orlando or beyond in search of a fine meal, we can vouch for **The Ravenous Pig** (565 W. Fairbanks Ave.; ☎ 407-628-2333; theravenouspig.com), **Kabooki Sushi** (3122 E. Colonial Dr.; ☎ 407-228-3839; kabookisushi.com), **Saigon Noodle & Grill** (101 N. Bumby Ave.; ☎ 407-532-7373; saigon noodleandgrill.com), **Pig Floyd's Urban Barbakoa** (1326 N. Mills Ave.; ☎ 407-203-0866; pigfloyds.com), **The Strand** (807 N. Mills Ave.; ☎ 407-920-7744; strandorlando.com), and **The Artisan's Table** (22 E. Pine St.; ☎ 407-730-7499; artisanstableorlando.com).

SHOPPING *at* UNIVERSAL ORLANDO

YOU'LL HAVE PLENTY of opportunities at Universal Orlando to take home overpriced dust magnets (oops, we meant to say priceless mementos) from your stay. And if you are staying on-site, you can charge them to your room using your hotel key card; just be prepared for the reckoning upon checkout.

If you return home and realize that you forgot something, a selection of Universal Orlando merchandise can be ordered online at shop .universalorlando.com.

SHOPPING AT UNIVERSAL STUDIOS FLORIDA

AS KANG AND KODOS OBSERVE at the end of The Simpsons Ride, it's apparently a state law that every Universal attraction must end in (or near) a gift shop. Most of these have the typical T-shirts and toys tied to the experience you just exited, though a few have offerings of note.

Chris Eliopoulos

The Universal Studios Store sits near the park's entrance: If you forgot to get a gift elsewhere in the park, you can probably find it here; while waiting in the checkout line, browse the selection of exclusive character-themed candy bars, including E.T.'s chocolate–peanut butter bar with Reese's Pieces, SpongeBob's white chocolate bar with pineapple bits, and Donkey's maple-flavored waffle bar. And if you forget to stop at the Studios Store, It's A Wrap straddles the exit, selling last season's souvenirs at discount prices, as well as serving as the park's package pickup point. If you prepurchased a My Universal Photos package, stop in **On Location** to activate it or pick up prints.

In **Production Central, Super Silly Stuff** at Despicable Me Minion Mayhem is decorated like the candy-colored amusement park from the film. You can access the Minion photo op at the attraction's postshow from the shop if the ride's queue is too long. There's a magic mirror and some other fun decor in **Shrek's Ye Olde Souvenir Shoppe.** Transformers' **Supply Vault** has pricey collectibles, as well as toy versions of the attraction's cybertronic stars, including an exclusive model of the EVAC ride vehicle. Directly across from the Transformers entrance sits **The Film Vault,** a movie nerd's nirvana with new products tied to vintage Universal films, from *Psycho* and *Scarface* to *Back to the Future* and *The Big Lebowski.* Nearby, the **Park Plaza Holiday Shop** sells hand-painted Universal ornaments, be it October or August. Beware the self-service bulk candies at **Studio Sweets**; they are priced per quarter-pound, and small bags can add up very quickly.

New York's postride shops are fairly pedestrian, though you'll find NBC apparel at **The Tonight Shop** and faux-Egyptian jewelry in Revenge of the Mummy's **Sahara Traders. Rosie's Irish Imports** has everything Emerald Isle expats (or just admirers) need, from coat of arms key chains to football club sweatshirts.

Shopping in **San Francisco** is limited to the **San Francisco Candy Factory** (sadly, Ghirardelli is just a facade) and the **Custom Gear** gift shop that guests must pass through while exiting Fast & Furious: Supercharged; pick out a personalized toy car, or just pose for a photo with the wax statue of Vin Diesel.

The Wizarding World of Harry Potter–Diagon Alley is groaning with great shopping opportunities, including **Weasleys' Wizard Wheezes** (toys and candy), **Borgin and Burkes** (spooky stuff), **Madam Malkin's Robes for All Occasions** (clothing), **Magical Menagerie** (stuffed animals), **Sugarplum's Sweet Shop** (cakes and candy), and of course **Ollivanders** (wands). See page 281 for more Diagon Alley shopping details.

Over in **Springfield: Home of the Simpsons,** the **Kwik-E-Mart** has a great selection of *Simpsons* collectibles and exclusive candy bars, like the Krusty Klump (from the "Homer Badman" episode) and Farmer Billy's Choco-Bacon. **MIB Gear** in **World Expo** has a trippy room full of glow-in-the-dark toys, but a chronic mildew issue makes it the smelliest store in the resort.

Woody Woodpecker's KidZone is home to **SpongeBob StorePants,** where the big yellow guy himself holds court daily; adults will appreciate the snarky signs inside. **E.T. Toy Closet** has toys from that Spielberg classic and others, plus two adorable photo ops (one on a flying bicycle and the other in a closet full of toys) that are included with My Universal Photos packages. The most notable thing about **The Barney Store,** aside from the world's largest collection of purpledinosaur videos, is the character meet and greet located in the adjoining playground.

Back in **Hollywood,** the **Hello Kitty** shop is as eye-poppingly adorable as the *kawaii* Japanese feline and her cartoon friends, who are represented here on clothing, housewares, pastries (don't miss the animal-shaped s'mores), and countless other Sanrio-sanctioned products. **The Betty Boop Store** stocks Boop-centric accessories and apparel, including nightgowns. **Studio Styles** stocks shirts and stuffed toys from *The Secret Life of Pets* and other films featured in the *Cinematic Celebration* lagoon show. **Cyber Image** carries comic book superhero swag, featuring both DC and Marvel characters; a display case showcases props from the park's former *Terminator 2: 3-D* attraction. Note that in Universal's Hollywood, the **Brown Derby** is a hat shop, not a restaurant.

Williams of Hollywood is perhaps the most special shop in all of Universal because it's the only place where you can purchase an actual piece of the theme parks. Props, posters, and pieces of ride vehicles from *Terminator, Disaster!, Beetlejuice Graveyard Revue,* and even Jaws have been sold to the public, for prices ranging from $50 up to $5,000; Seth took home a door from the *Twister* preshow and a YOU MUST BE THIS TALL TO RIDE sign for a couple Benjamins, but you'll need to drop some big bills if you want to take home a flying cow. Read the price tags carefully; items actually used in the parks will be clearly marked, while others are simply thrift store finds and reproductions used to fill out the shelves. Before buying a large artifact, you may also want to consider how you'll transport your treasure home; Universal will happily mail it for you, but the shipping cost may exceed the sale price.

Finally, **The NBC Media Center,** located inside the Garden of Allah Villas between Hollywood and KidZone, is like a shop in reverse. Instead of spending money, you can volunteer to watch a video—often from a potential NBC TV series—and answer a survey, in exchange for a gift card or modest amount of cash. It isn't always available, and you may have to meet certain demographic qualifications, but you can make $20 or more in less than an hour. For guests on a tight schedule, this is a poor use of park time, but if you are a local or are spending several days at Universal, it can be an interesting experience.

SHOPPING AT ISLANDS OF ADVENTURE

LIKE USF, IOA PLACES ITS BIGGEST RETAIL venue right near the entrance; **Islands of Adventure Trading Company** in **Port of Entry** has selections from every area of the park, especially The Wizarding World. Next to it sits the open-air **Ocean Trader Market,** which sells exotic clothing and crafts. For Grinch fans, the **Port of Entry Christmas Shoppe** celebrates the holiday season 365 days a year. **DeFoto's Expedition Photography** is this park's My Universal Photos headquarters, and **Port Provisions** is the last-chance gift discounter and package pickup location at the exit turnstiles.

The **Marvel Alterniverse Store** on **Marvel Super Hero Island** stocks life-size busts of the Avengers (does anyone really put these in their

Top Six Gift Shops at Universal Orlando

GIFT SHOPS WERE ONCE SEEN as a necessary evil at Universal Orlando, but over the past several years, they've become attractions in and of themselves. Here are the six best shops in Islands of Adventure (IOA) and Universal Studios Florida (USF), according to Derek "Saturday Six" Burgan:

6. KWIK-E-MART (USF) Located next to The Simpsons Ride, Kwik-E-Mart is filled with the self-deprecating humor found throughout Springfield: Home of the Simpsons. Signs above the merchandise include sales pitches like, "Today's merchandise at tomorrow's prices!," and "These items won't buy themselves!" Outside the store is a photo op with Milhouse sitting on a bench, as well as one of USF's hidden gems: the Simpsons pay phone. Walking by this phone will trigger it to ring, and picking up the receiver will treat you to a gag line by one of the various *Simpsons* characters.

5. HELLO KITTY (USF) The shop has several Hello Kitty photo ops, a meet and greet with the feline star herself, plus mash-up merchandise that merges Hello Kitty with Universal films, including *Jaws, Back to the Future, Jurassic Park,* and even Alfred Hitchcock's *Psycho*. Be on the lookout for the bakery case of elaborately themed Hello Kitty snacks available only at this location.

4. COMIC BOOK SHOP (IOA) The guys from the *Big Bang Theory* would have no problem spending some time in this store. A huge mural by one of the registers tells the shop's backstory in comic book form: X-Men villain Magneto amassed a huge treasure trove of Marvel comics and channeled the entertainment value of the items into pure energy. Storm defeated Magneto, allowing guests the opportunity to purchase their favorite Marvel products. Excelsior!

3. SPONGEBOB STOREPANTS (USF) Like his long-running cartoon series, SpongeBob's store caters to children, but there is much for adults to enjoy as well. The front of the store holds a dedicated meet and greet area with SpongeBob, Patrick, and Squidward. There are tons of sight gags and jokes, and you can enter SpongeBob's pineapple and get your picture taken with Gary the snail.

2. ISLANDS OF ADVENTURE TRADING COMPANY (IOA) This one-stop shop at IOA's exit separates itself from similar stores with the amount of theming found in and outside the building. By the registers, a GIANT skeleton of a mythical creature hangs from the ceiling. The rest of the store features tons of details evoking an old-world adventure theme.

1. WEASLEYS' WIZARD WHEEZES (USF) This store perfectly replicates the fun madness of the store (as seen in *Harry Potter and the Half-Blood Prince*) and contains a whole bunch of merchandise straight from the films (many of which are exclusive to the store). Walking through this gift shop feels like walking on the actual movie set, complete with Dolores Umbridge on a unicycle crossing the store above you (there's a smaller version you can buy). It's a dream come true for many Potter fans.

For more life-changing lists like this, be sure to check out the "Saturday Six" every week on the touringplans.com blog.

home?) and lets you pose for photos with Spidey himself, while the **Comic Book Shop** has a good selection of current releases and trade paperback classics, along with collectible figurines. For something superheroic yet still stylish, stop into the small **Marvel Boutique** for on-trend clothes and accessories highlighting edgier characters like Deadpool and the Guardians of the Galaxy.

The main drag of **Toon Lagoon** is made up of two stores: the **Betty Boop Store** and **Toon Extra**—selling toys and apparel tied to characters no one under age 40 has heard of. **WossaMotta-U** sells T-shirts and toys from *The Secret Life of Pets*.

Jurassic Park's post-splashdown shop **Jurassic Outfitters** specializes in beach towels (small wonder), and the Discovery Center's **Dinostore** sells semiprecious gems and semieducational toys. The gift kiosk at the exit of **Skull Island: Reign of Kong** is so small that it doesn't even have a name, though it does have some nice faux-vintage Eighth Wonder Expedition gear.

Before Diagon Alley opened, **The Wizarding World of Harry Potter–Hogsmeade** set the bar for theme park shopping. **Honeydukes** (candy), **Dervish and Banges** (toys, apparel), **Ollivanders** (wands), and **Filch's Emporium of Confiscated Goods** at the Forbidden Journey exit will sap your wallet as surely as a Dementor sucks souls. See page 326 for details.

The diminished **Lost Continent** still has a few curiosities in its Arabian bazaar, such as **The Coin Mint,** where you can watch money being made, and a **heraldry shop** with heavy armor. The most eclectic award goes to **Treasures of Poseidon,** where you can pick up a polo shirt, a potted plant, and a $16 pearl that's still inside a live oyster.

If you want a set of the Thing 1 and Thing 2 T-shirts you'll spot around Universal, **Cats, Hats and Things** at The Cat in the Hat ride exit in **Seuss Landing** is the spot. **Mulberry Street** has a small entrance door just for kids, but its limited edition prints and sculptures will appeal to adults. If your Theodor Geisel collection has any gaps, **All the Books You Can Read** can help fill it. And be warned: Upon exiting The High in the Sky Seuss Trolley Train Ride!, you may be forced to pass through **Snookers & Snookers Sweet Candy Cookers,** which is known to cause weight gain simply from staring at its case of fudge and candy apples. If Snookers doesn't snare you, **Honk Honkers** surely will, with its spun-to-order gourmet cotton candy, mixed with sprinkles and wrapped around a unicorn lollipop.

SHOPPING AT VOLCANO BAY

SHOPPING IS PROBABLY THE LAST THING on the minds of most guests splashing at the water park, unless they've forgotten some essential item. That explains why merchandise opportunities in Volcano Bay are minimal and mostly focused on beach apparel—hats, swimsuits, flip-flops—and accessories. **Waturi Marketplace,** located next to the ice cream stand to the left of the park entrance, is the main gift store; it consists of two adjoining huts hocking clothing with the park logo, plus live plants and tiki tchotchkes. **Krakatoa Katy's,** a smaller outpost on the beach to the right of the main entrance, has a more limited selection of shirts, focusing instead on towels, bags, and collectible cups. Both locations stock sundries like sunscreen.

SHOPPING AT UNIVERSAL CITYWALK

CITYWALK (citywalk.com) comprises 30 acres in a relatively compact area between the two Universal theme parks. CityWalk's focus is on food and entertainment, rather than high-dollar shopping sprees, so the store lineup is designed for causal browsing and impulse buys.

Our favorites include **Fresh Produce,** featuring swimwear and loungewear for women, kids, and infants; bags and accessories; and more. **Quiet Flight Surf Shop** sells merchandise from beachy brands such as Billabong, Hurley, Nixon, Oakley, Quiksilver, Reef, Rip Curl, Roxy, Volcom, and VonZipper. Quiet Flight sports an iconic surfboard photo op outside, and its inside connects with Island Clothing, forming a handy shortcut between the parking garage and Universal Studios Florida. **The Island Clothing Co.** features resort wear from designers such as Hurley, Honolua Surf Co., and Quiksilver.

Up for some ink? CityWalk also has a branch of **Hart & Huntington Tattoo Company.** For jewelry, **Fossil** has a notable collection of watches, as well as sunglasses and leather goods. **P!Q** (pronounced "pick") sells an oddball assortment of Pylones housewares, gag gifts, and novelty toys; think of it as Spencer's Gifts without the smut. **The Universal Studios Store** offers one-stop shopping for all theme park merchandise, including the best selection of Harry Potter products outside the parks. Finally, many of the restaurants—including Bubba Gump, Margaritaville, Hard Rock Cafe, Bob Marley, and Pat O'Brien's—have merchandise shops, in case you want memories of your meal to live on forever in your closet.

SHOPPING AT UNIVERSAL ORLANDO RESORT HOTELS

THOUGH THE LOEWS HOTELS HAVE every amenity you'll want during your Universal Orlando stay, there isn't much to get excited about in terms of resort shopping. Each of the on-site hotels has a main store near the central lobby carrying sundries, souvenirs, and branded apparel.

Hard Rock Hotel's Rock Shop carries hip brands such as Harajuku and English Laundry, sells the bed and bath linens used in guest rooms, and even has a touch screen video wall with info on the hotel's rock memorabilia collection. At **Portofino Bay Hotel,** you'll find resort-specific items in **Le Memories de Portofino** and a full array of Universal merch in the harbor promenade's **Universal Store,** along with **Alta Moda** resort wear and swim clothes, an **art gallery,** and a **family photography studio. Toko Gifts** and **Mas** are twin gift shops framing the **Royal Pacific Resort**'s entrance that cover all the essentials, while **Treasures of Bali** by the pool carries beach gear and island wear. **Cabana Bay Beach Resort,** the cheapest hotel, actually has one of the best stores, with retro clothes, custom candy, and even Jack LaLanne gear in the **Universal Gift Shop. Sapphire Falls Resort** has a **Universal Studios Store** of its own, as does **Aventura Hotel**; while both have a good selection of sundries and theme park souvenirs, those hotels' branded merchandise isn't nearly as eye-catching as Cabana Bay's.

SHOPPING *near* UNIVERSAL ORLANDO

IF YOU'VE EXHAUSTED Universal Orlando's shopping venues and want to venture off property, Central Florida's premier shopping experience is found only a couple exits east along I-4 at **The Mall at Millenia** (☎ 407-363-3555; mallatmillenia.com), anchored by **Bloomingdale's,**

Macy's, and **Neiman Marcus.** Other stores include **Anthropologie, Burberry, Cartier, Coach, Crate & Barrel, Gucci, Guess, J. Crew, Kate Spade, Louis Vuitton, Lululemon Athletica, Tiffany & Co., Tory Burch, Urban Outfitters,** and **Versace.** Hours are Monday–Saturday, 10 a.m.–9 p.m.; Sunday, 11 a.m.–7 p.m.

Artegon Marketplace, an artsy bazaar a few minutes south of Millenia on the north end of International Drive, is being converted into a vintage vehicle museum and adventure park, but the luxurious **Cinemark movie theater** (5150 International Dr.; ☎ 407-352-1042; cinemark.com) and **Bass Pro Shops Outdoor World** (5156 International Dr.; ☎ 407-563-5200; shops.basspro.com) attached to the failed mall are still in operation. **Gods & Monsters** (5421 International Dr.; ☎ 407-270-6273; godmonsters.com), our favorite former Artegon fixture, relocated its comic books and sci-fi collectibles across the street, adding a retro arcade and postapocalypse-themed pub.

On the south end of International Drive is **Pointe Orlando** (9101 International Dr.; ☎ 407-248-2838; pointeorlando.com), with a handful of stores. This complex gets a lot of its business from the convention center, less than a mile away, rather than from locals. Hours are October–May, Monday–Saturday, noon–10 p.m., and Sunday, noon–8 p.m.; June–September, Sunday–Thursday, noon–8 p.m., and Friday–Saturday, noon–9 p.m. (Bars and restaurants stay open later.) I-Drive is the heart of Orlando's tourist district, jammed with hotels, discount stores, and endless traffic; locals generally avoid the area or use Universal Boulevard (on the south end) and Grand National Drive (on the north end) to dodge the worst of the congestion.

OUTLETS NEAR UNIVERSAL ORLANDO

LIKE EVERY MAJOR TOURIST DESTINATION in the United States, Central Florida has hundreds of factory-outlet stores, most of them situated near major attractions. Having spent many hours checking prices and merchandise, we generally conclude that at most stores you'll save about 20% on desirable merchandise and up to 75% on last-season (or older) stock. Some stores in the outlet malls are full retail or sell a few brands at a 20% discount and the rest at full price.

Orlando Premium Outlets-International Drive (4951 International Dr.; ☎ 407-352-9600; premiumoutlets.com/outlet/orlando -international; open Monday–Saturday, 10 a.m.–11 p.m.; Sunday, 10 a.m.–9 p.m.), on the north end of I-Drive, features 180 of the world's hottest designers and brand names, among them **BCBG Max Azria, Dooney & Bourke, Hugo Boss Factory Store, Kate Spade, Michael Kors, Movado, Saks Fifth Avenue OFF 5TH, St. John, Under Armour, Victoria's Secret,** and the only **Neiman Marcus Last Call** in Central Florida. There's even a **Disney's Character Warehouse,** where unsold Walt Disney World souvenirs go to die; read Derek Burgan's monthly "Magic, Memories, and Merch" reports at tinyurl.com/burganmerch. You can reach the outlets by car (arrive early for any hope of free parking), taxi, or I-Ride Trolley (it's stop #1).

PART SEVEN

UNIVERSAL STUDIOS FLORIDA

WHEN UNIVERSAL STUDIOS BEGAN developing its first Orlando park, the park was originally envisioned along the lines of the Hollywood Studio Tour, with the majority of the guest experiences occurring during an extensive tram tour of the limited-access back lot, along with a handful of rides and shows in the front of the park. When Disney aped that exact game plan for Disney's Hollywood Studios park (which opened in 1989 as Disney–MGM Studios), Universal did a dramatic 180 with its designs, breaking out the tram tour's iconic encounters—King Kong, Earthquake, and Jaws—into their own headliner attractions, each of which easily exceeded its Disney contemporaries in technology and thrill (if not reliability) upon **Universal Studios Florida**'s (USF's) 1990 debut.

Despite that difference, during their first decade, the competing parks were roughly equivalent in many guests' minds. Both parks offered movie- and TV-themed rides and shows, while other attractions provided an educational, behind-the-scenes introduction to the cinematic arts. And both had working film- and TV-production facilities.

Since the turn of the millennium, the two parks have gone in different directions. Whereas Disney's Hollywood Studios (DHS) essentially abandoned its production facilities long ago, USF test-markets TV pilots to guests and has limited actual filming, some of which visitors can attend. More important, Universal has updated, upgraded, or entirely replaced nearly every attraction that opened in the 1990s, replacing Kong with Revenge of the Mummy, Back to the Future with The Simpsons Ride, Jaws with Harry Potter's Diagon Alley, and *Earthquake* (and its descendant *Disaster!*) with Fast & Furious: Supercharged. With each renovation came groundbreaking advancements in ride hardware and special effects. In contrast, DHS went a decade without adding any truly innovative attractions, and even after its Star Wars expansion opens in 2019, it will offer only 9 real rides, versus USF's 13 major moving attractions.

Watching USF's constant evolution has been thrilling, but it can also be disconcerting. If the last time you visited Universal was in the early 2000s, you literally won't recognize the majority of the park. USF celebrated its 25th anniversary in 2015, but precious little early history is left intact in the park for longtime visitors who loved long gone opening-day attractions such as *Alfred Hitchcock: The Art of Making Movies,* The Funtastic World of Hanna-Barbera, and *Ghostbusters Spooktacular.* (For a trip down memory lane, visit Universal's retired attractions tributes at tinyurl.com/uniretired.) Even so, there are no signs that Comcast is slowing down in its extreme makeover of USF, which welcomed Fast & Furious: Supercharged and the *Cinematic Celebration* lagoon show in 2018. A replacement for *Terminator 2: 3-D* will debut in 2019, and look for Woody Woodpecker's KidZone to get a makeover in the coming years.

NOT TO BE MISSED AT UNIVERSAL STUDIOS FLORIDA
PRODUCTION CENTRAL • Transformers: The Ride 3-D
NEW YORK • Revenge of the Mummy
THE WIZARDING WORLD OF HARRY POTTER—DIAGON ALLEY • Harry Potter and the Escape from Gringotts • Hogwarts Express
WORLD EXPO • Men in Black Alien Attack
SPRINGFIELD: HOME OF THE SIMPSONS • The Simpsons Ride
HOLLYWOOD • *Universal Orlando's Horror Make-Up Show*

GETTING ORIENTED *at* UNIVERSAL STUDIOS FLORIDA

USF IS LAID OUT in a P configuration, with the rounded part of the *P* sticking out disproportionately from the stem. Beyond the main entrance plaza (known as the **Front Lot**), a wide boulevard stretches past several shows and rides to the park's New York area. Branching off this pedestrian thoroughfare to the right are four streets that access other areas of the park and intersect a promenade circling a large, oval manmade lake, where the majority of the shows and attractions are located. The area of USF open to visitors is a bit smaller than Epcot.

Beginning at the park entrance and going clockwise, the first area you'll encounter is **Production Central,** which includes Despicable Me Minion Mayhem, Hollywood Rip Ride Rockit, Transformers: The Ride 3-D, and *Shrek 4-D.* At the top of the *P* is the **New York** area, including Race Through New York Starring Jimmy Fallon and Revenge of the Mummy. Next is **San Francisco,** the home of Fast & Furious: Supercharged; **The Wizarding World of Harry Potter—Diagon Alley** with Hogwarts Express–King's Cross Station and Harry Potter and the Escape from Gringotts; **World Expo** with Men in Black Alien Attack; **Springfield: Home of the Simpsons,** featuring, of course, The Simpsons Ride; and **Woody Woodpecker's KidZone,** containing E.T.

continued on page 262

Universal Studios Florida

Attractions

1. *Animal Actors on Location!* UX
2. Curious George Goes to Town
3. *A Day in the Park with Barney* UX
4. Despicable Me Minion Mayhem UX
5. E.T. Adventure UX
6. Fast & Furious: Supercharged UX VL
7. *Fear Factor Live (seasonal)* UX
8. Fievel's Playland
9. Harry Potter and the Escape from Gringotts UX ☑
10. Hogwarts Express: King's Cross Station UX ☑
11. Hollywood Rip Ride Rockit UX
12. Kang & Kodos' Twirl 'n' Hurl UX
13. Men in Black Alien Attack UX ☑
14. Ollivanders
15. Race Through New York
    Starring Jimmy Fallon UX VL

16. Revenge of the Mummy UX ☑
17. *Shrek 4-D* UX
18. The Simpsons Ride UX ☑
19. Transformers: The Ride–3-D UX ☑
20. *Universal Orlando's Horror
    Make-Up Show* UX ☑

New York

16

A M

5th Ave.

15

AA

57th St.

7th Ave.

South St.

Production Central

19

T

Plaza of the Stars

8th Ave.

11

N

D

4

17

Hollywood Blvd.

S

Rodeo Dr.

20

B

Stunt
Show
(opens 2019)

Hollywood

Counter-Service Restaurants

A. Ben & Jerry's
B. Beverly Hills Boulangerie
C. Bumblebee Man's Taco
   Truck
D. Cafe La Bamba (seasonal)
E. Chez Alcatraz
F. Duff Brewery
G. Fast Food Boulevard 👍
H. Florean Fortescue's
   Ice-Cream Parlour 👍

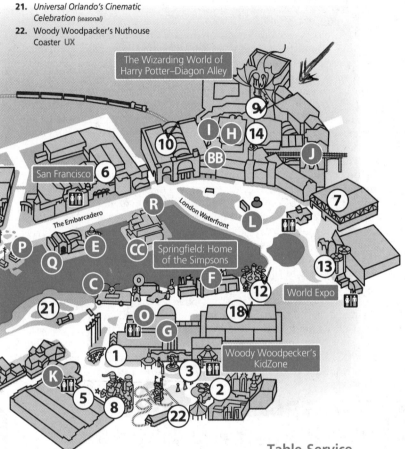

21. *Universal Orlando's Cinematic Celebration* (seasonal)
22. Woody Woodpacker's Nuthouse Coaster UX

The Wizarding World of Harry Potter–Diagon Alley

San Francisco 6

The Embarcadero

London Waterfront

Springfield: Home of the Simpsons

World Expo

Woody Woodpecker's KidZone

Table-Service Restaurants

I. Fountain of Fair Fortune	**Q.** Richter's Burger Co.	**AA.** Finnegan's Bar & Grill
J. The Hopping Pot	**R.** San Francisco Pastry Company	**BB.** Leaky Cauldron (counter service) 👍
K. KidZone Pizza Company		**CC.** Lombard's Seafood Grille
L. London Taxi Hut	**S.** Schwab's Pharmacy (seasonal)	
M. Louie's Italian Restaurant	**T.** Universal Studios' Classic Monsters Cafe	
N. Mel's Drive-In		
O. Moe's Tavern		
P. New York Craft Beer Cart		

UX Attraction Offers Universal Express   VL Virtual Line   ✚ First Aid Station   🚻 Restrooms

👍 Recommended Dining   ☑ Not to Be Missed   • • • Parade Route

continued from page 259

Adventure, an animal show, and several play areas. The last themed area, back near the front of the park, is **Hollywood,** featuring *Universal Orlando's Horror Make-Up Show.*

In most of USF, the line where one themed area begins and another ends is blurry because much of the architecture consists of boring boxlike soundstages barely concealed behind false fronts. No matter; guests orient themselves by the major rides, sets, and landmarks and refer, for instance, to "the waterfront," "over by E.T.," or "by Mel's Drive-In." In diametric contrast, The Wizarding World of Harry Potter—Diagon Alley (and, to a much lesser extent, the Springfield area around The Simpsons Ride) is an immersive themed area whose scope and scale point to the place-making potential of upcoming Universal lands.

Almost all guest services are found in the **Front Lot,** just inside the main entrance. Services and amenities include stroller and wheelchair rentals to the left as you enter; lockers, Lost and Found, and First Aid are to the right. You'll also find the **Studio Audience Center,** where you can sign up to be an audience member at any live TV productions that may be recording that day. Past series taped at USF have included game shows, talk shows, cooking shows, Telemundo's *La Voz Kids,* and TNA's *IMPACT Wrestling.* Call ☎ 407-363-8400 and select option 5 to find out what's scheduled during your visit.

A "secret" secondary entrance to USF is tucked under the Hollywood Rip Ride Rockit track, between Despicable Me Minion Mayhem and the Universal Studios Store. It doesn't open until late morning (usually around 10:30 a.m.), but it can save you a few minutes entering on a busy afternoon; follow the signs from CityWalk for the Blue Man Group theater to find it. It also makes an excellent egress when you want to exit toward the Hard Rock Cafe or Islands of Adventure.

UNIVERSAL STUDIOS FLORIDA ATTRACTIONS

PRODUCTION CENTRAL

AT THE FRONT OF USF, Production Central is the first land that guests see upon entering the park and passing through the Front Lot. It's a shame, therefore, that this is one of the most meh main streets of any theme park, with bland beige buildings broken up only by the incongruously colossal coaster tracks. Its underwhelming aesthetics don't seem to hurt the area's attractiveness to guests because Production Central holds three of the park's most popular attractions outside of Diagon Alley.

In addition to the rides, show, and counter-service restaurant, Production Central is home to **Music Plaza Stage,** a Hollywood Bowl–inspired amphitheater with an artificial turf viewing lawn (where you'll often find unconscious tourists sprawled on sunny days) that's used during Mardi Gras concerts and similar special events. There is also access (when applicable) from here to the soundstages used for TV production and Halloween haunted houses.

Despicable Me Minion Mayhem *(Universal Express)* ★★★★

APPEAL BY AGE PRESCHOOL ★★★½ GRADE SCHOOL ★★★★½ TEENS ★★★★
YOUNG ADULTS ★★★★ OVER 30 ★★★★ SENIORS ★★★½

What it is Motion-simulator 3-D ride. **Scope and scale** Major attraction. **When to go** Immediately after park opening or just before closing. **Comments** Child swap available (see page 188). Expect *long* waits in line. Great fun. **Duration of ride** 5 minutes. **Average wait in line per 100 people ahead of you** 7 minutes; assumes all simulators in use. **Loading speed** Moderate–slow.

DESCRIPTION AND COMMENTS Despicable Me Minion Mayhem is a 3-D motion-

Motion Sickness

simulator ride similar to Universal's The Simpsons Ride and Star Tours at Disney's Hollywood Studios. You're seated in a ride vehicle that faces a large video screen, onto which the attraction's story is projected. When the story calls for you to drop down the side of a building, your ride vehicle tilts forward as if you were falling; when you need to swerve left or right, your ride vehicle tilts the same way. This particular motion-simulator system premiered as The Funtastic World of Hanna-Barbera when the park opened in 1990; was used again in Jimmy Neutron's Nicktoon Blast, which replaced the former in 2003; and was refurbished for the attraction's third incarnation as Despicable Me Minion Mayhem, which opened in the summer of 2012.

As with its former incarnations, the main difference between Minion Mayhem and other simulators is that most other simulators usually provide one video screen per ride vehicle, while Minion Mayhem arranges all of its eight-person vehicles in front of one large IMAX-size video screen. The ride vehicles are set on raised platforms that get slightly higher toward the back of the theater, affording good views for all guests in the rear. Though the simulators have been updated, the most significant upgrade is incorporated in the projection system, which employs high-definition 3-D digital technology.

The ride's story serves as a mini-sequel to the original animated movie *Despicable Me,* starring Gru, the archvillain, along with his adopted daughters and his diminutive yellow Minions. The preshow area is inside Dr. Gru's house, where you see his unique family tree and other artifacts. Our favorite is the mounted lion's head (in the lion's mouth is a dog, in the dog's mouth is a cat, and in the cat's mouth is a mouse). The premise of the ride is that you are being turned into one of Dr. Gru's Minions. Once converted you must navigate the Minion Training Grounds, where your "speed, strength, and ability not to die" are tested. Something soon goes amiss, though, and your training turns into a frenetic rescue operation. The events of this ride take place exactly one year after the *Despicable Me* film; a subplot of the ride involves Gru's daughters (Edith, Agnes, and Margo) celebrating the anniversary of their adoption. In a brilliant marketing tie-in, the adorable gift that Agnes gives to Gru can be purchased in the Super Silly Stuff gift shop on your way out.

The ride itself (which lasts about 5 minutes) is a fast-paced series of dives, climbs, and tight turns through Gru's Rube Goldberg–esque machines. Like The Simpsons Ride, there are more sight gags and interesting things to see here than anyone possibly could in a single ride; luckily, it's Universal's least intense motion simulator, so re-rides are less likely to make you lose your lunch. Guests exit the ride into a disco party with interactive video screens and a photo op where they can boogie down with a Minion.

TOURING TIPS Despicable Me Minion Mayhem is unfortunately situated at the very front of the park, within a few yards of the entrance turnstiles, and usually begins operating before the official opening time. As a result, long lines develop as soon as the park opens. If you're among the first to enter and the wait is 20 minutes or less, get in line for Despicable Me, and then ride Hollywood Rip Ride Rockit. However, if the line for Despicable Me exceeds 20 minutes, try late afternoon or the hour before the park closes. Note that the posted standby time is just the wait to enter the building; you'll be watching preshows for an additional 10 minutes before you actually ride.

The 3-D perspective from simulators on the sides can be skewed, and the vehicles up front are a bit too close; for the best view, you want to be in the middle of one of the center rows. Stationary seating is available for those prone to motion sickness and for children less than 40 inches tall; ask an attendant for directions. On busy days they occasionally open up a queue with direct access to stationary seating, which can significantly slash your wait time.

Hollywood Rip Ride Rockit (Universal Express) ★★★★

APPEAL BY AGE	PRESCHOOL ★½	GRADE SCHOOL ★★★★	TEENS ★★★★½
YOUNG ADULTS ★★★★½		OVER 30 ★★★★	SENIORS ★★½

What it is High-tech roller coaster. **Scope and scale** Headliner. **When to go** The first hour after park opening or after 5 p.m. **Comments** 51″ minimum height requirement; child swap available (see page 188); single-rider line available. Expect long waits in line. Woo-hoo! (and ouch!). **Duration of ride** 2½ minutes. **Average wait in line per 100 people ahead of you** 6–8 minutes. **Loading speed** Moderate.

DESCRIPTION AND COMMENTS When it opened in the summer of 2009, Hollywood Rip Ride Rockit was USF's candidate for the most technologically advanced coaster in the world. Well, that distinction didn't last very long, but for sure this ride has some features we've never seen before. Let's start with the basics: Rip Ride Rockit is a sit-down X-Car coaster that runs on a 3,800-foot steel track, with a maximum height of 167 feet and a top speed of 65 miles per hour. Manufactured by German coaster maker Maurer AG, X-Car vehicles are more maneuverable than most other kinds and use less restrictive restraints, making for an exhilarating ride.

You ascend—vertically—at 11 feet per second to crest the 17-story-tall first hill, the highest point reached by any roller coaster in Orlando, until Mako in SeaWorld opened in 2016. The drop is almost vertical too, launching you into Double Take, a loop inversion in which you begin on the inside of the loop, twist to the outside at the top (so you're upright), and then twist back inside the loop for the descent. Double Take stands 136 feet tall, and its loop is 103 feet in diameter at its widest point. You next hurl (no, not that kind of hurl!) into a stretch of track shaped like a musical treble clef. As on Double Take, the track configuration on Treble Clef is a first. Another innovation is Jump Cut, a spiraling negative-gravity maneuver. Usually on coasters, you experience negative gravity on long, steep vertical drops; with Jump Cut you feel like you're in a corkscrew inversion, but you never actually go upside down. Other high points include a 95-degree turn, a downhill into an "underground chasm" (gotta love those Universal PR wordsmiths!), and a final incline loop banked at 150 degrees.

The ride starts in the Production Central area; weaves into the New York area near Race Through New York Starring Jimmy Fallon, popping out over the heads of guests in the square below; and then storms out toward the lagoon separating USF from CityWalk.

Each train consists of two cars, with riders arranged two across in three rows per car. Each row is outfitted with color-changing LEDs and high-end audio and video technology for each seat. Like Rock 'n' Roller Coaster at Disney's Hollywood Studios, the "Triple R" features a musical soundtrack, but in this case you can choose the genre of music you want to hear as you ride: classic rock, country, disco, pop, or rap. The ride has dozens of hidden songs in its catalog. Press the Rip Ride Rockit logo on the number pad for 10 seconds, then enter 113 to hear Led Zeppelin's "Immigrant Song." Press 902 to hear The Muppets sing "The Rainbow Connection." For the complete list, see tinyurl.com/rockitsongs, or download the Pocket Rockit Setlist app from the Apple or Android stores.

When it's over, Universal flogs both still photos and a DVD video of your ride, which intercuts stock footage of the coaster with clips of you screaming, as recorded by your seat-mounted camera. The DVD costs $35, or $40 with a 5-by-7-inch print; My Universal Photos members pay $20 for just the video.

From a Whalton, England, mom:

A fabulous, gut-wrenching coaster that thrilled the socks off my 8- and 9-year-olds. (Mum found it a bit too brutal to repeat.)

A perhaps-jaded Easton, Connecticut, coaster aficionado offers this:

The loud music blasting in our ears canceled out the sound of the coaster. If only they had a "None of the Above: Silence" selection. The singles line hint was a real time-saver.

When Hollywood Rip Ride Rockit premiered in 2009, it was pretty smooth. Alas, the wheels on the cars haven't held up well in the hot Florida sun, and though some of the cars have been overhauled to make the ride more comfortable, none of the fixes have helped much long-term. While perfectly safe, Rip Ride Rockit now subjects you to a lot of side-to-side jarring. To crib a phrase from Tina Turner, some folks like it easy . . . and some folks like it *rough.* This reader from Armonk, New York, definitely falls in the former category:

Despite the fact that I love roller coasters and always have, and I am in good physical shape with no issues, Hollywood Rip Ride Rockit hurt my back. My 17-year-old daughter who also loves all rides didn't love it either.

And from another reader in Belgium, Wisconsin:

I've ridden many roller coasters in my 35 years, including some over 400 feet tall and with speeds in excess of 120 mph, yet I've never ridden one that was as painful and rough as Rip Ride Rockit. With the beating that my head and neck took, I'll never ride that one again.

On the other hand, this family from Lancaster, Pennsylvania, thinks Rockit is worth riding:

Our 10-year-old son rode Rip Ride Rockit four times with almost no waiting. This was a ride we hadn't even included in our plan because we thought it would be too scary and the lines not worth the wait. It ended up being a favorite experience of the trip.

TOURING TIPS Rip Ride Rockit can put more trains on the tracks simultaneously than any other coaster in Florida, which means, on paper, that it should be able to handle about 1,850 riders per hour. In practice, you'll wait about 6–8 minutes for every 100 people in the queue ahead of you, indicating an hourly capacity of 1,500 riders. Because the ride is so close to the USF entrance, it's a crowd magnet, creating bottlenecks from park opening on. Your best chance to ride without a long wait is to be one of the first to enter the park when it opens, or use the single-rider entrance. You'll have to empty your pockets into a free locker and pass through a metal detector before queuing.

Shrek 4-D (Universal Express) ★★★½

APPEAL BY AGE	PRESCHOOL ★★★★	GRADE SCHOOL ★★★½	TEENS ★★★
YOUNG ADULTS ★★★	OVER 30 ★★★	SENIORS ★★★½	

What it is 3-D movie. **Scope and scale** Headliner. **When to go** Anytime after experiencing the rides. **Comments** Child swap available (see page 188). The snarkiest 3-D show in town. **Duration of show** 20 minutes. **Probable waiting time** 16 minutes.

DESCRIPTION AND COMMENTS An indoor 3-D film with moving theater seating, set between the franchise's first two films, *Shrek 4-D* follows the adventures of Shrek, Donkey, and Dragon as they attempt to rescue Fiona after she's kidnapped by Lord Farquaad. The preshow holding area is themed as Lord Farquaad's dungeon, where the Three Little Pigs and the Gingerbread Man warn riders about the pains and tortures in store for everyone, until the diminutive despot appears to deliver a monologue about his evil plan to reclaim his lost bride. The plan is posthumous because Lord Farquaad ostensibly died in the movie, and it's his ghost making the plans, but never mind.

Guests then move into the main theater, don their 3-D glasses, and recline in seats equipped with "tactile transducers" and "pneumatic air propulsion and water spray nodules capable of both vertical and horizontal motion." In English, that means the seats move, bump, and vibrate along with the action, like the D-BOX seats now found in local cinemas. The film's 3-D effects aren't bad, and the 3-D glasses you'll wear do a good job even if you're putting them over prescription glasses, but it relies on older polarized 3-D projection instead of the newer dichroic system used by Despicable Me. As far as the phrase *4-D* goes, physicists may point out that Earth's fourth dimension is time, but as far as theme parks go, the fourth dimension is water. Expect to get a mild spritz or three during the show. Guests are also subjected to leg ticklers and smells relevant to the on-screen action (oh, boy).

Technicalities aside, *Shrek 4-D* is a mixed bag. It's frantic, laugh-out-loud funny, and iconoclastic. Concerning the last, the film takes a good poke at Disney, with Pinocchio, the Three Little Pigs, and Tinker Bell (among others) all sucked into the mayhem. But the video quality and 3-D effects are dated by today's ultra-HD standards, the story line is incoherently disconnected from the clever preshow, and the bucking seats swiftly become a pain in the butt. On the upside, in contrast to Disney's *It's Tough to Be a Bug!*, *Shrek 4-D* doesn't generally freak out kids under age 7.

TOURING TIPS Universal claims that it can move about 2,400 guests per hour through *Shrek 4-D,* but the show's location at the front of the park and directly across from Despicable Me Minion Mayhem translates to heavy traffic in the morning. If you see lines longer than 20 minutes, try visiting during mealtimes or in the last 2 hours the park is open. There's not much in the film or preshow to scare small children. Stationary seating is available on request. Be aware that *Shrek 4-D* shuts down one of its two theaters in the fall to hold a haunted house for Halloween Horror Nights, greatly increasing wait times during an otherwise slow season. Universal Studios Hollywood closed its *Shrek 4-D* attraction in 2017, turning it into a DreamWorks

Animation theater showcasing a new *Kung Fu Panda* 4-D film. The Orlando version was still open at press time, but the rumor mill claims that it may be replaced by an elaborate animatronic-filled dark ride based on *The Secret Life of Pets*.

Transformers: The Ride—3-D *(Universal Express)* ★★★★½

APPEAL BY AGE	PRESCHOOL	★★½	GRADE SCHOOL	★★★★	TEENS	★★★★½
YOUNG ADULTS	★★★★		OVER 30	★★★★	SENIORS	★★★½

What it is Multisensory 3-D dark ride. **Scope and scale** Super-headliner. **When to go** First 30 minutes the park is open or after 4 p.m. **Comments** 40" minimum height requirement; child swap available (see page 188); single-rider line available. A breathtaking, deafening blur; not to be missed. **Duration of ride** 4½ minutes. **Average wait in line per 100 people ahead of you** 5 minutes. **Loading speed** Moderate–fast.

Motion Sickness

DESCRIPTION AND COMMENTS Transformers—those toy robots from the 1980s that you turned and twisted into trucks and planes—have been around long enough to go from commercial to kitsch to cool and back again. Thanks to director-producer Michael Bay's movie series (most recently represented by 2018's *Bumblebee* prequel), "Robots in Disguise" are again a blockbuster global franchise, and in 2013 Transformers fans finally received a USF attraction (cloned from earlier rides in Singapore and Hollywood) befitting their pop-culture idols. Recruits to this cybertronic war enlist by entering the N.E.S.T. Base (headquarters of the heroic Autobots and their human allies) beneath a 28-foot-tall statue of Optimus Prime. Inside an extensive, elaborately detailed queue, video monitors catch you up on the backstory. Basically, the Decepticon baddies are after the AllSpark, source of cybernetic sentience. We're supposed to safeguard the shard by hitching a ride aboard our friendly Autobot ride vehicle EVAC, presumably without getting smooshed like a Lincoln in a souvenir penny press every time he shifts into android form. Needless to say, Megatron and his pals Starscream and Devastator won't make things easy, but you'll have Sideswipe and Bumblebee (in his modern Camaro form; look for an old-school Volkswagen Beetle in the final scene) backing you up. For the ride's 4½ minutes, you play human Ping-Pong ball in an epic battle between these Made in Japan behemoths.

To do justice to this Bay-splosion-packed war of good versus evil, Transformers harnesses the same traveling simulator system behind Islands of Adventure's Amazing Adventures of Spider-Man ride, and it ups the ante with photo-realistic high-definition imagery, boosted by dichroic 3-D glasses that produce remarkably sharp, vivid visuals. The plot amounts to little more than a giant game of keep-away, and the uninitiated will likely be unable to tell one meteoric mass of metal from another, but you'll be too dazzled by the debris whizzing by to notice. Fanboys will squeal with delight at hearing original cartoon actors Peter Cullen and Frank Welker voicing the pugilistic protagonists, and then spill into the postride gift shop to purchase armloads of exclusive merchandise, while the rest of us might need a bench on which to take a breather afterward. We'll admit slight disappointment at not getting to see an actual four-story-tall animatronic transform, but the ride's mix of detailed (though largely static) set pieces and video projections was likely a much more maintenance-friendly solution for bringing these colossi to life. Either way, this is one of the most intense, immersive thrill rides found in any theme park. However, Transformers doesn't hold up as well after repeated rides as The Amazing Adventures of Spider-Man, as it lacks the humor, heart, and moving props of its predecessor. Two millennials had, shall we say, a visceral take on Transformers:

The illusion of being smashed through an office building is pretty convincing. If you've ever wondered what it would be like to be eaten, digested, and pooped out of a giant robot, this is the ride for you.

Hopefully, it's also a ride for those who don't exactly see Transformers as a ride down the alimentary canal. Robots poop? Who knew?

TOURING TIPS This ride draws crowds. Your only solace is that The Wizarding World of Harry Potter—Diagon Alley draws even larger throngs. Follow our touring plan to minimize waits. The single-rider line will get you on board faster, but as singles lines go, this is one of the slower ones and is closed off if it becomes backed up. Finally, it's hard to focus on the fast-moving imagery from the front row; center seats in the second and third rows provide the best perspective.

NEW YORK

THE CITY STREETS OF NEW YORK are re-created in the New York section of USF. Along with London and Hollywood, New York represents some of the best theming found in the park. Make sure to explore the crooked alleyways behind *The Blues Brothers* stage for some authentic-looking urban backdrops. Trivia note: The statue near the border with San Francisco has the body of Abraham Lincoln and the head of late MCA/Universal mogul Lew Wasserman.

New York has two attractions, one sit-down restaurant, one counter-service restaurant, an arcade, and a Starbucks coffee café. *The Blues Brothers Show* (see page 292) is also performed here. First Aid is located in the alley behind Louie's Italian Restaurant.

Race Through New York Starring Jimmy Fallon
(Universal Express) ★★★½

APPEAL BY AGE	PRESCHOOL ★★½	GRADE SCHOOL ★★★★	TEENS ★★★★
YOUNG ADULTS ★★★★	OVER 30 ★★★★	SENIORS ★★★★	

What it is Comedic 3-D simulator ride. **Scope and scale** Headliner. **When to go** According to your Virtual Line return time. **Comments** May require free Virtual Line reservation. 40" minimum height requirement; child swap available (see page 188). **Duration of ride** 4 minutes. **Average wait in line per 100 people ahead of you** 5 minutes. **Loading speed** Moderate.

DESCRIPTION AND COMMENTS Housed in a replica of NBC's historic 30 Rock offices in Manhattan, Race Through New York offers Virtual Line passes instead of a standby queue. Guests, except for those with Universal Express, are assigned a reservation time via Universal's mobile app or an automated kiosk. When your appointed time arrives, you return to the ride entrance, where you'll be directed to the first lobby of the NBC offices. An NBC page will hand you a color-coded card—hold on to it and take time to enjoy the lobby tributes to the previous hosts of *The Tonight Show*: Steve Allen (1954-1956), Jack Paar (1957-1962), Johnny Carson (1962-1992), Jay Leno (1992-2009 and 2010-2014), and Conan O'Brien (2009-2010).

Once you ascend to the second floor, you await your ride in a fancy lounge outfitted with couches and touch screen tables with video games inspired by *The Tonight Show Starring Jimmy Fallon*. The main attractions, however, are live appearances by some *Tonight Show* regulars: the Ragtime Gals, a male vocal quintet that performs tongue-in-cheek barbershop interpretations of pop hits; and Hashtag the Panda, a dancing fur character (celebrity guests who have worn the costume range from Chris Rock to Miley Cyrus).

When the color of the lights changes to match the color of your card, it's time to make your way to Jimmy Fallon's studio. The Roots, Fallon's house band, rap the safety instructions before you enter a 72-seat theater with a large screen. Next, you'll don 3-D glasses and race against Fallon in his souped-up Tonight Rider roadster. Starting at the *Tonight Show* studio, the competition sends you careening through the streets and subways of New York and eventually to, yes, the moon. Fans create wind effects, and there are faint pizza smells in addition to the obligatory water spray. (Hey, it's Universal!)

The queueless experience and preshow areas get a lot of points, and the ride itself has some of the sharpest visuals and smoothest movement in the Universal repertoire. But it breaks no new technical ground for the genre, and it relies on recognition of Fallon's stable of characters (like Ew! Girl and Tight Pants Man) for its jokes, which grow stale after several viewings. Race Through New York gets mixed reviews from our readers; this visitor from Crystal Lake, Illinois, represents the majority opinion:

> *I was surprised with how unimpressed I was with Race Through New York with Jimmy Fallon. Universal has raised the bar so much and has done such an amazing job with everything that I had big hopes for this ride. In the end, it was OK, but not as good as I expected.*

But others agree with this family from Vadnais Heights, Minnesota:

> *We went on it twice, and all the kids loved it. The kids really liked the games they could play before they went on the ride, and they had fun with Hashtag the Panda.*

TOURING TIPS Race Through New York typically opens with a regular standby queue for the first hour of the day before switching to Virtual Line–only operations. Reserve your Virtual Line pass through the Universal smartphone app for early afternoon, when other attractions generally have their longest lines. You can also grab a ticket from the kiosks outside the attraction after riding Revenge of the Mummy. If return times have run out for the day, check back at the attraction an hour or two before park closing, when walk-ins are usually accepted.

Request a free **studio tour** for a guided glimpse backstage, including a peek into the ride's control room, a visit to the private VIP balcony, and possibly a private audience with Hashtag. Tours are subject to staff availability; try asking at the attraction entrance around 10 a.m. or 4 p.m.

Revenge of the Mummy (*Universal Express*) ★★★★½

APPEAL BY AGE	PRESCHOOL	★½	GRADE SCHOOL	★★★½	TEENS	★★★★½
YOUNG ADULTS	★★★★½		OVER 30	★★★★½	SENIORS	★★★★

What it is Combination dark ride and roller coaster. **Scope and scale** Super-headliner. **When to go** The first 2 hours the park is open or after 4 p.m. **Comments** 48″ minimum height requirement; child swap available (see page 188); single-rider line available. Killer! Not to be missed. **Duration of ride** 3 minutes. **Average wait in line per 100 people ahead of you** 7 minutes. **Loading speed** Moderate.

Motion Sickness

DESCRIPTION AND COMMENTS It's hard to wrap your mind around this attraction, but trust us—you're in for a very strange experience. Here, quoting Universal, are some of the things you can look forward to: "authentic Egyptian catacombs"; "high-velocity show-immersion system" (Huh? Quickie baptism?); "magnet-propulsion launch wave system"; "a 'Brain Fire' [!] that hovers [over guests] with temperatures soaring to 2,000°F"; and "Canopic jars containing grisly remains."

When you read between the lines, Revenge of the Mummy is a high-tech hybrid indoor roller coaster/dark ride based on the Mummy flicks starring Brendan Fraser (with no references to the recent Tom Cruise reboot). The ride's premise is that a movie production crew has taken over New York's Museum of Antiquities to film a sequel titled *Revenge of the Mummy.* The queuing area serves to establish the story line: you're in a group touring a set from the Mummy films when you enter a tomb where the fantasy world of film gives way to the real thing. You'll notice lots of interactive details built into the queue, including hints that the movie filming isn't going according to plan. By the time you board your clunky, jeeplike ride vehicle, you've learned that the movie's villain, Imhotep, is trying to use the film crew's souls to become immortal. Only the mystical Medjay symbol can save you from certain doom (cue dramatic music).

The ride begins as a slow, very elaborate dark ride, passing through various chambers, including one where flesh-eating scarab beetles descend on you. Suddenly your vehicle stops and then drops backward and rotates. Here's where you're shot at high speed up the first hill of the roller coaster part of the ride. We won't give away any of Mummy's secrets, but here's what you need to know: it's mostly in the dark and there are no loops, inversions, or any kind of upside-downness; there are plenty of tight turns and high-speed drops and a maximum speed of around 45 miles per hour. Though it's a wild ride by anyone's definition, the emphasis remains as much on the visuals, robotics, and special effects as on the ride itself. The special effects are aging but still pretty good: video effects, animatronics, lighting, and enough fire-spewing gas vents to rotisserie a chicken. The endings (yes, plural) are pretty clever.

TOURING TIPS Try to ride during the first 2 hours the park is open. If lines are long, one fallback is to use the singles line, which can cut your wait to a third of the posted wait time and is often more expedient than Universal Express. If you must wait on a hot day, the consolation is that Mummy's air-conditioning system is one of the best in the park.

The front left seat gets the best view of the animatronic effects, while the back corner seats offer the most air time in the coaster sections. Request row three for extra legroom if you found the test seat outside the attraction entrance to be a tight fit. Concerning motion sickness, if you can ride Space Mountain without ill effect, you should be fine on Revenge of the Mummy. Finally, note that the Mummy's queue contains enough scary stuff to frighten little kids all on its own. While most grade-schoolers we surveyed who were plucky enough to ride the Mummy gave it high marks, one father feels our rating for that age group is inappropriate:

This ride should NOT be recommended for grade-schoolers, for which you rated the ride a 3½. My second-grader (who wasn't scared at all on Space Mountain) was terrified during this ride and cried afterward. I am really upset I encouraged her to ride it and worried she'll have nightmares. Even I thought it was quite scary, and other adults on our ride echoed the same. I think you should really consider a lower rating for grade-schoolers, in addition to a warning about the VERY frightening aspects of this ride.

However, this reader thinks we've oversold the Mummy's fright factor:

We disagree with you about Revenge of the Mummy. We read your description and were anticipating being scared. While the coaster aspect is a fun ride, otherwise it wasn't scary in the slightest.

Ask the greeter out front if you can have a free **production tour;** if it isn't too busy, they may escort you into the maintenance area, where you can watch the coaster cars fly by overhead.

SAN FRANCISCO

UNIVERSAL'S TRIBUTE TO Baghdad by the Bay is a bit too abbreviated to leave your heart in, but the designers did manage to squeeze in an attraction, along with a number of eateries and shops, into only a couple of blocks of brick and boardwalk. Be on the lookout for Bruce the shark; this trophy formerly stood in front of the Jaws ride and was transplanted to the Frisco wharf once that attraction sailed away.

Fast & Furious: Supercharged *(Universal Express)* ★★★

| APPEAL BY AGE | PRESCHOOL | ★★ | GRADE SCHOOL | ★★★ | TEENS | ★★★ |
| YOUNG ADULTS | ★★★ | OVER 30 | ★★★ | | SENIORS | ★★½ |

What it is Car chase motion simulator. **Scope and scale** Headliner. **When to go** After experiencing the other headliners. **Comment** 40" minimum height requirement; child swap available (see page 188); single-rider line available. Optional Virtual Line reservations available. **Duration of ride** 5 minutes. **Average wait in line per 100 people ahead of you** 3 minutes. **Loading speed** Fast.

DESCRIPTION AND COMMENTS Universal Studios Hollywood added a new finale to its classic back lot tram tour in 2015, incorporating the cast and plot of the $5 billion box office behemoth that is its long-running Fast and Furious franchise. That finale became a stand-alone attraction at USF in 2018.

Guests enter the attraction through the distressed facade of San Francisco's historic Oriental Warehouse, which was erected on the site of the park's former *Beetlejuice* stage show. The Fast & Furious experience starts in the elaborate queue, an industrial warehouse where you can check out some of the high-performance automobiles seen in the films. Gearheads will weep with envy, while anyone who isn't into exotic cars may feel like they're stuck in their local garage waiting for a lube job. The latter can amuse themselves by hunting for hidden references in the queue to the *Beetlejuice* and *Disaster* attractions that previously occupied the area.

Next, two preshows, featuring live hosts awkwardly interacting with prerecorded clips of Jordana Brewster (Mia Toretto) and Chris "Ludacris" Bridges (Tej), establish the backstory for anyone who hasn't yet seen all—or any—of the eight (and counting) Furious films.

After boarding specially designed 48-passenger tramlike "party buses," you're taken to an underground club, where a postrace rave party is in full swing until the feds crash the party, searching for a crucial crime witness hiding among the guests. Series stars Vin Diesel (Dominic "Dom" Toretto), Dwayne Johnson (Luke Hobbs), Michelle Rodriguez (Letty Ortiz), and Tyrese Gibson (Roman Pearce) appear in holographic form to rescue you from Luke Evans (Owen Shaw), the bad guy from *Fast & Furious 6*. In the attraction's climax, a 360-degree projection tunnel—filled with hydraulic platforms, 400-foot-long screens, and excessive sprays of smoke and water—make it appear as if your ride vehicle is in the midst of a high-stakes car chase, speeding at 100-plus miles per hour through a West Coast urban jungle.

Fast & Furious: Supercharged is similar to Skull Island: Reign of Kong in Islands of Adventure, but without the immersive 3-D or impressive animatronics. The dialogue and visual effects are shockingly cheesy even by theme park standards (some consider this part of the appeal), but it all goes by in such a nitro-fueled blur that it may not matter to fans of the flicks.

TOURING TIPS The free Virtual Line system for Supercharged kicks in a couple hours after park opening, letting you select your ride time via the smartphone app or by grabbing a ticket from the ride's kiosks, but due to the queue arrangement, you'll only save time if the standby wait is more than 30 minutes. Standard standby, Universal Express, and single-rider lines are also available; as a bonus, single riders bypass the embarrassing preshows.

The best views are from the center/right seats in the first bus; stay to the left when the queue splits before the loading dock. Though less scary than the King Kong ride, Supercharged has a slightly higher height requirement; luckily, the custom slot car racing game in the child swap room may be more fun than the actual attraction.

THE WIZARDING WORLD OF HARRY POTTER— DIAGON ALLEY

WHEN UNIVERSAL OPENED The Wizarding World of Harry Potter at Islands of Adventure (IOA), it created a paradigm shift in the Disney–Universal theme park rivalry. Not only did Universal trot out some groundbreaking ride technology, but it also demonstrated that it could trump Disney's most distinctive competence: the creation of infinitely detailed and totally immersive themed areas. To say that The Wizarding World was a game changer is an understatement of the first order.

It was immediately obvious that Universal would build on its Potter franchise success—but how and where? Universal isn't sitting on 27,000-plus acres like Disney, so real estate was at a premium. If Potterville was going to grow, something else had to go. Conventional wisdom suggested that The Wizarding World expansion would gobble up The Lost Continent section of IOA, and that may happen yet. But looking at the ledger, it was clear that the older USF theme park could use a boost.

It just so happened that a substantial chunk of turf at USF was occupied by the aging Jaws ride and its contiguous Amity-themed area. The space allowed for substantial development; plus, its isolated location—in the most remote corner of the park—was conducive to creating a totally self-contained area where Potter themes could be executed absent any distraction from neighboring attractions. In short, it was perfect.

So how would the new Potter area tie in to the original at IOA? And what Harry Potter literary icons could be exploited? It was pretty clear that a new suburb of Hogsmeade wasn't going to cut it. The answer was virtually shouting from the pages of the Harry Potter novels, which observe a clear dichotomy of place—plots originate in London and then unfold at distant Hogwarts.

Two London sites that figure prominently in the Potter saga brim with attraction possibilities: Diagon Alley, a secret part of London that is a sort of sorcerers' shopping mall; and the King's Cross railroad station, where wizarding students embark for the train trip to Hogwarts.

Following much deliberation and consultation with Warner Bros. and author J. K. Rowling, the final design called for a London waterfront street scene flanking Universal Studios Lagoon. The detailed facades, anchored by the **King's Cross railroad station** on the left and including **Grimmauld Place** and **Wyndham's Theatre,** recall West London scenes from the books and movies. **Diagon Alley,** secreted behind the London street scene, is accessed through a secluded entrance in the middle of the facade. Like Hogsmeade at IOA, Diagon Alley features shops and restaurants in addition to three attractions and live entertainment.

Diagon Alley covers 20 acres—about the same area as the Hogsmeade original—but offers about two-and-a-half times the pedestrian space because it doesn't have space- (and people-) eating outdoor roller coasters. With only one high-capacity ride (**Harry Potter and the Escape from Gringotts**), along with an enlarged version of the **Ollivanders** wand-shop experience in Hogsmeade and the **Hogwarts Express** train connecting the two Wizarding Worlds, the new area's increased elbowroom is somewhat offset by a relatively reduced hourly attraction capacity, making Diagon Alley's maximum capacity approximately 8,000 persons, about double Hogsmeade's occupancy limit.

In the attraction department, Universal once again came out swinging for the fences. As before with Harry Potter and the Forbidden Journey, the headliner attraction for the expansion is high-tech and cutting-edge—and once again a dark ride, but this time of the roller coaster genre. The labyrinthine passages and caverns of Gringotts Wizarding Bank, the financial institution of choice for the wizarding set, are the setting of this plot-driven 3-D dark ride–coaster.

Though the Gringotts attraction is Diagon Alley's headliner, the most creative element in the two-park Potter domain is Hogwarts Express, which re-creates the train trip from London to Hogwarts and vice versa. Serving as both an attraction and transportation between USF and IOA, the Express unifies the two disparately located Wizarding Worlds.

Diagon Alley in Detail

Diagon Alley and its London Waterfront are sandwiched between the San Francisco and World Expo areas of the park, about as far from USF's main entrance as you can get. From the park entrance, turn right on Rodeo Drive to Mel's Drive-In; from here, circumnavigate the lagoon counterclockwise, keeping it to your left until you reach the entrance to the London Waterfront, where wrought iron fencing surrounds a park-like promenade. Here you can access London through the gateway closest to the *Fear Factor Live* stadium. You can also access the London Waterfront from the San Francisco area by walking clockwise around the lagoon; usually you can enter from either end, but on the busiest days, you'll have to take a shoreline bypass along the embankment to the World Expo side of the Potter-themed area. Note that if you take Hogwarts Express from IOA, you'll debark into San Francisco just outside of the London Waterfront.

Having arrived at the London area, take a moment to spot Kreacher (the house elf regularly peers from a second-story window above 12 Grimmauld Place); dial MAGIC (62442) in the red phone booth for a message from the Ministry of Magic; poke your head in the back door of the triple-decker purple Knight Bus; and chat with the Knight Bus conductor and his Caribbean-accented shrunken head. For some Easter eggs from the attraction designers—including the first of several tributes to Jaws, the original occupant of this area—inspect the record albums in the music store window. You'll also find a couple of cabmen's shelters selling snacks (jacket potatoes, British crisps, and hot dogs in cylindrical buns) and London souvenirs, along with an exacting replica of the towering Shaftesbury Memorial Fountain from Piccadilly Circus.

Now enter Diagon Alley next to the Leicester Square marquee in the approximate center of the building facades. As in the books and films, the unmarked portal is concealed within a magical brick wall that is ordinarily reserved for wizards and the like. (Unfortunately, the wall doesn't actually move, due to safety concerns.) The endless parade of Muggles (also known as plain old humans) in shorts and flip-flops will leave little doubt where that entryway is, and just in case you're completely clueless, Universal positions attendants outside to obtrusively point the way.

Once admitted, look down the alley to the rounded facade of **Gringotts Wizarding Bank,** where a 40-foot fire-breathing Ukrainian Ironbelly dragon (as seen in *Harry Potter and the Deathly Hallows: Part 2*) perches atop the dome. The dragon doesn't move, but about every 10 minutes (weather permitting), he unleashes a jet of flame; get your camera ready when you hear him growl. To your left is the **Leaky Cauldron,** the area's flagship restaurant, serving authentically hearty British pub fare.

Intersecting Diagon Alley near the Leaky Cauldron is **Knockturn Alley,** a labyrinth of twisting passageways where the Harry Potter bad guys hang out. A covered walk-through area with a projected sky creating perpetual night, it features spooky special effects in the faux shop windows—don't miss the creeping tattoos and crawling spiders! Finally, to the right of Gringotts is **Carkitt Market,** a canopy-covered plaza where short live shows are staged every half hour or so. All the sections of Diagon Alley are crammed with elaborate signage, animated window displays, and endless hidden details to discover.

Discover is an important word in Diagon Alley because this overwhelmingly intricate area actually feels like a place you can explore and get lost in, much like, say, Epcot's Morocco Pavilion or Disneyland's New Orleans Square. We can't overstate how seamlessly Diagon's designers have rendered the illusion of a living world, topping even Disney California Adventure's Cars Land. *Immersion* is an often-overworked buzzword in themed entertainment, but this Wizarding World exemplifies it, enveloping fans in Potter's world to a degree that far exceeds Hogsmeade's high standards. And even if you aren't a follower of the franchise, you may find yourself falling for the fictional universal after experiencing Universal's incarnation.

Diagon Alley Attractions

Harry Potter and the Escape from Gringotts
(Universal Express) ★★★★★

APPEAL BY AGE **PRESCHOOL** ★★½ **GRADE SCHOOL** ★★★★½ **TEENS** ★★★★★
YOUNG ADULTS ★★★★★ **OVER 30** ★★★★½ **SENIORS** ★★★★

Motion Sickness

What it is Super-high-tech 3-D dark ride with roller coaster elements. **Scope and scale** Super-headliner. **When to go** First thing during early entry or in the late afternoon. **Comments** 42" minimum height requirement; child swap available (see page 188); single-rider line available. The ultimate realization of "Ride the Movies"; not to be missed. **Duration of ride** 4½ minutes. **Average wait in line per 100 people ahead of you** 4 minutes. **Loading speed** Moderate–fast.

DESCRIPTION AND COMMENTS Owned and operated by goblins, Gringotts is the Federal Reserve of the wizarding economy, as well as the scene of memorable sequences from the first and final Potter installments. It's known for its toppling column facade, chandelier-adorned lobby, and bottomless caverns (and the heart-stopping rail carts running through them). The theme park adaptation is the centerpiece of Diagon Alley and is the ultimate expression of the virtual reality rides that Universal has been refining since IOA opened.

Like Forbidden Journey at IOA, Harry Potter and the Escape from Gringotts incorporates a substantial part of the overall experience into its elaborate queue, which (like Hogwarts Castle) even nonriders should experience. You enter through the bank's lobby, where you're critically appraised by glowering animatronic goblins. Your path takes you to a "security checkpoint," where your photo will be taken (to be purchased afterward as an identity lanyard in the gift shop, natch), and past animated newspapers and office windows where the scenario is set up.

Unlike Forbidden Journey, Gringotts doesn't rush you through its queue but rather allows you to experience two full preshows before approaching the ride vehicles. In the first, goblin banker Blordak and Bill Weasley (Ron's curse-breaking big brother) prepare you for an introductory tour of the underground vaults. Then you're off for a convincing simulated 9-mile plunge into the earth aboard an "elevator" with a bouncing floor and ceiling projections. All this is before you pick up your 3-D glasses (shaped like magical goggles) and ascend a spiral staircase into the stalactite-festooned boarding cave where your vault cart awaits.

Also unlike Forbidden Journey, and indeed all the rest of The Wizarding World, Gringotts is not set in a nebulous "moment frozen in time," where incidents from various stories simultaneously coexist. Instead, visitors enter the bank at the exact moment that Harry, Ron, Hermione, and Griphook have arrived to liberate Helga Hufflepuff's Cup Horcrux from Bellatrix Lestrange's vault. Only in this retelling of *Harry Potter and the Deathly Hallows: Part 2*'s iconic action scene, you (as Muggles opening new bank accounts) are ingeniously integrated into the action. Familiar film moments featuring the vaults' guardian dragon play out in the ride's background as Bellatrix and Lord Voldemort appear to menace you with snakes and sinister spells, whereupon the heroic trio pauses its quest to save your hapless posteriors. The storytelling, which is much more coherent than Forbidden Journey's hodgepodge approach, may disorient scholars of the Potter canon, but it's an intelligent way to allow fans to relive a favorite adventure without merely rehashing the plot.

Gringotts's ornately industrial ride vehicles consist of two-car trains, each holding 24 people in rows of four. The ride merges Revenge of the Mummy's indoor coaster aspects with The Amazing Adventures of Spider-Man's seamless integration of high-resolution 3-D film (the finale dome completely surrounds your car) and massive sculptural sets (some of the rockwork inside is six stories tall), while adding a few new tricks, such as independently rotating cars and motion-simulator bases built into the track.

The result is a ride that, though it doesn't break completely new ground as Forbidden Journey and Spider-Man did, combines favorite innovations from its predecessors in an exhilarating new way. The visuals are sometimes murky and the dialogue difficult to discern. And it's slightly disappointing that no animatronic figures, moving set pieces, or actual pyrotechnics appear in the ride, though you will get spritzed with water, blasted with warm air, and sprayed with fog—this is Universal, after all. Finally, though Helena Bonham Carter and Ralph Fiennes reprised their screen roles, Daniel Radcliffe and Emma Watson did not. Harry and pals' computer-generated image stand-ins look OK, as they're never seen up close, but Hermione's voice double is dreadful.

Nitpicks aside, whether Escape from Gringotts is *the* greatest themed thrill ride of all time or merely *one* of the greatest can be happily debated by park fans until the next great leap forward comes along. To these New England honeymooners, there's not much to debate:

> *Gringotts is a terrific ride! Less intense than the Forbidden Journey but still full of surprises.*

TOURING TIPS Gringotts is the pot of gold at the end of Universal's rainbow that a kazillion crazed guests are racing toward. Though the interior line is gorgeous and air-conditioned, the mostly unshaded outdoor extended queue holds 4,000 guests—you don't want to be at the end of it. If you're a Universal resort guest and you qualify for early entry, use it; Express Passes aren't valid during early entry, so the line moves swiftly. When USF doesn't offer Early Park Admission, day guests who arrive before official opening may be allowed to queue for Gringotts before it begins running. Otherwise, try the attraction around lunchtime or in the late afternoon; wait times usually peak after opening but become reasonable later in the day. Just be aware that the queue may shutter to new arrivals before the park closes if the posted wait time exceeds the remaining operating hours by more than 60 minutes, or even earlier if the ride breaks down. Be warned that, as with any ride this advanced, Gringotts can be expected to experience some downtime almost daily. Most operational interruptions are brief and resolved within 10 or 15 minutes.

As far as physical thrills go, Gringotts falls somewhere between Disney's Seven Dwarfs Mine Train and Space Mountain, with only one short (albeit unique) drop and no upside-down flips. It was designed to be less intense (read: less nauseating) than Forbidden Journey and therefore more appealing to families, with fewer height, weight, and size restrictions. The restraints are similar to Revenge of the Mummy's, with bars across your lap and shins, but slightly more restrictive. Use the test seat to the left of the front entrance if you're unsure, and request the third or sixth row for additional legroom.

The ride feels noticeably different depending on the row in which you're seated. The front is closest to the action and has the scariest view of the drop; 3-D effects look better farther back. The sixth row gets the most coaster action, especially from the initial fall, but the screens are slightly distorted. The far right seat in row four is the sweet spot.

As is the case with most of Universal's thrill rides, you must leave your bags in a free locker. Luckily, unlike at Hogwarts Castle, the lockers are separated from the attraction entrance, greatly improving guest flow. Universal Express is accepted at this attraction, and the only part of the preshow experience that Express guests miss is the boring outdoor queue. If you don't have bags and don't mind breaking up your group, the singles line will cut your wait to about a third of the posted standby time, but you'll skip all the preshows past the lobby; we don't advise this option until after your first ride.

Hogwarts Express (Universal Express) ★★★★½

APPEAL BY AGE PRESCHOOL ★★★★½ GRADE SCHOOL ★★★★½ TEENS ★★★★½
YOUNG ADULTS ★★★★½ OVER 30 ★★★★½ SENIORS ★★★★½

What it is Transportation attraction. **Scope and scale** Headliner. **When to go** Late morning or just before park closing. **Comments** Requires a park-to-park ticket. A moving experience; not to be missed. **Duration of ride** 4 minutes. **Average wait in line per 100 people ahead of you** 7 minutes. **Loading speed** Moderate.

DESCRIPTION AND COMMENTS Part of the genius of creating Diagon Alley at USF is that it's connected to Hogsmeade at IOA (see Part Eight) by Hogwarts Express, just as in the novels and films. The counterpart to Hogsmeade Station in IOA is USF's King's Cross Station, a landmark London train depot that has been re-created a few doors down from Diagon Alley's hidden entrance. (It's important to note that King's Cross has a separate entrance and exit from Diagon Alley: you can't go directly between them without crossing through the London Waterfront.)

The passage to Platform 9¾, from which Hogwarts students depart on their way to school, is concealed from Muggles by a seemingly solid brick wall, through which you'll witness guests ahead of you dematerializing. (Spoiler: The Pepper's Ghost effect creates a clever but congestion-prone photo op, but you experience only a dark corridor with whooshing sound effects when crossing over yourself.)

Once on the platform, you'll pass a pile of luggage (including an owl cage with an animatronic Hedwig) before being assigned to one of the three train cars' seven compartments. The train itself looks exactingly authentic to the nth degree, from the billowing steam to the brass fixtures and upholstery in your eight-passenger private cabin. Along your one-way Hogwarts Express journey, you'll see moving images projected beyond the windows of the car rather than the park's backstage areas, with the streets of London and the Scottish countryside rolling past outside your window. The screen isn't 3-D, but it's slightly curved to conceal the edges and create a convincing illusion of depth. Even more impressive are the frosted-glass doors you enter through, which turn out to be amazing screens that make it seem as if someone is standing on the other side. You experience a different presentation coming and going, and in addition to pastoral scenery, there are surprise appearances by secondary characters (Fred and George Weasley, Hagrid) and threats en route (bone-chilling Dementors, licorice spiders), augmented by vibration and sound effects in the cars. Note that, as in Escape from Gringotts, two of the lead actors did not reprise their roles, to the ride's detriment, as this Middleton, Delaware, reader reports:

> Ron sounds like Ron, and Harry is decent, but Hermione sounds like they grabbed a worker's relative and put her in a sound booth. I wish they would change it already.

Hogwarts Express isn't an adrenaline rush in the same way that Escape from Gringotts is, but for those invested in Potter lore, it may be even more emotionally thrilling. And unlike most Potter attractions, it can be experienced by the whole family, regardless of size.

TOURING TIPS Because using the train for a one-way trip involves park-hopping, passengers need a valid park-to-park ticket. Disembarking passengers must enter the second park and, if desired, queue again for their return trip. You'll be allowed to upgrade your one-park Base Ticket at the station entrance.

If the line becomes too long, Universal could limit you to only one one-way ride per day. If you wish to take a same-day return trip, you could be relegated to a secondary queue that promises to be exponentially slower than the already glacial standby queue. (Thankfully, this has only been enforced a couple of times.)

Lines rarely exceed 15 minutes in the morning, though the queue may swell to an hour in midafternoon, or in the evening when one park closes before the other. The walk from one train station to the other is just under a mile and takes 20 minutes at a moderate pace. If the posted wait is 15 minutes or less, it is typically quicker to take the train than to walk to the other Wizarding World.

Guests exiting in Hogsmeade have a chance to take a photo with the locomotive before it backs out for its next run. Guests departing from Hogsmeade should pose with the static train outside the station before they queue up.

Ollivanders ★★★★

APPEAL BY AGE PRESCHOOL ★★★	GRADE SCHOOL ★★★★½	TEENS ★★★★½
YOUNG ADULTS ★★★★½	OVER 30 ★★★★	SENIORS ★★★★

What it is Combination wizarding demonstration and shopping op. **Scope and scale** Major attraction. **When to go** After riding Harry Potter and the Escape from Gringotts. **Comments** Audience stands. Enchanting. **Duration of presentation** 6 minutes. **Probable waiting time per 100 people ahead of you** 18 minutes.

DESCRIPTION AND COMMENTS Ollivanders, located in Diagon Alley in the books and films, somehow sprouted a branch location in Hogsmeade at IOA (see page 336). Potter purists pointed out this misplacement, but the wand shop stayed put with J. K. Rowling's blessing and became one of the more popular features of The Wizarding World. It also became a horrendous bottleneck, with long lines where guests roasted in an unshaded queue. In the Diagon Alley version, Ollivanders assumes its rightful place, and with much larger digs. At IOA, only 24 guests at a time can experience the little drama where wands choose a wizard (rather than the other way around). At USF, the shop has multiple cleverly concealed choosing chambers, changing it from a popular curiosity into an actual attraction. As for the IOA location, it continues to operate.

The actual show inside is identical to IOA's original outpost in script and special effects. Every few minutes, following a scene from the Potter books, a wand-selection show takes place, where a random customer (often a child dressed in Potter regalia) is selected to take part in a wand-choosing ceremony. Usually just one person in each group gets to be chosen by a wand, though occasionally siblings are selected together. This is one of the most truly imaginative elements of The Wizarding World: A Wandkeeper sizes you up and presents a wand, inviting you to try it out; your attempted spells produce unintended, unwanted, and highly amusing consequences. Ultimately, a wand chooses you, with all the attendant special effects.

The Celtic zodiac-inspired wands presented in the ceremony are detailed interactive models that interact with shop windows throughout The Wizarding Worlds (see below). After the presentation, guests exit into a greatly enlarged gift shop, where interactive wands are available for purchase, along with noninteractive "famous wizard" replica wands for a vast variety of characters.

TOURING TIPS Check out the self-sweeping broom (shades of *Fantasia*?) while waiting for the show. To increase your odds of being picked, be a cute kid, stand up front, and make eye contact. If your young 'un is selected to test-drive a wand, be forewarned that you'll have to buy it if you want to take it home.

Interactive Wands and Spell-Casting Locations in Diagon Alley

Interactive wands ($52) are available in 13 Ollivanders Original styles inspired by the Celtic calendar; interactive wands modeled after those wielded by a variety of characters (including Harry, Hermione, Dumbledore, Sirius Black, and Luna Lovegood) are also available. In addition, nonfunctional replica wands ($46) are sold at both **Ollivanders** outposts and in the smaller selection at **Wands by Gregorovitch** in Diagon Alley. The widest selection of wands is found in the two Ollivanders shops. Stores outside of The Wizarding World at the entrance of each park, as well as at CityWalk's Universal Studios Store and gift shops at each hotel, carry a limited variety of interactive and noninteractive wands, including toy "learner" wands ($28.95) for li'l wizards. Wands can also be ordered from Universal Orlando's merchandise website.

Medallions embedded in the ground designate a couple dozen locations split between the two Wizarding Worlds, where hidden cameras in storefront windows can detect the waving of these special wands and respond to the correct motions with special effects both projected and practical. You might use the swish and flick of Wingardium Leviosa to levitate an object or the figure-four Locomotor spell to animate another.

It can take some practice to get the hang of spell casting. Wizards wander around the area to assist novices and demonstrate spells (though they may not loan their wands), but queues to trigger certain effects can grow to a dozen deep at peak times. A map provided with each wand purchase details the location and movement for most effects, but there are some secret ones to uncover on your own. (Hint: One is in Scribbulus's window, and another is in the Slug & Jiggers storefront.) Look at your map under the ultraviolet lights in Knockturn Alley for another surprise.

Note that the price of the interactive wands includes unlimited activations of the hidden effects; you don't have to pay to recharge your wand on subsequent visits, or even replace a battery. Damaged wands are cheerfully repaired for free (even without the original box or receipt) at any Ollivanders, and globe-trotting wizards will be happy to know that their wands will also function at The Wizarding Worlds in Hollywood and Japan. If you encounter a spell-casting location with a sign saying CURRENTLY HAS AN ANTI-JINX IN PLACE, just move along to the next one; that's Potter-speak for "it's broken."

We've received positive feedback so far on the interactive wands, like this praise from a New York family:

We took our interactive wand and map . . . and explored all the many interactive surprises for well over an hour and had a fantastic time. An interactive wand is highly recommended. Our girls are 12 and 14, and they found every spot where something happened and had a blast making the wand motions and watching the windows come to life.

On the other hand, a cost-conscious dad from Rigby, Indiana, sends this advice:

If you don't want massive pressure from your kid to buy one of Universal's EXPENSIVE wands, don't do the wanding ceremony. If you do it anyway, speak to an attendant prior to entering the ceremony room, and advise him or her that your kids ARE NOT to be wanded! Not getting your kid one of Universal's expensive wands will not ruin their lives—honest. And from what we saw, about half of the users couldn't get their wands to work reliably. The kids get very frustrated when the 5-year-old in front of them can make things appear, move, talk, or whatever, but they can't!

Entertainment in Diagon Alley

An elevated area in **Carkitt Market,** between The Hopping Pot and the Gringotts Money Exchange, comes to life with short shows inspired by Rowling's stories. Though modest in scope, these are some of the best performances found at Universal, and well worth working into your touring plan if you have more than one day at the resort. Showtimes aren't listed in the park map, but performances usually start every 30 minutes on the hour and half hour.

Celestina Warbeck and the Banshees (★★★★) is a live musical showcasing the Ella Fitzgerald–esque Singing Sorceress with her comely backup crew, swinging to jazzy tunes with a 1940s big band feel. With song titles created by Harry Potter author J. K. Rowling ("You Stole My Cauldron But You Can't Have My Heart," "A Cauldron Full of Hot Strong Love," and "You Charmed the Heart Right Out of Me"), Celestina and her three Banshees perform a lively show that also uses audience participation. (Shy Muggles need not worry: the guest performers are asked ahead of time.) While the songs contain a plethora of references to the Potter books and movies that fans will love, guests who don't know (or care) about the Harry Potter universe will still enjoy the elaborate choreography, fantastic singing, and witty music and lyrics courtesy of Michael Weiner and Alan Zachary, the duo behind Disney Cruise Line's *Twice Charmed: An Original Twist on the Cinderella Story*. During the holiday season, a special Christmas version is performed with different songs and costumes. The show runs about 12–13 minutes.

Tales of Beedle the Bard (★★★½) recounts one of two wizard fables—"The Three Brothers" from *Harry Potter and the Deathly Hallows* or "The Fountain of Fair Fortune"—using puppets crafted by Michael Curry (Broadway's *The Lion King, Finding Nemo—The Musical*). The story is chosen "randomly" at the start of each performance. The puppets are gorgeous in a creepy kind of way, and the way the actors perform while maneuvering them is quite clever, though some of the dialogue can be difficult to understand, especially during the "Fountain" tale. Some preschoolers may be scared of the large Death puppet used in "The Tale of the Three Brothers." The show runs 10–12 minutes.

Shopping in Diagon Alley

Shopping is a major component of Diagon Alley in Potter lore; while Hogsmeade visitors went wild for the few wizardly shops there, Diagon Alley is the planet's wackiest mall, with a vastly expanded array of enchanted tchotchkes to declare bankruptcy over. Shops include:

WEASLEYS' WIZARD WHEEZES is a joke shop with many of the toys also found in Hogsmeade's Zonko's, plus new gags such as Skiving Snackboxes and Decoy Detonators. Look up through the three-story shop's glass ceiling for fireworks.

WISEACRE'S WIZARDING EQUIPMENT, at the exit of Harry Potter and the Escape from Gringotts, sells crystal balls, compasses, and hourglasses.

MADAM MALKIN'S ROBES FOR ALL OCCASIONS stocks school uniforms, Scottish wool sweaters, and dress robes for wizards and witches. The talking mirror will critique your ensemble if you stand in front of it.

MAGICAL MENAGERIE is the place to adopt a plush cat, rat, owl, or hippogriff; the adorable animatronic Kneazle is unfortunately not for sale.

SHUTTERBUTTON'S will film your family in front of a green screen and insert you into a DVD of Potter scenes ($70 in a souvenir case or $50 with a My Universal Photos package).

QUALITY QUIDDITCH SUPPLIES sells golden snitches and jerseys for your favorite Hogwarts house teams.

SCRIBBULUS carries quills, notebooks, and similar school supplies.

BORGIN AND BURKES in Knockturn Alley stocks objects from the dark side of magic (watch out for the mummified hand!).

SUGARPLUM'S SWEET SHOP tempts guests with fudge (including an unbearably sweet Butterbeer variety), pastries, no-melt ice cream (also known as a cup of icing), Potter-themed candies, and most of the other treats also found at Honeydukes in Hogsmeade.

GLOBUS MUNDI is a small travel agency–inspired shop in Carkitt Market that carries luggage tags, key chains, pins, and the like.

You can pay for all this loot in **Gringotts bank notes,** which you can purchase inside the **Gringotts Money Exchange** overseen by an imperious interactive animatronic goblin, and then spend it anywhere within Universal Orlando; see page 148 for details. Even if you don't want to exchange any of your Muggle money, take a moment to query the proprietor about his age, the current exchange rate, or almost anything you've ever wanted to ask a goblin (but were afraid to ask). In general, Diagon Alley's stores are larger and more plentiful than the tiny shops over in Hogsmeade, with carefully planned external and internal queues to corral waiting customers.

Diagon Alley Touring Strategy

During Diagon Alley's first few years of operation, experiencing the Harry Potter area without interminable waits was a major challenge, because in essence the area has only one-and-a-half rides (plus the various shops and shows) to entertain the expected masses. Now that newer attractions have helped redistribute USF's crowds, touring Diagon Alley is much more comfortable, but you'll still want to prepare a game plan if visiting on even a moderately busy day.

When Early Park Admission is offered, USF admits eligible on-site resort guests 1 hour before the general public, with the turnstiles opening up to 90 minutes before the official opening time. Early entry is a tremendous perk if you're staying on-property, but you'll still be competing with thousands of other resort guests, so arrive at least 30 minutes before early entry starts; during peak season, showing up on the very first boat or bus from your hotel is recommended. If you're a day guest visiting on an Early Park Admission day, Diagon Alley will already be packed when you arrive. Even when USF doesn't offer Early Park Admission, all guests may enter Diagon Alley from the front gates up to 15 minutes before park opening, and hotel guests in IOA will arrive via Hogwarts Express a little after that, though Harry Potter and the Escape from Gringotts doesn't begin operating until the official opening time.

If you aren't using early entry, leave Diagon Alley until late afternoon, or at least lunchtime when the early birds have exhausted themselves. Barricades and timed-return tickets have been used for crowd control on a handful of extraordinarily busy days, but you should almost always be able to waltz right into Diagon Alley without a wait. (Gringotts itself is, of course, another story.)

WORLD EXPO

THIS AREA STRETCHES around USF's central lagoon from Diagon Alley to The Simpsons Ride and somewhat clumsily incorporates several competing aesthetics. The World Expo name, as well as the theming of Men in Black Alien Attack in the area's center, is derived from the 1964 World's Fair's New York State Pavilion. The *Fear Factor Live* stadium, the area's only other attraction, appears to be themed to the style known as ugly warehouse. Though not exactly an attraction, the space-age Coca-Cola kiosk near Men in Black lets you type your name on a digital soda bottle and refill your Freestyle cup.

Fear Factor Live (Universal Express) ★★½

APPEAL BY AGE	PRESCHOOL ★★½	GRADE SCHOOL ★★★½	TEENS ★★★★
YOUNG ADULTS ★★★½	OVER 30 ★★★½	SENIORS ★★★½	

What it is Live version of the gross-out stunt TV show. **Scope and scale** Headliner. **When to go** 3–5 shows daily; crowds are smallest at the first and second-to-last shows. **Duration of show** 30 minutes. **Probable waiting time** None.

DESCRIPTION AND COMMENTS *Fear Factor Live* is a stage version of the uniquely stomach-turning reality show that ran on NBC 2001–2006 and again 2011–2012. In the theme park iteration, six volunteers compete for modest prizes, like

Universal T-shirts. Contestants must be 18 years or older (with a photo ID to prove it) and weigh at least 110 pounds. Those demented enough to volunteer should arrive at least 75 minutes before showtime to sign papers and complete some obligatory training for the specific competitive events. Anyone who doesn't wish to compete in the stage show itself can sign up for the Critter Challenge or the Food Challenge. With an adult's permission, volunteers as young as age 16 can compete in the latter.

The stage show is performed in a covered theater and consists of three different challenges. In the first, all six contestants are suspended two-and-a-half stories high in the air and try to hang on to a bar as long as possible. The difficulty is compounded by heavy-duty fans blasting the contestants' faces (as you can imagine, this stunt requires exceptional upper-body strength). Only four people go on to the next round, and the person who hangs on to the bar the longest gets to choose his or her partner for the next event.

Once the first two contestants are eliminated, it's time for a brief intermission called the Desert Hat Ordeal. This involves a brave audience member–lunatic who has signed up for the Critter Challenge. Prepared with eye goggles and a mouthpiece, the volunteer is put in a chair with a glass case over his or her head. A wheel is spun to determine what will be crawling over the volunteer's head; the creepy-crawly choices include spiders, snakes, roaches, and scorpions. The only incentive to participate is a free photo of the ordeal for contestants to take to their therapists.

Back at the main competition, the four remaining contestants are split into two teams to compete in the Eel Tank Relay. This consists of one team member grabbing beanbags out of a tank full of eels and throwing them to his or her partner to catch in a bucket. Audience members drench the contestants with high-powered water guns, further spicing up the event. The duo who buckets the most beanbags wins, going on to compete against each other in the final round for the prize package.

As the stage is prepared for the finale, the folks who volunteered for the Food Challenge are split into two teams and invited to drink a mixture of curdled milk, mystery meat, and various live bugs that are all blended together on stage. The team that drinks the most of the mixture within the time limit wins a glamorous plastic mug that says, "I Ate a Bug," a convenient euphemism for "I have the brain of a nematode."

In the last event the two remaining contestants scramble up a wall to retrieve flags, jump into a car that is lifted into the air, and then jump out of the car to retrieve more flags. When the required climbing, jumping, and flag-grabbing are accomplished, the first player to remove a rocket launcher from the backseat of the car and hit a target on the stage wall wins.

The above description may make the show sound more entertaining than it is. It's our duty to confess that this is one of our least favorite shows in any theme park, anywhere, ever. You have been warned.

TOURING TIPS If you've ever wanted a chance to test your mettle (sanity?), *Fear Factor Live* may be your big chance. Participants for the physical stunts are chosen early in the morning and between performances outside the theater, so head there first thing if you want to be a contestant. The contestants for the skeevier stunts, such as the bug-smoothie drinking, are chosen directly from the audience. Sit close to the front and wave your hands like crazy when it comes time for selection. Finally (and seriously), this show is too intense and gross for kids age 8 and under.

An extremely relevant query from two University of Iowa students:

> *We're thinking about volunteering to drink the bug smoothie and want to know if it's better to chew the bugs or just chug the*

*smoothie and hope they die after crawling around for a while in
your stomach. Also, do you recommend holding your nose?*

We recommend practicing both options at home, preferably while heavily medicated and under the supervision of a psychiatrist. *Fear Factor Live* mercifully goes on hiatus in the fall to turn its stadium over to Halloween Horror Nights, and rumors persist that it may permanently close for a Ministry of Magic–themed expansion of The Wizarding World.

Men in Black Alien Attack *(Universal Express)* ★★★★½

**APPEAL BY AGE PRESCHOOL ★★★½ GRADE SCHOOL ★★★★ TEENS ★★★★
YOUNG ADULTS ★★★★ OVER 30 ★★★★ SENIORS ★★★½**

Motion Sickness

What it is Interactive dark thrill ride. **Scope and scale** Headliner. **When to go** During the first 2 hours the park is open. **Comments** May induce motion sickness; 42″ minimum height requirement; child swap available (see page 188); single-rider line available. Buzz Lightyear's Space Ranger Spin on steroids; not to be missed. **Duration of ride** 4½ minutes. **Average wait in line per 100 people ahead of you** 5 minutes. **Loading speed** Moderate-fast.

DESCRIPTION AND COMMENTS Men in Black Alien Attack brings together Will Smith and Rip Torn (as Agent J and Men in Black [MIB] director Zed) for an interactive sequel to the hit sci-fi franchise. You'll notice that the ride's building pays homage to the architecture from the 1964 World's Fair, including the observation towers from the New York State Pavilion that featured in the 1997 film's finale. That theme is carried over to the attraction's preshow, which perfectly parodies the style of *Walt Disney's Carousel of Progress* before taking a surprise turn. The story line has you recruited as an MIB trainee. After an introduction warning that aliens "live among us" and articulating MIB's mission to round them up, Zed expounds on the finer points of alien spotting and familiarizes you with your training vehicle and your weapon, an alien zapper.

You then load up in a six-passenger spinning ride vehicle and are dispatched into an innocuous training room, which is a shooting gallery full of plywood targets shaped like aliens. Your training is cut short when it is revealed that a real alien spaceship has landed in New York and you must save the city. The meat of the ride consists of careening around Manhattan in your MIB vehicle and shooting aliens. There are more targets than anyone could possibly shoot, and they're presented at a fast pace. Each ride vehicle is paired with another ride vehicle running on a parallel track, and both vehicles compete to see who can shoot the most aliens. At a certain point during the ride, you'll be able to shoot at the "fusion exhaust port" of the opposing ride vehicle, causing it to spin momentarily. This disorients the other riders and causes them to lose precious time splatting the aliens. Of course, the other riders (and some of the aliens!) can shoot at you too.

Men in Black is interactive in that your marksmanship and ability to blast yourself out of some tricky situations will determine how the story ends. You're awarded both a personal score and a score for your car. There are about three dozen possible outcomes and literally thousands of different ride experiences determined by your pluck, performance, and, in the final challenge, your intestinal fortitude. Regardless of your score, all recruits are deemed not ready to join MIB, and everyone's memories of the game are wiped at the end of the ride.

TOURING TIPS Each alien figure has sensors that activate special effects and respond to your zapper. Aim for the eyes and keep shooting because you can score repeatedly on the same target. Your gun has auto-fire and unlimited ammo, so just keep the trigger depressed the whole ride; you'll even get a small number of points for missed shots. Targets above you score the most points: look for aliens behind second-story windows. At the ride's climax, listen carefully for Zed to instruct you to "push the red button," and hold it down when he says "push" to score a bonus 100,000 points. If you're good enough, you can max out with 999,999 points—trust us, it can be done.

The ride is packed with Universal in-jokes. Keep a sharp eye out for an alien seated on a park bench, hiding behind a newspaper. The head on a stick that the alien uses as a disguise bears an uncanny resemblance to Steven Spielberg, executive producer of the Men in Black films.

Visitors who are susceptible to motion sickness should heed this warning from a Missouri City, Texas, reader:

> This ride was WAY TOO MUCH fast spinning for me. I definitely got dizzy on that one.

Avoid a long wait and ride during the first 2 hours the park is open, or try the single-rider line if you don't mind splitting your group. However, the singles and Express queues skip the preshow, which is worth seeing at least once. You can re-ride by following the signs for the child swap at the top of the exit stairs.

If it isn't too busy, ask the attendant out front if you can have a free **immigration tour.** If you're lucky, they'll take you into the large preshow room below the queue, where you can take selfies sitting at an agent's desk and get a close-up look at the animatronic alien twins.

SPRINGFIELD: HOME OF THE SIMPSONS

BUTTING UP AGAINST Men in Black's modernist architecture is Springfield: Home of the Simpsons, the setting of the long-running animated sitcom *The Simpsons*. What started as just The Simpsons Ride and Kwik-E-Mart store was hugely expanded in 2013, with a fabulous re-creation of Moe's Tavern, the Jebediah Springfield statue (emblazoned with A NOBLE SPIRIT EMBIGGENS THE SMALLEST MAN), and other cartoon landmarks. Springfield, which has long been a de facto land unto itself but was still wedded to World Expo on park maps, officially gained its independence in 2016 in the park's little-noticed answer to Brexit.

Kang & Kodos' Twirl 'n' Hurl (*Universal Express*) ★★★

APPEAL BY AGE	PRESCHOOL ★★★★½	GRADE SCHOOL ★★★★	TEENS ★★★½
YOUNG ADULTS ★★★½	OVER 30 ★★★	SENIORS ★★½	

What it is Spinning ride. **Scope and scale** Minor attraction. **When to go** After The Simpsons Ride. **Comments** Child swap available (see page 188). Rarely has a long wait. The world's wittiest spinner. **Duration of ride** 1½ minutes. **Average wait in line per 100 people ahead of you** 21 minutes. **Loading speed** Slow.

DESCRIPTION AND COMMENTS The Twirl 'n' Hurl is primarily eye candy for Springfield, USF's *Simpsons*-themed area. Think of it as Dumbo with Bart's sense of humor: guests ride around in little flying saucers while the alien narrators, Kang and Kodos, hold pictures of *Simpsons* characters. Make the characters speak and spin by steering your craft to the proper altitude. All the while, Kang exhorts you (loudly) to destroy Springfield and makes insulting comments about humans. Preschoolers enjoy the ride, while older kids and *Simpsons* fans crack up over the gags.

TOURING TIPS Twirl 'n' Hurl rarely attracts long lines, but (like all rides in this style) it can be very slow loading. If you want to enjoy the jokes without the wait, you can easily hear them all from the sidelines. If you have folks who are hot to ride, get them on whenever there are 50 or fewer guests in line. Try before 11 a.m. It should take awhile for most guests to arrive in Springfield, especially with Diagon Alley, Transformers, and Despicable Me keeping guests busy elsewhere.

Twirl 'n' Hurl may stop running early on nights when the seasonal evening lagoon show starts before park closing, so as not to distract from the show.

The Simpsons Ride *(Universal Express)* ★★★★

| APPEAL BY AGE | PRESCHOOL ★★★ | GRADE SCHOOL ★★★★ | TEENS ★★★★ |
| YOUNG ADULTS ★★★★ | OVER 30 ★★★½ | SENIORS ★★★½ |

Motion Sickness

What it is Mega-simulator ride. **Scope and scale** Super-headliner. **When to go** During the first 2 hours the park is open or after 4 p.m. **Comments** 40" minimum height requirement; not recommended for pregnant women or people prone to motion sickness; child swap available (see page 188). Despicable Me Minion Mayhem with attitude; not to be missed. **Duration of ride** 4½ minutes, plus preshow. **Average wait in line per 100 people ahead of you** 5 minutes. **Loading speed** Moderate.

DESCRIPTION AND COMMENTS Another animated film coupled to a motion simulator, The Simpsons Ride is as much a satire of theme parks as it is a high-speed thrill ride through the Fox animated series that is now TV's longest-running sitcom. Featuring the voices of Dan Castellaneta (Homer), Julie Kavner (Marge), Nancy Cartwright (Bart), Yeardley Smith (Lisa), and other cast members, the attraction uses a visit to Krustyland—the absurdly unsafe amusement park owned by the show's cantankerous Krusty the Clown—as an excuse to skewer Disney, SeaWorld, and even Universal itself.

The queue area and preshows involve *Simpsons* video clips (both classic and newly created) that help define the characters for guests who are unfamiliar with the TV show and that mock virtually every classic Disney attraction from The Haunted Mansion (here as the Haunted Condo, with "999 unhappy teen employees") to *Hall of Presidents* (redone as *Hall of the Secretaries of the Interior*—wait time 0 minutes). Not even ride-safety videos are spared; The Simpsons's version is an outrageous gore-fest starring Itchy and Scratchy demonstrating how *not* to behave.

The attraction itself recycled the foundations of Universal's former Back to the Future ride; watch the queue video for a time-traveling cameo by Doc Brown. The simulator is similar to Star Tours at Disney's Hollywood Studios and Despicable Me Minion Mayhem (see page 263), but with a larger curved screen more like that of Soarin' at Epcot. The ride vehicles hold eight guests in two rows of four.

The story line has the conniving Sideshow Bob secretly arriving at Krustyland, the aforementioned amusement park, and plotting his revenge on Krusty and Bart for sending him to jail. Sideshow Bob gets even by making things go wrong with the attractions that the Simpsons (and you) are riding. While there are dozens of dips, turns, climbs, and drops during the ride, there are probably hundreds of one-liners and visual puns. Like the show on which it's based, The Simpsons Ride definitely has an edge and operates on several levels. There will be jokes and visuals that you'll get but will fly over your children's heads—and most assuredly vice versa.

TOURING TIPS Because the screen you sit in front of is a giant curved dome, anyone sitting outside the central sweet spot gets a distorted view, which may aggravate motion sickness. For the best experience, ask the attendant at the bottom of the ramps for Level 2, and then ask the next attendant you see for Room 6. Taller guests (6 feet or over) should sit in the front row to avoid bumping their heads.

As far as motion simulators go, The Simpsons Ride isn't as sickness-inducing as many. The wider screen seems to help, as this mom from Huntington, New York, said:

> I'm not a fan of wild motion simulators, but I was fine on this ride. The field of vision makes it very engrossing, like Soarin'. However, our family still rates Star Tours higher than The Simpsons Ride, as participating in the Star Tours simulation was most like actually being a character in the original Star Wars movie!

Though not as rough and jerky as its predecessor, The Simpsons Ride is a long way from being tame. Skip it if you're an expectant mom or prone to motion sickness. Some parents may find the humor too coarse for younger kids.

WOODY WOODPECKER'S KIDZONE

NAMED AFTER THE CLASSIC Walter Lantz cartoon character, Woody Woodpecker's KidZone is situated in a colorful cul-de-sac between Hollywood and World Expo. KidZone holds most of the park's child-themed attractions, including a pint-size roller coaster and several elaborate playgrounds.

KidZone nearly closed last year to make room for Super Nintendo World, featuring an interactive Mario Kart racing ride, a Donkey Kong Country roller coaster that seems to sail off of its rails, and numerous areas inspired by old-school console favorites to explore. However, that project appears to have been pushed off to the new theme park that Universal is developing on its expansion property, and different family-friendly themes—including Nintendo's Pokémon and DreamWorks' *Trolls*—are currently under consideration for KidZone's future. In the meantime, the SpongeBob SquarePants store, the *Animal Actors* stage, and E.T. Adventure appear to be safe, but the rest of the attractions are likely to join Jimmy Neutron and Biff Tannen in Universal's retirement home.

Animal Actors on Location! (Universal Express)   ★★★½

APPEAL BY AGE	PRESCHOOL ★★★½	GRADE SCHOOL ★★★★½	TEENS ★★★★
YOUNG ADULTS ★★★★	OVER 30 ★★★★	SENIORS ★★★★	

What it is Animal tricks and comedy show. **Scope and scale** Major attraction. **When to go** After you've experienced all rides. **Comment** Cute li'l critters. **Duration of show** 25 minutes. **Probable waiting time** None.

DESCRIPTION AND COMMENTS *Animal Actors on Location!* is a live show featuring performing dogs, birds, pigs, and a menagerie of other animals in a covered outdoor stadium. This show integrates video segments with live sketches, jokes, and animal tricks performed onstage. A human trainer acts as the host, explaining how the animals are conditioned to execute the tricks. Several of the animal thespians are veterans of TV and movies; many were rescued from shelters. The demonstration usually makes use of audience volunteers (mostly children) in a couple of segments. Sit in the center of the stadium about halfway up for the best chance to be selected.

If you've seen *Up! A Great Bird Adventure Show* at Disney's Animal Kingdom, you'll recognize many of the bird routines in *Animal Actors*. What sets *Animal Actors* apart is the use of varied and unusual kinds of animals, as well as the opportunity to see the animals being trained onstage. Pet owners (and parents) will note that the animals are trained using only positive reinforcement—that is, rewarding the animal when it performs the correct behavior—and no negative reinforcement (punishing for incorrect behavior).

TOURING TIPS Check the daily entertainment schedule for showtimes. You shouldn't have any trouble getting into the next performance. The stadium is covered but not enclosed, meaning that it is still hot during summer and cold during winter. Come to the front of the stage at the conclusion to snap a photo with some of the furry stars.

Curious George Goes to Town ★★½

APPEAL BY AGE	PRESCHOOL ★★★★½	GRADE SCHOOL ★★★★	TEENS ★★★
YOUNG ADULTS ★★	OVER 30 ★★★		SENIORS ★½

What it is Interactive playground. **Scope and scale** Minor attraction. **When to go** Anytime. **Comments** *The* place for rambunctious kids.

DESCRIPTION AND COMMENTS This interactive playground exemplifies the Universal obsession with wet stuff; in addition to innumerable spigots, pipes, and spray guns, two giant roof-mounted buckets periodically dump a thousand gallons of water on unsuspecting visitors below. Kids who want to stay dry can mess around in the foam-ball playground, also equipped with chutes, tubes, and ball blasters.

TOURING TIPS Visit after you've experienced all the major attractions.

A Day in the Park with Barney (Universal Express) ★★★

APPEAL BY AGE	PRESCHOOL ★★★★	GRADE SCHOOL ★★★	TEENS ★½
YOUNG ADULTS ★★½	OVER 30 ★★	SENIORS ★★★	

What it is Live-character stage show. **Scope and scale** Major children's attraction. **When to go** Scheduled showtimes. **Comments** A great hit with preschoolers. **Duration of show** 20 minutes, plus 5-minute preshow and character greeting after the show. **Probable waiting time** None.

DESCRIPTION AND COMMENTS Barney—the cuddly purple dinosaur of public-TV fame—leads his sidekicks Baby Bop and BJ in an audience sing-along of toddler classics, including "If You're Happy and You Know It" and "I Love You, You Love Me." A short preshow featuring a live actor playing Mr. Peek-a-boo gets the kids lathered up before they enter Barney's Park (the theater). The characters are supplemented with props—including cartoon cows, pigs, ducks, and skunks—during some of the songs. Interesting theatrical effects include wind, falling leaves, clouds and stars in the simulated sky, and faux snow.

After the show, Barney sometimes hangs out for a brief postshow dance party, where you can snap a selfie with the whole dino herd. On other days, Barney and a pal can be found posing for photos with parents and children in the indoor playground at the theater exit.

TOURING TIPS If your child likes Barney, this show is a must. There's also a great indoor play area nearby, designed especially for wee tykes. In the weeks around Christmas, this show becomes *A Barney Holiday Show,* featuring a cameo from Frosty the Snowman.

E.T. Adventure *(Universal Express)*   ★★★½

What it is Indoor adventure ride based on the beloved movie. **Scope and scale** Major attraction. **When to go** Within 30 minutes of ride opening or late afternoon. **Comments** 34″ minimum height requirement; child swap available (see page 188). A long, strange, happy trip. **Duration of ride** 4½ minutes. **Average wait in line per 100 people ahead of you** 5 minutes. **Loading speed** Moderate.

DESCRIPTION AND COMMENTS Inspired by Steven Spielberg's classic 1982 film (and the not-so-classic 1985 sequel novel *Book of the Green Planet*), this is the only ride at Universal that's remained essentially unchanged since opening day. Guests board bicycle-like ride vehicles (suspended from the ceiling) on an adventure returning everyone's favorite Extra-Terrestrial from Earth to his dying home planet.

After a brief video introduction from Mr. Spielberg himself, guests provide their first name to an attendant and receive a credit card–size interplanetary passport (more on this later) before wending their way through a dark forest of tall pine trees; this is one of the most evocative indoor ride queues in any park. As the ride itself starts, you're weaving through the woods, evading the moon-suited scientists and earthly law-enforcement officials trying to capture E.T. As in the film, you're airborne soon enough, flying your way over Los Angeles (a lovely tableau) and into a warp tunnel to E.T.'s home planet. You arrive just in time to allow E.T.'s healing touch to save everything, and the ride ends in a mash-up of colorful flowers, lighting, and aliens. Concerning the latter, where E.T. is reunited with family and friends, Len Testa likens it to *The Wizard of Oz*'s Technicolor transition, only restaged with a cave full of naked mole rats. (C'mon, Len, where's the love?)

Before you return home, E.T. bids each rider farewell by name, thanks to those passports you received earlier. The speech system was overhauled in 2014, allowing E.T. to say more than 20,000 names (though he misidentifies riders more often than not). A Baton, North Carolina, reader with perhaps too much time on his hands got to wondering:

> *Why do the inhabitants of E.T.'s home planet, who presumably have never visited Earth, speak better English than he does?*

While the attraction's premise is good, its sophistication has lost some luster over its almost 30-year run. The human animatronics in the first half look laughably like dime-store dummies, and some of E.T.'s pals in the acid-soaked second act are downright disturbing with their out-of-sync facial animation. Even so, because E.T. is one of Universal's only family-friendly dark rides that relies on sets and robotics instead of screens—a type of attraction the resort could use more of—we hope it sticks around for a long time to come.

TOURING TIPS Most preschoolers and grade-school children love E.T. We think it's worth a 20- to 30-minute wait, but no longer than that. The ride often doesn't open until 10 a.m., and lines build quickly within 30 minutes of opening; waits can reach 2 hours on busy days. Ride in the morning or late afternoon. On peak days, a time-saving single-rider line is occasionally opened.

A mother from Columbus, Ohio, writes about horrendous lines at E.T.:

> *The line for E.T. took 2 hours! The rest of the family waiting outside thought that we had really gone to E.T.'s planet.*

Fievel's Playland ★★★

APPEAL BY AGE PRESCHOOL ★★★★★ GRADE SCHOOL ★★★★½ TEENS ★★★½
YOUNG ADULTS   ★★★★   OVER 30   ★★½   SENIORS   ★★★★

What it is Children's play area with waterslide. **Scope and scale** Minor attraction. **When to go** Anytime. **Comment** A much-needed attraction for preschoolers. **Probable waiting time** 20–30 minutes for the waterslide; otherwise, none. **Loading speed** Slow for the waterslide.

DESCRIPTION AND COMMENTS A great place for the little ones to blow off some steam. The idea behind this whimsical playground is that you've been shrunk to the size of *An American Tail*'s rodent protagonist and let loose to explore the detritus in an Old West town. The playground features ordinary household items reproduced on a giant scale, as a mouse would experience them. Kids can climb nets, walk through a huge boot or 1,000-gallon cowboy hat, splash in a sardine-can fountain, sway along elevated wooden bridges, seesaw on huge spoons, and clamber onto a cow skull.

Most of the playground is reserved for preschoolers and grade-schoolers, but a combo waterslide and raft ride is open to all ages. The rafts of the three-story water-slide hold two people, so you should start faking that old war/football/child-bearing back injury to other adults in your group as soon as you get near the playland. You will get wet.

TOURING TIPS Most of Fievel's Playland requires no waiting, so you can visit anytime and stay as long as you want. Most of the play sets are designed for kids old enough to run, climb, and slide by themselves.

The waterslide is extremely slow-loading and carries only 300 riders per hour. During warmer months, it's possible for the waterslide to develop a wait of 20–30 minutes, and Express Passes are not honored. We don't think the 16-second ride is worth that kind of wait. If riding the slide is important to your child, try visiting right after lunch or dinner, when many other families are still eating.

Lack of shade is a major shortcoming of the entire attraction—the playground is scorching during the heat of the day.

Woody Woodpecker's Nuthouse Coaster *(Universal Express)* ★★½

APPEAL BY AGE PRESCHOOL ★★★★½ GRADE SCHOOL ★★★★ TEENS ★★★
YOUNG ADULTS   ★★★   OVER 30   ★★★   SENIORS   ★★★★

What it is Kids' roller coaster. **Scope and scale** Minor attraction. **When to go** Anytime. **Comments** 36" minimum height requirement; children 36"–48" must be accompanied by a supervising companion; child swap available (see page 188). A suitable starter thrill ride. **Duration of ride** 1 minute. **Average wait in line per 100 people ahead of you** 5 minutes. **Loading speed** *Slooow*.

DESCRIPTION AND COMMENTS Woody Woodpecker's Nuthouse Coaster is a short, relatively low roller coaster designed to introduce small children to this kind of amusement park ride. The Nuthouse Coaster is small enough for kids to enjoy but sturdy enough for adults, though its moderate speed might unnerve some smaller children (the minimum height to ride is 36 inches). The entire ride lasts about a minute, and at least 20 of those 60 seconds is spent cranking the train up the first (and only) lift hill. There are several tight turns, but the ride doesn't go upside down or even come close.

TOURING TIPS Visit after you've experienced all the major attractions. If your young child has never before experienced a roller coaster, this would be an appropriate first attempt.

HOLLYWOOD

THE HOLLYWOOD AREA RE-CREATES the glamour and energy of Southern California from the 1930s through the 1950s. Several areas surrounding Hollywood, including Beverly Hills and the Hollywood Hills, are represented. The faux Garden of Allah Villas (famed home of F. Scott Fitzgerald, Marlene Dietrich, and other Hollywood golden age legends), which were some of the best themed buildings in either park, have been converted into an **NBC Media Center** (see page 253), eliminating a convenient shortcut to KidZone.

Spy Stunt Show (opens 2019)

What it is Spy-themed stunt show. **Scope and scale** Major attraction. **When to go** Scheduled showtimes; after you've experienced all rides. **Comment** May frighten young children.

DESCRIPTION AND COMMENTS The long-running *Terminator 2: 3-D* attraction closed October 8, 2017, and will be replaced in 2019 with a new live-action experience inspired by a "high-energy Universal franchise." At press time, Universal had not officially confirmed the new attraction's theme, but all signs point to a stunt show inspired by Jason Bourne, the amnesiac super-spy portrayed onscreen by Matt Damon.

TOURING TIPS The previous show in this venue accommodated more than 700 patrons per performance, so its replacement should have similar capacity. Save it for the afternoon when the rides become crowded. Parents of young children should be aware that, while there won't be much blood and guts, they should expect the show to feature violent fisticuffs and loud firearms.

Universal Orlando's Horror Make-Up Show
(*Universal Express*) ★★★★½

APPEAL BY AGE	PRESCHOOL ★★★½	GRADE SCHOOL ★★★★	TEENS ★★★★½
YOUNG ADULTS ★★★★★	OVER 30 ★★★★½	SENIORS ★★★★½	

What it is Theater presentation on the art of makeup. **Scope and scale** Major attraction. **When to go** Scheduled showtimes; after you've experienced all rides. **Comments** May frighten young children. A gory knee-slapper; not to be missed. **Duration of show** 25 minutes. **Probable waiting time** None.

DESCRIPTION AND COMMENTS The *Horror Make-Up Show* is a brief but humorous look at how basic monster-movie special effects are done. The show includes onstage demonstrations of effects, such as blood-spurting fake knives and rubber limbs, plus how mechanical effects are combined with latex masks to transform human heads into wolf-shaped skulls. The hosts pay tribute to Universal makeup pioneers such as Lon Chaney, Jack Pierce, Tom Savini, and Rick Baker, while also poking fun at some of the studio's less successful spooks. Film clips are interspersed throughout the presentation, showing how computer-generated special effects are blended into live-action films like Tom Cruise's 2017 reboot of *The Mummy*. The finale involves an audience volunteer and a remote-controlled creature that isn't all he appears.

This may be Universal's most entertaining live show. While there's plenty of fake blood thrown around, the script is much more funny than scary funny. The hosts keep everything moving along at a fast pace (except when they start to improv and crack each other up like the old Carol Burnett show), and their running commentary about horror-filmmaking is interspersed with plenty of pop-culture jokes for the kids, along with some surprisingly subversive stabs at the hand that feeds them; after offering a dry towel to a damp volunteer, they'll demand cash, smiling, "Welcome to Orlando!"

TOURING TIPS The *Horror Make-Up Show* is the sleeper attraction at Universal, and one of the only theme park comedy shows we can watch over and over again. Its humor and tongue-in-cheek style transcend the gruesome effects, and most folks (including preschoolers) take the blood and guts in stride. But it's the exception that proves the rule, as this reader relates:

> My 7- and 9-year-olds were scared by the Horror Make-Up Show (despite me telling them that the guy was not really cutting any-one's arm off!). We ended up leaving before the show was over.

And from a New Orleans family:

> My husband and I really enjoyed the humor; it was just corny enough. The special effects with the audience member were pretty cool, and we thought the whole thing was fun. My kids were not quite as taken with this show. My son (5) hid his face against my arm most of the time, and my daughter (10) had her hands over her eyes a lot. The video montage of horror clips was especially upset-ting to them. As we were leaving the theater, they both commented that the show was really scary, and they didn't like it.

A good test is to take your child into the theater lobby between shows, where display cases filled with bloody props and monster masks act as a mini-museum of Universal horror history from *The Hunchback of Notre Dame* to *Hellboy.* If the static severed heads here send your kid into hysterics, the show itself may have you pay-ing therapy bills for decades to come.

Look for the second-story windows to the left of the theater marquee for a touching tribute to victims of the Pulse nightclub tragedy.

LIVE ENTERTAINMENT *at* UNIVERSAL STUDIOS FLORIDA

IN ADDITION TO THE SHOWS profiled previously, USF offers two major daily outdoor entertainments, along with a wide range of smaller street performances.

Costumed comic book and cartoon characters (Shrek and Don-key, SpongeBob SquarePants, Transformers) pose with guests at orga-nized meet and greets that are marked on the park maps. Others, like Scooby-Doo, along with look-alikes of movie stars (both living and deceased), roam the Hollywood and Front Lot areas for photo ops. See page 191 for more character information.

The Studio Brass Band (★★★) performs familiar TV and movie theme songs in a funky, high-energy style. You'll see them in the morn-ing as you enter, set up on the corner near the Hello Kitty shop. Show-times are listed in the map and usually end by early afternoon. The band may take five during slow seasons.

In New York and San Francisco several small-scale shows entertain the crowds. ***The Blues Brothers Show*** (★★★½) is a 12-minute rhythm and blues concert. Held on the corner of the New York area, across from the lagoon, *The Blues Brothers Show* features Jake and Elwood performing a few of the hit songs from the classic 1980 movie musical, including "Soul Man" and "Shake a Tail Feather." The brothers are joined on stage by Jazz the saxophone player and Mabel the waitress, who belts an Aretha Franklin cover to start the show.

Blues Brothers is one of the better musical performances in the Studios. The singers have captured many of the movie's dance moves and vocal styles, and the music's tempo keeps everyone's toes tapping. The concert is a great pick-me-up, and the short running time keeps the energy high. During the holiday season, a special *Blues Brothers Holiday Show* is performed, featuring songs such as "Blue Christmas" and "Run Rudolph Run," sung around a festive tree festooned with beer cans and cigarette packs. It's even better than the regular show.

Marilyn Monroe and the Diamond Bellas (★★½) perform a 4-minute song and dance routine (anachronistically lip-synched to the *Moulin Rouge* cover of her signature song) in front of the Macy's facade, followed by a photo op. Nearby, the ***Sing It!*** (★★½) show is an a cappella "competition" loosely inspired by the riff-off scene in *Pitch Perfect,* featuring earworm pop tunes performed by powerful vocalists. The **Beat Builders** (★★★) are a quartet of beefy guys who hang out on the scaffolding outside Louie's Italian Restaurant and turn their construction equipment into percussion instruments, in the tradition of *Stomp.*

All of these shows have performance times listed in the park map, and most are not worth going out of your way for. If you aren't on a tight touring plan and see one starting as you walk by, stop and watch until you get bored, but don't be surprised if some have been retired by the time you read this.

During peak seasons, you may find the **Street Breakz** (★★½) break-dancing corps demonstrating its skills in Hollywood or Woody Woodpecker's KidZone or a troupe of gymnasts in a random spot; it's impossible to say what kind of acts Universal will pull out when the parks get packed.

Universal Orlando's Cinematic Celebration (seasonal)
★★★★

APPEAL BY AGE	PRESCHOOL ★★★★½	GRADE SCHOOL ★★★★½	TEENS ★★★★★
YOUNG ADULTS ★★★★½	OVER 30 ★★★★½	SENIORS ★★★★	

What it is Fireworks, dancing fountains, and movies. **Scope and scale** Major attraction. **When to go** 1 show a day, usually at park closing. **Comments** Presented seasonally, when the park is open after dark. **Duration of show** 19 minutes. **Probable waiting time** None.

DESCRIPTION AND COMMENTS This is USF's big new nighttime event, shown on the lagoon in the middle of the Studios. The presentation pays tribute to favorite franchises featured around Universal's parks, including Jurassic World, Despicable Me, Transformers, and Fast & Furious. The scenes are projected onto multiple enormous "screens" made by spraying water from the lagoon into the air (similar to *World of Color* at Disney California Adventure), which are augmented by more than 120 illuminated fountains.

Highlights of the show include Harry Potter defeating a pack of Dementors with his Patronus; E.T.'s spaceship blasting into space; and a joyful Justin Timberlake tune from *Trolls*. (References to Kung Fu Panda and How to Train Your Dragon may be hinting at future attractions.) Each film series is showcased for a few minutes, before Gru and his Minions kick off a grand finale, gathering all of the characters together. Fireworks are deployed sparingly, in deference to the residential neighborhood across the street, but projection mapping (which makes the New York building facades appear to freeze or burst into flames) is used to good effect, as are moving lights and lasers.

Cinematic Celebration is easily the best nighttime show USF has offered in this century, and it's well worth sticking around until closing time to see it. While it isn't as breathtaking as Magic Kingdom's *Happily Ever After,* it's more exciting and accessible than *Rivers of Light* at Animal Kingdom, and better paced than Disney's Hollywood Studios' *Fantasmic.*

TOURING TIPS The terraced Central Park across the lagoon from San Francisco is the primary viewing location for this show, with additional viewing between Mel's and Transformers and near Duff Brewery. No reservations are required, and you should be able to get a good view by arriving about 15 minutes before showtime. The grassy field in the rear of Central Park provides the best perspective on the widescreen presentation.

Universal's Superstar Parade ★★★½

APPEAL BY AGE	PRESCHOOL	★★★★	GRADE SCHOOL	★★★½	TEENS	★★½
YOUNG ADULTS	★★★	OVER 30	★★★	SENIORS	★★★½	

What it is Parade with animated characters. **Scope and scale** Major attraction. **When to go** Check daily entertainment schedule for parade and showtimes. **Comments** Colorful but inconvenient. **Duration of presentation** 15–20 minutes. **Probable waiting time** None.

DESCRIPTION AND COMMENTS Universal's Superstar Parade features dancers and performers, four large and elaborate floats inspired by cartoons, and a very mixed bag of street-prowling Universal characters. The featured franchises are Dora the Explorer (with acrobatic monkeys swinging from her float); SpongeBob SquarePants (accompanied by a phalanx of in-line skating fish); Max, Duke, and their furry friends from The Secret Life of Pets movies (riding in a New York City apartment–size float filled with animatronic animals); and Gru's whole Despicable Me crew, from his adopted daughters to the adorable yellow Minions. The parade is not very long, but it stops twice—once in New York near Louie's Italian Restaurant and Revenge of the Mummy and again in Hollywood between the Hello Kitty store and Mel's Drive-In—for a highly choreographed ensemble number. Though impressive in its scope and coordination, the performance is well-nigh impossible to take in from any given viewing spot.

The parade, marked in the park map, begins at the Esoteric Pictures gate in Hollywood between *Universal Orlando's Horror Make-Up Show* and Cafe La Bamba. It turns right, then immediately makes a hard left around Mel's Drive-In, and follows the waterfront past Transformers toward San Francisco. From there it turns left at Louie's Italian Restaurant and proceeds along Fifth Avenue, past Revenge of the Mummy. At the end of Fifth Avenue, the parade takes a left onto 57th Avenue/Plaza of the Stars and heads toward the front of the park, where it makes another left onto Hollywood Boulevard, from whence it disappears backstage through the gate where it entered.

The same floats used in the parade are trotted out individually to the Character Party Zone (located in Hollywood at the corner near Mel's Drive-In) at scheduled times in the late morning and early afternoon for mini-shows and character meet and greets. These are a much better opportunity than the parade itself for your kids to get up close and personal with their favorite character.

TOURING TIPS The best viewing spots are along Fifth Avenue, on the front steps of faux buildings in New York. The wheelchair viewing area is in front of the Macy's facade. If you miss part of the parade in the New York area, you can scoot along the waterfront to Mel's Drive-In and catch it as it comes down Hollywood Boulevard. If, after watching the parade on the New York streets, you plan to leave the park, you can use the same route to access Hollywood Boulevard and the park exit before the parade arrives.

SPECIAL EVENTS *at*
UNIVERSAL STUDIOS FLORIDA

BEYOND ITS YEAR-ROUND OFFERINGS, USF also hosts some of the best seasonal events in the theme park industry, and most of them are included with any regular admission (including annual passes). For those events that aren't—Rock the Universe and Halloween Horror Nights—you'll need to purchase a separate ticket, and daytime Universal Express Passes (including those offered with hotel rooms) won't be honored.

ROCK THE UNIVERSE *(early February)*

UNIVERSAL ORLANDO BILLS Rock the Universe, its annual weekend of fist-pumping praise rock-and-roller coasters, as "Florida's biggest Christian music festival." This hard-ticket after-hours event attracts hordes of surprisingly rowdy church youth groups, who get access to the parks starting at 4 p.m. and keep boogying for the Lord until 1 a.m. It used to be held in September at the same time as Disney's eerily similar (and now extinct) Night of Joy event but was rescheduled to February for 2019.

Concerts take place across three stages inside Universal Studios Florida and start after the park closes to day guests at 6 p.m. Past acts have included Skillet, Jesus Culture, Lecrae, TobyMac, For King & Country, Family Force 5, Lauren Daigle, and Casting Crowns. Most of the park's thrill rides (*except* Diagon Alley) operate during Rock the Universe, and Hollywood Rip Ride Rockit is reprogrammed with Christian rock songs. There's also a Saturday night candle-lighting ceremony and a Sunday morning worship service in the *Fear Factor Live* stadium (we always pray at that show).

Single-night tickets start around $69, with a weekend pass with daytime park-to-park access Friday–Sunday going for about $169 for two-park access, or $219 including Volcano Bay. Attendees can buy discounted Rock Your Weekend tickets that combine both event nights with daytime park tickets. Universal Express Passes run an additional $20–$30 per night. Youth group leaders get a free ticket for every 10 their charges purchase, plus free access to Universal Express ride queues and lounges with free snacks. Learn more at rocktheuniverse.com.

MARDI GRAS *(early February–mid-April)*

YOU ARE NO DOUBT FAMILIAR with the gigantic Mardi Gras celebration in New Orleans, or at least the idea of it. Well, Universal Studios has a yearly festival as well. Sure, it's not quite as bawdy as its French Quarter compatriot, but it is exceedingly fun and probably a better event to bring the kids along.

Mardi Gras originated in the religious observation of Fat Tuesday (the literal translation of the name), which is the day before Ash Wednesday on the Catholic calendar and the start of Lent's 40 days of dietary restrictions. People bid "farewell to flesh" with a carnival where they indulge in the meat and drink they are about to forswear. Mardi Gras is the New Orleans variation on this tradition—which is echoed in other cities from Venice to Rio de Janeiro.

Over the centuries, the religious significance has been stripped away, and most Mardi Gras revelers attend for strictly secular reasons—namely, epic quantities of booze, beads, and bare breasts. Universal took a look at the festivities and said, "This will make a fine family-friendly event"—minus the bare breasts, of course—and amazingly it is. But that doesn't mean that it's inauthentic. Much like Universal partnered with Macy's for its holiday parade, Universal engages Kern Studios, the same company that's been building floats for the real deal since 1932, to create the park's parade platforms. And musicians and recipes imported from the Big Easy add to the French Quarter feel. Of course, the real Bourbon Street doesn't have concerts from big-name recording artists after the parade (on select nights), much less a high-speed roller coaster cruising by in the background.

In addition to the parade and headliner concerts, Universal carves a miniature Bourbon Street out of its New York back lot. Chef Steven Jayson and his culinary team pride themselves on the authentic N'awlins flavors they bring to the French Quarter Courtyard, an area between Revenge of the Mummy and Transformers, with temporary food and beverage booths that open at 4 p.m. each Mardi Gras concert night. The jambalaya, andouille sausage, and beignets are all pretty good. You can eat to the beat and enjoy live blues and zydeco musicians from Louisiana busking on the French Quarter corners. Universal started this tradition more than a decade ago to support New Orleans artists in the wake of Hurricane Katrina.

In 2019 the good times roll every evening February 9–April 4. Viewing of the parade and concerts are included with any valid admission, and all annual pass holders are admitted in the evening, except Seasonal Pass holders who are blocked out on concert nights. For more information, visit tinyurl.com/unimardigras.

Mardi Gras Parade

Universal's version of a Mardi Gras parade includes the crazy characters of the New Orleans version but is much more compact. Floats are updated every year with new themes—2018's additions were inspired by astrological constellations, from Virgo the Maiden to Orion the Hunter—but you can always count on the massive King Gator float and multistory Riverboat to roll down Universal's boulevards. The floats are each accompanied by dozens of strolling performers and stilt walkers, while costumed revelers ride upon them and toss colorful plastic beads to the crowds below.

The parade typically follows the same route as the daily Superstar Parade but in reverse, starting and ending at Hollywood's Esoteric Pictures gate near the *Horror Make-Up Show* and traveling clockwise around New York and the waterfront.

Viewing Tips: The parade takes about 15 minutes to pass by any one spot, and it lasts around 45 minutes. The parade generally begins at 7:45 p.m. Times may vary with operating hours, so check the park map for details. You can find good viewing anywhere along the parade route, and unless you insist on standing right up front, there's no need to save your spot more than 10 or 15 minutes in advance.

Special reserved viewing areas are also available for annual pass holders (near Mel's Drive-In), American Express card holders (across from Hollywood's Brown Derby), guests with disabilities (near Macy's in New York), and young Little Jesters and their families (in front of the Brown Derby).

If you really want to get in on the action, it's possible to volunteer as a bead-tossing float rider. Annual pass holders can sign up for themselves and a guest online; you must RSVP at least one week in advance. Slots are also saved for on-site resort guests; watch Universal's website for preregistration or inquire at your hotel's Ticket Center. If space is available, additional riders may be recruited from park guests in the afternoon. Some years, American Express members who used their card to purchase multiday admission are invited to ride the floats; receipt to prove purchase is required. All riders must be at least 18 years old (or accompanied by an adult) and 48 inches tall; space is limited and availability is not guaranteed.

Mardi Gras Live Concerts

Every Saturday night (and select Sundays) during the Mardi Gras event, after the parade concludes (approximately 45 minutes after it begins), a big-name concert kicks off on Music Plaza Stage underneath Hollywood Rip Ride Rockit. The concerts are a definite highlight of Universal's Mardi Gras celebration. With dozens of great musical acts entertaining the crowd at no extra cost, there is really no downside to these fantastic concerts, other than the extraordinary crowds that popular artists can draw. To get an idea of the quality of the acts, performers in recent years have included heavyweights from the past—The Beach Boys; Olivia Newton-John; Foreigner; Earth, Wind & Fire; REO Speedwagon; and Kool & the Gang—and present, such as Fifth Harmony, Macklemore, Jason Derulo, Jessie J, Yandel, and Phillip Phillips. In addition to the headliners, Universal also imports authentic New Orleans musicians to perform near the French Quarter stalls before the big show. (Musicians and limited food options are still offered on non-concert event nights.)

Viewing Tips: There is no additional charge for Mardi Gras concerts; they are included with park admission. All concerts are standing-room only and first come, first served; crowds can be enormous, and folks sometimes start lining up shortly after park opening for the hottest acts. There is no extra-cost VIP area available, but there is an ADA-accessible viewing section near the Race Through New York restrooms. Large video screens broadcast the stage to those standing in the far back, so consider watching from the New York Battery Park area if you aren't an überfan of the artist.

HALLOWEEN HORROR NIGHTS
(mid-September–early November)

THE GODFATHER (or is that gorefather?) of all Universal Orlando seasonal events, Universal Orlando's Halloween Horror Nights (or HHN, as it's known to its legions of bloodthirsty fans) is recognized as the nation's most popular and industry-awarded haunted theme park event. Originally a locals-friendly filler during a normally slow season, USF's Halloween celebration started in 1991 as a single weekend of Fright Nights and proved popular enough to almost single-handedly save Universal's financial skin during the park's lean early years. Over the last quarter century, HHN has grown so famous that the seven-week-long scare-abration can provide a substantial percentage of USF's annual attendance statistics. Much like visiting any of Orlando's theme parks during a peak holiday season, an evening at HHN can be tremendous fun if you go in with a solid plan and sane expectations. Without those things . . . well, you might be better off eaten by zombies! This reader, who traveled all the way from Belgium to attend the event, summarizes the sentiments of many haunt fans:

> *Halloween Horror Nights is truly the world's premier Halloween event. I recommend it to any adult or teen who is a Halloween fan. I've been twice and will certainly do it again; it's worth the money!*

We've been attending HHN every year since 1996, and it has become one of our favorite after-dark activities in any park, but it isn't for everybody. Before attending, make sure that Universal's brand of Halloween is right for you; this ain't Mickey's Not-So-Scary Halloween Party. Halloween Horror Nights is a gory, gruesome bacchanalia of simulated violence and tasteless satire, marinated with a liberal dose of alcohol and rock-and-roll. In other words, it's a heck of a party as long as you know what you're getting into. If the idea of copious blood, guts, and booze doesn't appeal to you, we advise staying far, far away. Needless to say, it is not appropriate for young children, though you will likely see many there.

The three basic elements of each year's event are haunted houses (or mazes), outdoor scare zones, and theater shows. Universal also makes many of its regular rides available during HHN, including Harry Potter and the Escape from Gringotts (though not the Hogwarts Express) in The Wizarding World of Harry Potter—Diagon Alley.

Planning for Halloween Horror Nights

Even more so than daytime touring, a successful Halloween Horror Nights visit requires a careful date selection. In 2018 HHN was held on 36 select nights September 14–November 3; visit orlando.halloween horrornights.com for the operational calendar. In short, you want to avoid all Saturdays (especially the final three Saturdays leading up to Halloween) like the plague. Fridays in October—particularly the last two Fridays before Halloween—aren't much better. Wednesday nights are usually the least crowded, followed by Thursdays (especially the first two) and Sundays (especially the first, but excluding the last). Opening weekend brings out all the local fans, so your best bets are the last two weeks of September or the first week of October. Halloween night itself and any nights after it are often extremely quiet. The price of Express Passes on a given night (as listed at tinyurl.com/HHN Express) is your best guide to how busy it will be: the larger the cost, the larger the crowds.

If you walk up to the box office on the night of the event, you'll pay $114.99—a frightening sum for as little as 6½ hours in the park—and likely wait in a ridiculously long line for the privilege. Instead, study the myriad online ticket options in advance and purchase before you leave home.

Deep discounts (up to $52 off) are offered on advance purchases of date-specific tickets. If you don't know exactly which night you want to attend, advance flex tickets valid on any one Sunday–Friday cost $81.99 ($89.99 for Sunday–Saturday). Annual pass holders are entitled to even deeper price breaks (up to $58 off advance tickets) and early event entry during pass-holder parties on select nights during the opening weekends. If you already have daytime admission to a Universal park, you can purchase an add-on ticket at the park that allows you to remain through the evening's event for a discounted price, depending on the night.

Finally, if you are a hard-core haunt fan and are spending more than a night in the area, you'll want a Frequent Fear (valid every Sunday–Thursday event night, with Fridays included in the Plus version for an extra fee) or Rush of Fear (valid every event night through the first three weekends) multiday pass. Universal also offers an Ultimate Frequent Fear Pass valid every event night, in case you feel like spending more than the cost of an annual pass for a few weeks of scares. Multiday passes cost about $23 less online than at the gate and are even cheaper for annual pass holders. If you come for an evening and like what you see, any single-night ticket (except the free one included with Premier Annual Passes) can be upgraded to a seasonal pass before you depart.

*un*official **TIP**
You can buy a Rush of Fear ticket and upgrade it to an Ultimate Frequent Fear ticket on or before its expiration date.

Universal Orlando's paid line-skipping service is a welcome luxury during the day but an absolute lifesaver at night. On peak event nights, queues for the haunted houses will approach 3 hours, and even on the slowest nights, they will hit 60 minutes. HHN Express Passes reduce that wait to 25%–33% of what it would otherwise be, which can make the difference between experiencing two or three houses in a night to visiting seven or more. The only catch is that Express starts at $79.99 per person and goes up to more than $159 depending on the night. Express is also available as an add-on for Rush of Fear or Frequent Fear multinight passes. Express Passes often sell out and may be more expensive or unavailable inside the park, so if you do want them, buy in advance. On off-peak nights it is possible to experience all the haunted houses and at least one show without Express, if you arrive early and stay until closing. On peak nights it is virtually impossible to do the same without Express Passes, and can be challenging even with them.

If you're feeling particularly flush and are fed up with any kind of queue, the **RIP guided tour** will whisk you to the head of every line for $159.99–$349.99 depending on the night, admission not included; half-night tours may be available for half price. A private RIP tour for you and up to nine of your friends starts at $1,799 and goes up to $3,999 (again, admission not included). When money is no object, the RIP tours are highly recommended. Call ☎ 866-346-9350 or email vipexperience@universalorlando.com for pricing and reservations.

For the superfans with extra spending money, Universal offers a choice of in-depth HHN experiences. Join one of Universal's designers on daytime lights-on trips through three houses on each of the two **Unmasking the Horror behind-the-scenes tours** ($79.99 and up for one tour, $129.99 for both). On event nights, ticket holders can start their night with a $49.99 Scareactor dinner, which includes an all-you-can-eat buffet and monster meet and greet. These upgrades can be booked online at tinyurl.com/HHNExtras.

To arm yourself with knowledge before braving Halloween Horror Nights, visit the official website (orlando.halloweenhorrornights.com), along with the fan-run websites horrornightnightmares.com, hhncrypt .com, hhnrumors.com, and hhnunofficial.com.

Halloween Horror Nights Touring Tips

Please note that the following information is based on 2018's Halloween Horror Nights (HHN) event, though the essentials of the following advice should still serve you well in 2019.

The event officially begins each evening at 6:30 p.m., but the front gates typically open as early as 6 p.m. If you have an HHN ticket but not daytime admission, you'll want to be outside the park gates, ticket in hand, by 5:45 p.m. at the latest on slow nights, and as early as 5 p.m. on peak nights. Be sure to leave ample time for I-4 traffic and parking, which is full price until 10 p.m. Valet parking is available, but remember that there is no free or discounted valet for annual pass holders on event nights.

After navigating the security screening in the parking hub, your goal is to secure a spot as close to the USF turnstiles as possible; don't be shy about lining up at the temporary entry scanners at the center gate. On-site hotel guests also get their own exclusive entrance on the far right end of the USF arches. (Note that the Express Unlimited access included with some resort rooms is not valid during HHN.) Early arrivals may also get a view of a gate-opening performance, which usually occurs just inside the main entrance. Don't worry if you miss this minor event; it's a nice touch but not essential.

Better yet, get a jump on the general public outside the gates by being inside the park before they open. The park closes to daytime guests at 5 p.m. on event nights, but anyone holding a ticket for that night's HHN is allowed to remain inside the park in designated holding areas. Anyone can access this opportunity if they have any valid daytime park ticket, including annual pass holders.

Note that the park is officially open for regular operations until 5 p.m., but you'll want to enter before 4:30 p.m. to avoid dealing with the arriving evening crowds. Between the park's closing and reopening, guests remaining in the park are confined to one of the following locations:

- The **Springfield** section near Fast Food Boulevard features priority access to the first two haunted houses that open each evening. Guests in this area can queue for the two houses with entrances in Woody Woodpecker's KidZone between 5:30 and 5:45 p.m. Guests are released from the area around 6 p.m. and can be the first to queue for the houses near the MIB Gear shop. A limited selection of Simpsons food and drink is available here after daytime guests have exited. Note that on the first two weekends, this area is restricted to annual pass holders who have registered online for an exclusive pass-holder event, during which three houses are opened as early as 5:30 p.m.

- The **New York** holding area includes Finnegan's Bar and Grill, which offers a full bar and table-service food, though reservations aren't accepted and tables are virtually impossible to secure on event afternoons. Guests here are released around 5:45 p.m., giving them first crack at the soundstage houses.

- A small overflow holding area is located in **Hollywood** near the Hello Kitty shop. There is no food or beverage available here, but you do get early access to the soundstage closest to the park entrance (which tends to attract the longest lines later).

- Finally, **Diagon Alley** is not a holding area for HHN, and the Hogwarts Express train stops running in both directions as soon as USF's closing time arrives.

The haunted houses (expanded to 10 for 2018) are the signature attractions at HHN and quickly develop wait times ranging from moderate to absolutely ridiculous. Four haunted mazes are housed in the huge production soundstages located behind Hollywood Rip Ride Rockit; four are located in warehouses and large sprung tents erected backstage behind Springfield and World Expo; one is wedged between Men in Black and the *Fear Factor Live* stadium; and one takes over one of the two theaters inside the *Shrek 4-D* attraction. Each year, due to theme or location, some houses seem to attract longer queues than others. In 2018 the houses near the front entrance based on films and TV shows (including Stranger Things, Poltergeist, and Halloween) were the most popular, while the original-concept mazes in the rear of the park drew shorter lines than average. Keep this in mind when deciding whether to bite the bullet and queue up for a particular maze.

Even the least popular houses, however, will have peak waits of 30 minutes or more, even on less busy nights. Your first hour at the event is therefore essential to making the most of the evening, and your initial plan of attack is determined by which location you start your night from:

- **Springfield Holding Area:** If you are among the first inside the Springfield holding area, queue up for the first available house as soon as allowed. The exit of that maze should lead directly to the entrance of the second house to open. Alternatively, if you are late entering the holding area, the queue for the first house may already be posted at an hour or more. In that case, do the second maze first, saving the first for later in the early-entry period (the wait should diminish rapidly) or late in the evening. Guests should be released from the Springfield area around 6 p.m. and can line up for the second tent house near MIB Gear, or cross the park to the open soundstage houses.

- **Finnegan's Bar and Grill Holding Area:** Enter the New York holding area between 4 and 5 p.m. (the earlier the better, especially if you want to get food or drink), receive a wristband, and relax until released around 5:45 p.m. You will have a short head start on everyone else for the first of the soundstage houses to open. Once the general public is admitted through the front gates (as early as 6 p.m.), queues at the soundstage houses will swiftly build; see as many as you can until waits exceed 30 minutes, and then proceed to the houses in the back of the park.

- **Hollywood Holding Area:** Check into the holding area outside the Hello Kitty shop before park closing, and work your way through the plaza as close to Despicable Me Minion Mayhem as possible. Guests will be released shortly before the front gates open, and make a mad dash across the street to the first soundstage entrance. By the time the first holding area guests exit the haunted house, the line behind them may be an hour or more, so you should head toward Springfield immediately afterward.

- **General Admission:** If you are among the first folks through the gates when they open around 6 p.m., head straight to the open soundstage houses and jump in line if it is still 15 minutes or less. Otherwise, the majority of guests will mob the four houses located in the soundstages near the front of the park. You should avoid the horde by heading in the opposite direction, toward Springfield, which should have processed the majority of guests who were already in the park by now. You can also continue through Springfield to the houses outside MIB Gear and in the Men in Black extended queue.

This reader from Highlands Ranch, Colorado, followed our Halloween touring advice with great success:

Being a day guest at the park gave us a tremendous head start on Halloween Horror Nights. Using the recommendations in the guide, we waited in the Springfield holding area, which gave us access to several of the houses that opened before the official 6:30 start. We were thus able to see four houses in roughly an hour and still catch the first show.

After the haunted houses, the *Academy of Villains* live show, held inside the *Fear Factor Live* stadium, is the top draw. As seen on *So You Think You Can Dance* and *America's Got Talent,* this talented high-energy dance troupe pulls off athletic choreography and gravity-defying acrobatics to a blistering horror-rock soundtrack. The first and last performances of the night are always the least crowded, but you shouldn't have trouble finding a seat if you show up 15–20 minutes in advance of any showing.

unofficial **TIP**
Don't waste time at the beginning of the evening queuing for a house that hasn't yet opened when you could be enjoying short waits at the mazes that are operating. Houses that don't open until after 6:30 p.m. will accumulate a large backlog of guests before they begin operating, so save them for the end of the night instead.

After the sun sets (around 7:30 p.m.) and the waits for the houses become unbearable, begin exploring the scare zones, which have evolved from open-air haunted mazes (minus the conga-line queues) into social media–friendly selfie opportunities. Just as much fun as getting scared yourself is finding a vantage point to stand still and see others getting spooked; this is some of the best people-watching you'll ever find. Be on the lookout for staged scenes, in which actors attack planted "victims" within the crowd.

By the midpoint of the evening, standby waits for all the houses will be substantial, and lines for the rides will be astronomical on Saturdays, but experiencing several top attractions should still be manageable using single-rider queues. Men in Black Alien Attack, Revenge of the Mummy, Escape from Gringotts, Transformers: The Ride–3-D, and Fast & Furious: Supercharged all have fairly efficient single-rider operations. Hollywood Rip Ride Rockit has a single-rider line, but it is often as long as the standby queue. On off-peak nights, you may find ride queues shockingly short; just be aware that most rides shut down an hour or two before the event ends.

Even on a slow night, Horror Nights crowds can drive you to drink, and many of your fellow guests will doubtlessly be imbibing. Temporary bars serve beer and overpriced premixed cocktails on seemingly every spare square foot of sidewalk, but for serious in-park boozing, we prefer Finnegan's Bar in New York or Duff Brewery in Springfield. Better yet, if the park is open past 1 a.m., get out of Dodge for an hour or so and retreat to CityWalk. Most HHN passes include admission to CityWalk's clubs, or you can grab a drink at Antojitos or NBC Sports Grill & Brew without a cover charge.

As the evening's event approaches its final hour, wait times at the haunted mazes drop dramatically. If you are interested in the headliner show and didn't catch an earlier showing, show up 15–20 minutes before the last performance on peak nights (or 5–10 minutes before showtime off-peak). Otherwise, use the final hours to catch up on the houses you missed earlier. The last 30–60 minutes before park closing is the best time to hit the most popular houses. If you didn't see the most popular mazes at the start of the night, step into line for one of them about 15–20 minutes before closing; you should be allowed to stay in the queue until you're through, barring technical difficulties.

Unless you leave significantly before closing time, you're best off dawdling in the park or CityWalk on the way out. The parking garage exits will be at a standstill, so you might as well grab a seat outside and relax rather than breathing fumes in a traffic jam.

HOLIDAYS AT UNIVERSAL STUDIOS
(early December–early January)

UNIVERSAL ORLANDO CELEBRATES the holiday season every year from the first Friday of December through the Saturday after New Year's. Universal Orlando holidays might not have quite the nostalgic lure of Mickey's merrymaking, but its options are every bit as expertly produced and have the benefit of all being included with regular park admission (unlike the extra-cost hard-ticket nighttime parties at the Magic Kingdom).

USF's holiday festivities feature seasonal decoration on the front archway and throughout the park, holiday songs broadcasting from speakers in the streets, and a giant tree that is ceremoniously lit every evening at sunset. Several park attractions, such as *The Blues Brothers Show,* get into the spirit with special versions tied to the season. Universal also celebrates the holidays Harry Potter–style with **Christmas in The Wizarding World.** Diagon Alley's streets and shops are adorned with holiday decor, and seasonal snacks are served inside the Leaky Cauldron. But the star of the holidays at Universal Studios is undoubtedly **Universal's Holiday Parade Featuring Macy's.**

USF has been bringing elements of Macy's famous New York parade down to Orlando for a post-Thanksgiving encore every December for more than a decade. For 2017 Universal renamed and revamped the procession, adding elaborate new floats featuring characters from Shrek, Madagascar, and Despicable Me. But Macy's balloons are still a big part of the fun: while the largest balloons you've seen sailing through Manhattan on TV can't make it down the narrower streets of USF, several of the smaller ones are paraded through both productions, and more of the classic king-size inflatables (such as Garfield and Grover) can be seen on stationary display around the park.

Universal's Holiday Parade begins each evening around 5 p.m. (subject to change; check the show schedule in your park map) near the *Horror Make-Up Show,* continues down Hollywood Boulevard toward the park entrance, travels past Despicable Me Minion Mayhem and *Shrek 4-D* toward New York, and then turns near Revenge of the Mummy and again past Transformers, exiting through the gate it originally entered.

You can get a good view of the parade from anywhere along the route, but ideal viewing spots are near Mel's Drive-In at the beginning of the route and near the large tree in New York toward the end. Reserved viewing areas are marked on the park map for guests with disabilities (in front of Macy's in New York), for annual pass holders (near Mel's Drive-In), and for young Little Stars and their families (near Hollywood's Brown Derby).

If you've always fantasized about guiding a giant inflatable animal down Fifth Avenue, you can volunteer to participate in the parade as a balloon handler for free. Volunteers must be 18 years or older, at least 48 inches tall and 125 pounds, English speaking, and able to walk the mile-long route for up to an hour. Sign-up is held daily 2 hours before the parade starts in Woody Woodpecker's KidZone near E.T. Adventure. A limited number of spots are available for guests each day, and you'll have to sign a waiver to participate.

After the parade on select nights, USF's Music Plaza Stage hosts live concerts by **Mannheim Steamroller.** The electrified orchestra usually performs its amped-up holiday classics on the first two Saturdays and Sundays of the season. These shows can be popular, so arrive at least 45 minutes early if you want a close-up view.

UNIVERSAL STUDIOS FLORIDA TOURING PLANS

OUR STEP-BY-STEP touring plans are field-tested for seeing *as much as possible* in one day with a minimum of time wasted in lines. They're designed to help you avoid crowds and bottlenecks on days of moderate to heavy attendance. Understand, however, that there's more to see at USF than can be experienced in one day during peak season. If you are visiting on days of lighter attendance (see "Trying to Reason with the Tourist Season," page 27) or using Universal Express (see page 57), our plans will save you time but won't be as critical to successful touring as on busier days.

In general, most visitors find that they can be far more flexible with their touring plans at Universal than at Disney and still see everything they want to see. But if you are at the parks on a busy day, you will want to stick to the script, at least until you get the most popular attractions out of the way. Afternoon touring at USF is largely dependent on Universal's ever-shifting show schedule, so check showtimes on the park map as soon as you arrive and shuffle the steps accordingly.

Before using any of our Universal Orlando touring plans, first become familiar with Universal's park-opening procedures, as described on page 51. Purchase your admission ahead of time, and call ☎ 407-363-8000 or check universalorlando.com the day before you go to verify official operating hours. If you are eligible for Early Park Admission (see page 54), arrive at USF 90–120 minutes before the official park opening time. If you are not eligible for early entry, arrive at the park 30–45 minutes prior to opening time.

If you are using TouringPlans' Lines smartphone app, you can select any of the following premium touring plans, copy it to your list of personalized plans, and optimize the plan steps to your preferences. Once you arrive at the park, select the appropriate plan in the app to make it active, and track your progress during the day by marking each attraction as complete after exiting. Optimize the plan repeatedly during your day to refine it with the latest wait-time information. If you are following a two-park plan, a link to part two will appear at the top of the plan; switch to the second part when moving to the second park, and then return to part one when you return to the original park.

Once you're admitted into the park, move quickly from attraction to attraction, following your chosen touring plan exactly. If you're not interested in an attraction it lists, simply skip that attraction and proceed to the next. When you encounter a very long line at an attraction that the touring plan calls for, skip the attraction in question and go to the next step, returning later to retry. Don't worry that other people will be following the plans and render them useless. Fewer than 2 in every 100 people in the park will have been exposed to this info.

CHOOSING THE APPROPRIATE TOURING PLAN

WE PRESENT THREE USF touring plans:

- Universal Studios Florida One-Day Touring Plan for Adults
- Universal Studios Florida One-Day Touring Plan for Parents with Small Children
- Universal Studios Florida One-Day Touring Plan for Seniors

In addition, we have three Universal Orlando touring plans that combine both USF and IOA, for guests with park-to-park admission:

- Universal Orlando Highlights One-Day/Two-Park Touring Plan
- Wizarding World One-Day/Two-Park Touring Plan
- Universal Orlando Comprehensive Two-Day/Two-Park Touring Plan

If you have two days at Universal Orlando, the Comprehensive Two-Day/Two-Park Touring Plan is by far the most relaxed. The two-day plan takes advantage of early morning, when lines are short and the park hasn't filled with guests. This plan works well year-round and eliminates much of the extra walking required by the one-day plans. No matter when the park closes, our two-day plan guarantees the most efficient touring and the least time in lines. The plan is perfect for guests who wish to explore the attractions and the atmosphere of USF and IOA, with an emphasis on both Wizarding Worlds.

If you have only one day to visit USF and do not have park-to-park tickets, then use the One-Day Touring Plan for Adults. It's exhausting, but it packs in the maximum. If you have one-day park-to-park passes, the Universal Orlando Highlights Touring Plan will help you pack in all of the best thrill rides at USF and IOA, including The Wizarding

World ones, at the expense of most shows and a lot of shoe leather. Alternatively, Harry Potter superfans who have one-day park-to-park passes and zero interest in anything at Universal outside Hogsmeade and Diagon Alley (a mistake in our estimation, but it's your money) can follow the Wizarding World One-Day/Two-Park Touring Plan to maximize their magical immersion.

If you have young ones in tow, adopt the One-Day Touring Plan for Parents with Small Children. It's a compromise, blending the preferences of younger children with those of older siblings and adults. The plan includes many children's rides but omits roller coasters and other attractions that frighten young children or are off-limits because of height requirements greater than 40 inches. Or use the One-Day Touring Plan for Adults and take advantage of child swap, a technique whereby children accompany adults to the loading area of a ride with age and height requirements but don't board (see page 188).

If you have three days at Universal Orlando, use the Comprehensive Two-Day/Two-Park Touring Plan on the first two days, and use the Universal Orlando Highlights One-Day/Two-Park Touring Plan or Wizarding World Touring Plan on your last day. With four or more days, you can pretty much explore the parks at your leisure, using any of the plans as a general guideline.

ONE-DAY TOURING PLAN FOR ADULTS *(page 387)*

THIS PLAN IS FOR GUESTS without park-to-park tickets and includes every recommended attraction at USF. If a ride or show is listed that you don't want to experience, skip that step and proceed to the next. Move quickly from attraction to attraction, and if possible, hold off on lunch until after experiencing at least six rides.

ONE-DAY TOURING PLAN FOR PARENTS WITH SMALL CHILDREN *(page 388)*

THIS PLAN IS FOR GUESTS without park-to-park tickets and eliminates all rides with a minimum height requirement greater than 40 inches. The plan includes a midday break of at least 2 hours back at your hotel. It's debatable whether the kids will need the nap more than you, but you'll thank us later, we promise.

ONE-DAY TOURING PLAN FOR SENIORS *(page 389)*

THIS PLAN IS FOR GUESTS without park-to-park tickets and is specifically designed for seniors and grandparents, taking walking distances and attraction ratings from this group into account. This plan focuses on shows and family-friendly attractions and avoids thrill rides.

UNIVERSAL ORLANDO HIGHLIGHTS ONE-DAY/ TWO-PARK TOURING PLAN *(pages 393–394)*

THIS PLAN IS FOR GUESTS with one-day park-to-park tickets who wish to see the highlights of USF and IOA in a single day. The plan uses Hogwarts Express to get from one park to the other and then back again;

you can walk back to the first park for the return leg if the line is too long. The plan includes a table-service lunch at Mythos (make reservations online a few days before your visit) and dinner at the Leaky Cauldron; during holiday periods, you may need to substitute a quick-service snack for one or both meals to fit in all of the plan's attractions.

WIZARDING WORLD ONE-DAY/TWO-PARK TOURING PLAN *(pages 395–396)*

THIS PLAN IS FOR GUESTS with one-day park-to-park tickets who wish to experience The Wizarding World of Harry Potter to the exclusion of everything else Universal has to offer. The plan uses Hogwarts Express to get from one park to the other and then back again; you can walk back to the first park for the return leg if the line is too long. The plan includes lunch at Three Broomsticks and dinner at the Leaky Cauldron; during holiday periods, you may need to substitute a quick-service snack for one or both meals to fit in all of the plan's attractions.

UNIVERSAL ORLANDO COMPREHENSIVE TWO-DAY/ TWO-PARK TOURING PLAN *(pages 397–400)*

THIS PLAN IS FOR GUESTS with multiday park-to-park tickets who wish to explore USF and IOA in-depth over two days. The plan includes one Hogwarts Express trip between parks per day. Incidentally, all the water rides are concentrated in the morning of the second day, so if bad weather is in the forecast, consider flipping the plan days.

PART EIGHT

UNIVERSAL'S ISLANDS *of* ADVENTURE

UNIVERSAL STUDIOS FLORIDA HAD BARELY opened before planning began on Project X, the second theme park that would provide Universal with enough critical mass to actually compete with Disney. Originally envisioned as Cartoon World, with areas devoted to DC Comics superheroes and Looney Tunes characters, the concept evolved into **Islands of Adventure** (IOA), a fully themed fantasy park inspired by family-friendly literature.

From its very inception, IOA was designed to directly compete with Disney's Magic Kingdom. The park has kid-friendly rides and cartoon characters (like Fantasyland), thrill rides in a sci-fi city (like Tomorrowland), and a jungle river with robot creatures (like Adventureland). Its layout—a central entry corridor leading to a ring of connected lands—even mimics the classic Disneyland model, with one major exception: instead of a hub and castle in the center, Universal built a large lagoon, whose estuaries separate the park's thematically diverse "islands" (actually peninsulas).

IOA debuted in 1999 as a state-of-the-art park competing with a Disney park decades older, but it didn't initially do gangbuster business, thanks partly to a botched marketing rollout and Universal's failure to add any major

> *unofficial* **TIP**
> Thrill rides at Islands of Adventure are the real deal—not for the faint-hearted or for little ones.

attractions during IOA's first decade. That all changed in 2010, which marked IOA's coming-out party. In one of the greatest seismic shifts in theme park history, Universal opened the first Harry Potter–themed area within the park. Harry P. is possibly the only fictional character extant capable of trumping Mickey Mouse, and Universal went all out, under J. K. Rowling's watchful and exacting eye, to create a setting and attractions designed to be the envy of the industry.

BEWARE OF THE WET AND WILD

THOUGH WE'VE DESCRIBED IOA as a direct competitor to the Magic Kingdom, know this: whereas most Magic Kingdom attractions are designed to be enjoyed by guests of any age, attractions at IOA are created largely for an under-40 population. The roller coasters at Universal are serious with a capital *S*, making Space Mountain and Big Thunder Mountain Railroad look about as frightening as Dumbo. In fact, six of the top eight attractions at IOA are thrill rides; of these, three will not only scare the crap out of you but will also drench you with water. And about that water: it ain't exactly Evian, as a reader from New York learned the hard way:

> *The amount of water dumped on us at Popeye & Bluto's Bilge-Rat Barges was incredible, and the chlorine was so bad that one of us could not see.*

After your chemical baptism, you may be tempted by the heated full-body drying booths strategically positioned near the exit of each drenching attraction, but this Pennsylvania reader has a warning:

> *The People Dryers are a waste of $5. We used one and were no drier than before, just poorer.*

If you get soaked, you're better off just walking off the wetness in warm weather, or packing a change of clothes if it's cool.

For families, there are three interactive playgrounds as well as six rides or shows without height restrictions that young children can enjoy. Of the thrill rides, only The Amazing Adventures of Spider-Man, Skull Island, and the two in Toon Lagoon (described later) are marginally appropriate for little kids, and even on these rides, your child needs to be fairly hardy.

GETTING ORIENTED *at* UNIVERSAL'S ISLANDS *of* ADVENTURE

LAID OUT MUCH LIKE Epcot's World Showcase—arranged in a large circle surrounding a lagoon—IOA evinces the same thematic continuity present in the Magic Kingdom. Each "land," or "island" in this case, is self-contained and visually consistent in its theme.

You first encounter **Port of Entry,** a mélange of Middle Eastern and Asian architecture where you'll find Guest Services, lockers, stroller and wheelchair rentals, ATM banking, Lost and Found, and shopping. From the Port of Entry, moving clockwise around the lagoon, you access **Marvel Super Hero Island, Toon Lagoon, Skull Island, Jurassic Park, The Wizarding World of Harry Potter—Hogsmeade, The Lost Continent,** and **Seuss Landing.** There is no in-park transportation to move you between lands.

As you enter IOA, lockers and rentals are to your left, and First Aid and Guest Services are to your right. Before bolting through Port of Entry

NOT TO BE MISSED AT ISLANDS OF ADVENTURE
MARVEL SUPER HERO ISLAND
• The Amazing Adventures of Spider-Man   • The Incredible Hulk Coaster
TOON LAGOON   • Popeye & Bluto's Bilge-Rat Barges
SKULL ISLAND   • Skull Island: Reign of Kong
JURASSIC PARK   • Jurassic Park River Adventure
THE WIZARDING WORLD OF HARRY POTTER–HOGSMEADE
• Harry Potter and the Forbidden Journey   • Hogwarts Express

to your first adventure—or at least on your way out before leaving—take a few moments to appreciate the details that Universal lavished on this area, from the fountain made of giant leaves, to the sounds of gamblers from an upstairs casino, to the jail that's been broken and the fire station that burned down. Also listen for the original background music, which is synchronized throughout the park and changes as you move from island to island. Port of Entry doesn't have any attractions, but it does have dining (including a Starbucks) and shopping options.

UNIVERSAL'S ISLANDS *of* ADVENTURE ATTRACTIONS

MARVEL SUPER HERO ISLAND

THIS ISLAND, WITH ITS FUTURISTIC and retro-future design and comic book signage, offers shopping, dining, and two of Orlando's best thrill rides, all based on Marvel Comics characters. The architecture, which some fault as flat, seeks to re-create the Pop Art look of comic book backgrounds; some buildings have Chrome Illusion paint that changes colors depending on the angle of sunlight. Look for the meteor impact sculpture covered in hundreds of Marvel characters, as well as communication booths delivering messages from S.H.I.E.L.D.

Several times a day on a published schedule, Marvel heroes parade in on all-terrain vehicles and take over the streets greeting guests; the activity can make it tough to navigate through the area. Between the Hulk's roar and the bass beats surrounding the Spider-Man building, Super Hero Island is also one of the loudest sections of the park; seek refuge along the water behind Captain America Diner.

In case you were curious: Yes, Disney now owns Marvel Comics, but Universal locked up the theme park rights to certain character groups—the Avengers, Spider-Man, the Fantastic Four, and X-Men—in perpetuity on the East Coast. You may see Iron Man and Captain America in Disneyland or in Mickey's international parks, but they are exclusive to IOA in Orlando (and Universal Studios Japan) for the indefinite future. The Guardians of the Galaxy, who are getting their own roller coaster at Epcot, are an exception to this restriction.

continued on page 314

Universal's Islands of Adventure

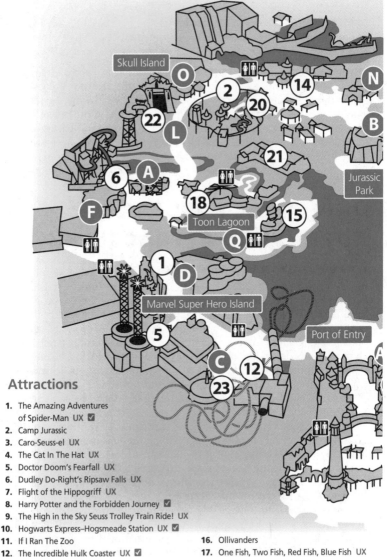

Attractions

1. The Amazing Adventures of Spider-Man UX ☑
2. Camp Jurassic
3. Caro-Seuss-el UX
4. The Cat In The Hat UX
5. Doctor Doom's Fearfall UX
6. Dudley Do-Right's Ripsaw Falls UX
7. Flight of the Hippogriff UX
8. Harry Potter and the Forbidden Journey ☑
9. The High in the Sky Seuss Trolley Train Ride! UX
10. Hogwarts Express–Hogsmeade Station UX ☑
11. If I Ran The Zoo
12. The Incredible Hulk Coaster UX ☑
13. Jurassic Park Discovery Center
14. Jurassic Park River Adventure UX ☑
15. Me Ship, *The Olive*

16. Ollivanders
17. One Fish, Two Fish, Red Fish, Blue Fish UX
18. Popeye & Bluto's Bilge-Rat Barges UX ☑
19. *Poseidon's Fury* UX
20. Pteranodon Flyers VL

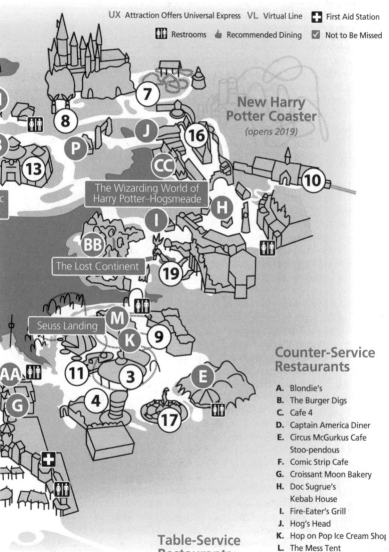

UX Attraction Offers Universal Express   VL Virtual Line   ✚ First Aid Station

🚻 Restrooms   👍 Recommended Dining   ☑ Not to Be Missed

New Harry
Potter Coaster
(opens 2019)

The Wizarding World of
Harry Potter–Hogsmeade

The Lost Continent

Seuss Landing

Counter-Service Restaurants

A. Blondie's
B. The Burger Digs
C. Cafe 4
D. Captain America Diner
E. Circus McGurkus Cafe Stoo-pendous
F. Comic Strip Cafe
G. Croissant Moon Bakery
H. Doc Sugrue's Kebab House
I. Fire-Eater's Grill
J. Hog's Head
K. Hop on Pop Ice Cream Shop
L. The Mess Tent
M. Moose Juice, Goose Juice
N. Pizza Predattoria
O. Thunder Falls Terrace 👍
P. The Watering Hole
Q. Wimpy's *(seasonal)*

Table-Service Restaurants

AA. Confisco Grille
BB. Mythos Restaurant 👍
CC. Three Broomsticks *(counter service)* 👍

21. Raptor Encounter
22. Skull Island: Reign of Kong UX ☑
23. Storm Force Accelatron UX

continued from page 311

The Amazing Adventures of Spider-Man *(Universal Express)*
★★★★★

APPEAL BY AGE PRESCHOOL ★★★ GRADE SCHOOL ★★★★½ TEENS ★★★★½
YOUNG ADULTS ★★★★½ OVER 30 ★★★★½ SENIORS ★★★★½

What it is Indoor adventure 3-D simulator ride. **Scope and scale** Super-headliner. **When to go** During the first 40 minutes the park is open. **Comments** 40" minimum height requirement; child swap available (see page 188); single-rider line available. One of the best attractions anywhere; not to be missed. **Duration of ride** 4½ minutes. **Average wait in line per 100 people ahead of you** 5 minutes. **Loading speed** Fast.

Motion Sickness

DESCRIPTION AND COMMENTS Widely regarded as one of the best theme park attractions in Orlando, and one of our favorite rides anywhere in the world, The Amazing Adventures of Spider-Man has fended off Kong and Potter, maintaining its position at the top of IOA's must-do list. The attraction moves a spinning, tilting ride vehicle through 13 scenes (covering 1.5 acres) of mayhem, which fuse 4K 3-D digital projections almost seamlessly with actual sets and props, accompanied by special effects including fog, water, and fire. In many instances guests cannot tell until the action begins whether they're looking at a movie screen or an actual brick wall.

The total package is astonishing—frenetic yet fluid, and visually rich. The ride is wild yet very smooth. Though the attraction opened 20 years ago, Spider-Man is still technologically ahead of almost everything at Walt Disney World outside Pandora: The World of Avatar or Star Wars: Galaxy's Edge—which is to say that it will leave you in awe.

The story line is that you're visiting the *Daily Bugle* newspaper (where Peter Parker, also known as Spider-Man, works as a mild-mannered photographer) when crime reports start coming in. The Sinister Syndicate—consisting of Spidey's archenemies Doctor Octopus, Hobgoblin, Electro, Hydro-Man, and Scream—have used an antigravity gun to steal (we promise we're not making this up) the Statue of Liberty. You're drafted on the spot by cantankerous editor J. Jonah Jameson to get the story. You board a 12-passenger SCOOP vehicle—a mobile open-top motion simulator identical to the cars used in Universal Studios Florida's (USF's) Transformers—and follow the "Spider Signal" straight into an epic battle between the web-slinger and his foes.

The Amazing Adventures of Spider-Man combines your ride vehicle's motion so smoothly with the film sequences that you quickly believe you're part of the action. Without giving away too much of the surprise, one part of the attraction has you raised high above the city skyline. After speeding around, you experience a 400-foot sensory drop from a skyscraper roof all the way to the pavement. The blending of 3-D film and pitching of the ride car is so convincing that, during our first ride, we were sure that we were being lifted inside the building; we had to ride a second time, with our glasses off, to see how the effect was done while keeping the car on the ground.

Even though Spidey's cybertronic sibling in USF has proven popular, the original 3-D dark ride has held its ground as the first and still favorite in its genre. It's less frantic and frenetic than Transformers and features more dialogue and humor. And despite using similar systems, some folks who get motion sick on Transformers find that they can tolerate this ride better.

Marvel Comics founder Stan Lee makes a cameo appearance in any film featuring the characters he helped create, and The Amazing Adventures of Spider-Man ride is no exception. Lee appears as the truck driver who swerves to miss your

SCOOP vehicle early in the ride; outside the theater as Spidey and Doc Ock duke it out; in the street after your vehicle falls to the ground; and finally with the cops as the stolen Statue of Liberty is being flown back into place. He is also the voice who bids you farewell before disembarking.

TOURING TIPS If you were on hand for Early Park Admission, ride after experiencing The Wizarding World, Skull Island: Reign of Kong, and The Incredible Hulk Coaster. If you elect to bypass The Wizarding World congestion, ride after Hulk.

Seats in the first row are the most immersive, but we find that the 3-D effects focus better from a row or two back. The rear corners get the most movement, while the center of the second row is the most stable. There is an on-ride photo, but the camera is in an odd position, so everyone comes out facing the wrong way.

The standby and Express queues both wind through portions of the *Daily Bugle* newsroom; Express cuts through Peter Parker's darkroom (look for Spidey's glowing handprints on the ceiling), while standby passes by J. J.'s trophy case, with hidden tributes to the designers. The single-rider option, when available, can greatly cut your wait as long as the line doesn't reach the stroller parking area.

Doctor Doom's Fearfall (*Universal Express*) ★★★

APPEAL BY AGE	PRESCHOOL	★½	GRADE SCHOOL	★★★½	TEENS	★★★★
YOUNG ADULTS	★★★★		OVER 30	★★★½	SENIORS	★★★

What it is Tower launch and free fall. **Scope and scale** Headliner. **When to go** During the first hour the park is open or in the last 2 hours before closing. **Comments** 52" minimum height requirement; child swap available (see page 188); single-rider line available. More bark than bite. **Duration of ride** 40 seconds. **Average wait in line per 100 people ahead of you** 18 minutes. **Loading speed** Slow.

DESCRIPTION AND COMMENTS Here you are (again), strapped into a seat with your feet dangling and blasted 200 feet up in the air and then allowed to partially free-fall back down. Imagine the midway game where a macho guy swings a sledgehammer, propelling a metal sphere up a vertical shaft to ring a bell—on this ride, you're the metal sphere.

That prospect sounds worse than it actually is. The scariest part of the ride is the apprehension that builds as you sit, strapped in, waiting for the ride to launch. Blasting up and falling down are actually pleasant, with one exhilarating, fleeting moment of negative-gravity "air time" at the top. Riders in chambers three and four get a great view of the park, while those in one and two look out over I-4 and International Drive.

TOURING TIPS We've seen glaciers that move faster than the line for Doctor Doom's Fearfall, though the ominous queue and satirical propaganda films compensate slightly. If you want to ride without investing half a day, be one of the first to ride. If you're on hand at opening time, being among the first isn't too difficult (mainly because The Wizarding World, Hulk, and Spider-Man attractions are bigger draws). Alternatively, the ride often has no wait near the end of the operating day, and the view is especially nice at night.

Fortunately, Doctor Doom also has a singles line that's nearly always open; look for the stairwell to the left of the ride's entrance.

The Incredible Hulk Coaster (*Universal Express*) ★★★★½

APPEAL BY AGE	PRESCHOOL	★½	GRADE SCHOOL	★★★★½	TEENS	★★★★★
YOUNG ADULTS	★★★★★		OVER 30	★★★★½	SENIORS	★★★½

What it is Roller coaster. **Scope and scale** Super-headliner. **When to go** During the first 40 minutes the park is open. **Comments** 54" minimum height requirement; child swap available (see page 188); single-rider line available. A coaster-lover's coaster; not to be missed. **Duration of ride** 2¼ minutes. **Average wait in line per 100 people ahead of you** 9 minutes. **Loading speed** Moderate.

Motion Sickness

DESCRIPTION AND COMMENTS The Incredible Hulk's towering loops, which are some of the most iconic elements of the IOA skyline, were completely disassembled in 2016 and rebuilt from scratch. Now, the big green guy has roared back to life with a brand-new track (which follows the same path as the original) and trains featuring lights flashing to a synchronized soundtrack composed by Fall Out Boy's Patrick Stump. A revamped entryway stars a statue of the Hulk himself holding a coaster car overhead—the marquee is made of salvaged track from the original version—and the queue building received a modern makeover with dramatic lighting and the world's largest plasma display. (Ask a team member for a **gamma tour** to examine the Marvel Comics Easter eggs hidden along the line.) The upgrades are underpinned by a new story line that has you volunteering for General Thaddeus "Thunderbolt" Ross's experimental attempt to create super-soldiers via gamma ray bombardment. (We're pretty certain that it isn't covered by Obamacare.) The story falls apart almost as soon as the ride starts, but you'll be too scared to notice.

What you need to know about this attraction is simple. You'll be shot like a carrier-launched jet from 0 to 40 miles per hour in 2 seconds, flung upside down into a zero gravity barrel roll 100 feet off the ground (which will, of course, induce weightlessness), and then thrown immediately into a pair of cobra rolls and a vertical loop of more than 100 feet, into a belowground tunnel, no less! Two more rolls and another loop follow, for a total of seven upside-down experiences in a ride of a little more than 2 minutes. At the end of the ride, you may be just as green as the Hulk.

Seriously, the Hulk is a great roller coaster, one of the best in Florida, providing a ride comparable to that of Kumba or Montu (Busch Gardens) with the added thrill of an accelerated launch, instead of the more typical uphill crank. We had hoped that the complete reconstruction of the Hulk's track would eliminate the headbanging it had developed over the years, but while more comfortable than before the refurb, the coaster isn't exactly opening-day smooth (it's still a far cry from the side-to-side shaking of Hollywood Rip Ride Rockit next door). We're also a little sad to see the famously hollow steel filled with sand, muting the track's once-mighty roar, though a recorded growl now blares with every launch. The video screen in the launch tube doesn't make much impact, and the audio from the in-seat speakers is sometimes too low to understand, but the driving orchestral rock soundtrack successfully makes the ride feel faster than ever.

TOURING TIPS Our advice is to skip The Wizarding World attractions in the early morning and ride The Incredible Hulk Coaster first thing. Alternatively, if you insist on going to Hogsmeade at rope drop (or if you are eligible for Early Park Admission), you should ride Hulk immediately after you've enjoyed Harry Potter and the Forbidden Journey, Flight of the Hippogriff, and Reign of Kong.

Universal provides electronic lockers near the entrance of the Hulk to deposit any items that might depart your person during the ride. Use the lockers for anything—and we mean anything—that could be dislodged during your ride: hats, glasses, cell phones, camera bags, and toupees. The lockers are free for the duration of your wait, and use of these lockers is enforced; be prepared to pat down your pockets for loose change, or you'll be pulled aside for a TSA-style wanding after triggering the metal detectors.

At the boarding area is a separate line for those who want to ride in the first row. Riders in the front row of Hulk get a spectacular, brief view of the park. If you get to Hulk early enough and the line is short enough, opt for the special front-row line near the boarding area. It's worth waiting an extra 5 or 10 minutes. The back left seat gets the best zero gravity effect from the opening inversion.

The singles line is almost always open.

Storm Force Accelatron *(Universal Express)* ★★½

APPEAL BY AGE	PRESCHOOL ★★★★½	GRADE SCHOOL ★★★★	TEENS ★★★★
YOUNG ADULTS ★★★½	OVER 30 ★★★½		SENIORS ★★★½

What it is Covered spinning ride. **Scope and scale** Minor attraction. **When to go** Anytime. **Comments** Child swap available (see page 188). May induce motion sickness. **Duration of ride** 1½ minutes. **Average wait in line per 100 people ahead of you** 21 minutes. **Loading speed** Slow.

Motion Sickness

DESCRIPTION AND COMMENTS Storm Force Accelatron is a spiffed-up version of Disney's nausea-inducing Mad Tea Party. In Storm Force Accelatron, up to five people are seated in a round plastic ride vehicle that has a metal wheel mounted in the center. Turning the metal wheel causes the ride vehicle to spin on its central axis. While that's happening, each ride vehicle is part of a group of three similar vehicles, also spinning around a common axis. And the entire group of 12 ride vehicles is simultaneously spinning around the Accelatron's center.

In Universal's take on this carnival classic, you spin to the accompaniment of a simulated thunderstorm. Flashing lights and loud music either really enhance the experience or make it much, much worse, depending on your stomach. A story line involving the X-Men heroine Storm loosely ties this midway-type ride to the Marvel Super Hero Island area, but it's largely irrelevant and offers no advice on keeping your lunch down.

Young children, teens, and masochists like to lure the unsuspecting onto the ride, and then turn the wheel like maniacs. It's also effective for determining if you've recently developed any kind of inner-ear disorder.

TOURING TIPS Storm Force is hidden behind Hulk's locker banks and is largely overlooked by the crowds. During the off-season, the ride is typically a walk-on, and even on the busiest days the wait rarely tops 20 minutes. If you're prone to motion sickness, keep your distance.

TOON LAGOON

WHIMSICAL AND GAILY COLORED, with rounded and exaggerated lines, Toon Lagoon translates cartoon art into real buildings and settings. King's Row and Comic Strip Lane, the main drags of Toon Lagoon, are the domains of such vintage Sunday-funnies favorites as *Beetle Bailey, The Family Circus,* and *Blondie*—in other words, intellectual property that Universal could get for cheap. Across a bridge lies Sweethaven, home to Popeye and Olive Oyl, and a mountain dedicated to Dudley Do-Right looms around the corner.

The island's King Features Syndicate and Jay Ward comic characters, though classic, are probably unrecognizable to anyone born after 1980, but that doesn't stop kids from enjoying the resort's two wettest water rides, both of which are found here. Entering Toon Lagoon from Marvel Super Hero Island, you'll have to pass a midway of unthemed carnival games and an enormous amphitheater that sits empty 99% of the time, making this transition the biggest eyesore in an otherwise exquisite park. There are some great photo ops here, especially the sideways sign where you can snap a gravity-defying shot with Marmaduke the Great Dane.

If your kids want to get wet but are too small for the water rides (or you don't want to wait in line), send them to the splash pads at either entrance to Toon Lagoon. A few minutes frolicking in fountains of sulfurous water should satisfy them.

Dudley Do-Right's Ripsaw Falls *(Universal Express)* ★★★½

APPEAL BY AGE PRESCHOOL ★★★½ GRADE SCHOOL ★★★★½ TEENS ★★★★½
YOUNG ADULTS ★★★★½ OVER 30 ★★★★ SENIORS ★★★★

What it is Flume ride. **Scope and scale** Major attraction. **When to go** Before 11 a.m.
Comments 44″ minimum height requirement; child swap available (see page 188). **Duration of ride** 5 minutes. **Average wait in line per 100 people ahead of you** 9 minutes. **Loading speed** Moderate.

Motion Sickness

DESCRIPTION AND COMMENTS Dudley Do-Right's Ripsaw Falls features characters spun off from the old Rocky and Bullwinkle TV show. Dudley is a cheerfully incompetent Canadian Mountie who pursues Snidely Whiplash, his nemesis, throughout the Great White North. Snidely inevitably tries to kidnap Nell, the girl of Dudley's dreams, and Dudley (with trusted horse, Horse) rescues her, usually in spite of himself. The original cartoons parodied everything from the implausible plots of early silent movie melodramas to the "friendly Canadian" trope, complete with really bad Quebecois accents. Being fans of the show, we think this attraction may have been inspired by Dudley's "Saw Mill" cartoon circa 1962.

Story line aside, IOA's tribute to the cartoon is a flume ride similar to the Magic Kingdom's Splash Mountain. Riders sit single file in loglike boats and bob along a man-made river, floating past mostly static scenes telling the story of Snidely kidnapping Nell, with Dudley's eventual rescuing.

As far as log flume rides go, Ripsaw Falls is pretty good. There are several medium-size drops during the 5-minute ride, and a heart-stopping 75-foot one near the end. Universal claims that this is the first flume ride to "send riders plummeting 15 feet below the surface of the water"; you're just plummeting into a tunnel, but it's a nifty effect. The ride queue and loading area have some visual gags that would make the original show's writers proud, and the on-board ride audio is also good.

That being said, the theming and visuals of Ripsaw Falls aren't in the same league as Disney's Splash Mountain attraction, to which everyone inevitably compares it. Most of Ripsaw Falls's effects are nonmoving statues, whereas Splash Mountain is loaded with moving animatronics, water effects, and gorgeous scenery. Dudley's defects are partly intentional, in keeping with the cartoon's satirical spirit, like an exposed view of backstage following the "scenic overlook" that is cheekily labeled "overlooked scenery." But the flaws are mostly due to the ride's rushed completion (it opened a year earlier than originally scheduled), resulting in a potential classic that was never properly finished.

TOURING TIPS This ride will get you wet, but on average not as soaked as on Popeye & Bluto's Bilge-Rat Barges. If you want to stay dry, however, arrive prepared with a poncho. If you're going to ride both Ripsaw Falls and Bilge-Rat Barges, see them one after another during the morning (if it's sunny enough to dry you off) or at the end of the day before slogging back to your hotel. After riding, take a moment to gauge the timing of the water cannons that go off along the exit walk. This is where you can really get drenched. Ride this after experiencing all of the Marvel Super Hero rides.

This is one of the few single-file log flumes that uses lap bar restraints, and it makes for a mighty tight fit. Make sure that you try the test seat outside the queue before waiting in line. If you don't want to ride, you can pump quarters into the water sprayers along the bridge leading to Skull Island and amuse yourself by dousing guests who just survived the big drop.

Me Ship, *The Olive*   ★★½

APPEAL BY AGE PRESCHOOL ★★★★★ **GRADE SCHOOL** ★★★★ **TEENS** ★★★★
YOUNG ADULTS ★★★★ **OVER 30** ★★★½ **SENIORS** ★★★★½

What it is Interactive playground. **Scope and scale** Minor attraction. **When to go** Anytime. **Comments** Colorful and appealing for kids.

DESCRIPTION AND COMMENTS *The Olive* is Popeye's beloved boat come to life as a three-floor interactive playground. *The Olive* offers a chance for kids to run around and expend some of the energy they've pent up in lines. Besides slides, stairs, and climbing platforms, kids can play with props, including the ship's wheel, bell, and throttle. Those who climb to the second floor will find water cannons that can reach riders on the nearby Bilge-Rat Barges. A separate play area, called Swee'Pea's Playpen, is available for smaller children.

TOURING TIPS Usually opens at 10 a.m., or an hour after the park opens. If you're into the big rides, save this for later in the day. Also, take a few minutes to explore the shoreline pathways behind the ship; you'll find some punny Popeye props and a little peace and quiet.

Popeye & Bluto's Bilge-Rat Barges
(Universal Express) ★★★★

APPEAL BY AGE PRESCHOOL ★★★½ **GRADE SCHOOL** ★★★★½ **TEENS** ★★★★
YOUNG ADULTS ★★★★½ **OVER 30** ★★★★½ **SENIORS** ★★★★

What it is Whitewater rapids raft ride. **Scope and scale** Major attraction. **When to go** Before 11 a.m. **Comments** 42″ minimum height requirement; child swap available (see page 188). Bring your own soap; not to be missed. **Duration of ride** 4½ minutes. **Average wait in line per 100 people ahead of you** 5 minutes. **Loading speed** Moderate.

DESCRIPTION AND COMMENTS Hands down our favorite whitewater raft ride on the East Coast, Bilge-Rat Barges is only bested in its genre by Grizzly River Run at Disney California Adventure. Bilge-Rat Barges seats 10 riders at a time on a circular raft down a man-made canyon of gushing rapids, waterfalls, twists, turns, and dips. Some of the scenery is visually interesting, such as the 18-foot octopus crammed into a cave two sizes too small, but the minimally moving props along the side don't quite make for an immersive story line.

TOURING TIPS If you didn't drown on Dudley Do-Right, here's a second chance. You'll get a lot wetter from the knees down on this ride, so use your poncho or garbage bag and ride barefoot with your britches rolled up. Each raft has a covered center console into which you can place backpacks, socks, and shoes; lockers or zip-top bags are strongly suggested for anything electronic.

This ride usually opens an hour later than the rest of the park, typically 10 a.m. Experience the barges in the morning after the Marvel Super Hero attractions and Dudley Do-Right. Some people ride Bilge-Rat Barges and Dudley Do-Right's Ripsaw

Falls consecutively, right before leaving the park, to avoid sloshing around in wet clothes most of the day.

Some children may be frightened more by the way the rapids look, and by the screams coming from the ride as it passes through Toon Lagoon, than by the roughness of the ride itself. These are screams of laughter. If your child is apprehensive about riding, take them to any of the platforms overlooking the ride to see how much fun everyone is having.

SKULL ISLAND

WE'RE NOT ENTIRELY SURE how Skull Island qualifies as its own land on IOA's map when it consists of a single attraction and a couple of kiosks, but that's a question for Universal's crack cartographers. While it's the smallest stand-alone section of this (or perhaps any) park, Skull Island makes a big visual impact on guests passing through to Jurassic Park, with which it shares an aesthetic kinship.

Skull Island: Reign of Kong *(Universal Express)* ★★★★½

APPEAL BY AGE PRESCHOOL ★★½ GRADE SCHOOL ★★★★ TEENS ★★★★½
YOUNG ADULTS ★★★★ OVER 30 ★★★★½ SENIORS ★★★★

What it is Indoor–outdoor truck safari with 3-D effects. **Scope and scale** Super-headliner. **When to go** Immediately after park opening or just before closing. **Comments** 36" minimum height requirement; child swap available (see page 188); single-rider line available. The King has returned; too dark and scary for small children; not to be missed. **Duration of ride** About 6 minutes. **Average wait in line per 100 people ahead of you** 4 minutes. **Loading speed** Fast.

Motion Sickness

DESCRIPTION AND COMMENTS Skull Island: Reign of Kong is both an attraction and an entire "island" unto itself, located between Toon Lagoon's Dudley Do-Right's Ripsaw Falls and the Thunder Falls Terrace restaurant in Jurassic Park. This attraction isn't exactly based on the 2005 King Kong remake (though director Peter Jackson did consult on the design), nor is it directly tied to the *Kong: Skull Island* film released in 2017. Rather, the ride is an original adventure set in the 1930s, casting guests as explorers with the Eighth Wonder Expedition Company, which has set up its jungle base camp in an ancient temple inhabited by a hostile Kong-worshipping indigenous tribe. That may seem like a foolish place to pitch your tent, but it makes for a phenomenal queue experience, featuring both lifelike animatronic figures and live haunted house–style actors who aggressively startle unwitting guests.

The winding skeleton-strewn path eventually leads to your transportation: an oversize 72-seat open-sided "expedition vehicle" that superficially resembles Disney's Animal Kingdom's Kilimanjaro Safari trucks. It's helmed by one of five different animatronic tour guides, each with a unique personality and backstory, which lends the attraction additional re-ridability. Your ride begins with a short loop outside through the jungle (which may be bypassed in inclement weather, abbreviating the experience by almost 2 minutes), ending at the massive torch-framed doors in the center of Skull Island's imposing stony facade. The doors open, allowing you passage into a maze of caves; there, you're swiftly assaulted by all manner of icky prehistoric bats, bugs, and beasties, brought to gruesome life through a mix of detailed physical effects and razor-sharp 3-D screens (even better than the ones in Harry Potter and the Escape from Gringotts and Transformers). After barely surviving a preliminary series of multisensory near misses, you're thrust into the center of a raging battle between vicious *V. Rex* dinosaurs and the big ape himself, in a climactic sequence similar (though not identical) to the *King Kong 360 3-D* attraction on Universal Studios Hollywood's (USH's) tram tour. Finally, just when you think it's all over, you'll have one last face-to-face encounter with the "eighth wonder of the world," only this time in the fur-covered flesh.

Reign of Kong is a remarkable achievement in immersive attractions, stimulating every sense (including olfactory) along the epic journey. However, some small but crucial creative missteps hold it back from being a grand slam, resulting in a ride that sits slightly behind Harry Potter and the Forbidden Journey and The Amazing Adventures of Spider-Man with second-tier E-tickets. The queue's atmosphere is unimpeachable, but muffled radio reports do an inadequate job of establishing the plot and characters before boarding. Once you are rolling, the initial scenes introduce a crisis that is completely abandoned once Kong arrives mid-ride, and though the 360 centerpiece has been noticeably upgraded since its original USH incarnation, an entirely original animation could have made for a more coherent connection to the opening. Finally, while the coda's animatronic Kong has stunningly fluid facial expressions, his movements are anticlimactically passive, resulting in an attraction that seems oddly brief despite being (at nearly 6 minutes) one of the longest in the resort. There's no shame in being among the top half-dozen rides in Universal Orlando's impressive lineup, but Kong's long-awaited return turned out to fall slightly short of the world-beating game changer his faithful fans may have expected.

TOURING TIPS Skull Island is epic in every sense, from the monumental exterior to the extensive lines it attracts. On the plus side, Kong draws some guests away from The Wizarding World of Harry Potter, helping rebalance the park. Hit Skull Island first thing in the morning after The Incredible Hulk and The Amazing Adventures of Spider-Man, or immediately following the Hogsmeade attractions if you're using Early Park Admission. A single-rider queue can help cut your wait, but it misses all the preshow elements and closes intermittently.

Kong's minimum height requirement is just 36 inches—one of the lowest in the resort—and is designed to be physically accessible to most members of the family. However, on a sensory and psychological level, it's extremely intense; the standby queue alone is enough to reduce fearful kids to tears, though the Express line bypasses most of the scares. If you or your little one has a fear of darkness, insects, or man-eating monsters, you may want to forgo the monkey. A child swap room (with benches and a TV showing clips of the 2005 film) is available, but you are directed to navigate the scary standby queue to reach it; if needed, ask a team member if you can access it via the accommodation line instead. And you don't have to be a small fry for Skull Island to leave you shaken, as this honest reader admitted:

> Being the grown-up I am, I wasn't expecting to be scared by any rides. However, Skull Island: The Reign of Kong was absolutely terrifying. When you're sitting on the very edge and a 3-D dinosaur looks like it's going to eat you, you lose all the bravery you realize you never had.

For those brave enough to board, the experience is far better in the back half of the truck (ideally, rows seven, eight, or nine), with guests on the right side getting the best view of the finale. If directed to one of the first few rows, politely ask to wait for the next truck so you can sit toward the rear. Sitting at either end of a row reveals the edges of the screens, so sacrifice the enjoyment of your friend or family member by forcing them to sit in the outside seat. The ride uses the same

3-D glasses as Spider-Man and Transformers; don't put them on until you enter the first interior scene, and remove them after the 360 projection tunnel to best appreciate the ending's animatronic.

Ask at the entrance for a **temple tour** to learn technical details about the ride's self-driving trucks, hear about tributes hidden in the queue, and (if you're lucky) skip the standby line.

JURASSIC PARK

JURASSIC PARK IS A STEVEN SPIELBERG film franchise about a theme park with real dinosaurs. Jurassic Park at IOA is a real theme park (or at least a section of one) with fictitious dinosaurs. The iconic visitor center from the original film is one of the first things guests will see across the lagoon after walking through Port of Entry. The amount of space within Jurassic Park is deceptively large, and the entire area is completely immersive as you walk through it (except where Harry Potter's Hogwarts intrusively pokes above the trees).

There are two main entrances to this island, one coming from Toon Lagoon via Skull Island and another from The Wizarding World of Harry Potter. A third way in is the bridge between Lost Continent and Jurassic Park, which allows guests to bypass Hogsmeade on busy days.

IOA's Jurassic Park is overdue for an update, and some preparations have been made for a new roller coaster that would repurpose the old Triceratops Encounter area next to the Discovery Center, but don't count on that hatching before 2020 at the earliest.

Camp Jurassic ★★★½

| APPEAL BY AGE | PRESCHOOL ★★★★★ | GRADE SCHOOL ★★★★ | TEENS ★★★★½ |
| YOUNG ADULTS ★★★★ | OVER 30 ★★★½ | SENIORS ★★★★ |

What it is Interactive play area. **Scope and scale** Minor attraction. **When to go** Anytime. **Comments** Creative playground, confusing layout.

DESCRIPTION AND COMMENTS Camp Jurassic is the most elaborate kid's play area at Universal, and one of the best theme park playgrounds you'll find anywhere. A sort of dinosaur-themed Tom Sawyer Island (minus the rafts), it allows kids to explore lava pits, caves, mines, and a rain forest. Explore and you'll find an echo cavern, bat caves, amber-bound bugs, and dilophosaurus heads that double as water blasters. The playground is big enough for many kids to spend a solid hour just running around. You may end up having to go into Camp Jurassic just to get the little nippers out, if you can find them. A parent from Rugby, Indiana, wrote in praise of the playground:

> For kids up to age 11 (depending on size and maturity), Camp Jurassic is an absolutely WONDERFUL experience! It was hilarious to see the 4-year-old enjoying shooting BIG water cannons at people, and his utter incredulity when they started shooting back! The (very!) high rope bridges were adventurous yet safe for all ages. The caves, hidden places, and twisting paths added mystery to the experience. If you have kids 10 and under, this is the place to let them go crazy, as they can safely experience everything.

Most of CJ is accessible to wheelchairs, excepting the ropes and higher platforms. Even the cave paths were navigable for a powered scooter. There are very few sitting spots inside CJ, so adults may want to wait outside in the nice, mostly shaded sitting area at CJ's front entrance. However, there are a couple of hard-to-find-but-there ways in and out, and if your child is easily disoriented, younger, or prone to panic if they lose their adults, they may need an adult to stay with them within CJ.

TOURING TIPS Camp Jurassic will fire the imaginations of the under-13 set. If you don't impose a time limit on the exploration, you could be here awhile. The layout of the play area is confusing and intersects the queuing area for Pteranodon Flyers. It's easy for kids and parents to get disoriented. If you think your children may get lost, you may end up having to climb, crawl, and slide along with them. Your chiropractor will thank you.

Jurassic Park Discovery Center ★★½

APPEAL BY AGE	PRESCHOOL ★★★½	GRADE SCHOOL ★★★★	TEENS ★★★
YOUNG ADULTS ★★★½	OVER 30 ★★★	SENIORS ★★★½	

What it is Interactive natural history exhibit. **Scope and scale** Minor attraction. **When to go** Anytime. **Comments** Definitely worth checking out.

DESCRIPTION AND COMMENTS This interactive educational exhibit mixes fiction from the Jurassic Park movies, such as using fossil DNA to bring dinosaurs to life, with skeletal remains and other paleontological displays. The best exhibit here lets guests watch an animatronic raptor being hatched, with a young witness getting to name the newborn. You never know quite when one will emerge, but ask an attendant if you should stick around. Other exhibits allow you to digitally "fuse" your DNA with a dinosaur's to see what the resultant creature would look like, play a cheesy game show with dino trivia, or "be a saurus" by seeing through the eyes of a life-size animatronic (if they happen to be working).

TOURING TIPS The center usually opens later than the rest of the park and may close earlier as well; typical hours are 10 a.m.–5 p.m. Cycle back after experiencing all the rides or on a second day. Most folks can digest this exhibit in 10–15 minutes. Behind the Discovery Center is a gorgeous waterfront terrace where you can get away from the crowds—at least when it isn't being used for a special event or as a Hogsmeade holding area. If it isn't busy, ask a lab assistant for a **nursery tour** to go inside the raptor hatchery and get an up close look at props that were used in the films.

Jurassic Park River Adventure *(Universal Express)* ★★★★

APPEAL BY AGE	PRESCHOOL ★★½	GRADE SCHOOL ★★★★	TEENS ★★★★½
YOUNG ADULTS ★★★★½	OVER 30 ★★★★	SENIORS ★★★★½	

What it is Indoor-outdoor river-raft adventure ride. **Scope and scale** Headliner. **When to go** Before 11 a.m. **Comments** 42" minimum height requirement; child swap available (see page 188); single-rider line available. Aging but still exciting; not to be missed. **Duration of ride** 6½ minutes. **Average wait in line per 100 people ahead of you** 5 minutes. **Loading speed** Fast.

DESCRIPTION AND COMMENTS One of IOA's original headliner attractions, Jurassic Park River Adventure is inspired by a scene in author Michael Crichton's original *Jurassic Park* novel. Guests board tour boats for an aquatic ride through the grounds of Jurassic Park. Everything is tranquil as the tour begins, as the boat floats among large herbivorous dinosaurs such as ultrasaurus and stegosaurus, along with prehistoric-looking plants and the occasional geyser.

To no one's surprise, something goes horribly wrong, and your tour boat is nudged off course by a dinosaur at exactly the most inopportune time: just as you're floating past the vicious raptor enclosure, whose gates have been mysteriously unlocked and left open. Before you have time to ask what OSHA's inspectors really do during the day, your boat is climbing through the inside of the raptor facility amid the destruction and carnage wrought by the escaped animals. Your first face-to-face encounter with a *T. Rex* is also your last, as you find rescue by plunging 85 feet (the tallest water descent in the world when it was built) into the river below.

The drop is a doozy; the scenery, background music, and ride narration are all done well; and Jurassic Park River Adventure is overall one of the more immersive attractions in the entire resort. But the dinosaurs look increasingly arthritic, especially in comparison to this ride's California cousin, which is being rethemed to the Jurassic World franchise during 2019. Hopefully, the Florida version will get an upgrade of its own before too long.

TOURING TIPS Riders don't get as wet on River Adventure as they do on Bilge-Rat Barges or Dudley Do-Right's Ripsaw Falls. Though the boats make a huge splash at the bottom of the 85-foot drop, you can stay relatively dry if you are sitting in an interior seat; sitting behind a larger person and keeping your arms down can help. Still, bring a poncho or plastic bag if you want to keep as dry as possible; paid lockers are located inside the queue. There's a viewing area to the left of the ride's final, big drop, where you can see how wet riders are getting before you decide to ride.

A Honolulu reader thinks Jurassic Park doesn't pass the smell test:

> *The Jurassic Park ride is a lot of fun—so fun, in fact, that you won't realize how truly HEINOUS the water that drenches you during the climactic splashdown is until much later. We sat in the front row for the ride and got soaked. Three hours later, my girlfriend and I realized that we reeked.*

Young children must endure a double whammy on this ride. First, they're stalked by giant, salivating (sometimes spitting) reptiles, and then sent catapulting over the falls. Unless your children are fairly hardy, wait a year or two before you spring the River Adventure on them.

Because the Jurassic Park section of IOA is situated between The Wizarding World of Harry Potter—Hogsmeade and Skull Island: Reign of Kong, the boat ride may experience heavy crowds earlier in the day. Try to ride before 11 a.m., or use the single-rider queue, which often has little to no wait.

Pteranodon Flyers ★★

APPEAL BY AGE PRESCHOOL ★★★★½ GRADE SCHOOL ★★★★ TEENS ★★★
YOUNG ADULTS ★★½ OVER 30 ★★★½ SENIORS ★★★

What it is Kiddie suspended coaster. Scope and scale Minor attraction. When to go In the first or last 30 minutes of the day, or (better yet) not at all. Comments 36" minimum height requirement; adults and older children must be accompanied by a child 36"–56" tall; child swap available (see page 188). All sizzle, no steak. Duration of ride 1¼ minutes. Average wait in line per 100 people ahead of you 28 minutes. Loading speed Slower than a hog in quicksand.

DESCRIPTION AND COMMENTS This is IOA's biggest blunder. Engineered to accommodate only 170 persons per hour, the ride dangles you on a swing below a track that passes over a small part of Jurassic Park. We recommend skipping this one. Why? Because the next ice age will probably end before you reach the front of the line! And your reward for all that waiting? A 1-minute-and-15-second ride.

TOURING TIPS This attraction is designed for children 36–56 inches in height. An adult or older child over 56 inches in height must accompany a child meeting the 36- to 56-inch height requirement.

We're amazed that the ride still exists, given its low capacity and long lines. Rumors of its demise have run rampant for years, but none (unfortunately) have panned out yet. We don't think Pteranodon Flyers is worth the wait, and Universal Express isn't valid on the attraction. If your children insist on riding and abject bribery fails, get in line as quickly as possible after opening, or look for Virtual Line kiosks outside Camp Jurassic that dispense timed-return tickets for Pteranodon Flyers. When in use, you must retrieve a return ticket to ride; the total wait time before your turn arrives won't be much shorter than under the old system, but at least your kids can play in the caves instead of stewing in the standby line. If all return tickets run out for the day, the ride usually reverts to a regular standby queue 2 hours before the park closes.

Raptor Encounter ★★★½

**APPEAL BY AGE PRESCHOOL ★★★ GRADE SCHOOL ★★★½ TEENS ★★★★½
YOUNG ADULTS ★★★★½ OVER 30 ★★★★½ SENIORS ★★★★½**

What it is Photo op with lifelike dinosaur. **Scope and scale** Minor attraction. **When to go** Check park map or attraction for appearance times. **Comments** Clever girl! Sure to scare the spit out of small kids. **Duration of encounter** About a minute. **Average wait in line per 100 people ahead of you** 30 minutes. **Queue speed** Very slow.

DESCRIPTION AND COMMENTS Just when everyone thinks that Disney has a lock on the meet and greet market, between its talking Mickeys and *Frozen* sisters, Universal does the impossible—breeds a live velociraptor and makes it pose for pictures! OK, it isn't actually a real dinosaur on display just outside the Jurassic Park Discovery Center. In fact, it's an amazingly realistic puppet, created by Michael Curry (who created designs for Disney's *Lion King* and *Finding Nemo* musicals, as well as Diagon Alley's *Tales of Beedle the Bard* show) and brought to life by talented performers.

Several times each hour, the blue siren lights around the sunken predator paddock signal the arrival of Blue, Jurassic World's semitame saurian star. A game warden briefs one family at a time regarding proper safety procedures (convey calm assurance, move in slowly, and try not to smell like meat) before they step up for a photo. Don't peer too closely over the edge of the raptor enclosure; you'll spot the cleverly camouflaged legs of the puppeteer inside and spoil the illusion. A Universal photographer will take your picture with his or her camera (included with My Universal Photos packages) or your own, and selfies are also encouraged—just don't be surprised if the dino snaps when you say, "Smile!"

Raptor Encounter isn't among IOA's major attractions, and the queue can move at a crawl, but this crew from Calgary, Canada, says you shouldn't overlook it:

> I was really intrigued by the Raptor Encounter. We probably would have missed it if it hadn't been for the guide. It was one of the highlights of our day! Blue the raptor tried to eat [my 15-year-old son's] hat. It was super fun.

TOURING TIPS The Raptor Encounter has become quite popular, and with limited capacity and little shade, this can become an unpleasant wait. Appearances begin around 10 a.m. and run continuously until 6:45 p.m., with brief breaks about every 20 minutes to rotate raptors. Ask a team member stationed outside the paddock entrance approximately how long your wait will be before queuing. Universal installed greenery at the exit to block passersby from snapping photos, so if you want to see the dino, you'll have to deal with the line. Don't try to touch the raptor, or you may come home minus a hand; surreptitiously feeding your offspring to the dinosaurs is also discouraged by management.

THE WIZARDING WORLD OF HARRY POTTER—HOGSMEADE

THE 20-ACRE WIZARDING WORLD is an amalgamation of landmarks, creatures, and themes that are faithful to the films and books. You access the area through an imposing gate that opens onto **Hogsmeade,** depicted in winter and covered in snow. This is The Wizarding World's primary shopping and dining venue. Exiting Hogsmeade, you first glimpse the towering castle housing **Hogwarts School of Witchcraft and Wizardry,** flanked by the **Forbidden Forest** and **Hagrid's Hut.** The grounds and interior of the castle contain part of the queue for the super-headliner **Harry Potter and the Forbidden Journey.**

Universal went all out on the castle, with the intention of creating an icon even more beloved and powerful than Cinderella Castle at Disney's Magic Kingdom, and very nearly succeeded—if only they'd added a bit more brick and rockwork to conceal the big honking soundstage that holds the land's groundbreaking ride.

Hogsmeade in Detail

THE WIZARDING WORLD OF HARRY POTTER—Hogsmeade is in the northwest corner of IOA, between The Lost Continent and Jurassic Park. From the IOA entrance, the most direct route there is through Port of Entry and then right, through Seuss Landing (staying to the left of Green Eggs and Ham) and The Lost Continent, to the Hogsmeade main gate. The alternative route is to cross the bridge connecting The Lost Continent with Jurassic Park, and then turn right after entering the latter area. Note that the bridge is closed on slower days.

For the moment, though, let's begin our exploration at The Wizarding World's main entrance, on The Lost Continent side. Passing beneath a stone arch, you enter the village of **Hogsmeade.** The **Hogwarts Express** locomotive sits belching steam on your right. The village setting is rendered in exquisite detail: stone cottages and shops have steeply pitched slate roofs, bowed multipaned windows, gables, and tall, crooked chimneys. Add cobblestone streets and gas streetlamps, and Hogsmeade is as reminiscent of Sherlock Holmes as it is of Harry Potter.

Your first taste—literally—of the Harry Potter universe comes courtesy of **Honeydukes.** Specializing in Potter-themed candy such as Acid Pops (no flashbacks, guaranteed), Tooth Splintering Strong Mints, and

Fizzing Whizbees, the sweet shop offers no shortage of snacks that administer an immediate sugar high. There's also a small bakery inside; while we recommend avoiding the prepackaged Cauldron Cakes, which look much better than they taste, the big draw is the elaborately boxed Chocolate Frogs. The chocolate inside isn't anything special, but the packaging looks as if it came straight from a Harry Potter film, complete with lenticular wizard trading card.

Next door to Honeydukes and set back from the main street is **Three Broomsticks,** a rustic tavern serving English staples such as fish-and-chips, shepherd's pie, Cornish pasties, and turkey legs; kids' fare includes the obligatory mac and cheese and chicken fingers. To the rear of the tavern is the **Hog's Head pub,** which serves a nice selection of beer as well as The Wizarding World's signature nonalcoholic brew, Butterbeer (see page 203). Three Broomsticks and the Hog's Head were carved out of The Lost Continent's popular Enchanted Oak Tavern, which was Potterfied pretty effectively in its reincarnation, though a good deal of seating capacity was sacrificed. To dine at Three Broomsticks anytime from its opening until roughly 8 p.m., you'll have to wait in a long queue during busier times of year, with waiting times exceeding 30 minutes on busy days.

Roughly across the street from the pub, you'll find benches in the shade at the **Owlery,** where animatronic owls (complete with lifelike poop) ruffle and hoot from the rafters. Next to the Owlery is the **Owl Post,** where you can have mail stamped with a Hogsmeade postmark before dropping it off for delivery (an Orlando postmark will also be applied by the real USPS). The Owl Post also sells stationery, toy owls, and magic wands. Here, once again, a nice selection of owls preens on the timbers overhead. You access the Owl Post in either of two ways: through an interior door following the wand-choosing demonstration at **Ollivanders** (see page 336) or through **Dervish and Banges,** a magic-supplies shop that's interconnected with the Owl Post. You can't enter through the Owl Post's front door on busy days, when it serves exclusively as an exit. Because it's so difficult to get into the Owl Post, IOA often stations a team member outside to stamp your postcards with The Wizarding World postmark.

At the far end of the village, the massive **Hogwarts Castle** comes into view, set atop a rock face and towering over Hogsmeade and the entire Wizarding World. Follow the path through the castle's massive gates to the entrance of Harry Potter and the Forbidden Journey. Below the castle and to the right, at the base of the cliff, are the **Forbidden Forest, Hagrid's Hut,** and the **Flight of the Hippogriff** children's roller coaster. In the village, near the gate to Hogwarts Castle, is **Filch's Emporium of Confiscated Goods,** which offers all manner of Potter-themed gear, including Quidditch clothing, magical-creature toys, film-inspired chess sets, and, of course, Death Eater masks (breath mints extra).

In keeping with the stores depicted in the Potter films, the shopping venues in Hogsmeade are small and intimate—so intimate, in fact, that they feel congested when they're serving only 12–20 shoppers. With so many avid Potter fans, lines for the shops can develop on busy days by 9:30 or 10 a.m., creating a phenomenon we've never seen in all our years of covering theme parks: the lines for the shops are sometimes nearly as long as the waits for the attractions. Filch's Emporium is the only shop in The Wizarding World that you can enter during high season without waiting in line; the problem is that it doubles as the exit for Forbidden Journey. As throngs of riders flow out continuously, trying to enter Filch's is not unlike swimming upstream to spawn; still, it's a whole lot better than standing in lines for the other shops. Because the stores are so jammed, IOA sells some Potter merchandise, including wands, through street vendors and in Port of Entry shops.

At the end of the village and to the left is the bridge to **Jurassic Park,** the themed area contiguous to The Wizarding World. This is the best vantage point to get your photo with Hogwarts Castle in the background, as the hordes of people posing in the middle of the walkway will attest.

Entertainment in Hogsmeade

Hogsmeade raised "retail theater" in theme parks to unprecedented levels, as nearly every shop space and storefront window sport some sort of animatronic or special effects surprise. At **Dervish and Banges,** the fearsome *Monster Book of Monsters* rattles and snarls at you as Nimbus 2001 brooms strain at their tethers overhead. At the **Hog's Head** pub, the titular porcine part, mounted behind the bar, similarly thrashes and growls when the barkeep receives a gratuity.

Two brief street entertainments are staged in a raised outdoor alcove at the Forbidden Journey end of Hogsmeade. Showtimes aren't listed in the park map, but performances usually start every 30 minutes on the hour and half hour.

The *Frog Choir* (★★★) is composed of four singers, two of whom are holding large amphibian puppets sitting on pillows. Inspired by a brief scene in *Harry Potter and the Prisoner of Azkaban,* the group sings a cappella three or four wizard-related songs, including "Hedwig's Theme" and "Something Wicked This Way Comes." The 10-minute show is followed by a photo op. Though cute, the *Frog Choir* isn't much more than filler for IOA's attraction list and probably is not worth going out of your way for. A special set of Yuletide tunes is performed during the annual Christmas in The Wizarding World celebration.

The *Triwizard Spirit Rally* (★★★) showcases a group of three men, who perform martial arts–type moves including jumps, kicks, and simulated battle with sticks; and a group of four women, who perform simple rhythmic gymnastic moves with ribbons. The entire performance lasts about 6 minutes. After each show, the students of Beauxbatons Academy of Magic and the Durmstrang Institute are available for group photos. Though marginally more exciting than the *Frog Choir,* this is only a must-do for major Potter fans.

On select evenings throughout the year, *The Nighttime Lights at Hogwrds Castle* show (★★★★) brings the Forbidden Journey facade to life with colorful spells and magical creatures cavorting to John Williams's stirring film score, all thanks to the Muggle miracle of digital projection mapping. Powerful video projectors (some cleverly disguised as owl roosts) are hidden around Hogsmeade, all pointing at Hogwarts and the mountain on which it sits, and twinkle lights in the trees change colors to complement the castle. While the Sorting Hat narrates, each of the school's four houses gets a chance to unfurl its banners and show off its mascot; watch out for Slytherin's snapping snake. The brief 5-minute celebration is capped with a quick burst of pyrotechnics.

During the holiday season's Christmas in The Wizarding World event, a special *Magic of Christmas at Hogwarts* version of the projection show is presented. About 2 minutes longer, it features additional fan-favorite characters like the Weasley twins, who transform the castle's turret into a big Boggart Banger. It's well worth seeing even if you've already experienced the year-round version.

The best viewing area for either castle show is located in front of the *Frog Choir* stage or on the bridge to Jurassic Park. The show is repeated every 15–20 minutes from sunset to park closing; the first couple showings are the most crowded, and the last is the least attended. Prior to showtime, the bridge to Jurassic Park is restricted to exiting traffic only, and guests entering Hogsmeade through The Lost Continent are held in front of Ollivanders (where there is no view of the show) once the courtyard around the castle is full. Our recommendation is to make your way into Hogsmeade shortly before the first performance of the evening, and enjoy Forbidden Journey and Flight of the Hippogriff during the first couple showings. You'll be able to walk freely between the rides, and lines should be nonexistent. Then wait for the crowd to begin exiting after a show, and grab a good spot for one of the later runs.

Hogsmeade Touring Strategy

Crowds at IOA's Wizarding World are still large during the summer and holidays, and you'll encounter lines for the attractions even at slower times of year.

When IOA offers Early Park Admission, on-site hotel guests are allowed into Hogsmeade 1 hour before the general public (either via the front gate or Hogwarts Express). If you have early-entry privileges for The Wizarding World, use them, arriving as early during the early-entry period as possible. Otherwise, we suggest leaving The Wizarding World for late in the day, as the area will be occupied by hotel guests by the time the first day guests arrive.

unofficial **TIP**
If you leave The Wizarding World while the entrance barriers are in place and you wish to return, you'll either have to wait in line to get another pass (provided they haven't all been distributed) or wait until late in the day, when the barricades come down as crowds disperse.

Universal uses a flexible system of basic crowd-control options predicated on the expected level of attendance for any given day.

(Similar procedures are in place at Diagon Alley; see page 282 in Part Seven.) On most days of the year, from the slowest off-season through the busiest summer weeks, you can enter and depart The Wizarding World—Hogsmeade as you please. The waits for the rides will still be more than an hour at times, but gaining entry to the themed area itself is not an issue.

On days when the park is busiest, such as during spring break or December 25–January 1, access to Hogsmeade may be limited for part of the day. Barricades are placed at both entrances to The Wizarding World—Hogsmeade once the area reaches maximum occupancy. You can then go to touch screen ticket kiosks outside the Jurassic Park Discovery Center and obtain a free return ticket (not unlike the old paper FastPasses at Walt Disney World) to come back during your choice of designated time windows. You do not need your admission ticket to receive a timed-return ticket, and one person can retrieve a time for your entire party (up to nine people). At the specified time, return to The Lost Continent entrance and present your pass to the barricade crew to gain entry.

The return time on your pass depends on crowd conditions and how many Universal resort guests are in Hogsmeade before the park opens to the general public. Depending on demand, your possible return times may be many hours in the future, and it's possible (though extremely rare) for return tickets to run out entirely. Another factor that will affect your wait is how well Harry Potter and the Forbidden Journey is operating because this is what those in line are waiting for. If the ride comes up on schedule and runs trouble-free, everything runs smoothly. If Forbidden Journey experiences problems, though, especially first thing in the morning, it gums up the works for everyone.

On these peak days, a standby queue may also be erected in the waterfront landing behind the Jurassic Park Discovery Center; because more guests can enter only as others leave, this line can be painfully slow, so a return ticket is strongly suggested. It is common for the entrance barricades to be removed during the last hour or two the park is open, thus presenting the opportunity to come and go as you please.

Once admitted to The Wizarding World—Hogsmeade, you'll still have to wait for each ride, store, and concession, as well as for the area's one restaurant. Because Hogsmeade has less elbowroom than Diagon Alley, it reaches maximum occupancy and requires return tickets on days when Diagon does not, and feels more crowded once you finally get inside.

Note that guests arriving on the Hogwarts Express disembark outside Hogsmeade and must still retrieve a ticket before entering. The timed-return tickets are neither needed nor accepted for Hogwarts Express.

Waits for the rides finally dissipate about an hour or so before closing, even on the busiest days, but the streets become even more crowded after dark on nights when the Hogwarts Castle projection show is scheduled. A bonus of visiting late is enjoying the exquisite lighting and magical nighttime personality of The Wizarding World. Forbidden

Journey will accommodate anyone already in line at park closing, and many of the Hogsmeade shops stay open awhile after closing.

However complicated, it's all doable, as a multigenerational Grosse Pointe, Michigan, family attests:

> *Convinced of your rectitude, we went without fear to Universal. We made it to Harry Potter by 8:05, were out of the Forbidden Journey and on the Hippogriff by 8:30, and had our Butterbeer by 9.*

Flight of the Hippogriff *(Universal Express)* ★★★

APPEAL BY AGE	PRESCHOOL	★★★★	GRADE SCHOOL	★★★★	TEENS	★★★½
YOUNG ADULTS	★★★½		OVER 30	★★★½	SENIORS	★★★½

What it is Kiddie roller coaster. **Scope and scale** Minor attraction. **When to go** First 90 minutes the park is open or after 4 p.m. **Comments** 36" minimum height requirement; child swap available (see page 188). A good beginner coaster. **Duration of ride** 1 minute. **Average wait in line per 100 people ahead of you** 14 minutes. **Loading speed** Slow.

DESCRIPTION AND COMMENTS Below and to the right of Hogwarts Castle, next to Hagrid's Hut, the Hippogriff is short and sweet but not worth much of a wait. An outdoor, elevated coaster designed for children old enough to know about Harry Potter but not yet tall enough to ride Forbidden Journey, the ride affords excellent views of the area within Wizarding World and of Hogwarts. The theming is also very good, considering that this isn't a major attraction. As a children's coaster only slightly taller and longer than the Magic Kingdom's Barnstormer, there are no loops, inversions, or rolls: it's just one big hill and some mild turns, and almost half of the 1-minute ride time is spent going up the lift hill. Unfortunately, Orlando's Hippogriff has become increasingly rough in recent years, and it is not as pleasant to ride as the identically named coaster at Universal Studios Hollywood.

For fans of Harry Potter, there are two gorgeous items in this attraction that you will want to see. The first is a faithful re-creation of Hagrid's Hut in the queue (complete with the sound of Fang howling), while the second is an incredible animatronic of Buckbeak that you pass by while on the ride. Remember that when Muggles encounter hippogriffs such as Buckbeak, proper etiquette must always be maintained to avoid any danger. Hippogriffs are extremely proud creatures and must be shown the proper respect by bowing to them and waiting for them to bow in return.

TOURING TIPS Have your kids ride soon after the park opens while older siblings enjoy Forbidden Journey.

Hagrid's Magical Creatures Coaster *(opens 2019)*

What it is Roller coaster. **Scope and scale** Super-headliner. **When to go** First 30 minutes the park is open or at park closing. **Comments** Minimum height requirement; child swap available (see page 188). **Duration of ride** About 4 minutes. **Loading speed** Moderate.

Motion Sickness

DESCRIPTION AND COMMENTS In September 2017 Universal Orlando decommissioned the Dragon Challenge inverted roller coasters (originally known as the Dueling Dragons) in favor of a new family-friendly thrill ride. The yet-unnamed replacement, scheduled to open in 2019, will also be a roller coaster, but a highly themed one without huge hills or upside-down loops. Instead, it will focus on multiple high-speed launches through the heavily forested terrain during outdoor segments, and close encounters with animatronic beasties inside and between the ride's indoor show buildings.

The 14-passenger trains from Intamin are inspired by Hagrid's motorcycle and sidecar, and the original coaster's load station is being transformed into an immersive new queue. Highlights of the adventure include an indoor vertical tunnel that leads into a backward helix, followed by a dropping track in the darkness. Fantastic beasts and familiar figures from the Potter world—such as the flying Ford Anglia, Fluffy the three-headed dog, and Hagrid himself—will make appearances during your experience.

TOURING TIPS The new ride will have a lower height requirement than Forbidden Journey, so we expect it to take the crown as the park's most popular ride. Because hourly capacity will be limited, visit as early as possible or shortly before closing.

Harry Potter and the Forbidden Journey
(Universal Express) ★★★★★

APPEAL BY AGE	PRESCHOOL ★★	GRADE SCHOOL ★★★★½	TEENS ★★★★★
YOUNG ADULTS ★★★★★	OVER 30 ★★★★½	SENIORS ★★★★	

What it is Motion-simulator dark ride. **Scope and scale** Super-headliner. **When to go** Immediately after park opening or in the last hours before closing. **Comments** Expect *long* waits in line; 48″ minimum height requirement; child swap available (see page 188); single-rider line available. Marvelous for Muggles; not to be missed. **Duration of ride** 4¼ minutes. **Average wait in line per 100 people ahead of you** 4 minutes. **Loading speed** Fast.

Motion Sickness

DESCRIPTION AND COMMENTS This ride provides the only opportunity at Universal Orlando to come close to Harry, Ron, Hermione, and Dumbledore as portrayed by the original actors. Half the attraction is a series of preshows, setting the stage for the main event, a thrilling dark ride. You can get on the ride in only 10–25 minutes using the singles line, but everyone should go through the main queue at least once. The characters are incorporated into the queue and serve as an important element of the overall experience, not merely something to keep you occupied while you wait for the main event.

From Hogsmeade you reach the attraction through the imposing Winged Boar gates and progress along a winding path. Entering the castle on a lower level, you walk through a sort of dungeon festooned with various icons and prop replicas from the Potter flicks, including the Mirror of Erised from *Harry Potter and the Sorcerer's Stone*. You later emerge back outside and into the Hogwarts greenhouses. The greenhouses compose the larger part of the Forbidden Journey's queuing area, and despite some strategically placed mandrakes, there isn't much here to amuse. If you're among the first in the park and in the queue, you'll move through this area pretty quickly. Otherwise . . . well, we hope you like plants. The greenhouses are not air-conditioned, but fans move the (hot) air around. Blessedly, there are water fountains but, alas, no restrooms.

unofficial **TIP**
Even if your child meets the height requirement, consider carefully whether Forbidden Journey is an experience he or she can handle—because the seats on the benches are compartmentalized, kids can't see or touch Mom or Dad if they get frightened.

Having finally escaped horticulture purgatory, you reenter the castle, moving along its halls and passageways. One chamber you'll probably remember from the films is a multistory gallery of portraits, many of whose subjects come alive when they take a notion. You'll see for the first time the four founders of Hogwarts: Helga Hufflepuff holding her famous cup, Godric Gryffindor and Rowena Ravenclaw nearby, and the tall, moving portrait of Salazar Slytherin straight ahead. The founders argue about Quidditch and Dumbledore's controversial decision to host an open house at Hogwarts for Muggles (garden-variety mortals). Don't rush through the gallery—the effects are very cool, and the conversation is essential to understanding the rest of the attraction.

Next up, after you've navigated some more passages, is Dumbledore's office, where the wizard principal appears on a balcony and welcomes you to Hogwarts. The headmaster's appearance is your introduction to Musion Eyeliner technology—a high-definition video-projection system that produces breathtakingly realistic, three-dimensional, life-size moving holograms. The technology uses a special foil that reflects images from HD projectors, producing holographs of variable sizes and incredible clarity. After his welcoming remarks, Dumbledore dispatches you to the Defence Against the Dark Arts classroom to hear a presentation on the history of Hogwarts.

As you gather to await the lecture, Harry, Ron, and Hermione pop out from beneath an invisibility cloak. They suggest you ditch the lecture in favor of joining them for a proper tour of Hogwarts, including a Quidditch match. After some repartee among the characters and a couple of special effects surprises, it's off to the Hogwarts Official Attraction Safety Briefing and Boarding Instructions Chamber—OK, it's actually the Gryffindor Common Room, but you get the picture. The briefing and instructions are presented by animated portraits, including an etiquette teacher. Later on, even the famed Sorting Hat gets into the act. All this leads to the Room of Requirement, where hundreds of candles float overhead as you board the ride.

After all the high-tech stuff in your queuing odyssey, you'll naturally expect to be wowed by your ride vehicle. Surely it's a Nimbus 3000 turbo-broom, a phoenix, a hippogriff, or at least the Weasleys' flying car. But no, what you'll ride on the most technologically advanced theme park attraction in America is . . . a *bench*? Yep, a bench.

A bit anticlimactic, perhaps, but as benches go, this one's a doozy, mounted on a Kuka robotic arm. When not engaged in Quidditch matches, a Kuka arm is a computer-controlled robotic arm similar to the kind used in heavy manufacturing. If you think about pictures you've seen of automotive assembly plants, Kuka arms are like those long metal appendages that come in to complete welds, move heavy stuff around, or fasten things. With the right programming, the arms can handle just about any repetitive industrial tasks thrown at them (see kuka-robotics.com for more info).

Bear with us for a moment; you know how we Unofficials like techno-geekery. When you put a Kuka arm on a ride platform, it provides six axes—six degrees of freedom, with synchronized motion that can be programmed to replicate all the sensations of flying, including broad swoops, steep dives, sharp turns, sudden stops, and fast acceleration. Here's where it gets really good: until now, when Kuka arms and similar robotic systems have been employed in theme park rides, the arm has been anchored to a stationary platform. In Forbidden Journey, the arm is mounted on a ride vehicle that moves you through a series of live sets and action scenes projected all around you. The movement of the arm is synchronized to create the motion that corresponds to what's happening in the film. When everything works right, it's mind-blowing.

High-tech hijinks aside, is the attraction itself ultimately worthy of the hype? In a word, *yes*! Your 4¼-minute adventure is a headlong sprint through the most thrilling moments from the first few Potter books: you'll soar over Hogwarts Castle, narrowly evade an attacking dragon, spar with the Whomping Willow, get tossed into a Quidditch match, and fight off Dementors inside the Chamber of Secrets. Scenes alternate between enormous physical sets (complete with animatronic creatures), elaborate lighting effects, and high-definition video-projection domes that surround your field of view, similar to Soarin' or The Simpsons Ride. Those Kuka-powered benches really do "levitate" in a manner that feels remarkably like free flight, and while you don't go upside down, the sensation of floating on your back or being slung from side to side is certainly unique.

The seamless transitions between screens and sets, and the way the domes appear to remain stationary in front of you while actually moving (much like Dreamfinder's dirigible in the original Journey into Imagination at Epcot), serve to blur the boundary between actual and virtual better than any attraction before it. The greatest-hits montage plotline may be a bit muddled, but the ride is enormously effective at leaving you feeling as though you just survived the scariest scrapes from the early educational career of The Boy Who Lived.

We have two primary bones to pick. First, the staff rush you through the queue. To understand the story line and get the most out of the attraction, you really need to see and hear the entire presentation in each of the preshow rooms. This won't happen unless, contrary to the admonishments of the team members, you just park yourself and watch a full run-through of each preshow. Try to find a place to stop where you can let those behind you pass and where you're as far away from any staff as possible. As long as you're not creating a logjam, the team members will leave you alone as often as not.

Another gripe: The dialogue in the preshows is delivered in English accents of varying degrees of intelligibility, and at a very brisk pace. Add an echo effect owing to the cavernous nature of the preshow rooms, and it can be quite difficult for Yanks to decipher what's being said. This is especially evident in the staccato repartee between Harry, Ron, and Hermione in the Defence Against the Dark Arts classroom.

TOURING TIPS Harry Potter and the Forbidden Journey quickly became the most popular attraction at IOA, and one of the most in-demand theme park attractions in America. While much of the attention has turned toward Gringotts at USF, the best way to ride Forbidden Journey with a reasonable wait is to be one of the first through the turnstiles in the morning, use Universal Express, or visit in the final hours of the evening, especially during the projection show.

Upon approaching Forbidden Journey's front gates, all guests may be directed into an extended outdoor queue if the mandatory lockers are overcrowded. If you don't need to stow your stuff and want to be sneaky, you can enter the castle through Filch's gift shop and cut through the lockers to reach the ride queue. Our wait-time research has shown that, in some cases, not needing a locker can save you as much as 30 minutes of standing in line.

Universal warns you to secure or leave behind loose objects, which most people interpret to mean glasses, purses, hats, and the like. However, the ride makes a couple of moves that will empty your trousers faster than a master pickpocket—ditto and worse for shirt pockets. When these moves occur, your stuff will clatter around like quarters in a slot machine tray. It's much better to use the small compartment built into the seat back for keys, coins, phone, wallet, and pocket Bible. Be prepared, however: team members don't give you much time to stow or retrieve your belongings.

The single-rider line is not clearly marked, so relatively few guests use it. Whereas on most attractions the wait in the singles line is one-third the wait in the standby line, at Forbidden Journey it can be as much as one-tenth. Because the individual seating separates you from the other riders whether your party stays together or not, the singles line is a great option, as this wife from Edinburgh, Scotland, discovered:

> Trust me, sitting next to hubby on Forbidden Journey, romantic though it may be, is not as awesome as having to wait only 15 minutes as a single rider.

To get there, enter the attraction gates and keep left all the way into the castle. Past the locker area, take the first left into the singles line.

If you see a complete iteration of each preshow in the queue and then experience the ride, you'll invest 25–35 minutes even if you don't have to wait. If you elect to skip the preshows (the Gryffindor Common Room, where you receive safety and loading directions, is mandatory) and use the singles line, you can get on in about 10–25 minutes at any time of day. At a time when the posted wait in the regular line was 2 hours, we rode and were out the door in 15 minutes using the singles line.

Forbidden Journey is one of our favorite rides in the world, and it's a big hit with our readers, like this mother of three from Crystal Lake, Illinois:

> I was in awe from the minute I stepped into line, [and] from the minute I began "flying," I was like a little kid. The integration of movement, video screens, and real scenery was so seamless that I truly felt like I was part of the movie. Here I was, a 40-year-old woman, and I literally walked off the ride with tears in my eyes and happiness in my heart. It was the most amazing ride I had ever been on, and I believe any ride would be hard-pressed to bring about the same feeling of joy!

But much as we enjoy Forbidden Journey, it behooves us to pass along this warning from a mom in St. Louis:

> A security person at Universal told me that Harry Potter and the Forbidden Journey is THE most motion sickness–inducing ride in the two Universal parks. My husband and daughter went on the ride, and then somehow convinced me to try it. I should have listened to the security person!

The ride's videos were upgraded in 2018 to 4K, 120 frames per second, creating a smoother, sharper image that's easier to watch for those with a weak stomach. Universal has also toned down the Kuka programming since the ride opened and added fans to each seat that blow cool air on rider's foreheads in a somewhat successful effort to reduce motion sickness. We nonetheless recommend that you not ride with a full stomach. If you start getting queasy, fix your gaze on your feet and try to exclude as much from your peripheral vision as possible.

In response to many larger guests being denied rides when Harry Potter and the Forbidden Journey first opened, the end seats on each flying bench were redesigned to accommodate a wider variety of body shapes and sizes. Though these modified seats allow many more people to ride, it's still possible that guests of size can't fit in them. The best way to figure out whether you can fit in a regular seat or one of the modified ones is to sit in one of the test seats outside the queue or just inside the castle. After you sit down, pull down on the safety harness as far as you can. One of three safety lights will illuminate: A green light indicates that you can fit into any seat, a yellow light means that you should ask for one of the modified seats on the outside of the bench, and a red light means that the harness can't engage enough for you to ride safely.

In addition, IOA team members select guests of all sizes "at random" to plop in the test seats, but they're really looking for large people or those who have a certain body shape. Team members handle the situation as diplomatically as possible, but if they suspect you're not the right size, you'll be asked to sit down for a test. For you to be cleared to ride, the overhead restraint has to click three times; once again, it's body shape rather than weight (unless you're over 300 pounds) that's key.

Most team members will let you try a second time if you don't achieve three clicks on the first go. Passing the test by inhaling sharply is not recommended unless you can also hold your breath for the entire 4-plus minutes of the ride.

Hogwarts Express *(Universal Express)* ★★★★½

APPEAL BY AGE	PRESCHOOL ★★★★½	GRADE SCHOOL ★★★★½	TEENS ★★★★½
YOUNG ADULTS ★★★★½	OVER 30 ★★★★½	SENIORS ★★★★½	

What it is Transportation attraction with special effects. **Scope and scale** Headliner. **When to go** Immediately after park opening until midafternoon. **Comments** Requires park-to-park admission. A moving experience; not to be missed. **Duration of ride** 4 minutes. **Average wait in line per 100 people ahead of you** 7 minutes. **Loading speed** Moderate.

DESCRIPTION AND COMMENTS The counterpart to USF's King's Cross is Hogsmeade Station, which sits on the border between IOA's Hogsmeade and Lost Continent. See Part Seven, page 277, for a full review of the Hogwarts Express experience.

TOURING TIPS Because the Hogsmeade Station doesn't include the cool Platform 9¾ effect found at the King's Cross end, you'd expect waits for the one-way trip to be shorter here. Surprisingly, lines can be longer here than at USF on slower days, though King's Cross is the busier end during peak periods. Lines are usually less than 20 minutes through the morning but can build later in the day. Hogsmeade Station also lacks other King's Cross amenities, such as air-conditioning and an in-queue snack stand.

On most days, disembarking guests will be allowed directly into Hogsmeade, less than a minute's walk away. On peak days when the area reaches capacity, they'll be directed to the bridge between The Lost Continent and Jurassic Park, where they'll have to either queue to enter Hogsmeade or obtain a free timed-return ticket to visit The Wizarding World at a specified time.

If you wish to experience the train, do so before the queue builds in midafternoon. If the line grows very long, guests wishing to ride a second time in one day may be relegated to a slower re-ride queue.

Ollivanders ★★★★

APPEAL BY AGE	PRESCHOOL ★★★★	GRADE SCHOOL ★★★★½	TEENS ★★★★½
YOUNG ADULTS ★★★★½	OVER 30 ★★★★	SENIORS ★★★★½	

What it is Combination wizarding demonstration and shopping op. **Scope and scale** Minor attraction. **When to go** In the first or last 30 minutes of the day. **Comments** Audience stands; identical to USF version but with a much slower line. Enchanting but inefficient. **Duration of presentation** 6 minutes. **Average wait in line per 100 people ahead of you** 36 minutes.

DESCRIPTION AND COMMENTS Next to the Owl Post is Ollivanders, a musty little shop stacked to the ceiling with boxes of magic wands. Inside you'll find the same intimate wand-choosing ceremony found in the Diagon Alley attraction of the same name (see page 278). It's great fun, but the tiny shop can accommodate only about 24 guests at a time. After the show, the whole group is dispatched to the Owl Post and Dervish and Banges to make purchases.

The wand experience is second in popularity only to Harry Potter and the Forbidden Journey. Lines build quickly after opening, and there's little to no shade. The average wait time during summer and other busy periods is 45–85 minutes between 9:30 a.m. and 7:30 p.m. If you're just looking to buy a wand without the interactive features, a cart is usually set up near the *Frog Choir* stage, with little to no wait.

TOURING TIPS Due to its very low capacity (about 150 guests per hour), long lines for the show at Ollivanders form quickly upon park opening and last until just before the park closes. If you need to see this show, and you can't go to the USF branch, go first thing in the morning or as late as possible.

You do not need to see the wand-selection show to purchase a wand at Ollivanders—just enter the store directly rather than wait in the long outdoor queue. Also, interactive wands and other Harry Potter merchandise are available online and at other stores in The Wizarding World, as well as at Islands of Adventure Trading Company.

Interactive Wands and Spell-Casting Locations in Hogsmeade

Interactive wands sold in either park come with a map that shows Diagon Alley spell-casting locations on one side and Hogsmeade locations on the other. All of the spells in Hogsmeade are found in the central village, not near Hogwarts Castle or Hogwarts Express. Effects aren't as numerous or as elaborate in Hogsmeade as they are in Diagon Alley, and several are adaptations of older effects that previously ran automatically. There are also no hidden effects in Hogsmeade (as far as we know). On the other hand, there usually aren't quite as many kids trying to trigger effects here. If you are only visiting IOA, it probably isn't worthwhile to buy an interactive wand, but if you are visiting both parks, make sure to test out your purchase from USF's Ollivanders here.

THE LOST CONTINENT

THE LOST CONTINENT WAS ONCE among IOA's largest areas, until its medieval Merlinwood section was repurposed into The Wizarding World of Harry Potter—Hogsmeade, leaving only the Arabian and Ancient Greek portions intact. What's left of Lost Continent is extremely well themed and features the park's only attractions that aren't tied to a licensed intellectual property. Lost Continent can be reached directly from Hogsmeade or Seuss Landing, or on busy days via a bypass bridge to Jurassic Park.

The Lost Continent was home to *The Eighth Voyage of Sindbad Stunt Show,* which set sail for uncharted shores in September 2018, with no imminent plans announced for a replacement. Proposals have been floated to turn the entire land into the Isle of Berk (from How To Train Your Dragon) or Hyrule (from Legend of Zelda), and there are always advocates for expanding The Wizarding World, but we predict that Universal will direct its efforts elsewhere for a couple years once Hogsmeade's new coaster debuts.

The best attraction in Lost Continent may be the **Mystic Fountain,** an interactive talking fountain. A team member behind the scenes controls the fountain and is able to talk to and hear from anyone who approaches. Many kids seem mesmerized by it. Parents can grab a quick snack or drink while the little ones are entertained by the fountain mere steps away. The park's second First Aid station is also located here, behind the coin vendor.

Poseidon's Fury (Universal Express) ★★★½

What it is High-tech theater attraction. **Scope and scale** Headliner. **When to go** After experiencing all the rides. **Comments** Audience stands throughout. Dumb but dazzling. **Duration of show** 17 minutes, including preshow. **Probable waiting time** 25 minutes.

DESCRIPTION AND COMMENTS Greek god Poseidon dukes it out with an evil wizardlike guy—named Lord Darkenon, of all things—with Poseidon as the heavy. The two fight with fire, water, lasers, and smoke machines.

   As you might have inferred, the story is somewhat incoherent, but the special effects are still amazing, as is the theming of the preshow area. The plot unfolds in installments as you pass through a couple of antechambers and finally into the main theater. Though the production plods a bit at first, it wraps up with quite an impressive flourish.

TOURING TIPS Catch *Poseidon* after getting your fill of the rides. The attraction opens 1 or more hours after the rest of the park (usually at 10 a.m.) and closes 30 minutes or more before park closing. Check the daily entertainment schedule for showtimes.

   If you're still wet from Dudley Do-Right's Ripsaw Falls, Popeye & Bluto's Bilge-Rat Barges, or the Jurassic Park River Adventure, you might be tempted to cheer the evil wizard's flame jets in hopes of finally drying out. Our money, however, is on Poseidon—it's legal in Florida for theme parks to get guests wet, but setting them on fire is frowned upon.

   While most of the action takes place on movie screens, *Poseidon's Fury* can frighten many small children. The entire theater is thrown into total darkness many times during the show, and many of the special effects involve fire, loud noises, and flashing lights.

   As impressive as the facade of *Poseidon's Fury* is, this Massachusetts mom of a family of four thinks the attraction itself is a letdown:

> The one attraction we wished we'd skipped was Poseidon's Fury. The posted wait time was 10 minutes. After waiting 30 minutes, we were ushered into a series of rooms with no chairs to watch a set of poorly executed special effects. I'm 5 feet tall and saw none of it because everyone was standing, and the floor was poorly slanted. At the end, we were all tired and wanted to go home.

Finally, from a woman in New York State:

> The show was really annoying. I am short and couldn't see anything.

SEUSS LANDING

THIS 10-ACRE THEMED AREA is based on Dr. Seuss's famous children's books. Buildings and attractions replicate a whimsical, brightly colored cartoon style with exaggerated features and rounded lines. The odd-shaped facades were carved from Styrofoam and sprayed with concrete, and the impossibly bent palm trees were salvaged from Hurricane Andrew, resulting in a land without a single straight line or right angle. Sadly, the unmistakable Green Eggs and Ham Cafe is now permanently shuttered, but its namesake sandwich made a much better photo opportunity than meal anyway.

Featuring many of Dr. Seuss's most beloved characters (including the Lorax, the Grinch, Thing 1 and Thing 2, Sam-I-Am, and the Cat in the Hat), *Oh! The Stories You'll Hear!* (★★★) is a fun singing and dancing show staged in an outdoor area between Circus McGurkus Cafe Stoo-pendous and All the Books You Can Read. After each 9-minute show, the characters separate for individual meet and greets and autographs. Showtimes are listed in the park map. During inclement weather, the show takes place within the Circus McGurkus Cafe Stoo-pendous restaurant nearby. During Grinchmas, the show relocates to a stage between One Fish, Two Fish, Red Fish, Blue Fish and The Cat in the Hat ride.

Look for a photo op with top-hatted dignitaries outside the Mulberry Street Store; the figure with the beard and glasses is Dr. Theodor "Seuss" Geisel himself.

Caro-Seuss-el *(Universal Express)*   ★★★

APPEAL BY AGE	PRESCHOOL ★★★★★	GRADE SCHOOL ★★★★	TEENS ★★★
YOUNG ADULTS ★★★½	OVER 30 ★★★	SENIORS ★★★★	

What it is Merry-go-round. **Scope and scale** Minor attraction. **When to go** Anytime. **Comments** Child swap available (see page 188). Ride is outside but covered. Wonderfully whimsical. **Duration of ride** 2 minutes. **Average wait in line per 100 people ahead of you** 9 minutes. **Loading speed** Slow.

DESCRIPTION AND COMMENTS Totally outrageous, this full-scale, 56-mount merry-go-round is made up entirely of Dr. Seuss characters, each of which has an interactive effect (wagging tongues, blinking eyes) that the rider can control. While you turn, a Seussian orchestra of ridiculous instruments plays like a cacophonous calliope.

TOURING TIPS A gentle ride, even for the smallest children. If you are too old or don't want to ride, Caro-Seuss-el is still worth an inspection. If you do want to ride, waits are usually not too long, even in the middle of the day.

The Cat in the Hat *(Universal Express)*   ★★★½

APPEAL BY AGE	PRESCHOOL ★★★★½	GRADE SCHOOL ★★★★	TEENS ★★★
YOUNG ADULTS ★★★	OVER 30 ★★★½	SENIORS ★★★½	

What it is Indoor cartoon dark ride. **Scope and scale** Major attraction. **When to go** Before 11:30 a.m. or after 4 p.m. **Comments** 36" minimum height requirement; child swap available (see page 188). Dr. S. would be proud. **Duration of ride** 3¾ minutes. **Average wait in line per 100 people ahead of you** 5 minutes. **Loading speed** Moderate.

DESCRIPTION AND COMMENTS Universal's answer to Disney's vintage Fantasyland dark rides, this indoor, sit-down attraction recounts the entire *Cat in the Hat* story from beginning to end in a little less than 4 minutes. Guests ride on "couches" through 18 different sets inhabited by animatronic Seuss characters. Of course, mayhem ensues when Cat brings Thing 1 and Thing 2 over to play, as the beleaguered goldfish tries to maintain order in the midst of bedlam, but the entire mess is cleaned up just before Mom gets home.

The audio narration is clear, and each scene is crammed with the kind of crazy furniture and bizarre housewares found in the book. The ride is straightforward enough, but we wish it had more sophisticated animatronics and better effects.

TOURING TIPS This is fun for all ages. Try to ride early, or ride late in the day after families with young children have started to depart.

We think there's almost nothing here to frighten small children beyond some loud noises. A father of three from Natick, Massachusetts, disagrees:

> *The Cat in the Hat ride has quite the fright potential. My wife took my fairly advanced 3½-year-old daughter on the ride, and she was screaming her head off. Nearly two years later, she still reminds me of the scary Cat in the Hat ride (it hasn't affected her love for the books, though!).*

The High in the Sky Seuss Trolley Train Ride!
(Universal Express) ★★★½

APPEAL BY AGE	PRESCHOOL ★★★★½	GRADE SCHOOL ★★★★	TEENS ★★★
YOUNG ADULTS ★★★½	OVER 30 ★★★½	SENIORS ★★★★	

What it is Elevated train. Scope and scale Major attraction. When to go Before 11:30 a.m. or just before closing. Comments 36″ minimum height requirement; child swap available (see page 188). A relaxed look at the park. Duration of ride 3½ minutes. Average wait in line per 100 people ahead of you 9 minutes. Loading speed Molasses.

DESCRIPTION AND COMMENTS An elevated train ride through and around the buildings in Seuss Landing, the Trolley Train putters along elevated tracks while a voice reads a Dr. Seuss story over the train's speakers. As each train makes its way through Seuss Landing, it passes a series of simple animatronic characters in scenes that are part of the story being told.

The slow ride around Seuss Landing is pleasant and affords great views of most of the park, including Marvel Super Hero Island. Little tunnels and a few mild turns make this a charming attraction, but a bizarrely high minimum height requirement (recently reduced to 36″) means that many in the trolley's target demographic are banned from riding.

Note that you can choose from two different train tracks at the boarding station. As you face the platform, to your left is the Beech track, which is aquamarine; to your right is the Star track, which is purple. If you're riding with a large group, keep your group together if you all want the same experience because the track on each side offers different visuals and two randomly selected ride soundtracks.

TOURING TIPS The line for this ride is much less charming than the attraction. The trains are small, fitting about 20 people, and the loading speed is glacial. Save High in the Sky for the end of the day or ride first thing in the morning. There is no on-ride photo, but a photo op is available in the standby queue.

If I Ran the Zoo ★★★

APPEAL BY AGE	PRESCHOOL ★★★★★	GRADE SCHOOL ★★★½	TEENS ★★★★
YOUNG ADULTS ★★★★½	OVER 30 ★★★	SENIORS ★★★★½	

What it is Play area. Scope and scale Diversion. When to go Anytime. Comments Kids may get wet. A nice break for parents.

DESCRIPTION AND COMMENTS An interactive play area and outdoor maze themed to Dr. Seuss rhymes and filled with fantastic animals and gizmos from the stories.

TOURING TIPS Tour anytime. Note that much of the play area is unshaded; bring a drink and hat for the little ones.

One Fish, Two Fish, Red Fish, Blue Fish
(Universal Express)   ★★★

APPEAL BY AGE	PRESCHOOL ★★★★½	GRADE SCHOOL ★★★★	TEENS ★★★
YOUNG ADULTS ★★★	OVER 30 ★★★	SENIORS ★★★½	

What it is Wet version of Dumbo the Flying Elephant. **Scope and scale** Minor attraction. **When to go** Before 11:30 a.m. **Comments** Child swap available (see page 188). Plan on getting wet. Who says you can't teach an old ride new tricks? **Duration of ride** 2 minutes. **Average wait in line per 100 people ahead of you** 9 minutes. **Loading speed** Slow.

DESCRIPTION AND COMMENTS Imagine a mild spinning ride similar to Disney's Magic Carpets of Aladdin, TriceraTop Spin, and Dumbo rides, only with Seuss-style fish for ride vehicles, and you have half the story. The other half involves yet another opportunity to drown.

Guests board a fish-shaped ride vehicle mounted to an arm attached to a central axis, around which the ride vehicles spin. Guests can raise and lower their fish 15 feet in the air while traveling in circles and trying to avoid streams of water sprayed by other fish mounted to "squirt posts" around the ride's perimeter.

You can avoid most of the spray by going up or down at the right time. If you pay attention to the color of your vehicle and listen to the song played in the background, you can (eventually) figure out when to move your fish.

TOURING TIPS We don't know what it is about this theme park and water, but you'll get wetter than at a full-immersion baptism. Lines can build in the afternoon, so ride early while you'll still have time to dry off.

SPECIAL EVENTS *at* UNIVERSAL'S ISLANDS *of* ADVENTURE

IOA DOESN'T HOST NEARLY AS MANY special events throughout the year as USF, but the one it has is first-rate and included with standard admission.

GRINCHMAS *(early December–early January)*

YOU'LL FIND CHRISTMAS DECOR throughout IOA's Port of Entry, and Hogsmeade now celebrates **Christmas in The Wizarding World** with festive ornamentation, holiday treats, and a spectacular light show on Hogwarts Castle. But the epicenter of the holiday at IOA is obviously Seuss Landing. The star, naturally, is the Grinch, the iconic icky-green grump who famously stole Christmas from the Whos, only to return it when his undersized heart finally grew.

The Grinch is normally represented in the park by a masked representation of the cartoon character, but during Grinchmas, a speaking actor wearing professional prosthetic makeup impersonates Jim Carrey's live-action film incarnation. The Grinch meets and greets guests during the day inside the All the Books You Can Read store; he takes time to interact before each photograph, usually to hilarious effect, which results in a very slow-moving line. If meeting the Grinch is a priority, make this your first stop in the morning.

In addition to greeting guests, the Grinch stars in his own *Grinch-mas Who-liday Spectacular,* a 30-minute musical performed six to eight times each day inside a soundstage located behind Circus McGurkus Cafe Stoo-pendous. The show, which blends the original book and cartoon with elements from the Carrey flick and musical accompaniment arranged by Chip Davis of Mannheim Steamroller, is a must-see for Grinch fans. It features a first-rate cast (some of whom have appeared on Broadway), expansive set, and even an appearance by a live canine as the Grinch's faithful pet, Max.

Showtimes are listed in the park map and typically begin between 10:45 a.m. and noon and continue until around 6 p.m. Line up near the One Fish, Two Fish ride a minimum of 30–45 minutes before showtime, as performances fill to capacity early on busy days. You will be directed to a seat once inside, but the venue is shallow enough that even the back row has an acceptable view.

The **Grinch character breakfast** is held in Circus McGurkus Cafe Stoo-pendous on select mornings during December. It costs $34.99 (plus tax and gratuity) for adults, $20.99 for kids age 9 and under. Theme park admission is required; see "Character Meals" on page 198 for information.

UNIVERSAL'S ISLANDS *of* ADVENTURE TOURING PLANS

DECISIONS, DECISIONS

WHEN IT COMES TO TOURING IOA efficiently in a single day, you have two basic choices, and as you might expect, there are trade-offs. The Wizarding World of Harry Potter—Hogsmeade sucks up guests like a Hoover vacuum, and the 20-acre section of the park is quickly overrun by crowds on days of moderately heavy attendance. Because of Harry Potter and the Forbidden Journey's several preshows, it takes about 25 minutes to experience, even if you don't have to wait, which compounds the challenge of creating an optimal touring plan.

If you're intent on experiencing **Harry Potter and the Forbidden Journey** first thing, be at the turnstiles waiting to be admitted at least 30 minutes before the park opens. Once you're admitted, move as swiftly as possible to The Wizarding World and then ride Forbidden Journey, followed by Flight of the Hippogriff, in that order.

If the rides operate as designed, you're golden. You can get Hogsmeade out of the way in about an hour, and be off to other must-see attractions before the park gets crowded. Then come back to The Wizarding World late in the day to explore Hogsmeade and the shops. If, on the other hand, the ride suffers technical difficulties, you may be stuck in line a long while, during which time the crowds will have spread to other areas of IOA. By the time you exit Forbidden Journey, there will be long lines for all of the park's other popular attractions.

Unless you have Early Park Admission (EPA) privileges at IOA, a much better choice (and the path we follow in our recommended touring plans) is to skip Potterville first thing. Instead, enjoy other attractions in IOA, starting at Marvel Super Hero Island and Skull Island. The good news is that The Wizarding World usually clears out in the afternoon, and its queues are often empty in the last hour, even on busy days. You can ride Forbidden Journey with a minimal wait if you step in the queue shortly before closing time.

Even if you do take advantage of early entry, Forbidden Journey frustratingly runs only a small fraction of its available benches during the EPA hour, often making what should be a nominal wait stretch to 30 minutes or more. As a consequence, Forbidden Journey's wait is sometimes longer during EPA than it will be later that same afternoon. Unless you want to waste your entire early-entry hour standing in the Gryffindor Common Room, make sure you are one of the first families of the day inside Hogwarts Castle's halls, or save Forbidden Journey until after it has been brought up to full speed. Otherwise, you risk missing the rope drop rush toward Skull Island.

ONE-DAY TOURING PLAN FOR ADULTS (page 390)

THIS TOURING PLAN IS FOR GUESTS without park-to-park tickets and is appropriate for groups of all sizes and ages. It includes thrill rides that may induce motion sickness or get you wet. If the plan calls for you to experience an attraction that doesn't interest you, simply skip it and go to the next step. Be aware that the plan calls for some backtracking. If you have young children in your party, customize the plan to fit their needs and take advantage of child swap at thrill rides.

ONE-DAY TOURING PLAN FOR PARENTS WITH SMALL CHILDREN (page 391)

THIS PLAN IS FOR GUESTS without park-to-park tickets and elimi-nates all rides with a minimum height requirement greater than 40 inches. The plan includes a midday break of at least 2 hours back at your hotel. It's debatable whether the kids will need the nap more than you, but you'll thank us later, we promise.

ONE-DAY TOURING PLAN FOR SENIORS (page 392)

THIS PLAN IS FOR GUESTS without park-to-park tickets and is specifically designed for seniors and grandparents, taking walking dis-tances and attraction ratings from this group into account. This plan focuses on shows and family-friendly attractions and avoids thrill rides.

Also see pages 307–308 in Part Seven for our multiday and multi-park touring plans.

PART NINE

UNIVERSAL'S VOLCANO BAY

WET 'N WILD WAS STARTED in 1977 by SeaWorld creator George Millay as the world's first modern water park. It was independently owned until 1998, when it was sold to Universal Orlando, which also purchased the land under and around the park in 2013. That venerable park permanently closed December 31, 2016, and the property now holds Universal's Endless Summer Resort, while the water park's upstart successor opened May 25, 2017, as Universal's first on-property water park option.

Universal Orlando describes **Volcano Bay**'s 28 acres as "a lush, tropical oasis that unfolds before you, instantly transporting you to a little-known Pacific isle." Unlike the former Wet 'n Wild, whose only themes appeared to be concrete and plastic, Volcano Bay showcases a scenic, man-made mountain and a colorful atmosphere that goes toe to toe with those of Disney's water parks. In fact, Universal bills this water park as its third theme park, which is both technically correct and an act of marketing hubris on par with the initial advertising of The Wizarding World of Harry Potter as a "theme park within a theme park."

In practical terms, the park looks like an upscale resort in the South Pacific, with lush palm trees, thatched roofs, and tiki carvings (created by some of the same craftsmen behind Trader Sam's bar at Disney). As long as you're at ground level, you'll hardly guess that there's a busy interstate only yards away. The park is beautifully landscaped and contains many of the small details and inventive technology expected from the Universal theme park division. However, it is not substantially different from any other water park in style, no matter what the marketing suggests.

The park has an elaborate backstory (detailed at tinyurl.com/waturi) based on the fictional Waturi tribe, an ancient Polynesian people who set out on their outrigger canoes to find a new home with the mantra "Water is Life. Life is Joy." The Waturi visited many Polynesian islands, drawing elements from each culture, until they caught sight of the legendary fish Kunuku playing in the waves of Volcano Bay and settled there. The Waturi legend also influenced the unpronounceable names of most of the attractions, but that's about as far as the theming goes on the slides—don't expect any animatronic figures or elaborate effects.

Nomenclature notwithstanding, no one can deny that Universal opened Volcano Bay before it was really ready for prime time. The park premiered in a semi-incomplete state, and guests who paid full price for an unfinished attraction loudly lambasted Volcano Bay on websites like Yelp and TripAdvisor. Today, the park has worked out most (but not all) of its operational quirks and offers a good variety of activities. If you're staying on-site (or temper your attraction-riding expectations) and can relax into the park's immersive atmosphere, Volcano Bay may just be your slice of paradise alongside I-4.

GETTING ORIENTED *at* VOLCANO BAY

ONCE DROPPED OFF at Volcano Bay's bus plaza, guests are ushered through an ornate underground tunnel (seemingly hewn from stone) before ascending an escalator into the park's entryway. Here, fountains burble beside an Easter Island–style statue that occasionally speaks; you'll also find more prosaic objects like an ATM, lockers, and Guest Services window outside the park's turnstiles.

Volcano Bay is divided into four primary areas (also known as lands), each with a unique theme, but because all of the areas sport the same lush South Seas scenery, it's impossible to tell where one section ends and another begins without a map. Guests enter the park at **Wave Village,** which is dominated by the **Waturi Beach** multidirectional wave pool and **The Reef** leisure pool. Paths from there lead clockwise to **Rainforest Village,** home to the park's densest collection of thrill rides, including **TeAwa the Fearless River,** and counterclockwise to **River Village,** which has family-friendly attractions like the signature **Krakatau Aqua Coaster** and **Kopiko Wai** lazy river. The heart of the park puts **The Volcano** in Volcano Bay: 200-foot-tall **Krakatau,** home to hidden caverns with cascading waterfalls and special effects triggered by your TapuTapu band.

While there are signposts throughout the park, the winding walkways can make it confusing to find your way. Blissfully, many of the cement sidewalks are cooled by sprinklers, so at least you won't burn your bare feet while wandering in circles.

TAPUTAPU AND VIRTUAL LINES

UNIVERSAL BOASTS THAT it has eliminated the biggest hassles at water parks—standing in long lines for slides—by replacing queues with a Virtual Line mandatory reservation system. Where it differs from Universal Express or Disney's FastPass+ is that there is no standby line at all; all guests save their places in line with their TapuTapu wearables, allowing them to do other things as they await their turns.

Universal's Volcano Bay

Attractions

1. Honu Slide
2. ika Moana Slide
3. Kala & Tai Nui Serpentine Body Slides
4. Ko'okiri Body Plunge
5. Kopiko Wai Winding River
6. Krakatau Aqua Coaster
7. Maku Round Raft Ride
8. Ohyah and Ohno Drop Slides
9. Puihi Round Raft Ride
10. Puka Uli Lagoon
11. Punga Racers
12. The Reef
13. Runamukka Reef
14. Taniwha Tubes: Tonga & Raki
15. TeAwa the Fearless River
16. Tot Tiki Reef
17. Vol's Caverns
18. Waturi Beach

Restaurants

A. Bambu
B. The Feasting Frog
C. Kohola Reef Restaurant & Social Club
D. Whakawaiwai Eats

➕ First Aid Station   🚻 Restrooms   🔳 Cabanas

Every visitor is issued a waterproof TapuTapu wristband (think a slightly bulkier Apple Watch with a rubber wristband) that you use to claim your place in the Virtual Lines, as well as reserve and open lockers, and make payments throughout the park. The TapuTapu bands also trigger special effects throughout Volcano Bay, such as controlling streams of water in Tot Tiki Reef or shooting water cannons at other guests who are enjoying the Kopiko Wai Winding River.

To enter Volcano Bay, you must first register a ticket with an online account and assign it to your name; setting up a credit card charge account (with a secure PIN and custom spending limits for each family member) is optional. Attendants will assist you with this at the turnstiles, but your entry will be far smoother if you set everything up ahead of time through universalorlando.com or the official Universal smartphone app when purchasing your tickets in advance.

Every attraction that uses Virtual Lines has a tiki totem outside its entrance with a digital display. For the first hour or so after opening, most slides will show "Ride Now," indicating that there is little to no wait to ride. Once its queue begins to build, each attraction activates its Virtual Line, and the totem displays a wait time; by 11 a.m., most slides will report at least an hour virtual wait.

Tap your TapuTapu band against the glowing symbol below any of the touch screens surrounding the tiki, and you'll be assigned an approximate time when you can return. Your actual return time may be earlier than expected if other guests skip their return times, or later if the attraction temporarily closes due to weather or technical problems; your TapuTapu will notify you of any changes. You can hold a reservation for only one ride at a time, and TapuTapu will alert you when it's time to return with a minimal wait (typically 5–15 minutes, but we've experienced Over 30 minutes during technical difficulties).

Reservations don't expire once they become active, so you don't have to rush to ride, but you can't get in another Virtual Line until you use or cancel your first ride. However, you may jump into any queue displaying "Ride Now" without losing your place in a Virtual Line. Conversely, if a tiki says "Ride Full," all the day's reservations are claimed, but don't lose hope; closed Virtual Lines often reopen in the hours before closing as other guests exit, abandoning their spots.

In theory, Volcano Bay's Virtual Line system should allow guests to enjoy wait-free attractions like the wave pool and lazy river instead of standing in hot queues. In reality, guests who don't enter early spend a lot of time baking on the beach and may only get to ride four or five slides on a busy day. We love the idea of the Virtual Line and being able to relax while waiting our turn. The problem so far has come in the execution, which has not been as smooth as Universal would have liked. The park's initial months were plagued by multihour waits for most of the slides, with popular attractions completely filling up for the day by midmorning. Thankfully, TapuTapu's implementation has made great strides since opening day, and we were able to experience everything we wanted to during our recent visits. However, the system still has too many glitches to feel seamless, so we recommend visiting Volcano Bay with measured expectations of how many slides you'll ride in a day.

One final hitch: Though the TapuTapu wristband has two snaps to hold it more securely, it has a habit of coming loose, especially in TeAwa the Fearless River. If your TapuTapu takes a swim, swing by Guest Services for a free (though time-consuming) replacement.

Volcano Bay Universal Express Passes, which bypass the Virtual Lines and provide immediate access to the slides' boarding queues, are sold in advance online and inside the park at the concierge huts; quantities are limited and sell out on busy days. Universal Express at Volcano Bay is not free for anyone (even those staying in the top three on-site hotels), and it is available only for one-time use, not unlimited. However, it is cheaper than purchasing Express at the theme parks, especially if you go for the version valid only on select slides. See page 60 for details.

CABANAS AND PREMIUM SEATING

YOU CAN UPGRADE YOUR VISIT with reserved padded loungers ($49.99 and up per pair), 6-person cabanas ($199.99 and up), or 16-person Family Suite cabanas ($599.99 and up). While they're not a necessity, we recommend the private loungers for their included shade canopy, locking storage box, and attendant to deliver food and drink orders. The locker's mechanism can only be activated by one TapuTapu at a time and is frustratingly finicky; carefully align your wristband with the sensor, and firmly push down until you hear it click.

The cabanas get all the same perks, plus towel service, free fruit and bottled water, the ability to order upscale appetizers (such as conch fritters and coconut shrimp) that aren't offered on the regular menus, and a private kiosk for making TapuTapu reservations. However, many of the cabanas don't offer much privacy, and the attendants get mixed reviews on their attentiveness, making them a dubious value.

The private loungers and cabanas are yours to use all day, even if you exit and return to the park, but they sell out early. Call ☎ 877-489-8068 (for loungers) or 877-801-9720 (for cabanas) up to 60 days in advance for reservations, and bring a printout of your confirmation to the park. When selecting a seat location, keep in mind that Wave Village is nearest to the entrance and gets the most morning sun; River Village is closest to the kids' playgrounds and smoking areas; and Rainforest Village is right up against the interstate. Upon arriving, head to a concierge hut to be checked in and walked to your reserved area; most guests make a beeline to the concierge closest to the entrance, while there's rarely a wait at the one in River Village.

LOCKERS AND TOWELS

RESTROOM AND CHANGING FACILITIES with large banks of lockers are located around the park; the ones in Wave Village closest to the park entrance are always the most crowded, while the ones at the back of the park in River Village are rarely busy. Lockers come in three sizes and cost between $8 and $16. (Note that you'll need a credit card—either in hand or linked to your TapuTapu account—to rent directly at the locker; see an attendant to pay with cash or a hotel key.) Lockers are yours for the full day and are opened and closed with your TapuTapu. Up to four other members of your party can also be assigned access to your locker; follow the prompts on the locker kiosk's touch screen to add additional authorized users. A bank of large all-day lockers ($15) is located immediately outside the park, but we don't recommend using them because you must return your TapuTapu and forfeit any Virtual Line reservations each time you exit.

Towels are not provided free (as they are at some other water parks), but you can rent one for $5 at any concierge hut. You'll have to dry it in the sun between swims because that fee doesn't include swapping out wet towels (unless you luck into a sympathetic employee). Souvenir towels are also sold for around $25.

UNIVERSAL'S VOLCANO BAY ATTRACTIONS

THE BULK OF VOLCANO BAY'S SLIDES are hidden from the view of guests as they enter behind the mountain's blown-out back side. Attractions range from mild family-friendly raft rides (all with convenient conveyer belts that carry your craft uphill for you) to heart-seizing drop slides from the caldera's summit. Read the posted warnings carefully before you climb 20 stories to the top, and be prepared for a discreet weigh-in before most slides to ensure safety.

THE VOLCANO

THE 200-FOOT VOLCANO **Krakatau** lies at the center of the park. Inside, guests can explore hidden caverns with cascading waterfalls.

Vol's Caverns ★★★

APPEAL BY AGE	PRESCHOOL ★★★★½	GRADE SCHOOL ★★★★½	TEENS ★★★
YOUNG ADULTS ★★★	OVER 30 ★★½	SENIORS ★★★	

What it is Interactive walk-through. **Scope and scale** Diversion.

The volcano contains a network of caverns concealed behind waterfalls and curtains of steam; look for entrances near the queues for Krakatau Aqua Coaster, Ko'okiri Body Plunge, and Kala & Tai Nui Serpentine Body Slides. Once inside, you'll find colorful fountains surrounding Vol, the spirit of the mountain who converses with guests through a digital projection, similar to the Mystic Fountain in Islands of Adventure. Make sure you trigger the light display depicting Kunuku, the mythical fish, on the cave wall.

RAINFOREST VILLAGE

THIS VILLAGE HOUSES the park's densest collection of thrill rides.

Kala & Tai Nui Serpentine Body Slides ★★★★½

APPEAL BY AGE	PRESCHOOL ★★★½	GRADE SCHOOL ★★★★½	TEENS ★★★★★
YOUNG ADULTS ★★★★★	OVER 30 ★★★★½	SENIORS ★★★★	

What it is Two extreme twisting body slides. **Scope and scale** Headliner. **Comments** 48" minimum height requirement; 275-pound maximum weight requirement per rider. **Duration of ride** About 25–30 seconds.

After falling through a drop door, two riders go down 124-foot body slides simultaneously. Their paths cross several times as they hurtle down translucent intertwining tubes. The blue Kala slide is intense enough, but the green Tai Nui side is like The Incredible Hulk Coaster of slides: it starts fast and gets even faster as it goes. These slides are sometimes "Ride Now" even when other attractions have long virtual waits, perhaps because they are so intimidating. Note that you must climb more than 200 steps to reach the top of these slides.

Maku Round Raft Ride ★★★

APPEAL BY AGE PRESCHOOL ★★★½ GRADE SCHOOL ★★★★½ TEENS ★★★★½ YOUNG ADULTS ★★★★½ OVER 30 ★★★★½ SENIORS ★★★★

What it is Mild family raft ride. **Scope and scale** Major attraction. **Comments** 42" minimum height requirement; 48" minimum height requirement if riding alone; 1,050-pound maximum weight requirement per raft. **Duration of ride** About 30–40 seconds.

Maku and Puihi are Waturi for "wet" and "wild," respectively, making this pair of group raft slides a subtle tribute to Volcano Bay's predecessor. North America's first "saucer ride," the six-person Maku round raft plunges riders through bowl-like formations that are surrounded by erupting geysers before ending in a pool. Unfortunately, the advertised fountains usually fail to deliver on the slide's name, making it one of the park's bigger busts. On the plus side, there's rarely a long wait for Maku, and the tower it shares with Puihi has one of the park's only elevators, for those unable to climb stairs.

Ohyah and Ohno Drop Slides ★★★½

APPEAL BY AGE PRESCHOOL ★★ GRADE SCHOOL ★★★★ TEENS ★★★★½ YOUNG ADULTS ★★★★½ OVER 30 ★★★★ SENIORS ★★★½

What it is Two twisting body slides with drop endings. **Scope and scale** Minor attraction. **Comments** 48" minimum height requirement. **Duration of ride** About 15 seconds.

Two short but intense twisting slides launch guests 4 and 6 feet above the water at the end, guaranteeing that splashdown sends water straight up your sinuses. Ohno is the taller of the two and typically has a longer wait; the extra 2 feet of free fall isn't worth an additional 20 minutes.

Puihi Round Raft Ride ★★★★½

APPEAL BY AGE PRESCHOOL ★★★★½ GRADE SCHOOL ★★★★½ TEENS ★★★★½ YOUNG ADULTS ★★★★½ OVER 30 ★★★★½ SENIORS ★★★★

What it is Thrilling family raft ride. **Scope and scale** Major attraction. **Comments** 42" minimum height requirement; 48" minimum height requirement if riding alone; 850-pound maximum weight requirement per raft. **Duration of ride** About 45 seconds.

Maku's mate, Puihi, is the far more frightening slide of the pair: a six-person raft launches down a dark, winding tunnel before shooting up a banked curve; riders glimpse the highway below and momentarily experience zero gravity prior to sliding back down. Among the park's family raft slides, this is second only to Honu for making riders scream in terror.

Puka Uli Lagoon ★★½

APPEAL BY AGE	PRESCHOOL ★★★★	GRADE SCHOOL ★★★★★	TEENS ★★★
YOUNG ADULTS ★★	OVER 30 ★★½	SENIORS ★★★	

What it is Kiddie pool with fountains. **Scope and scale** Diversion.

This shallow pool near the Ohyah and Ohno Drop Slides is framed by towering tikis and windmill-like contraptions that spray water when TapuTapu sensors are activated. The area around Puka Uli is a great spot to set up camp if you are keeping an eye on young kids, but not so much if you're looking for peace and quiet.

Punga Racers ★★★½

APPEAL BY AGE	PRESCHOOL ★★½	GRADE SCHOOL ★★★★	TEENS ★★★★
YOUNG ADULTS ★★★★	OVER 30 ★★★½	SENIORS ★★★½	

What it is Side-by-side mat slides. **Scope and scale** Minor attraction. **Comments** 42″ minimum height requirement; 48″ minimum height requirement if riding alone. **Duration of ride** About 20 seconds.

Guests on racing mats shaped like manta rays go down enclosed slides across four lanes and through "underwater sea caves" (also known as plastic tubes). For a swifter ride, face forward, hold your mat in front of you, and jump forward onto it when given the signal, then pull back on the handles as you slide. The orange slide in the center feels the fastest, while the two outside tubes are twistier; tuck your elbows in on the turns or you may be bruised.

Taniwha Tubes: Tonga & Raki ★★★★

APPEAL BY AGE	PRESCHOOL ★★★	GRADE SCHOOL ★★★★	TEENS ★★★★½
YOUNG ADULTS ★★★★½	OVER 30 ★★★★½	SENIORS ★★★★	

What it is Four intertwined two-passenger raft slides. **Scope and scale** Major attraction. **Comments** 42″ minimum height requirement; 48″ minimum height requirement if riding alone; 300-pound maximum weight requirement per rider; 450-pound maximum weight requirement per raft. **Duration of ride** About 25–30 seconds.

One tower sports four Easter Island–inspired waterslides with rafts for single or double riders, who sit single file bobsled-style. The slides are similar but not identical—bear left to Tonga (the green slides) with more open-air sections if you get claustrophobic, or go right to Raki (the blue ones) if you like enclosed slides with lots of twists. The best thing about Taniwha Tubes is that they are almost always "Ride Now," and you'll rarely wait more than a few minutes for your turn, so you can try out all four slides to find your favorite.

TeAwa the Fearless River ★★★★½

APPEAL BY AGE	PRESCHOOL ★★½	GRADE SCHOOL ★★★★½	TEENS ★★★★½
YOUNG ADULTS ★★★★½	OVER 30 ★★★★½	SENIORS ★★★★	

What it is Rapids river. **Scope and scale** Headliner. **Comments** 42″ minimum height requirement; 48″ minimum height requirement if riding alone; everyone must wear approved life vest.

On this racing-torrent river, guests hang tight in their mandatory life vests amid roaring whitewater rapids as they surf beneath the slides inside Krakatau. This is the best attraction of its kind that we've experienced outside of Atlantis in the Bahamas, but if you're looking for a lazy river, this ain't it! A tip for hopeful surfers: Paddle upstream as you exit from under the volcano long enough to catch a curl from the wave generator.

RIVER VILLAGE

NAMED AFTER THE WATERWAY that winds through it, River Village features family-friendly attractions.

Honu Slide ★★★★★

APPEAL BY AGE PRESCHOOL ★★★★½ **GRADE SCHOOL** ★★★★½ **TEENS** ★★★★½
YOUNG ADULTS ★★★★½ **OVER 30** ★★★★½ **SENIORS** ★★★★

What it is Extreme family raft ride. **Scope and scale** Headliner. **Comments** 42″ minimum height requirement; 49″ minimum height requirement if riding alone; 700-pound maximum weight requirement per raft. **Duration of ride** About 35–40 seconds.

Honu and ika Moana are two separate slides attached to the same tower, where guests board multiperson animal-themed rafts (a sea turtle and a whale, respectively) before speeding down into a pool. Honu is a blue raft slide that sends two to five riders vertically up two giant sloped walls before sliding back down, giving a terrifying taste of what skateboarders call hang time at the top. It's the scariest group raft ride in the park, and our pick as the best. It's also the most popular, along with Krakatau Aqua Coaster, so make it one of your top priorities on arrival.

ika Moana Slide ★★★

APPEAL BY AGE PRESCHOOL ★★★★½ **GRADE SCHOOL** ★★★★½ **TEENS** ★★★★½
YOUNG ADULTS ★★★★½ **OVER 30** ★★★★½ **SENIORS** ★★★★

What it is Moderate family raft ride. **Scope and scale** Major attraction. **Comments** 42″ minimum height requirement; 48″ minimum height requirement if riding alone; 800-pound maximum weight requirement per raft. **Duration of ride** About 45 seconds.

Though both are boarded from the same platform, don't confuse ika Moana with its neighbor, Honu. Ika Moana (no relation to the Disney princess) is a much gentler journey in and out of twisting green tunnels, on a raft that's supposed to spray water from its center. Much like Maku and Puihi, ika Moana isn't necessarily a bad ride; it's simply upstaged by its sibling.

Ko'okiri Body Plunge ★★★★½

APPEAL BY AGE PRESCHOOL ★★½ **GRADE SCHOOL** ★★★½ **TEENS** ★★★★½
YOUNG ADULTS ★★★★½ **OVER 30** ★★★★½ **SENIORS** ★★★

What it is High-speed vertical drop slide. **Scope and scale** Headliner. **Comments** 48″ minimum height requirement; 300-pound maximum weight requirement per rider. **Duration of ride** About 20 seconds.

Hop on this 125-foot slide, featuring a drop door with a 70-degree-angle descent, straight through the heart of the mountain. Drumbeats building up to the drop get your heart pounding, but the plunge itself is over before you have time to scream. You won't be able to see much with all the water in your face, but other guests can watch your splashdown through a clear tube located between Waturi Beach's wave pool and The Reef pool. As with all body slides, cross your ankles, fold your arms across your chest, and arch your back for the best ride. Ko'okiri commands the longest waits of the extreme body slides, so daredevils should make it their first stop. Note that you must climb more than 200 steps to reach the top of this slide.

Kopiko Wai Winding River ★★★★

APPEAL BY AGE PRESCHOOL ★★★★½ **GRADE SCHOOL** ★★★★½ **TEENS** ★★★★
YOUNG ADULTS ★★★★ **OVER 30** ★★★★½ **SENIORS** ★★★★★

What it is Lazy river. **Scope and scale** Headliner. **Comments** Children under 48" must wear an approved life vest and be accompanied by a supervising companion.

This gentle, lazy river passes through the park's landscape and into the volcano's hidden caves. The highlight is Stargazer Cavern, a mist-filled grotto with constellations of pinpoint lights blanketing the rocky ceiling. Beware of spots where guests on dry land can target you for soaking by triggering TapuTapu-activated fountains. You're allowed to swim along without an inner tube, but snag one for maximum relaxation.

Krakatau Aqua Coaster ★★★★★

APPEAL BY AGE	PRESCHOOL ★★★★½	GRADE SCHOOL ★★★★★	TEENS ★★★★★
YOUNG ADULTS ★★★★★	OVER 30 ★★★★★	SENIORS ★★★★½	

What it is Roller coaster-style family raft ride. **Scope and scale** Super-headliner. **Comments** 42" minimum height requirement; 48" minimum height requirement if riding alone; 700-pound maximum weight requirement per raft. **Duration of ride** 1⅓ minutes.

Guests board a specially designed canoe that seats up to four. The ride uses linear induction motor technology, which launches the canoe uphill as well as downhill as you twist and turn around the volcano's blown-out interior. It's similar to Crush 'n' Gusher at Typhoon Lagoon but far longer and more thrilling, delivering delightful moments of air time like a real roller coaster. It's a shame that Universal didn't make Krakatau a full-blown dark ride by including indoor scenes or special effects, but this is still the best waterslide on which we've ever been. Krakatau is the park's starring headliner and can only service about 700 guests per hour, so take advantage of "Ride Now" at rope drop or get your Virtual Line reservation as early as possible.

Runamukka Reef ★★★½

APPEAL BY AGE	PRESCHOOL ★★★★★	GRADE SCHOOL ★★★★	TEENS ★★★★
YOUNG ADULTS ★★★	OVER 30 ★★★	SENIORS ★★★½	

What it is Wet playground. **Scope and scale** Minor attraction. **Comments** 48" maximum height requirement for slides.

This three-story water playground for older children inspired by the coral reef includes twisting slides, sprinklers, and more. Even though it's intended for kids, parents will want to clamber around the structure too.

Tot Tiki Reef ★★½

APPEAL BY AGE	PRESCHOOL ★★★★★	GRADE SCHOOL ★★★★	TEENS ★★★★
YOUNG ADULTS ★★★	OVER 30 ★★★	SENIORS ★★★½	

What it is Infant splash area. **Scope and scale** Diversion. **Comments** 48" maximum height requirement for slides.

A small toddler play area with spraying Maori fountains, slides, and a kid-size volcano. Visually imaginative but hardly expansive, this is little more than a glorified splash pad, but it's entertaining enough for the swim-diaper set. Speaking of which, swim diapers are mandatory for all babies and may be bought at Whakawaiwai Eats.

WAVE VILLAGE

LOCATED AT THE BASE of Krakatau, Wave Village contains wave and leisure pools, as well as the park's largest beach.

The Reef ★★★

APPEAL BY AGE	PRESCHOOL	★★★★	GRADE SCHOOL	★★★★	TEENS	★★
YOUNG ADULTS	★★½	OVER 30	★★★	SENIORS	★★★★	

What it is Calm pool with a view. **Scope and scale** Minor attraction. **Comments** Children under 48″ must wear an approved life vest.

Leisure pool with calm waters and its own waterfall. Relax and watch braver souls shoot down the Ko'okiri Body Plunge through a clear tunnel where the pool meets Waturi Beach.

Waturi Beach ★★★★

APPEAL BY AGE	PRESCHOOL	★★★	GRADE SCHOOL	★★★★	TEENS	★★★★
YOUNG ADULTS	★★★★½	OVER 30	★★★★	SENIORS	★★★½	

What it is Wave pool. **Scope and scale** Super-headliner. **Comments** Children under 48″ must wear an approved life vest.

The central swimming lagoon at Volcano Bay, situated at the foot of Krakatau Lagoon and fed by waterfalls cascading off the volcano's peak, contains a cutting-edge wave pool capable of cycling through different types of surf. Every 10 minutes a musical fanfare sounds as the sign above the pool rotates, indicating a shift in the seas: from calm waters, to moderate multidirectional chop, to powerful unified breakers.

UNIVERSAL'S VOLCANO BAY TOURING STRATEGY

DUE TO THE NATURE of the Virtual Line system, it's impossible for us to provide a precise touring plan for Volcano Bay like we do for other parks. We can share basic touring strategies to maximize the number of attractions you experience during your visit, which worked out well for these readers from Lee's Summit, Missouri:

> We had no clue how to do [Volcano Bay], so we followed the touring advice exactly. The park closed due to capacity, but we did everything and did not feel like it was too hard to ride things. We were done and chilling out when it got busy.

Just remember that your enjoyment of Volcano Bay is not dictated by the quantity of slides you ride. Simply vegetating in a lounge chair or lazy river all day is perfectly valid:

1. Purchase your admission in advance, and create an online account at universalorlando.com or through the Universal Orlando smartphone app to register your tickets and members of your party. You can also set up a credit card for charging purposes if you wish.

2. Arrive at Volcano Bay as early as possible, at least 75 minutes before the park's official opening, leaving extra time for parking and transportation.

3. Upon entering, secure seats and a locker, if needed. The loungers on Waturi Beach are the first to be claimed, but you'll find plenty of options around the rear side of the volcano until midmorning.

4. Tackle the most popular slides while the queues are in "Ride Now" mode, starting with Krakatau Aqua Coaster, Honu, and Ko'okiri Body Plunge (for thrill seekers only), in that order.

5. Circle counterclockwise from River Village to Punga Racers; ride a couple times if there's no line, then tackle Puihi in Rainforest Village.

6. By now you've experienced the majority of the major slides, and the Virtual Line system has probably been activated. Get a return time for Ohyah or Ohno (whichever is sooner). While waiting, ride Kala & Tai Nui (if you're brave and they still show "Ride Now") or relax in the Puka Uli Lagoon.

7. After using your Ohyah or Ohno return time, backtrack clockwise to experience Maku, which should still say "Ride Now."

8. Cross the park back to River Village and ride ika Moana. Check one of the park's wait time boards while walking there; if ika Moana is "Ride Now," you can use TapuTapu to get a return time for your second ride on Krakatau Aqua Coaster, Ko'okiri Body Plunge, or Honu along the way.

9. You've now conquered all of the park's slides save for Taniwha Tubes, which you can experience at any time. Virtual Line waits may be in the triple digits by now, so enjoy the wave pool, Fearless and Winding Rivers, and any other slides still showing "Ride Now" while waiting for your next return time. Also take time to explore the volcano's caverns and search for interactive TapuTapu effects.

10. Lines for food at Volcano Bay build early and move slowly. Order an early lunch before 11 a.m. or wait until after 3 p.m. It's important to stay hydrated, so feel free to visit the bars early and often. Restaurants begin to shutter 2 hours prior to park closing; Kohola Reef and Dancing Dragons typically stay open the latest.

11. During the summer, you can count on a thunderstorm sweeping through in midafternoon. Everyone is ushered out of the water as soon as lightning strikes within 5 miles, and many guests flee for the parking buses once a downpour starts. Sit tight; Orlando showers are usually short-lived, and you'll have the slides to yourself once the all clear is given.

12. As closing time approaches, Virtual Line waits will begin to drop, and some queues that were formerly full may reopen, so secure your last re-rides on any favorites.

13. Try to stay in the park past sunset to see the volcano erupt with crimson water. Don't forget to return your TapuTapu wristbands on your way out.

PART TEN

UNIVERSAL ORLANDO CITYWALK

MUCH LIKE THE STORY OF UNIVERSAL ORLANDO'S parks, the story of its nightlife offerings is one of punches and counterpunches. Back in the 1970s and '80s, developer Bob Snow's Church Street Station attracted tourists and locals alike to downtown Orlando with the area's first themed nightclub complex. Disney took aim at Church Street throughout the 1990s with its now-demolished Pleasure Island, which slowly smothered the once-successful Station. Finally, Universal Orlando opened CityWalk with Islands of Adventure in 1999 and essentially put Disney out of the nightlife business. Though downtown has bounced back a bit, and Disney has remade its former Downtown Disney into the upscale Disney Springs, CityWalk is still the most popular spot among area visitors (and many residents) for post-park partying.

CityWalk is a shopping, dining, and entertainment venue that doubles as the entrance plaza for the Universal Studios and Islands of Adventure theme parks. Situated between the parking complex and the theme parks, CityWalk is heavily trafficked all day but truly comes alive at night. The complex is arrayed in a crescent shape around the waterway that connects Universal's two theme parks with the resort's top three hotels. Along its streets, CityWalk offers a number of nightclubs to sample, and many of those entertainment and restaurant venues depend on well-known brand names. You'll find a Hard Rock Cafe and concert hall; Jimmy Buffett's Margaritaville; a Bubba Gump Shrimp Co.; a branch of New Orleans's famous Pat O'Brien's club; an NBC sports bar; and a reggae club that celebrates the life and music of Bob Marley. Places that operate without big-name tie-ins include The Red Coconut Club, a lounge and nightclub; The Groove, a high-tech disco; Toothsome Chocolate Emporium, a fanciful chocolate-themed restaurant; and CityWalk's Rising Star, a karaoke club with a live backup band.

Another CityWalk distinction is that most of the clubs are also restaurants, or alternatively, several of the restaurants are likewise clubs. Though there's a lot of culinary variety, restaurants and nightclubs are different animals. Room configuration, acoustics, intimacy, sight lines, and atmosphere—important considerations in a nightclub—are not at all the same in a venue designed to serve meals. Though it's nice to have all that good food available, the club experience is somewhat dulled.

Red Coconut Club, The Groove, and CityWalk's Rising Star are more nightclub than restaurant, whereas Margaritaville is more restaurant than club. Bob Marley's and Pat O'Brien's are about half-and-half. The Hard Rock Cafe, Antojitos, Vivo, NBC Sports Grill & Brew, Toothsome Chocolate Emporium, and The Cowfish are restaurants, profiled in Part Six. The venue for the Blue Man Group is strictly a performance space, though a full bar and snack food are available.

ARRIVING *and* PARKING

CITYWALK VISITORS PARK in the same garage as Universal park guests. Self-parking is free after 6 p.m. (except during Halloween and special events); prime and valet parking are also available. See Part Three for detailed driving directions and parking information.

Universal Orlando on-site hotel guests can reach CityWalk using the same water taxis, buses, and walking paths that lead to the parks. The water taxi hub is located along the waterfront path before the bridge to Universal Studios Florida (USF). Guests walking from the Hard Rock and Portofino Bay Hotels enter CityWalk closest to USF near Hard Rock Cafe, while guests walking from the other hotels enter CityWalk near Jimmy Buffett's Margaritaville.

As you enter CityWalk from the parking structure, you'll see a concierge kiosk beneath the escalator outside Starbucks, offering information, guide maps, restaurant menus, and dining reservations. Guest Services, the restrooms, an ATM, and First Aid are all located to your left, immediately past Cold Stone Creamery. A secondary ticket window where you can purchase Party Passes is located near The Groove.

ADMISSION PRICES

CITYWALK'S **Party Pass All-Club Access** is $11.99 plus tax, which gets you into all the clubs: Bob Marley, The Groove, Margaritaville, Pat O'Brien's, Red Coconut, and Rising Star. You can pay an individual cover charge of $7 (tax included) at each club. Given that, getting the all-access pass makes the most sense if you plan to visit more than one club in an evening, though if you arrive before the cover charge kicks in (typically 10 p.m.), you can enjoy your first club for free.

Complimentary admission to the aforementioned clubs is also included with any on-site hotel stay or multiday Universal theme park ticket (valid for 7 consecutive nights, starting the first time the ticket

continued on page 360

Universal Orlando CityWalk

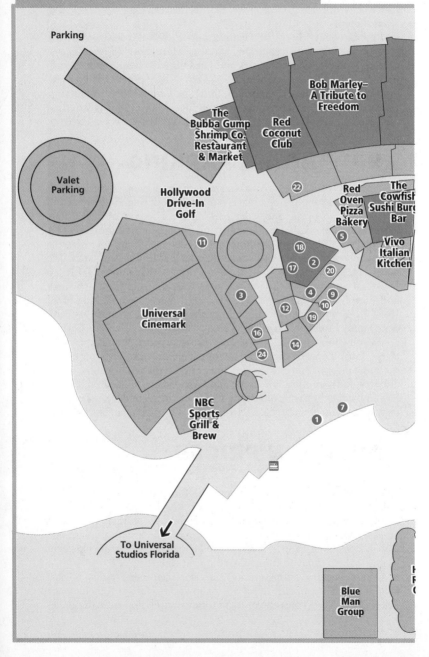

Parking

Valet
Parking

Hollywood
Drive-In
Golf

The
Bubba Gump
Shrimp Co.
Restaurant
& Market

Red
Coconut
Club

Bob Marley–
A Tribute to
Freedom

22

Red
Oven
Pizza
Bakery

The
Cowfish
Sushi Burg
Bar

Vivo
Italian
Kitchen

5

11

18

17   2   20

3

12

4   9

10

16

19

24

14

Universal
Cinemark

NBC
Sports
Grill &
Brew

1   7

To Universal
Studios Florida

Blue
Man
Group

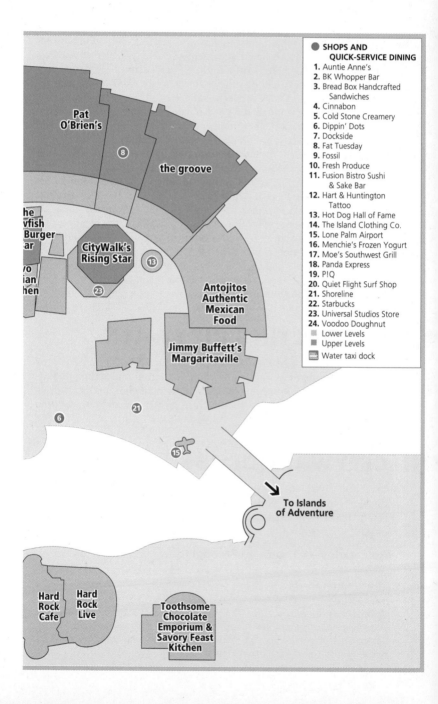

SHOPS AND QUICK-SERVICE DINING

1. Auntie Anne's
2. BK Whopper Bar
3. Bread Box Handcrafted Sandwiches
4. Cinnabon
5. Cold Stone Creamery
6. Dippin' Dots
7. Dockside
8. Fat Tuesday
9. Fossil
10. Fresh Produce
11. Fusion Bistro Sushi & Sake Bar
12. Hart & Huntington Tattoo
13. Hot Dog Hall of Fame
14. The Island Clothing Co.
15. Lone Palm Airport
16. Menchie's Frozen Yogurt
17. Moe's Southwest Grill
18. Panda Express
19. P!Q
20. Quiet Flight Surf Shop
21. Shoreline
22. Starbucks
23. Universal Studios Store
24. Voodoo Doughnut

Lower Levels
Upper Levels
Water taxi dock

Pat O'Brien's

the groove

CityWalk's Rising Star

the ~~vfish~~ Burger ~~ar~~

~~vo~~ ~~ian~~ ~~hen~~

Antojitos Authentic Mexican Food

Jimmy Buffett's Margaritaville

To Islands of Adventure

Hard Rock Cafe

Hard Rock Live

Toothsome Chocolate Emporium & Savory Feast Kitchen

continued from page 357

is used). Premier Annual Pass holders also get free club admission for themselves, as well as for a guest, Sunday–Thursday. Preferred and Premier Pass holders get 20% off additional Party Passes (up to four per night). Party Passes (free or otherwise) are only valid during regular operating hours and not during special events such as New Year's Eve.

Nightclubs not enough for you? If you're hungry for more, City-Walk's concierge desk offers a number of combination tickets that could save you a few dollars, providing you choose carefully. For $21.95 (tax and gratuity included) the **Meal & Movie Deal** includes cinema admission with dinner at Bob Marley, Fusion Bistro Sushi, Margaritaville, or Pat O'Brien's. Or for $21 (tax and gratuity included), the **Meal & Party Deal** combines dinner with a CityWalk Party Pass. You get an entrée and soft drink but must order from a very limited menu. If you like Jamaican curry, fish sandwiches, spicy tuna rolls, or jambalaya, the meal portion of these deals (valued at around $14, including a 15% gratuity) can save you up to $10 on dinner, depending on what you order.

Finally, the **Meal & Blue Man Group Deal** combines—what else?—dinner at one of the above restaurants with a ticket to see the Blue Man Group (see page 363), saving you about $9 versus eating à la carte.

CONTACTING CITYWALK

CONTACT CITYWALK GUEST SERVICES at ☎ 407-224-2691, or visit its website at citywalk.com/orlando. Keep in mind, though, that CityWalk personnel may not be up on individual club doings, so your best bet may be to contact specific clubs directly when you reach the Orlando area.

CITYWALK CLUBS

THE FOLLOWING NIGHTCLUB VENUES are mostly located along the elevated curving pathway that sits behind and above CityWalk's central plaza. At most of these venues, you must be 21 or older (passport or photo ID required) to enter after 10 p.m.

Bob Marley—A Tribute to Freedom

What it is Reggae restaurant and club. **Hours** Daily, 4 p.m.–2 a.m. **Cuisine** Jamaican-influenced appetizers and main courses. **Entertainment** Live reggae bands and DJ in the outdoor gazebo every night. **Cover** $7 after 10 p.m. nightly (more for special acts).

This club is a re-creation of Marley's home in Kingston, Jamaica, and contains a lot of interesting Marley memorabilia. The open-air courtyard is the center of action. Must be age 21 or older after 9 p.m. Sunday is Ladies Night, with no cover charge for women before midnight and drink specials.

CityWalk's Rising Star

What it is Karaoke club with live band and backup singers Tuesday–Saturday (Sunday–Monday, sing to recorded tracks with live backup singers). **Hours** Nightly, 8 p.m.–2 a.m. **Cuisine** Red Oven Pizza delivery. **Entertainment** Karaoke. **Cover** $7 (no extra charge to sing).

With live musicians backing you up, you can pretend that you've hit the big time at this opulent karaoke. The good news is that, instead of a canned "tiny orchestra," Rising Star gives you a full live backing band to perform with on Tuesday–Saturday nights, and a live host and backup singers (with prerecorded music) on Sundays and Mondays. The bad news is that the song list is rather short, with only a little more than 200 options instead of the thousands you may be used to back home. Even so, this is an extremely popular spot; be sure to put your selections in as early in the evening as possible if you want to get on stage. While waiting your turn, you can get your courage up with one of its supersweet specialty cocktails; pizza delivery from Red Oven is available if stage fright makes you hungry. Guests age 18 and older are welcome Sunday–Thursday, but the club is restricted to age 21 and up on Friday and Saturday.

The Groove

What it is High-tech disco. **Hours** Nightly, 9 p.m.–2 a.m. **Cuisine** No food. **Entertainment** DJ plays dance tunes. **Cover** $7 after 10 p.m.

Guests must be age 21 or older to enter this *très* chic club designed to look like an old theater in the midst of restoration. There are seven bars and several themed cubbyholes (the ultramodern Blue Room, laid-back Green Room, and brothel-like Red Room) for getting away from the thundering sound system. Dancers are barraged with strobes, lasers, and heaven knows what else. Friday nights feature DJ Chino, and DJ M-Squared spins every Saturday. VIP reserved tables with premium bottle service is available for those with money and liver cells to burn; call ☎ 407-224-2166 to book your party. Attire is casual chic with no hats or tank tops permitted for men.

Jimmy Buffett's Margaritaville

What it is Key West–themed restaurant and club. **Hours** Sunday–Thursday, 10:30 a.m.–midnight; Friday–Saturday, 10:30 a.m.–2 a.m. **Cuisine** Caribbean, Florida fusion, and American. **Entertainment** Live rock and island-style music. **Cover** $7 after 10 p.m. (select nights only).

Jimmy's is a big place with three bars that turns into a nightclub after 10 p.m. Jimmy Buffett covers are popular (no surprise), as is island music and light rock. If you eat dinner here, you'll probably want to find another vantage point when the band cranks up on the main stage around 9 p.m. There's always an acoustic guitarist strumming on the Porch of Indecision from 5 p.m. daily. If you are already inside the restaurant eating dinner before the cover charge kicks in, you won't be kicked out when the band kicks off.

Pat O'Brien's Orlando

What it is Dueling piano sing-along club and restaurant. **Hours** Daily, 4 p.m.–2 a.m. **Cuisine** Cajun. **Entertainment** Dueling pianos and sing-alongs. **Cover** $7 after 10 p.m. for piano bar only.

A clone of the famous New Orleans club of the same name. A solo pianist starts playing a little after 5 p.m., and he or she is joined by a second starting around 9 p.m. These are some of the most talented singing musicians in town and will happily handle nearly any request you throw at them (even—gasp!—Disney tunes) as long as you write it on a generous gratuity. You can dine in the courtyard or on the terrace without paying a cover. You must be age 21 or older to hang out here after 9 p.m.

The Red Coconut Club

What it is Modern lounge and nightclub. **Hours** Nightly, 8 p.m.-2 a.m. **Cuisine** Appetizers; Red Oven Pizza delivery after 10 p.m. **Entertainment** Lounging and dancing, with live music on Friday and Saturday. **Cover** $7 after 10 p.m.

This nightspot is billed as a nightclub and ultra-lounge, advertising talk for "hip place to be seen." The eclectic mix of decor—part 1950s, part tiki—and three bars on two levels would make it a great later-day hangout for the Rat Pack, if Frank and Dean happened to be resurrected in Orlando. There is a dance floor, and the bar serves signature martinis and mojitos. An evening here can quickly add up, with VIP bottle service starting at $100 (call ☎ 407-224-2425 for reservations), but a nightly happy hour 8-10 p.m. offers $6 cocktails and appetizers. On weekends, a live band swings 8 p.m.-midnight, after which a DJ closes out the night.

CITYWALK ENTERTAINMENT

BEYOND THE NIGHTCLUBS, CityWalk's attractions include an array of separately ticketed entertainment venues. None of the following attractions are included in basic Party Passes or park tickets.

UNIVERSAL CINEMARK 20 WITH XD

IF YOU WANT TO TAKE A BREAK from "riding the movies" inside Universal's parks and just want to watch one instead, the 20-screen Universal Cinemark at CityWalk has you covered. Originally one of the nicer theaters in town, the Cineplex had faded under AMC's management, but Cinemark took over in late 2018 and began a full refurbishment. When complete in early 2019, all 20 screens will be outfitted with La-Z-Boy–like Luxury Loungers, featuring oversize cupholders and motorized footrests. All screens also have digital projection and surround sound, as well as stadium seating. An upgraded snack bar will serve hot foods (along with the usual overpriced cinema standards, including Coke Freestyle sodas) and alcohol.

The Cinemark's digital XD theater was added by retrofitting a wall-to-wall screen into an existing room, along with new multichannel speakers and an advanced projector that generates 35 trillion colors. It's bigger than the standard screens and delivers more impact in 3-D films but isn't ginormous like the true IMAX screen at Pointe Orlando on I-Drive.

Tickets for showings starting after 6 p.m. (4 p.m. on Saturday, Sunday, and holidays) cost $11 for adults; 3-D and XD films cost $3.50 extra. Early bird matinees starting before 1 p.m. cost $7.50 for everyone, and all shows between 1 and 6 p.m. (4 p.m. on Saturday, Sunday, and holidays) are $9.50. Tickets for kids ages 1–11, seniors age 62 and up, and all Universal seasonal and annual pass holders cost $8 at all times. Students and military with valid ID pay $9.50. On Discount Tuesday, all showings are just $5 (not valid on holidays or opening day of new films). Note that children under age 6 are not permitted to attend R-rated films after 6 p.m., thanks to Cinemark's distraction-free environment policy.

Visit cinemark.com/florida/cinemark-orlando-and-xd or use Cinemark's mobile app to see showtimes and buy tickets, or call ☎ 407-354-3374 to hear a recording of what's playing. Tickets can be retrieved from automated kiosks located to the right of the box office. You can save the $1 or $2 online service fee and watch a free movie each month by joining Cinemark's Movie Club for $8.99 (cinemark .com/movieclub).

BLUE MAN GROUP

NO PIECE OF ENTERTAINMENT better encapsulates the "Universal Difference" than the Blue Man Group's nightly performances at CityWalk. Blue Man Group, now owned by Cirque du Soleil, is intimate, offbeat, and occasionally ornery (in comparison to its opulent, elegant, and universally appealing corporate parent), with elements of avant-garde performance art that are as likely to provoke a loud "WTH?" as applause.

The three blue men of the Blue Man Group are just that—blue—and bald and mute. Wearing black clothing and skullcaps slathered with bright-blue grease paint, they deliver a fast-paced show that uses music (mostly percussion) and multimedia effects to make light of contemporary art and life in the information age. The Universal act is just one expression of a franchise that started with three friends in New York's East Village. Now you can catch their zany, wacky, smart stuff in New York, Las Vegas, Boston, Chicago, and Berlin, among other places. The 1-hour, 45-minute Orlando production reflects cultural changes in the use of technology in daily life; it includes some segments similar to those seen in other cities but isn't identical.

Funny, sometimes poignant, and always compelling, Blue Man Group pounds out vital, visceral tribal rhythms on complex instruments (made of PVC pipes) that could pass for industrial intestines, and makes seemingly spontaneous eruptions of visual art rendered with marshmallows and a mysterious goo. The weekly supplies include 25½ pounds of Cap'n Crunch, 60 Twinkies, 996 marshmallows, and 9½ gallons of paint. If all this sounds silly, it is, but it's also strangely thought-provoking and deals with topics such as the value of modern art, the ubiquity and addictive nature of tablet devices, the way rock music moves you, and how we're all connected. (*Hint:* It's not the internet.)

A live percussion band backs Blue Man Group with a relentless and totally engrossing industrial dance riff. The band resides in long, dark alcoves above the stage. At just the right moments, the lofts are lit to reveal a group of pulsating neon-colored skeletons.

Audience participation completes the Blue Man experience. The blue men often move into the audience to bring guests on stage. At the end of the show, giant glowing balloons drop from the rafters for the audience to bat around like beach balls. And a lot of folks can't help standing up to dance and laugh. Magicians for the creative spirit that resides in us all, Blue Man Group makes everyone a coconspirator in a joyous explosion of showmanship.

This show is decidedly different and requires an open mind to be appreciated. It also helps to be a little loose because, like it or not, everybody gets sucked into the production and leaves the theater a little bit lighter in spirit. If you don't want to be pulled onstage to become a part of the improvisation, don't sit in the first half-dozen or so rows.

The Blue Man Group Box Office (☎ 888-340-5476 or 407-BLUE-MAN [258-3626]) is open 7 a.m.–7 p.m. EST, or you can buy tickets online at bluemanorlando.com. Advance tickets at the Universal Orlando website run $60–$110 for adults, $30–$57 for children ages 3–9; tickets purchased at the box office cost $10 more. The show isn't recommended for kids under age 3, but they may attend without a ticket if they sit on a lap. AAA members and all annual pass holders (even seasonal pass holders) save 20% on up to six tickets, and students with school ID can buy two tickets for $36 on the day of the show, if any are left. If you're also eating at CityWalk or visiting the theme parks, you can save a few bucks on the bundle with a Blue Man Group combo ticket (see page 360). All Blue Man Group tickets include free CityWalk club admission after the show. Blue Man Group also partners with Autism Speaks to offer periodic sensory-friendly shows with modifications such as reduced sound and light levels; visit blueman.com/autismspeaks for details.

A VIP option ($199 for adults, $149 for children) combines premium seating for the show with a guided backstage tour of the theater, starting 1 hour prior to the performance, and a meet and greet with the Blue Man Group after the show.

The show is staged in the Sharp Aquos Theatre, which was originally the Nickelodeon soundstage (look for "green slime" tiles in the outside restrooms). It can be accessed from CityWalk by following the path between Hard Rock Cafe and Hollywood Rip Ride Rockit, or by exiting Universal Studios Florida through the side gate near Despicable Me Minion Mayhem. Center seats in rows B–F go for a premium price; we recommend center seats in rows G–L, at least 11 rows back from the stage.

CITYWALK STAGE

AT VARIOUS TIMES OF THE YEAR Universal offers free concerts and DJ performances on a stage located in the plaza at CityWalk. The stage may be positioned in front of the water feature between Vivo and the Universal Studios Store or it may be located closer to the waterline at the bottom of the amphitheater. Performances are almost exclusively at night, though the space has been used for live tapings of morning talk shows. When *Ant & Dec's Saturday Night Takeaway* taped its 2018 finale here, they drew huge crowds, but there's normally no problem getting a view. The entertainment is usually free, but on New Year's Eve and a few other occasions, the entire area is reserved for those purchasing special-event tickets.

HARD ROCK LIVE

LOCATED ACROSS THE LAGOON from most of CityWalk, adjoining the Hard Rock Cafe and separate from the Hard Rock Hotel, this theater hosts concerts, contests, and various private events. Musical acts, both nationally known and up-and-coming, as well as stand-up comedians, appear regularly. Recent shows have run the gamut from Death Cab for Cutie and Alice in Chains to Jim Jefferies and *Mystery Science Theater 3000*. Great acoustics, comfortable seating (for up to 3,000), and good sight lines make this the best concert venue in town.

Hours vary with live shows; performances usually begin 7–9:30 p.m. Ticket prices vary depending on the act, ranging from $24 to more than $200. There is a full liquor bar, and (depending on the event) you can order food from the restaurant's kitchen. Floor viewing is from removable chairs, or sometimes standing-room only depending on the act, while guests in the VIP balcony can get cocktail service delivered to their leather armchairs. Annual pass holders save $5 on tickets to the Classic Albums Live series, where talented studio musicians re-create records from the 1970s through 1980s note for note; their renditions of Queen and Pink Floyd are flawless.

If seeing a show here, be sure to leave plenty of time for parking and security. You'll be inspected again before entering the venue, and the line can be agonizingly slow. Also note that there's normally no reentry allowed once you exit the venue.

For information and an events calendar, call ☎ 407-351-7625 or see hardrock.com/live/locations/orlando/calendar.aspx. To purchase tickets for an event at Hard Rock Live, call ☎ 407-351-LIVE (5483) or visit ticketmaster.com/Hard-Rock-Live-Orlando-tickets-Orlando/venue/278539. (*Warning:* Exorbitant service fees apply.)

HOLLYWOOD DRIVE-IN GOLF

SO THIS IS WHAT MONEY and imagination can do. On one edge of the CityWalk entertainment complex, these 18-hole courses are awash in elaborate settings, props, and even audio. The theme is a drive-in movie showing two features: *Invaders from Planet Putt* and *The Haunting of Ghostly Greens*. Players can choose a single (18 holes) or double (36 holes) feature.

The Invaders from Planet Putt course entertains with nonfrightening statues and props such as rocket ships and little green men; a pretend newspaper box shows the *Roswell [New Mexico] Register* of July 8, 1947, with the blaring headline, "UFO SIGHTINGS CONTINUE."

The Haunting of Ghostly Greens course features a giant spider, a graveyard, and a basement-lab scene. This course is particularly nice at night but may creep out younger golfers. At various holes, the sound effects are a mooing cow, a chain saw, and a ray gun (we guess, as we've never actually heard a ray gun).

The courses are quite easy, and the greens are in superb condition. We rank Hollywood Drive-In as the best mini-golf in Orlando, along with Disney's Fantasia Gardens and Congo River in Kissimmee. Note that one of the courses is fully wheelchair accessible, while the other requires navigating some stairs.

Hollywood Drive-In is located at the entrance to CityWalk, between the Universal Cinemark and the valet parking loop. As you exit the parking garages and moving sidewalks, Hollywood Drive-In Golf is on your immediate right, down one level.

The course is open daily, 9 a.m.–2 a.m. For 18 holes, it costs $15.99 for adults, and $13.99 for children ages 3–9. For 36 holes, it costs $28.98 for adults, and $24.98 for children ages 3–9. Preferred and Power Annual Pass holders, Florida residents, military, adults age 62 and older, and AAA members all save 10% on 18 holes for up to five players; Premier Pass holders save 15%. You can purchase online at hollywooddriveingolf.com in advance, saving up to 10%, but online tickets aren't refundable if unused.

Before 6 p.m., you must pay the usual parking fee to play at Hollywood Drive-In, which drastically boosts the price of playing these courses if you aren't already visiting Universal Orlando.

Call ☎ 407 802-4848 or visit the website above for more information. You can download a free scorecard app for Apple and Android in preparation for your putting.

APPENDIX

READERS' QUESTIONS
to the AUTHORS

FOLLOWING ARE QUESTIONS from *Unofficial Guide* readers.

QUESTION:

When you do your research, are you admitted to the parks for free? Do the Universal people know you're there?

ANSWER:

We pay the regular admission, and usually the Universal people don't know we're on-site. Similarly, both in and out of Universal Orlando, we pay for our own meals and lodging.

QUESTION:

How often is The Unofficial Guide revised?

ANSWER:

We publish a new edition once a year in the late fall.

QUESTION:

Where can I find information about what's changed at Universal Orlando in between published editions of The Unofficial Guide?

ANSWER:

We post important information online at touringplans.com.

QUESTION:

Do you write each new edition from scratch?

ANSWER:

We do not. When it comes to a destination the size of Universal Orlando, it's hard enough to keep up with what's new. Moreover, we put a lot of effort into communicating the most useful information in the clearest possible language. For future editions, if an attraction or hotel has not changed, we're reluctant to tinker with its coverage for the sake of freshening the writing.

QUESTION:

How many people have you surveyed for your age-group ratings regarding the attractions?

ANSWER:

Since the first *Unofficial Guide* containing Universal coverage was published in 1992, we've interviewed or surveyed thousands of Universal Orlando patrons. Even with such a large survey population, however, we continue to find that certain age groups are underrepresented. Specifically, we'd love to hear more from seniors about their experiences with coasters and other thrill rides.

█ READERS' COMMENTS

OUR READERS LOVE TO SHARE TIPS. An Iowa City, Iowa, couple offers this observation about being in touch with your feelings:

We didn't build rest breaks into our plans but were willing to say, "OK, I'm just not having fun right now—we should leave the park," and go on to something else (like a water park, hotel pool, or shopping trip). This is a skill I would like to see more people develop. I can't count the number of people or families I saw who were obviously not having fun.

A Norwalk, Ohio, mom searched for happy feet:

On the subject of footwear, support is just as important as comfort. On one trip I wore Keds—big mistake. My shins ached unbelievably before the end of the second day. From then on I was a die-hard tennis shoe girl, until I discovered FitFlops [go to fitflop.com for stores]. You get the support of a tennis shoe with the comfort of a flip-flop.

A woman from Mount Gretna, Pennsylvania, had some questions about theme park attire:

There wasn't a section that addressed whether you could wear dresses on rides. Quite a few amusement parks have security straps or bars that come up between one's knees, making it very difficult and immodest to wear dresses or skirts. Many women want to wear dresses for convenience, comfort, or cultural/religious convictions. I was concerned as I was packing whether this would limit any rides I could get on. I was quite pleased that it did not.

A Columbia, Missouri, woman offers advice for wives with anxious husbands:

A smartphone is the best thing in the world for keeping your husband busy in line. As long as mine had that phone, he could check email, check dinner plans, and take and send pictures of the kids to family back home. He never complained about waiting in line, ever.

All for the love of Mom, writes a woman from Haddon Heights, New Jersey:

I was traveling with my mother, who has an artificial knee, a herniated disc, and bad feet. My mantra was, "Try not to kill your mother." Without the book, I would have undoubtedly come home an orphan.

Finally, a Somerville, Alabama, woman is succinct if nothing else:

Everything, other than my husband, was perfect.

And so it goes. . . .

INDEX

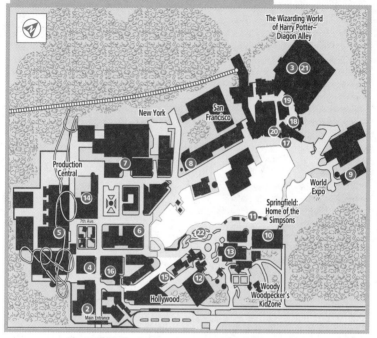

UNIVERSAL STUDIOS FLORIDA ONE-DAY TOURING PLAN FOR ADULTS

1. Buy admission in advance. Call ☎ 407-363-8000 the day before for the official opening time.

2. Arrive at USF 90–120 minutes before the official opening time if Early Park Admission is offered and you're eligible, or 30–45 minutes before opening for day guests. Get a park map as soon as you enter.

3. Early-entry guests should ride Harry Potter and the Escape from Gringotts if it's operating. If it's not, enjoy the rest of Diagon Alley but don't get in line.

4. Before early entry ends, hotel guests should exit Diagon Alley and ride Despicable Me Minion Mayhem. Day guests should wait in the Front Lot until permitted to ride Despicable Me.

5. Ride Hollywood Rip Ride Rockit.

6. Experience Transformers: The Ride 3-D.

7. Ride Revenge of the Mummy in New York. After riding, retrieve a Virtual Line return time for Race Through New York Starring Jimmy Fallon nearby.

8. Ride Fast & Furious: Supercharged. Virtual Line reservations shouldn't be necessary, but use the single-rider line if the standby wait time exceeds 20 minutes.

9. Ride Men in Black Alien Attack in World Expo.

10. Ride The Simpsons Ride in Springfield.

11. Ride Kang & Kodos' Twirl 'n' Hurl if 50 or fewer people are in line.

12. Ride E.T. Adventure in Woody Woodpecker's KidZone.

13. Work in *Animal Actors on Location* around lunch

(we recommend Fast Food Boulevard), according to the daily entertainment schedule. If you're running behind, skip *Animal Actors*.

14. Experience Race Through New York Starring Jimmy Fallon according to the Virtual Line reservation you made earlier.

15. See *Universal Orlando's Horror Make-Up Show* according to the daily entertainment schedule.

16. See *Shrek 4-D* in Production Central.

17. On your way into Diagon Alley, chat with the Knight Bus conductor and his shrunken head. Also look for Kreacher in the window of 12 Grimmauld Place, and listen to the receiver in the red phone booth.

18. See the *Celestina Warbeck and the Banshees* and *Tales of Beedle the Bard* shows.

19. See the wand ceremony at Ollivanders and buy a wand if you wish.

20. Tour Diagon Alley. Browse the shops, explore the dark recesses of Knockturn Alley, and discover the interactive effects. If you're hungry, try the Leaky Cauldron or Florean Fortescue's Ice-Cream Parlour.

21. Ride Harry Potter and the Escape from Gringotts. If this is your first ride, take the standby queue. For re-rides, use the single-rider line.

21. Revisit any favorite attractions, time permitting, and (if scheduled) watch *Universal Orlando's Cinematic Celebration* from Central Park (between Hollywood and Woody Woodpecker's KidZone).

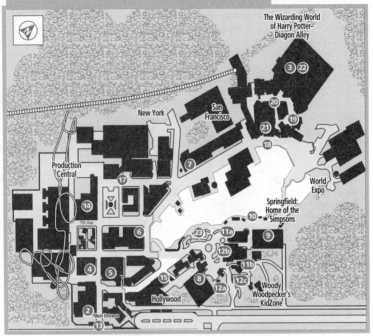

The Wizarding World
of Harry Potter–
Diagon Alley

New York

San
Francisco

Production
Central

World
Expo

7th Ave.

Springfield:
Home of the
Simpsons

Hollywood

Woody
Woodpecker's
KidZone

Main Entrance

UNIVERSAL STUDIOS FLORIDA ONE–DAY TOURING PLAN
FOR PARENTS WITH SMALL CHILDREN

1. Buy admission in advance. Call ☎ 407-363-8000 the day before for the official opening time.

2. Arrive at USF 90–120 minutes before the official opening time if Early Park Admission is offered and you're eligible, or 30–45 minutes before opening for day guests. Pick up a park map as soon as you enter. Rent a stroller if needed.

3. Early-entry guests should ride Harry Potter and the Escape from Gringotts, and use child swap or exit after the elevators. Or just enjoy Diagon Alley.

4. Before early entry ends, hotel guests should exit Diagon Alley and then ride Despicable Me Minion Mayhem. Day guests should wait in the Front Lot until permitted to ride Despicable Me.

5. See *Shrek 4-D* in Production Central.

6. Experience Transformers: The Ride 3-D if your kid can handle the noise and explosions.

7. Ride Fast & Furious: Supercharged. Ask for a Virtual Line return time if the wait exceeds 30 minutes.

8. Ride E.T. Adventure in Woody Woodpecker's KidZone.

9. Ride The Simpsons Ride in Springfield.

10. Experience Kang & Kodos' Twirl 'n' Hurl.

11. See *Animal Actors on Location* (**11a**) and *A Day in the Park with Barney* (**11b**) according to the daily entertainment schedule. Get a snack on Fast Food Boulevard while waiting for the shows to start.

12. Between shows, work in Woody's Nuthouse Coaster (**12a**) and time in Fievel's Playland (**12b**) and Curious George Goes to Town (**12c**).

13. Take a break from the park for at least 2 hours,

depending on how late the park is open. Before exiting, retrieve a Virtual Line return time for Race Through New York Starring Jimmy Fallon. If staying nearby, return to your room for a nap. Otherwise, take a rest at CityWalk or a resort hotel.

14. Return to the park a couple hours before Universal's Superstar Parade and use your Virtual Line reservation for Race Through New York.

15. If your kids are brave, see *Universal Orlando's Horror Make-Up Show* according to the daily entertainment schedule.

16. Greet characters such as Shrek, SpongeBob, and the Transformers at locations shown on the park map.

17. See the late afternoon Superstar Parade from the New York area near Revenge of the Mummy.

18. On your way into Diagon Alley, chat with the Knight Bus conductor and his shrunken head. Also look for Kreacher in the window of 12 Grimmauld Place, and listen to the receiver in the red phone booth.

19. See the *Celestina Warbeck and the Banshees* and *Tales of Beedle the Bard* shows.

20. See the wand ceremony at Ollivanders.

21. Tour Diagon Alley. If you're hungry, try the Leaky Cauldron or Florean Fortescue's Ice-Cream Parlour.

22. Ride Harry Potter and the Escape from Gringotts from the standby queue (if you didn't earlier), and use child swap or exit after the elevators.

23. Revisit any favorite attractions, time permitting, and (if scheduled) watch *Universal Orlando's Cinematic Celebration* from Central Park (between Hollywood and KidZone).

Universal Studios Florida

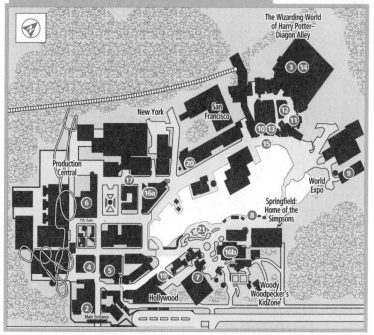

The Wizarding World of Harry Potter–Diagon Alley

New York

San Francisco

Production Central

World Expo

Springfield: Home of the Simpsons

7th Ave.

Hollywood

Woody Woodpecker's KidZone

Main Entrance

UNIVERSAL STUDIOS FLORIDA ONE-DAY TOURING PLAN FOR SENIORS

1. Buy admission in advance. Call ☎ 407-363-8000 the day before for the official opening time.

2. Arrive at USF 90–120 minutes before the official opening time if Early Park Admission is offered and you're eligible, or 30–45 minutes before opening for day guests. Get a park map as soon as you enter. Rent a wheelchair or ECV if needed.

3. Early-entry guests should ride Harry Potter and the Escape from Gringotts. Exit after the elevators if you don't wish to experience a mild roller coaster. Or enjoy the rest of Diagon Alley.

4. Before early entry ends, hotel guests should exit Diagon Alley and then ride Despicable Me Minion Mayhem. Day guests should wait in the Front Lot until permitted to ride Despicable Me. Stationary seating is available on request.

5. See *Shrek 4-D* in Production Central. Stationary seating is available on request.

6. Experience Race Through New York Starring Jimmy Fallon. If simulated motion bothers you, enjoy the preshow but exit before the ride.

7. Ride E.T. Adventure in Woody Woodpecker's KidZone.

8. Ride Kang & Kodos' Twirl 'n' Hurl in Springfield if 50 or fewer people are in line.

9. Ride Men in Black Alien Attack in World Expo if you can tolerate some moderate spinning.

10. Have an early lunch at Leaky Cauldron.

11. See the *Celestina Warbeck and the Banshees* and *Tales of Beedle the Bard* shows.

12. See the wand ceremony at Ollivanders and purchase a wand if you wish.

13. Tour Diagon Alley. Browse the shops, explore the dark recesses of Knockturn Alley, and discover the interactive effects. If you're still hungry, try Florean Fortescue's Ice-Cream Parlour.

14. Experience Harry Potter and the Escape from Gringotts via the standby queue (if you didn't earlier), and exit after the elevators if you don't wish to experience a mild roller coaster.

15. Chat with the Knight Bus conductor and his shrunken head. Also look for Kreacher in the window of 12 Grimmauld Place, and listen to the receiver in the red phone booth.

16. See *The Blues Brothers Show* (**16a**) and *Animal Actors on Location* (**16b**) according to the daily entertainment schedule. If time is short, skip *Animal Actors*.

17. See the late afternoon Superstar Parade.

18. Have an early dinner inside the park at Fast Food Boulevard, Finnegan's Bar, or Lombard's Seafood.

19. See *Universal Orlando's Horror Make-Up Show* according to the daily entertainment schedule.

20. Ride Fast & Furious: Supercharged if you can handle a bumpy bus ride. Use the single-rider line if the standby wait exceeds 20 minutes.

21. Revisit any favorite attractions, time permitting, and (if scheduled) watch *Universal Orlando's Cinematic Celebration* from Central Park (between Hollywood and KidZone).

Universal's Islands of Adventure

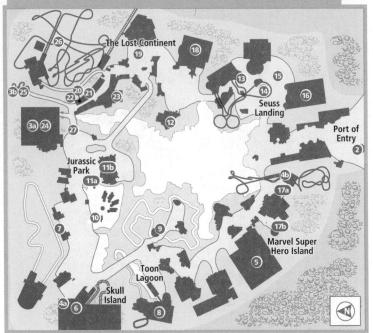

UNIVERSAL'S ISLANDS OF ADVENTURE ONE-DAY TOURING PLAN FOR ADULTS

1. Buy admission in advance. Call ☎ 407-363-8000 the day before for the official opening time.

2. Arrive at IOA 75–90 minutes before the official opening time if Early Park Admission is offered and you're eligible, or 30–45 minutes before opening for day guests. Get a park map as soon as you enter.

3. Early-entry guests should ride Harry Potter and the Forbidden Journey (**3a**). Ride Flight of the Hippogriff (**3b**) as well if you have time.

4. Early-entry guests can exit Hogsmeade into Jurassic Park as early entry ends and ride Skull Island: Reign of Kong (**4a**) as soon as it opens, then continue to Marvel Super Hero Island to ride The Incredible Hulk Coaster (**4b**). Guests without early entry should start at this step with the Hulk.

5. Ride The Amazing Adventures of Spider-Man.

6. Experience Skull Island: Reign of Kong (if you haven't already).

7. Take the Jurassic Park River Adventure. Put your belongings in a pay locker here and leave them through the next two water rides.

8. Reverse course to ride Dudley Do-Right's Ripsaw Falls in Toon Lagoon.

9. Ride Popeye & Bluto's Bilge-Rat Barges. Retrieve your property from Jurassic Park.

10. Explore Camp Jurassic.

11. If time permits before lunch, meet Blue at the Raptor Encounter (**11a**) and/or check out the exhibits in the Jurassic Park Discovery Center (**11b**).

12. Eat lunch. A good sit-down choice is Mythos. Make reservations through Zomato.

13. Ride The High in the Sky Seuss Trolley Train Ride! in Seuss Landing.

14. Enjoy the Caro-Seuss-el.

15. Ride One Fish, Two Fish, Red Fish, Blue Fish.

16. Experience The Cat in the Hat.

17. Return to Marvel Super Hero Island to ride Storm Force Accelatron (**17a**) and Doctor Doom's Fearfall (**17b**) using the single-rider line. Skip them if you're short on time.

18. In Lost Continent, experience *Poseidon's Fury.*

19. Chat with the Mystic Fountain.

20. Enter The Wizarding World of Harry Potter—Hogsmeade, and see the *Frog Choir* or *Triwizard Spirit Rally* perform on the small stage outside Hogwarts Castle.

21. See the wand ceremony at Ollivanders and buy a wand if you wish.

22. See the stage show you didn't see earlier. Pose for a picture with the Hogwarts Express conductor, and explore the shops and interactive windows around Hogsmeade.

23. Have dinner at Three Broomsticks.

24. Ride Harry Potter and the Forbidden Journey during the first Hogwarts Castle nighttime light show (performed seasonally).

25. Ride Flight of the Hippogriff.

26. Ride the Magical Creatures roller coaster (opens 2019).

27. Watch the last Hogwarts Castle light show before closing, or revisit any favorite attractions.

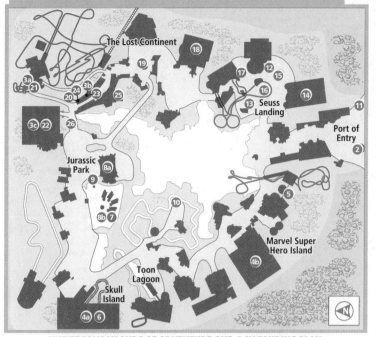

UNIVERSAL'S ISLANDS OF ADVENTURE ONE-DAY TOURING PLAN FOR PARENTS WITH SMALL CHILDREN

1. Buy admission in advance. Call ☎ 407-363-8000 the day before for the official opening time.

2. Arrive at IOA 75–90 minutes before the official opening time if Early Park Admission is offered and you're eligible, or 30–45 minutes before opening for day guests. Get a park map as soon as you enter. Rent a stroller if needed.

3. Ride Flight of the Hippogriff (**3a**), see the wand ceremony at Ollivanders (**3b**), and tour the queue (but exit before boarding) at Harry Potter and the Forbidden Journey (**3c**).

4. Early-entry guests can exit Hogsmeade into Jurassic Park as early entry ends and ride Skull Island: Reign of Kong (**4a**) as soon as it opens (if your kids are brave enough), then continue to Marvel Super Hero Island to ride The Amazing Adventures of Spider-Man (**4b**). Guests without early entry should start at this step with Spider-Man.

5. Ride Storm Force Accelatron.

6. Experience Skull Island: Reign of Kong if you dare (and haven't already).

7. Continue to Jurassic Park. Get a timed-return ticket for Pteranodon Flyers if your child is 36–56 inches tall.

8. Let the kids explore the Jurassic Park Discovery Center (**8a**) and play in Camp Jurassic (**8b**) until their time comes to ride Pteranodon Flyers.

9. Meet Blue at the Raptor Encounter.

10. Return to Toon Lagoon. Explore Me Ship, *The Olive*.

11. Take a break from the park for at least 2 hours, depending on how late the park is open. If staying

nearby, return to your room for lunch and a nap. Otherwise, take a rest at CityWalk or a resort hotel.

12. Return to the park. See the next scheduled show of *Oh! The Stories You'll Hear!* in Seuss Landing.

13. Explore If I Ran the Zoo while waiting for the show.

14. Ride The Cat in the Hat.

15. Ride One Fish, Two Fish, Red Fish, Blue Fish.

16. Enjoy the Caro-Seuss-el.

17. Ride The High in the Sky Seuss Trolley Train Ride.

18. See *Poseidon's Fury* in The Lost Continent.

19. Chat with the Mystic Fountain.

20. Enter The Wizarding World of Harry Potter–Hogsmeade, and see the *Frog Choir* or *Triwizard Spirit Rally* perform on the small stage outside Hogwarts.

21. Ride Flight of the Hippogriff (if you didn't earlier).

22. If you didn't already, walk through the queue of Harry Potter and the Forbidden Journey.

23. See the wand ceremony at Ollivanders and buy a wand if you wish.

24. See the stage show you didn't see earlier. Pose for a picture with the Hogwarts Express conductor, and explore the shops and interactive windows around Hogsmeade.

25. Have dinner at Three Broomsticks.

26. Watch the Hogwarts Castle light show, or revisit any favorite attractions.

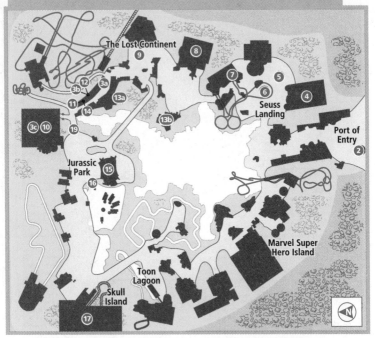

UNIVERSAL'S ISLANDS OF ADVENTURE ONE-DAY TOURING PLAN FOR SENIORS

1. Buy admission in advance. Call ☎ 407-363-8000 the day before for the official opening time.
2. Arrive at IOA 75–90 minutes before the official opening time if Early Park Admission is offered and you're eligible, or 30–45 minutes before opening for day guests. Get a park map as soon as you enter. Rent a wheelchair or ECV if needed.
3. Early-entry guests should explore the shops of Hogsmeade (**3a**), see the wand ceremony at Olli-vanders (**3b**), and walk through the queue at Harry Potter and the Forbidden Journey (**3c**) (ask for the exit before boarding).
4. Exit Hogsmeade before early entry ends, and head to Seuss Landing to ride The Cat in the Hat. Guests without early entry should start at this step.
5. Ride One Fish, Two Fish, Red Fish, Blue Fish.
6. Enjoy the Caro-Seuss-el.
7. Ride The High in the Sky Seuss Trolley Train Ride!
8. Experience *Poseidon's Fury* in The Lost Continent.
9. Chat with the Mystic Fountain.
10. Enter Hogsmeade and walk through the queue of Harry Potter and the Forbidden Journey (if you didn't earlier).
11. See the *Frog Choir* or *Triwizard Spirit Rally* perform on the small stage outside Hogwarts.

12. See the wand ceremony at Ollivanders (if you didn't earlier) and buy a wand if you wish.
13. Have lunch at Three Broomsticks (**13a**) or Mythos (**13b**).
14. After lunch, see the stage show you didn't see earlier. Pose for a picture with the Hogwarts Express conductor, and explore the shops and interactive windows around Hogsmeade. Make sure you sample (or at least smell) some sweets at Honeydukes.
15. Cross the bridge to Jurassic Park and see the exhibits in the Jurassic Park Discovery Center.
16. Meet Blue at the Raptor Encounter.
17. Ride Skull Island: Reign of Kong, or at least request a temple tour through its elaborate queue.
18. Walk counterclockwise around the park, paying attention to the quiet paths along the waterfront in each island.
19. Revisit any favorite attractions, or remain in Hogsmeade to watch the Hogwarts Castle light show. Or exit the park for an early dinner in CityWalk.

Universal Studios Florida

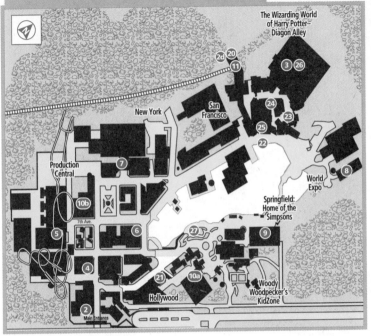

The Wizarding World
of Harry Potter–
Diagon Alley

New York

San
Francisco

Production
Central

7th Ave.

World
Expo

Springfield:
Home of the
Simpsons

Woody
Woodpecker's
KidZone

Hollywood

Main Entrance

UNIVERSAL ORLANDO HIGHLIGHTS ONE-DAY/TWO-PARK TOURING PLAN
(Assumes: 1-Day Park-to-Park Ticket)

1. Buy admission in advance. Call ☎ 407-363-8000 the day before for the official opening time.

2. Arrive at USF 90–120 minutes before the official opening time if Early Park Admission is offered and you're eligible, or 30–45 minutes before opening for day guests. Pick up a park map as soon as you enter. **Alternative:** If only IOA is open for Early Park Admission and you're eligible, arrive at IOA's turnstiles 75–90 minutes before the official opening time (**2a**). Ride Harry Potter and the Forbidden Journey (**2b**). Ride Flight of the Hippogriff (**2c**) as well if you have time. Take the Hogwarts Express to King's Cross Station (**2d**) before USF officially opens for the day, and continue at the next step.

3. Early-entry guests will be led directly to Diagon Alley. Ride Harry Potter and the Escape from Gringotts if it is operating. If Gringotts is not operating, enjoy the rest of Diagon Alley but don't get in line.

4. Before early entry ends, hotel guests should exit Diagon Alley and return to the front of the park

to ride Despicable Me Minion Mayhem. Day guests should wait in the Front Lot until permitted to ride Despicable Me.

5. Ride Hollywood Rip Ride Rockit.

6. Ride Transformers: The Ride 3-D in Production Central.

7. Ride Revenge of the Mummy in New York. After riding, retrieve a Virtual Line return time for Race Through New York Starring Jimmy Fallon nearby.

8. Walk through San Francisco and past the London Waterfront to ride Men in Black Alien Attack in World Expo.

9. Ride The Simpsons Ride in Springfield.

10. Ride E.T. Adventure (**10a**) in Woody Woodpecker's KidZone if you have small children. If not, experience Race Through New York Starring Jimmy Fallon (**10b**) according to the Virtual Line reservation you made earlier.

11. Ride the Hogwarts Express from King's Cross Station to IOA. Have your park-to-park ticket ready.

(continued on next page)

Universal's Islands of Adventure

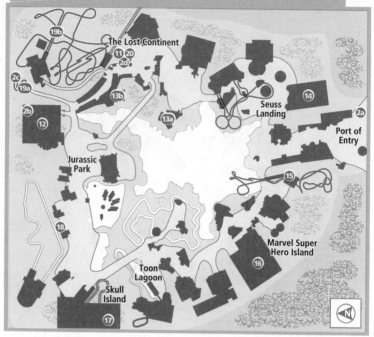

UNIVERSAL ORLANDO HIGHLIGHTS ONE-DAY/TWO-PARK
TOURING PLAN *(continued)*

(continued from previous page)

12. Ride Harry Potter and the Forbidden Journey. If the wait is more than 30 minutes, use the single-rider line.

13. Eat lunch at Mythos in Lost Continent (**13a**) or Three Broomsticks in Hogsmeade (**13b**).

14. Ride The Cat in the Hat in Seuss Landing.

15. Ride The Incredible Hulk Coaster on Marvel Super Hero Island.

16. Ride The Amazing Adventures of Spider-Man.

17. Ride Skull Island: Reign of Kong.

18. Continue clockwise, and take the Jurassic Park River Adventure.

19. Enter Hogsmeade, and ride Flight of the Hippogriff (**19a**) if the wait isn't too long, followed by the Magical Creatures coaster (opens 2019) (**19b**). Use the single-rider line if the wait is over 30 minutes.

20. Return to USF via Hogwarts Express, or walk back to the other park if the posted wait exceeds 20 minutes.

See map on previous page for the following steps.

21. See the next showing of *Universal Orlando's Horror Make-Up Show* upon returning to USF. Also

remember your return time for any remaining Virtual Line reservations you made. If you couldn't get a return time, check at the attractions an hour or two before closing.

22. On your way into Diagon Alley, chat with the Knight Bus conductor and his shrunken head. Also look for Kreacher in the window of 12 Grimmauld Place, and listen to the receiver in the red phone booth.

23. See the *Celestina Warbeck and the Banshees* and/or *Tales of Beedle the Bard* shows.

24. See the wand ceremony at Ollivanders and buy a wand if you wish.

25. Tour Diagon Alley. Browse the shops, explore the dark recesses of Knockturn Alley, and discover the interactive effects. If you're hungry, try the Leaky Cauldron or Florean Fortescue's Ice-Cream Parlour.

26. Ride Harry Potter and the Escape from Gringotts. If this is your first ride, take the standby queue. For re-rides, use the single-rider line.

27. If scheduled, watch *Universal Orlando's Cinematic Celebration* from Central Park (between Hollywood and Woody Woodpecker's KidZone), or revisit any favorite attractions.

Universal Studios Florida

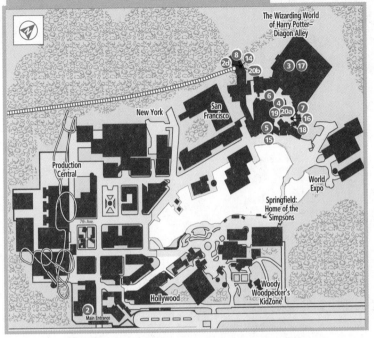

The Wizarding World of Harry Potter–Diagon Alley

New York

San Francisco

Production Central

7th Ave

World Expo

Springfield: Home of the Simpsons

Woody Woodpecker's KidZone

Hollywood

Main Entrance

WIZARDING WORLD ONE–DAY/TWO–PARK TOURING PLAN
(Assumes: 1-Day Park-to-Park Ticket. Excludes: All non-Potter attractions.)

1. Buy admission in advance. Call ☎ 407-363-8000 the day before for the official opening time.

2. Arrive at USF 90–120 minutes before the official opening time if Early Park Admission is offered and you're eligible, or 30–45 minutes before opening for day guests. Pick up a park map as soon as you enter. **Alternative:** If only IOA is open for Early Park Admission and you're eligible, arrive at IOA's turnstiles 75–90 minutes before the official opening time (**2a**). Ride Harry Potter and the Forbidden Journey (**2b**). Ride Flight of the Hippogriff (**2c**) as well if you have time. Take the Hogwarts Express to King's Cross Station (**2d**) before USF officially opens for the day, and continue at the next step.

3. Early-entry guests should ride Harry Potter and the Escape from Gringotts if it is operating. If Gringotts is not operating, enjoy the rest of Diagon Alley but don't get in line.

4. See the wand ceremony at Ollivanders and buy a wand if you wish. Gringotts may have a long line by the time the park officially opens if Early Park Admission was offered, so day guests should begin with Ollivanders if the posted wait time for Gringotts is more than 30 minutes.

5. Have breakfast at the Leaky Cauldron or Florean Fortescue's Ice-Cream Parlour (hey, you're on vacation!).

6. Tour Diagon Alley. Browse the shops, explore the dark recesses of Knockturn Alley, and discover the interactive effects.

7. See one of the two *Tales of Beedle the Bard* shows.

8. Exit Diagon Alley and ride the Hogwarts Express from King's Cross Station to IOA. Have your park-to-park ticket ready.

(continued on next page)

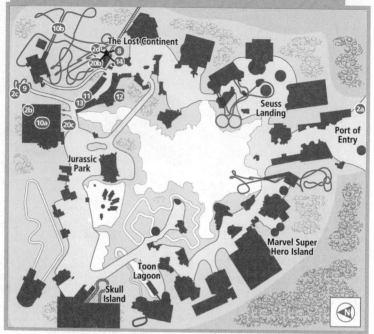

The Lost Continent

Seuss Landing

Port of Entry

Jurassic Park

Marvel Super Hero Island

Toon Lagoon

Skull Island

WIZARDING WORLD ONE-DAY/TWO-PARK TOURING PLAN *(continued)*

(Assumes: 1-Day Park-to-Park Ticket. Excludes: All non-Potter attractions.)

(continued from previous page)

9. Enter Hogsmeade and ride Flight of the Hippogriff.

10. Ride Harry Potter and the Forbidden Journey (**10a**), followed by the new Magical Creatures roller coaster (opens 2019) (**10b**).

11. See the *Frog Choir* or *Triwizard Spirit Rally* perform on the small stage outside Hogwarts.

12. Have lunch at Three Broomsticks.

13. After lunch, see the stage show you didn't see earlier. Pose for a picture with the Hogwarts Express conductor, and explore the shops and interactive windows around Hogsmeade. Make sure you sample (or at least smell) some sweets at Honeydukes.

14. Return to USF via Hogwarts Express.

See map on previous page for the following steps.

15. Chat with the Knight Bus conductor and his shrunken head. Also look for Kreacher in the

window of 12 Grimmauld Place, and listen to the receiver in the red phone booth.

16. Reenter Diagon Alley and catch the *Tales of Beedle the Bard* show that you didn't see earlier.

17. Ride Harry Potter and the Escape from Gringotts. If this is your first ride, take the standby queue. For re-rides, use the single-rider line.

18. See the *Celestina Warbeck and the Banshees* show.

19. Have dinner at the Leaky Cauldron, or just eat dessert from Florean Fortescue's Ice-Cream Parlour or Sugarplum's Sweet Shop.

20. Stay in Diagon Alley (**20a**) until closing time, enjoying the atmosphere. The fireworks of the nighttime show look fantastic over the Gringotts dragon. Alternatively, take Hogwarts Express (**20b**) back to IOA and watch the light show on Hogwarts Castle (**20c**) (performed seasonally).

Universal Studios Florida

UNIVERSAL ORLANDO COMPREHENSIVE TWO-DAY/TWO-PARK TOURING PLAN: DAY ONE
(Assumes: Multiday Park-to-Park Ticket)

1. Buy admission in advance. Call ☎ 407-363-8000 the day before for the official opening time.

2. Arrive at USF 90–120 minutes before the official opening time if Early Park Admission is offered and you're eligible, or 30–45 minutes before opening for day guests. Get a park map as soon as you enter.

3. Early-entry guests should ride Harry Potter and the Escape from Gringotts if it is operating. If Gringotts is not operating, enjoy the rest of Diagon Alley but do not get in line.

4. Before early entry ends, hotel guests should exit Diagon Alley and ride Despicable Me Minion Mayhem. Day guests should wait in the Front Lot until permitted to ride Despicable Me.

5. Ride Hollywood Rip Ride Rockit.

6. Experience Transformers: The Ride 3-D in Production Central.

7. Ride Revenge of the Mummy in New York.

8. Experience Fast & Furious: Supercharged. Virtual Line reservations shouldn't be necessary, but use the single-rider line if the standby wait time exceeds 20 minutes.

9. Walk past the London Waterfront to ride Men in Black Alien Attack in World Expo.

10. Ride The Simpsons Ride in Springfield.

11. Ride Kang & Kodos' Twirl 'n' Hurl if 50 or fewer people are in line.

12. Ride E.T. Adventure in Woody Woodpecker's KidZone.

13. Work in *Animal Actors on Location* around lunch (we recommend Fast Food Boulevard), according to the daily entertainment schedule.

14. Ride the Hogwarts Express from King's Cross Station to IOA. Have your park-to-park ticket ready.

(continued on next page)

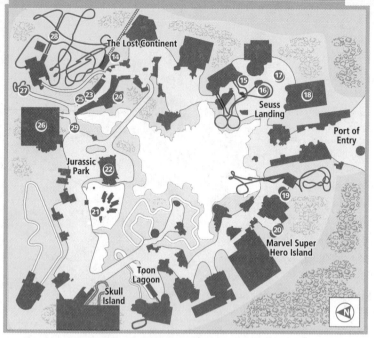

UNIVERSAL ORLANDO COMPREHENSIVE TWO-DAY/TWO-PARK TOURING PLAN:
DAY ONE *(continued)*
(Assumes: Multiday Park-to-Park Ticket)

(continued from previous page)

15. Ride The High in the Sky Seuss Trolley Train Ride! in Seuss Landing.

16. Enjoy the Caro-Seuss-el.

17. Ride One Fish, Two Fish, Red Fish, Blue Fish.

18. Experience The Cat in the Hat.

19. Cross through Port of Entry to Marvel Super Hero Island and ride Storm Force Accelatron.

20. While in Marvel, ride Doctor Doom's Fearfall.

21. Walk through Toon Lagoon to Jurassic Park and explore Camp Jurassic.

22. Check out the exhibits in the Jurassic Park Discovery Center.

23. Enter Hogsmeade, and see the *Frog Choir* or *Triwizard Spirit Rally* perform on the small stage outside Hogwarts.

24. Have dinner at Three Broomsticks.

25. After dinner, see the stage show you didn't see earlier. Pose for a picture with the Hogwarts Express conductor and explore the shops and interactive windows around Hogsmeade. Make sure you sample (or at least smell) some sweets at Honeydukes.

26. Ride Harry Potter and the Forbidden Journey during the first Hogwarts Castle nighttime light show (performed seasonally).

27. Ride Flight of the Hippogriff.

28. Ride the new Magical Creatures roller coaster (opens 2019).

29. Watch the last Hogwarts Castle light show before closing, or revisit any favorite attractions.

(Day Two is on next page.)

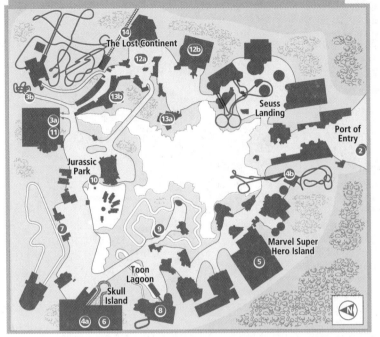

UNIVERSAL ORLANDO COMPREHENSIVE TWO-DAY/TWO-PARK TOURING PLAN: DAY TWO

(Assumes: Multiday Park-to-Park Ticket) (Day One is on previous pages.)

1. Buy admission in advance. Call ☎ 407-363-8000 the day before for the official opening time.

2. Arrive at IOA 75–90 minutes before the official opening time if Early Park Admission is offered and you're eligible, or 30–45 minutes before opening for day guests. Get a park map as soon as you enter.

3. Early-entry guests should ride Harry Potter and the Forbidden Journey (**3a**). Ride Flight of the Hippogriff (**3b**) as well if you have time.

4. Early-entry guests can exit Hogsmeade into Jurassic Park as early entry ends and ride Skull Island: Reign of Kong (**4a**) as soon as it opens, then continue to Marvel Super Hero Island to ride The Incredible Hulk Coaster (**4b**). Guests without early entry should start at this step with the Hulk.

5. See The Amazing Adventures of Spider-Man.

6. Experience Skull Island: Reign of Kong (if you haven't done so already).

7. Take the Jurassic Park River Adventure. Put your

belongings in a pay locker here and leave them through the next two water rides.

8. Reverse course to ride Dudley Do-Right's Ripsaw Falls in Toon Lagoon.

9. Ride Popeye & Bluto's Bilge-Rat Barges. Now that you've achieved maximum soakage, retrieve your property from Jurassic Park.

10. Get your photo taken at the Raptor Encounter if the wait isn't overwhelming.

11. Ride Harry Potter and the Forbidden Journey if you didn't ride earlier.

12. Stop and chat with the Mystic Fountain (**12a**) on your way to experience *Poseidon's Fury* (**12b**) in The Lost Continent.

13. Eat lunch at Mythos in Lost Continent (**13a**) or Three Broomsticks in Hogsmeade (**13b**).

14. After lunch, take the Hogwarts Express from Hogsmeade Station to USF, or walk back to the other park if the posted wait exceeds 20 minutes. Have your park-to-park ticket ready.

(continued on next page)

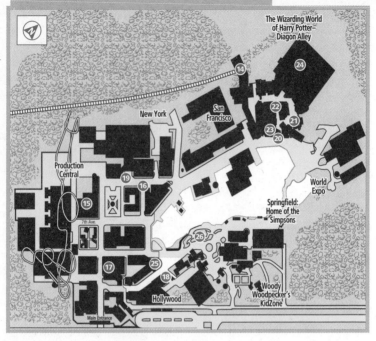

UNIVERSAL ORLANDO COMPREHENSIVE TWO-DAY/TWO-PARK TOURING PLAN:
DAY TWO *(continued)*
(Assumes: Multiday Park-to-Park Ticket)

(continued from previous page)

15. Retrieve a Virtual Line reservation for Race Through New York Starring Jimmy Fallon.

16. Work in *The Blues Brothers Show* and *Sing It!* show around your Jimmy Fallon return time according to the daily entertainment schedule. If time is short, skip *Sing It!*

17. See *Shrek 4-D* in Production Central.

18. See *Universal Orlando's Horror Make-Up Show* according to the daily entertainment schedule.

19. If you have time, see the late afternoon parade.

20. On your way into Diagon Alley, chat with the Knight Bus conductor and his shrunken head. Also look for Kreacher in the window of 12 Grimmauld Place, and listen to the receiver in the red phone booth.

21. See the *Celestina Warbeck and the Banshees* and *Tales of Beedle the Bard* shows.

22. See the wand ceremony at Ollivanders and buy a wand if you wish.

23. Tour Diagon Alley. Browse the shops, explore the dark recesses of Knockturn Alley, and discover the interactive effects. If you're hungry, try the Leaky Cauldron or Florean Fortescue's Ice-Cream Parlour.

24. Ride Harry Potter and the Escape from Gringotts. If this is your first ride, take the standby queue. For re-rides, use the single-rider line.

25. Revisit a favorite attraction, or browse the Williams of Hollywood prop shop.

26. If scheduled, watch *Universal Orlando's Cinematic Celebration* from Central Park (between Hollywood and Woody Woodpecker's KidZone)..